HUMAN SOCIETIES

An Introduction to
Macrosociology

The cover of this book reflects the changes that have occurred in human societies over the last 10,000 years. It includes a cave drawing from the Old Stone Age, a painting from ancient Egypt, and the plaque designed for the Pioneer 10 and 11 spacecraft, humanity's first ventures into the universe beyond our own solar system. This plaque and other materials aboard Pioneer 10 and 11 carry into deep space basic information about ourselves and the planet we inhabit.

FOURTH EDITION

HUMAN SOCIETIES

An Introduction to Macrosociology

Gerhard Lenski

Jean Lenski

McGraw-Hill Book Company

New York St. Louis San Francisco Auckland
Bogotá Hamburg Johannesburg London Madrid
Mexico Montreal New Delhi Panama
Paris São Paulo Singapore Sydney Tokyo Toronto

HUMAN SOCIETIES: An Introduction to Macrosociology

Copyright © 1982, 1978, 1974, 1970 by McGraw-Hill, Inc. All rights reserved. Printed in the United States of America. Except as permitted under the United States Copyright Act of 1976, no part of this publication may be reproduced or distributed in any form or by any means, or stored in a data base or retrieval system, without the prior written permission of the publisher.

4 5 6 7 8 9 0 D O D O 8 9 8 7 6 5 4 3

This book was set in Optima by Black Dot, Inc. The editors were Eric M. Munson and David Dunham; the designer was Joseph Gillians; the production supervisor was Charles Hess. The photo editor was Inge King. New drawings were done by Danmark & Michaels, Inc.
R. R. Donnelley & Sons Company was printer and binder.

ISBN 0-07-037176-8

See Picture Credits on pages 486–488.
Copyrights included on this page by reference.

Library of Congress Cataloging in Publication Data

Lenski, Gerhard Emmanuel, date
    Human societies.

    Includes bibliographical references and indexes.
    1. Sociology. 2. Social evolution. I. Lenski,
Jean. II. Title.
HM51.L357 1982   301   81-8235
ISBN 0-07-037176-8   AACR2

Contents

Preface

This volume is an introduction to macrosociology, the study of the largest, most inclusive, and most complex of all social systems: human societies. Interest in macrosociology has increased considerably in recent years as it has become apparent that the most critical problems of the contemporary world are essentially problems of malfunctioning societies.

Macrosociology is the only branch of science that specializes in the study of human societies per se. *Micro*sociology studies social systems within societies, and other social sciences study such varied aspects of them as their economies, their polities, their histories, and the psychic processes of their members. But it falls to macrosociology to integrate the great mass of relevant material and to provide theories capable of illuminating these most complex and vital of social entities.

As interest in macrosociology has grown, so has appreciation of its value in teaching. Because it is concerned with the largest and most inclusive social systems, a macrosociological perspective can accommodate and integrate many of the more detailed materials of microsociology. In fact, when entities such as labor unions, churches, communities, families, and individuals are studied within the context of the society of which they are a part, their own structure and functioning become clearer and more meaningful.

The theoretical perspective that shapes our analysis is best described as *structural-functional-ecological-evolutionary*. Although, for the sake of convenience, we refer to it as *ecological-evolutionary*, or simply as *evolutionary*, the perspectives of functionalism and structuralism are an essential element. The great virtue of evolutionary theory, in our judgment, is its remarkable capacity for incorporating the insights of the other three perspectives within a framework that makes a critical contribution of its own: insight into the most fundamental processes of societal change and development.

We have been extremely pleased with the reactions of students and instructors to the previous editions of *Human Societies*, most pleased of all, perhaps, that it has proved helpful in illuminating the processes of change in the contemporary world. One of our basic assumptions is that macrosociology is an essential tool for citizens in a modern democratic society. They need not understand all of the discipline's research techniques, but they should be aware of the findings of that research and they should understand the theories that interpret and give meaning to those findings.

Since no single volume can cover fully every facet of a subject as extensive as macrosociology, most instructors will wish to supplement the text in one area or another. For this reason, we have tried to incorporate all the major topics into our analysis, thus providing points of departure for more extended discussions. The instructor who wants to develop *socialization* more fully, for example, will find opportunities in Chapters 1, 2, 3, 5, 6, 7, 9, 10, and 12. Similarly, instructors can introduce additional materials on such subjects as population control, the role of women, environmental problems, and social stratification at numerous points, and in the context of societies of the past, present, and future.

The book is organized into three sections. In the first, human societies are established as bio-sociocultural systems, part of the natural world, and units involved in a unique evolutionary process. In the second section, we survey the first 99.9 per cent of human experience, tracing the successive transformations of human societies from the remote prehistoric era to the eve of the Industrial Revolution. In the final section, we examine the industrial and industrializing societies of the modern era, analyze their more serious problems, and conclude with a look at the future and the alternatives it holds for humanity.

In Parts II and III, we focus primarily on five major types of societies—hunting and gathering, horticultural, agrarian, industrializing, and industrial—and analyze them in terms of their basic technology, demographic patterns, economy, polity, social stratification, religion and ideology, and kinship. We believe that this holistic approach—viewing societies as systems of interrelated elements—is far more productive than the traditional approach, which examines a succession of institutions more or less independently of one another and of the larger social system of which they are a part.

Changes since the Last Edition

Although the basic theory is unaltered, we have made many changes since the last edition. Our chief objective has been to make more visible to students the linkages between the analyses of empirical materials in Parts II and III and the basic theory developed in Part I. We have also tried to make the text as clear, as readable, and as interesting as possible, to achieve a smoother flow of ideas, and to add new material where it is useful for purposes of clarification or interest. Finally, we have endeavored to update factual material on contemporary societies and to cover certain topics which we had omitted in earlier editions.

All of the changes are detailed in our *Instructor's Manual* (available from McGraw-Hill), but the more important of them can be listed here. At the end of Chapter 2 we have expanded the unit "Reassembling the System" to include a discussion of the important concept of institutions and to emphasize the dynamic qualities of human societies. Chapter 3 has been substantially overhauled, primarily to disentangle the explanation of the process of social and cultural change in individual societies from the explanation of change in the world system as a whole. In Chapter 4, we have added a unit to explain the need for measurement and statistics in sociology and to introduce several basic statistics used later in the volume.

One of the most important changes in the text is the addition of units at the ends of Chapters 5, 6, 7, 12, and 13 that serve to place the type of society that has been examined in a larger theoretical perspective. In Chapters 5, 6, and 7, the discussion is accompanied by a flowchart that links the characteristics of the particular societal type to general theory and clarifies the causal relationships among those characteristics. We have also introduced, in Chapter 6, an important new hypothesis about the causes of the shift from hunting and gathering to horticulture, and, in Chapter 7, a flowchart to explain the slow rate of technological innovation in the agrarian era. The concluding unit of Chapter 8, which summarizes sociocultural evolution up to the eve of the Industrial Revolution, does so now in terms of the basic trends in human history presented initially in Chapter 3, a format that should prove useful to students.

There is a considerable amount of new and revised material in Chapter 9, including a new flowchart showing the causes of the Industrial Revolution, and the analysis of the causes of the continuing revolution is now more firmly grounded in theory. In Chapter 10, we have included democracy in our discussion of the major new ideologies of the industrial era, and introduced an important distinction between democratic socialism and revolutionary socialism. The unit on the economy is now included in this chapter and addresses some new points (e.g., the shift from labor-intensive to capital-intensive industry, the emergence of the world economic system) and expands on others (e.g., the comparison of Marxist and non-Marxist economies). Similarly, Chapter 11 has more comprehensive discussions of Marxist polities and of sex stratification in industrial societies, both Marxist and non-Marxist. The unit on the family in industrial societies (Chapter 12) contains a great deal of new material on the causes of change in family life and on the disruption of the nuclear family. There is also a new section on the mass media, a more comprehensive discussion of the problems of industrial societies, and a new closing unit that analyzes the consequences of industrialization.

A similar unit in Chapter 13 sets industrializing societies and their problems more explicitly within the framework of ecological-evolutionary theory and offers a critical analysis of both modernization and dependency theories. Finally, the analysis of the future (Chapter 14) has been almost totally rewritten.

We hope that the reaction of the majority of instructors to these changes will be as favorable as the reactions of the several who were kind enough to review the manuscript prior to publication. For we remain committed to the belief that the introductory course in sociology should provide students with a systematic theoretical perspective that is capable of organizing and explaining the vast body of information that sociology has acquired. Without such a framework, students leave the course with bits and scraps of information that are soon forgotten. With it, however, they have a tool that they can use throughout their lives to order and organize the otherwise confusing flood of information with which members of modern industrial societies are inundated.

Acknowledgments

It is not possible to acknowledge all our intellectual debts in the brief space available. Those who read this volume will almost certainly recognize the influence of Thomas Malthus, Charles Darwin, Herbert Spencer, Karl Marx, Max Weber, Thorstein Veblen, William Graham Sumner, Albert Keller, William Ogburn, V. Gordon Childe, George Peter Murdock, R. H. Tawney, Sir Julian Huxley, George Gaylord Simpson, Leslie White, Julian Steward, and C. Wright Mills, to name but a few. The note citations at the end of this volume should be regarded as further acknowledgments of indebtedness and appreciation.

Quite a number of scholars have been kind enough to provide us with critical comments and suggestions for one or more of the four editions of *Human Societies* to date. Those to whom we owe a real debt in this connection include E. Jackson Baur, William Catton, Jr., Ronald Cosper, Alfred E. Emerson, David Featherman, George Furniss, Walter Goldschmidt, Amos Hawley, Paul Heckert, Joan Huber, Donald Irish, Peter Kott, Philip Marcus, Patrick Nolan, Ross Purdy, Leo Rigsby, Norman Storer, Edward O. Wilson, and Everett K. Wilson.

We also thank our editor at McGraw-Hill, Eric Munson, for all he has done to facilitate the publication of this edition. And we owe a special word of appreciation to Anna Tyndall for her outstanding work in preparing the manuscript for the publisher. Her unfailing skill and good humor, in the face of illegible copy and a succession of urgent deadlines, helped to preserve our faith in the ability of humanity to overcome almost any obstacle.

Gerhard Lenski
Jean Lenski

PART I

Theoretical Foundations

CHAPTER 1

Starting Points

The twentieth century has been a time of revolutionary change for every aspect of human life. New technologies, new problems, and new beliefs and values confront people everywhere. This is reflected in our language, which is shot through with words and phrases that either did not exist or had very different meanings only a short time ago:

. . . the pill . . . the bomb . . . nuclear power . . . solar energy . . . strip mining . . . synfuel . . . air pollution . . . acid rain . . . the energy crisis . . . the population explosion . . . the Third World . . . germ warfare . . . genetic engineering . . . organ transplants . . . pacemakers . . . kidney dialysis . . . open-heart surgery . . . automation . . . the computer . . . silicon chips . . . data banks . . . electronic surveillance . . . instant replay . . . racism . . . sexism . . . gay liberation . . . transsexuals . . . hard rock . . . grass . . . the drug culture . . . the generation gap . . . living wills . . . pulling the plug . . .

What caused this revolution? Where is it taking us? And most important, how can we control it? How can we be sure it does not culminate in a nuclear holocaust, an ecological disaster, or an Orwellian 1984?

Questions like these force us to face the unpleasant fact that we are like people hurtling through time and space in an enormous rocket ship on which their survival depends. The ship is our society and, though it seems familiar to us because we have lived in it since birth, our knowledge of the forces acting on it and of the mechanisms for controlling it is dangerously limited. We obviously have a vested interest in learning more about our own society, as well as about the other societies that are hurtling into the future alongside us.

Sociology is the branch of science that specializes in the study of human societies.* Its interests are broad: sociologists study every aspect of societal life from marriage relations to international relations. This volume provides an introduction to the field from the perspective of *macro*sociology—which simply means that our primary focus and our ultimate concern will be human societies themselves. Smaller social units (e.g., families, religious groups, work organizations, governmental bureaucracies) will also be important in our inquiry, but they will be studied in the context of the total society of which they are part.

As we study human societies, we will do so within the framework of *ecological-evolutionary theory*. As its name suggests, this theory is concerned with two very important things. First, it seeks to understand the ecology of human societies—that is, the relations of societies to their environments, both biophysical (i.e., terrain, climate, natural resources, and so on) and social (i.e., the other societies with which they interact). Second, it seeks to understand their evolution—how and why societies change, why they are different from one another, and what lies behind the rapid pace of change in societies today.

At this point, it may be useful to clarify the meanings of two words we have just used: *science* and *theory*. Many people are inclined to think of science as being primarily a body of facts, and they are not sure what theory means, or whether it should even be considered a part of science. Carl Sagan, the astronomer, addressed this question, noting that "Science is a way of thinking much more than it is a body of knowledge. Its goal is to find out how the world works, to seek what regularities there may be, to penetrate to the connections of things from subnuclear particles . . . to living organisms, the social community, and thence to the cosmos as a whole."[1] As a means of attaining these goals, every branch of science from high energy physics to macrosociology constructs theories.

A theory is essentially an explanation of some aspect of the world around us, an explanation that reveals both the "connections" among things and the "regularities"—the natural laws or causes—that underlie them. Every part of such an explanation, each individual hypothesis, must be repeatedly scrutinized and tested under new conditions, and it must be altered, if necessary, in the light of new evidence and new insights. To gain widespread acceptance in the scientific community, a theory or hypothesis must be capable of explaining not only what has been learned through past observation and research, but evidence gleaned from current research as well.

Since the subjects to which scientists address themselves range from infant behavior to the movement of stellar galaxies, the techniques of research,

---

*Definitions of this and other terms are provided in the Glossary on pages 443–448, and readers are urged to consult unfamiliar terms frequently.

measuring, and testing vary enormously from one discipline to another, and so does the form theory takes. But in every branch of science, there is a continuing search for "connections" and "regularities," and an endless process of theoretical refinement and revision.*

Human Societies: Their Place in Nature

The first thing required by this view of science, as well as by ecological-evolutionary theory, is that we consider the relationship of human societies to the other parts of the world of nature. This relationship is widely misunderstood, largely because of a tendency to exaggerate the uniqueness of human societies and to treat them as if they existed in a world apart from the rest of nature. But this is a mistake: *societies, human and nonhuman alike, are part of the natural order.*[2]

As many scholars have observed, the world of nature is structured rather like a system of wheels within wheels, with all the parts ultimately related. Thus, when we examine any object carefully, we discover it is made up of various differentiated parts which are, in turn, composed of still smaller parts. Similarly, when we look in the other direction, we see that our original object is part of a larger, more inclusive system, which is, itself, part of an even larger, more inclusive one.

Figure 1.1 provides a necessarily oversimplified view of this complex system of organization. Elementary particles, such as protons and electrons, form the lowest level. These are combined in various ways to form atoms, such as carbon and radium. Atoms, in turn, are organized into molecules, such as water, salt, amino acids, and proteins. Though Figure 1.1 does not show it, molecules constitute more than a single level in the hierarchy, because some of the simpler molecules, the amino acids, for example, are the building blocks for more complex and more inclusive molecules, such as the proteins.

Once we go beyond the level of molecules, we encounter the important division between living and nonliving things. Since our concern is with human societies, there is no need to consider all the levels of nonliving matter. Suffice it to note that the structure leads by degrees to the level of the giant galaxies that wheel through space and ends with the universe itself.

Societies, however, are part of the biotic world: they are one of the ways in which living things are organized. More specifically, they are a form of organization found in some species of multicellular organisms. Because many kinds of multicellular organisms do *not* have societies, however, there is also a line in Figure 1.1 that bypasses that block and directly connects multicellular organisms to species. This brings us to the question of why some species are organized into societies while others are not.

---

*For one example of theoretical revision in macrosociology, see the discussion of the origins of horticulture in Chapter 6, pages 134–136.

6

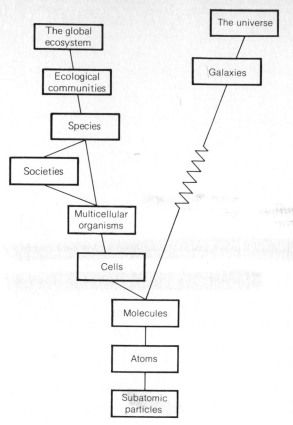

FIGURE 1.1 Levels of organization in the world of nature.

The Basic Function of Societies

The development of the societal mode of organization has been called "one of the great steps in evolution, as important as the emergence of the cell, the multicellular organism, and the vertebrate system."[3] Actually, societies evolved not once, but a number of times, independently and in widely scattered lines of the animal kingdom. They are concentrated in three areas: (1) many species of vertebrates, especially among mammals, birds, and fish; (2) the social insects (ants, termites, and many species of wasps and bees); and (3) the colonial invertebrates (such as corals, sponges, and Portuguese man-of-war).[4]

Why did so many and such diverse species develop this particular mode of organization? Quite simply, because being organized this way helped these species survive. In other words, the societal mode of life became common in the animal kingdom for the same reason characteristics like wings, lungs, and protective coloring became common: they are all important *adaptive mechanisms*.

But societal organization is different from adaptive mechanisms that enable species to perform some particular activity—the way wings, for example, enable creatures to fly, or lungs enable them to exchange oxygen and

FIGURE 1.2 Elephant society as an adaptive mechanism: adult members forming a protective ring around their young.

other gases with the air. What distinguishes social species from all the rest is a characteristic that has the potential for being used in a great variety of ways. For every social creature has *an enhanced capacity for cooperation.*

To those who study animal behavior, "cooperation" means simply that the individuals in a given species associate with and interact with one another for their mutual benefit. It does not mean they cooperate in every activity, nor does it imply that they are never competitive or antagonistic toward one another.

The types of cooperative activities in which the various social species engage include reproduction, nurture of their young, securing food, and defense against predators and other dangers.* Some social species rely on cooperative behavior in virtually every facet of life. Others are less involved in, or less dependent on, social activities. But every social species benefits

---

*Even *non*social animals display cooperative activity in the area of reproduction (i.e., they reproduce sexually). But a species is not classified as "social" if its cooperative activity is limited to this single, though important, area.

substantially from the fact that its members are genetically programmed to try to solve at least some of their problems by acting together instead of individually.

Once we recognize that human societies are, first and foremost, adaptive mechanisms that are vital to the survival of our species, we see why we cannot divorce our study of them from the study of the rest of the biotic world.* We see, too, why it is imperative that students of human societies have a clear understanding of the biological foundations of the societal mode of organization in general and of human societies in particular.

A Definition of Human Societies

A prominent zoologist recently defined a society as "a group of individuals belonging to the same species and organized in a cooperative manner."[5] This definition has the virtue of simplicity and, at the same time, encompasses the fundamental points of concern to biologists.

Sociologists, however, need to add something to this definition before it can be applied to human societies. Virtually every human society of which we have knowledge has had subgroups within it—families, communities, and specialized associations of various kinds—and the definition above does not differentiate between these subgroups and the larger societies of which they are a part. To accomplish this, we need to specify that human societies are *autonomous groups*, that is, free from outside political control. Thus, a human society may be defined as *an autonomous group of people engaged in a broad range of cooperative activities*. This clearly applies to American society, Soviet society, or Brazilian society, while excluding such subgroups as America's AFL-CIO, Soviet Jewry, and the population of Rio de Janeiro. None of the latter is autonomous: all are politically subordinate to the societies of which they are part.

Sometimes it is difficult for biologists to say for certain whether a particular group of animals does or does not comprise a society. This is because social species, as we noted, engage in cooperative behavior in varying degrees. For example, apart from the nurture of their young, many mammals expend little time or energy on social activities, while some of the social insects are immersed in them. Thus, between the extremes represented by completely solitary animals and the most social ones, there is a scale or continuum with countless fine gradations along which all the others are ranged.

In the case of human societies, there are gradations not only in terms of the cooperative behavior displayed by their members, but also in terms of the *autonomy* of the groups. Consider, for example, a more or less typical American Indian society of the sixteenth or seventeenth century, an autonomous group whose members were caught up in a complex system of social

---

*This is not to suggest that the study of human societies can be swallowed up by the biological sciences. It simply means it is necessary to take the biological foundations of human life fully into account when analyzing human societies.

activity. In time, the group established trade relations with Europeans or Americans and eventually came under their political control. This process often involved the gradual absorption of the Indian society by the larger, more powerful society, but it would be impossible, in such a case, to say precisely at what point the Indian society ceased to exist (i.e., lost its autonomy) and became merely a subgroup within the other society. Autonomy is clearly not an "all or nothing" quality. Rather, like cooperative behavior (and like many other phenomena, such as weight and temperature), its existence is a matter of degree.

The Biological Foundation of Human Societies

The foundation of every society in the biotic world is the genetic heritage of the creatures who form it—which explains why the structure of a termite society and the activities that go on within it are so different from those of a society of wolves or birds. If we want to understand the structure of human societies and what goes on in them, we obviously have to begin with the genetic heritage of humans. Thus, we will spend the rest of this chapter examining this heritage. Our goal is not to understand how we, as individuals, differ from one another, but to understand those more fundamental and important characteristics that we all possess simply because we are members of Homo sapiens and not some other species.

During the last hundred years, there has been a lot of confusion and controversy on this subject of human nature. One view was popularized by some of Charles Darwin's more enthusiastic followers, who argued that science had proved Homo sapiens was not, after all, the exalted being humans so long imagined themselves to be, but merely an animal that could be understood in purely biological terms.

Most scholars have since rejected this view on the grounds that it involves what a leading evolutionary theorist, George Gaylord Simpson, once termed the "nothing but" fallacy. In his words:

> To say that man is nothing but an animal is to deny, by implication, that he has essential attributes other than those of all animals. This would be false as applied to any kind of an animal; it is not true that a dog, a robin, an oyster, or an amoeba is nothing but an animal. As applied to man the "nothing but" fallacy is more serious than in application to any other sort of animal, because man is an entirely new kind of animal in ways altogether fundamental for understanding of his nature. It is important to realize that man is an animal, but it is even more important to realize that the essence of his unique nature lies precisely in those characteristics that are not shared with any other animal.[6]

In reacting against the "nothing but" fallacy, however, many social scientists backed into an equally unsatisfactory position. By ignoring or minimizing the biological foundation of human societies, they seemed almost to deny our animal heritage. Happily, however, there is a third view which recognizes that our species has some characteristics in common with all living things, some that we share with certain other species but not with all, and some that are uniquely human. In the pages that follow, we will consider each of these in turn so that we may better understand the biological foundation on which all human societies rest.

Characteristics Humans Share with All Other Species

When we first consider the world of living things in all its diversity and variety, it is hard to imagine that there are any characteristics which *all* plants and animals share. Yet beneath their obvious and immense differences, the human, the slime mold, the rose, and the amoeba are alike in some very important ways.

To begin with, all living things have *the same underlying structure*.[7] For every organism is composed of one or more cells, and all cells are composed of the same basic materials: water, mineral solids, and organic compounds such as carbohydrates, fats, proteins, nucleotides, and their derivatives. What is more, every cell contains everything that is necessary (genes, enzymes, etc.) for performing the most basic life functions. Therefore, *the same basic activities* go on in every organism, whether it is single-celled or highly complex. First, there is metabolism, a complex set of activities that might be said to "run the machinery of life."*[8] Second, every organism responds in a self-preserving way to internal and external stimuli. And third, every organism has a capacity for reproducing itself.

Why are the basic structure and functioning of such diverse forms of life fundamentally alike? Simpson answers that it is because

> . . . all living things are brothers in the very real, material sense that all have arisen from one source and been developed within the divergent intricacies of one process.[9]

In other words, the *most* basic thing shared by all forms of life is *involvement in the process of biological evolution*.

Biological evolution is the process of gradual genetic change and development through which every species of plant or animal has developed out of a preexisting species.[10] This process has been going on for approximately 3.5 billion years, ever since life began on our planet. Every change in the characteristics of a species—whether it has involved appearance or behavior†—has been a manifestation of change in its genetic makeup. The enormous complexity and diversity of plants and animals today testify to an incredible number of such changes.

Genes, the basic units of heredity, are complex chemicals that are present

---

*Metabolism consists of three processes: *nutrition*, which provides the organism with the raw materials (nutrients) it requires; *respiration*, which uses the nutrients to produce energy; and *synthesis*, which uses them for tissue repair and growth.

†"Behavior" refers to *any response by an organism to internal or external stimuli*. Thus, behavior includes chemical processes like digestion and suntanning, and activities like hearing and thinking, as well as overt movements like crawling or biting.

FIGURE 1.3 "Broderick, what do you know about evolution?"

in every cell of every organism. An organism may have as many as 3 or 4 million genes in every cell. Rather like sets of built-in commands, genes trigger a variety of chemical processes in various parts of a plant or animal and, in so doing, determine its structure, how it functions, and how it differs from other organisms. When it reproduces, the organism passes on to its offspring precise copies of some or all of its own genes.* This is why the basic life processes are so orderly and predictable—why elephants do not give birth to butterflies, mushrooms do not grow as tall as oaks, and pigs do not produce chlorophyll.

To understand how evolutionary change occurs, we must focus on a *population*. This term refers to an aggregation of organisms of the same species that tend to interbreed because of geographic proximity. A herd of bison, the sparrows on an offshore island, and the earthworms in a local patch of forest are all examples of a population. Although most reproductive activity takes place *within* a population, there is almost always occasional interbreeding with nearby populations of the same species.

The members of a population are fundamentally alike in both appearance and behavior, but they are not identical. This means that some genes in a population are found in every member, while others are found in varying proportions of the population. Since the genetic heritage of a population consists of all these varied individual heritages, biologists have coined the term *gene pool* to refer to the genes of all the members considered collectively.

The ultimate origin of genetic variation, and of every gene in biotic history, is *mutation*. A mutation is essentially an accident: a slight alteration occurs in the chemical structure of a gene as it is being replicated, with the result that the "copy"—the gene that is transmitted to the offspring—does not carry the same chemical message as the original—the gene of the parent.

Mutations occur continually in every population,† but they are never purposive. For example, a new gene in a white moth population does not arise

---

*The copies are precise, that is, except in the event of mutation (see below).
†The cause of most mutations is unknown, although some are known to result from exposure to such agents as x-rays and certain chemicals.

for the purpose of making the insects a color that blends with the tree bark on which they alight, thus making them safer from predators. Rather, mutations are *random*, or chance, occurrences. Most of them, in fact, are actually harmful to the genetic makeup of the offspring into which they are introduced —much the way a random bit of metal substituted for a small part in a smoothly running machine is far more likely to harm than improve its operation. But every now and then, a mutation *does* produce an "improved" gene, a gene that gives its bearer an advantage (usually a very slight one) in its efforts to survive and reproduce. In this way, some new genes eventually become established in a gene pool and may even become part of the genetic makeup of every individual in the population.

But mutations are only the beginning of genetic variation in species that reproduce sexually, as nearly all species do. Because this mode of reproduction involves the genes of two individuals, genes and sets of genes are, in effect, shuffled and reshuffled over the generations, creating ever new combinations, or *recombinations*, as they are called.

Just as important in the evolutionary process as a genetically varied population is the *environment*. This term refers to everything external to a population that influences it or is influenced by it. Its environment includes inorganic matter, physical phenomena (such as climate), other living things (among them, other populations of the same species), and everything the population requires to survive: food, moisture, air, light, and so on.

This relationship between population and environment is the most basic one in the biotic world. It is an intimate and dynamic relationship in which each contributes to, and is affected by, change in the other. And it is *this relationship that shapes evolution*.

We can understand how this happens if we focus on the gradual change that takes place in a population's genetic attributes—or, more precisely, on the change in the composition of its gene pool. Over a period of time, some genes become more frequent, others become less so, and some become rare or even disappear. This happens because some members of the population are reproducing their genes more frequently than others.

In most populations, the great majority of organisms do not reproduce at all. They die before reproductive age because of the universal tendency of living things to have more offspring than the environment can support. (An oyster, for example, lays more than a million eggs per season, a tapeworm 120,000 per day.[11]) The rest of the population, meanwhile, not only have different numbers of offspring, but offspring with different genetic potential for surviving and reproducing themselves.

Over the long run, the thing that determines this differential reproduction is the adaptive value of the various genes and sets of genes in the population. The genetic traits that "work best" for a particular species in a particular environment are "selected" for reproduction through a natural process (i.e., one not contrived by humans): hence the term *natural selection*. Each new generation of individuals in a population is essentially like the parental type, and it must cope with essentially the same environment. But each new generation also has a supply of genetic innovations that will be put to the test, and discarded or used in the never-ending process of maintaining an adequate relationship with the environment or achieving a better one.

All the populations of a species normally change in unison—that is, the species *as a whole* evolves. This is what we would expect of reproductive units that share with one another, at least occasionally, their different genetic "solutions" to the challenges of similar environments. A population that is well adapted to its environment is more likely to reject genetic alterations than to accept them, and the same is true of the species as a whole: it tends to resist change. As a result, a species does not usually experience major structural change during its span on earth. Its change is gradual and not dramatic.

The story may be different, however, during *speciation*, the process by which a new species splits off from its parental line. Speciation usually occurs in a small population that has become reproductively isolated from others of its kind. This is typically a consequence of a growth in numbers that causes the parent population to spread over such a wide area that some of its populations are struggling to survive on the outer fringe of the geographical area to which the species is adapted. Eventually, one of these peripheral populations may be completely cut off from the rest.

In a small, marginal population like this, one that barely manages to relate to its environment to obtain its basic needs, any useful new genetic trait (mutation or recombination) spreads rapidly. In effect, the rate of natural selection speeds up because of the peculiar circumstances. If such a population survives (and most do not), it will probably change more quickly than the other populations of its species, and not in unison with them. In a span of time that by evolutionary standards is very brief indeed (i.e., only hundreds or thousands of years), it may become so different genetically from the parental stock that effective interbreeding would no longer be possible if the separated populations were reunited. Two species would exist where there was one before.

Over the mind-boggling expanse of time since life first appeared on our planet, these same natural forces have been constantly at work, producing genetic variation purely at random, and then selecting from it through a process that is *not* random, but is guided by the relation of living things to their environments. The genetic heritage of every extant species, *including our own*, is thus quite literally the product of billions of years of biological experimentation.

Characteristics Humans Share Only with Some Other Species

We humans obviously have more in common with most living things than the heritage of living cells and the fact that we are all caught up in the process of biological evolution. As the preceding explanation of evolutionary theory would lead us to expect, the closer our biological kinship with other species, the greater the range of characteristics we share with them. Thus, we have more in common with other members of the animal kingdom than with plants, and more in common with other vertebrates than with invertebrates.

For the same reason, we are more like other mammals than like nonmammalian vertebrates, such as reptiles, birds, and fish. We share with all mammals a wide assortment of traits that include warm-bloodedness; body hair; lungs; four limbs (or vestiges of them) with nails; claws, hoofs, or digits; external genitalia; internal fertilization; teeth that come in only twice and that are differentiated according to use; a bony palate that permits breathing and chewing at the same time; a relatively elaborate brain; a marked capacity for learning; and, in the female, mammary glands that secrete milk. In addition, all mammals are social animals: there is, at a minimum, the cooperative behavior displayed by mothers in the nurture of their young, and in many mammalian species patterns of cooperation go far beyond this (e.g., hunting by a pack of wolves, or grouping for mutual defense by a herd of elephants).

When we compare ourselves only to other primate species, our common traits are even more striking. In addition to those we share by virtue of being mammals are such characteristics as upright posture and flexible arms, flexible hands with separated fingers and opposable thumbs, year-round sexual readiness, prolonged immaturity, greater reliance on the sense of sight than of smell, an enlarged neocortex, and a high order of intelligence. As the author of a leading biology text recently wrote, ''Primates are the most intelligent and also the most curious, inventive, mischievous, and destructive of the mammals.''[12]

One cannot compare humans with other species this way without recognizing the extent to which basic patterns of human life are rooted in our genetic systems. For it is not just a matter of similarities between our anatomy and physiology and that of the other primates: it is a matter of basic behavioral tendencies and predispositions. If we humans are cooperative and live in societies, it is clearly not because we choose to be social creatures but because of our genetic heritage. Similarly, if we rely on learning as a basic mode of adaptation to the world we live in, it is not because we decided it was the best thing to do, nor did we invent learning. Rather, these are basic expressions of our mammalian and primate heritage.

Modern research has shed a good deal of light on the way we and the rest of the primate line came to be distinguished by the particular characteristics that set us apart from other species. The basic elements in our package of adaptive traits began to be forged about 65 million years ago when a mouse-sized ancestor of modern primates moved into a new environmental niche and began living in trees.[13] Manual dexterity and good vision were clearly of greater importance for tree-dwellers than for their cousins on the ground. Safe movement from tree to tree depended far more on sight than on smell, which had long been more important to the survival of ground-dwelling mammals. At the same time, as a consequence of the dangers inherent in arboreal life, there was a developing solicitude for the young which gradually led to stronger social ties between mothers and their offspring. The small individual whose agility, good vision, and vigilant mother kept him safely in the treetops would be more likely to reproduce the genes governing these critical traits than would the youngster, slightly less well endowed in these respects, who fell to the ground. The forces of natural selection thus began shaping the emerging primate line.

FIGURE 1.4   All mammalian species have a marked capacity for learning: among primates, this is enhanced by the prolonged physical immaturity of the young. Chimpanzee family, with sister nuzzling brother in mother's arms.

That basic combination of traits (i.e., manual dexterity, excellent vision, and stronger social ties) apparently provided the foundation for further genetic change, particularly growth of the forebrain and increasing reliance on learning and intelligence as basic adaptive mechanisms. Although these traits are found in some degree in all mammals, the evolution of nonprimates took them in other directions, and quite different traits became critical components of their genetic makeup. Great strength, stealth, and fecundity, for example, are important supplements to the ability to learn among, respectively, elephants, cats, and mice. But the primate line came to rely primarily on intelligence and learning. In fact, when the anatomy and physiology of primates are compared to that of other mammals, they are considered to be relatively unspecialized except for a single organ: the brain.[14]

Learning is the process by which an organism acquires, through experience, information with behavior-modifying potential.[15] This means that when it comes to solving problems, an animal that can learn is not completely dependent on the behavioral repertoire provided by its genetic heritage. Instead, its own experiences become a factor shaping its behavior. In the case of humans and some of the higher primates, the evolution of the forebrain has reached the point where they are able to store such a wide range of memories that they can learn by *insight*; in other words, they can see into a situation, as it were, and analyze the factors involved, thereby avoiding the time-consuming and often costly and painful process of trial and error.[16]

The adaptive value of the ability to learn is greatly enhanced when animals live together in groups. This gives the individual animal more opportunity to observe, and to communicate with, others of its kind. In effect, a social animal benefits from the experience of its fellows as well as from its own. Social life thus multiplies the amount of information available to a population. In the words of two leading students of primate life, "The [primate] group is the locus of knowledge and information far exceeding that of the individual member. It is in the group that experience is pooled."[17]

The adaptive value of the ability to learn is also greatly enhanced among primates by the prolonged physical immaturity of their young. The young of most species are genetically equipped to fend for themselves from the moment of birth. For mammals and birds, however, there is a period in which the young depend on sustained contact with one or both parents. In the case of primates, this period of dependence is especially prolonged, a fact which is linked both with their enhanced capacity for learning and with their dependence on a societal mode of life.

Characteristics Unique to Humans

We do not require science to tell us that our species is unique. Only humans build skyscrapers, set off nuclear explosions, philosophize, compose symphonies, travel in space, and do a thousand other things no other species can do. This seems to suggest that our genetic makeup must be profoundly different from that of every other species.

Such is not the case, however: recent immunological research has shown that chimpanzees are as close genetically to humans as horses are to zebras, and closer than dogs are to foxes. One estimate is that humans and chimpanzees share 99 per cent of their genetic materials, and other research suggests that gorillas may be even more closely related to us than that.[18]

Since there can be no doubt that a species' behavior is intimately related to its genetic makeup, why is it that the behavior and the activities of these great apes are not more like our own? The explanation is that at some point in the evolution of one primate line, there occurred a series of genetic changes, which, although relatively minor, had revolutionary consequences for behavior.

These critical changes occurred in the structure of the brain. Although they are not fully understood, it is certain that one change involved the relocation of the center of vocalization. In every other species, including chimpanzees and gorillas, this voice-control center lies in an old part of the mammalian brain that is intimately involved with instinct and strong emotion. But in the hominid line,* the processes of biological evolution had shifted this center to the neocortex, the newer part of the brain, where learning takes place and where learned information is stored.[19] In effect, a new and far more intimate relationship had been forged between the past experiences of an

---

*Hominid refers to humanlike creatures. There were once a number of different hominid species, but ours is the only one that exists today.

individual and the sounds which that individual produced. The consequence of such changes in brain structure was that *hominids could create symbols.*

Because of this unique ability to create and use symbols, and eventually to develop symbol systems, or *languages,* our ancestors' capacity for learning, and for sharing what they learned with others of their kind, was increased tremendously. And this enormous capacity for learning was, in turn, the foundation for a totally new kind of adaptive mechanism, one without parallel in the biotic world: *culture.*[20]

Because culture is such a basic and crucial feature of human life, it is important that we understand precisely what it is. This term has been defined in a variety of ways over the years, but implicit in every definition has been a recognition that culture rests upon our species' great capacity for learning. Scientists, both social and biological, have increasingly come to speak of culture in terms of a *learned heritage* that is passed on from generation to generation. Moreover, they recognize that a human society's cultural heritage is as important to its survival as its genetic heritage. The essential distinction between them is in the way they are transmitted: one is passed on through genes, the other through symbols. Thus, we can best define culture by saying that it consists of *symbol systems and the information they convey.**

What are symbols that they have made such a difference to our species? After all, the members of other species also communicate among themselves, using *signals* to convey information. In other words, both signals and symbols are *information conveyers.* But there is a vital difference: the meaning of a signal is wholly or largely determined by the genetic makeup of those who use it; the meaning of a symbol is not.

The best way to understand this distinction is to look at examples of the two kinds of information conveyers, beginning with signals.[22] Animals signal with movements, sounds, odors, color changes, and so on, and the signals they produce vary greatly in the amount of information they convey. The simplest type of signal is one that is used by an organism in only a single context and that has only one possible meaning—the sexually attractive scent released by the female moth, for example. In contrast, some species are able to transmit more complex information by varying the frequency or intensity of a signal or by combining different signals simultaneously or in sequence. Thus, a foraging honeybee returns to her hive and performs the "waggle dance" to direct fellow workers to the food source she has located.[23] By varying the movements and vibrations that comprise the dance, she communicates enough information about direction and distance to enable her sisters to land remarkably near the target, and at the same time adds a comment on the quality of the food supply and the state of the weather.

In some species, especially birds and mammals, the use of and response to

---

*A number of anthropologists and sociologists have included behavior and material artifacts in their definitions of culture, but it seems more appropriate to regard these as *products* of culture. This is in keeping with the recent trend described by Milton Singer in his article on culture in the *International Encyclopedia of the Social Sciences.* He reports that increasingly, in definitions and analyses of culture, "behavior, observed social relations, i.e., social structure, and material artifacts . . . are not themselves considered the constituents of culture."[21]

signals is partially learned. The young of certain species of birds, for example, must learn some elements of their territorial songs from adults.[24] Humans, too, communicate with signals, such as yawns and laughter, that we learn to modify and use in different ways. Thus, we learn to smother a yawn deliberately to indicate boredom. But whether it is simple or complex, and whether or not there is learning involved, a signal is essentially *an information conveyer whose form and related meaning are both determined genetically*.

Symbols, by contrast, are not genetically determined. The ability to create and use symbols does depend on genetics, but the form of a symbol and the meaning attached to it do not. Thus, a symbol is *an information conveyer whose form is arbitrary and whose meaning is determined by those who use it*.

Humans share the ability to create symbols with no other creature. Over the course of history, however, a variety of animals from plow horses to circus seals have been trained to recognize, respond to, and even use, in a fashion, a number of symbols. In recent years, chimpanzees and gorillas have proved to have a remarkable ability in this regard, learning to use up to two hundred different symbols, and even combining a few of them to convey a more complex meaning.

It is important to recognize, however, that none of these animals has ever created a symbol, has ever assigned its own original meaning to a gesture, sound, or object. Rather, the symbols they use were designed especially for them. What is more, these creatures show no prelanguage features in the wild.[25] Thus, while they appear to be fairly well along the way to a neurological level that would make symbol creation possible for them, they provide a strong contrast to the human situation with respect to symbols.[26] For we not only quickly master the language of the group into which we are born but are capable, at a very early age, of devising new symbols and even entire symbol systems. Small children concoct names for their stuffed animals and sometimes go on to make up "secret codes." And at least one case has been well documented in which a set of twins, first thought to be retarded because no one understood their speech, proved to have invented an entirely original and complex language by which they communicated with one another.

We can appreciate the significance of symbols only when we understand their "genetic independence." Take the sound of the third letter of our alphabet, for example. We use that sound to refer to the act of perceiving, to a bishop's jurisdiction, and to a large body of water, as well as to the letter itself. Spanish-speaking people, meanwhile, use it to say "yes," and French-speaking people to say "yes," "if," "whether," or "so." Obviously there is no connection between these various meanings, nor is there any genetically determined connection between the meanings and the sound. They are simply arbitrary usages adopted by the members of certain societies.

Further evidence that symbols are determined by their users and not by genes is the ease with which we alter them. When Chaucer wrote "Hir nose tretis, hir yen greye as glas . . . sikerly," he meant to say—in fact, he did say—"Her nose well-formed, her eyes gray as glass . . . certainly." English-speaking people have simply altered many of their symbols since his day. Slang is created by the reverse procedure: the symbol itself remains unchanged, but it is given a new meaning. The words "bread" and "dough," for example, have both come to be used to refer to money.

Although linguistic symbols are the most basic and important, they are not the only kind we use. For not only sounds, but anything to which humans assign a meaning, becomes a symbol. Thus, the cross has become a symbol of Christianity, the hammer and sickle a symbol of Russian communism. Every nation in the world today has a flag to represent it, and standardized symbols communicate basic traffic directions on our highways.

Because they are not genetically determined, symbols can be combined and recombined indefinitely to form symbol systems of fantastic complexity, subtlety, and flexibility. There are no intrinsic limits to the amount and variety of information they can handle. The only limits are set by the physical characteristics of those who use them, that is, by the efficiency and capacity of the human brain and nervous system and the accuracy of our senses. And symbol systems help overcome even these limitations. For example, our species' memory (i.e., its capacity for storing information) has been greatly increased by the use of written symbols and written records.

In the final analysis, the importance of symbol systems lies not in what they are, but in what they have made it possible for our species to become. Although we are all born into the human family, we become truly human only through the use of symbols. Without them, we cannot develop the unique qualities we normally associate with humanness. For symbols are more than a means of communication: they are the basic tools with which we think and plan, dream and remember, create and build, calculate, speculate, and moralize.

The difference between a human mind without symbols and that same mind with them is eloquently described in accounts of Helen Keller's early life. Miss Keller became both deaf and blind before she learned to talk. By the age of seven, after years devoid of meaningful communication with other people, she had become very much like a wild animal. Then a gifted teacher, Anne Sullivan, began trying to communicate with Helen by spelling words into her hands. Helen learned several words, but she did not yet comprehend the real significance of symbols. Then, in a moment that both women later described in moving terms, Helen suddenly realized that *everything* had a name, that *everything* could be communicated with symbols! In her own words, she felt "a thrill of returning thought."[27] The world that exists only for symbol users began to open to Helen Keller.

Miss Keller's experience helps us understand why the ancients, in their accounts of creation, so often linked the beginning of language with the beginning of the world. One of the oldest written texts from Egypt, for example, tells how Ptah, the creator of the world and the greatest of the gods, "pronounced the names of all things" as a central part of his act of creation.[28] Language also figures prominently in Chinese and Hindu creation myths. The book of Genesis tells us that the first thing Adam did after he was created was to name all the beasts and birds; and the Gospel According to St. John opens with the famous lines "In the beginning was the Word, and the Word was with God, and the Word was God." Significantly, the original Greek for "word" was *logos,* which meant not merely word, but meaning and reason. And *logos* is the root of our own word *"logic,"* and of the suffix *-logy,* used to denote science, as in biology or sociology.

In more recent times, the German scientist Alexander von Humboldt said, "No words, no world." And it is certainly true that the *human* world, the world of human societies, would not exist without words. Without symbols, human societies would lack their most distinctive feature: *culture.* With symbols, however, each of them has developed a rich cultural heritage to supplement its genetic heritage.

The Common Genetic Heritage of Humans

Attributes we share with the amoeba, attributes we share with the ape, attributes we share with no other living thing—these are the elements that make up our species' common genetic heritage. We have examined some facets of this heritage in detail, and we have barely alluded to others. Now it is important to look at this heritage *as a whole* and consider its implications. For the complex cluster of traits that is part of every human is also *the biological foundation of every human society.*

Summarizing these traits is not as easy as it might seem, however, for two reasons. First, there is no way to observe and study humans (except possibly newborn infants) *apart* from culture. After that, cultural influences become so pervasive that it is extremely difficult to distinguish between their effects and those of genetics.

The other reason it is so hard to identify our common traits is because of the *complexities* of human genetics. For example, an observable trait (i.e., a behavioral or physical characteristic) does not typically result from one particular gene, as we might suppose, but reflects the interaction of a number of genes. Any given gene, meanwhile, usually affects not a single trait, but a number of different traits. What is more, most traits are not determined by heredity alone, but by both genetic endowment and environmental factors. Because of these complexities, many things are still poorly understood. Which genes or sets of genes are common to us all? Which are variable (i.e., either not present in everyone, or present in different forms)? And what is the relative contribution of inheritance and environment to the variance observed in a particular trait? Answers are beginning to emerge in all these areas, but they are still just that—a beginning.

Enough is now known, however, to put to rest some older views of human nature. One of these, the "tabula rasa" hypothesis, held that the newborn infant's mind is like a blank page and that the eventual content is supplied entirely by the environment.[29] This view was extremely popular among philosophers and social scientists in the eighteenth, nineteenth, and early twentieth centuries because it provided the basis for a highly optimistic view of the future. For if babies are so malleable, it should be possible, with careful planning and proper education, to eliminate most of society's evils, such as war, crime, and economic exploitation. Events of the twentieth century, however, have raised grave doubts about human malleability and perfectibility.[30]

Meanwhile, the work of scientists and scholars in widely scattered disciplines has produced a clearer understanding not only of the human brain but of many other components of our common genetic heritage. At the risk of oversimplifying an extremely complex and still controversial subject, we will try to identify those elements that are most relevant to the study of human societies.

First, all humans have *the same fundamental needs*. To begin with, there are those basic physical requirements (for food, water, sleep, oxygen, elimination, etc.) that must be satisfied if we are merely to survive. We also have a variety of other common needs, needs whose satisfaction is not essential for individual survival or whose intensity varies greatly from one stage of life to another. These include sexual needs, the need for play, the need for new experience, and the need for social experience.[31] That these needs have as much of a genetic base as our "survival needs" has been well documented. The need for new experience, for example, is evident in the newborn infant, who exhibits a decided preference for visual variety and contrast and has "a bias to explore" that it begins to satisfy almost from the moment of birth.[32] The newborn also has such a fundamental need for social contact and stimulation that, if it is not satisfied, the child may not even survive.[33]

Second, we all develop a *variety of derivative needs*. Our common genetic makeup provides us with the potential for developing certain individual needs and desires in addition to those above, needs and desires that are largely the result of our social and cultural experiences. Because this experience varies from one society to another and among individuals in the same society, and also because genetic variations play a role in their development, the intensity of these needs varies greatly. But all of us have the potential for at least minimal development of any number of needs beyond those required for our mere survival. These include the need to control people and events, to possess things, to give and receive affection, to express one's self aesthetically and in other ways, to be respected and admired, to have emotional, aesthetic, or religious experiences, and to discern order and meaning in life.

Third, we all have *the same basic resources to use in satisfying our needs*. To begin with, we have such obvious physical equipment as legs, fingers, teeth, ears, bowels, heart, brain, and so on. Our brain is a particularly impressive resource: it provides us with the means of recording "memory traces" equivalent to the content of a thousand twenty-four-volume sets of the *Encyclopaedia Britannica* and is ten thousand times more densely packed with information than a computer.[34] In addition, we are genetically programmed for the automatic performance of a variety of activities (e.g., digestion, growth, ovulation, circulation, etc.) and have many valuable response sets and reflex actions (e.g., we pull away when we touch something hot). Paradoxically, some of our resources are hard to distinguish from our needs. This is true, for example, of the "exploring tendency," which is at one and the same time an expression of an innate need for new experience and a resource (i.e., an attribute that serves us in our efforts to satisfy other needs).

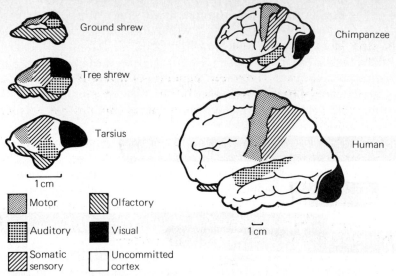

Ground shrew

Tree shrew

Tarsius

Chimpanzee

Human

1 cm

	Motor		Olfactory
	Auditory		Visual
	Somatic sensory		Uncommitted cortex

1 cm

FIGURE 1.5   The human brain is an impressive resource: it can record "memory traces" equivalent to 1,000 twenty-four-volume sets of the *Encyclopaedia Britannica*. Compare the size of the cerebral cortex of humans with that of other primates.

Because we all have essentially the same resources to use in satisfying the same basic needs, we behave in strikingly similar ways and develop strikingly similar social patterns. For example, because of the universal need for sleep, and because our eyes, unlike those of many species, are poorly designed for seeing in the dark, every human society has been geared to the same basic cycle of heightened daytime activity and reduced activity at night.

Fourth, we are all *dependent on the societal mode of life*, especially during our formative years. The human infant is born in a condition of extreme immaturity and helplessness. In fact, for its first year it experiences growth patterns (e.g., bone ossification, brain growth) that are part of *fetal* development in other primate species.*[35] Maturation proceeds at a slow pace: children require much longer to reach maturity than the young of other species (e.g., even the anthropoid apes reach sexual maturity by about the age of nine). And even as adults, most people cannot satisfy all their basic needs except through cooperative activities.

Fifth, as we have already observed, we all have *the capacity to create and use symbol systems*. This uniquely human ability, on which all culture rests, is compounded of a variety of genetic attributes, including such organs of speech as lips, tongue, palates, sinuses, and vocal cords. Far more important, however, are peculiarities of the human brain, specifically those unique areas of our cerebral cortex that control speech and abstract thought.[36] A growing number of linguists believe that despite the great variability of our 3,000

*The reason humans enter the world in an essentially embryonic state is apparently related to our brain. If the infant were to develop *in utero* an additional seven to twelve months, its increased head size would make birth impossible.

spoken languages—differences in vocabularies, in the sounds and combinations of sounds used, and in grammar, or the way words are "put together"—there is a "deep structure" common to them all.[37] This is thought to be the only explanation for the amazing speed and ease with which all normal human young learn language.[38] In other words, our genetic heritage does not bestow on us a vague, generalized capacity for speech (i.e., for communicating with oral symbols) but appears actually to determine the basic structure this speech will assume.

Sixth, related to our use of symbols, we all have *an immense capacity for learning, and for modifying our behavior in response to what we learn*. The result is a remarkable behavioral flexibility that frees us from the limitations of a single, hereditary set of behaviors or response sets. We are able to devise alternative patterns of behavior for virtually every circumstance of human life and develop new ways of satisfying our needs.

Seventh, we all have *a fully developed self-awareness*, an acute consciousness of ourselves and of our situation with respect to the rest of the world.* This aspect of human nature has been called both a blessing and a curse, and rightly so. Because of it, we are able to picture ourselves in situations we have never experienced, and thus we have the capacity to *plan*, individually and collectively, for the future, and to develop purposes and goals. Because of it, we are able to imagine things that have never been, and thus we have the capacity to *create*. But with our awareness and our foresight comes the realization that we are responsible for our actions, and thus we acquire the capacity for making moral judgments and *creating moral orders*, which all human societies are. Theodosius Dobzhansky, the late geneticist, once remarked that no other animal has to bear anything comparable to the tragic discord that self-awareness has created in the human soul.[40]

Eighth, and finally, we all have *a genetically rooted motivation to satisfy our needs and, when necessary, to put their satisfaction ahead of those of others*. The reason for this becomes evident when we consider the true social insects, whose societies are remarkably free from the discord so characteristic of our own. Their social relationships are harmonious because they are programmed genetically to respond to other members of the society in a wholly cooperative and altruistic manner. The worker bee cannot alter its activities or vary its routine; nor can it choose between its way of life and that of the drone. Individuality is automatically suppressed with these creatures and cooperative behavior is unavoidable. The social behavior of mammals is not genetically regulated to anything like the same extent, and individuality is consequently far more pronounced. Thus, in mammalian societies, cooperative behavior is to a large degree *learned* behavior, and self-assertive, self-seeking tendencies are never entirely suppressed.

In human societies, the infant begins life exclusively concerned with the satisfaction of his or her own basic needs. Gradually, the child becomes aware

---

*Human consciousness and self-awareness evolved with the development of those lobes of our brain that control abstract thought. This permits us to think in a new time dimension: the future. Even the apes have only a rudimentary conception of that important dimension of existence.[39]

of the needs of other people, and is trained to be more considerate of them. With even the best of us, however, our innate selfishness does not—indeed, it cannot—disappear. Rather, two things happen that dull its sharp edge.

First, we learn that cooperative behavior is essential if we are to attain the things we want; that in order to get, we must also give. Second, through social and cultural experience, the scope of our needs expands and some of our new needs cause us actually to *become* less self-centered, while others cause us to *behave as if we were* less self-centered. We really become less self-centered when we develop the desire to please people who love us or satisfy our needs, for example, or when we seek to protect our children or others with whom we identify very closely.* We may even develop a social conscience that compels us to attend to the needs of underprivileged or suffering people with whom we have no personal ties. On the other hand, we often simply give *the appearance* of being unselfishly motivated as a means to other ends, such as gaining popularity or respect, for example. Thus, most of our behavior continues to reflect self-seeking tendencies. And yet, because our needs have been modified, and because we have learned to satisfy our needs through cooperative means, human behavior is compatible with relatively harmonious social life.

One manifestation of our innate self-centeredness is the *expansive* quality of our socially derived needs and desires. We have all, at various times in our lives, been convinced that to attain a particular thing—some material possession, the attention of an individual we admired, or a passing grade in a difficult course—was all we required to be happy. Thus, we were highly motivated to attain that goal. But once we achieved it, we became just as eager for something more.[41]

Abraham Maslow, a psychologist, theorized that there is an inborn hierarchy of human needs in which our physiological needs are the most basic, followed by the need for safety, and then, in turn, by the need to belong and be loved, the need for esteem and respect, and the need for "self-actualization."[42] The more basic needs, according to Maslow, remain dominant in a person's life until they are satisfied, but the more fully they are satisfied the stronger the higher needs become. Thus, the most urgent need of one accustomed to having all of his or her physical and safety needs met will be the need to be loved and accepted by others. And the person whose needs are satisfied in every other respect may be driven by the need for "self-actualization"—the need for self-expression, perhaps, or for power, or for aesthetic experience. Although Maslow's theory is hardly definitive, it certainly appears consistent with what can be observed of human behavior.

By now it should be clear why we had to examine our biological heritage before we could examine our societies. When a single species combines such diverse and often contradictory attributes as ours does, we can expect its societies to be complex and difficult to understand, and what we have established in this chapter will illuminate what we encounter in those that follow.

As many of the great novelists and poets have recognized, a tremendous

---

*Unfortunately, the development of a capacity to care for others carries with it the potential for an enhanced capacity to inflict harm on those *outside* the circle of one's loyalties.

tension is built into the very fabric of human life: Homo sapiens is, by nature, both a social animal and an individualistic, self-seeking animal. It is this, more than anything else, which creates the drama in human life, and the uncertainties. And it is this which justifies one early sociologist's classic description of human societies as systems of "antagonistic cooperation."[43]

Excursus: A Brief History of Sociology

Before going further in our analysis of human societies, it may be well to pause and take a closer look at sociology itself—its origins and history, its recent trends and current status. This brief excursus will also provide an opportunity to consider the relationship between sociology and the other social sciences.

Though sociology is a relatively recent addition to the scholarly world, its roots can be traced back to the writings of Plato and Aristotle. Philosophers then were already speculating about their own societies—comparing one with another and trying to understand the forces that shaped them.

The more immediate origins of modern sociology, however, lie in the sixteenth, seventeenth, and eighteenth centuries. This was a period during which the peoples of Western Europe, especially the educated minority, were confronted with a tremendous amount of new information that could not be assimilated into their traditional belief systems. They learned that their earth was not, as they had long supposed, the center of the universe. And they also learned, through the discovery of whole new continents populated by peoples with cultures radically different from their own, that Western Europe was not the center of the earth. At the same time, European societies were themselves changing. The Protestant Reformation had divided Western Europe, and the bitter religious wars that followed undermined much of the moral and intellectual authority of the clergy. Meanwhile, urban populations were growing in size and influence. All this contributed to the questioning of older theories and to renewed speculation about the nature of human life.

Among the consequences were two more or less independent developments, which laid the foundation for modern sociology. The first of these was the revival of interest in the systematic study of man and society, fostered by writers such as Thomas Hobbes, John Locke, Jacques Rousseau, Adam Smith, and Thomas Malthus. Before the eighteenth century ended, these men had established the independence of social theory from theology and had laid the foundations of the modern social sciences. Some of them even went so far as to identify the phenomenon of sociocultural evolution—long before Darwin's day—and to formulate explanations for it.[44]

During this same period, others began making systematic, quantitative studies of various social phenomena. Birth and death rates were an early object of research; later there were studies of class, family income, jury verdicts, election results, and a variety of other phenomena. Sometimes those who were involved in developing theory were also involved in research, though this was usually not the case. By the end of the century, the quantitative tradition was firmly established; ties to theory were still imperfectly developed, but a basis had been established for the eventual integration of these two essentials of science: theory and research.[45]

The term "sociology" first appeared in the 1830s in the writings of a Frenchman, Auguste Comte. As a result, Comte is often referred to as the founder of modern sociology. This is an unmerited honor, however, since his writings were in an already established tradition and his own distinctive contribution was not that important.

The most famous nineteenth-century sociologist, and the most influential in his own day, was an English scholar, Herbert Spencer. Through his writings, which were translated into nearly all of the major languages, he brought sociology to the attention of the educated classes throughout the world. Like others before him, Spencer was profoundly interested in sociocultural evolution, though he saw it as merely one manifestation of a universal cosmic process linking the physical, biotic, and human worlds. Interest in evolution was further stimulated in that period by the writings of Charles Darwin, a contemporary of Spencer.

Another major contributor to the study of human societies in the nineteenth century was Karl Marx. Unlike Spencer, he stood apart from the emerging discipline of sociology, with the result that the relevance of his work to the discipline went unrecognized for many years. With the passage of time, however, this has changed. One reason has been the belated appreciation of the importance of the material base of human life—people's need for food, shelter, and the like, and the techniques for meeting these needs. Most of the other pioneer social scientists neglected or underestimated this factor.

Ironically, despite its European origins, sociology found more rapid acceptance in the United States. A number of leading American universities established professorships even before the turn of the century, and by the early decades of the present century, many institutions had established full-fledged departments of sociology. During the period between the two world wars, sociology continued to expand in the United States but failed to do so in Europe, partly because of attacks by totalitarian governments, especially in Germany and the Soviet Union, partly because of greater resistance to change and innovation by the faculties of European universities. As a result, sociology became primarily an American enterprise.

Following World War I, sociology underwent a number of important changes. Under American leadership the discipline became increasingly concerned with contemporary American society. Interest in other societies declined, as did interest in the historical dimension of human experience. To a large extent these changes reflected the desire of a new generation of sociologists to make the discipline more scientific. The result was a greatly heightened interest in field research, especially studies of local communities and their problems—crime, poverty, divorce, juvenile delinquency, illegitimacy, prostitution, the problems of immigrants, and so forth.

With this shift in the focus of interest, sociologists gradually abandoned the earlier evolutionary approach. In part, this was because of criticisms leveled against it, but primarily it was because the older approach seemed irrelevant to the concerns of the newer generation. Sociologists were forced to find a substitute for evolutionary theory—some new theoretical approach that could organize the growing but diffuse body of information on American society. By the late 1930s, *structural-functional* theory emerged as the apparent successor to evolutionary theory.

Structural-functional theory is, in effect, the sociological counterpart of anatomy and physiology in biology. Like anatomists, structural-functionalists are concerned with the identification and labeling of the many different parts of the things they study and with the structural relations among them (e.g., the structural patterns formed within business organizations, families, etc.). Like physiologists, they are interested in the functions each of the parts performs. Just as physiologists are concerned with the

functions of organs, such as the liver, heart, and spleen, structural-functionalists are interested in the functions of institutions, such as the family, and of moral rules, such as the taboo against incest.

Talcott Parsons, an American professor, was especially instrumental in developing structural-functional theory. Building on foundations laid around the turn of the century by Max Weber in Germany and Emile Durkheim in France, Parsons developed a theoretical system that was carried by his students into leading universities throughout the country.

Since World War II, sociology has grown substantially not only in the United States but in Europe, Japan, and Canada, and it has begun to take root in other areas as well. One significant development has been the changing attitude of Communist authorities. During the Stalin and Mao eras, sociology was outlawed throughout the communist world. Now, however, restrictions have been removed and interest in the subject is growing, especially in Poland, Yugoslavia, and Hungary.[46] The growth of sociology in other countries has reduced the unhealthy concentration of the discipline in the United States that characterized the decades of the 1930s and 1940s.

Another notable development has been the movement of sociology beyond the confines of the academic community. Prior to the 1940s, sociologists were employed almost entirely by universities and colleges. Beginning in World War II and continuing to the present, there has been a growing demand for their services by government, industry, and other kinds of organizations.

Intellectually, too, sociology has made substantial progress. Two of the most important developments have been the increasing use of quantitative techniques and the emergence of *ecological-evolutionary* theory. The first of these was a natural outgrowth of efforts to achieve greater precision in describing social phenomena and greater rigor in analysis. This trend was given an enormous boost by the invention of computers, which enable researchers to handle large volumes of data and carry out complex statistical analyses that would otherwise be impossible.

The new ecological-evolutionary theory developed in response to a growing recognition among sociologists that structural-functional theory alone does not provide an adequate basis for studying and explaining two crucial aspects of life in human societies: change and conflict.[47] Although these have, of course, been experienced by every society in history, never have they been more important than in our own century. A variety of events—the civil rights movement, the women's movement, the population explosion, the environmental crisis, the energy crisis, the continuing technological revolution, ferment and unrest in the Third World, a succession of wars, growing threats to world peace—have contributed to the dissatisfaction with a purely structural-functionalist approach to human societies, and to the development of the newer, more comprehensive theory.

Sociology and the Other Social Sciences

The study of human societies has never been exclusively a sociological concern. All the social sciences have been involved in one way or another. Most of the others, however, have focused on some particular aspect of the subject. Economics and political science limit themselves to a single institutional area. Human geography studies the impact of the physical and biotic environments on societies. Social psychology is concerned with the impact of society on the behavior and personality of individuals.

Only sociology and anthropology have been concerned with human societies per se. That is to say, only these two disciplines have interested themselves in the full range of social phenomena, from the family to the nation and from technology to religion. And only these two disciplines have sought to understand societies as entities in their own right.

In matters of research, there has been a fairly well established division of labor between the two disciplines. Sociologists have, for the most part, studied modern industrial societies; anthropologists have concentrated on preliterate societies of both the past and present. This division of labor has made good sense, since the skills needed to study a remote tribe in the mountains of New Guinea are very different from those needed to study a modern industrial society such as our own.

From the standpoint of teaching and the development of theory, however, the separation of sociology and anthropology has been far less satisfactory. Many problems, especially those involving long-term evolutionary processes, require the contributions of both disciplines. Ignoring either leads to incomplete or biased interpretations and conclusions. As a consequence, there has been a long tradition of intellectual "borrowing" between sociology and anthropology, and this volume follows that tradition.

With the revival of evolutionary theory,[48] scholars in these fields came to recognize that both disciplines were neglecting agrarian societies—those societies which occupy the middle range in the evolutionary scale between primitive preliterate societies and modern industrial societies. In recent years, therefore, both sociologists and anthropologists have begun research on these groups in Southeast Asia, the Middle East, and Latin America.

The growing concern with agrarian societies has also led to increased cooperation between sociologists and historians. Since history is the study of written records of the past, historians have been the experts on agrarian societies of earlier centuries. Much of the older work by historians, with its heavy emphasis on the names and dates of famous men and events, is of limited value to students of human societies. But that discipline has been changing too, and historians today are increasingly concerned with the basic social processes and patterns that underlie the more dramatic but usually less significant events on which their predecessors focused. As a result history and sociology are becoming more valuable to each other.

This trend toward interdisciplinary cooperation is evident today in all the social sciences, and even beyond. Scholars are coming to recognize that no discipline is sufficient unto itself. To the degree that any field cuts itself off from others, it impoverishes itself intellectually. Conversely, to the degree that it communicates with other disciplines, it enriches itself and them.

CHAPTER 2

Human Societies as Sociocultural Systems

One of the fascinations of human societies is their diversity. In any other social species, one society is remarkably like the next in size, complexity, and the activities of its members. This is hardly surprising, however, in view of the fact that one society is also remarkably like the next in its genetic heritage and that this heritage determines the great majority of the species' characteristics.

Why, then, are human societies, which *also* have similar genetic heritages, so different from one another in so many ways? Why are some huge and organizationally complex, while others are small and simple? And why are the activities of their members often so varied? Why, for example, are the members of some societies warlike, while the members of others are relatively peaceful? Why are some puritanical in relations between the sexes, while others are much more permissive?

The explanation of the tremendous variations among human societies is that their similar genetic heritages enable them to develop very *dissimilar* cultural heritages. Without their cultures, human societies, too, would all be essentially alike. But with culture comes an extraordinary potential for creating diversity.

Because our societies, unlike those of other species, are both social *and* cultural units, sociologists and other social scientists often refer to them as *sociocultural* systems. This contraction of the two words is partly a convenience. But it is more than that: it is a reminder that the social and cultural aspects of human life are inextricably intertwined. In this chapter we will begin to explore the many implications of this fact.

Human Societies as Systems

The term *system*, which we have just linked with "sociocultural" and which appears frequently in sociological writing, is a simple word with a profound meaning. It can be applied to a wide variety of things, many of them in the world of nature. There are physical systems such as the solar system, star systems, weather systems, and systems of lakes and rivers. Every living organism is a system. And there are systems *within* organisms (digestive, reproductive, etc.), systems *among* organisms (populations, societies), and systems that include organisms and their environments (ecosystems). Among the systems created by humans are a multitude of mechanical systems (cars, pianos) and a variety of such dissimilar ones as political, linguistic, mathematical, irrigation, and transportation systems. In every instance, the term is appropriate because *a system is an entity made up of interrelated parts*.

The key word in this definition is "interrelated." In the words of one expert, a system is a "bundle of relations."[1] For this reason, what happens to one of the component parts of a system has implications for other parts and for the system as a whole. Too much beer in the stomach has repercussions for the brain, for example, just as the alignment of an automotive system's wheels affects its steering. Francis Thompson, the poet, captured the systemic qualities of the total universe in his line, "Thou canst not stir a flower without troubling of a star."[2]

The meaning of the concept *system* is best understood, however, if we focus on a smaller, more specific "bundle of relations," such as the mechanism of a clock. In working order, this entity is a mechanical system. Each of its components (gears, dial, hands, springs, etc.) is also an entity—and each remains an entity even if the mechanism is dismantled. But when the relations among these components have been destroyed, the entity that is *the system* ceases to exist. A system, then, is clearly more than the sum of its parts: it is the sum of its parts *plus the relations among them*.

Systems vary a great deal in their internal coordination, that is, in the degree to which the functions of the parts are coordinated with one another and with the functioning of the system as a whole. Using this as a criterion, mechanical systems are among the most nearly "perfect" systems there are. Consider the clock mechanism again. Each component exists, and each functions, for one purpose only: the purpose for which *the system* exists and functions (i.e., to mark the passage of time). Moreover, each component relates only to the other parts of its own system, and its operation is totally dependent upon theirs.

It should come as no surprise to note that, insofar as *systemic* qualities are concerned, the societies of some species resemble the clock mechanism more than they resemble human societies. The activities that go on in the honeybee's social system are as beautifully coordinated as gears and dials; they all serve the interests of the system (i.e., the society as a whole) rather than the interests of any individual or caste; and they demonstrate a nearly total interdependence among the parts. That species' heritage might be thought of as a genetic blueprint for a harmonious social system.

The situation is quite different in human societies. For one thing, the coordination among their component parts is frequently poor. For another, their components do not always function in ways that are conducive to the well-being of the system itself (i.e., the society). For example, their members are individualistic and often self-assertive, resist efforts to coordinate and control their behavior, and do not readily subordinate their needs to the needs of the group. In short, a genetic blueprint that is very different from the honeybee's, but just as compelling, *prevents* human societies from achieving the strict ordering of relations that characterizes some systems.

System-Needs of Human Societies

Human societies make it possible for humans to satisfy their needs. But, being systems, however imperfect, societies have needs of their own. In short, certain conditions must exist if the particular "bundle of relations" that comprises a sociocultural system—or any other kind of system, for that matter—is not to disintegrate. The conditions necessary for societies to survive are sometimes called *functional requisites.*[3]

Although there is a great similarity between the needs of a society's members and those of the society, or system, itself, they are not precisely the same. For example, it is not fatal to an individual if he or she fails to reproduce. But the situation is different for a society, as we will see below.

The first of the system-needs of a human society is for *communication among its members*. This is the *sine qua non* of every social organization, human or nonhuman, because if its members are unable to communicate (i.e., unable to exchange information among themselves), social behavior is impossible. Thus, every human society has, at a minimum, a spoken language.

Second, there must be *production of goods and services* to satisfy both the physical and psychic needs of the members. This requires a substantial store of information—not only on the subject of the production of material goods (i.e., about tools, techniques, location of resources), but also about the responsibilities that the members should assume and the contributions they should make toward the satisfaction of one another's needs. For in human societies, production, whether of food or of affection, is largely a cooperative effort.*

Third, there must be *distribution of the goods and services that are produced*. Producers and consumers are never precisely the same in any society: at a minimum, the essentials must be provided for the young. In human societies, the solutions to problems of distribution, like those of

---

*Although hermits and other isolated individuals sometimes provide entirely for their own basic material needs apart from society, even they are dependent on some society's accumulated store of information.

production, are essentially cultural solutions and vary tremendously from one society to the next.*

Distribution is an especially serious problem in societies where production is so highly specialized that there is little overlap between those who produce a given product or service and those who use it. This situation requires multiple and often highly complex cultural answers. A society must develop mechanisms that facilitate exchange between producers and consumers (e.g., systems of barter, monetary systems). It must also have mechanisms for moving goods and services from one place to another (i.e., transportation systems). And, perhaps most important, it must have mechanisms for determining who receives how much of the various things that are produced (i.e., stratification systems).

Fourth, there must be *protection of the members* from threats posed by the environment. These include physical hazards (storms, heat, cold, flood, etc.), other organisms (germs, wild animals, crop-destroying insects), and other human societies. To enable its members to protect themselves, individually and collectively, a society's culture contains a diversity of techniques, ranging from techniques for building shelters and making clothing to techniques of healing and warfare.

No society can be entirely successful in defending its members against hostile forces, for every individual dies eventually. For the *society* to survive, however, it is only necessary that enough of its members live long enough and in good enough health to carry on its functions and to raise the next generation to adulthood.

Fifth, because death is the ultimate fate of every individual, *members must be replaced.* This need is partially satisfied by biological reproduction, which perpetuates the society's *genetic* heritage. But this is not enough. If the society is to survive, its *cultural* heritage must also be perpetuated. This is accomplished by means of the socialization process.

Socialization is the process through which individuals become functional members of their society. This complex process, which begins at birth and extends over many years, consists of social and cultural experiences that result in substantial modification of behavior. Through socialization, we develop in our earliest years those qualities we associate with "being human," but which are only potentialities in the newborn infant. Later, we learn to assume responsibility for our own behavior and to satisfy many of our own needs through a variety of learned activities, both solitary and cooperative. Finally, as we reach adulthood, we take on a broad range of responsibilities, for ourselves and others, including the task of transmitting our society's culture to the next generation.

Sixth, there must be *some control and regulation of the behavior of the members.* There are two reasons why this must be done if a society is to survive

---

*This is not true in other animals' societies, where genetics provide solutions to the fundamental problems of production and distribution. The wild dogs of Africa, for example, on returning from a successful hunt, regurgitate some of the fresh meat they consumed to feed the mothers and pups that were unable to accompany them.[4] This does not vary from individual to individual or group to group, thus indicating the genetic basis of the practice.

as a system: (1) to ensure that the vital work of the society gets done; and (2) to prevent conflicts among the members from disrupting societal life.

Both of these ends are, *to some extent*, accomplished through genetic mechanisms. Consider one of society's most vital needs, for example: the production of new members. Genetically based mechanisms (i.e., physical attraction, sex drives) help to ensure that mating will occur and babies be born. Even the subsequent problem of caring for those infants is partially answered by our genetic makeup, as evidenced by the fact that the great majority of mammalian mothers, including human ones, demonstrate an eagerness to be near and to nurture their babies (though prior social experiences also affect this relationship). Moreover, studies of nonhuman primate societies have shown that infants are very attractive not only to their mothers,

FIGURE 2.1   Socialization occurs in play as well as in situations where adults attempt to train the young.

but to other members of the society as well (see Figure 1.4).[5] A similar innate appeal on the part of human infants probably helps ensure that they, too, will be looked after and protected.

The same basic principle applies in the case of avoiding conflict among the members of society: biological mechanisms provide part of the answer. For example, genetically determined signals, such as certain facial expressions, postures, noises, and gestures, can serve to inform others about our mood or our reaction to what they do. Such emotions as fear or anger, for example, may be "written all over us." Simply knowing, through such signals, what another person is prepared to do in a tense situation (e.g., stand up and fight, or back off) has often prevented violence in human societies, just as similar biological mechanisms do in the societies of some other species.

In human societies, however, the potential both for the neglect of socially necessary tasks and for socially disruptive behavior is so great that genetic mechanisms of control must be supplemented with cultural mechanisms. These mechanisms, called *social controls*, help order societal life by rewarding some types of behavior and penalizing others. The specific actions that are encouraged or suppressed, as well as the way this is done, vary from one society to the next. But every system of social control has two basic components. First, there is always a set of *norms* to define what kind of behavior is good or bad, better or worse, under various circumstances. Norms take the form of laws, rules, regulations, customs, guidelines, standards, and so forth. Second, there is always a set of *sanctions* to motivate people to behave in ways approved by their society. Sanctions are rewards and punishments, and they range all the way from a simple word of encouragement to a large monetary prize or appointment to an important office, from a fleeting frown on someone's face to the death penalty.

As sociologists have long noted, no system of social control can be effective if it depends exclusively on *external* rewards and punishments—that is, on sanctions that the members impose on each other. Rather, every individual must assume a large degree of responsibility for his or her own conduct and therefore must be able to impose *internal* sanctions (e.g., guilt feelings or self-congratulation). This is why one of the major objectives of the socialization process is to internalize the standards and values of the group so that they become also the personal standards and values of the members. Although no society ever achieves this goal completely, it must at least approximate it. The alternative is anarchy, and the end of the society as a system.

The final system-need is for what might be termed *group-direction*. First of all, there must be mechanisms that make it possible for the group to make decisions. This is necessary to ensure that, even in the face of divergent views among its members, the group as a whole will be able to respond to external changes or threats (e.g., drought, a hostile neighboring society) in time to avert disaster. Thus, every society requires a system of leadership—and a culturally defined means of determining which of its members will serve in that capacity. Equally important, if the members are to accept direction and work together in an effort to solve common problems, they must have some sense of a common or shared identity, the perception that they all belong to a unique and important entity. For this reason, every culture includes information about the name, origin, and history of the society, as well as elements of art, music, folklore, religious beliefs, and other things that are uniquely its own.

One could easily expand this list of the system-needs of human societies by breaking them down into a more detailed list. This simplified list, however, serves to suggest the diversity and variety of the things human societies require if they are to survive. It also provides us with an excellent basis for understanding the basic components of sociocultural systems.

Basic Components of Sociocultural Systems

Every human society, because it is a system, is made up of various components and the relations among them. Even the simplest of these systems is so complex that it would be impossible to identify each of its component parts and detail all their relationships. Our goal in this chapter is to examine the most basic components that comprise every human society: (1) population, (2) culture, (3) material products of culture, and (4) social structure.

Population

The first component of sociocultural systems is population, a term that refers to *the members of a human society considered collectively*. As this suggests, in studying human societies we are primarily concerned with the characteristics of the group, rather than with those of its individual members. Viewed in this way, there are three aspects of a population that must be taken into account: (1) genetic constants, (2) genetic variables, and (3) demographic variables.

Genetic Constants The genetic constants of a population are those of its attributes which are rooted in our species' common genetic heritage. They are the same for the population of every human society and, for all practical purposes, the same from one generation to the next. Since we have already discussed this subject at length in Chapter 1, nothing need be added here beyond the observation that this heritage includes not only the ability to reason and to devise cultural solutions to problems, but also powerful emotions and appetites that evolved in our prehuman ancestors and are preserved in that portion of our brain which many physiologists refer to as "the old brain."[6] Thus, the genetic constants are at one and the same time every society's most precious resource and the cause of many of its most serious problems.

Genetic Variables In addition to that central core of traits that comprises the major portion of every individual's genetic heritage, each of us also has thousands of genes that are variable—that is, they are absent or occur in different forms in other individuals. Because these genes are not necessarily distributed equally among societies, there is a *variable* genetic aspect to population as well as a constant one. Such variables range from traits like skin color, hair texture, and eye shape to blood type, incidence of color blindness, and taste sensitivity.[7] From the standpoint of their impact on the life of human societies, genetic variables, relative to genetic constants, are of minor importance. And yet, because so much attention has been focused on certain of them (i.e., racial variables), it may be useful to examine this subject in some detail.

Although human populations have frequently been reproductively isolated, none has ever been cut off long enough to become a separate species—that is, so genetically different that its members could not mate with other human populations and produce fertile offspring. During those periods of isolation, however, as the processes of mutation and natural selection continued to fit each human group to its particular environment, populations developed gene pools (see Glossary) in which the frequency of certain genes varied significantly. Among these genes were the ones responsible for the highly visible characteristics on which the concept of *race* is built, such as the color of skin, hair, and eyes, hair type, body build, and shape of face and head. A race, in other words, is simply a breeding population in which one or more of these traits occur with a frequency that is appreciably different from other breeding populations.[8]

Members of modern societies often have difficulty appreciating the adaptive value of racial variables, because we no longer depend on them for our survival or well-being. When we encounter unpleasantly strong sunlight, for example, we adapt *culturally*: we create artificial shade, or we apply artificial "pigment" to our eyes (sunglasses) and, if we are lightly pigmented, to our skin (suntan oil). Until relatively recently, however, a population's *genetic* attributes were its primary means of adapting to the hazards of its environment, and even minor variations in relevant characteristics, such as the ability to store body fat as an insulation against extreme cold, could determine which individuals survived and which did not.

This explains why many genetic variables, from skin color to body and facial form, are not randomly distributed across the globe, but occur in discernible geographical patterns.[9] For example, the pigment in our skin determines how dark it is and protects underlying cells from exposure to ultraviolet light. And darker skin is universal in hot, sunny regions,[10] with the heaviest pigmentation of all in the African Sudan, where solar radiation is the most intense and constant.[11]

The "sickling gene," found chiefly in populations of Africa, the Middle East, and India, in areas where a particularly deadly form of malaria occurs, provides a somewhat different illustration of the adaptive value of genetic variables. An individual who inherits this gene from both parents will develop sickle-cell anemia, a disease normally fatal before adolescence. But a far greater number of people in the population inherit the gene from only one parent, develop only mild symptoms of the anemia, and are also likely to be highly resistant to certain virulent forms of malaria. In areas with a high incidence of malaria, the sickling gene clearly has adaptive value: its benefits to a population outweigh its costs.[12]

Most variable traits are not as easy to identify as the ones we have discussed so far. This is because most of our characteristics result from the action of more than one gene and, in addition, are not determined by genes alone. Genes provide the *potential*, but the reality is determined by the interaction of genes and environment. And environment includes that of the prenatal period, even the preconception experience of sperm and egg. This dual determinancy of genetics and environment has been dramatically illustrated many times, as in the case of Jewish children born in Israeli kibbutzim and Japanese children born in America who tower over parents born, respectively, in the ghettos of Europe and in Japan. It is clear that most biological characteristics, from longevity to musical aptitude, are shaped by both genes and environment. But so far, at least, efforts to separate the two and measure their relative influence have generally proved frustrating and unprofitable.

One thing has been clarified, however: the relation between racial and nonracial genetic variables. Studies have been made, for example, of color blindness and blood characteristics, which are variables that can be precisely identified and are minimally affected by environmental factors, and whose gene frequency in a population can therefore be precisely calculated. When the distributions of these genes are plotted geographically, they cut across racial lines.[13] For example, the frequency of the gene for type B blood is essentially the same in the gene pools of the South Chinese, the Russians, and the West Africans.[14] Findings like these make it clear that the traits used to define race are an extremely limited set of variables that are not correlated to any appreciable degree with other genetic variables that have been carefully analyzed.

Demographic Variables   The demographic properties of a population include such things as its size; its density; how it is dispersed or concentrated (e.g., to what extent its members are concentrated in a few areas or spread out more evenly over its entire territory); the patterns of migration into and out of the society; its composition in terms of age and sex; and its birth and death rates. These characteristics, like certain clusters of genes, vary from one society to another. But these variations, unlike most genetic variations, have clear, demonstrable, and far-reaching consequences for human societies.

Population size is by far the most variable of the demographic properties of human societies, which have ranged in numbers from twenty members or less (in some preliterate societies of the recent past) to nearly a billion (China's current population). Variations in other demographic characteristics often appear insignificant beside such variations in size. For example, two societies with stable populations (i.e., neither growing in size nor declining) and with annual death rates of 14 per 1,000 and 40 per 1,000, respectively, may not seem very different. But this variation actually means that the average life-span of the members of the first society is seventy-one years, and in the second barely twenty-five years.

Similarly, the birthrate in the United States in recent years has been approximately 15 births per 1,000 population, while in neighboring Mexico it has been about 43. This seemingly modest difference, however, has meant that a far smaller proportion of Mexico's population has been of an age to be economically productive (see Figure 2.2). As a consequence, that society has been unable to improve substantially the standard of living for its rapidly growing population. This, in turn, has had implications for the demography of

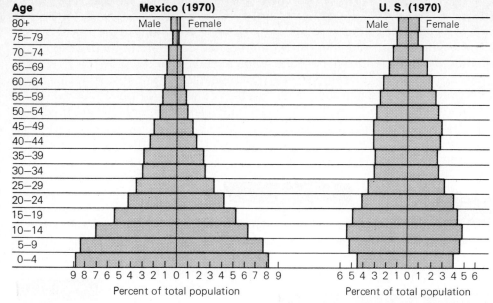

FIGURE 2.2 Population pyramids of Mexico and the United States compared: the broad-based Mexican pyramid is typical of Third World societies today with their high birthrates and large proportion of young people, while the narrow-based pyramid of the United States is typical of advanced industrial societies with their low birthrates.

Mexico's neighbor, as it has stimulated a massive migration into the United States.

In later chapters, we will have frequent occasion to consider demographic variables, since they play an important part in the evolution of human societies. By contrast, we will have very little to say from here on about the genetic variables discussed in the previous section, since there is little to indicate that they have played a significant role in sociocultural evolution.

Culture

The second basic component of sociocultural systems is culture, a *society's symbol systems and the information they convey.* As we saw in Chapter 1, symbols are information conveyers that enable us to handle information in ways impossible for other creatures. We can *extract* more information from an experience (i.e., *learn* more), because symbols permit us thought processes denied other species. We can *share* more information, because symbols enable us to express so much more of the subtlety, complexity, and diversity of our experiences. We can, in fact, do more with information *whatever* is involved: in recording it, accumulating it, storing it, combining it, or applying it, symbol users have a fantastic advantage over signal users.

The symbol systems and store of information that comprise a society's culture are like a foundation laid down by previous generations. Because each new generation has this base on which to build, it can avoid repeating many of the experiences of earlier generations. If the members of a society constantly had to debate the norms regulating relations between the sexes, for instance, there would be that much less time for other activities. Similarly, if a group has already learned how to make and use fire, or invented the plow, or devised a system of numbers, its members need not repeat the time-consuming and often unrewarding experiences by which that particular element of culture was first acquired. Rather, they can turn to new challenges, which may result in further enrichment, or modification, of their culture.

We will examine both of the basic parts of culture in some detail, beginning with symbol systems.

Symbol Systems   The most basic symbol system in any society is its *spoken language*. No matter how many other symbol systems a society may create, this remains the one with which its members develop their capacity for speech and are socialized, the one employed in their basic thought processes, and the one that bears the major burden of transmitting information among them.

At the heart of every spoken language is a mass of social conventions, or customary practices, that govern its vocabulary and its grammar. A vocabulary is a set of sounds with meanings attached to them, and the relationship between a sound and its meaning is embedded in the history of its use by those who share that language. To those who speak English, the word "bed" means a place to sleep, not because of any logical or necessary connection between the sound and the activity, but because this is the convention that has evolved in English-speaking populations. Similarly, grammatical conventions tell us how words must be combined if they are to be meaningful and intelligible to those who use our vocabulary. It means one thing to say, "The bear ate Jack," something quite different to say, "Jack ate the bear," and nothing at all to say, "The ate bear Jack."

Until we study a foreign language, most of us have the impression that there is something natural—even inevitable—about the way our own society and its language separate experience and thought into the bits of meaning we call words, and that learning another language is only a matter of learning the sounds another society applies to those same "units of experience." Yet as people conversant in two or more languages are well aware, words in one do not necessarily have an equivalent in the other. Americans and Russians were reminded of this some years ago during talks between President Kennedy and Chairman Khrushchev. Kennedy repeatedly said that the Russians should not miscalculate the will and intentions of the American people, and every time the word "miscalculate" was translated, Khrushchev flushed angrily. Kennedy later learned that the Russian language has no precise equivalent of this word, and the translator had seized on a Russian word, normally applied to a small child or uneducated person, meaning "unable to count." Khrushchev naturally assumed that Kennedy was implying he was not very bright![15]

One reason languages separate experience into different units is because the experiences of the people who *create and use* the languages are so different. For example, gauchos, the famous horsemen of the Argentine prairies, have 200 words to denote the different colors of horses, but only 4 for all the plants known to them: *pasto*, fodder; *paja*, bedding; *cardo*, wood; and

---

GREEN HEAD CAUSES RED FACES

For a moment the bustle of activity at the Afro-Arab summit meeting in Cairo in March 1977 was brought to a halt by the announcement of the arrival of "The Prime Minister of Green Head." Confused delegates stared blankly at one another until finally someone figured out that the official concerned was the Prime Minister of the Cape Verde Islands and his mangled title the result of a sequence of literal translations from Portuguese to Arabic to English.

Source: *The Washington Post,* March 8, 1977.

---

yuyos, all others.[16] Meanwhile, the Eskimos have numerous terms to refer to the various phenomena that we call simply "snow." They have one word for dry-wind-driven snow, one for dry-packed-suitable-for-cutting-into-blocks-and-building-igloos snow, another for ice-crust-surface snow, and so on.[17] In yet another part of the world, the Dugum Dani, Stone Age horticulturists on the island of New Guinea, have seventy different words that refer to sweet potatoes, their staple crop;[18] and in the Middle East, Arabic is reputed to have a thousand words for sword, indicative of that culture's stress on poetry and emphasis on synonyms and figures of speech.[19] English is a language rich in numbers and units of measurement, perfect for describing and recording mathematical and scientific data. In short, a language reflects the needs and concerns of those who use it.

Another reason languages differ in the way they categorize and classify experience is the haphazard and spontaneous manner in which they evolve. Consider the evolution of the word "bureau," for example. A bureau was originally something made of baize, a thick green cloth. Because these bureaus were often put on writing tables and chests of drawers, the word was eventually extended to mean the furniture as well as the cloth. Later, because many government offices were equipped with bureaus, or writing tables, the offices themselves came to be known by that term (e.g., the Federal Bureau of Investigation).[20]

This process of change in language is so much a matter of chance that it is highly unlikely that the same pattern would occur in two societies. Even if two societies begin with the same language, as when a small group separates from the parent group to settle a new territory, linguistic differences are bound to develop unless a remarkably high level of communication is maintained between them. There is probably no better example of this in the modern era than in the differences between English as it is spoken in England, Australia, and the United States.*

So far we have talked about spoken language as if it were merely a neutral

---

*Another interesting example is provided by the differences that are reported to be developing between East and West Germans. For an earlier period there are the differences that developed between the Saxons who settled in England and those who remained on the Continent. Because of the break in communication that developed, their speech is no longer mutually intelligible.

and passive vehicle for transmitting information. But as political leaders, propagandists, and advertisers have long recognized, individual words often acquire, through the process of association, powerful emotional connotations that enable them to convey a great deal of information beyond what is embodied in their formal definitions. Words like "communist," "racist," and "sexist," for example, have such strong negative associations for many Americans that they respond unthinkingly to the emotional content of the symbol. Words can also acquire strong positive associations, and these, too, may be used to manipulate emotions. For example, linking kinship terms with organizations, as in "Mother Russia," "Mother Church," or "Uncle Sam," can stimulate warm feelings of affection.

A leading linguist of the last generation, Edward Sapir, went so far as to claim that the way people perceive reality "is to a large extent unconsciously built upon the language habits of the group," and that as a result, different societies live in different worlds, "not merely the same world with different labels attached."[21] Though few scholars today would go this far, they recognize that language is more than a passive instrument of communication.[22] Language is, itself, part of our experience, and therefore it helps to determine what we feel, what we perceive, and what we do.

Supplementing the spoken language of every society is a repertoire of conventional gestures and facial expressions that are widely used and whose meanings are evident to members of the group. This "body language" should not be confused with the many facial expressions and body movements that are genetically determined, such as our involuntary reaction when we touch something hot, or the way we pucker up when we taste something bitter. True body language is symbolic, just as words are, for the form and meaning of the gestures and expressions are determined by those who use them. Consider, for example, the shrug of the shoulders. Americans, and a number of other peoples as well, use it to convey indifference, uncertainty, or a lack of information on the subject in question, with the specific meaning being indicated by the context in which it is used.

Body language may well be the oldest type of symbol used by our species, and it probably once played a relatively greater role in communication than it does today. Yet even now, it can be an invaluable source of information: people convey so much with a smile or frown, a tilt of the head, a movement of the hands. This is one reason many of us avoid the telephone when we have an emotionally charged message to deliver, such as the death of a loved one. We know we can communicate our own feelings more effectively, and read those of others more clearly, when words, body language, and signals are all involved.

A third kind of symbol system in many societies is written language, a relatively recent development in human history. Some of the oldest written records in existence today were prepared thousands of years ago by temple authorities in Mesopotamia to enable them to keep a record of their business transactions.[23] These priests were stewards of their god's resources, and when they loaned out his animals or grain, it was imperative to get them back again. Even though the priest who made a loan might die, the god expected it to be recovered. To keep track of their god's property and thereby avoid incurring his wrath, the priestly community devised a primitive system of writing that involved a mixture of numerals, pictographs, and ideograms.

The arbitrary (i.e., symbolic) nature of this writing is clear. Even when a pictograph (essentially a picture) was used to represent a bull, it was a stylized representation that excluded many of the animal's features that might have been included. Moreover, the same features were used consistently, indicating that conventional forms of notation had already been established. Similarly, from a very early date, the pictograph of a jar came to represent a certain quantity of grain, rather than the jar itself. And finally, among these early examples of writing are a number of ideograms, which are "pure" symbols, in effect, for they are completely arbitrary and based solely on convention. They lack any visual resemblance to the objects they represent (sheep, for example) just as our dollar sign bears no resemblance to the dollar.

As new uses for writing were discovered, new efforts were made to translate spoken language into written form. At an early date, kings and princes were recording their successes for posterity, priests their sacred rites and traditions. At first, as the Mesopotamian priests' experience makes clear, a society's written symbols could express only a small part of what was possible with its verbal symbols. Gradually, however, written languages developed until they were capable of conveying the same information as spoken ones, and writing came into its own as a means of storing information, for communication across the barriers of space and time, and eventually as a medium of artistic expression, education, and entertainment.

As societies have acquired more information, it has frequently become necessary to go beyond such basic symbols as letters and numerals. Thus, new symbol systems have evolved that greatly facilitate the handling of specialized kinds of information. For example, musicians devised musical notation so they could express the units of information that they create and use, and mathematicians and scientists developed a wide variety of symbol systems to express abstract ideas, complex numbers, and so on. The specialized symbol systems now found in modern societies include languages for the deaf, the blind, engineers, stenographers, computer scientists, and others too numerous to mention.

Over the course of history, the relative importance of the three basic types

FIGURE 2.3 Two sides of a limestone tablet found in Mesopotamia, bearing some of the oldest known picture writing (about 3500 B.C.). Included are symbols for head, hand, foot, threshing sledge, and some numerals.

of language—body, spoken, and written—has altered considerably. Body language, including symbolic gestures and facial expressions, may well have been dominant at an early date, declining only when true speech evolved. Then, until quite recently, verbal symbols remained the primary means of transmitting information from one person to another and from one generation to the next. With the invention of the printing press and the subsequent spread of literacy, however, written language steadily increased in relative importance, largely because it could overcome space and time, the historic barriers to communication. During the last 100 years, thanks to such devices as the telephone, radio, motion pictures, and television, the spoken language, too, has overcome those barriers, altering the balance once again. And in the most recent, most dramatic development of all, a plethora of languages have been written for computers, enabling them to handle fantastic amounts of information of widely diverse kinds. More important than these shifts in the relative importance of different types of language, however, is the fundamental trend that has persisted from early prehistoric times: *the human population has steadily expanded its capacity to handle information.*

Information   Cultural information is *knowledge acquired through experience and conveyed through symbols.* A society's information is, in effect, a product of its experience: its experiences in the remote past, and in the recent past; its experiences with its environment, and with itself. Needless to say, no society's culture includes every thought of every member during its entire history. Rather, out of the flow of information, a society gleans what it considers valuable and attempts to preserve it.

Because every society has a unique past, every culture is unique. We can say this another way: out of diverse experience, diverse information emerges. This means that human societies not only have different amounts of information on a given subject; they frequently have different "facts" as well. Since we know that human senses and intellect are limited and fallible, this comes as no surprise. Even hard scientific "facts" in modern societies must often be revised in the light of subsequent research.

Cultural information is not limited to the kind of ideas whose truth or accuracy is capable of being proved or disproved, however. Rather, it includes a group's total perception of reality: its ideas about what is real, what is true, what is good, what is beautiful, what is important, what is possible. When we discussed symbol systems, we saw that they, too, are so rooted in subjective experience that even individual symbols may be "units of experience"—which explains why a word like "mother" can be so emotionally charged. We also saw that the kind of information conveyed by symbol systems ranges from historical and statistical data to concepts of deity, attitudes toward horses (*and* plants), characteristics of snow, poetic inclinations, even music itself. Cultural information includes, quite literally, *everything humans are capable of experiencing and able to translate into symbolic form.*

Because all human societies have certain fundamental kinds of experiences in common, and because they all have the same basic needs to satisfy, all cultures include information on certain basic subjects:

- Every culture has a substantial store of information about the biophysical environment to which the society must adapt, including its plant and animal life, its soils and terrain, its mineral resources and water supply, its climate and weather conditions.

- Every culture includes information about its social environment, the other human societies with which the group has contact.

- Every culture contains information about the society itself: its origin, its people, its heroes, its history.

- Every culture contains information that explains the ultimate causes of events in this world.

- Every culture has a lot of information that enables the members to cope with recurring problems, from feeding themselves to resolving intragroup conflict.

- Every culture contains information that guides individuals in making judgments about what is good and what is right and what is beautiful.

- Every culture has information created solely to satisfy culturally activated and intensified needs, such as the desire for artistic expression, for example, or for ritual.

FIGURE 2.4   All cultures contain information created solely to satisfy culturally activated and intensified needs, such as the desire for artistic expression and ritual: Indonesian dancers performing the sacred dance drama of The Witch and The Dragon.

Although this list is neither exhaustive nor detailed, it conveys something of the breadth of culture.

A great deal of the information we have just mentioned is ideological in nature. We might say it is information that results from efforts to make sense out of human experiences.[24] For *ideology* is *information used to interpret experience and help order societal life*. Because humans are users of symbols and creatures of culture, life can be overwhelming. We think, feel, hope, enjoy, and suffer as no other creatures can. We imagine what we cannot know and yearn for what may not exist. We live simultaneously in three worlds: the past, the present, and the future. We alone, apparently, live out our lives aware that death is inevitable. To make things more difficult, we create for ourselves a profusion of cultural alternatives, in the face of which our genetic heritage is an inadequate guide. It is not surprising, therefore, that, as individuals, we need help in interpreting experience, finding meaning, and making choices. And, as we have seen, societies as a whole need help in regulating and ordering our collective life.

Medieval Christianity is a good example of a highly developed and comprehensive ideology, the kind that answers virtually all of these individual and societal needs.* At its center was a vision of a universe inhabited by various kinds of spiritual beings (seraphim, cherubim, humans, demons, devils, etc.) mostly under the dominion of God. God was perceived as the King above all earthly kings, but because His authority was challenged by Satan, the prince of darkness, people were confronted with a choice as to which to serve. Those who chose God (who would ultimately prevail) were obliged to subscribe to the Church's doctrines and conform to its code of morality. The latter enjoined Christians to be charitable to one another, honest, sober, hardworking, monogamous (better yet, celibate), obedient to all in authority, and regular in devotions and worship. Since no one could adhere perfectly to these requirements, the Church provided opportunities for people to confess their sins, do penance, and obtain absolution.

When we look closely at medieval Christianity, we find the three basic elements that comprise *every* ideology. First, there is a system of *beliefs* about the kind of world we inhabit. Second, there is a system of generalized *moral values* that emanate from, or are justified by, those beliefs. Finally, there is a system of *norms* that apply those general values to specific situations and spell out how the members of the group are to act in various circumstances, what they should and should not do.

There are two basic kinds of norms in every society and they have evolved in very different ways. Some of them are part of official or legal codes of behavior that are systematically enforced by an authority, such as a government, a church, or other kind of organization. These norms are what we usually refer to as *laws*, *regulations*, or simply *rules*, and they are sometimes accompanied by more or less explicit statements of the sanctions that will be

---

*Marxism is an example of a well-developed and comprehensive *non*theistic ideology. Some other ideologies, such as capitalism, address themselves only to certain limited facets of human life.

used to punish those who violate them. A city ordinance, for example, may set a fine of $25 for littering streets or sidewalks.

In contrast, many norms are informal and unofficial, and violations of them are not officially sanctioned. Thus, every society and every subgroup in a society, from corporations to families, has numerous informal rules, or *customs*, which are, in effect, the group's definition of desirable or acceptable behavior. They may apply to such diverse things as modes of dress, hairstyles, food preparation, the selection of marriage partners, the performance of various tasks, proper grammar, and attitudes toward children or older people —to name only a few. These informal norms are as important in shaping behavior as more formal ones. As we saw on page 33, norms and their related sanctions (i.e., rewards and punishments) are the basic components of every system of social control.

Sometimes it is difficult to determine, or even to imagine, how certain elements of ideology originated, or what they can possibly tell us about the

---

INDIA'S SACRED COWS: THE ADAPTIVE VALUE OF AN IDEOLOGY

In a society where tens of millions of people go to sleep hungry every night, devout Hindus, who constitute the vast majority of India's population, would not dream of killing any of that country's 54 million cows for food. To a Hindu, even murder is not as great a sacrilege as killing a cow.

Marvin Harris, a leading proponent of ecological-evolutionary theory, examined this seeming paradox in an effort to find a rational explanation. He rejected the view that an ideology evolves arbitrarily, unrelated to the rest of societal life or to the experiences of its members in the past. Rather, he suspected that any belief that has been as widespread and as persistent as the Indian taboo against cow slaughter must have significant adaptive value for the society.

In a volume titled *Cows, Pigs, Wars and Witches: The Riddles of Culture*, Harris reported the results of an analysis of this subject. He found, first of all, that the cow is of enormous value to the members of Indian society in meeting their basic needs. A peasant's cow is, in effect, a factory that provides food (milk, butter); fertilizer; fuel for cooking (dried manure is excellent for this purpose, producing a clean, low heat); flooring material (a paste of manure and water hardens into a smooth surface that holds down dust and can be swept clean); and, most important of all, oxen to pull the peasant's plow. Harris also found that less than 20 per cent of the food consumed by Indian cattle is edible by humans. In short, the cow converts substances of little worth to the peasant into extremely valuable products.

Although Indian peasants recognize that a living, productive cow is vastly more valuable to them and to their children than the same cow consumed as food, it would be only natural for them to ignore this fact when they are desperately hungry. The religious taboo against killing cows is a powerful cultural mechanism that serves to protect these animals even in times of famine and thereby preserve an invaluable resource. In short, Hinduism's conception of the cow as sacred is based on the experience of countless generations of the Indian people.

past experience of a society. This is true, for example, of one of the central beliefs of Hinduism, the belief in the sacredness of the cow. The boxed insert on the preceding page explains how this seemingly strange belief has, for centuries, helped the members of Indian society cope with some of their basic and recurring problems in a highly adaptive way.

Another crucial body of information in every culture is *technology*. This is *information about how to use the material resources of the environment to satisfy human needs.* Compared to ideology, technology seems to be a rather prosaic and uninteresting subject. Historians and social scientists have tended to ignore it,[25] and until recently people seldom came to blows over the relative merits of different technologies. As we will see in the next chapter, however, the influence of technological information on the course of history and on the process of societal change and development has been out of all proportion to the recognition usually accorded it.

In every society, a large component of technological information concerns food: where and how to get it and how to process it for consumption or storage. There is also information about the other material resources available to the society and how they may be converted into useful forms—into fuel for heat, cooking, and other purposes; into clothing and shelter; into tools, weapons, ornaments, and other things the group needs or values.

Because a distinctive body of information tends to build up in response to each set of human needs, we sometimes speak of different technologies in the same society, such as its military technology or its communications technology. More often, however, we speak of a society's technology in the singular, because there is an underlying unity to this store of information. The principles of metallurgy, for example, are used in virtually every area of technological activity in a modern industrial society, and the same is true of other basic elements of technology.

Material Products of Culture

The third component of sociocultural systems consists of the material products of culture, the result of the use of technological information to convert environmental resources into things that the members need or want. These range from perishable items that are consumed within hours of production (such as certain foods) to things that may endure for centuries, such as pyramids, cathedrals, and plastic containers. They range, too, from purely utilitarian objects like hammers, bombs, and gasoline to frivolous items like jewelry or Frisbees. And they include products, such as works of art, whose significance may persist beyond a single generation or extend beyond a single society.

Among the most important material products of every society are its *capital goods.* These are things that are devoted to the production of other things. Thus, the more capital goods a society possesses, the more goods of various kinds it is able to produce, and the wealthier it tends to become.

The first capital goods were simple tools made of stone, wood, and bone, which enabled our ancestors to produce such essentials as fire, food, shelter, and more tools. Later, as the store of cultural information increased and as new environmental resources became available, the character of tools changed. Metals were especially important in this respect because they combined strength and durability with malleability. This culminated in the last 200 years in the production of the kinds of capital goods that are vital in modern industrial societies: machines and instruments of diverse kinds, railroads, motorized vehicles, electrical power systems, factory complexes, and so forth.

Early in human history another environmental resource was gradually transformed by human societies into what we might call *living* capital: domesticated animals. Their contribution to production has been crucial in every society which depended upon oxen or horses to pull plows and wagons, cattle or goats to provide milk and cheese, or sheep to provide wool. Domesticated animals have often been a society's primary capital investment and its medium of exchange as well. This was true, for example, in ancient Greece and Rome. Our word "pecuniary," which means "relating to money," derives from *pecus*, Latin for cattle.

As the mention of plows and wagons reminds us, energy is a critical factor in production. In fact, *energy itself is every society's most important product.* For in producing food, a society produces the energy that underlies every physical or mental activity of its members. No society can survive without a steady, minimal input of energy, and every social and cultural activity beyond mere survival requires an additional input. Thus, information about new sources of energy or new ways of increasing the flow of energy has always been of particular importance.

Social Structure

The fourth basic component of sociocultural systems is social structure. This refers to *the network of relationships among the members of a society*. These relationships make it possible for the members to satisfy their own individual needs as well as the system-needs of the society.

The kinds of relationships found in human societies are, to some extent, biologically determined. Social relationships in all mammalian societies, for example, are organized to take account of age and sex differences. Human societies, however, rarely stop there. In most instances, they go much further, developing elaborate kinship networks and other complex social arrangements that reflect cultural influences. Thus, as we think about social structure in human societies, we should view it as an organizational and behavioral product of the interaction of culture and genetics.

Individuals   The two basic building blocks in every social structure are the individuals who make up the society and the roles they fill. Little need be added to what we have already said concerning the nature of individuals. Each person has a genetic heritage that is partly distinctive and partly shared, and each has a cultural heritage that is also partly distinctive and partly shared. From society's standpoint this is sometimes an asset and sometimes a liability. On the one hand, it ensures a high rate of individuality as a consequence of ever new recombinations of genetic and cultural elements in different individuals. This can have great adaptive value for a society, especially when it is confronted with new circumstances to which it must adjust. On the other hand, intrasocietal conflict results from this individuality, as we have seen. Whatever else is true of the members of human societies, they are certainly not just interchangeable cogs in a social machine.

Roles The term *role* means in sociology the same thing it means in the theater—*a position that can be filled by an individual and that has certain distinctive behavioral requirements and expectations attached to it.*[26] Thus, just as a man may play the role of Macbeth on the stage, so he may "play" the roles of husband, father, and doctor in his home and community. In both instances, people expect him to act in certain ways, and not in others, simply because of the roles he occupies. If he fails to live up to their expectations—if he flubs his lines, for example, or neglects his family or patients—he will probably be criticized, censured, or worse. The audience may boo him, his wife and patients leave him. On the other hand, if he fulfills the requirements of his roles and satisfies people's expectations, he will probably be applauded, loved, and well paid.

The behavioral requirements and expectations that are attached to "real life" roles are nothing other than the *norms* we discussed on pages 33 and 44. As we saw in our earlier discussion, norms may be extremely formal, as in the case of laws regarding murder or embezzlement, for example, or quite informal, as in the case of a neighborhood's expectations concerning property maintenance. They may involve anything from fundamental moral issues to details of etiquette. Norms also vary widely in the scope of their application. Some, for example, apply to all the people in a certain geographical area, who are told to "keep off the grass." Others direct the actions of only a relatively few, such as the rules that govern a Catholic priest in celebrating the Mass.

We get an idea of how a large number of norms *combine* to shape a role if we return to the man in our earlier illustration. His role as doctor is defined by a variety of formal norms that deal with moral issues (e.g., the Hippocratic oath) or are part of legal codes (e.g., the license to practice medicine). But his role will also be shaped by less formal norms, such as local customs regarding house calls and what fees to charge for various services. Similarly, his behavior is shaped to his roles within the family by a great variety of norms, from laws that govern monogamy and child abuse to local customs that dictate how much time parents are expected to devote to such things as parent-teacher organizations or Little League baseball.

The fact that real life, unlike the stage, normally demands that an individual fill a number of roles simultaneously, does not necessarily present a problem. A young woman, for example, may easily combine the roles of daughter, sister, niece, friend, college student, church member, and citizen. Later, however, when she tries to coordinate the requirements and expectations of new roles, such as wife, mother, and career woman, difficulties may well arise.

In a situation like this, an individual has several options. The first is to continue in the conflicting roles, disregarding or violating the norms of one or more of them and hoping that the penalties will not be too severe. Thus, the woman in this case might neglect some of her friends or her parents, or attend church less often. A second option is to abandon one of the roles. The woman could give up her job, for example; or she might file for divorce, though that would probably do little to resolve her basic role conflict if she were the mother of a small child. A third possibility is to try to alter the norms attached to one of the roles so that it is more compatible with the others. Thus, the young woman might try to get some change made in her hours of employment. Or she might attempt to change her husband's and children's expectations of her, perhaps by altering their definition of the role of "mother" to mean a person who shares responsibilities for child care with a *father*. Her chances of success in changing her own family's perception of the role would obviously be influenced by developments in other families, since expectations for a role such as mother tend to develop on a societywide basis.

The options mentioned above are not available in every instance of role conflict. For example, it is sometimes virtually impossible to abandon a role. This is especially true in the case of *ascribed* roles, which are roles that are assigned us with little or no choice on our part. In every society, every individual has an age role and a sex role, and in many societies a racial or an ethnic role as well. (There are no racial or ethnic roles in societies where everyone is of the same racial or ethnic stock.) Thus, in American society, one may be an adolescent white female, for example, or an elderly black male, or a middle-aged Hispanic, whether one likes one's roles, and the expectations associated with them, or not. People sometimes try to change ascribed roles, as in the case of an older man who darkens his hair and understates his age, or a transvestite who misrepresents her sex. But deceptions involving ascribed roles are fraught with the risk of serious embarrassment, or worse, if they are discovered.

Redefining a role's requirements and expectations may also be impossible or, at best, extremely difficult. The reason is clear in the example we cited: changing the norms attached to the mother's role would simultaneously alter the norms attached to the father's. In short, every individual has a vested interest in minimizing the costs and maximizing the benefits of the roles he or she occupies, and efforts to shift responsibilities (through redefining a role or simply through neglecting its obligations) naturally engender resistance. For roles are not isolated entities; they are elements in the complex web of social relationships that form the social structure of a society.

Roles serve many functions in societies, but four of these functions are of crucial importance. First, and most basic, roles are an important mechanism of social control. They harness people's energies to those tasks that must be accomplished if the system is to survive and the needs of the members are to be met. Roles also ensure the performance of less essential tasks that the society as a whole, or its more powerful members or subgroups, regard as necessary or desirable.

A second function of roles is to encourage specialization. This tends to increase the efficiency of the members' efforts, since no one can do everything well. Third, role specialization, in turn, increases the level of interdependence among the members, which strengthens the group.

Finally, roles are a mechanism for cultural transmission, for passing traditions on from one generation to the next. Individuals are mortal; roles are not: they can persist indefinitely. The role of rabbi, for example, has existed for over 2,500 years, contributing immeasurably to the survival of the Jewish group and to the preservation of its cultural heritage.

Groups   In most societies, the members are divided into a variety of units we call groups. These range from small family units and cliques to giant corporate entities of various kinds. In popular usage, the term "group" is often applied indiscriminately to any aggregation of people, regardless of their other characteristics. Sociologists, however, limit the term to *an aggregation whose members (1) act together in a common effort to satisfy common, or complementary, needs, (2) have common norms, and (3) have a sense of common identity*.

As this definition suggests, human aggregations differ in their *degree* of "groupishness." While some aggregations clearly qualify as groups (e.g., Jehovah's Witnesses) and others just as clearly do not (e.g., all the redheads in the United States), many are on the borderline (e.g., Americans of Irish descent). This last example reminds us that the degree of "groupishness" of an aggregation is not permanently fixed. Aggregations may take on more of the qualities of a group, or they may lose some. Their members may come to work together more closely; develop new, stronger, and more generally shared norms; and acquire a stronger sense of common identity; or just the opposite may occur, as has happened with Irish-Americans during the last hundred years.

Despite the exclusion of aggregations such as redheads, the concept "group" still includes such a wide variety of organizations that it is necessary to differentiate among them. The most familiar way of doing this is by their basic function in society. Thus, we differentiate between families, churches, schools, political parties, and so forth.

Sociologists have also found it useful to differentiate among groups on the basis of their size and the intensity of the social ties among their members. Small groups in which there are face-to-face relations of a fairly intimate and personal nature are known as *primary groups*. Larger, more impersonal groups are known as *secondary groups*. Primary groups are of two basic types, *families* and *cliques*. In other words, they are organized around ties of either kinship or friendship.

Secondary groups are also of two basic types, associations and communities. An *association* is a formally organized secondary group that performs some relatively specialized function or set of functions. A political party, a church, a labor union, a corporation, and a governmental agency are all associations. *Communities*, by contrast, are less formally organized and perform a wider range of functions. Basically, there are two types of communities, geographical and cultural. *Geographical communities* are those whose members are united primarily by ties of spatial proximity, such as neighborhoods, villages, towns, and cities. *Cultural communities* are those whose members are united by ties of a common cultural tradition, as in racial and ethnic groups. A religious group (an association) may also be considered a

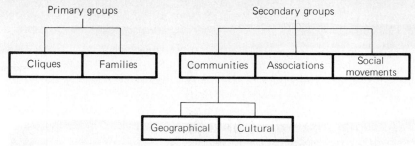

FIGURE 2.5 **Types of human groups.**

cultural community if its members are closely integrated by ties of kinship and marriage and if the group has developed a distinctive subculture of its own.

As this last example indicates, associations may give rise to communities. The opposite can also happen: communities can give rise to associations (for example, in the United States during the 1960s, black political associations, such as CORE, emerged from the larger black community). When either of these developments occurs, the membership of the community and the membership of the association overlap to some extent. Usually, however, the community is larger because its membership requirements are less stringent, with membership often being automatically conferred by virtue of birth.

In addition to associations and communities, there are several other types of secondary groups, the most important of which are *social movements.* These are loose-knit groups that hope to change society in some way. The antiwar movement which developed in the United States in opposition to the Vietnam War is a good example of such a group.

Statuses Up to this point in our discussion of social structure, we have considered only the *horizontal* dimension: the functional differences between roles and between groups. There is a second dimension, however—a *vertical* dimension. Individuals, roles, and groups can be ranked in a variety of ways, such as by income, wealth, or education. This ranking is the *status* of the unit. Sociologists are especially concerned with statuses that reflect power, privilege, and prestige, since these are extremely important characteristics in shaping societal life.

As a rule, the various statuses of a given unit are fairly consistent. People who are wealthy and well educated, for example, also tend to be powerful and to have considerable prestige. There are exceptions, however, and these are often interesting and important. A leader of the Mafia, for example, may enjoy great power and wealth in the community at large but have little prestige except in the Mafia itself. Or a member of an ethnic minority who has low status in that role may enjoy high status in the occupational system.

The status of a unit often changes with the passage of time. When this occurs, the unit is said to be *upwardly mobile* or *downwardly mobile,* as the case may be. For example, when an individual is promoted, he or she is upwardly mobile; when a family fortune is dissipated, the family is downwardly mobile.

Classes The term *class* is used in two different, though related, ways.[27] Sometimes it refers to an aggregation or group of people whose *overall* status is fairly similar. In this case, we usually speak of upper, middle, and lower classes; or, if we divide the hierarchy more narrowly, of upper-middle, lower-middle, and so on. Members of the same class have roughly the same degree of power, privilege, and prestige in their community or society.

"Class" can also be used to mean an aggregation or group of people who are alike with respect to something that affects their *access* to power, privilege, and prestige. In other words, people can be classified according to such basic resources as education, occupation, ethnic background, wealth, and political position, all of which either help or hinder individuals in their efforts to attain greater status. This use of the concept of class is generally more precise than the one described in the previous paragraph. It enables us to identify such specific entities within a society as the working class, the governing class, and the propertied class, to name a few; and it makes it possible for us to refer to the nobility and the peasantry of a society in the past or to the rich and the poor of a contemporary society.

One question that arises at this point is whether classes are groups. The answer is both yes and no. In many instances, classes are simply aggregates whose members, though in a similar position with respect to some important resource, have no sense of common identity, have no common behavioral expectations, and do not act together to satisfy common, or complementary, needs. This is the situation of American office workers, a rapidly growing occupational class that does not constitute a group. On the other hand, American blacks, a racial-ethnic class, *are* a group: they have long been a cultural community with a strong sense of common identity.

Taken together, all the classes within a society form what sociologists call a *system of stratification*. The basic function of such a system is to distribute the things of value that society produces. These "valuables" include not only *material products* but also *services* (e.g., education and medical care) and *psychic gratifications* (e.g., prestige and popularity).

Because no society has yet been able to produce enough of all these things to satisfy fully the needs and desires of every individual, systems of stratification usually generate dissatisfaction and even conflict. This problem is impossible to resolve to everyone's satisfaction, because there is no obviously "right" way to distribute things that are produced by the cooperative actions or efforts of many different people. It is equally reasonable to argue, for example, that a given product should be distributed on the basis of (1) how much a person needs it, (2) how much effort a person invests in producing it, or (3) how much skill a person contributes, to name only three possibilities.

Even if a society settles on one of these principles, disputes are still likely. If the members apply the principle of effort, for example, they must still decide how to measure effort. Should it be calculated by the hours spent on the job, by the foot-pounds of energy expended, or by how hard a person tries? Or, if the group adopts a different criterion, how do they measure and compare such dissimilar skills as those of a nurse, a statesman, and a computer programmer? In brief, there is no simple way, no one "right" way, to handle distribution in human societies, and arbitrary standards are inevitable. But arbitrary or not, fair or not, there must *be* standards. Given our natural tendency to put the satisfaction of our own needs and those of our immediate families ahead of other people's, the only alternative is anarchy.

Not surprisingly, the subject of social stratification and inequality has given rise to one of the major controversies in modern sociology.[28] The issue is whether distributive systems develop in response to system-needs of society or in response to the power of elite groups. One school of sociologists stresses the inevitability of inequality, sometimes arguing that inequality is needed to motivate the abler members of society to seek the more important positions, and sometimes arguing the need for a decision-making elite. A second group argues that most inequality is simply the result of force and fraud on the part of the more powerful and clever. A third group sees elements of truth in both views and tries to synthesize them.[29] Though we cannot hope to resolve this controversy here, there will be materials in later chapters that should help readers develop more informed views on this important subject.

Conclusion   By way of conclusion, we can say that social structures are built primarily on two principles: (1) the principle of the division of labor and (2) the principle of stratification. Because it is more efficient and more rewarding for the members of a society to divide up the tasks that are necessary for their survival and well-being, a system of functionally differentiated roles and groups gradually evolves. But as this process of *functional* differentiation takes place, it is accompanied by a process of *status* differentiation. Thus, individuals, roles, and groups come to be differentiated in terms of status as well as in terms of the functions they perform. This, in turn, often leads to the formation of classes. In some human societies, these possibilities have been realized in only the most limited way, but in others, social structures have become enormously complex.

Reassembling the System

When we began this chapter, we observed that a system is not so much a matter of parts per se as of *relationships among parts*. Thus, although it is necessary to separate the parts of a system in order to study them, as we have done in this chapter, it is important to remember that they do not normally exist except in relation to one another. We must not, in other words, become so intrigued with the components that we lose sight of the system.

Strange as it may seem, this can happen. Modern scientists have often been content merely to dismantle and dissect systems (biological, sociocultural, and others), in the apparent belief that this would ultimately tell them everything they want to know. In his book *So Human an Animal*, the distinguished biologist René Dubos maintains that the philosophical heroes of modern science have been Democritus and Descartes, both of whom "taught that the way to knowledge is to separate substances and events into their ultimate components and reactions."[30] According to Dubos, this process, known as *reductionism*, leads the scientist

. . . to become so involved intellectually and emotionally in the elementary fragments of the system and in the analytical process itself, that he commonly loses interest in the phenomena or the organisms which had been his first concern. For example, the biologist who starts with a question formulated because of its relevance to human life is tempted, and indeed expected, to progress seriatim to the organ or function involved, then to the single cell, then to subcellular fragments, then to molecular groupings or reactions, then to the individual molecules and atoms.[31]

Maintaining that this has been a profound mistake, Dubos argues that "The most pressing problems of humanity . . . involve . . . situations in which systems must be studied as a whole in all the complexity of their interactions. This is particularly true of human life."[32] Dubos goes on to say that to be fully relevant to life, the biological sciences must deal with the responses of total biotic systems to their total environments.

Dubos's advice, though aimed at biological scientists, is equally applicable to social scientists. It is easy for us, too, to become so absorbed in "the elementary fragments of the system"—individuals, roles, symbols, norms, and all the rest—that we neglect sociocultural systems themselves. To say this is not to minimize the importance of understanding these components. It only means that we cannot stop there. We must find some means of studying human societies *without* stripping them of the rich and complex network of interrelationships that make them the systems they are. Fortunately, there is a concept in sociology that serves just this purpose.

Institutions and Institutional Systems

Because human societies have so many needs, and because these needs persist over long periods of time, every society develops more or less standardized and traditional ways of dealing with them. These "continuing answers" to "continuing problems" are known as institutions and institutional systems.*

An institution may be defined as *a system of social relationships and cultural elements that develops in a society in response to some set of basic and persistent needs.* Such a system always involves a significant segment of all four of a society's basic components: some of the members of its *population*, who act within the framework of a *social structure* of stable and well-defined roles, statuses, and groups, using elements of their *culture* (symbols, as well as various kinds of information, including beliefs, values, and norms) and some of its *material products*. And these relationships and these activities all exist because of important and continuing needs of society.

We can best understand the concept of "institution" through an illustration. A society's institutions of higher learning are systems in which certain

---

*The term "institution" tends to be used to refer to more specific "answers," or those of more limited scope (e.g., marriage, the family), while "institutional system" is usually applied to larger and more inclusive patterns (e.g., kinship).

individuals, their roles defined as students, faculty, and administrators (among others), and their relationships structured into departments, classes, and fraternities (among others), use such things as mathematical symbols, information about the physical world, information about the human past, and literature, as well as things like books, laboratories, buildings, and calculators, to satisfy a set of important and persistent needs: the students' need for advanced education, the staff's need for employment, and society's need for educated members and for the products of faculty research.

Because it utilizes and integrates the major components of a sociocultural system, an institution is rather like a wedge of the larger "pie" that is the total society. To put it another way, focusing on an institution or institutional system is like viewing the total sociocultural system from one particular angle. It follows, then, that if we study all of the institutional systems of a society, as well as the relationships among them, we have come close to studying the society as a whole. All that is missing are the society's responses to less important and less persistent needs.

Kinship is the oldest institutional system of all. Thousands of years ago, as societies became more complex, economic, political, and religious institutions evolved out of it and became separate and identifiable systems in their own right. More recently, education, science, health, and other systems have emerged in many societies. In later chapters, we will rely heavily on institutions and institutional systems in analyzing the various types of human societies.

Human Societies as Dynamic Systems

What are human societies? In Chapter 1, we said that they are autonomous groups whose members engage in a broad range of cooperative activities. This is a good basic definition because it helps us see how a society is different from groups like communities and associations (which are *parts* of society), and because it directs attention to the essential role of cooperation in human societies.

Now, however, we have seen that human societies are actually systems that contain a great variety of subsystems and sub-subsystems, vastly more complex entities than any simple definition could possible indicate. Moreover, another dimension must be added to the picture: human societies are not static, stable entities like so many systems with which we are familiar. A mechanical system, for example, does not change during its lifetime. A clock may be repaired and some of its parts replaced, but because the new parts are functionally identical to the old, *the system* remains the same.

A human society, in contrast, is a dynamic, changing, evolving entity. As its store of information changes, so do the relations among its various components. In other words, *the system itself changes over time*. Were we to ignore this process of change, we would miss one of the most basic characteristics of human societies. For this reason, we turn now to that process of societal change and development known as *sociocultural evolution*.

CHAPTER 3

Sociocultural Evolution

Although the word "evolution" refers to change, it does not follow that all change is evolutionary. Some change is essentially random, haphazard, and unpatterned, as appears to be the case with day-to-day weather conditions in many parts of the world. And some change is essentially cyclical, with the same series of events being repeated at regular intervals, as in the changing seasons, the menstrual cycle, and the ocean tides.

Evolutionary change is different from both of these kinds of change, for it is essentially a process of *cumulative* change by which a succession of new phenomena develop, more or less gradually and over an extended period of time, out of phenomena that already exist. Both biological and sociocultural evolution provide dramatic examples of what this kind of change can accomplish. Biological evolution began about 3.5 billion years ago with a tiny, cell-like bit of material and, through the process of "descent with modification," has produced literally millions of fascinatingly diverse species of plants and animals. Sociocultural evolution, beginning far more recently, has produced thousands of human societies with highly diverse characteristics (in size, beliefs, material products, etc.) and has endowed humans with the ability to do countless things that biological evolution did not equip us to do. It is almost as if, for our species, sociocultural evolution picked up where biological evolution left off. This, as a matter of fact, very well describes what actually did happen, as an acquaintance with the basic mechanisms underlying both these kinds of evolutionary change reveals.

The Basis of Evolutionary Change: Encoded Information

During the last several decades, our understanding of how the two evolutionary processes work to effect change has altered dramatically. It is now clear for the first time that, in both the biotic world and the world of human societies, evolutionary change is cumulative change based on *systems of encoded information*.

This surprising similarity between the two kinds of evolution has come to be recognized only in the years since World War II, as a consequence of major advances in the field of genetics. Although biologists used the concept ''gene'' to refer to the basic unit of heredity as long ago as the 1860s, they had no idea what a gene actually was. During the nineteen-fifties, however, geneticists determined that a gene is composed of minute bits of the chemical molecule deoxyribonucleic acid, or DNA.[1] Within the two intertwined strands of this molecule, information is encoded in the many varied sequences of four nitrogen bases. These four (adenine, guanine, cytosine, and thymine, or A, G, C, and T, as they are known) are like the letters of our alphabet, which can be combined to convey virtually unlimited amounts of information.* With those four nitrogen bases, a fantastic amount of information is recorded in *genetic code* within the cells of every living thing, and it is this which is translated into the chemical ''messages'' that guide and control an organism's development and behavior. For example, scientists have recently found that sickle-cell anemia is caused by the shift of a single letter—a T instead of an A—in the seventeenth position in the sequence of 438 As, Cs, Gs, and Ts making up the beta-globin molecule.[2]

The four letters of the genetic alphabet have, to paraphrase a noted geneticist, written all the words and all the sentences that comprise billions of years of biological history.[3] During much of that time, this was the *only* form in which information was available to living things. Later, as we saw on page 15, some species acquired the ability to *learn*: drawing on individual experience, they could obtain information beyond what was genetically programmed in them, and store this new information in memory systems by means of electrochemical codes.

Then, when our species emerged, able to create symbols, the potential for handling learned information took a tremendous leap forward. The reason is that symbol systems, like the genetic alphabet, can handle an unlimited amount and variety of information. Both the genetic alphabet and symbol systems thus provide populations of living things with the means of acquiring, storing, transmitting, and using enormous amounts of information. And both the genetic alphabet and symbol systems are mechanisms through which evolutionary change occurs. In short, *symbol systems are the functional equivalent of the genetic alphabet.*

---

*Because our alphabet contains twenty-six symbols, it might be supposed that it could handle more information than the four-unit genetic code. This is not true, however, as becomes obvious when we consider the Morse code, which, with just two basic units (dots and dashes), can handle as much information as the twenty-six unit alphabet.

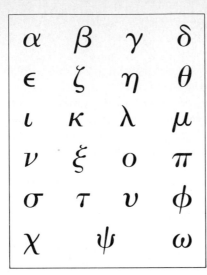

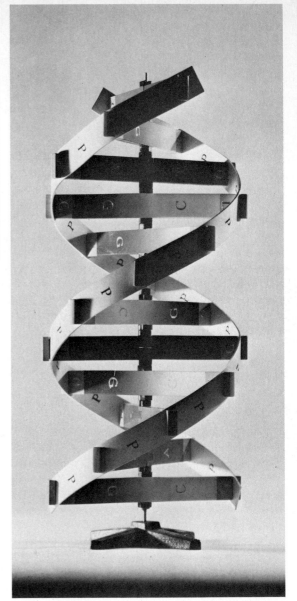

FIGURE 3.1 Symbol systems are the functional equivalent of the genetic alphabet. Both provide populations of living things with the means of acquiring, storing, transmitting, and using information, and both are mechanisms through which change occurs. The Greek alphabet and the DNA molecule.

It is hardly surprising, then, that there is a fundamental similarity in the way the two evolutionary processes operate. In each case, what happens is this: first, *new information is produced*, and second, *there is a process of selection which results in the retention of some of the new information and the elimination of the rest.*

Despite these fundamental similarities, there are a number of important differences in the way the two modes of evolution operate. Some of these are of special significance for students of human societies, such as the difference that results from the way information is transferred and spread in the two evolutions. The only way genetic information can be transmitted is through the process of reproduction. Because different species cannot interbreed, they cannot share genetic information with one another.* Thus, biological evolution is characterized by continued differentiation and diversification, a process rather like the branching of a tree or shrub. Cultural information, by contrast, is easily exchanged between the members of different sociocultural systems. Not only can human societies exchange information, but two or more can merge into a single system—the equivalent, were it possible, of the merging of separate species in biological evolution. Thus, sociocultural evolution is likely to eventuate in fewer and less dissimilar societies than exist today.

This is related to a second important difference. In biological evolution, the emergence of more complex species of plants and animals has not had the effect of eliminating, or reducing the number of, simpler species. One-celled organisms thrive alongside, and indeed *inside*, complex multicellular organisms. In sociocultural evolution, on the other hand, the emergence of new and more complex kinds of societies has usually led to the extinction of older, simpler ones, as illustrated by the destruction of thousands of small American Indian societies since 1492. Thus, while biological evolution produces the pattern of a richly branched shrub, sociocultural evolution more nearly approximates the pattern of a pine tree that gradually loses its lower branches as new, higher branches appear and overshadow them.

Another basic difference involves a population's ability to incorporate into heritable form the useful information its members have acquired through the process of individual *learning*. In sociocultural systems, this is easily done; it is, as we have seen, the basis of their evolution. But it has no counterpart in biological evolution. Most biologists prior to Darwin believed that something analogous *did* occur in the biotic world. Jean Baptiste Lamarck, Darwin's most famous predecessor, argued that if an organism continually repeats a certain behavior, not only will this produce structural change in the organism, but the change will be inherited by its offspring.[4] It has long since been clear that biological evolution does not work that way: giraffes do not have long necks because their ancestors stretched day after day to reach high leaves, but because long necks were such an asset in their ancestors' environment that the genes responsible for long necks were selected for. In the cultural world, however, a kind of Lamarckian evolution does occur. Just about anything a population learns and considers worth preserving can be incorporated into its cultural heritage.

Springing from the easy flow of cultural information among societies and the ease with which it is incorporated into heritable form is yet another way in which sociocultural evolution differs from biological: it has a capacity for much higher rates of change in our species. An evolution whose mechanism is genetic change is necessarily a slow process in a species that has a long

---

*Closely related species do occasionally interbreed, as when lions and tigers produce "ligers" or "tiglons." Hybrids are usually sterile, however, at least in the animal kingdom, and therefore their importance in the total process of biological evolution has been minimal.

generation span and relatively few offspring. But cultural information, relative to genetic, can be rapidly acquired, exchanged, recombined, and accumulated, with the result that substantial alterations in a society's culture may occur within a single generation. Moreover, sociocultural evolution does not require that every society go through step-by-step sequential stages of development, which are the essence of biological evolution. Rather, a society may compress or even skip stages.[5] In the Third World today, for example, some nations have gone directly from human porters and pack animals to trucks and airplanes as the primary movers of goods, largely bypassing the stage of dependency on wagons and railroads that was part of the evolutionary experience of those societies in which the newer methods of transportation were first developed.

One other important difference involves the conditions under which major evolutionary change occurs. In the biotic world, most *major* change happens when a population becomes reproductively isolated and cannot receive new genetic information from other populations (i.e., during speciation; see page 13). In contrast, human societies that are isolated almost invariably experience a *low* rate of cultural change. In short, isolation tends to have opposite effects in the two modes of evolution.

Finally, sociocultural evolution has a much greater potential than biological evolution has for being brought under rational human control. So far, however, this process is far from complete. One of humanity's most urgent tasks in the years ahead is to increase our understanding of the dynamics of sociocultural evolution so that we can find the means of controlling its direction and make it more responsive to human needs and ideals.

A Definition of Sociocultural Evolution

It is now clear that *sociocultural evolution is the process of change and development in human societies that results from cumulative change in their stores of cultural information.* Although sociocultural evolution is an extraordinarily complex process, it becomes easier to understand when we think of it in terms of the two subprocesses that comprise it. There is, first of all, a process of *innovation*, which produces variations. Then, there is a process of *selection*, which determines the fate of these variations.

It is important to recognize that this dual process goes on at two different levels simultaneously. First, innovation and selection occur in *each individual society*. The variations that are produced are cultural elements, and the selective process determines which ones survive and the role each plays in the life of the society. Second, sociocultural evolution also proceeds at the level of *the world system of societies*. In this case, the variations are not cultural elements, but entire societies. And the process of selection at this level determines their fate—which survive, which become extinct, and the role each plays in the life of the world system of societies.

The consequences of social and cultural change have been very different for different human societies: when we look at them individually, we see many different patterns of change. But when we look at the world system, we see that sociocultural evolution at that level has produced *one dominant pattern*. For this reason, we must examine the processes of variation and selection at these two levels in separate sections.

The Process of Change in Individual Societies

New elements of culture—new ideas, new customs, new bits of information of various kinds—are constantly being produced in every society. How do they emerge? What determines the rate at which these variations are produced? And what factors determine how widely a cultural element will be accepted in the society, or when it is no longer of any value? To answer such questions, we must consider, first, cultural innovation, and then, cultural selection.

Innovation: Source of Social and Cultural Variation in a Society

Both *chance* and *conscious, purposive action* play a part in producing new cultural elements. The members of modern industrial societies are so accustomed to innovations that are the product of careful planning and rational effort (e.g., a treaty, a play, an invention) that it is often difficult for us to appreciate the role of chance in the innovative process. Yet its role has been a significant one from the earliest times to the present. As we have seen in previous chapters, the important relations between symbols and their meanings, for example, have developed through what has been a largely unplanned and random process in every language.

Many elements of belief systems have also originated by chance, often because of an incorrect inference about a causal connection between two events which happen to coincide. Thus, in a primitive society, someone with a high fever may dream of a visit by a long-dead grandfather and awaken to find the fever abated. Nothing would be more natural, under the circumstances, than for the individual to assume that the "visit" by the grandfather was the cause of the cure and, in future illnesses, to pray to him for help. Should such prayers be followed by further cures, the practice might be tried by other people, and eventually become a permanent feature of the society's culture.

Chance has also played a role in technological innovation. Random strikes of lightning, for example, were almost certainly an important part of the process through which humans first learned about fire and became aware of its uses and dangers. Only after countless random occurrences of this kind had provided early human societies with a good bit of information on the subject (e.g., that roasted meat was not only edible but tender) were they able to take the first conscious and deliberate steps toward using and controlling fire for their benefit.

There are some innovations that could hardly be called "purposeful," yet neither can they be said to be merely the result of chance. For example, many new cultural elements develop spontaneously as a consequence of continuing interaction among the members of a society. As they live and work together, they gradually develop new ways of relating to one another and form new expectations concerning one another's conduct. This is the origin of most of the informal norms of societies and, indirectly, of many formal ones as well: they began as *unintended by-products* of ongoing human relationships.

Unintended innovations may occur even when people consciously try to prevent them. In societies that lack a written language and rely on word-of-mouth transmission of stories, songs, and legends to preserve their traditions, changes often occur simply because of the fallibility of human memory. People may forget details or confuse different stories, for example, losing or transforming important elements in the process.

While chance and unplanned occurrences play a role in the process of innovation, so does deliberate, purposive action. Much technological innovation, in fact, seems to involve both accident and purpose. For example, the great scientist Louis Pasteur discovered the principle and technique of immunization only after he accidentally injected a stale bacterial culture of chicken cholera into some animals. When, unexpectedly, they survived, it occurred to Pasteur that a weakened culture might immunize against disease.[6] Similarly, a key problem in the development of modern photography was solved when Louis Daguerre put a bromide-coated silver plate into a cupboard where, unknown to him, an open vessel of mercury was standing. When he returned the following day, he found that a latent image had begun to develop and surmised that fumes from the mercury were responsible.

Human purpose and rationality combine with forces beyond human comprehension or control to produce *non*technological innovations as well. It was the inexplicable coincidence of dream and cure that planted the seed of a new idea—a new explanation of the "connection" among things, as it were—in the mind of the individual in our earlier example. But at some point, conscious, purposive thought and action also came into play.

FIGURE 3.2 **"If this doesn't result in one or two first-class inventions, nothing will."**

Why have the members of human societies always been intimately involved in the process of innovation? What, in other words, makes people alert to the possibilities inherent in a new idea, or interested in trying a new way of doing something? The fundamental reason, of course, is *human needs and desires*. This force is so potent because those needs and desires, as we saw in Chapter 1, are potentially limitless in both scope and number. They may include anything from the most basic survival needs common to all humans (e.g., the need for oxygen) to highly individualized or very complex needs (e.g., the need to understand, the need to control others). Nor does the satisfaction of one need or set of needs satisfy most people for long; instead, it serves as the catalyst for new needs and new desires.

Closely related to this underlying cause of innovation is another: *the biophysical environment*. Because it provides the material resources on which their very survival depends, the members of a society are extremely conscious of the potential inherent in their environment and quick to exploit that potential. The importance of this factor in the innovative process is evident in the many cultural differences that distinguish primitive societies of the arctic from those of both the tropics and temperate regions, and the latter from one another—cultural differences that stem directly from differences in flora, fauna, and climate. Significant change in the biophysical environment is an even more compelling force for innovation. Archaeologists have found, for example, that changes in climate have often led to significant changes in diet, technology, and probably other areas as well.[7] But even when it is not changing, a society's environment still provides a continuing challenge to the members to develop new and better ways of using its resources and adapting to its conditions.

A society's *social environment*—the other societies with which it has contact—may also be a source of innovation, and in two ways. The society may simply borrow new elements of culture from those societies, a process known as *diffusion*. Or, it may be stimulated to make *independent* innovations on its own if neighboring societies provide it with new opportunities for trade and commerce, or if they pose a military or economic threat. As this suggests, change in a society's social environment, like change in the biophysical, can upset long-established social and cultural patterns and make innovation an absolute necessity.

Finally, the *systemic nature of human societies* is an underlying cause of innovation. Because a society is not a mere aggregation of unrelated parts but a sociocultural system, change in one component is likely to generate pressure for change in another, thereby stimulating innovation. Growth in the size of a society's population, for example, creates the need for more food, clothing, housing, and other material products. Similarly, a cultural innovation of one variety may stimulate cultural innovation of quite a different kind. The invention of the automobile, for example, stimulated the development of a whole new body of law. Television led to innumerable innovations in literally dozens of areas, including advertising, regulatory laws, political campaign styles, family life, even diet (e.g., TV dinners). And the technological innovations and advances that reduced the infant death rate stimulated further innovations both in technology (e.g., new methods of contraception) and in ideology (e.g., new values on ideal family size, new norms on sterilization and abortion). Clearly, just about any kind of new cultural element can lead to further innovation of one kind or another.

All cultural innovations do not generate the same degree of pressure for change in the rest of the system, however. Some create very little pressure for further innovation or change; others make it inevitable. A new technique of painting, for example, may have no discernible impact on a society outside a small circle of artists and critics, and perhaps a few manufacturers of artists' materials. A new religious doctrine could have far greater consequences, depending on the number of people espousing it, their position in society, the seriousness with which they regard it, and the practical consequences it entails—that is, whether it involves norms and sanctions that could significantly alter the patterns of societal life. But one kind of innovation that never fails to have far-reaching consequences is change in a society's basic subsistence technology. For *any change that alters the way a society obtains the material necessities of life generates pressure for change in virtually every part of the sociocultural system.*

It is not difficult to see why this is so. A society's store of technological information—the cultural information that helps its members to utilize the material resources of the biophysical environment—is essentially an extension of, and a supplement to, the genetic information that provides us with the physical equipment we use for that purpose. Thus, when a society experiences a major change in its technology, it is as if there had been an important modification in the genetic makeup of its members. When bands of hunters acquired the spear, it was as if they had grown a deadly new extension to their bodies. When societies acquired the wheeled cart, it was as if their members had grown much stronger and could carry far heavier loads. When societies learned to harness the energy inherent in wind and water, and later in petroleum products, the implications for the strength and endurance of their members was even more dramatic. And just as major biological differences between species are inevitably accompanied by significant differences in every aspect of their lives, so major technological change in a society is always accompanied by significant changes in every aspect of societal life.

It is a serious matter, of course, when such pervasive change occurs in a system, for it means that fundamental relationships shaped over long periods of time have been disturbed. This is true of the relationship of the society to its environment, and it is true of the various relationships among the component parts of the sociocultural system. As a result, new problems confront any society that has experienced major changes in its technology. As someone has said, reversing the old proverb, "Invention is the mother of necessity." For while it is true that human need produces innovation, it is equally true that innovation creates new needs and new problems.

The Rate of Innovation When we compare different societies, we find that they produce innovations at greatly differing rates. Some, such as American society, have experienced extremely high rates of innovation. In other societies, innovation has been almost imperceptible.

There are a number of reasons for this difference, but one of the most important is *how much information a society already possesses.*[8] This is true because one of the most basic and important modes of innovation—*invention*—is essentially a combination of existing cultural elements. For example, all that the inventor of the automobile, Gottlieb Daimler, did was to combine in a new way a number of elements of technology that were already part of the cultural heritage of all western nations (e.g., the gasoline engine, the carriage body, running gears, the drive shaft). The "only" thing new was *the combination of elements*, the automobile itself.

As this illustration suggests, technological information in particular lends itself to being manipulated in this way. Because inventions use cultural elements it already has, a society's potential for invention is a simple mathematical function of the number of available technological elements. This is easily illustrated: Table 3.1 shows the number of combinations that are possible for various numbers of units or elements. Though two units can be combined in only one way, three units can be combined in four ways, and four units in eleven ways. In other words, *the addition of each new unit more than doubles the number of possible combinations*. Thus a mere fivefold increase in the number of units from two to ten leads to a *thousandfold* increase in the number of possible combinations, and when the number of units reaches twenty, over a million combinations are possible!

Of course, not all elements, even of technology, can be combined in a useful way. It is difficult, for example, to imagine a useful combination of the hammer and the saw. The number of potential combinations, therefore, is much greater than the number of *fruitful* ones. This does not, however, affect the relationship between the number of units and the number of combinations. Thus, the amount of available technological information is a major factor in a society's rate of innovation.

A second cause of variation in the rate of innovation is *population size.*[9] Because every member of a society has somewhat different needs and abilities, the more people there are, the more new ideas and information are likely to be produced. Larger populations, especially when they are more complex, are also likely to generate more varied patterns of social interaction, leading to

TABLE 3.1   Number of Combinations Possible for Various Numbers of Units

No. of Units	2 at a Time	3 at a Time	4 at a Time	5 at a Time	6 at a Time	7 at a Time	8 at a Time	9 at a Time	10 at a Time	Total
2	1	0	0	0	0	0	0	0	0	1
3	3	1	0	0	0	0	0	0	0	4
4	6	4	1	0	0	0	0	0	0	11
5	10	10	5	1	0	0	0	0	0	26
6	15	20	15	6	1	0	0	0	0	57
7	21	35	35	21	7	1	0	0	0	120
8	28	56	70	56	28	8	1	0	0	247
9	36	84	126	126	84	36	9	1	0	502
10	45	120	210	252	210	120	45	10	1	1,013

Total Number of Combinations

more new customs, norms, laws, and other kinds of information required to control and regulate relationships. In the case of technological innovations, the more people there are who are aware of a problem and looking for a solution, the more quickly it will be found, other things being equal. Since societal populations vary so greatly in size, this is another factor of considerable importance.

A third factor affecting the rate of innovation is *the stability of the environment to which a society must adapt*. The greater the rate of environmental change, the greater the pressure for change in culture or social structure. This is true with respect to both the biophysical and the social environment. And any change in the latter that upsets the balance of power among societies (e.g., large-scale migrations, empire building, a new weapons system) is an especially potent force for innovation and change.

A fourth factor influencing the rate of innovation in a society is *the extent of its contact with other societies*. The greater the amount of its interaction, the greater its opportunities to appropriate their innovations. In effect, contact enables one society to take advantage of the brainpower and cultural information of other societies through diffusion.

The importance of diffusion was beautifully illustrated some years ago by an anthropologist, Ralph Linton, who wrote:

> Our solid American citizen awakens in a bed built on a pattern which originated in the Near East but which was modified in Northern Europe before it was transmitted to America. He throws back covers made from cotton, domesticated in India, or linen, domesticated in the Near East, or wool from sheep, also domesticated in the Near East, or silk, the use of which was discovered in China. All of these materials have been spun and woven by processes invented in the Near East. He slips into his moccasins, invented by the Indians of the Eastern woodlands, and goes to the bathroom, whose fixtures are a mixture of European and American inventions, both of recent date. He takes off his pajamas, a garment invented in India, and washes with soap invented by the ancient Gauls. He then shaves, a masochistic rite which seems to have been derived from either Sumer or ancient Egypt. . . .

Linton follows this individual as he goes through his daily round of activities using cultural elements that originated in other societies. As the day comes to a close and "our friend has finished eating," Linton writes,

> he settles back to smoke, an American habit, consuming a plant domesticated in Brazil in either a pipe, derived from the Indians of Virginia, or a cigarette, derived from Mexico. If he is hardy enough he may even attempt a cigar, transmitted to us from the Antilles by way of Spain. While smoking he reads the news of the day, imprinted in characters invented by the ancient Semites upon a material invented in Germany. As he absorbs the accounts of foreign troubles, he will, if he is a good conservative citizen, thank a Hebrew deity in an Indo-European language that he is 100 per cent American.[10]

A fifth factor in a society's rate of innovation is *the character of its biophysical environment*. As we have seen, the potential for development and change in some societies has been severely limited by environmental factors over which they have no control. Thus, desert and arctic societies have been unable either to develop the techniques of plant cultivation themselves or to learn them from others. The absence of vital resources, such as an adequate water supply or accessible metallic ores, can also hinder innovation, as can endemic diseases and parasites that deplete people's energy.[11] Topography has played an important role in shaping patterns of intersocietal communication. Such features as oceans, deserts, and mountain ranges have prevented or seriously impeded the flow of information between societies, while other features, such as navigable rivers and open plains, have facilitated it. Considering the importance of diffusion, enormous differences in the rate of innovation can be explained by this factor alone.

Sixth, the rate of innovation is greatly influenced by *"fundamental" discoveries and inventions*. Not all discoveries and inventions are of equal importance: a few open the way for literally thousands of others, while the majority have no such effect.[12] The invention of the plow and the steam engine and the discovery of the principles of plant cultivation, animal domestication, and metallurgy were all fundamental innovations. So, too, were the inventions of writing and of money.

Sometimes a fundamental innovation will cause the rate of innovation to rise because it involves a principle that can be applied, with minimum effort and imagination, in hundreds, even thousands, of areas. This was true, for example, of the steam engine, metallurgy, and printing. Sometimes, however, an invention or discovery can be called "fundamental" because it so drastically alters the conditions of human life that hundreds or thousands of other changes become either possible or necessary. This was the case with the principles of plant cultivation, which, as we shall see in a later chapter, led to revolutionary changes in every area of human life.

A seventh factor influencing the rate of innovation is *the society's attitude toward innovation*. In many societies, there has been such a powerful ideological commitment to the past and to traditional ways of doing things that innovation of any kind has been discouraged. By contrast, most modern societies have a much more positive attitude toward innovation.

Though the problem has not been studied as systematically as it deserves, a society's attitude toward innovation seems to be greatly influenced by its prior experience with change. A society that has benefited from change is usually more receptive to innovation than a society that has not. Attitudes toward innovation also vary according to the nature of the dominant ideology in the society. Some ideologies generate a very conservative and anti-innovative outlook; Confucianism is a classic example of such a faith. Capitalism and Marxism, by contrast, have been much more supportive of innovation and change.

Before we leave the subject of the rate of innovation, it is important to note a tendency that is especially evident where technological innovation is concerned: it will sometimes "snowball," or occur at an accelerating pace. Figure 3.3 depicts this speed-up in the rate of technological innovation for human societies as a whole during one 900-year period. The majority of

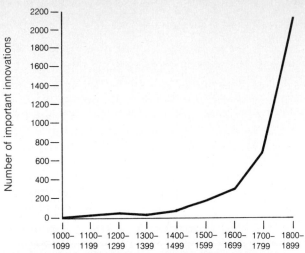

FIGURE 3.3   Number of important technological innovations by century, 1000 to 1900 A.D. Technological innovations tend to occur at an accelerating pace, because each new element increases the probability of acquiring more.

societies have never experienced such an acceleration. But those that have experienced it have had an influence on human history out of all proportion to their numbers.

The explanation of the snowballing effect lies in the fact that *each new bit of useful technological information acquired by a society increases the probability it will acquire still more.* This is partly a function of the superior potential of technological elements, relative to other cultural elements, for being recombined in new ways (see page 65). But in addition, technological advance tends to *mutually reinforce* a number of the basic factors that are responsible for the rate of innovation. Throughout history, for example, advances in a society's subsistence technology have typically led to an increase in the size of its population, which, in turn, contributed to further innovation (since there were more people aware of problems and alert to possible solutions). Similarly, technological advance has led to increased intersocietal contact, resulting in greater diffusion and thus enhancing the rate of technological innovation. And, to cite a final example, a society's impact on its biophysical environment grows with technological advance, and ensuing changes in that environment then provide their own pressures for technological changes in the society.

In short, technological innovation and advance tend to make *further* technological innovation and advance increasingly likely, a process that can easily snowball. It is hardly surprising, therefore, that societies in which this happens come to be increasingly differentiated from societies in which it does not.

The process of selection determines several things: which of the new social and cultural elements that become available to a society are actually incorporated into its social structure and culture; which existing elements will be preserved, or continue somewhat altered by being combined with new elements; and which will be replaced and thus become extinct. In some cases, the fate of extinction is averted when a cultural element is replaced functionally by a newer element, but comes to be valued for a different reason. For example, stories that were once important elements in a society's process of socializing the young may survive as elements of folklore. Similarly, a society may replace an older element of technology, yet retain information about it and even some examples of the material product itself (e.g., butter churns, Model T Fords, and other collector and museum items).

The process of selection is like the process of innovation in that it, too, can be rational and deliberate, as when a governing body replaces an old,

FIGURE 3.4 Sociocultural selection may happen almost imperceptibly, as one element of technology gradually replaces another: the horseless carriage gradually replaced the horse-drawn carriage in the United States in the first several decades of the present century.

outdated law with a new one. Or, again like innovation, selection may occur without conscious intent and with little evidence of deliberation. This kind of selection may occur swiftly, as when a nation of television viewers switches channels and thereby relegates another new show to oblivion. Or it may happen almost imperceptibly, as one element of technology, or one mode of dress, gradually replaces another.

Although it is the members of a society that make the choices that shape and alter their society, everyone does not have an equal voice. "Who decides" depends on the kind of decision involved and the nature of the relevant power structure. For example, the teenaged members of an industrial society may choose, at one level, which pop recordings make it into the top ten, but their range of choices has already been substantially narrowed by the people who control the recording industry and who pay disc jockeys to promote certain records and otherwise manipulate the selective process. Similarly, all of the members of a democratic society may have equal opportunities to cast their votes for certain public officials, yet the choices presented to them, of issues and of candidates, have already been narrowed by the mass media and other elites in the political power structure.

This raises the question of whether or not a society's body of cultural information can be considered to be truly adaptive. The answer to this is that, while much of it is adaptive for the society as a whole (i.e., it satisfies the basic needs of the system and its members), much of it is selected by and for the benefit of special segments of the society and is "adaptive" only, or largely, for them. Thus, the process of selection may result in the retention of many elements that are *nonadaptive* or even *maladaptive* for the society as a whole. Drug pushers and users select elements that they find rewarding, but which create serious problems for society (e.g., crime and illness). Similarly, major corporations make decisions that lead to the adoption of maladaptive elements in a society, such as sugar-coated cereals, tobacco, and cars that give poor gas mileage.

Because sociocultural change is *cumulative* change, it rarely involves the abrupt elimination of a large proportion of the social and cultural elements of a society and their replacement by new ones. Even in a society that appears to be changing very rapidly, most of its elements are *not changing*. Most of its symbols and their meanings, and most of its store of information and how it is used, continue to exist, and to exist unaltered. Rather, there is the gradual addition of new elements to a continuing base. This persistence of social and cultural elements in a society is called *continuity*.

Evidence of social and cultural continuity is all around us. The alphabet and the modern processes of papermaking, printing, and bookbinding used to produce this book, for example, contain numerous elements that originated hundreds of years ago, while the concept of books is over three thousand years old. Other elements, such as the concept of God, the calendar, and certain tools and techniques of plant cultivation and metallurgy, to name only a few, are even older than that. Even after a society experiences a political revolution that promises sweeping changes, many aspects of life remain more or less unchanged. For example, as various observers have noted, "Governments come and go, but the bureaucracy goes on forever."

There are a number of reasons for this persistence of social and cultural elements in a society, but one of the most important is *conscious recognition of their adaptive value*. People are naturally reluctant to do away with something they depend on when they have nothing better to take its place. Thus, every society preserves its spoken language, its basic medical, military, and subsistence technologies, and many of its norms and customs because they are widely recognized to be workable solutions to some very important needs of the *society as a whole*. Cultural elements are also preserved if they are perceived by enough people as useful in answering their *individual* needs. This accounts for the persistence of elements of art, music, literature, and religion that satisfy these needs, and for the persistence of a great variety of customs and norms, including even such antisocial patterns of behavior as speeding or using drugs.

Sometimes elements of culture are preserved not because they are superior solutions to problems but simply because they ensure *standardized behavioral responses* in situations where these are essential. For example, although driving a car on the right side of the road is inherently neither safer nor easier than driving on the left, this choice cannot be left to the individual. Every society must have a norm to ensure that all of its drivers follow the same procedure.

Another cause of continuity is *the cost involved in changing*. Change can be financially expensive; no one knows how many millions of dollars it will cost Americans to change to the metric system, for example. But change can also be costly in terms of time and energy, and it takes both to learn new rules and techniques, new ways of relating to others and of performing one's job.

Change also exacts a *psychic* toll. This can affect people at any age when they encounter new environments, as when a child moves to a new neighborhood or a young woman enters boot camp. But *new information* can be even more threatening. People in the past were reluctant to believe the world was round because it contradicted the evidence of their senses; people today are often just as loathe to part with the comfortable thought that our earth is the center of the universe or that the world was created in six days. For new information can threaten one's view of life to the extent that it is necessary to restructure one's thinking on many other subjects in order to accomodate it.

Not surprisingly, the longer one lives with a set of ideas and beliefs, the more difficult and traumatic such a "restructuring" becomes. This is why older people tend to be more conservative—that is, less open to new information and less eager for change—than young people. *The process of aging* is thus a very real force for continuity in a society. Moreover, its effects are magnified by the fact that, in most societies, people middle-aged and older have the greatest power and influence in the selection, or decision-making, process. The net result is a considerable resistance to change.

But aging is not the only process that makes the members of a society conservative. This is also accomplished through *socialization*, probably the greatest force of all for continuity in a society. For it is through this process that the members of a society acquire the belief that their culture is a precious resource and worth preserving. During their prolonged immaturity, children are obliged to master some of the most basic elements of their culture. This is essential for their survival, and their only road to any degree of independence. Before they learn to talk, for example, children are almost totally dependent on other people; after they learn, they have acquired an invaluable tool to help them get what they want. The same is true of other elements of culture: it pays the child to master them. Thus, the desire of members of the adult generation to preserve their culture by transmitting it to their offspring is more than matched by their offspring's eagerness to learn it, especially during the formative years. Since this is necessarily a cycle that repeats itself as each generation matures, the result is a tremendous force against change.

These efforts to pass culture on to the next generation are reinforced by most *ideologies*. One of their chief functions is to preserve for the future basic insights of the past. Since these insights usually include the belief that the existing social order is a moral order and ought to be preserved, a society's values, norms, and leadership all acquire an aura of the sacred and thus become less vulnerable to efforts to alter them. Ironically, even revolutionary ideologies like Marxism eventually acquire a sacred and conservative character: once they win acceptance, they, too, become a force for continuity—and against change.

Finally, the *systemic nature of human societies* is a major force for continuity, just as it is for innovation. The reason for this, as we saw on page 63, is because most of the elements in a sociocultural system are linked to other elements in such a way that change in one area is likely to make change in other areas necessary. As a result, the members of a society *do not embrace change casually*, especially in cases where they are aware of how extensive— and expensive—that change may ultimately be. When Sweden shifted to driving on the right-hand side of the road, for example, this "simple" change meant not only that cars and other vehicles had to be redesigned, but that traffic signals and road signs throughout the country had to be relocated, traffic laws revised, and the deeply ingrained habits of millions of people altered. A society naturally hesitates to make changes that might have such far-reaching consequences, and this is a considerable force for preserving the status quo.

As we saw at the end of Chapter 2, the systemic nature of human societies is most apparent in its institutions and institutional systems, and it is there that we can see most clearly many of the basic forces for continuity and conservatism. A British sociologist, in fact, once referred to institutions as "frozen answers to fundamental questions."[13] Although "frozen" is too strong a characterization, institutions are associated with conservatism and are resistant to change, because they are systems whose importance is recognized by the members of society.

In summary, the selective process within a society constantly tests the various social and cultural elements that have been introduced through the process of innovation. This testing may be conscious and deliberate or spontaneous and completely unplanned, and the outcome may reflect either the interests of the society as a whole or only certain segments of it. But whatever the nature of the selective process, the end result is the preservation and continuation of some elements of the sociocultural system and the elimination of others.

Societal Development, Stasis, and Regression

Every human society has experienced some change during its lifetime, but the amount has varied tremendously. Some societies have undergone profound change. In other societies the same cultural and social patterns have persisted for centuries.

How can we account for this difference? The answer of ecological-evolutionary theory is that *the pattern of change in a society, as well as its other characteristics, can be explained by two basic factors: (1) its environment, both biophysical and social; and (2) its store of information, especially technological and ideological.* For as Figure 3.5 shows, these are the factors that determine what happens during the processes of innovation and selection. As a result, one of three patterns will ensue: the society will grow and develop, it will remain essentially the same, or it will regress.

Societal Development   As strange as it may seem to the members of modern industrial societies, societal growth and development has not been the typical pattern. Throughout history, in fact, most societies have consisted of only a single community with less than a hundred members. Even two or three centuries ago, the majority of societies still fit that description. Societies that have grown larger and have experienced development in all of their components are the exceptions to the rule. And they have all had one thing in common: an expanded store of information about how to utilize the resources of their environments to satisfy their basic needs.

As we saw on page 64, any change that affects the way a society obtains its material necessities generates pressure for change in other parts of the

FIGURE 3.5   Determinants of basic pattern of change in a society.

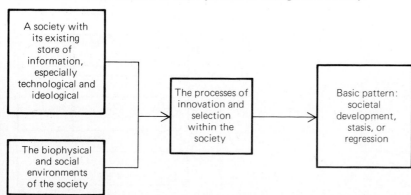

sociocultural system. And we noted on page 68 some of the changes that typically accompany technological advance, such as population growth and further technological innovation. But as the model of a developing sociocultural system makes clear, the impact is even greater than that.

Figure 3.6 shows that technological advance in a society has consequences in every area. It leads to changes in demography (e.g., growth in size, new patterns of population distribution); growth and change in the society's store of nontechnological information, including its beliefs, values, and norms; an increase in both the variety and quantity of its material products; and growth and change in its social structure. But the model barely hints at the number and diversity of the changes that occur in a sociocultural system as a consequence of a significant advance in technology. For example, "growth in complexity of social structure" could involve the creation of new, more specialized occupations; the formation of specialized associations, such as churches, businesses, labor unions, political parties, and schools; an increasing division of labor both within communities and between different communities and regions; the development of a variety of status systems; and the emergence of classes, bureaucracies, and social movements. Similarly, changes in a society's ideological information may involve new beliefs, values, and norms that have far-reaching consequences for the society's kinship system, polity, economy, religion, education, and other institutional areas. The greater the change in its technology and the faster it occurs, the greater and more rapid the change in the rest of the system is likely to be.

An important feature of the model is the role of *feedback*, indicated by the dotted arrows. Feedback is a special kind of causal relationship in which a part of the effect produced by an initial cause or event reverts back to its source. For example, weakness might cause an ill person to miss a number of meals, and the lack of food would then reinforce the original weakness. Similarly, population growth that results from technological advance has a feedback effect that produces still further technological innovation and advance. Other

FIGURE 3.6   Model of a developing sociocultural system.

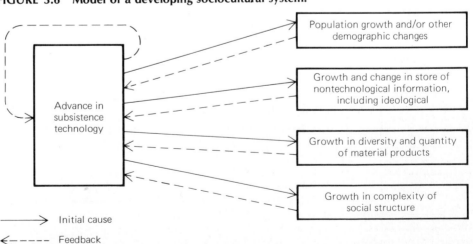

consequences of technological advance also have feedback effects, as shown in the model.

Societal Stasis Stasis is a word borrowed from the ancient Greeks, for whom it meant the condition of standing still. This term applies to societies that for a considerable period of time, or even for their entire history, show little or no evidence of growth or development. As we have seen, this applies to the vast majority of societies in human history. Typical of these societies are the small, isolated, technologically primitive groups that were found until recently in areas like the Canadian arctic, the Amazonian rain forest, and most of the Australian continent.

Societies like these apparently achieved a stable equilibrium with their environments, both biophysical and social. Their biophysical environments provided them with resources, their technology enabled them to use those resources, and neither other societies nor changes in the biophysical environment did anything to interfere with or disrupt the status quo. Changes did, of course, occur in these societies. There might, for example, be changes in the content of stories or legends, in the way words were pronounced, or in the rules governing kinship relationships. But changes like these could not alter the group's basic means of adapting to its environment or produce any significant growth in its population size or structural complexity. The condition of stasis would thus be preserved for centuries.

Societal Regression Occasionally, a society has actually regressed, losing important cultural elements, declining in size, or becoming less developed in other ways. One society, for example, lost the technique of canoe making, with serious consequences for its subsistence.[14] Another is believed to have abandoned farming and reverted to hunting and gathering.[15]

Regression can also occur in larger, more advanced societies. This is especially likely to happen as a result of military defeat, but it can also be a consequence of plagues and other disasters. Germany and Japan in the years immediately following World War II, and Rome in the last decades of its existence, are examples of the former. Many of the societies of Western Europe in the years following the Black Plague experienced some degree of social and cultural regression: enormous losses of population in many areas led to the abandonment of numerous communities, substantial reductions in productivity, and a variety of other reversals.[16] In these more advanced societies, however, the process of regression is likely to be temporary unless, as in the case of Roman society, it eventuates in the collapse of the entire sociocultural system.

Technology's Role in Societal Change

The importance of technology in the process of societal change should, by now, be clear. Technological change, more than any other kind of change, stimulates and even necessitates change in other parts of a sociocultural system. We partially explained this by saying technology is a lot like an extension of, or supplement to, the store of genetic information that helps us satisfy our most basic needs.

But technology goes even further. It helps us satisfy socially and culturally derived needs as well. For example, people's needs for aesthetic experience and for self-expression lead them to apply their society's store of technological information to the creation of musical instruments and fine fabrics. Similarly, the need to understand the world around them has led people to apply their technology to the production of scientific instruments. Such applications of technology to meet needs *beyond* our basic ones can create a multitude of new needs and new interests in a society. Without the instruments that have peered into space, for example, there would be no space programs, no movies or books based on the new store of information, no culturally derived need to learn more about worlds and galaxies beyond our own.

It is thus clear that technology's ability to extend and enhance our genetic capabilities carries with it not only the potential for altering a society's mode of subsistence, with all that this implies for the development of a sociocultural system. Technology also has the potential for creating more diverse populations, both within and among societies. This is a fundamental cause of the differences found even among societies that have similar technologies and similar environments.

As this suggests, a society's characteristics are not *determined* by its technology; rather, they are made *possible* by it. For technology affects a society and its patterns of change and development in two basic ways. First, *a society's technology sets limits on what is possible in the rest of the sociocultural system*. Thus, a society with a limited store of technological information cannot build cities or develop complex social structures, such as large corporations. Second, *a society's technology determines the relative economic costs of the options available within those limits.*[17] The technology of a Third World nation, for example, might provide its members with several possible solutions to the problem of hunger. Their options might include importing more food, importing more farm machinery and fertilizer, developing industries to manufacture more farm machinery and fertilizer at home, and developing a program to reduce the rate of population growth. The society's technology would not only make all of these alternatives possible, but it would determine which would be the most expensive and which the least.

Ideology's Role in Societal Change

Although technology's influence on the process of societal change is substantial, it is never total. A society's beliefs and values also play a role. Whether there will be more guns or more butter, better housing for the masses or more splendid public monuments, more nonessential products or cleaner air, are decisions that reflect, to a greater or lesser degree, the ideological information of the society as a whole or of its more influential members.

We have just seen that a society's technology determines the relative economic costs of available options, and it is in this context that the role of ideology can be seen most clearly. For ideological reasons, a society may choose *not* to adopt the least costly solution to a problem. In the case of hunger in Third World nations, it is clear that most of them have rejected the least expensive solution—population limitation—because of their members' beliefs about birth control and the desirability of having many children. Similarly, Iranian society under the Ayatollah Khomeini knowingly sacrificed much of its oil revenue in an effort to create a social order that its leaders believed would conform more closely to Islamic ideals.

Because modern industrial societies have greater economic resources to work with, there is more scope in them for ideological influence on many issues than in less advanced societies. But no society has unlimited resources. When a costly solution to one of its problems is adopted, it invariably means there will be fewer resources available for solving the rest.

How great a role ideology plays in the selection process depends in large part on the kind of choice involved. In the more utilitarian aspects of life, ideology is unlikely to have an appreciable impact, because competing elements of technology can be evaluated and judged in terms of their relative efficiency and because there is so little sentiment attached to most elements of technology. As a result, the tools and techniques used by steelmakers in the Soviet Union are likely to be very similar to those used by steelmakers in the United States, despite the ideological differences that divide the two societies. For similar reasons, ideology has rarely influenced women who have had the opportunity to choose between scrubboards and washing machines, or men who have had a choice between horsedrawn plows and tractors.

The situation is very different, however, in many other areas of human life. In art, religion, politics, and morality, for example, it is difficult to demonstrate the relative intrinsic value of specific cultural elements, and as a result it is almost impossible to evaluate the alternatives accurately and objectively. To the choices he or she must make in such areas, each individual brings ideological information that reflects his or her personal experiences, a set of beliefs and values not quite like that of any other individual. Thus, when large numbers of individuals become involved in a decision, there is likely to be a tremendous diversity of "scales" on which the alternatives are weighed.

Ideologies provide people with different information even on such a basic issue as whether there should *be* any change in their society. Some ideologies, as we have seen, lead the members of the society, or those in positions of power, to oppose change, while other ideologies encourage it. Among the latter, ideology also helps to determine *how such change should be brought about*. Some ideologies, such as Marxism, advocate collectivist methods of dealing with societal problems. Others, such as Christianity and capitalism, place the responsibility for change primarily on the individual. These differences can also be very important in shaping the choices a society makes within the limits set by its technology.

The Process of Change in the World System

Because human societies interact with one another and relationships develop among them, there is a world system of societies. Change occurs in this world system, and like change in any individual society or sociocultural system, it is the result of a process of *selection* operating on a set of competing *variations*. In this case, however, it is not the social and cultural elements of individual societies that are the variations: it is the societies themselves.

Variation: A Diversity of Societies

Over the course of human history, there have been an incredible number of societies. For example, it is estimated that the world system of societies around 7000 B.C. included at least 100,000 of them.[18] When our species first emerged, and for a long time afterward, societies were all very much alike with respect to size, structural complexity, technology, and other basic characteristics. Up until about 10,000 B.C., the world system remained relatively homogeneous; it contained no significant variations for the process of selection to work on.

Eventually, however, as the processes of innovation and selection continued to work *within* societies, greater variation was produced and increasingly dissimilar societies came to be part of the same world system. This trend continued until, in recent centuries, the world system has included every type of human society that ever existed, from small nomadic bands of a few dozen hunters and gatherers to enormous and complex industrial nations.

The Process of Intersocietal Selection

Why does one society in a world system survive while others are eliminated? The members of American, Canadian, Australian, Brazilian, and Soviet societies need not look far for the answer to this question: it is in their own history books. For in the not too distant past of each of these societies, much of the territory they now occupy was occupied by thousands of societies that no longer exist. Most of those societies were tiny and had very limited stores of technological information.* And in the vast majority of cases, they failed to survive because they lacked sufficient military resources and people to defend their territorial bases. The same thing has happened in other centuries, and in other parts of the world. For the harsh fact of history is that, when struggles have developed between a society that is technologically more advanced—and thus militarily more powerful—than its neighbors, the former has survived and the latter have not.

Many people today believe that peace is the normal state of relations among nations, and that hostility and war are abnormal. As much as we might wish this were true, the historical record says otherwise. A study of eleven European countries, for example, covering periods of from 275 to 1,025 years,

---

*A very few were larger and more advanced, such as Estonia, Latvia, and Lithuania, all once independent nations in what is now Soviet territory, but all small in comparison with that society.

The most important underlying cause of intersocietal conflict is essentially the same that underlies competition in the rest of the biotic world: the limited supply of resources. A finite supply of resources, no matter how great, will not suffice for a population with an infinite capacity for expansion. Unless its growth is curtailed, every population, human or animal, eventually exhausts its supply of resources and encroaches on the territory of neighboring populations.

In the case of our species, of course, the problem is greatly intensified by culture, which, as we have seen, *multiplies* human needs. Once a society is able to produce more than the necessities of life, its members strive to produce and acquire nonessentials because of their prestige value.[20] Since prestige is a relative thing, it is impossible to satisfy the demand for goods and services it generates, and scarcity is inevitable, regardless of how much technology advances and production is increased. Many wars have been fought to provide, not the necessities of life for the masses, but glory and luxuries for their leaders.

Nonmilitary forms of power can also affect intersocietal selection. Indian society, for example, has been gradually destroying, through cultural absorption, scores of primitive societies along its borders.[21] In most instances, members of these tribes, or their leaders, are envious of the advantages afforded by membership in Indian society. This leads them to abandon the traditional culture of their own group and adopt Hindu ways. Even when only part of a tribe does this, it can be enough to undermine the autonomy of the group and bring about its eventual destruction. Other cases of nonviolent extinction have involved disasters such as epidemics. Certain American Indian societies, for example, were so decimated by smallpox that they could not function independently and the survivors were absorbed by neighboring societies. It is important to note that, even in cases like these, technological advance is not irrelevant. More advanced societies, with their larger populations, could have survived the loss of half or even more of their members, as a number of European societies did during the plagues of the Middle Ages.[22]

In summary, then, we can say that *intersocietal selection has overwhelmingly favored societies with greater stores of technological information*, which survive while the less advanced disappear. Nor should this surprise us when we recall that it is technology that sets the limits of what is possible in a society.

A Model of Sociocultural Evolution in the World System of Societies

Building on what we have learned about the process of selection in the world system, we can now construct a model of the evolutionary process that explains the basic trends in the history of human societies over the last 10,000 years. As Figure 3.7 indicates, the model is based on two things. The first is the variation among human societies that is produced by the processes of change

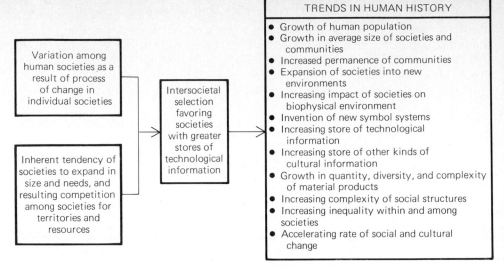

FIGURE 3.7 **Model of sociocultural evolution in the world system.**

in individual societies. The second is the inherent tendency of populations to develop increasing needs for resources, either because of growth in numbers or because of the growth of culturally based needs and desires. The combination of these two conditions sets the stage for a deadly process of competition that results in the survival of some societies and the extinction of others.

Because technologically advanced societies have the advantage in this process of intersocietal selection, their characteristics have increasingly come to be the characteristics of the world system as a whole. Thus, because technologically advanced societies tend to be larger than other societies, the average size of societies has been increasing for the last 10,000 years. Similarly, because technologically advanced societies are structurally more complex than other societies, the trend in the world system has been in the direction of increasingly complex societies. The same logic applies to all of the trends shown in Figure 3.7.

There is, of course, nothing inevitable or unalterable about these trends. A number of factors could disrupt them. For example, a deadly new disease could sweep through human societies and, in a short period of time, reverse most of the trends of the last 10,000 years. The Black Plague of the fourteenth century had this effect in a number of societies, and it is not inconceivable that something comparable could happen on a global scale. An unpredictable catastrophe involving the biophysical environment could also reverse the trends of history. But a more likely possibility than either of these is that disaster will result from modern military technology. Both nuclear warfare and biochemical warfare have the potential for producing a global catastrophe, and there is no technological antidote for either one of them. Thus, ecological-evolutionary theory provides no grounds for complacency regarding the future.

Although we cannot predict the future, we can say that, so far, the process of intersocietal selection has favored technologically advanced societies. Like the old game of musical chairs, it has eliminated first one, then another, of the societies with small populations and limited stores of technological information. The result is a world system that, with the passage of time, increasingly consists of what were once the exceptions: developing societies.

CHAPTER 4

Types and Varieties of Societies

The basic aim of science is to explain how the world works. To this end, scientific research—whether it is focused on butterflies, galaxies, or human societies—seeks to discover the patterns and regularities that underlie the universe we inhabit. This entails countless observations that are designed to reveal how phenomena are similar to one another, how they differ, and why—a process of *systematic comparison*. The entire enterprise of science depends upon this process.

Classifying Human Societies

Over the years, the process of scientific comparison has given rise to a variety of classificatory systems, in sociology and in other fields (e.g., the periodic table in chemistry, the Linnaean taxonomy and its successors in biology). A classificatory system, or *typology*, helps to order and organize the wealth of information that is available to the researcher in a given field of study; serves as a guide to suggest new lines of research and new comparisons that ought to be made; and, above all, promotes the development of theory that can explain the patterns and regularities that are observed.

The typology we will use to classify human societies is based on *subsistence technology*, the technology that the members of a society use to acquire the material necessities of life. The origins of this typology, like the origins of ecological-evolutionary theory itself, lie in the work of seventeenth- and eighteenth-century European scholars who responded to the discovery of less advanced societies in the New World, Africa, and Asia by rethinking the age-old questions about our species' origins and early development. This led, quite naturally, to comparisons of societies and efforts to differentiate among them and classify them. As early as the eighteenth century, a number of scholars recognized the crucial importance of subsistence technology and based their systems of classification on it.[1]

The next eight chapters will be devoted to an examination and analysis of ten basic types of societies, each defined according to a basic mode of subsistence:[2]

Hunting and gathering societies

Simple horticultural societies

Advanced horticultural societies

Simple agrarian societies

Advanced agrarian societies

Fishing societies

Maritime societies

Simple herding societies

Advanced herding societies

Industrial societies

There are, in addition, a variety of *hybrid* types, but we need to consider the basic types first.

Figure 4.1 illustrates how the various types of societies are related to one another. The vertical dimension indicates the degree of overall technological advance: the higher the societal type, *the greater its store of information about how to utilize the material resources of its environment.* Hunting and gathering societies are the least advanced in this respect, industrial societies the most. As the diagram indicates, societies may reach comparable technological levels by following different evolutionary paths, that is, by developing different but equally advanced subsistence technologies. Because of this, the categories cannot all be neatly ranked, one ahead of the other. Maritime and agrarian societies, for example, are roughly equal in terms of overall technological advance, even though their subsistence technologies differ considerably.

For a typology to be useful, it must be as simple and unambiguous as the data permit. For this reason, the criteria used to classify societies have been held to a minimum. In most instances, a single criterion is used to differentiate between two adjacent categories (i.e., categories with a common boundary in Figure 4.1). For the same reason, the criteria used are things that can be easily ascertained—the use of plows in a society, for example.

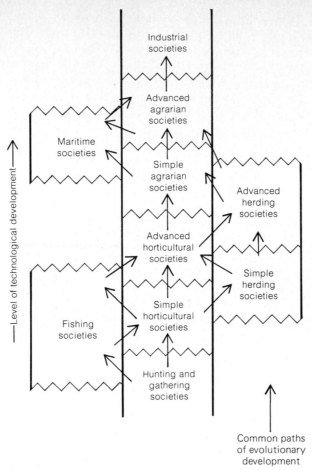

FIGURE 4.1   Relationships among basic types of societies.

A society is classified as hunting and gathering when these are its primary means of subsistence. This does not mean that the group never gets any of its material necessities by other means. Most of the hunting and gathering societies studied in the last century have, in fact, relied on fishing or part-time horticulture to some degree. But when hunting and gathering are the *primary* means of subsistence, that is the basis of classification.

The four categories of horticultural and agrarian societies constitute an evolutionary sequence of societies that depend on plant cultivation. We could lump them all together, but in doing so we would lose many valuable insights into the nature of the evolutionary process. The best way to describe the relationship among the four types is to list the *minimal* criteria for each. Horticultural societies have no plows: they work the soil only with hoes and digging sticks. Advanced horticultural societies, however, make many of their tools and weapons of *metal*, while simple horticulturists have only stone and wooden ones. All agrarian societies have plows, but advanced have *iron* for

**FIGURE 4.2   Bushmen of Southwest Africa: members of a contemporary hunting and
gathering society.**

their tools and weapons, while simple ones have only copper and bronze,
which are softer metals and less plentiful.

Fishing, herding, and maritime societies are different from the other types
of societies in that they are *environmentally specialized* types. Each of these
three is distinguished from other societies at roughly the same level of
development, not so much in terms of the technological information they
possess, but rather in terms of what part of it they *use* in their subsistence
activities. Each relies disproportionately on those elements in its technology

TABLE 4.1   Criteria for Classifying Human Societies

Type of Society	Plant Cultivation*	Metallurgy*	Plow*	Iron*	New Energy Sources†
Hunting and gathering	−	−	−	−	−
Simple horticultural	+	−	−	−	−
Advanced horticultural	+	+	−	−	−
Simple agrarian	+	+	+	−	−
Advanced agrarian	+	+	+	+	−
Industrial	+	+	+	+	+

*The symbol + means that the trait is present in the type of society indicated; the symbol − means
it is absent.
†The symbol + means that coal, petroleum, natural gas, nuclear power, and the other, newer
inanimate forms of energy are the dominant energy sources in the type of society indicated; the
symbol − means they are not.

that are especially suited to the distinctive features of its particular environment. Thus, a fishing society relies primarily on the part of its technology that is most useful to a people located on a body of water. A herding society relies disproportionately on those elements of its technology that enable it to subsist on open grasslands with sparse rainfall. Maritime societies, like fishing societies, utilized their proximity to water, though in a different way: being technologically more advanced, they adapted their technology to the use of waterways for trade and commerce at a time when the movement of most goods was much cheaper by water than by land.

Technologically, there is more variation among herding societies than among either of the other specialized types. For this reason, the category is divided into simple and advanced types. The basic distinction is that the latter employ horses or camels for transportation in work and warfare, while the former lack this important resource.

Industrial societies were the most recent variety to appear. The key to their emergence was the development of a technology capable of harnessing a growing variety of inanimate energy sources (i.e., neither human nor animal) to power a growing variety of complex machines. During the eighteenth century, coal was added to the inanimate energy sources that had previously been available: wind, water, and wood. Subsequently, petroleum, natural gas, hydroelectric power, and, most recently, nuclear power came into use. *A society is classified as industrial when it derives most of its wealth and income from productive activities involving machines powered by inanimate energy sources.*

The jagged lines along the upper and lower boundaries of the various types of societies in Figure 4.1 indicate that a few of the most advanced groups within one type may be a bit more advanced overall than the least advanced societies in the next higher type. This seeming contradiction exists because of our decision to base the system of classification on the fewest possible criteria. As a result, a society that lacks a key differentiating element (e.g., the plow) may possess enough other technological elements to make it somewhat more advanced *overall* than a few of the least advanced societies that have the key element. Despite occasional incongruities of this kind, the benefits of a simple method of classification far outweigh the drawbacks.*

Finally, a word about *hybrid* societies. These are omitted from Figure 4.1 because they would clutter the diagram and make it difficult to read. Hybrid societies are those that rely substantially on two or more basic modes of subsistence. In most cases these societies are on the boundary between adjacent societal types. For example, a society might rely as much on fishing as on hunting and gathering. In another society, at a certain time in its history,

---

*The chief advantages are that (1) the information needed to classify a society is most likely to be available when few criteria are used and (2) with fewer criteria, fewer categories are required and fewer societies will be unclassifiable because of contradictory characteristics (i.e., some characteristics pointing to one classification, others to another).

FIGURE 4.3 Hybrid societies rely substantially on elements of technology from two or more basic societal types. Contemporary India, an industrializing agrarian society, combines elements of the older agrarian technology and the newer industrial.

a basic innovation like the plow may have spread to the point where roughly half the population uses it, while the other half still relies on the hoe. Neither society can be put in a single category, and we have to classify them as hybrids.

In some instances, the pattern of hybridization is more complex. This is particularly true when highly advanced societies come into contact with substantially less developed groups and crucial elements of technology diffuse from the former to the latter. Most contemporary African societies south of the Sahara are good examples of this: they are best described as industrializing horticultural societies (see Chapter 13).[3]

Societal Types through History

Throughout most of our species history, the entire human population lived in hunting and gathering societies. This period of relative technological uniformity ended only within the last 10,000 to 12,000 years. The first new kind of society to emerge was probably fishing (see Figure 4.4). Though the practice of fishing seems to have developed thousands of years earlier, the invention of fishhooks, nets, traps, boats, and paddles was required before any society

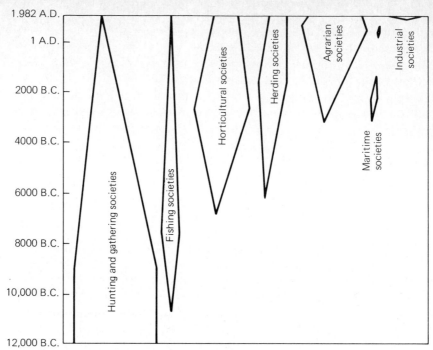

FIGURE 4.4   Societal types from 12,000 B.C. to the present: the relative size of the figures indicates in an approximate way the number of each of the types of societies in existence at different dates.

could make the shift from hunting and gathering to fishing and gathering as its primary means of subsistence.[4]

Simple horticultural societies probably came next, first appearing in the Middle East around 7000 B.C.[5] Though people began to use copper within the next 1,500 years,[6] it was not until nearly 4000 B.C. that metal tools and weapons became common enough to permit us to call any of these societies *advanced* horticultural.[7]

The plow was invented late in the fourth millennium, and this innovation also occurred in the Middle East.[8] By 3000 B.C. it was used widely enough by societies in Mesopotamia and Egypt to justify calling them simple agrarian.

Iron was discovered early in the second millennium B.C. but, like copper, did not become the dominant material in tools and weapons for a long time.[9] Thus, the first *advanced* agrarian societies did not appear until the early years of the first millennium B.C.

The origin of herding societies remains something of a mystery. Evidence of animal domestication dates from about 9000 B.C., but evidence from the earliest site suggests a hybrid technology.[10] While we cannot say for certain when any society first relied on herding as its chief means of subsistence, it was probably sometime after horticultural societies appeared.

Maritime societies date from the end of the third millennium B.C. Minoans on the island of Crete were apparently the first people to rely on overseas commerce as their primary economic activity.[11] Unlike other major societal types, maritime societies have not had a *continuous* history. After flourishing in the Mediterranean world for 2,000 years, they were destroyed by the growth of Roman power. During the Middle Ages, they enjoyed a brief revival for a few centuries, only to disappear once more.

The last major societal type is industrial. Although the basic inventions that mark the beginning of the modern technological revolution occurred in the eighteenth century, it was not until early in the nineteenth that Britain, which pioneered in industrialization, reached the point where it could be classified as a truly industrial society. Since then numerous others have followed Britain's lead.

Historical Eras

As Figure 4.4 makes clear, the types of human societies in existence have been changing constantly during the last 10,000 years. There was a time when every society was at the hunting and gathering level of development; today, we have everything from hunting and gathering to industrial societies.

To understand the problems that confront a given society, past or present, it is not always enough to know what type of society it is or was. It is equally important to know when it existed, since this tells us a great deal about its social environment, and thus about its chances for survival. For example, the situation of hunting and gathering societies today is far more precarious than the situation of hunting and gathering societies 10,000 years ago. In the modern world such a group usually finds itself in the unenviable position of interacting with far more advanced, and hence far more powerful, societies. No matter where it is located, agents of industrialism have penetrated, using their vast resources to transform the conditions of life for the less advanced group. This may be done with the best of intentions—as in the case of medical, educational, or religious missions—but that makes little difference. The ultimate effect is to transform and eventually destroy the sociocultural systems of technologically primitive peoples.

For analytical purposes, therefore, it is often necessary to specify the historical era to which one is referring. The various eras are named according to the type of society that was politically and militarily dominant in them. Thus, the long period in which all human societies were hunting and gathering societies is designated as the hunting and gathering era, while the period in which we live today is the industrial era.

From the standpoint of ecological-evolutionary theory, the four major eras in human history have been:

1. The hunting and gathering era (from the origins of our species to approximately 7000 B.C.);

2. The horticultural era (from approximately 7000 B.C. to approximately 3000 B.C.);

3. The agrarian era (from approximately 3000 B.C. to approximately 1800 A.D.);

4. The industrial era (from approximately 1800 A.D. to the present).

As Figure 4.5 suggests, the best way to learn what sociocultural evolution has meant is to examine in sequence the four types of societies whose dominance in successive eras has defined the upper limits of technological advance. In them, we can trace all the basic trends in population, culture, the material products of culture, and social structure, not simply those in subsistence technology.

The reason for these trends, as Figure 4.5 reminds us, is that the rise of the technologically more advanced societies contributed directly to the decline of technologically less advanced societies. For when horticultural societies appeared, the chances for survival of neighboring hunting and gathering societies were substantially reduced unless they also adopted the new technology. The same was true for both hunting and gathering and horticultural societies when agrarian societies appeared. The less advanced societies lacked both the numbers and weapons needed to defend themselves against the more advanced societies that coveted their territories and other resources. Those that managed to survive did so only in remote and isolated areas protected by oceans or other geographical barriers, or in territories judged undesirable by members of the more advanced societies (e.g., deserts, tropical rain forests, mountainous areas). In more recent times, the pattern of military conquest and expansion has declined considerably, but the pattern of cultural penetration by technologically more advanced nations has certainly not declined. If anything, it has become more pronounced, as we will see in later chapters.

FIGURE 4.5   The sequence of historical eras resulting from the increasing store of technological information in human societies.

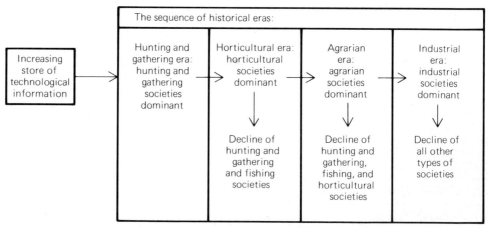

Differences among Types of Societies

The classification of human societies on the basis of their level of technological development is of tremendous value when it is used in conjunction with ecological-evolutionary theory. For the theory provides us with testable hypotheses about how differences in the *technological information* available to societies are linked to differences in their *other attributes*.

In Chapters 5 through 13, we will examine each of the major types of societies in detail. This will provide an extended test of the adequacy of both evolutionary theory and the system of classifying societies derived from it. Meanwhile, there is a simpler and quicker way to check the essential validity of our system of classification. Some years ago, George Peter Murdock assembled data on certain basic characteristics of approximately one thousand preindustrial societies. His work provides us with the information necessary both to classify those societies according to their subsistence technology and to use them to test several hypotheses derived from ecological-evolutionary theory.[12]

Population Size of Societies and Communities

One of the most basic consequences of technological advance, according to evolutionary theory, is growth in the size of both societies and the communities within them. Table 4.2 confirms both of these predictions. In hunting and gathering societies, communities are extremely small, averaging only about forty inhabitants apiece. Since these groups are nearly always autonomous—that is, independent societies in their own right—the average hunting and gathering society also contains only about forty people. In simple horti-

TABLE 4.2 Median Size of Communities and Societies, by Type of Society

Type of Society	Median Size of Communities	Median Size of Societies	No. of Societies*
Hunting and gathering	40	40	93–62
Simple horticultural	95	95	48–45
Advanced horticultural	280	5,800	107–84
Agrarian	Not ascertained	Over 100,000	58–48
Fishing	60	60	20–22
Herding	55	2,000	17–22

Source: See note 12, page 454.
*This column indicates the number of societies for which data were available and on which the statistics are based. The first of the two figures indicates the number of cases on which the median size of communities is based, the second, the number for the median size of societies.

SCIENCE AND MEASUREMENT

Science requires the precise and accurate comparison of phenomena. In most cases, it is not enough simply to say, for example, that X is larger than Y, or that it is hotter, or faster, or growing more rapidly. For this reason, scientists in every field use mathematical tools to measure things, and the precise language of mathematics to describe them and the relationships among them.

Sociology is no exception. In comparing different human societies, for example, it is not enough to say merely that one type of society is larger than another; this could mean that it is 1 per cent larger or 1,000 times larger. Such vague and imprecise statements do little to clarify the true nature of relationships that exist among phenomena and thus hamper the search for patterns and their explanation.

Sociologists and other social scientists make great use of a set of mathematical tools known as *statistics*, the most basic of which are called *summary measures*. A summary measure reduces a number of different measurements to a single measure that "summarizes" them all. The most widely used are *measures of central tendency*—or what are popularly known as "averages."

The most familiar measure of central tendency is the *arithmetic mean*. The arithmetic mean is determined by adding the measurements of the individual units and dividing the total by the number of units. For example, if 5 hunting and gathering societies have 25, 32, 39, 48, and 56 members respectively, the sum of the individual measurements is 200; and when this is divided by the number of societies—5—we obtain the mean of 40.

Another widely used measure of central tendency is the *median*. We determine the median by arranging all of the individual measurements in order and identifying the one that is in the middle. In the example above, the median is 39. The median is often a more meaningful measure of central tendency than the mean, because it minimizes the effect of a single, highly discrepant case. If the sizes of the 5 societies in the example above had been 25, 32, 39, 48, and 156 (instead of 56), we would have obtained a mean of 60, which would have been a poor "summary" of the actual facts. But the median remains 39, a more accurate reflection of the size of most of the societies.

There is one other statistical tool that we will have occasion to use in this volume: *the correlation coefficient*. This is a measure of the degree to which two sets of measurements are related to one another. For example, we may need to know the degree to which the size of societies is linked to their standards of living.

The computation of the correlation coefficient is more complex than that of the mean or the median and need not concern us here. What is important is to understand its meaning and how to interpret it. Correlation coefficients range in value from $+1.0$ to -1.0. A coefficient of $+1.0$ means that the two sets of measurements being considered are perfectly "co-related": an increase in one is matched by a predictable increase in the other (e.g., a 10 per cent increase in X is always matched by a 25 per cent increase in Y). A coefficient of -1.0 also means that the two variables are perfectly correlated with one another, but in this case an increase in one is always accompanied by a predictable *decrease* in the other. A coefficient of 0.0, in contrast, means that there is *no* relationship between the two variables, and that an increase (or decrease) in one will have no predictable effect on the other. Correlation coefficients usually fall somewhere between 0.0 and plus or minus 1.0, indicating an *imperfect* relationship between the two variables. The closer the coefficient is to $+1.0$ or -1.0, the stronger the relationship between them, while the closer it is to 0.0, the weaker the relationship.

cultural societies, communities average nearly a hundred, and there, too, these groups are usually autonomous, so that community and society are the same size.

Among advanced horticultural societies, however, the picture changes. Not only are communities larger, but multicommunity societies are the rule. Thus, though the average advanced horticultural *community* is only three times larger than its simple horticultural counterpart, the average advanced horticultural *society* is sixty times larger than its counterpart. The trend continues in agrarian societies, where urban communities are common and the average society includes even more communities. Since 60 per cent of the agrarian societies for which we have data fall into Murdock's top cateogry of "100,000 or more,"[13] it is not possible to give an exact figure for them. But it is clear that they are substantially larger on the average than even their nearest rivals among the less advanced types.

Table 4.2 is also relevant to our earlier discussion of the relative technological levels of fishing, herding, and horticultural societies. Fishing societies stand between hunting and gathering and simple horticultural societies in size. In community size, herding groups are in the same position, but for societal size, which is more important, they stand between simple and advanced horticultural. It may seem strange that although herding communities are no larger than fishing communities, herding *societies* are more than thirty times the size of fishing societies. The explanation seems to be that fishing communities generally occupy especially favorable environmental niches with respect to food, enabling them to build up greater local population densities than are normal for communities at their level of technological development, while herding peoples' environments are just the opposite. At the societal level, however, the technological superiority of herding societies permits them to expand geographically and develop politically to a degree that is impossible for the less advanced fishing groups. Moreover, political expansion is easier in the open steppe and prairie environments of herders than in the coastal and river territories of fishing peoples, where there are often a multitude of natural barriers.

Permanence of Settlements

Ecological-evolutionary theory also predicts that technological advance leads societies to establish more permanent settlements. Because the hunting of wild animals and the gathering of wild vegetable products soon depletes the supply of foodstuffs in the immediate area surrounding human settlements, hunter-gatherers are forced to move about with considerable frequency. In contrast, societies that practice horticulture or agriculture should, according to our theory, be able to establish more permanent settlements.

Murdock's data confirms that this is so. Of the 147 hunting and gathering societies for which data were available, *only 10 per cent* were reported to have permanent settlements, and these only because of unusually favorable environmental conditions or partial reliance on horticulture, fishing, or other more advanced technologies. Meanwhile, *96 percent* of the 377 horticultural and agrarian societies had permanent settlements.

Complexity of Social Structure

A third important prediction which ecological-evolutionary theory allows us to make is that technological advance will be linked to greater complexity of social structure. Murdock's data permit us to test this hypothesis in two ways. First, we can compare societies on the basis of the degree of their occupational specialization, and second, we can compare them on the basis of the complexity of their status systems. Thus, we can test the complexity of both the vertical *and* the horizontal dimensions of social structure (see page 51).

Table 4.3 shows the frequency with which several kinds of occupational specialists are found in seven different types of societies. In hunting and gathering societies, technologically the least advanced, there are no specialists in the six areas indicated. Specialization in those areas occurs in a tiny minority of simple horticultural societies, but becomes considerably more common in advanced horticultural and agrarian societies. In industrial societies, there are specialists in all of these fields. In fishing societies, the level of occupational specialization is comparable to that in simple horticultural societies, while in herding societies it more closely resembles advanced horticultural societies.

Figure 4.6 shows the relationship between subsistence technology and the complexity of status systems. Once again, as ecological-evolutionary theory would lead us to expect, there is a steady progression from hunting and gathering to industrial societies, with complex status systems totally absent in the former and universally present in the latter. The three intermediate types of societies occupy intermediate positions on the scale, with the technologically more advanced also the more likely to have complex status systems.

TABLE 4.3   Frequency of Craft Specialization,* by Type of Society (in percentages)

Type of Society	Metalworking	Weaving	Leather Working	Pottery	Boat Building	House Building	Average
Hunting and gathering	†	0	0	0	0	0	0
Simple horticultural	†	0	3	2	4	2	2
Advanced horticultural	100	6	24	24	9	4	28
Agrarian	100	32	42	29	5	18	38
Industrial‡	100	100	100	100	100	100	100
Fishing	†	0	0	0	9	4	2
Herding	95	11	22	†	†	0	21

Source: See note 12, page 454.
*The term "craft specialization" as used here includes Murdock's category of industrial specialization.
†The activity in question is seldom found in this type of society.
‡The figures for industrial societies are not from Murdock's data but are added simply for comparative purposes.

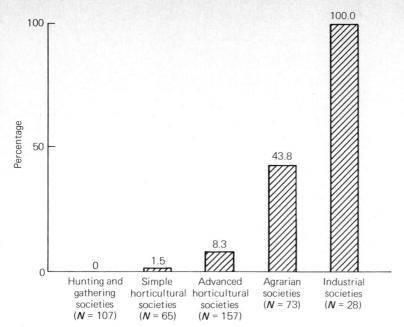

FIGURE 4.6 Percentage of societies having complex status systems, by type of society.

Ideology

Finally, our theory leads us to expect that technologically advanced societies will differ from less advanced societies in matters of ideology. Here again, Murdock's data give us the information we need to test this hypothesis with respect to at least one aspect of ideology: the religious beliefs of preindustrial societies.

As Table 4.4 indicates, the basic religious beliefs of the technologically least advanced societies—hunting and gathering, simple horticultural, and fishing—tend to be quite different from those of the more advanced, especially agrarian and herding societies. Few societies in the first group have even developed the concept of a Supreme Creator, and those that have usually assume him to be remote and indifferent to human concerns. By contrast, the majority of advanced horticultural societies believe in a Supreme Creator, but they, too, see him as inactive or indifferent to the affairs of humans. Finally, the majority of agrarian and herding societies believe not only in a Supreme Creator, but in one who is actively concerned with this world and provides support for those patterns of conduct he finds pleasing.[14]

Technological Determinism?

Today, as in the past, efforts to understand the role of technology in human life have been hindered by the tendency of some scholars to take extreme positions on the subject. Over the years, one group has argued the case for technological

**TABLE 4.4   Beliefs Concerning God, by Type of Society
(in percentages)**

Type of Society	Beliefs*				Percentage Total	No. of Societies
	A	B	C	D		
Hunting and gathering	60	29	8	2	99	85
Simple horticultural	60	35	2	2	99	43
Advanced horticultural	21	51	12	16	100	131
Agrarian	23	6	5	67	101	66
Fishing	69	14	7	10	100	29
Herding	4	10	6	80	100	50

Source: See note 12, page 454.
*A—no conception of Supreme Creator; B—belief in a Supreme Creator who is inactive or not concerned with human affairs; C—belief in a Supreme Creator who is active in human affairs but does not offer positive support to human morality; D—belief in a Supreme Creator who is active and supports human morality.

determinism, saying, in effect, that technology explains almost every sociocultural pattern.[15] To combat this exaggerated view and to uphold the importance of ideological factors, other scholars have minimized or even denied the importance of technology.[16] The unreasonableness of *both* positions has apparently escaped many social scientists, with the result that sociology and anthropology have been slow in coming to a realistic assessment of technology's role in the evolutionary process.

Much of the confusion results from the failure to think in *probabilistic* and *variable* terms. Few, if any, significant social patterns are determined by a single factor. Where human societies are concerned, one can rarely say that A, and A alone, causes B. Usually B is due to the combined effect of a number of factors, and, although A may be the most important, it alone is not likely to be strong enough to determine the outcome. The most we can say, as a rule, is that if A is operative, B will occur *with some degree of probability*.

The problem is further complicated because so many of the B's we deal with are *variables*. For example, when we talk about a society's population, we are not interested in whether it exists, but in its relative size. The same is true of most of the other things we are concerned with—the *degree* of occupational specialization, the *frequency* of warfare, the *extent* of the authority vested in leaders, and so forth. To think in categorical, either-or terms about such matters is bound to be misleading.

Clearly, then, the controversy over technological determinism has been a false issue. Technological factors are obviously incapable of explaining all social and cultural phenomena. On the other hand, the evidence indicates that they explain a great deal. How much they explain varies from subject to subject. We can see this in Table 4.5, which is a measure of the explanatory power of the societal typology we have used in analyzing Murdock's data.

To understand what this table means, look again at Table 4.4. In column D, which shows the percentage of societies of various types that believe in a

TABLE 4.5 Range of Differences for Selected Variable Characteristics in Six Basic Types of Societies* (in percentages)

Variable Characteristics	Range
Specialization in metalworking	100
Leather working: wholly or largely a female activity	96†
Boat building practiced	91
Nomadic communities	87
Median size of communities 100 or more	80
Belief in Creator God as active and moral force	78
Slavery practiced	74
Two or more levels of government above the local community	71
Pottery made	71
Urban communities of 5,000 or more	67
Bride price or bride service required	56
Weaving practiced	56
House construction: predominantly male activity	51
Premarital virginity enforced for women	49
Weaving: predominantly male activity	46†
Specialization in leather working	42
Gathering: predominantly female activity	31
Specialization in pottery making	29
Specialization in fishing	29
Fishing: predominantly male activity	22†
Specialization in house construction	18
Specialization in boat building	9
Boat building: predominantly male activity	8†
Polyandry	1
Hunting: predominantly male activity	0†

*The societal types are those shown in Table 4.4. Industrial societies are not included.
†Percentage difference based on those societies in which the specified activity is carried on and for which data on sexual specialization are available.

Supreme Creator who is active in human affairs and supports the moral order, we see that the highest figure is 80 per cent (herding societies) and the lowest is 2 per cent (both hunting and gathering and simple horticultural societies). The difference between these extremes is 78 percentage points, and this is the figure which appears in the sixth row from the top of Table 4.5 beside the heading, "Belief in Creator God as active and moral force." All the other figures in Table 4.5 were obtained in the same way from tables similar to Table 4.4, but dealing with other topics. Industrial societies were not included in the calculations, since Murdock's data on them were often inadequate.

The chief fact that emerges from a study of Table 4.5 is that the influence of technology on the other characteristics of human societies is *highly variable*. In fact, it covers the full range of our scale, from 0, where there is no relationship between the subsistence technology of a society and the other characteristic, to 100, where there is a perfect relationship. Most relationships fall somewhere between these extremes.

In summary, modern ecological-evolutionary theory does *not* take a deterministic view of technology's role: it views subsistence technology as but one force in a field of forces that, together, determine the total pattern of societal characteristics. Its position can be stated briefly in two propositions:

1. Technological advance has been the chief determinant of that set of global trends—in population, culture, the material products of culture, and social structure—which defines the basic outlines of human history.

2. Subsistence technology is the most powerful single variable influencing the social and cultural characteristics of societies, individually and collectively—not with respect to the determination of each and every characteristic, but rather with respect to the total set of characteristics.

These propositions suggest that the first step in analyzing *any* society should be to determine its basic technology. This assures that we take into account, at the start of our analysis, the most powerful single factor influencing the total life of that society.

Our basic task for the rest of this volume will be to apply these propositions in a broadly comparative study of human societies. We will examine each of the major societal types that have emerged in the course of history, seeing how technological innovations have influenced developments in population, culture, social structure, and material products, and how developments in these areas have fed back on technology and influenced its development. We will, for obvious reasons, give special attention to the industrial and industrializing societies of our own day. Our ultimate goal is to understand the basic forces responsible for sociocultural evolution, in the hope that this will help us better understand and better control the processes of change that are such striking, and at times, threatening, features of the contemporary world.

PART II

Preindustrial Societies

CHAPTER 5

Hunting and Gathering Societies

Hunting and gathering societies are unique, for they alone span the whole of human history. From the emergence of our first hominid ancestors down to the present, there have always been societies obtaining their livelihood in this way, but the effects of industrialization make it unlikely that any will survive into the twenty-first century. Because these peoples add so much to our understanding of the development of human societies, we must be grateful that they survived long enough for trained observers to live among them and record their way of life.

For several decades, these modern hunting and gathering societies were the focus of a major controversy among social scientists. Some scholars saw them as the living counterparts of prehistoric hunting and gathering societies. Others denied this, arguing that these modern groups are products of an evolutionary process just as lengthy as that of any modern industrial society.

Though the latter view prevailed for a time, there has been a substantial reversal. Many archaeologists now refer to the hunting and gathering peoples of prehistoric and modern times as "analogous peoples" and acknowledge that inferences drawn from ethnographic studies (i.e., studies of *contemporary* primitive societies) benefit archaeological studies.[1] A leading British archaeologist summed up the current view when he wrote that the archaeologist learns from the ethnographer

. . . how particular peoples adapt themselves to their environments, and shape their resources to the ways of life demanded by their own cultures: he thus gains a knowledge of alternative methods of solving problems and often of alternative ways of explaining artifacts resembling those he recovers from antiquity. Study of ethnography will not as a rule . . . give him straight answers to his queries. What it will do is to provide him with hypotheses in the light of which he can resume his attack on the raw materials of his study. In fact, the great value of ethnography to the [archaeologist] is that it will often suggest to him what to look for. . . . By constant reference to the culture of living or recently living societies, the [archaeologist] should be able to enrich and fortify his interpretation of the past, as well as bring into the open problems calling for further research.[2]

In our analysis, we will not assume that hunting and gathering societies of both eras are alike, but will, instead, follow the conservative procedure of presenting the findings of archaeology and ethnography separately. Only after we have done this will we explore the question of whether they provide consistent or contradictory images of hunting and gathering societies.

Hunting and Gathering Societies Prior to 35,000 B.C.

It is easy to speak of "the dawn of human history," but it is not so easy to assign a date to it, or even to say precisely what it means. The same evolutionary process that produced our species, Homo sapiens, first produced a number of others (e.g., Ramapithecus and Homo erectus) that were, to widely varying degrees, "humanlike." Thus, it is impossible to say that human history began at some particular point. What *is* possible is to identify the patterns that gradually began to form during the long era of "morning twilight" that ultimately produced *fully* human creatures and *truly* human societies.

Our species, Homo sapiens, is part of the genus *Homo*, which is, in turn, part of the family *Hominidae*, better known as the hominids. This family split off from the ancestors of the modern chimpanzees and gorillas at least 4 million years ago, according to the best available evidence,[3] and has subsequently pursued a separate, distinct, and increasingly unique evolutionary course. The process of natural selection, operating on the populations of a succession of hominid species, gradually shaped this line in certain fundamental and important ways that culminated in Homo sapiens, the sole surviving member of the hominid family.

If we could look across the abyss of space and time to a grass-covered plain in Africa several million years ago, we would see that hominids were already on an evolutionary course distinct, in a number of important respects, from that of other primates. By then, according to fossil evidence, they had abandoned their ancestors' arboreal and largely herbivorous life for a bipedal, terrestrial, and omnivorous one. In other words, our ancestors had come out of the trees, were walking on two feet and moving about much as we do today, and were eating fruits, vegetables, and meat obtained by hunting smaller animals or scavenging the remains of larger ones that had died or been killed by carnivores.[4]

This drastic set of changes had involved many genetic modifications, especially in cranium, dentition, hips, and limbs. The most critical of these was the new upright stance, for this meant that hominids' hands were no longer required to propel their bodies through trees or over ground, but were freed for other kinds of activity—to manipulate sticks, stones, and other objects as tools, and eventually to fashion tools of their own invention.[5] This was a major factor contributing to the evolution of our brain, for much of the development of that organ was a response to what hominids did with their hands during that long era.

Throughout hominid evolution, the attributes being selected as elements in their basic genetic heritage developed more or less in concert, not independently of one another. These included not only greater overall brain size, but an enlarging cerebral cortex (see Figure 1.5, page 22); larger physical size (the earliest hominids appear to have weighed only about fifty pounds); improvement in hand-eye coordination; a variety of other advances in the nervous system; and increased cooperation and communication.

The hominids' shift to an omnivorous diet, interestingly, seems to have had implications for the emergence of important new elements of social structure in hominid societies. To begin with, hunting probably played a role in the early evolution of the division of labor. Because of pregnancy, lactation, and care of the young, females were probably somewhat handicapped in hunting activities. This may have led, at a fairly early date, to the beginnings of a pattern found in every hunting and gathering society of modern times: males have primary responsibility for providing meat, females for vegetables, fruits, shellfish, and other materials that may be more easily "gathered." This hypothesis is supported by recently discovered evidence that, as early as 2 million years ago, hunter-scavengers in east Africa transported their meat from the place where they obtained it to an "eating-place."[6] This practice, which is so unlike that of any living species of nonhuman primate, suggests a division of labor in acquiring food, as well as the sharing of food and the organization of activities around a "home base."

Division of labor along sexual lines may well lie behind yet another development in hominid societal life that distinguished hominids from other primates: the formation of more durable bonds between males and females. Other primate societies are basically organized around the ties between groups of mothers and their offspring; adult males do not maintain sustained contact with the group. The sustained association between the sexes that is such a fundamental part of human life may thus have had its origin in that ancient diversification of hominid diet.

The scavenging, and later hunting, of large animals also confronted hominids with the problem of how the meat should be distributed. Recent studies of chimpanzees have shown that the time they communicate the most intensely is when they are dividing up meat,[7] and it is not unreasonable to assume that our ancestors reacted much the same way. Their increasing dependence on meat may thus have been an early factor in stimulating the development of hominid symbol use as a supplement to signals.

As the ages passed, hominids came to be more like humans, both in appearance and behavior. But the rate of change was extremely gradual.

Archaeologists speak of the "almost unimaginable slowness of change" during this period.[8] Eventually, however, as a consequence of their increasing use of, and dependence on, tools, and as a result of the further evolution of their brains, hominids reached a point where, as the "brainiest" of the mammals, they began to make more effective use of the resources of their environment.

One of the manifestations of this was the beginning of big-game hunting, an activity with numerous repercussions on hominid societies. First of all, a shift to the pursuit of larger animals would have required a greater capacity for planning, maneuvering, remembering, communicating, and cooperating, and the males that did this best were likeliest to survive and reproduce. Thus, there appears to be an important link between this activity and continuing evolution of the brain, especially in its development of more memory units and interconnecting nerve cells.[9] Symbol use, too, would have been further stimulated.

There is also good reason to believe that the greater degree of cooperation demanded by big-game hunting strengthened the social bonds that united the adult members of hominid societies. Adult males could no longer be as independent of one another as they tend to be in most primate societies. And the new activity probably served to reinforce the division of labor between the sexes. Females would have been even more disadvantaged in this kind of hunting, because, as the hominid brain increased in size, their hips had

FIGURE 5.1   Fire was the first great natural force to be brought under human control. Artist's conception of cave-dwelling, fire-using hunters near Beijing, China, about 500,000 B.C.

become wider to enable them to accommodate the infant's head at birth; running had thus become slower and more awkward for them.

The use of fire was another significant technological innovation of this period. Fire was the first great natural force to be, in any sense, brought under control. Although humans may not have been able to generate fire during this era, they could preserve it after it was started by natural causes. And fire did far more than warm these societies. It set humans apart from all other animals, giving them some control over the cycle of day and night, and giving them a little more freedom of movement. It was also important for protection, and was a powerful weapon for driving predators away from camp or out of an especially good cave that humans wanted to use. Fire was also used to harden the points of wooden spears, and possibly to kill large animals by driving them over cliffs or into swamps.

The use of fire for cooking may have further affected the evolution of our teeth, and even the shape of our faces, since cooked food requires so much less chewing than raw. It was probably also involved in the beginnings of religious experience, as a basis of ritual, even as an object of worship. But most important, fire strengthened the network of interrelationships within these societies, drawing the group together at the end of a day to communicate, to remember, and to plan.

No one can say with any certainty when Homo sapiens first appeared on the scene, but the best evidence available indicates that it was somewhere between 250,000 and 500,000 years ago.[10] If we look for some dramatic change in human societies at this point, however, we are in for a disappointment. Though the archaeological record for this period is sparse, there is nothing to suggest that there were any significant new developments until much later. Living remained precarious, and life expectancy short. An authority who analyzed the remains of forty individuals who lived as recently as 50,000 to 100,000 years ago found that only one of them apparently reached the age of fifty, and only 10 per cent the age of forty. Half of them died before their twentieth year.[11]

Within the last 100,000 years, hominids began to bury their dead, often placing in the grave with them artifacts that strongly suggest belief in life after death: food, flowers, implements, and red ocher, which some scholars suspect was felt to have the life-giving properties of blood.[12] At least one grave held animal bones and cinders, suggesting either burnt offerings or the remains of a funeral feast. This era also provides us with our first evidence of intraspecies violence. Several skeletons have been found with wounds that were almost certainly inflicted by other humans (e.g., a flint projectile in a rib cage and a pelvis with a spear hole in it.)[13]

Although human societies of this era were clearly becoming more dependent upon culture, cultural change was still not as important in their adaptive response as genetic change. But the situation altered later. Since our subspecies (Homo sapiens sapiens) emerged, about 35,000 years ago, there has been no major genetic change in human evolution: cultural evolution has taken its place.

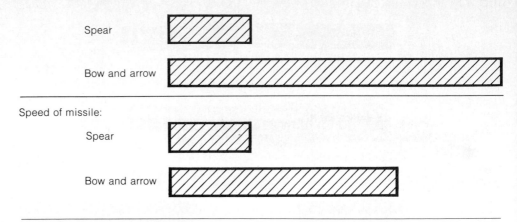

Effective wounding range:

Spear

Bow and arrow

Speed of missile:

Spear

Bow and arrow

FIGURE 5.2   Two comparisons of the spear and the bow and arrow.

Hunting and Gathering Societies from 35,000 to 7000 B.C

The clearest indication of the quickening pace of sociocultural evolution is the rapid proliferation of new and improved tools and weapons. The spear, for example, had been in use for hundreds of thousands of years, with no significant improvements except for the use of fire to harden the point. Then, in the period from 35,000 to 7000 B.C., hunters made several further improvements. First, they developed the spear-thrower, which, because it applies the principle of the lever, doubles the distance a spear can be hurled.[14] Second, at the other end of the spear they began using sharpened bone points to increase the penetrating power. Finally, they added barbs to the spearhead to create a much more serious wound.[15]

The most important innovation in weapons, however, was the bow and arrow. Utilizing the principle of the concentration of energy, hunters in this period created a weapon of great usefulness and versatility. Its effective wounding range is roughly four times that of the spear and twice that of the spear thrown with the aid of a spear-thrower.[16] Furthermore, an arrow travels two and a half to three times faster than a spear. This is important not only because of the time advantage it affords the hunter, but also because the force of the blow is a function of the missile's speed.* Finally, unlike the spear, the bow and arrow permit the hunter to sight the missile at eye level, which greatly increases the accuracy of the hunter's aim.

Other technological improvements, though less dramatic, were no less important. As one writer puts it, people of this era "began to make the tool fit the task with an altogether new precision."[17] Innovations included such diverse tools as pins or awls, needles with eyes, spoons, graving tools, axes,

---

*These advantages are partly offset by the greater weight of the spear, which means that it might remain best for hunting animals with thick hides.

**FIGURE 5.3   Artist's reconstruction of a settlement of
mammoth hunters in Czechoslovakia.**

stone saws, antler hammers, shovels or scoops, pestles and grinding slabs (for grinding minerals to obtain coloring materials), and mattocks.

In colder regions, people usually lived in caves. This was not always possible, however, as in the case of the mammoth hunters who ranged from Czechoslovakia to Siberia and whose way of life forced them to remain in caveless country even during the winter. Figure 5.3 shows a modern reconstruction of one of their settlements. Some societies also built true earth houses.[18]

FIGURE 5.4   The stag hunt: cave wall painting, Spain.

The discovery of such settlements has provided us with information on the size of human societies in that era. In general, they were quite small, many with as few as six to thirty persons. One was spread out along a two-mile stretch of river in France and may have housed as many as 400 to 600 persons, but this was exceptional and reflected unusual fishing opportunities.[19]

The best-known innovation of that period is its art. The drawings on the walls of caves in Western Europe (see Figure 5.4) are world famous, but they are only one of the new art forms developed at that time. There was sculpture of various kinds (Figure 5.5), as well as bone and ivory carvings, often on the handles of weapons and tools (Figure 5.6).[20]

It would be hard to exaggerate the importance of these artistic remains, for they provide many insights into the evolution of human thought, and the rapidly growing body of nontechnological information. Drawings of men dressed to resemble animals strongly suggest magical or religious practice and

FIGURE 5.5 The Venus of Willendorf, Germany.

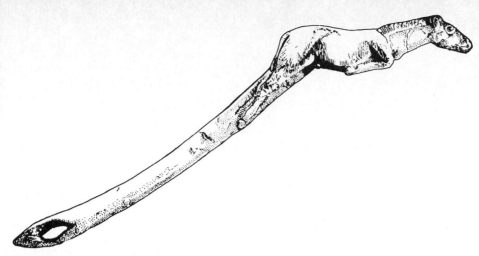

FIGURE 5.6   **Spear-thrower carved in the form of a horse, France.**

a belief in sympathetic magic. This belief—that anything done to an image, or a part, of a person or animal will affect that person or animal—is further suggested by the fact that a great number of the drawings have spears or darts drawn or scratched into animals' flanks.[21] Sympathetic magic was apparently also used to produce fertility, in both humans and animals. At least this is the most likely explanation for the numerous female figures with exaggerated evidences of pregnancy (see Figure 5.5). Most scholars think it is no coincidence that the artist ignored the facial features and devoted all his attention to the symbols of fertility.

Many examples of the art of this period indicate the development not only of new beliefs, but of ceremony and ritual. This is suggested by the drawings of men dancing and by engravings of processions of men standing before animals, heads bowed and weapons resting on their shoulders in a non-threatening position. It has been suggested that they are following the practice of some modern hunters and are asking the forgiveness of the animals they plan to kill.[22] In short, the art of this era reveals the growth of human consciousness and people's efforts to understand and control their environment, and it attests to the gulf developing between them and the animal world.

By the close of the hunting and gathering era (about 7000 B.C.), human societies possessed a far greater store of cultural information than they possessed 30,000 years before. They had, in fact, acquired more information in those last 30,000 years than in all the previous millions of years of hominid history.

Table 5.1 shows how dramatic the change was in the rate of technological innovation alone. It lists all the known technological innovations of importance from the beginnings of the hominid family to the end of the hunting and gathering era. The four time intervals involved correspond to the periods which archaeologists label the Lower Paleolithic, Middle Paleolithic, Upper Paleolithic, and Mesolithic, and it should be noted that they differ tremendous-

TABLE 5.1   The Rising Rate of Technological Innovation: 4,000,000 to 7,000 B.C.

Time Periods and Their Major Technological Innovations		No. of Major Innovations	Rate of Innovation*
4,000,000 to 100,000 B.C.		5	1
Hand ax	Wooden spear		
Use of fire	Constructed shelters		
Fire-hardened spear point			
100,000 to 35,000 B.C.		3	36
Use of bone for tools	Skin clothing (probable)		
Built-in handles on tools			
35,000 to 10,000 B.C.		16.5†	515
Spear-thrower	Bow and arrow		
Lamps	Harpoon heads		
Fish gorgets	Pins or awls		
Needles with eye	Antler hammers		
Shovels or scoops	Mattocks		
Stone saws	Graving tools		
Spoons	Stone ax with hafted handle		
Separate handles	Pestles and grinding slabs		
Boats (?)			
10,000 to 7,000 B.C.		15.5†	4,030
Boats (?)	Fishhooks		
Fish traps	Fishnets		
Adzes	Sickles		
Plant cultivation	Domestication of sheep		
Basketry	Domestication of dog		
Grinding equipment	Leather-working tools		
Paving	Sledge		
Ice picks	Combs		

Sources: This table is based on data in Grahame Clark and Stuart Piggott, *Prehistoric Societies* (New York: Knopf, 1965); S. A. Semenov, *Prehistoric Technology* (New York: Barnes and Noble, 1964); John Pfeiffer, *The Emergence of Man*, 2d ed. (New York: Harper & Row, 1972); and Jacquetta Hawkes, *Prehistory*, UNESCO History of Mankind, vol. 1, part 1 (New York: Mentor, 1965).
*All rates are calculated as multiples of the rate for the earliest period, which is set arbitrarily at one.
†Since the date for the invention of boats is uncertain, half credit has been assigned to each of the latest periods.

ly in their duration (from 3,000 years to 3.9 *million* years).* By dividing the number of innovations by the approximate time required to produce them, and by adjusting the results to make the earliest figure unity, or one, we arrive at the figures in the right-hand column, which are rough measures of the relative *rate* of innovation during the successive periods.

The 4,000-fold acceleration shown in this table cannot be explained by genetic change alone. For one thing, our genus, Homo, had already appeared more than a million years before the close of the first time period, while our species, Homo sapiens, was around for the whole of the second. But far more important is the fact that our subspecies, Homo sapiens sapiens, existed throughout the entirety of the third and fourth time periods, when the most dramatic acceleration occurred. Since there was no important genetic change

*We have set the point of hominid origins at the latest possible date, judging from current evidence, thus making our estimates of the rise in the rate of technological innovation low and conservative.

during that time (i.e., from 35,000 B.C. to 7,000 B.C.), it is clear that the explanation lies elsewhere. As we saw in Chapter 3 (page 65), inventions are essentially recombinations of existing elements of technology, and the potential for invention is therefore an exponential function of the number of technological elements available at any given time. What we see in Table 5.1, then, is a striking demonstration of this principle—and evidence of the beginnings of a trend that has continued to our own day.

Hunting and Gathering Societies of the Recent Past

Even after the emergence of more advanced types of societies, hunting and gathering societies continued to flourish in many parts of the world. A hundred years ago, there were still large numbers of them in both the New World and Australia, and smaller numbers in Southwest Africa, in parts of the rain forest in central Africa, in certain remote areas in Southeast Asia and neighboring islands, and in Arctic Asia.[23] As recently as 1788 there were probably 5,000 hunting and gathering societies in Australia alone[24] and almost certainly as many more in North America. Although the settlement of these areas by Europeans and the spreading influence of industrialization are now destroying the last of them, we have detailed descriptions of many of these groups.

In our review, we will concentrate on hunting and gathering groups whose way of life had been least affected by contact with agrarian and industrial societies at the time they were studied. Our primary concern will be with the more remote and isolated groups, and with groups that were studied before social contacts and cultural diffusion transformed or destroyed their traditional social patterns.

Even with these limitations, the societies in our sample are by no means all alike. Of the 151 hunting and gathering societies in Murdock's sample (see page 91), 13 per cent relied on hunting and gathering for their entire subsistence, while 11 per cent relied on these techniques for only about half. Most groups (80 per cent) depended on fishing to some extent, and a few (15 per cent) obtained nearly half their food from this source. A minority (23 per cent) derived part from horticulture, and a few (less than 5 per cent) almost half. In short, some were pure hunting and gathering societies, but most of them incorporated limited elements of fishing or horticulture or both.

Population

Size and Density   Despite these variations in subsistence technology, modern hunting and gathering societies* have a lot in common. For example, none of them can support a large or dense population. Even in the most favorable environments, such as north central and northern California prior to white

*When referring to "modern" hunting and gathering societies, we mean those which survived into the modern era (i.e., the last several hundred years). In writing about these societies, the present tense is usually used for convenience even though most of the studies were conducted some years ago.

settlement, the population density for small localities rarely reaches 10 people per square mile and, over larger areas, seldom exceeds 3 per square mile. In less favorable environments, such as Australia, much of which is desert, population density drops well below 1 person per square mile.[25] Communities, therefore, are necessarily small. And, since communities are almost always autonomous, societies are equally small. The average size of those that survived into the modern era is somewhere between twenty-five and fifty.[26] As ecological-evolutionary theory would lead us to expect, the more completely societies depend for their subsistence on hunting and gathering, the smaller they tend to be, while those that incorporate fishing, horticulture, or herding as secondary means of subsistence are larger (see Table 5.2).

The rate of population growth in hunting societies is so low as to be virtually nonexistent. The number of births each year seems to be matched by the number of deaths. In part, this is because of high death rates from natural causes, such as accidents and disease.[27] But it is also the result of biological processes which slow the birthrate: women who are nursing infants and women with little body fat are both less likely to ovulate than other women.[28]

The most important factor in producing an equilibrium in population size may be cultural, however, rather than biological. Infanticide and abortion are extremely widespread in these societies. One study revealed that infanticide was practiced in 80 of 86 hunting and gathering societies examined, while another study found that abortion was practiced in 13 of 15 societies studied.[29] Some scholars estimate that between 15 and 50 per cent of all live births end in infanticide in societies at this level of technological development.[30]

The members of hunting and gathering societies are not, of course, less loving than the members of other societies. Their norms and values, like those of every society, simply reflect the past experiences of the group. And this has taught them that any other course of action can be disastrous. When a mother already has one child at the breast, and may have to keep it there for several years because there is no safe alternative,[31] a second child can mean death for both children. This is especially likely to be true if the food supply is at all variable, that is, if hunting and gathering provide a glut of food at some times and a shortfall at others. If, in addition, the mother must participate regularly in the search for food and watch over her children at the same time, and if she must carry all her possessions as well as her children to a new campsite every few weeks or months (the usual practice), the logic of abortion and infanticide

TABLE 5.2 Average Size of Hunting and Gathering Societies, by Percentage of Food Supply Obtained through Hunting and Gathering

Percentage of Food Supply Obtained through Hunting and Gathering	Median Size	Number of Societies
86–100*	29	32
50–85*	48	61

Source: See note 12, page 454.
*These figures are estimates made by Murdock and his associates, based on nonquantitative statements in ethnographic sources.

**FIGURE 5.7 Bushman girl gathering berries,
Southwest Africa.**

becomes obvious. They are simply measures that ensure the health and survival of mothers and children, and thus the survival of the society.

Nomadism Modern hunting and gathering societies are usually nomadic. Some groups are reported to remain in an area for periods as short as a week.[32] On the other hand, a few occupy permanent settlements, but all of these either rely on fishing or horticulture as important secondary sources of subsistence or are located in areas with high concentrations of game and other food resources.[33]

The nomadic character of most hunting and gathering communities is an inevitable result of their subsistence technology. One anthropologist described the basic problem when he said of a group of African Pygmies that "after a month, as a rule, the fruits of the forest have been gathered all around the vicinity of the camp, and the game has been scared away to a greater distance than is comfortable for daily hunting."[34] He went on to say that since "the economy relies on day-to-day quest, the simplest thing is for the camp to move."

Hunters and gatherers may also change campsites for other reasons. A recent study of the Hadza in east Africa, for example, indicates that they often move to the place where a large animal has been killed simply to avoid carrying the meat.[35] Since their possessions are few, such a move requires little effort. The Hadza also move to a new site when someone dies, or even when a member becomes sick or has a bad dream.

Many hunting and gathering groups disperse for a part of the year, with individual families striking out on their own. This pattern has been observed in such widely scattered groups as the Bushmen of Southwest Africa, the Eskimo, and the Australian aborigines. Sometimes seasonal changes in flora and fauna make it more advantageous for the group to split up and do their hunting and foraging in smaller groups. Sometimes the splitting up of the group seems to be a response to controversies and conflicts that require a cooling-off period— after which the attractions of greater opportunities for socializing bring the group back together again.[36]

Despite their nomadism, hunters and gatherers usually restrict their movements to a fairly well-defined territory. When the society moves, it usually settles in or near some former campsite. There may even be a regular circuit of sites that the group uses year after year. A group is deterred from entering new territories if only because they are usually occupied already by others. Moreover, hunters and gatherers normally have a strong attachment to their traditional territory, which has often acquired a sacred or semisacred character that is maintained through song and legend.

Kinship

Ties of kinship are vitally important in most hunting and gathering groups. It is hard for members of modern industrial societies to appreciate the tremendous significance of these ties, because so much of our own social interaction is organized independently of kinship, in terms of roles such as teacher and student, clerk and customer, or friend and friend.

In contrast, social interaction in hunting and gathering societies is usually organized around kinship roles. A student of the Australian aborigines reports that "in a typical Australian tribe it is found that a man can define his relations to every person with whom he has any social dealings whatever, whether of his own or of another tribe, by means of the terms of [kinship]."[37] Another writer says of these people that "every one with whom a person comes in contact is regarded as related to him, and the kind of relationship must be ascertained so that the two persons concerned will know what their mutual behavior should be."[38] He adds that kinship ties are the anatomy and physiology of aboriginal society and "must be understood if the behavior of the aborigines as social beings is to be understood." Though there are exceptions to this, *kinship is usually the basic organizing principle in hunting and gathering societies.*[39]

Viewed in evolutionary perspective, the family has often been described as the matrix, or womb, from which all other social institutions have evolved. This points to a basic truth: in hunting and gathering societies, kin groups perform many of the functions that are performed by schools, business firms, governmental agencies, and other specialized organizations in larger, more advanced, and more differentiated societies.

Kin groups in hunting and gathering societies are of two types, nuclear and extended families. A nuclear family includes a man, his wife or wives, and their unmarried children. Polygyny is widespread; only 12 per cent of the hunting and gathering groups in Murdock's data set are classified as monogamous. It does not follow, of course, that 88 per cent of the *families* in a society are polygynous: this is impossible, given the roughly equal numbers of men and women. Usually only one or two of the most influential men have more than one wife, and they seldom have more than two or three. This limited polygyny is possible because girls usually marry younger than boys, and some men are obliged to remain bachelors. Multiple wives appear to be an economic asset in these societies and, to some extent, a status symbol as well.

Divorce is permitted in virtually all hunting and gathering societies and is fairly common in some.[40] In others, however, it is made relatively difficult. The most we can say is that there is great variability in this matter.

The nuclear family is usually part of a larger, more inclusive, and more important kin group known as the extended family.[41] The extended family typically includes a group of brothers and their families or a father and his married sons with their families. In any event, in hunting and gathering societies it is usually organized around kinship ties among *males*. This practice probably reflects the peculiar requirements of hunting.[42] Successful hunting often calls for extremely close cooperation—cooperation that presupposes years of close association in the activity and enables every individual to anticipate the moves of every other. Gathering has no such requirement. Since plants are stationary, no cooperation is required; if women go food-gathering in groups, it is largely for companionship. Furthermore, since animals, unlike plants, move about, hunters must have an intimate knowledge of the local environment. This kind of familiarity is acquired from early childhood on, and it is not readily transferable from one locale to another. Since marriage usually means one of the young pair must move from his or her extended family and more familiar land, the group has developed the answer that is best for its survival. Finally, the practice of keeping married sons within the family probably reflects, to some extent, simple male dominance and male preference.

The extended family is also important because the ties of kinship among its members encourage the practice of sharing. When the daily acquisition of food is as uncertain as it is in many hunting and gathering societies, a nuclear family could easily starve if it had to depend exclusively on its own efforts. A family might be surfeited with food for a time and then suddenly have nothing. Or all the adult members of the family could be ill or injured at the same time. In either case the family would be dependent on the generosity of others. Although sharing can, and does, take place between unrelated persons, kinship ties strengthen the tendency. In this connection, it is interesting that many hunting and gathering peoples create what we would call fictional ties of kinship when there is no "real" relationship by blood or marriage. These ties are just as meaningful to them, however, as "true" kinship ties and serve to tighten the bonds within the group.

Through marriages with people in nearby groups (a practice known as exogamy), a society gradually establishes a web of kinship ties with neighboring groups. According to one anthropologist, "One of the important functions of exogamy is that of opening up territories so that peaceful movements can take place among them, and particularly so that any large temporary variations in food resources can be taken advantage of by related groups."[43] This is also the explanation for the custom of wife lending, practiced by hunting and gathering peoples as diverse as the Eskimo and the Australian aborigines.[44] As in the case of exogamy, the purpose seems to be to strengthen, restore, or create bonds between the men involved. Thus, if two individuals or two groups have had a quarrel, they may settle it by lending one another their wives. The practice is predicated on the assumption that women are prized possessions that one does not share with everyone. It would be a mistake to suppose, however, that women are merely property in these societies; they often have considerable influence in the life of the group and are far removed from the position of chattels.

The Economy

Economic institutions are not highly developed in hunting and gathering societies. One reason is that the combination of a primitive technology and a nomadic way of life makes it impossible for most hunting and gathering peoples to accumulate many possessions (see Figure 5.8). In describing the Negritos of the Philippines, one observer reports that "the possessions of a whole settlement would not be a good load for a sturdy carrier."[45] The situation is the same among the Bushmen of southwest Africa. As one ethnographer explains, "It is not advantageous to multiply and accumulate in this society. Any man can make what he needs when he wants to. Most of the materials he uses are abundant and free for anyone to take. Furthermore, in their nomadic lives, without beasts of burden, the fact that the people themselves must carry everything puts a sharp limit on the quantity of objects they want to possess."[46] The few hunting and gathering groups able to establish permanent settlements may accumulate more possessions, but even they are severely limited by their primitive technology.[47]

The quest for food is an important activity in every hunting and gathering society. Since most of these societies have no way to store food for extended periods, the food quest is fairly continuous. Moreover, unlike the situation in more advanced societies, every member of the group participates and makes a contribution in this most basic part of the economy.

Until recently, most studies of hunting and gathering societies emphasized the uncertainty of the food supply and the difficulty of obtaining it.[48] A number of more recent studies, however, paint a brighter picture. Reports from the Pygmies of the Congo, the aborigines of Australia, the Tasaday of the Philippines, and even the Bushmen of the Kalahari Desert in southwestern Africa indicate that they all secure an ample supply of food without an undue expenditure of time or energy.[49] This has led some anthropologists to swing to the other extreme and refer to hunters and gatherers as "the most leisured people in the world" and to their way of life as "the original affluent society."[50]

FIGURE 5.8   Home and possessions of Paiute family in southern Utah in the 1870s.

Neither view does justice to the diversity and changeability of the situations reported by the numerous observers who have lived among these peoples. Conditions vary considerably from group to group, and within a group they may vary from season to season. For example, the Indians of northern California usually had an abundance of food, and yet they occasionally encountered a shortage so severe that some of them starved.[51]

A very few societies, such as the recently discovered Tasaday, do not practice hunting. For the rest, hunting usually provides less food, in terms of bulk, than gathering. Yet hunting is valued more highly in virtually all these groups. There are several reasons for this. To begin with, meat is generally preferred to vegetables.[52] Whether this reflects a genetically based need or preference, we do not know; certainly not everyone feels this way. In some groups, preference for meat may simply reflect its scarcity. Hunting may also be valued because it provides excitement and challenge and an opportunity for the individual to excel. Added to all this is the fact that meat, unlike vegetables, is commonly shared beyond the immediate family, so success in hunting may be rewarded by widespread respect and deference. One leading anthropologist even suggests that sharing meat "is basic to the continued association of families in any human group that hunts."[53]

Because of the primitive nature of its technology, the division of labor in a hunting and gathering economy is largely limited to distinctions based on age and sex. Hunting and military activity fall to the male, as do most political, religious, ceremonial, and artistic activities. The collection and preparation of vegetables and the care of children are women's responsibilities.[54] Some activities, such as constructing a shelter, may be defined as either men's or women's work, depending on the society.[55] Still other activities may be considered appropriate for both sexes. Further division of labor results because both the very young and the aged are limited in their capabilities.

There are no full-time occupational specialties in hunting and gathering societies, although there is usually some part-time specialization. For example, most groups have at least a headman and a shaman or medicine man. When their services are required, they function in these specialized capacities, but, as one writer says of the headmen of the Bergdama and the Bushmen, "when not engaged on public business they follow the same occupations as all other people."[56] He adds that this is most of the time.

Within hunting and gathering societies, the family or kin group is normally the only significant form of economic organization. Sometimes, when the practice of sharing is widespread and hunting and gathering are carried on as communal activities, even the kin group ceases to be economically important.

With respect to subsistence, each society is virtually self-sufficient. Trade often occurs, but except where contacts have been established with more advanced societies, the bartered items tend to be nonessentials, primarily objects with status or aesthetic value. Such exchanges usually involve things that are scarce or nonexistent in one group's territory but fairly abundant in the other's (e.g., certain kinds of shells, stones, or feathers).

Trade with advanced societies is more likely to involve economically important items. For example, many groups obtain metal tools and weapons this way.[57] In the past, these imports were seldom on a scale sufficient to alter the basic character of these societies.* In recent years, however, as contacts with industrialized and industrializing societies have increased, the volume and importance of the items have often greatly distorted traditional patterns of economic life and done much to undermine the sociocultural system as a whole.

The Polity

The political institutions of modern hunting and gathering societies are very rudimentary. As we have seen, most local communities are autonomous and independent entities (i.e., they are, in fact, societies as well as communities) even though they have populations of fewer than fifty people. Because they are

---

*The introduction of the horse and the gun among the Plains Indians of the United States was an important exception to the usual pattern.[58]

so small, hunting and gathering societies have not developed political mechanisms of the kind required to control and coordinate large or diverse populations.

The primitive nature of the political systems of these societies can be seen most clearly in the limited development of specialized political roles and the equally limited authority vested in them. In most cases, there is simply a headman, who provides minimal leadership for the group.[59] The late Allan Holmberg, who lived among the Siriono of eastern Bolivia, wrote a description of their headmen that is close to being a portrait of the "typical" headman in a hunting and gathering society.

> Presiding over every band of Siriono is a headman, who is at least nominally the highest official of the group. Although his authority theoretically extends throughout the band, in actual practice its exercise depends almost entirely upon his personal qualities as a leader. In any case, there is no obligation to obey the orders of a headman, no punishment for nonfulfillment. Indeed, little attention is paid to what is said by a headman unless he is a member of one's immediate family. To maintain his prestige a headman must fulfill, in a superior fashion, those obligations required of everyone else.
>
> The prerogatives of a headman are few. . . . The principal privilege . . . if it could be called such, is that it is his right to occupy, with his immediate family, the center of the [communal] house. Like any other man he must make his bows and arrows, his tools; he must hunt, fish, collect, and plant gardens. He makes suggestions as to migrations, hunting trips, etc., but these are not always followed by his [people]. As a mark of status, however, a headman always possesses more than one wife.
>
> While headmen complain a great deal that other members of the band do not satisfy their obligations to them, little heed is paid to their requests. . . .
>
> In general, however, headmen fare better than other members of the band. Their requests more frequently bear fruit than those of others because headmen are the best hunters and are thus in a better position than most to reciprocate for any favors done them.[60]

There are similar reports on most other hunting and gathering societies.[61] In a number of instances it is said that the headman "held his place only so long as he gave satisfaction."

Occasionally the headman enjoys a bit more power and privilege. For example, among the Arunta of Australia the headman "has, ex officio, a position which, if he be a man of personal ability, but only in that case, enables him to wield considerable power. . . ."[62] Among the Bergdama of Southwest Africa, the headman "is treated with universal respect, being specified as a 'great man' by adults and 'grandfather' by children; he usually has the most wives (sometimes three or more); he has the pick of all wild animal skins for clothing himself and his family, and only his wives wear necklaces or girdles of ostrich eggshell beads; and he receives portions of all game killed in the chase, and tribute from men finding honey."[63]

At the opposite extreme are a number of hunting and gathering societies, including 12 per cent of those in Murdock's data set, that do not even have a headman. In these societies, decisions that affect the entire group are arrived at through informal discussions among the more respected and influential members, typically the heads of families.[64]

The limited development of political institutions in hunting and gathering societies stands in sharp contrast to the situation in more advanced societies (see Table 5.3). It stems from the primitive nature of the groups' subsistence technology, and the resultant small size and relative isolation that make it possible for them to handle their political problems very informally. Consensus is achieved much more readily in a small, homogeneous group of a few dozen people (of whom only the adults, and often only the adult males, have a voice) than in a larger, more heterogeneous community of hundreds or thousands. A headman is valuable to such a small group only if he contributes special knowledge, insight, or skills.

Even if the leader of a hunting and gathering band were ambitious and eager to increase his power, he would not get very far. Unlike leaders in technologically more advanced societies, he would find it impossible to build and maintain an organization of dependent retainers to do his bidding, or to obtain a monopoly of the more powerful weapons. Every man is able to provide for his own material needs. The materials for making weapons lie ready at hand, and every man is trained to make and use them. If worse comes to worst, a man can usually leave the band he is in and join another.[65] Thus, there are no opportunities for building political empires, even on a small scale.

Given the rudimentary nature of political institutions in hunting and gathering societies, one might suppose that there are few restrictions on an individual. In one sense this is true; there *are* few imposed by political authorities—no court, no police, no prisons. The individual is hardly free, however, to do as he wishes. No society is indifferent to the actions of its members, and even in the absence of formal political authority, the group controls their conduct through a system of norms and sanctions.

Though there are minor variations from one hunting and gathering society to another, similar patterns of social control have developed in groups as far apart as the Kaska Indians of the Canadian Northwest, the Andaman Islanders of Southeast Asia, the Bushmen of southwest Africa, and the Punan of Borneo.[66] First, there is the custom of blood revenge, whereby the injured party, aided, perhaps, by his kinsmen, punishes the offender himself. As one student of the Bushmen put it, "when disputes arise between the members of the band . . . there is no appeal to any supreme authority [since] . . . there is no such authority. . . . The only remedy is self-help."[67] This mode of social control is usually invoked only when the victim of the offense is a single individual or a family. In contrast, when an entire band suffers because of a

TABLE 5.3 Degree of Power of Political Leaders, by Societal Type

Societal type	Degree of power (in percentages)			No. of Societies
	Substantial	Moderate	Slight	
Hunting and gathering	9	18	73	11
Horticultural	50	33	17	24
Herding	88	13	0	8

Source: Derived from data in Leo Simmons, *The Role of the Aged in Primitive Society* (New Haven, Conn.: Yale, 1945).

FIGURE 5.9 Bushman hunter.

member's actions, group pressure is used to sanction the individual. For example, if a man refuses to do his fair share in providing food, he is punished by losing the respect of others.[68] In the case of more serious offenses, the penalty may be ostracism or even banishment. The third method of control is a deterrent that applies primarily to violations of ritual prescriptions. In such cases, the group's fear of spontaneous supernatural sanctions provides the needed restraint. Bushmen, for example, believe that girls who fail to observe the restrictions imposed on them at puberty turn into frogs.[69] All three methods of social control are very informal and would not be sufficient except in small, homogeneous groups in which ties among the members are intimate and continuous, and contradictory ideas are absent.

Stratification

The rudimentary nature of the political system and the primitive nature of the economic system contribute to yet another distinctive characteristic of modern hunting and gathering societies: minimal inequality in power and privilege. Differences between individuals are so slight, in fact, that a number of observers have spoken of a kind of "primitive communism." To some extent this is justified. As we have seen, political authority with the power to coerce is virtually nonexistent. Differences in *influence* exist, but only to the degree permitted by those who are influenced, and only as a result of their respect for another individual's skills or wisdom. Should that individual lose this respect, he also loses his influence.

The chief exceptions to the near equality in wealth and economic privilege occur among the handful of nonnomadic groups, where some modest inequalities are reported.[70] In most societies, differences in wealth are very minor. Many factors are responsible for this. For one thing, as we have seen, the nomadic way of life prevents any substantial accumulation of possessions. Moreover, the ready availability of most essential resources (e.g., wood for bows, flint for stone tools, etc.) precludes the need to amass things, while technological limitations greatly restrict what can be produced. Finally, there is the widespread practice of reciprocity, or sharing, in most of these groups.

As a general rule, the concept of private property has only limited development among hunting and gathering peoples. Things that an individual uses constantly, such as his tools and weapons, are always recognized as his, but fields and forests are the common property of the entire society (see Table 5.4). These territorial rights of societies are often taken quite seriously, and outsiders are frequently obliged to ask permission to enter another group's territory to seek food.[71] Animals and plants are normally considered the common property of the entire society until they are killed or gathered, when they become the property of the individual. Even then, however, his use of them is hedged about by the rule of sharing.[72]

A successful hunter does not normally keep his kill for himself alone or even, in most cases, for his family.[73] The reason for this is the same as the one that underlies insurance systems in industrial societies: *it is an effective method of spreading risks*. As we have seen, poor hunting conditions, ill health, or just a streak of bad luck can render any individual or family incapable of providing for itself, and sharing food greatly enhances the entire group's chances of survival.

Despite the near equality of power and wealth, there is inequality in prestige in most hunting and gathering societies. The interesting thing about this, from the viewpoint of a member of an industrial society, is the extent to which prestige depends on the *personal* qualities of an individual rather than on such impersonal criteria as the offices or roles he occupies or the possessions he controls. This is, of course, a natural consequence of the limited development of specialized offices and roles and the limited opportunities for accumulating possessions and wealth. But it sharply differentiates these societies from our own.

TABLE 5.4 Frequency of Private Ownership of Land, by Societal Type

Societal type	Frequency of Private Ownership of Land (in percentages)				No. of Societies
	General	Frequent	Rare	Absent	
Hunting and gathering	0	0	11	89	9
Horticultural	36	23	23	18	22

Source: Derived from data in Leo Simmons, *The Role of the Aged in Primitive Society* (New Haven, Conn.: Yale, 1945).

Writing of the Andaman Islanders, A. R. Radcliffe-Brown reports that they accord honor and respect to three kinds of people: (1) older people, (2) people endowed with supernatural powers, and (3) people with certain personal qualities, notably "skill in hunting and warfare, generosity and kindness, and freedom from bad temper."[74] Although he does not say so explicitly, men are apparently more likely than women to become honored members of the group. These same criteria are usually employed by other hunting and gathering peoples, with skill in oratory often honored as well.[75]

Because personal criteria are so important, the systems of stratification in these groups have an openness about them not found in more advanced societies. Almost no organizational or institutional barriers block the rise of talented individuals. For example, even where the office of headman is inherited, as it is in approximately half the societies,[76] others can surpass him in achieving honor, and he himself may fail to win even a modicum of it. The study of the Siriono Indians quoted earlier tells of a headman who was a very poor hunter and whose status, as a result, was low. The importance attached to age also contributes to the openness of the system. Almost anyone who lives long enough will probably end up with a fair degree of honor and respect.

Religion

In almost every carefully studied hunting and gathering society of the modern era, there is evidence that its members have grappled with the task of explaining the world around them, especially those aspects of it that influence their own lives. Up to a point, their explanations and their interpretations of reality are the same as ours: animals run when they are frightened, people are hungry when they do not have enough to eat, serious illness can cause death.

Because their store of information is so much more limited than ours, however, they more quickly reach the limits of their ability to explain things in naturalistic terms. Insufficient food causes hunger; but why is there insufficient food? Illness is the cause of a death; but what caused the illness? To answer these "ultimate" questions, the members of hunting and gathering societies, like people in every society confronted with what they do not fully understand, have developed a set of explanations. Their explanations invoke the concepts of a type of religion known as *animism*.[77]

The central element in animism is the belief that spirits inhabit virtually everything that can be seen in the world of nature: rocks, stones, trees, lakes, and other nonliving things, as well as animals and humans. These spirits are constantly intervening in human affairs, sometimes helping, sometimes harming. They cause the arrow to strike the deer, or they warn the animal so it bolts; they enter the body to heal a wound, or they settle in the intestines to twist and burn them. What is more, these spirits can be influenced in their actions by humans who know the proper rituals, sacrifices, and magic charms. Some humans, however, are more skillful at this than others, and when people fail in their efforts to appease a spirit, as when an ill child fails to improve, they turn to the expert in such matters, the *medicine man* or *shaman*.

Shamans are not specialists in the strict sense of the term, any more than

FIGURE 5.10   Bushman shaman in a trance.

headmen are specialists. They are individuals who spend most of their time doing the same things as others of their sex (most shamans are men, but some are women), serving in their more specialized role only when the need arises.

While a shaman uses his powers in various ways, one of the most common is in healing.[78] He may also use them to ensure the success of hunting expeditions, to protect the group against evil spirits and other dangers, and generally to ensure the group's well-being. Shamans do not always use their special powers for the benefit of others, however. Sometimes they employ them to punish people who have personally offended them.[79]

Because of their role, shamans usually command respect and often are more influential than the headman.[80] Sometimes, as with the Northern Maidu in California, the headman "was chosen largely through the aid of the shaman, who was supposed to reveal to the older men the choice of the spirits."[81] The role of shaman tends to be profitable, since others are usually happy to offer gifts in exchange for help or to maintain goodwill. One early observer of the Indians of Lower California wrote that successful shamans in that area were even able "to obtain their food without the trouble of gathering it . . . for the silly people provided them with the best they could find, in order to keep them in good humor and to enjoy their favor."[82]

Socialization of the young in hunting and gathering societies is largely an informal process in which children learn both through their play and through observing and imitating their elders. Colin Turnbull, who lived among the Pygmies of the Congo, writes:

> For children, life is one long frolic interspersed with a healthy sprinkle of spankings and slappings. Sometimes these seem unduly severe, but it is all part of their training. And one day they find that the games they have been playing are not games any longer, but the real thing, for they have become adults. Their hunting is now real hunting; their tree climbing is in earnest search of inaccessible honey; their acrobatics on the swings are repeated almost daily, in other forms, in the pursuit of elusive game, or in avoiding the malicious forest buffalo. It happens so gradually that they hardly notice the change at first, for even when they are proud and famous hunters their life is still full of fun and laughter.[83]

At a relatively early age, boys are allowed to join the men on the hunt, participating in any activities of which they are capable. Fathers commonly make miniature bows as soon as their sons can handle them, and encourage the boys to practice. Girls assist their mothers in their campsite duties and in gathering vegetables and fruits. Thus the children prepare for their future roles.

This informal socialization is often supplemented by a formal process of initiation that marks the transition from childhood to manhood or womanhood.[84] Initiation rites vary considerably from one society to another, though girls' ceremonies are usually linked with their first menstruation. The rites for boys commonly involve painful experiences (e.g., circumcision, scarification, or knocking out a tooth), which prove their courage and thus their right to the privileges of manhood. As a rule, these rites are also the occasion for introducing young men to their group's most sacred lore, and this combination of experiences helps to impress on them its value and importance.

Compared with horticultural and herding societies, hunting and gathering societies put more stress on training the child to be independent and self-reliant, less on obedience (see Table 5.5). This is apparently a cultural response to a subsistence economy in which it is imperative to have venturesome, independent adults who can take initiative in finding and securing food.[85] By contrast, venturesomeness and independence are much less necessary in technologically more advanced horticultural and herding societies.

TABLE 5.5 Child-Rearing Emphases, by Societal Type, in percentages

Societal Type	Self-Reliance Stressed More than Obedience	Self-Reliance and Obedience Stressed Equally	Obedience Stressed More than Self-Reliance	Total	No. of Societies
Hunting and gathering	72	14	14	100	22
Horticultural and herding	11	3	87	101	39

Source: Adapted from Herbert Barry, III, Irving L. Child, and Margaret K. Bacon, "Relation of Child Training to Subsistence Economy," *American Anthropologist* 61 (February 1959), table 2.

Modern hunting and gathering peoples have produced a variety of artistic works. Some are strikingly similar to the cave drawings and carvings of hunters and gatherers of the prehistoric era. The motivation behind these efforts is not always clear, but in some cases it is plainly religious, in others, magical.[86] And sometimes it appears to be purely aesthetic.

Music, too, plays a part in the lives of at least some hunters and gatherers. Turnbull has written in detail of Pygmy hunter festivals, in which songs and the music of a primitive wooden trumpet are central.[87] These festivals have great religious significance and express the people's devotion to, and trust in, the forest. And, as with the visual arts, music may be used purely for aesthetic purposes, self-expression, and enjoyment.[88] Dancing is another valued feature in the life of many of these societies, and, again, the motives for it are varied.

Another popular leisure activity is storytelling. Turnbull reports that the Pygmies "are blessed with a lively imagination."[89] Stories range from accounts of the day's hunt (often embellished to hold the listeners' attention) to sacred myths and legends passed down over many generations. Legends commonly deal with the origins of the world and the group, which are often considered identical. Stories about the exploits of great heroes of the past are popular and are often used to explain the group's customs. Sacred myths and legends, as we have seen, frequently enter into initiation rites, especially for boys, and they are sometimes accompanied by music and dance. This complex interweaving

FIGURE 5.11   Contemporary cave art by an Australian hunter: the water snake and turtle illustrate a religious legend.

SONG OF THE ELEPHANT HUNTERS

The following song was sung by Pygmy hunters just before they set out on an elephant hunt. The headman was joined in the choruses by the entire group. The song was recorded by a visiting French missionary.

In the weeping forest, under the evening wind,
The night, all black, lies down to sleep, happy.
In the sky the stars escape trembling,
Fireflies flash and go out,
Up high, the moon is dark, its white light is out.
The spirits are wandering,
   Elephant hunter, take up your bow!
     Chorus: Elephant hunter, take up your
     bow!

In the timid forest the tree sleeps, the leaves
   are dead,
The monkeys have closed their eyes, hanging
   high from the branches,
The antelopes glide by with silent steps,
They nibble the cool grass, cocking their ears,
   alert,
They raise their heads and listen, a little fright-
   ened,
The cicada falls silent, cutting off his grating
   sound,
   Elephant hunter, take up your bow!
     Chorus: Elephant hunter, take up your
     bow!

In the forest that the great rain lashes,
Father elephant walks heavily, baou, baou,

Carefree and fearless, sure of his strength,
Father elephant whom nothing can vanquish,
Among the tall forest trees that he breaks, he
   stops and moves on,
He eats, trumpets, and searches for his mate,
Father elephant, we hear you from afar,
   Elephant hunter, take up your bow!
     Chorus: Elephant hunter, take up your
     bow!

In the forest where nothing moves through but
   you,
Hunter, lift up your heart, glide, run, leap, and
   walk,
The meat is in front of you, the huge piece of
   meat,
The meat that walks like a hill,
The meat that rejoices the heart,
The meat that will roast at your hearth,
The meat your teeth sink into,
The beautiful red meat and the blood that we
   drink steaming,
   Yoyo, Elephant hunter, take up your bow!
     Chorus: Yoyo, Elephant hunter, take up
     your bow!

From Carleton S. Coon, *The Hunting Peoples* (Boston: Little, Brown, 1971), pp. 114–115. Reprinted by permission of Little, Brown and Company in association with the Atlantic Monthly Press.

of art, religion, entertainment, and education provides a strong foundation for tradition and for sociocultural continuity.

Hunters and gatherers, like people everywhere, also enjoy gossip, small talk, and other nonessential activities. Games are played in virtually all these societies, but it is interesting to note that games of strategy are rare or unknown, while games of chance are more common than in any other type of society (see Table 5.6). Since a society's games, like the rest of its culture,

TABLE 5.6 Types of Games, by Societal Type

| Type of Society | Percentage of Societies Having Games of: | | | No. of Societies |
	Physical Skill	Chance	Strategy	
Hunting and gathering	96	83	0	117
Simple horticultural	83	33	7	30
Advanced horticultural	90	37	68	41
Agrarian	92	60	60	25
Fishing	93	63	3	30
Herding	89	44	56	9

Source: See note 12, page 454.

reflect its experiences, hunters and gatherers apparently feel less sense of control over the events in their lives than the members of more advanced societies feel.

Tribal Ties: Links between Societies

As we have noted a number of times, local hunting and gathering bands are usually autonomous. Rarely are even two of them brought under a single leader, and when this does happen, it usually involves groups no longer completely dependent on hunting and gathering.

Despite the virtual absence of formal political structures beyond the level of the local community, there are often informal social and cultural ties. The most inclusive of these, and one that is nearly universal, is the *tribe*—a group of people who speak a distinctive language or dialect, share a culture that distinguishes them from other peoples, and know themselves, or are known, by a definite name.[90] Unlike a society, a tribe is not necessarily organized politically. On the contrary, few are, at least among hunting and gathering peoples.

Most tribes appear to have been formed by the process of societal fission or division. When the population of a hunting and gathering band grows too large for the resources of the immediate area, it divides. Division may also occur because of conflict within a band.[91] In either case, although a new group is formed, its members will naturally continue to share the culture of the parent group. Normally the new group locates somewhere near the old one, if for no other reason than because its technology and accumulated experience become less relevant the further it moves and the more the environment differs from the one its members have been used to. As this process of fission occurs, it creates a cluster of autonomous bands with the same language and similar stores of information, and a new tribe is formed.

As this suggests, among hunters and gatherers the tribe is more important as a cultural unit than as a social unit. One writer, describing the Bushmen, reports that the tribe "has no social solidarity, and is of very little, if any, importance in regulating social life. There appears to be no tribal organization among the Bushmen, nothing in the nature of a central authority whose decisions are binding on all the members of the tribe, nor is collective action ever taken in the interests of the tribe as a whole. The tribe, in fact, is merely a loose aggregate of hunting bands which have a common language and name."[92] This description applies to most tribes of hunters and gatherers. Sometimes, as in Australia, an entire tribe comes together occasionally for some important event, but this is not typical.

From the structural standpoint, the chief significance of these tribal groupings lies in their evolutionary potential: with technological advance, they may become political units. Even among societies still on the hunting and gathering level, there is some evidence of movement in this direction. In a few of the more favorably situated sedentary groups, for example, several villages have been brought together under the leadership of a single individual.[93] Such a step would be impossible, of course, without a common cultural heritage.

Hunting and Gathering Societies in Theoretical Perspective

Archaeological and Ethnographic Evidence Compared

Now that we have completed our review of both the archaeological and the ethnographic evidence, we can consider the relationship between prehistoric hunting and gathering groups and contemporary ones. Though indiscriminate comparisons of the two can be misleading, our evidence indicates that careful comparisons are not only valid but extremely valuable.[94] To begin with, we must recognize that we cannot equate modern hunters and gatherers with early hominid hunters and gatherers of a million or more years ago—before *Homo sapiens sapiens* had evolved and before the basic tools and weapons of modern hunters and gatherers had been invented. We can, however, reasonably compare modern hunters and gatherers with those that lived during the last 15,000 years.

We can see why, now that we are familiar with both sets of evidence. The similarities between these two sets of hunters and gatherers are many and basic; the differences are fewer and much less important. The societies of the two periods are similar in such crucial matters as subsistence technology, size of local groups, relative equality,* and minimal occupational specialization. In addition, similarities in art suggest similarities in religious belief and practice.

The differences are largely of three types. First, in many modern hunting and gathering societies there are certain elements that originated in more advanced societies (e.g., metal tools and some religious ideas). Second, modern hunters and gatherers have had no opportunity for territorial expan-

---

*This is indicated by the absence of differentiation in burial remains prior to about 5000 B.C. In contrast, in more advanced societies of later eras one finds clear evidence of distinctions between rich and poor, the former having many rare and costly objects buried with them.

sion, which means that population growth has been impossible for them and their deaths and births must balance. Prehistoric hunters and gatherers were not always subject to this harsh restriction. Finally, technologically advanced societies have often forced modern hunters and gatherers out of territories that were suitable for farming and herding.*

As we have seen, the archaeological record is much less complete than the ethnographic, being silent on many subjects about which the latter provides a wealth of information. Therefore, when the ethnographic record shows patterns that are consistent for all or most modern groups and when these patterns do not depend on conditions peculiar to the industrial era, archaeologists now tend to regard them as applicable to most of the hunting and gathering societies of the last 15,000 years. This reflects the growing awareness of the *limiting* nature of a hunting and gathering technology,[95] and the realization that the range of variation in the basic characteristics of societies that depend on it will inevitably be very small. In short, except where relevant conditions have changed significantly, we can probably assume substantial similarity between the advanced hunting and gathering societies of the late prehistoric era and those of recent centuries.

A Model of Limited Development

In Chapter 2, we saw that human societies are systems of interrelated parts. In Chapters 3 and 4, we established that subsistence technology is the most powerful single variable influencing the other characteristics of a society. Now that we have completed our analysis of the first of the major societal types, we are in a better position to appreciate both the systemic nature of societies and the role of technology.

Figure 5.12 portrays the systemic qualities of a hunting and gathering society, and the relationships among its most important characteristics. The key element is the subsistence technology on which the members of these societies depend for their survival and well-being. Because of their dependency on a hunting and gathering technology, such groups are destined to be small, and usually to consist of only a single community; to be, in most cases, nomadic; to produce limited goods and services; to have a minimal division of labor, almost entirely along the lines of age and sex; and to emphasize independence in socializing their children. In addition, their contact with other societies will be quite limited relative to that of technologically more advanced societies. Although they have direct contact with other societies in their immediate area, they seldom have contact with more distant ones (except when more advanced societies establish the contact, which has often been a prelude to disaster for the hunting and gathering way of life).

---

*The importance of this may not have been as great as we would imagine, however, because territory that farmers and herders consider marginal may provide a good living for hunters and gatherers. Moreover, hunters and gatherers in both the New World and Australia still occupied good farming and herding lands until fairly recently, so we are not entirely without information on societies that existed under such conditions.

These characteristics of a hunting and gathering society lead, in turn, to others. Nomadism and a limited production of goods and services combine to limit the accumulation of property, which in *its* turn helps to ensure minimal inequality and reinforces the emphasis on independence training. Small size and limited contact with other societies have a negative influence on the rate of innovation. As Figure 5.12 reveals, there are numerous other indirect effects and consequences of a hunting and gathering technology, including the widespread pattern of food-sharing and the infrequency of warfare. In the end, the slow rate of technological innovation ensures the persistence of the same subsistence technology for very long periods of time—usually, in fact, for the life of the society.

The causal relationships specified in Figure 5.12 may actually *understate* the degree to which the various characteristics of a hunting and gathering society are interrelated; some arrows that should be included may not have been. The important point, however, is not the completeness of the model, but that it attests to the systemic nature of these societies and to the consequences

FIGURE 5.12 A model of limited development: systemic relations among the characteristics of hunting and gathering societies.

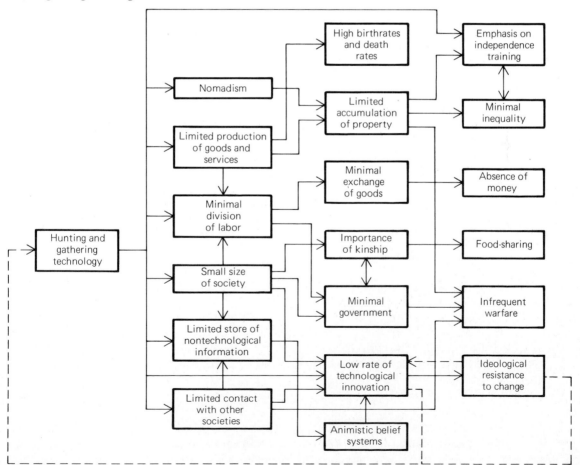

of their technology for every component of the system, including many of their basic beliefs, values, and norms.

Ecological-evolutionary theory asserts that technology sets limits on "the range of the possible" for a society, and in the case of hunting and gathering societies, it is clear that that range is a remarkably narrow one. We do, of course, find differences among these societies, but not in their basic character-istics. Many of the differences, as in modes of dress and housing, simply reflect the kind of environment in which their technology is used. Other social and cultural characteristics are not related to environmental variations, but neither are they determined by technology. This is true, for example, of certain marriage practices. In the matter of divorce, every possibility from its com-plete absence to its most casual practice has been observed. Similarly, both polygynous and monogamous marriages occur in hunting and gathering societies, with 12 per cent of these groups permitting only monogamy. In cases like these, we have to assume that a hunting and gathering technology sets broad limits on what is possible, and that it is the varied and unknown past experiences of individual societies that have led them to develop differences in some of their beliefs, values, and norms.

But where the basic characteristics and structural development of hunting and gathering societies are concerned, technology sets strict and inviolable limits. These limits are widest when the technology is applied to a particularly favorable environment. A society's biophysical environment, for example, may be especially rich in the resources on which it depends, or its social environment may provide limited competition for those resources. But the only way the limits set by its technology can be *expanded* is for a hunting and gathering society to expand its technology, as some of them have done by incorporating elements of fishing and horticulture. It is because they so beautifully illustrate the fact that subsistence technology defines the limits of societal development that hunting and gathering societies are so valuable in establishing the basic principles of ecological-evolutionary theory.

The Last Hunting and Gathering Societies

In the summer of 1975, death came to the last full-blooded member of the Ona, a tribe of hunters and gatherers that had inhabited the southern tip of South America since at least the days of Ferdinand Magellan, the famed sixteenth-century explorer, and probably for centuries or even millennia before that.[96] It is estimated that in Magellan's day there were 2,000 Ona, divided into about thirty societies. Despite the remoteness and harshness of their homeland, the Ona were destroyed not by that, but by their contacts with technologically more advanced societies. Disease, loss of territory, and loss of members to other societies all took their toll. The last Ona society died years ago; now the last member is also dead.

The experience of the Ona has been the experience of tens of thousands of hunting and gathering societies during the 9,000 years since hunters and gatherers first began competing for territories and other resources with techno-logically more advanced societies. Hunters and gatherers have had only one

FIGURE 5.13 One of the last photographs of the Ona of Tierra del Fuego, a tribe of hunters and gatherers that is now extinct.

defense: retreat to lands that other groups regarded as worthless or inaccessible.

Today, even this defense is crumbling and the last outposts of this ancient way of life appear doomed. The speed of the process is demonstrated by the experience of an anthropologist who pioneered in the study of the Bushmen of the Kalahari Desert in Southwest Africa. She reports that to reach them in 1951 required an arduous trip across the desert by truck, lasting eight days from the final outposts of civilization until she made contact with the Bushmen.[97] There was no road of any kind, not even a track across the sand and bush country. When she returned in 1962, only eleven years later, she reached them in one day over a well-cleared track. As Bushmen come more and more in contact with, and under the influence of, more advanced societies, their traditional way of life is doomed. According to a recent report, less than 5 per cent of the 30,000 Kung Bushmen are still hunters and gatherers.[98]

By the end of this century, perhaps sooner, the last hunting and gathering society will have vanished—and with it, an irreplaceable link to our past. For hundreds of thousands of years, these societies maintained a highly successful relationship with their environments. Relying entirely on cultural information that they could carry in their brains, hunters and gatherers adapted to a wide variety of biophysical environments; and, until the advent of societies with larger populations and more sophisticated technologies, they also adapted successfully to their social environments. The process of change in each part of these sociocultural systems occurred slowly enough that answering changes could occur in other parts without serious social unrest or upheaval. In short, this dying way of life served our species extremely well.

133

CHAPTER 6

Horticultural Societies

Before the hunting and gathering era ended, nine thousand years ago, human societies had accumulated substantial stores of information about plants and animals. People were as familiar with the behavior patterns of some animals as they were with their own, and probably understood them almost as well. They had identified hundreds of varieties of edible plants and become familiar with their processes of growth, fructification, and decay. Some hunters and gatherers in the Middle East even harvested wild grains with stone sickles. Thus, shifting from hunting animals to herding them and from gathering fruits and vegetables to cultivating them would not have been as great, or as difficult, a step as one might imagine.[1]

But what induced societies to take that step? Why, after hundreds of thousands of years of hunting and gathering, did the members of some societies abandon that ancient and time-hallowed way of life? Above all, why did they do it when the new way meant more work and less freedom?

Causes of the Shift from Hunting and Gathering to Horticulture

Until fairly recently, scholars tended to answer such questions by pointing out that the replacement of a less advanced technology with a more advanced one

brought obvious benefits to those involved. By shifting from hunting and
gathering to horticulture*—that is, plant cultivation without plows—societies
traded a precarious and marginal existence for a more secure and satisfying
one, or so they reasoned. Some scholars also hypothesized that the shift to
horticulture might have been stimulated by climatic changes that altered the
biophysical environment, especially the flora and fauna on which hunters and
gatherers depended.

In the last decade, however, doubts have been cast on these explanations.
New evidence shows that hunting and gathering societies had experienced
substantial changes in climate many times before without abandoning their
traditional mode of subsistence.[2] What is more, studies of modern hunting and
gathering societies have made it clear that their members put a high value on
the freedom of movement and other benefits their way of life affords.

During the 1970s, some interesting new evidence emerged, pointing the
way to a new hypothesis. It has been established that, between about 20,000
B.C. and 5000 B.C., three important and interrelated things were happening:

1. There were substantial advances in subsistence technology.

2. There was a rapid decline in both the numbers and the variety of big-game
    animals in various parts of the world.

3. There were significant changes in human diet in various parts of the world.

There is no need to repeat our earlier discussion of the technological
advances of this period (see pages 106–111). The decline of big-game animals
and the shift in human diets, however, require comment. In North America, for
example, thirty-two genera (sets of species) of large mammals became extinct
between 13,000 and 7000 B.C.[3] Included were horses, giant bison, oxen,
elephants, camels, antelopes, pigs, ground sloths, and giant rodents. The
pattern was similar in northern Europe, where the woolly mammoth, woolly
rhinoceros, steppe bison, giant elk, European wild ass, and a whole genus of
goats vanished.[4] In the Middle East during that period, people were no longer
hunting giant wild cattle and red deer, but smaller species, such as sheep,
goats, and antelope; and they relied increasingly on fish, crabs and other
shellfish, birds, snails, nuts, and wild grains and legumes.[5] Finally, a recent
study in northern Spain provides striking evidence that, around 8500 B.C.,
there was significant substitution of fish and shellfish for the meat of big-game
animals in peoples' diet, and that there was also an apparent decrease in the
average size of the shellfish caught, indicating overkill and the potential
depletion of that resource.

Putting this and other evidence together, it now appears that the shift from
hunting and gathering to horticulture may not have been a matter of choice but

---

*Horticulture is derived from the Latin words *cultura* (cultivate) and *hortus* (a garden).

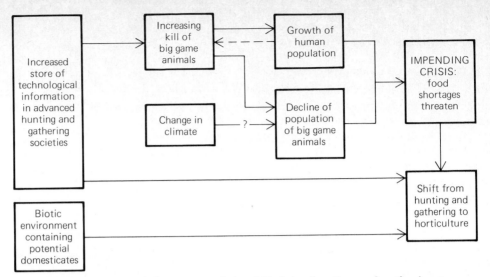

FIGURE 6.1   Model of the causes of the shift from hunting and gathering to horticulture.

of necessity. Figure 6.1 summarizes what probably happened.[6] The most basic factor in the process appears to have been the striking advances in weapons technology that began about 20,000 years ago. This would have led to increasing kills of big-game animals, whose meat has always been highly prized in hunting and gathering societies. The increased kill provided more food, leading, in turn, to growth in the size of populations. Population growth then had a feedback effect on the kill of big game, since more mouths to feed meant a need for even greater kills. As a consequence of these developments, perhaps in combination with changes in climate, things eventually reached the point where the modest reproductive rates of the larger mammals could no longer match the rate of kill, and one species after another was exterminated. This development, combined with larger populations, spelled food shortages of crisis proportions. Faced with a choice between widespread hunger, even starvation, and a change in lifestyle, people opted for the lesser evil wherever possible—that is, wherever the local flora and fauna included plants or animals that could be domesticated.

Despite the extra labor and other costs it entailed, plant cultivation, in particular, was attractive because it yielded so much more food per unit of land. Thus, it was possible for human societies to feed their swollen populations. In fact, as the store of information about domesticated plants and their growing requirements increased, so did the food yield, producing still further growth in the size of populations.

As with hunting and gathering societies, our discussion of horticultural societies begins with the evidence from archaeology. Then, provided with an historical perspective, we will move on to the evidence from ethnology, which answers a number of questions archaeology cannot. Finally, we will consider all of the evidence in the light of ecological-evolutionary theory.

In Asia Minor, Palestine, and the hill country east of the Tigris River, archaeologists have found the remains of ancient settlements, dating from about 7000 B.C., in which horticulture was apparently the primary means of subsistence.[7] During recent years our knowledge of these early horticultural societies has been advanced substantially by developments in the field of archaeology, including the excavation of new sites and the more extensive exploration of older ones. Biologists and geologists have contributed a great deal to our understanding of the biophysical environment during that era. Most important of all, greatly improved techniques for dating archaeological remains have been developed since World War II. With these techniques, prehistoric materials up to about 50,000 years of age can now be dated with a substantial degree of accuracy, and many once unanswerable questions can now be resolved.[8]

In traditional archaeological usage, the period in which simple horticultural societies were dominant in a region was known as the Neolithic, or New Stone Age. This name was chosen because in early research in Europe and the Middle East, some strata in excavated sites yielded distinctive stone axes, adzes, and hammers that, unlike earlier stone tools, had been smoothed by grinding or polishing. Prior to the discovery of radiocarbon dating, these tools were one of the best indicators of the relative age of the stratum and its place in evolutionary history.

As research progressed, however, and more and more sites were excavated, it became increasingly clear that these tools were neither the most distinctive feature of Neolithic societies nor their greatest technological achievement. Rather, their most important innovations were in the area of subsistence technology: for the first time in history, people were practicing horticulture, and hunting and gathering had been relegated to a secondary role. In this connection, it is important to recognize that these early horticultural societies had a mixed economy. Horticulture was their basic means of subsistence, but it was supplemented by herding, hunting, or gathering in various combinations.[9] The presence of livestock in many of these early societies was especially important, as we will soon see.

The First Great Social Revolution

Although many scholars today describe the emergence of horticultural societies as the first great social revolution in human history, it would be wrong to assume that the rate of change seemed revolutionary to those involved. As far as we can judge today, the process was so gradual that the changes occurring during a lifetime were neither very numerous nor overwhelming. For example, people in the Middle East had been using cereal grains for a thousand years or more before the horticultural era began. Techniques of harvesting, storing, grinding, and cooking grains were well established long before the techniques of cultivation were adopted. Furthermore, as we have noted, hunting, and to some extent gathering, continued to play an important part in the lives of the early horticulturists. There was undoubtedly considerable continuity in other areas of life as well, especially in kinship, religion, and politics. The survival of fertility cults, indicated by the widespread presence of female figurines in Neolithic remains, is one evidence of this.[10] Our use of the term "revolutionary" in connection with the rise of horticultural societies, then, is based primarily on our awareness of the long-term consequences of the change.

Permanence of Settlements   An immediate and very important consequence of the shift to horticulture was the greater permanence of settlements. No longer did groups of people have to move about constantly in search of food; on the contrary, the practice of horticulture forced them to stay in one place for extended periods. In the Middle East and in southeastern Europe, truly permanent settlements seem to have been established. In other areas, simple horticulturalists usually have had to move their settlements every few years, because their methods of cultivation seriously depleted the soil.[11] Why this was not necessary in the Middle East and southeastern Europe is still a mystery, since modern research indicates that only fertilization (by alluvial deposits or by man), irrigation, the use of the plow, or crop rotation permits land to be kept under continuous cultivation,[12] and so far there is no evidence of any of these practices. We do know, however, that these early horticulturalists kept livestock, and it is possible that the value of manure was discovered at an early date.[13] This practice may not have spread to other areas simply because of the greater availability of arable land elsewhere.

In any case, the shift from hunting and gathering to horticulture substantially increased the permanence of human settlements, thereby enabling people to accumulate many more possessions than ever before. This is evident in the archaeological remains left by horticulturalists of the Neolithic era. Tools and weapons are much more numerous and varied than in older sites,

FIGURE 6.2   Artist's reconstruction of a farmhouse of the horticultural era, Iraq (5500 to 5000 B.C.).

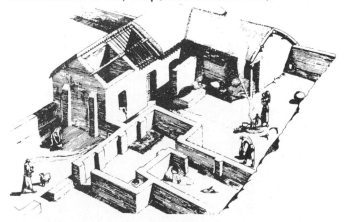

FIGURE 6.3 **Archaeological excavation at Çatal Hüyük.**

and for the first time there are large, bulky objects such as stone cups and bowls and pottery.[14] Dwellings also became more substantial. Some buildings contained several rooms and a small courtyard (see Figure 6.2) and were made of materials like sun-dried clay blocks, capable of lasting for as long as two generations.[15] Even more noteworthy is the appearance of such things as religious shrines or ceremonial centers, village walls, and occasional paved or timbered (corduroy style) roadways or alleys; though none of these is typical of simple horticultural communities, neither are they rare.[16]

The change from hunting and gathering to horticulture also resulted in larger settlements and denser populations. Jarmo, one of the oldest horticultural villages yet discovered, contained twenty to twenty-five houses and an estimated population of 150,[17] nearly four times that of the average hunting and gathering band. Neolithic villages in Europe had from eight to fifty houses, suggesting populations ranging up to at least 200.[18] In several cases there were even more striking concentrations of population. One of the most famous was a town located on the site of Jericho 5,000 years before the days of Joshua. Excavations there uncovered a community that apparently housed 2,000 to 3,000 inhabitants.[19] More recent excavations of Çatal Hüyük, in what is now Turkey, revealed a community occupying an even larger area with, presumably, a larger population (see Figure 6.3).[20]

Growth of Trade and Commerce These two communities, though obviously exceptional, illustrate another development associated with the rise of horticultural societies—the rapid expansion and growing importance of trade and commerce.[21] Modern scholars feel that the "great" size of Jericho and Çatal Hüyük was not simply the result of the practice of horticulture. As one writer has put it, "It is . . . most unlikely that [horticulture] should have flourished more at Jericho, 200 metres below sea-level, than elsewhere in Palestine. Some other resource must have existed, and this was probably trade."[22] As he points out, Jericho commanded the resources of the Dead Sea, including salt, bitumen,* and sulfur, all useful materials in simple horticultural societies and not available everywhere. This view of Jericho as an early center of trade is supported by the discovery there of products such as obsidian from Asia Minor and cowrie shells from the Red Sea. In the case of Çatal Hüyük, obsidian (i.e., volcanic glass, a material much sought after for use in weapons and other things) seems to have been the key local resource responsible for its growth. Even in small villages far removed from such centers as Jericho and Çatal Hüyük, there is evidence of trade. For example, shells from the Mediterranean have been found in the sites of horticultural villages and in graves throughout the Danube Basin and far down the Oder, Elbe, and Rhine river valleys in northern Europe.[23]

The growth in trade and commerce, combined with the increasing quantity of material products, may well have led to the beginnings of formal record keeping. Archaeologists have found a variety of clay tokens in horticultural sites from modern Turkey to Iran, but until recently no one could identify their use. Then it was discovered that the markings on many of the tokens were remarkably similar to symbols used in the oldest forms of writing (which date from the early years of the agrarian era) for such words as "sheep," "wool," "cloth," "bread," "bed," and a variety of numerals.[24] This strongly suggests that the tokens were used to represent those same objects and numbers. Since they were often stored in small clay containers, they were probably records of early business transactions (e.g., outstanding loans). But whatever their precise use in the societies of the time, those tokens tell us of a major breakthrough in the ability of human societies to store information.

Another probable consequence of the growth in trade and commerce was an increase in occupational specialization, at least in the chief commercial centers. Direct evidence of this has been found at several sites. For example, excavation of a community south of Jericho yielded a number of small workshops where such specialized craftsmen as a butcher, a bead maker, and a maker of bone tools worked.[25] This kind of specialization, however, was limited.[26] Most communities remained largely self-sufficient, and most families still produced nearly everything they used.[27] Important innovations continued in the domestic arts, with the invention of pottery and weaving being the most important of these.[28]

Increase of Warfare   There is little evidence of warfare in early horticultural societies. Graves rarely contain weapons, and most communities had no walls or other defenses.[29] Some, it is true, had ditches and fences, but these were

---

*Bitumen was used to fix blades in handles, mend pottery, etc.

more suitable for protection against marauding animals than against human enemies. Later in the horticultural era the picture changed drastically and warfare became increasingly common. In this period battle-axes, daggers, and other arms appear in the grave of every adult male. The reason for this change is not clear, but some scholars think it was linked with the growth of population and the resulting scarcity of new land suitable for horticulture. It may also have been related to declining opportunities for hunting, a traditional male activity. Warfare, with its demands for bravery and skill in the use of arms, would be a natural substitute, and if women were doing most of the work of tending the gardens, as is the case in most modern horticultural societies, men would have had substantial time on their hands to spend in this activity.[30] Moreover, the frictions created by growing pressure for land would provide a ready-made justification. Finally, some experts suspect that the increase in warfare was linked with the increase in wealth, especially in the form of cattle, which could be stolen so easily.[31]

One consequence of horticulture was that, as more and more societies adopted the new technology, it became increasingly difficult for other societies in the same area to continue hunting and gathering. As the population grew in a horticultural society, new settlements would form on the outer fringes. When they moved into territory occupied by hunters and gatherers, the horticultural- ists would, by remaining in one place for a number of years, reduce the supply of game to the point that it could no longer support the hunters. Were the latter tempted to fight for their "rights," they would usually find themselves outnumbered by a ratio of more than two to one, if the populations of contemporary groups are any indication.[32]

The Chinese Experience   The horticultural societies of China are of special interest because there the shift to that mode of subsistence began late enough, and writing developed early enough, that some memory of the horticultural era was preserved in legends that were eventually written down. For a long time scholars thought this material was entirely fictional, but modern archaeologi- cal research has substantiated enough of it that it is now regarded as an intermingling of fact and fiction.[33]

According to the legends, China's earliest inhabitants were hunters, but the increase of population eventually forced a shift to horticulture. As one source recounts, "The ancient people ate meat of animals and birds. At the time of Shen-nung [an early legendary ruler and culture hero] there were so many people that the animals and birds became inadequate for people's wants and therefore Shen-nung taught the people to cultivate."[34] Other legends relate that Shen-nung introduced pottery and describe the era as a period of peace and self-sufficiency. "During the Age of Shen-nung people rested at ease and acted with vigor. They cared for their mothers, but not for their fathers. They lived among deer. They ate what they cultivated and wore what they wove. They did not think of harming one another." This preference for mothers is intriguing, because it is so contrary to the later Chinese tradition, yet conforms to one of the distinctive features of contemporary horticultural societies (see page 153). Finally, there is a legend describing the Age of Shen-nung as the last era in which people were free from coercive political authority. "People were administered without a criminal law and prestige was built without the use of force. After Shen-nung, however, the strong began to rule over the weak and the many over the few."

The Ubaid Culture   During the horticultural era, technological progress was almost continuous, especially in the Middle East. In addition to the invention of pottery making and weaving, metals were discovered and the basic principles of working them were developed. Thus many of the simple horticultural societies of the latter part of the era were appreciably more advanced than their predecessors 3,000 years earlier.

The societies that flourished throughout Mesopotamia around 4000 B.C. illustrate how far these simple horticulturists had advanced. These groups apparently shared a common culture, known today as the Ubaid culture, named after one of the sites where its remains are found. This culture was notable in many ways. To begin with, large settlements were relatively common. This is indicated by the size of cemeteries (one of which contained more than 1,000 graves) as well as by the large temples that dominated these communities.[35] A variety of technical skills were highly developed. Some copper tools and weapons were used, as well as sickles and other tools made from clay fired at high temperatures, a process that produced a remarkably efficient substitute for the stone that was unavailable in that area.[36] Trade became extensive throughout Mesopotamia, facilitated by simple sailboats plying the myriad waterways.[37] This undoubtedly contributed to the wide diffusion of Ubaid culture. As one writer says, "Never before had a single culture been able to influence such a vast area, if only superficially."[38]

Advanced Horticultural Societies in Prehistoric Asia and Europe

Each of the inventions and discoveries of the horticultural era increased, to some degree, the ability of human societies to utilize the resources in their environments. But none had such far-reaching effects as *the use of metal in weapons and tools*. This is why metallurgy is used as the basic criterion for differentiating between simple and advanced horticultural societies. To be more specific, societies are classified as advanced horticultural only when the use of metal weapons and/or tools was widespread. Societies in which they were rare, or in which metals were used only for artistic and ceremonial artifacts (as in some pre-Columbian South and Central American Indian societies where gold was the only metal known), are better classified as simple horticultural, since the impact of metallurgy on societal life was limited.

The Shift from Stone to Metals

To the nontechnically inclined, the shift from stone to metal may suggest a radical break with the past and the introduction of something completely new.

Actually, however, the use of metals evolved from the use of stone by a series of surprisingly small steps.

For thousands of years, people had been aware of differences among rocks and stones. They had learned that some were better for tools and weapons because they were harder and held a cutting edge longer. They were also aware of the colors in rocks and used the more unusual for beads and other ornaments, and also as a source of pigments.

This interest in unusual rocks undoubtedly attracted people to copper. In its native form, copper appears as purplish green or greenish black nuggets which, when scratched or rubbed, show the yellowish kernel of pure copper. At first, copper was simply hammered cold into small tools and ornaments such as awls, pins, and hooks. A few articles made by this method have been found in Middle East sites dating from the seventh millennium B.C.[39] Later, between 5000 and 4000 B.C., the technique of annealing was discovered.[40] By being alternately heated and hammered, copper was made less brittle and thus could be used for a wider variety of purposes. The heat from a simple wood fire was sufficient for this process. Later still, people discovered techniques for extracting copper from various kinds of ores by means of smelting, as well as ways to melt "pure" copper and cast it in molds.[41]

These discoveries illustrate again the cumulative nature of technological progress. Both smelting and melting copper require higher temperatures than a simple wood fire can produce. This strongly suggests that these important discoveries came after the invention of pottery and the pottery kiln.[42] And these inventions, in turn, presupposed settled communities where heavy and bulky objects could be accumulated. Figure 6.4 summarizes the complex chain of causation involved and reminds us again of the systemic nature of human societies.

As far as we can judge, the use of copper tools and weapons increased

FIGURE 6.4 Apparent chain of causation leading from the adoption of horticulture to the widespread use of copper in the manufacture of tools, weapons, and other artifacts.

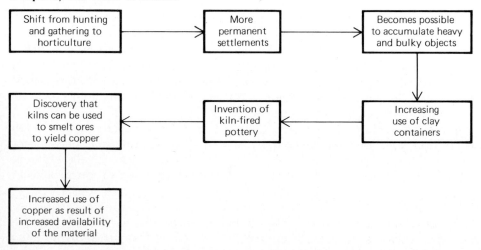

rather slowly, for a variety of reasons.[43] For one thing, until smelting was discovered, the supply of copper was extremely limited; for another, it often had to be carried some distance by primitive and costly methods of transportation. In addition, metal working (particularly smelting and casting) was probably mastered by only a few specialists, who may have treated their skills as a kind of magic (as smiths in modern horticultural societies often do) to protect a lucrative monopoly. Finally, since any man could make his own tools and weapons out of stone, people were undoubtedly reluctant to switch to the costlier product.[44] Thus, though copper was discovered as early as the seventh millennium B.C., no truly advanced horticultural society (i.e., one in which metal tools and weapons were widespread) seems to have developed until about 4000 B.C.[45]

The archaeological record provides an inadequate picture of European and Middle Eastern societies at the advanced horticultural stage of development. To see what the widespread adoption of metal tools and weapons meant for the life of a horticultural society, we must turn to China.

Consequences of Metal Tools and Weapons

Advanced horticultural societies flourished in China from the middle of the second millennium B.C. to the middle of the first.[46] The plow, for reasons that are unclear, was slow to appear in China, thus delaying the emergence of agrarian societies. This prolongation of the advanced horticultural era was undoubtedly a major reason why the overall level of technological development in China's horticultural societies surpassed most other horticultural societies.

One indication of this is the fact that the dominant metal in China during most of this era was not copper, as in the Middle East and Europe, but bronze. This is significant, because bronze, whose manufacture represents an important advance in metallurgy (involving, as it does, the principle of alloying), is a great deal harder than copper and thus can be used for many purposes for which copper is unsuitable. In the Middle East, the technique of making bronze was not really understood until the early part of the third millennium B.C., some time *after* the first agrarian societies had made their appearance.[47] These variations in the sequence of such major innovations as bronze and the plow warn us of the inadequacy of *unilinear* theories of evolution, which assume that all societies follow exactly the same evolutionary path. Some variation is the rule, not the exception.

When the advanced horticultural era in China is compared with the simple horticultural period, the differences are striking. During the earlier era, northern China was covered with numerous small, largely self-sufficient, autonomous villages. In the later period, the villages were no longer autonomous, and a few had become urban centers of some size and substance.

The emergence of these urban centers was largely the result of the military success of villages that had one important advantage: the possession of bronze weapons. As one scholar summarized this period, "In the course of a few centuries the villages of the plain fell under the domination of walled cities on whose rulers the possession of bronze weapons, chariots, and slaves conferred a measure of superiority to which no [simple horticultural] community could aspire.''[48]

The importance of this development can hardly be exaggerated. For the first time in Chinese history, people found the conquest of other people a profitable alternative to the conquest of nature. Much the same thing happened in other parts of the world during this stage in societal development. Thus, beginning in advanced horticultural societies and continuing in agrarian, we find almost as much energy expended in war as in the more basic struggle for subsistence. One might say that bronze was to the conquest of people what plant cultivation was to the conquest of nature. Both were decisive turning points.

From the military standpoint, China's advanced horticulturalists enjoyed a great advantage over simple horticulturalists. Recently excavated burial remains show that their warriors wore elaborate armor, including helmets, carried shields, and were equipped with spears, dagger-axes, knives, hatchets, and reflex bows capable of a pull of 160 pounds.[49] In addition, they used horse-drawn chariots carrying teams of three men (see Figure 6.5).

These societies also enjoyed *numerical* superiority over simple horticultural societies: every victory brought more people under their control, enabling them to enlarge their armies still further.[50] This could not have been

FIGURE 6.5 Chariots, together with bronze weapons, gave the advanced horticulturalists of China a great advantage over their simple horticultural neighbors. Burial remains of a warrior with his horses and chariot, from eleventh century, B.C.

accomplished by a hunting and gathering society, whose primitive technology would make it impossible for conquerors to incorporate a defeated people into the group. At that level of development, the *economic surplus* (i.e., production in excess of what is needed to keep the producers healthy and productive) was small and unpredictable. But with the introduction of horticulture, the situation changed dramatically. *For the first time, the conquest, control, and exploitation of other societies had become possible—and profitable.* All that was needed to transform this possibility into a reality was an advance in military technology that would give one society a definite advantage over its neighbors. That advance was bronze. It tipped the balance of military power decisively in favor of the advanced horticulturalists.

The earliest advanced horticultural society in China of which we have any knowledge was established around 1600 B.C., and its structure was basically feudalistic.[51] In most regions, especially those remote from the capital, power was in the hands of a warrior nobility that ruled the people in their immediate area. They paid tribute to the king and supported him militarily, but otherwise enjoyed great autonomy.[52] They were so independent, in fact, that they often waged war among themselves.

Marked social inequality was the rule in these societies. There were two basic classes, the small warrior nobility and the great mass of common people.[53] The warrior nobility was the governing class and lived in the walled cities which served as their fortresses. It was they who enjoyed most of the benefits of the new technology and the new social system. The chief use of bronze was to manufacture weapons and artistic and ceremonial objects for the exclusive benefit of this elite class. Almost none of this relatively scarce material was available to the common people for farm tools.[54] The situation was much the same in the Middle East and Europe for 2,000 years or more. As one writer put it, this was a world in which metals played a major role in the military, religious, and artistic spheres, but not in subsistence activities.[55]

Kinship was extremely important in the political systems of advanced horticultural China. Membership in the governing class was largely hereditary, and as far as possible leading officials assigned the major offices under their control to kinsmen.[56] The origins of these noble families are unknown, but it seems likely that they were descendants of village headmen of the simple horticultural era, and of close associates of early conquerors.

The walled towns where the aristocracy lived, small by modern standards, were nonetheless an important innovation. One recently excavated town, probably the capital of an early state, covered slightly over one square mile.[57] The size of the walled areas, however, does not tell the full story of these towns, especially in the earlier period, for many of the common people had their homes and workshops outside the protected area and cultivated nearby fields.

The walled area, while basically a fortress and place of residence for the governing class, was also a political and religious center. Religious activities were quite important and were closely tied to the political system—so closely, in fact, that one writer describes the state as "a kind of theocracy."[58] Though this appears to be an overstatement, ancient inscriptions prove that the ruler

FIGURE 6.6 The Great Wall of China. This 1,500-mile-long fortification, begun late in China's horticultural era, illustrates the growing ability of political elites to mobilize labor on a large scale.

did perform major religious functions and was what we today would call the head of both church and state.

The physical structure of those early urban centers was impressive and reflected the evolution of the state and its newly achieved ability to mobilize labor on a large scale. One scholar estimates, for example, that it required the labor of 10,000 men working eighteen years to build the wall around the capital of an early state. Such massive undertakings apparently utilized large numbers of captives taken in war, many of them subsequently used as human sacrifices.[59]

Not much is known about the daily life of the common people, but their chief functions were obviously to produce the economic surplus on which the governing class depended and to provide workers and armed forces for the various projects and military campaigns. Not all labor was of the brute, physical type, however. Some people were craft specialists who provided the new and unusual luxury goods that the governing class demanded for display and for ceremonial purposes; others produced military equipment.[60] Although many of these specialists were probably part-time farmers, the growth of occupational specialization was undoubtedly accompanied by a significant growth in trade.

Despite their increasingly exploitative character, the advanced horticultural societies of China made important advances in a number of areas. The more important innovations included writing, money, the use of the horse,

147

probably irrigation, and possibly the manufacture of iron at the very end of the horticultural era. In addition, there were lesser innovations too numerous to mention, some of them Chinese inventions or discoveries, others the result of diffusion. In most cases, it is impossible to determine which are which.

Horticulture in the New World: Testing Ground for Ecological-Evolutionary Theory

No one knows for certain when humans first settled the New World. Using radiocarbon dating techniques, archaeologists have calculated remains from one site in Alaska to be about 27,000 years old, and experts believe there may have been human settlements in the New World as early as 40,000 years ago.[61] In any case, the original settlers were almost certainly hunters and gatherers who migrated from Asia by means of the land bridge that once connected Siberia and Alaska.

When the last Ice Age ended and the waters locked in the glaciers were largely freed, the level of the oceans rose and the land bridge was submerged. As a result, the inhabitants of the New World were cut off from the inhabitants of the Old World during those crucial millennia associated with the horticultural revolution. Thus, there was no way that information about the techniques of plant cultivation could have spread to the Americas.

Despite this, horticultural societies did develop in the New World, and some of them achieved a level of technological sophistication comparable to that of agrarian Mesopotamia and Egypt. Space limitations prevent us from tracing these developments in detail, and much of the account would be repetitive if we did. But in the New World, as in the Old, the shift from hunting and gathering to horticulture was preceded by a massive killing of big game, and led to more permanent settlements, larger and denser populations, more substantial dwellings, increased wealth and possessions, the development of pottery and later of metallurgy, the beginnings of full-time craft specialization, the appearance of permanent markets and increased trade, the beginnings of urbanism, the establishment of permanent religious centers, the construction of massive temples and temple complexes (see Figure 6.7), and a marked increase in both militarism and imperialism.[62]

There were also some differences: New World horticulturalists were not as successful in domesticating animals, for example, nor was their metallurgy as advanced. On the other hand, they developed a numerical system that included the concept of zero centuries before this was invented in the Old World. But overall, the similarities far outweigh the differences.

The fact that horticulture developed at all in the isolated New World is the important point, however, for it provides an independent test of some basic ideas. For a long time, scholars debated whether the similarities between the process of societal development in the Middle East, China, and Europe were the result of the operation of basic laws of sociocultural evolution or merely the result of diffusion. The issue was impossible to resolve when only Old World societies were involved, because the possibility of diffusion could never be ruled out. The New World, however, is a different matter. Its contacts with

FIGURE 6.7 Mayan temple at Tikal, Guatamala. Some horticultural societies in the New World achieved a level of technological sophistication approaching that of ancient Egypt and Mesopotamia in the early agrarian era.

the Old World ended several thousand years before horticulture began there, and contact was not resumed until about 1000 A.D., when Leif Ericson briefly visited Vinland, somewhere on the northeast coast of North America.*

---

*Though attempts have been made to prove other contacts, they have not been successful. Moreover, careful studies of the evolution of plant cultivation in the New World convince scholars that this was entirely an indigenous process. For example, the transformation of maize, or corn, from a wild plant to a cultivated plant took much longer than one would expect if the process had been guided by information on the techniques of plant cultivation brought from the Old World.[63]

FIGURE 6.8 Sixteenth-century sketch of a village of simple horticulturalists in North Carolina.

In short, the New World has been a kind of "Second Earth," where ideas about sociocultural evolution suggested by studies of the Old World can be put to the test.[64] And the remarkable parallels between developments in the New World and the Old strongly indicate that much more was involved than either mere accident or purposive human choice. Apparently there is a necessary sequence in the progression of the more basic technological innovations. People must know certain things about both fire and rocks, for example, before metallurgy is possible, and a society must possess the hoe before it can invent the plow. In addition, major technological innovations have fairly predictable consequences for other aspects of sociocultural systems—especially for social structure, the demographic variables, and material production.

This is not to say that sociocultural evolution compels societies to march in lockstep. But it does indicate that there is a considerable element of predictability in the critical early stages of societal development beyond the hunting and gathering level. Marvin Harris, a major contributor to ecological-evolutionary theory, stated the matter as well as anyone when he wrote, *"Similar technologies applied to similar environments tend to produce similar arrangements of labor in production and distribution, and these in turn call* forth similar kinds of social groupings, which justify and coordinate their activities by means of similar systems of values and beliefs.''[65]

151

Horticultural Societies

Simple Horticultural Societies in the Modern Era

In recent centuries, simple horticultural societies have been confined almost exclusively to the islands of the Pacific and the New World. All of these societies have practiced some version of *slash-and-burn* or *swidden* horticulture. This involves the periodic clearing of new land to replace gardens that have lost their fertility and been abandoned. Clearing is typically done by girdling or cutting trees and undergrowth and, after they have dried, setting them on fire. The ashes fertilize the ground, and the garden is then planted amid the stumps and debris (see Figure 6.9). The basic tools are wooden hoes and digging sticks. In many horticultural societies, women have the primary responsibility for the routine tasks of gardening, men for the occasional and more strenuous tasks, such as clearing the land. Usually within a few years weeds take over and the soil loses its fertility, so new gardens must be cleared. The old ones are allowed to revert to jungle or forest and remain unused for decades until nature restores the soil's fertility. Then, the villagers return to the area and repeat the cycle all over again.

In most matters where comparisons are possible, the simple horticultural societies of modern times are strikingly similar to those of prehistoric times. In other words, they are usually small, largely self-sufficient, politically autonomous villages with populations ranging from a few dozen to a few hundred.[66] Compared with modern hunting and gathering societies, their settlements are larger and much more permanent, as we saw in Chapter 4.[67] As in prehistoric times, their relative permanence permits a greater accumulation of goods and the construction of more substantial buildings.[68] There is also a more diversified production of goods and services and an increase in trade.[69] Finally, as in the simple horticultural societies of the later horticultural era, warfare is fairly common.[70]

The Continuing Importance of Kinship

As with hunting and gathering societies, the ethnographic record not only supports the view provided by archaeology but broadens and enriches it. For example, modern studies show that kinship ties are extremely important in simple horticultural societies. In most instances, these ties provide the basic framework of the social system.[71] This is hardly surprising in view of the small size of these groups: almost everyone is related in some way to almost everyone else. Kinship obligations must be constantly taken into account in relations between individuals. The virtual absence of competing social structures (e.g., craft guilds, political parties, etc.) further enhances the importance of kinship.

Kinship systems in these societies are sometimes very complex, with

FIGURE 6.9   Women planting taro in a simple horticultural society in New Guinea. Note the tree stumps in the cultivated area: most horticulturalists do not clear the land as thoroughly as agriculturalists, who use the plow.

intricate systems of rules governing relations between numerous categories of kin. Extended kin groups, or *clans*, are common and usually very important, since they perform a number of essential functions for their members.[72] Above all, they function as mutual aid associations, providing the individual with protection against enemies and with economic support. Although both these functions are important, the former is critical, for the political system is too primitive at this level to provide police services. Clans also perform important regulatory functions in the area of marriage, and they sometimes have important religious functions as well. Finally, the most powerful or respected clan often assumes leadership of the entire community, with its head serving as headman for the village.

In horticultural societies, both simple and advanced, the concept of the kin group includes the dead as well as the living. This manifests itself in many ways, but especially in the form of religious rituals designed to appease the spirits of dead ancestors. Nowhere is ancestor worship more common than in horticultural societies (see Figure 6.10).

The reason for such a high incidence of ancestor worship among horticulturalists, relative to hunters and gatherers, is probably tied to the greater permanence of their settlements. Because of this, the living remain in close physical proximity to their buried dead and carry on their daily activities in the very same settings in which their ancestors once lived. Under such circumstances, ancestors are less easily forgotten. In agrarian societies, more awesome and more powerful polytheistic and monotheistic deities usually displaced ancestors from the central position they occupied in most horticultural societies, though ancestor worship was important in many of them (e.g., China, Rome).

Another distinctive feature of kinship systems in horticultural societies is the importance many of them attach to ties with the mother's relatives. This can be seen clearly in Murdock's data set, where the percentage of societies

FIGURE 6.10 Incidence of ancestor worship, by societal type.

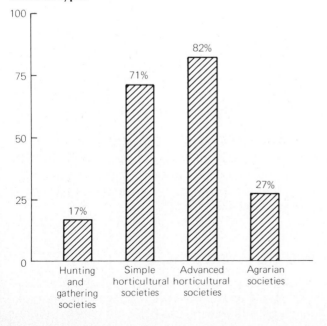

FIGURE 6.11   Leisure among the Yanamamö of South America. The man in the hammock is the boy's maternal uncle, and the relationship between them is an especially intimate one, as in many horticultural societies.

having *matrilineal kin groups* (i.e., descent traced through the maternal line) is as follows:[73]

Hunting and gathering societies	10%
Simple horticultural societies	26%
Advanced horticultural societies	27%
Agrarian societies	4%

This unusual pattern is apparently linked with women's contribution to subsistence in horticultural societies: in many of these groups, women do most of the work of cultivation (see Table 6.1). In societies where men also make a substantial contribution—by hunting or herding, for example—matrilineal patterns are not as likely to develop (see Table 6.2).[74]

Developments in Polity, Stratification, and Warfare

Though village autonomy is still the rule, multicommunity societies are much more common than at the hunting and gathering level.[75] When societies do consist of more than one community, there are usually only a few, seldom

TABLE 6.1   The Division of Labor between the Sexes in Horticultural and Agrarian Societies

Type of Society	Percentage Distribution				
	Cultivation Primarily a Female Responsibility	Both Sexes Share Equally	Cultivation Primarily a Male Responsibility	Total	Number of Societies
Simple horticultural	37	49	14	100	51
Advanced horticultural	50	27	23	100	142
Agrarian	7	37	56	100	43

Source: See note 12, page 454.

more than ten.[76] Most such societies were formed by a process of confederation by villages that belonged to the same tribe,[77] and the motivation to consolidate was a military one.

The power of political leaders remains quite limited in nearly all simple horticultural societies. Even in the larger, multicommunity societies, local villages enjoy virtual autonomy except in matters of war and relations with other societies. Both the village headman and the tribal chief depend more on persuasion than on coercion to achieve their goals. This is partly because of the limited development of the governmental system: a leader has few subordinates so dependent on him that they are obliged to carry out his instructions. Also important is the fact that there are no weapons that a governing class could monopolize to control the rest of the population.

In some simple horticultural societies, shamans also serve as headmen or chiefs because of the awe or respect in which they are held.[78] In some, secular leaders assume important religious functions and become quasi-religious figures. As one writer notes, a "chief's influence is definitely enhanced when he combines religious with secular functions."[79] In short, in many simple horticultural societies of the modern era, just as in the prehistoric past, "church" and "state" are closely linked and sometimes almost become one.

TABLE 6.2   Matrilineality among Simple Horticultural Societies, by Percentage of Subsistence Obtained from Hunting and Herding

Percentage of Subsistence Obtained by Hunting and Herding*	Percentage of Societies Matrilineal	Number of Cases
26 or more	13	16
16 to 25	25	28
Less than 15	39	23

Source: See note 12, page 454.
*These figures are estimates made by Murdock and his associates and are based on qualitative statements in ethnographic reports.

The only other important basis of political power in these societies is membership in a large and prosperous kin group. As we noted earlier, the senior member and leader of the largest, most powerful, or most respected lineage group often becomes the village headman or the tribal chief.[80] He can usually count on the support of his kinsmen, and that is a substantial political resource in a society with such limited political development.

Social inequality is generally rather limited in most simple horticultural societies of the modern era. Although extremes of wealth and political power are absent, substantial differences in prestige are not uncommon. Political and religious leaders usually enjoy high status, but this depends far more on their achievements than on mere occupancy of an office. There are few sinecures in these societies. Other bases of status include military prowess (which is highly honored in nearly all societies), skill in oratory, age, lineage, and in some cases wealth in the form of wives, pigs, and ornaments.[81] Each society has its own peculiar combination of these criteria.

The more advanced the technology and economy of one of these groups, the greater its social inequality tends to be. Societies that practice irrigation, own domesticated animals, or practice metallurgy for ornamental and ceremonial purposes are usually less egalitarian than groups without these characteristics. We can see this when we compare the villagers of eastern Brazil and the Amazon River basin with their more advanced neighbors to the north and west who, in pre-Spanish days, practiced irrigation and metallurgy (they used gold, which is too soft for tools and weapons, and therefore cannot be considered advanced horticulturalists). Hereditary class differences were absent in the former groups but quite common in the latter, where a hereditary governing class of chiefs and nobles was set apart from the larger class of commoners.[82]

Ethnographers have found warfare to be much more common among horticulturalists than among hunters and gatherers (see Table 6.3). This finding parallels the evidence from archaeology, where all the signs indicate that warfare increased substantially during the horticultural era. Now, as in the past, combat appears to serve as a psychic substitute for the excitement, challenge, and rewards which hunting previously provided and which were so important in the lives of men in hunting and gathering societies.

Warfare also functions as an important mechanism of population control in these groups. In addition to the direct loss of life in combat, warfare provides an important stimulus for female infanticide, which appears to be an even greater check on population growth.[83] In societies in which warfare is the normal state of affairs, it is imperative that the group be able to field the largest

TABLE 6.3   Incidence of Warfare, by Societal Type (in percentages)

Type of Society	Perpetual	Common	Rare or Absent	Total	No. of Societies
Hunting and gathering	0	27	73	100	22
Simple horticultural	5	55	41	101	22
Advanced horticultural	34	48	17	99	29

Source: Adapted from data in Gregory Leavitt, "The Frequency of Warfare: An Evolutionary Perspective," *Sociological Inquiry*, 14 (January 1977), appendix B.

FIGURE 6.12 In horticultural societies, combat appears to serve as a psychic substitute for the excitement, challenge, and rewards which hunting previously provided. Yanamamö men intoxicated on ebene, a hallucinogenic drug, prepare for a "friendly" duel with a neighboring village with which they are allied. Such duels often turn violent and lead to war.

possible number of warriors, and female infanticide seems to be the best method of accomplishing this. By reducing the number of girls, the group can devote its resources to the care and nurture of a larger number of boys. A recent survey of studies of 609 "primitive" societies found that the sex ratio among the young was most imbalanced in those societies in which warfare was current at the time of the study and most nearly normal in those societies in which warfare had not occurred for more than twenty-five years.[84] In the former group, boys outnumbered girls by a ratio of seven to five on the average, indicating that nearly 30 per cent of the females born in these societies had died as a result of female infanticide or neglect. If allowance is made for some degree of male infanticide (as in the case of male babies born with deformities or born before an older male sibling can be weaned), the actual rate of female infanticide may be 40 per cent or more.

When warfare grows in importance in a society, several new patterns develop. Above all, there is the cult of the warrior, which heaps honors on successful fighters. Record keeping and publicity are no less important to these warrior heroes than to modern athletes, and, in the absence of statisticians and sportswriters, they invent techniques of their own—especially trophy taking. Some of the more popular trophies are skulls and shrunken heads, which are preserved and displayed like modern athletic trophies (see Figure 6.13).[85]

Ceremonial cannibalism, a surprisingly widespread practice among sim-

FIGURE 6.13 **Record keeping and publicity are no less important to horticultural society warriors than to modern athletes. The Jivaro Indians of South America collected heads as trophies of their prowess and developed a special technique for shrinking and preserving them.**

ple horticultural societies, may have developed as a by-product of trophy collecting. Utilitarian cannibalism, or eating other humans to avoid starvation, is an ancient practice, traceable to distant prehistoric times, but ceremonial cannibalism seems to be a more recent innovation. The basic idea underlying it is that one can appropriate the valued qualities of a conquered enemy by eating his body. Ceremonial cannibalism is usually surrounded by a complex, and often prolonged, set of rituals, as the following account from South America indicates.

The prisoners taken by a Tupinamba war party were received with manifestations of anger, scorn, and derision, but after the first hostile outburst, they were not hampered in their movements nor were they unkindly treated. Their captors, whose quarters they shared, treated them as relatives. The prisoners generally married village girls, very often the sisters or daughters of their masters, or, in certain cases, the widow of a dead warrior whose hammock and ornaments they used. They received fields for their maintenance, they were free to hunt and fish, and they were reminded of their servile condition by few restrictions and humiliations.

The period of captivity lasted from a few months to several years. When, finally, the date for the execution had been set by the village council, invitations were sent to nearby villages to join in the celebration. The ritual for the slaughter of a captive was worked out to the most minute detail. The club and cord which figured prominently in the ceremony were carefully painted and decorated in accordance with strict rules. For three days before the event, the village women danced, sang, and tormented the victim with descriptions of his impending fate. On the eve of his execution a mock repetition of his capture took place, during which the prisoner was allowed to escape but was immediately retaken; the man who overpowered him in a wrestling match adopted a new name, as did the ceremonial executioner.

The prisoner spent his last night dancing, pelting his tormentors, and singing songs which foretold their ruin and proclaimed his pride at dying as a warrior. In the morning he was dragged to the plaza by old women amidst shouts, songs, and music. The ceremonial rope was removed from his neck and tied around his waist, and it was held at both ends by two or more men. The victim was once more permitted to give vent to his feelings by throwing fruit or potsherds at his enemies. The executioner, who appeared painted and dressed in a long feather cloak, derided the victim, who boasted of his past deeds and predicted that his relatives would avenge him.

The actual execution was a cruel game. The prisoner was allowed sufficient freedom of movement to dodge the blows aimed at him; sometimes a club was put in his hands so that he could parry the blows without being able to strike back. When at last he fell, his skull shattered, everyone shouted and whistled. Old women rushed in to drink the warm blood, children were invited to dip their hands in it, and mothers smeared their nipples so that even infants could have a taste. While the quartered body was being roasted on a babracot the old women, who were the most eager to taste human flesh, licked the grease running from the sticks. Certain delicate or sacred portions, such as the fingers and the grease around the liver, were given to distinguished guests.[86]

The high incidence of warfare in simple horticultural societies helps to keep the channels of vertical mobility open. Almost every boy becomes a warrior and thus has a chance to win honors and influence. Nevertheless, the channels of vertical mobility are somewhat more restricted in horticultural societies, because status advantages can more easily be passed from parent to child than in hunting and gathering societies. This is partly due to the greater amount of private property in horticultural societies, and its increased importance. In addition, there are the beginnings of inequality among kin groups: it is a distinct advantage to be born into a large, powerful, and wealthy clan. Finally, the institutional structures of these societies frequently evolve to the point where they can, to some extent, supplement the personal attributes of their leaders. No longer need a headman be the best man in his group; he need only be competent, because he now has assistants who can support and help him. As a consequence, such positions are more likely to be inherited than was the case in hunting and gathering societies. This growth in the heritability of status, though modest in scope and of limited importance in simple horticultural societies, marks the beginning of a trend destined to become of tremendous importance in more advanced societies.

Advanced Horticultural Societies in the Modern Era

For several centuries, advanced horticultural societies have been limited to two parts of the world, sub-Saharan Africa and Southeast Asia. Until recently, they occupied almost all of sub-Saharan Africa; other types of societies—hunters and gatherers, herders, and fishers—were relatively scarce. In Southeast Asia, on the other hand, agrarian societies occupied most of the land.

These advanced horticulturalists of modern times differ in one important respect from those of prehistoric times: the dominant metal in their societies has been iron, not copper or bronze. This is important, because iron ore is so much more plentiful than copper and tin* that it can be used for ordinary tools as well as weapons. However, because it is so much more difficult to reduce the ore to metal, the manufacture of iron was a later development.

The history of Africa proves once again that the evolutionary process does not compel societies to follow exactly the same pattern of development. Bronze was never the dominant metal in most of Africa below the Sahara. During the period when bronze was dominant in the Middle East, cultural contacts between Egypt and the territories to the south were minimal. By the time there was sufficient contact to permit diffusion of specialized skills like metallurgy, iron had become dominant.[87]

Increased Size and Complexity

Compared with hunting and gathering or simple horticultural societies, advanced horticultural societies are usually larger and more complex. Table 4.2 (page 91) summarizes the evidence from Murdock's data set. Communities in advanced horticultural societies are three times larger than those in simple horticultural societies and seven times larger than those in hunting and gathering societies. A comparison of *societies* is even more striking: on the average, advanced horticultural societies are 60 times the size of simple horticultural and 140 times the size of hunting and gathering societies.

As one would expect, advanced horticultural societies are also structurally more complex. Of those in Murdock's data set, some have as many as *four* layers of government above the local community; no simple horticultural society in the data set has more than *two*. These data also show that village autonomy is the rule in simple horticultural societies, the exception in advanced. In 79 per cent of the former, villages are autonomous; in 71 per cent of the latter, they are *not*.

Another evidence of structural complexity is the extent of occupational specialization. Table 4.3 (page 94) shows that craft specialization is much more common in advanced horticultural societies than in simple ones. In six kinds of activities, craft specialization occurred only 2 per cent of the time in simple horticultural societies, but 28 per cent of the time in advanced.

Murdock's data also show that social inequality increases rather markedly at this level of societal development. For example, slavery is found in 83 per

---

*Tin is an essential component of bronze.

**FIGURE 6.14   Craft specialization is much more common in advanced
horticultural societies than in simple ones. Basket weaver at work beside his home
in Guinea.**

cent of the advanced horticultural societies, but in only 14 per cent of the
simple. Hereditary systems of inequality are found in 47 per cent of the former,
but in only 15 per cent of the latter. And finally, classes are reported in 54 per
cent of the advanced horticultural societies and only 17 per cent of the simple.

One consequence of the more fully developed economy and stratification
system in advanced horticultural societies is their increased emphasis on the
economic aspect of marriage. In almost every one of these societies, marriage-
able daughters are viewed as a valuable property, and men who want to marry
them must either pay for the privilege or render extended service to their
prospective in-laws. Fortunately for young men with limited resources, extended kin groups usually view marriage as a sensible investment and are
willing to loan suitors part of the bride price. This economic approach to
marriage is much more common in advanced horticultural societies than in
either hunting and gathering or simple horticultural societies (see Table 6.4).

Political Development

The growth in social inequality is closely linked with the growth of government. A generation ago, Meyer Fortes, one of the pioneers in the study of
African political systems, argued that most traditional African societies fell into

TABLE 6.4   Association of Economic Transaction with Marriage, by Societal Type

Type of Society	Percentage of Societies Requiring Economic Transaction with Marriage	Number of Societies
Hunting and gathering	49	148
Simple horticultural	61	74
Advanced horticultural	97	265

Source: See note 12, page 454.

one of two basic categories: those "which have centralized authority, administrative machinery, and judicial institutions—in short, a government—and in which cleavages of wealth, privilege, and status correspond to the distribution of authority," and those which have none of these attributes.[88] Though recent studies suggest that this twofold division was something of an oversimplification, they confirm that African societies differ in the ways Fortes described and that there is a strong relationship between the development of the state and the growth of social inequality.[89]

African societies afford a valuable opportunity to study the early stages of political development. A leading student of east African political systems suggests that a critical step in the process occurs when the head of a strong extended kin group begins to take on, as retainers, men who are not related to him, thus overcoming one of the traditional limitations on power and its expansion.[90] These retainers are usually individuals who have been expelled from their own kin groups for misconduct or whose groups have been destroyed in war or some natural disaster, and they offer their allegiance and service in exchange for protection and a livelihood.

Since there is a natural tendency for men in this position to turn to the strongest families, power begins to pyramid. This is reinforced by the wealth of such a group, which permits it to buy more wives to produce more sons and warriors, and by the development of myths that explain the group's success by attributing magical powers to its leader. The final link in this chain of *state building* is forged when less powerful families, and even whole communities, are brought under the control of the head of a strong kin group—either by conquest or by the decision of the weaker groups to put themselves under the strong group's protection. When this happens, each of the subordinate groups is usually allowed to retain its land, and its leader his authority within the group, but the group is compelled to pay tribute. The leader of the dominant group then uses these revenues to support his kinsmen and retainers, thereby increasing their dependence on him and, he hopes, their loyalty to him as well.

Sometimes the state-building process is stimulated by intrafamily and interfamily feuds that get out of hand. Where there is no strong political authority, feuds are a serious matter. Individuals and families are forced to settle their own grievances, which often sets off a deadly cycle of action and reaction. More than one east African group has voluntarily put itself under the authority of a strong neighboring leader just to break such a cycle and reestablish peace among its members.

One might suppose that these processes, once set in motion, would have continued until eventually all Africa came under a single authority. But powerful countervailing forces prevented this. Technological limitations, especially in transportation and communication, were most important. Advanced horticulturalists in Africa, as in the New World, had no knowledge of the wheel and used no draft animals until contact with Europeans. As a result, the farther a ruler's power came to be extended into outlying areas, the weaker it became. These areas were vulnerable to attack by other societies, and, even more serious, they were likely to revolt. From the territorial standpoint, Songhay was probably the largest kingdom that ever developed in sub-Saharan Africa. In the early fourteenth century, it controlled approximately 500,000 square miles in the western Sudan (i.e., twice the size of present-day France).[91] Most African kingdoms were much smaller.

By the standards of modern industrial societies, the governments of Africa's advanced horticultural societies were extremely unstable. Revolts were a common occurrence, not only in outlying provinces but even in the capitals. These were seldom, if ever, popular risings. Rather, they were instigated by powerful members of the nobility, often the king's own brothers. This pattern was so common that the Zulus had a proverb that "the king should not eat with his brothers lest they poison him."[92]

In virtually every politically advanced society of horticultural Africa there was a sharply defined cleavage between a hereditary nobility and the mass of

FIGURE 6.15 In virtually every politically advanced society of horticultural Africa there was a sharply defined cleavage between a hereditary nobility and the mass of common people. Early bronze casting of Dahomean chief and his entourage of relatives and retainers. Note the fine workmanship. (For a modern scene similar to this, see Figure 13.9, page 396.)

common people. Historically, this distinction grew out of the state-building process.[93] Nobles were usually descendants either of past rulers and their chief lieutenants, or of hereditary leaders of subordinated groups. They comprised a warrior aristocracy supported by the labor of the common people. Below the commoners there was often a class of slaves, many of them captives taken in war, and, as in other horticultural societies, they were frequently slaughtered as human sacrifices.

In the advanced horticultural societies of Africa, as in the New World and elsewhere, religion and politics were intimately related. In many instances the king was viewed as divine or as having access to divine powers.[94] This undoubtedly served to legitimate tyrannical and exploitative practices. It also helps explain why no efforts were made to establish other kinds of political systems: given their ideological heritage, such a thing was inconceivable. These beliefs did not protect a ruler against attacks from his kinsmen, however, because they shared his special religious status and thus were qualified to assume the duties and privileges of the royal office—if they could seize it.

A comparison of the politically complex societies of sub-Saharan Africa with those which remained autonomous villages shows that the former were more developed in other ways as well. They were far likelier to have full-time craft specialization, for example, and they were also more likely to have urban or semiurban settlements—a few with populations of 20,000 or more.[95]

Before concluding this discussion of advanced horticultural societies in the modern era, a brief comment on those in Southeast Asia is necessary. The striking feature of these societies is their relative backwardness, especially from the standpoint of political development. In most instances they remain on the level of village autonomy, and when multicommunity societies have developed they are invariably small.[96] Urban or semiurban settlements are absent.

The reason appears to be ecological. Centuries ago, after this region came under the domination of more powerful agrarian societies, horticultural societies survived only in hill country where transportation was difficult and the land unsuited for the plow and permanent cultivation. This combination of more powerful neighbors and the deficiencies of their own territories apparently prevented all but the most limited development and caused these groups to be looked down upon, and often exploited, by their agrarian neighbors. Ecological factors of a different type had a similar effect in certain parts of Africa: political development was quite limited in the tropical rain forests. Apparently the lush vegetation and other hindrances to the movement of armies and goods made it impossible to build and maintain extensive kingdoms.[97]

Horticultural Societies in Theoretical Perspective

Few events in human history have been as important as the shift from hunting and gathering to horticulture. It is no exaggeration to say that the adoption of horticulture in the realm of technology was comparable to the creation of symbols in the realm of communication in that each was a decisive break with

FIGURE 6.16   Contemporary view of the old city of Kano in northern Nigeria. Kano has been an important commercial and political center for more than 500 years. Although the photograph is recent, the style of architecture remains much as it was centuries ago.

the animal world. Hunting and gathering, like the use of signals, are basically techniques our species inherited from its prehuman ancestors. But horticulture and symbols are uniquely human.

Of all the changes in human life that resulted from the horticultural revolution, the most fundamental—the one with the greatest repercussions for other change—was the creation of *a stable economic surplus*. Hunting and gathering societies were rarely able to create such a surplus: food producers and their dependents usually consumed all the calories those groups were able to provide. With nothing left over to support *non*producers of food, only the most limited occupational specialization was possible. There could be no governmental or religious institutions staffed by full-time officials and priests, nor could there be full-time artisans and merchants. And this, in turn, ruled out the development of towns and cities, since these are based on populations that are freed from the necessity of producing their own food.

The shift from hunting and gathering to plant cultivation provided societies with the means of establishing an economic surplus, but only if the growth in productivity was not nullified by a corresponding growth in population size. To translate the potential for a stable surplus into a reality, a society needed an ideology that would motivate the people producing food to turn over part of their harvest to an individual in authority who could dispense it as he saw fit.

Religious beliefs often answered this need. In a number of societies, people were already accustomed to offering sacrifices, and nothing was more natural than that they should continue this practice as they shifted to plant cultivation, putting part of its yield into the hands of a priest. With greater productivity, rituals became more elaborate and more frequent, and priestly activities became full-time, for one man at first, and eventually for others. In this way, small proto-urban communities began to develop around important shrines—communities that could exist only if a stable economic surplus was maintained.

In other societies, the development of a stable surplus appears to have evolved out of a tradition of turning over to the headman part of the fruits of the hunt to distribute to the families of hunters who were unsuccessful that day. Here, too, the increase in productivity resulting from the shift to plant cultivation made full-time employment possible, first for a headman, later for his aides. Thus, the foundation was laid for the emergence of the state as a specialized entity, in some sense separate from the rest of society.

In either case, the outcome was the same: the potential of an economic surplus became a reality, opening up important new possibilities for the organization of societal life. The possibilities would not all be realized in horticultural societies, however. The most dramatic and the most revolutionary would be realized only in agrarian and industrial societies, where the size of the economic surplus would be many times greater.

It is important to note that in horticultural societies we are seeing, for the first time, ideology play a significant role in shaping evolution. In hunting and gathering societies, the limits set by technology are so narrow that ideology's role is negligible (i.e., it does not influence selections that are capable of generating change and development throughout the system). But the picture changes with horticultural societies, where ideological differences among societies may be reflected in differences in their overall development.

Figure 6.17 summarizes the effects of the shift from hunting and gathering to horticulture for many societies. Not all of these consequences occurred in every horticultural society, but the model indicates the possibilities inherent in the new subsistence technology.

At a minimum, the shift to horticulture meant more permanent settlements and an increased production of goods and services. These, in turn, were likely to lead to the adoption or spread of ancestor worship, increased accumulation of possessions, growth in population, and the possibility of a sustained economic surplus. If that possibility became a reality, there would probably be a series of further developments, including growth of the state, the emergence of urban communities, the greater accumulation of weapons, a greater division of labor, increased warfare, expansion in societal size as a result of conquest, development of the cult of the warrior, increased female infanticide, increased trade and commerce, and, in some societies, the invention of a system of

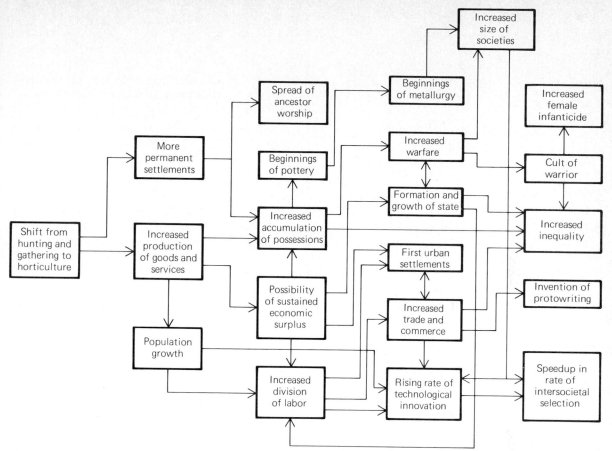

FIGURE 6.17   Model of the long-term effects of the horticultural revolution.

protowriting. Even in societies that did not establish a stable economic surplus and whose increased production of goods and services was totally consumed by population growth, some of these developments—including an increase in warfare, the cult of the warrior, and increased inequality—were still likely to occur, though they were not likely to be as pronounced.

Figure 6.17 also traces the causal connections from more permanent settlements to the beginnings of metallurgy, and from there *to the speedup in the rate of intersocietal selection.* The latter proved to be one of the most critical developments of the horticultural era, for two reasons. It meant the beginning of the decline of hunting and gathering societies. And it meant that all of the basic historical trends shown in Figure 3.7 (page 80) were now underway.

Before concluding this summary, a brief comment on the ethical consequences of the horticultural revolution is needed, lest anyone still suppose that the technological and structural advance of horticultural societies implies ethical progress. As numerous scholars have noted, it is one of the great ironies of evolution that progress in technology and social structure is often linked with ethical *regress.* Horticultural societies provide several striking examples.

FIGURE 6.18 **Human sacrifice, from carving on the Mayan Temple of the Jaguars, Chichén Itzá, Mexico.**

Some of the most shocking, by the standards of our own culture, are the increases in head-hunting, cannibalism, human sacrifice, and slavery, all more common in the technologically progressive horticultural societies than in the more primitive hunting and gathering groups.

Another development many would regard as ethical regression is the decline in the practice of sharing and the growing acceptance of economic and other kinds of inequality. This is not as simple a matter as it seems on the surface, however. Although inequality is an inevitable accompaniment of an economic surplus, the establishment of that surplus seems to have been a prerequisite for the development of civilization—with all that implies—and for subsequent improvements in the standard of living. In other words, without an economic surplus, all the benefits of technological advance would have been consumed by population growth, and there would simply have been more people living at the subsistence level. Our judgment of this growth in inequality, therefore, depends largely on whether we take a short-term or a long-term view.

CHAPTER 7

Agrarian Societies

"The thousand years or so immediately preceding 3000 B.C. were perhaps more fertile in fruitful inventions and discoveries than any period in human history prior to the sixteenth century, A.D."[1] So wrote V. Gordon Childe, the most influential archaeologist of the twentieth century. The innovations of that period included the invention of the wheel and its application to both wagons and the manufacture of pottery, the invention of the plow, the harnessing of animals to pull wagons and plows and their use as pack animals, the harnessing of wind power for use in sailboats, the invention of writing and numerical notation, and the invention of the calendar.[2]

Collectively, these innovations were the basis for a revolutionary transformation of the conditions of life in the Middle East, and ultimately for societies throughout the world. With these new cultural resources, societies expanded their populations, increased their material products, and developed social structures far more complex than anything known before.

Simple Agrarian Societies

Technology

Although all of the innovations to which Childe refers were important, the *plow* surpassed the rest in its potential for social and cultural change. To a modern city dweller, the plow may not sound very exciting, yet without it, we

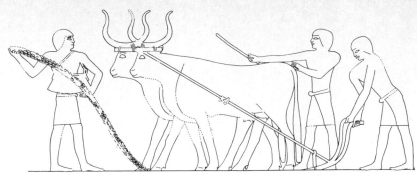

FIGURE 7.1 Early Egyptian ox-drawn plow (about 2700 B.C.). Note the primitive method of harnessing the animals—a simple bar attached to the horns.

would still be back in the horticultural era. To appreciate the importance of the plow, we need to keep in mind two basic problems that confront farmers everywhere: controlling weeds and maintaining the fertility of the soil.[3] With traditional horticultural tools and techniques, both problems grow more severe the longer a plot is cultivated. Weeds multiply faster than horticultural-ists with their hoes can root them out, while the soil's nutrients seep deeper into the ground, below the reach of plants and too deep to be brought back to the surface with hoes or other simple tools. Within a few years, the yield usually becomes so small that the cultivator is forced to abandon the plot and move elsewhere.*

The plow, if it did not eliminate these problems, at least reduced them to manageable proportions. Because it turns the soil over to a greater depth than the hoe, the plow buries weeds, not only killing them but adding humus to the soil. Deeper cultivation also brings back to the surface the nutrients that have seeped below root level. This made permanent cultivation of fields a common practice for the first time in history and led to the replacement of horticulture (from the Latin *hortus*, or garden) by agriculture (from *ager*, or field).

The invention of the plow also paved the way for the harnessing of animal energy.[4] As long as the digging stick and hoe were the basic tools of cultivation, men and women had to supply the energy. But the plow could be pulled, and it did not take long for people to discover that oxen could do the job. The importance of this discovery can hardly be exaggerated, since it established a principle with broad applicability. In Childe's words, ''The ox was the first step to the steam engine and the [gasoline] motor.''[5]

More immediately, however, the harnessing of animal energy relieved people of one of the most exhausting forms of labor required by the new mode of food production and led to greatly increased productivity. With a plow and a pair of oxen, a farmer could cultivate a far larger area than was possible with a hoe.[6] In addition, the use of oxen led, in many societies, to feeding them in stalls, and this in turn led to the use of manure as a fertilizer.[7] In short, the shift

---

*In a few instances, horticulturalists have been able to maintain continual cultivation because of irrigation (natural or artificial) or fertilization.

from hoe to plow not only meant fields kept permanently under cultivation and larger crops; it also meant the potential for a much larger economic surplus and new and more complex forms of social structure.[8]

The earliest evidence of the plow comes from Mesopotamian cylinder seals and Egyptian paintings dating from a little before 3000 B.C.[9] Modern research indicates that the plow, like so many other innovations in the last 10,000 years, presupposed certain earlier inventions and discoveries—underlining again the cumulative nature of technological change. The first plows of the Mesopotamians and the Egyptians were simply modified versions of the hoe, the basic farm implement of all advanced horticultural societies. In the earliest period, the plow was probably pulled by men, but before long, cattle and oxen began to be used. These plows, like all plows in simple agrarian societies, were made of wood, sometimes with a bronze plowshare at the cutting edge to provide greater strength.

The plow and related techniques of agriculture apparently spread by diffusion until agrarian societies were eventually established throughout most of Europe and much of North Africa and Asia. For reasons that are still not fully understood, use of the plow did not spread to sub-Saharan Africa until the period of European colonialism. In the New World, too, it was unknown until introduced by Europeans.

The full impact of the new technology was not felt immediately in either Mesopotamia or Egypt. Even so, the shift to agriculture was quickly followed by several important developments, notably the invention of writing, the rise of urban communities,[10] and the beginnings of empire building (which in Egypt led to the unification of the entire country under a single ruler for the first time in history). This was the period that historians have often referred to as "the dawn of civilization."

Similar developments occurred (though at later dates) in horticultural societies in China and Mexico, proving that an agrarian technology was not a necessary precondition for literacy, urbanism, and large-scale imperialism. But the rarity of these phenomena in horticultural societies and their frequency in agrarian societies indicate that the shift to agriculture, by increasing productivity, greatly increased the probability that they would occur.

Religion and the Growth of the Economic Surplus

In the earliest simple agrarian societies, religion was an extremely powerful force. Mesopotamian theology held that "man was . . . created for one purpose only: to serve the gods by supplying them with food, drink, and shelter so that they might have full leisure for their divine activities."[11] Each temple was believed to be, quite literally, the house of a particular god, and each community had its own special deity. Priests and other attendants constituted the god's court or household, and their chief task was to minister to his needs. Another responsibility was to mediate between the god and the community, trying to discover his will and appease his anger. In order to perform these tasks, temples and their staffs had to be supported by a steady flow of goods. Over the years, the temples were continually enlarged and

FIGURE 7.2   The temple of Luxor, Egypt.

became increasingly costly. In fact, they became, in many respects, substantial business enterprises, a development that apparently provided the stimulus for *the invention of true writing*, which was originally a means of recording the temple's business activities.[12] Many scholars have described the early Mesopotamian city-states as theocracies, since the local deity was regarded as the real ruler and the king merely as his "tenant farmer."[13]

Egypt was also a theocracy, but of a different type. One scholar compared the Egyptian and Mesopotamian patterns this way:

Egypt's theocracy was of a totally different kind from that of [Mesopotamia];

instead of the earthly ruler being but the chosen representative and the "tenant farmer" of the sovereign deity, Pharaoh was himself a god, and his government was divine simply because it was Pharaoh's. The other gods did not and could not dispute his authority. To whatever deity of the Egyptian pantheon the local temple might be dedicated, yet Pharaoh's statues adorned it, and, likely as not, the reliefs on the walls celebrated Pharaoh's exploits.[14]

To his subjects Pharaoh "was the incarnation, the living embodiment, of the god of any district he happened to be visiting; he was their actual God in living form, whom they could see, speak to, and adore."[15] Like the gods of the Mesopotamian city-states, he was theoretically the owner of the land and entitled to a portion of all that was produced, and, as in Mesopotamia, his revenues supported a small army of specialists (e.g., officials, craftsmen, soldiers).

In later years there was a secularizing trend, especially in Mesopotamia.[16] By then, however, societies had developed other institutional arrangements— notably political ones—to ensure the continued transfer of the economic surplus from the peasant producers to the governing class. Nevertheless, religion continued to play an important role as a legitimizing agency: it provided a rationale to justify the operation of the political system and its economic consequences.

The experience of Mesopotamia and Egypt thus supports the impression gained from horticultural societies concerning the importance of religion in the formation of an economic surplus. *Technological advance creates the possibility of a surplus, but to transform that possibility into a reality requires an ideology that motivates farmers to produce more than they need to stay alive and productive, and persuades them to turn that surplus over to someone else.* Although this has been accomplished on a number of occasions with secular and political ideologies, a system of beliefs that defined people's obligations with reference to the supernatural was best suited to play this critical role in societies of the past.

Population: Growth in Size of Communities and Societies

In the first few centuries after the shift to agriculture, there was striking growth in the size of a number of communities, especially in Mesopotamia.[17] These became *the first full-fledged cities in history*. The largest of them were the capitals of the largest and most prosperous societies. Although it is impossible to determine exactly the size of the cities and towns of the third and second millennia B.C., scholars believe that one or more of these cities passed the 100,000 mark.[18]

Egypt was the largest of the simple agrarian societies of ancient times and politically the most stable. She enjoyed the unique distinction of being a united and independent nation throughout almost the entire simple agrarian era. This achievement was due to her unique environmental situation: no other society had such excellent natural defenses and was so little threatened by powerful neighbors.

In the second half of the second millennium, Egypt embarked on a program of expansion that brought under her control all the territory from Syria to the Sudan. There were also other important empires in this era, especially those established by the Babylonians in the eighteenth century B.C. and the Hittites in the thirteenth century B.C. Babylonia succeeded briefly in uniting most of Mesopotamia, while the Hittites conquered much of what is now Turkey and Syria.

The Polity: Growth of the State

These conquests posed serious organizational problems for the rulers of early agrarian societies. Traditional modes of government based on ties among the members of an extended kin group proved totally inadequate for administering the affairs of societies whose populations now sometimes numbered in the millions. Though rulers continued to rely on relatives to help them perform the most essential tasks of government, they were forced to turn increasingly to others. One solution was to incorporate a conquered group as a subdivision of the state, leaving its former ruler in charge, but in a subordinate capacity. Eventually, however, all of the more successful rulers found it necessary to create new kinds of governmental structures, not based on kinship.

We can see these newer patterns evolving in both military and civil affairs. For example, the first armies in agrarian societies, like those in horticultural, were simply militia made up of all the able-bodied men in the society.[19] During this period, wars were of short duration and were fought only after the harvest was in. In fact, the period following the harvest came to be known as the "season when kings go forth to war." This limitation was essential because, with the shift to agriculture, men's responsibilities in farming were much greater.

As long as wars were brief and limited to skirmishes with neighboring peoples, this system was adequate. But once rulers became interested in empire building, it was no longer workable, and a new variety of specialists emerged. As early as the middle of the third millennium in Mesopotamia, would-be empire builders established small, but highly trained, *professional armies*. For example, Sargon, the famous Akkadian king, had a standing army of 5,400 men who "ate daily before him."[20] As far as possible, recruits were

FIGURE 7.3 Egyptian painting of soldiers attacking a fortress (about 1940 B.C.).

sons of old soldiers, and thus a military caste was gradually created. The Egyptians followed a similar policy except that they relied chiefly on foreign mercenaries. These new armies soon came to be *royal*, rather than national, armies. Their expenses were paid by the king out of his enormous revenues, and the profits resulting from their activities were his also. Not only were these armies useful in dealing with foreign enemies, they also served as a defense against internal threats.[21]

In civil affairs, too, the casual and informal practices of simpler societies proved inadequate. As states expanded and the problems of administration multiplied, new kinds of governmental positions were created, and a *governmental bureaucracy* began to take shape.[22] In addition to the many officials who comprised the royal court and were responsible for administering the king's complex household affairs, there were officials scattered throughout the countryside to administer the affairs of units ranging from small districts to provinces with hundreds of villages and towns. Each official had a staff of scribes and other lesser officials to assist him, and written records became increasingly important as administrative problems grew more complex.[23]

Throughout most of the history of the simple agrarian societies of antiquity, writing was a complex craft mastered by only a few individuals after long apprenticeships.[24] This is easily understood, considering the intricate preal-

FIGURE 7.4   Model of a royal granary, found in an Egyptian tomb (about 2000 B.C.). Note the scribes by the doorway recording the deliveries of grain.

phabetic systems of writing then in use. Even after a 2,000-year process of simplification, cuneiform script still had between 600 and 1,000 distinct characters. Before a person could learn to read or write, he had to memorize this formidable array of symbols and learn the complex rules for combining them. The Egyptian hieroglyphic and hieratic scripts were equally complicated. Thus, those who could write formed a specialized occupational group in society—the scribes—and their services were much in demand. For the most part, this occupation was filled by the sons of the rich and powerful, since only they could afford the necessary education.[25] Because of the political importance of their skill and the limited supply of qualified personnel, most scribes were at least marginal members of the governing class.

One consequence of the growth of empires and the development of bureaucracy was the establishment of the first formal legal systems. Over the centuries every society had developed certain concepts of justice, as well as informal techniques for implementing them. The most common solution, as we saw in the survey of hunting and gathering societies, was to rely on blood revenge by the injured party and his relatives. Because of anarchic tendencies in such a system, people began to seek settlement by arbitration, and quite naturally turned to the most respected and powerful members of the community. In this way, headmen and other political leaders gradually acquired judicial powers (i.e., the power to judge and to administer justice). Then, as empires grew, peoples of diverse cultures were brought within the framework of a single political system. In many instances, the official appointed to rule over an area was not a native and was therefore unfamiliar with local conceptions of justice (which varied considerably from place to place). This generated pressure to clarify and standardize judicial practice, which eventually led to the promulgation of the first *formal codes of law*. The most famous of these was the Code of Hammurabi, the great Babylonian empire-builder of the early second millennium.

The Economy: The Beginnings of Monetary Systems and the Expansion of Trade

Money as we know it was absent in the first simple agrarian societies. There were, nevertheless, certain standardized media of exchange. Barley served this function in ancient Mesopotamia, wheat in Egypt. Wages, rents, taxes, and various other obligations could be paid off in specified quantities of these grains.[26]

As media of exchange, grains were less than ideal, since they were both perishable and bulky. So, from a fairly early date, various metals, particularly silver and copper, were adopted as alternatives.[27] Initially, they were circulated in the form of crude bars of irregular size and weight, and their use was restricted to major transactions, since metal was still relatively scarce. Later, as metals were easier to obtain, smaller units were made to facilitate local trade, and their sizes and weights were gradually standardized. As the last stage in the process, governments assumed the responsibility for manufacturing metallic currencies, and full-fledged monetary systems took shape. This did not occur, however, until the very end of the simple agrarian era.

The growth of monetary systems had tremendous implications for societal development. *Money has always acted as a lubricant, facilitating the movement, the exchange, and ultimately the production of goods and services of every kind.* A money economy greatly enlarges the market for the things each individual produces, because, where there is money, products can be sold even to people who produce nothing the producer wants in exchange. Thus the demand for goods and services is maximized.

One immediate consequence of the emergence of a money economy is the growth of opportunities for *merchants*, or middlemen, who purchase goods which they do not want for themselves, but which they know are in demand. Once a class of merchants has come into being, they serve not only to satisfy existing demands but to create new ones. By displaying new and unusual articles, they generate new needs and desires and thereby stimulate economic activity.

In the long run, a money economy subverts many of the values of simpler societies, especially the cooperative tendencies of extended kin systems. It fosters instead a more individualistic, rationalistic, and competitive approach to life, and lays a foundation for many of the attitudes and values that characterize modern industrial societies.

All of these developments were still very limited, however, in the simple agrarian societies of the ancient Middle East. The newly emerging monetary economies barely penetrated the rural villages, where most of the people lived. Even in the cities and towns, the role of money was quite limited compared with what we are accustomed to. The major impact of money still lay in the future.

Stratification: Growing Social and Cultural Cleavages

In every simple agrarian society of the ancient world, social and cultural differences emerged that separated the members and had the potential for creating hostility, and even conflict, among them. These differences were especially serious in three areas. First, there was a cleavage between the small governing class and the much larger class of people who, having no voice in political decisions, had to turn over all or most of their surplus to the governing class. Second, there was a division between the urban minority and the far more numerous peasant villagers. Finally, there was a cleavage between the small literate minority and the illiterate masses.

Because these three lines of cleavage tended to converge, their effect was concentrated and the consequences for society were magnified. As a result, the small urban governing class lived in a very different world from that of the illiterate, rural, peasant majority—despite the fact that they were all members of the same society. The invention of writing had served to intensify the great social cleavage between the governing class and the governed, promoting the formation of two increasingly distinct *subcultures*.[28]

The subculture of the common people was a mixture of primitive superstition and the practical information they needed in their daily lives. It was extremely parochial in outlook and knew little of the world beyond the village. The subculture of the governing class, by contrast, incorporated many of the refinements we identify with "civilization." It included elements of philoso-phy, art, literature, history, science, and administrative techniques, and, above all, a contempt for physical labor of any kind (except warfare) and for those who engaged in it. In short, the governing class possessed a body of cultural information that differed radically from that of the peasant class.

In many respects the differences within simple agrarian societies were greater than those between them. Apart from the problems of language, an Egyptian peasant in the latter half of the second millennium B.C. could have adapted far more easily to the life of a Babylonian peasant than to the life of a member of the governing class of his own society. As this gulf widened, members of the governing class found it increasingly difficult to recognize the ignorant, downtrodden peasants as fellow human beings. The scribes of ancient Egypt were fond of saying that the lower classes were "without heart" (meaning that they lacked intelligence) and therefore had to be driven with a stick like cattle.[29]

Slowdown in the Rate of Technological Innovation

Another significant development in these societies was a marked slowdown in the rate of technological innovation and progress, beginning within a few centuries after the shift from horticulture to agriculture. Childe described the change this way:

> Before the [agrarian] revolution comparatively poor and illiterate communities had made an impressive series of contributions to man's progress. The two millennia immediately preceding 3,000 B.C. had witnessed discoveries in applied science that directly or indirectly affected the prosperity of millions of [people] and demonstrably furthered the biological welfare of our species by facilitating its multiplication. We have mentioned the following applications of science: artificial irrigation using canals and ditches; the plow; the harnessing of animal motive-power; the sailboat; wheeled vehicles; orchard husbandry; fermentation; the production and use of copper; bricks; the arch; glazing; the seal; and—in the earliest stages of the revolution—a solar calendar, writing, numerical notation, and bronze.
>
> The two thousand years after the revolution—say from 2,600 to 600 B.C.—produced few contributions of anything like comparable importance to human progress. Perhaps only four achievements deserve to be put in the same category as the fifteen just enumerated. They are: the "decimal notation" of Babylonia (about 2,000 B.C.); an economical method for smelting iron on an industrial scale (1,400 B.C.); a truly alphabetic script (1,300 B.C.); aqueducts for supplying water to cities (700 B.C.).[30]

Childe went on to note that two of these four innovations, the smelting of iron and the development of the alphabet, "cannot be credited to the societies that had initiated and reaped the fruits of the urban revolution" but rather were the products of somewhat less advanced neighboring societies.[31]

At first glance this slowing of the rate of cultural innovation seems an unlikely development. Larger populations, increased intersocietal contacts, and the greater store of information available to potential innovators should have produced still higher rates of innovation, especially in technology. The fact that they did not poses an interesting problem.

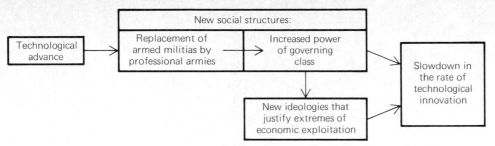

FIGURE 7.5   Model of the causes of the decline in the rate of technological innovation during the first two millennia of the agrarian era.

To explain this unusual development, we need to return to the concept of feedback. This, as we saw on page 74, is the effect produced when some part of an initial force reverts back to, and influences, the initial force itself. Until now, however, we have seen examples only of *positive feedback*, in which the secondary effect enhances or strengthens the original force. This is the type of feedback that has been involved in all of the major social and cultural changes we have examined so far. Now we are seeing one of the rare instances in sociocultural evolution in which major technological advances generated *negative feedback*. In other words, this is a case in which the secondary effect diminished or weakened the original force.

As Figure 7.5 indicates, changes in social structure and ideology that were themselves consequences of technological advance had the effect of *slowing down* the rate of technological innovation and advance. As the older system of an armed militia that included all able-bodied men was replaced by a system of professional armies, there was a substantial increase in the power of the governing class, which controlled the new armies. New beliefs and values emerged that served to justify the new system, and at the same time served to perpetuate it and make it even worse. Thus, the governing class found it increasingly easy to extract most of the economic surplus from the peasants, so that they were left with little more than the barest necessities of life.[32]

As a result, the peasants lost all incentive for creativity, knowing that any benefits that resulted from their inventions and discoveries would simply be appropriated by the governing class.* At the same time, the governing class, though it had a vested interest in a more productive economy, no longer had the necessary knowledge of, and experience with, subsistence technology and thus was in no position to make creative innovations. In short, *expertise and incentive were inadvertently divorced*, with disastrous results for technological progress.

Under the circumstances, it is hardly surprising that members of the governing class turned increasingly to warfare and conquest as the best way to increase their wealth. Warfare was something they understood; moreover, in their system of values, waging war was one of the few occupations considered appropriate for their class. The energies of this powerful and influential class

---

*It is possible that the problem was more complicated: the mental capacities of many peasants may also have been impaired by protein-deficient diets and by environments not conducive to learning in early childhood.

were thus turned *from the conquest of nature to the conquest of man.*[33] And this, thanks to the new, more productive technology, could be a highly profitable enterprise. With vast numbers of peasants producing more than they needed to survive and remain productive, there was a great economic surplus, in the form of taxes, tithes, and rents, steadily flowing in to support the host of servants and artisans that catered to the whims of the governing class, as well as the army of soldiers and officials that ensured the flow of revenues.

These developments help explain the growing complexity of social structures during this period. Having cut themselves off from the sweaty world of work and directed their efforts instead to conquest, members of the governing class found a new challenge for their creative talents in the area of social organization. The exercise of power and the manipulation of others were activities in keeping with their dignity. Furthermore, they were rewarding: the better organized an army or government, the greater its chances of success in struggles with other groups.[34]

By the end of the period when simple agrarian societies were dominant, substantial changes had occurred in societies that had adopted the new technology. The largest of these societies were substantially larger than any horticultural society had ever been, and substantially more complex. There was a much greater division of labor within them, and social inequality had also increased. But as impressive as they were, these changes were only the prelude to what was yet to come in the remainder of the agrarian era.

Advanced Agrarian Societies

Technology

During the period in which simple agrarian societies dominated the Middle East, the most important technological advance was the discovery of the technique of smelting iron. Prior to this, bronze had been the most important metal. But since the supply was always limited* and the demands of the governing class always took precedence over the needs of peasants, bronze was used primarily for military and ornamental purposes. It never really replaced stone and wood in ordinary tools, certainly not in agricultural tools, and so its impact on the economy was limited.

People knew of iron at least as early as the first half of the third millennium B.C., but apparently only in its meteoric form, which is very scarce.[35] Sometime during the second millennium, the Hittites of Asia Minor discovered iron ore and invented a technique for smelting it. For centuries they kept this a closely guarded secret, which brought them a considerable economic advantage. Then, about 1200 B.C., their nation was destroyed. This led to the rapid dispersal of both the Hittite people and the technique of iron smelting.

As one would expect, in view of the nature of the class structure of simple agrarian societies, the initial use of iron was limited largely to the governing class. Some of the earliest iron objects recovered from Egypt were a dagger, a

---

*This was because of the scarcity of tin, an essential component.

FIGURE 7.6 Throughout the agrarian era, societies depended on humans and animals as their chief sources of energy: Indian peasants raising water from a ditch to irrigate the field. The man on the post steps back on the crossbeam to raise the water, while the man below empties the container and lowers it again into the drainage canal.

bracelet, and a headrest found in the tomb of the pharaoh Tutankhamen. Prior to the military collapse of the Hittites, iron was five times more expensive than gold, forty times more than silver. It was not until about the eighth century B.C. that iron came into general use for *ordinary tools*. Thus, not until this period were there true advanced agrarian societies, although many Middle Eastern societies of the previous three or four centuries were certainly transitional types.

During this transitional period two further discoveries greatly enhanced the value of iron. First it was found that if the outer layers of the iron absorbed some carbon from the fire during the forging process, the metal became somewhat harder. Later it was discovered that this carburized iron could be hardened still further by quenching the hot metal in water, thus producing steel. With these developments, iron became not only more common than bronze but also more useful for both military and economic purposes. As one writer has said, "After the discovery of quench-hardening, iron gradually passed into the position from which it has never subsequently been ousted; it became the supremely useful material for making all the tools and weapons that are intended for cutting, chopping, piercing, or slashing."[36]

From its point of origin in the Middle East, iron-making spread until eventually it was practiced in nearly all of the Old World, even in many horticultural societies. By the time of Christ, advanced agrarian societies were firmly established in the Middle East, throughout most of the Mediterranean world, and in much of India and China. Within the next thousand years, the advanced agrarian pattern spread over most of Europe and much of Southeast Asia, and expanded further in India and China. Still later it was transplanted to the European colonies in the New World.

Compared with simpler societies, advanced agrarian societies enjoyed a very productive technology. Unfortunately, the same conditions that slowed the rate of technological advance in simple agrarian societies continued to operate. As a result, their progress was not nearly what one would expect on the basis of their size, the degree of contact among them, and, above all, their store of accumulated information.[37]

Nevertheless, over the centuries quite a number of important innovations were made. A partial list would include the catapult, the crossbow, gunpowder, horseshoes, a workable harness for horses, stirrups, the wood-turning lathe, the auger, the screw, the wheelbarrow, the rotary fan for ventilation, the clock, the spinning wheel, porcelain, printing, iron casting, the magnet, water-powered mills, windmills, and, in the period just preceding the emergence of the first industrial societies, the workable steam engine, the fly shuttle, the spinning jenny, the spinning machine, and various other power-driven tools. As a result of these and other innovations, the most advanced agrarian societies of the eighteenth century A.D. were considerably superior, from the technological standpoint, to their predecessors of 2,500 years earlier.

The level of technological development was not uniform throughout the agrarian world, despite diffusion. Information still spread slowly in most cases, and some areas were considerably ahead of others. During much of the advanced agrarian era, especially from 500 to 1500 A.D., the Middle East, China, and parts of India were technologically superior to Europe.[38] In part, this was simply a continuation of older patterns: the Middle East had been the center of innovation for more than 5,000 years following its shift to horticulture. An even more important factor in Europe's relative backwardness, however, was the collapse of the Roman Empire. For centuries afterward, Europe was divided into scores of petty kingdoms and principalities that had only enough resources to maintain the smallest urban settlements and the most limited occupational specialization. Therefore, Europeans were inactive on many of the most promising and challenging technological frontiers of the time. Though they made relative gains during the later Middle Ages—thanks

largely to the diffusion of knowledge from the East—they did not really catch
up until the sixteenth century and did not take the lead until even later.

183

Agrarian Societies

Population: Continuing Trends

Size of Societies and Communities   The populations of advanced agrarian
societies were substantially larger than those of any societies that preceded
them. This was due partly to advances in agricultural technology that permitted greater population densities and partly to advances in military technology
that aided the process of empire building. The largest simple agrarian society,
Egypt, probably had fewer than 15 million members.[39] By contrast, the largest
advanced agrarian society, mid-nineteenth-century China, had approximately
400 million.*[40] While that was exceptional, India reached 175 million in the
middle of the nineteenth century, and the Roman and the Russian empires each
had at least 70 million people.[41]

Similar differences are found in communities. The populations of the
largest cities in simple agrarian societies were probably not much over
100,000, if that. By contrast, the upper limit for cities in advanced agrarian
societies was about a million (see Table 10.5, page 280).[42] Only the capitals of
major empires ever attained such a size, and they maintained it but briefly.
Cities of 100,000 were more numerous than in simple agrarian societies,
though still quite rare.

Fertility and Mortality   Birthrates in both simple and advanced agrarian
societies have averaged 40 or more births per 1,000 population per year, nearly triple that of modern industrial societies.[43] In general, there seems to
have been little interest in limiting the size of families, since large families,
particularly ones with many sons, were valued for both economic and
religious reasons. From the economic standpoint, children were viewed by
peasants as an important asset, a valuable source of cheap labor.[44] The
members of modern industrial societies are usually unaware of the amount of
work required on a peasant farm. Children were also important as the only
form of old-age survivor's insurance available to peasants. Religion added
another incentive for large families, either by encouraging cults of ancestor
worship in which perpetuation of the family line was essential, or simply by
declaring large families to be a sign of God's favor.[45] The chief deterrent to
large families was probably the way women felt about the strains and risks of
repeated pregnancies; but because they were subordinate to their husbands,
their feelings usually counted for little.[46]

Despite their high birthrates, advanced agrarian societies grew slowly.
Sometimes they failed to grow at all or even declined in size. The reason, of
course, was that death rates were almost as high as birthrates and sometimes
higher. Wars, disease, accidents, and famine all took their toll. Infant mortality
was especially high before the development of modern sanitation and medi-

---

*Growth in China's population *after* the middle of the nineteenth century was increasingly
due to the beginnings of industrialization. The same is true of India.

cine. Recent studies show that the average child born in Rome 2,000 years ago could not expect to live more than twenty years.[47] Even as recently as the seventeenth century, the children of British queens and duchesses had a life expectancy of thirty years, with nearly a third dead before their fifth birthday. Youngsters of the elite who survived the dangerous infant years still had a total life expectancy of only a little more than forty years.[48] For the common people, conditions were even worse. With death rates averaging nearly 40 per 1,000 per year, life expectancy could not have been much over twenty-five years.

The larger cities were notoriously unhealthy places, especially for the common people. The citizens of Rome, for example, had a shorter life expectancy than those in the provinces.[49] England in the early eighteenth century presented a similar situation. During the first half of that century, there were an estimated 500,000 more deaths than births in London.[50] Some of the reasons for this become clear when we read descriptions of sanitary conditions in medieval cities. As one historian depicts them:

> The streets of medieval towns were generally little·more than narrow alleys, the overhanging upper stories of the houses nearly meeting, and thus effectually excluding all but a minimum of light and air . . . In most continental towns and

FIGURE 7.7 The narrow streets of medieval towns effectively excluded all but a minimum of light and air. View of Dubróvnik, Yugoslavia from the city wall.

some English ones, a high city wall further impeded the free circulation of air . . . Rich citizens might possess a courtyard in which garbage was collected and occasionally removed to the suburbs, but the usual practice was to throw everything into the streets including the garbage of slaughter houses and other offensive trades . . . Filth of every imaginable description accumulated indefinitely in the unpaved streets and in all available space and was trodden into the ground. The water supply would be obtained either from wells or springs, polluted by the gradual percolation through the soil of the accumulated filth, or else from an equally polluted river. In some towns, notably London, small streams running down a central gutter served at once as sewers and as water supply . . . In seventeenth century London, which before the Fire largely remained a medieval city, the poorer class house had only a covering of weatherboards, a little black pitch forming the only waterproofing, and these houses were generally built back to back. Thousands of Londoners dwelt in cellars or horribly overcrowded tenements. A small house in Dowgate accommodated 11 married couples and 15 single persons . . . Another source of unhealthiness were the church vaults and graveyards, so filled with corpses that the level of the latter was generally raised above that of the surrounding ground. In years of pestilence, recourse had to be made to plague pits in order to dispose of the harvest of death.[51]

This account calls attention to one of the striking demographic characteristics of advanced agrarian societies: the disasters that periodically overtook them and produced sharp peaks in their death rates.[52] The most devastating of all, the Black Plague that hit Europe in the middle of the fourteenth century, is

FIGURE 7.8 Sanitary standards were low in most agrarian societies: open-air butcher shop in the Middle East.

said to have killed a third of the population of France and England, half that of Italy, and to have left the island of Cyprus almost depopulated.[53] Crop failures and famines seldom affected such large areas, but they were much more frequent and could be just as deadly in the area affected. One Finnish province lost a third of its population during the famine of 1696–1697, and many parts of France suffered comparable losses a few years earlier.[54] Even allowing for a considerable margin of error in the reports of such disasters, it is clear from other kinds of evidence—for example, the severe labor shortages and the abandonment of farms that followed plagues and famines—that the number of deaths was huge. Because of these disasters, the growth of advanced agrarian populations was anything but continuous.

The Economy: Increasing Differentiation

Division of Labor   The growth in both geographical and population size that came with the shift from the simple to the advanced agrarian level brought with it an increase in the division of labor. For the first time, there was significant economic specialization by regions and by communities, and this was accompanied by increased occupational specialization.

The Roman Empire provides a good illustration of both regional and local specialization. North Africa and Spain were noted as suppliers of dried figs and

FIGURE 7.9   Occupational specialization in an advanced agrarian society: Middle Eastern silversmith in his shop.

olive oil; Gaul, Dalmatia, Asia Minor, and Syria for their wine; Spain and Egypt for salted meats; Egypt, North Africa, Sicily, and the Black Sea region for grain; and the latter for salted fish as well.[55] The tendency toward specialization at the community level is illustrated by a passage from a manual for wealthy farmers, written in the second century B.C., which advised:

> Tunics, togas, blankets, smocks and shoes should be bought at Rome; caps, iron tools, scythes, spades, mattocks, axes, harness, ornaments and small chains at Cales and Minturnae; spades at Venafrum, carts and sledges at Suessa and in Lucania, jars and pots at Alba and at Rome; tiles at Venafrum, oil mills at Pompeii and at Rufrius's yard at Nola; nails and bars at Rome; pails, oil urns, water pitchers, wine urns, other copper vessels at Capua and at Nola; Campanian baskets, pulley-ropes and all sorts of cordage at Capua, Roman baskets at Suessa and Casium.[56]

Similar patterns are reported in other agrarian societies.[57] Even at the village level a measure of specialization was not uncommon. In the agricultural off-season, peasants often turned to handicrafts to make ends meet, and certain villages gradually developed a reputation for a particular commodity.

In the larger urban centers, occupational specialization reached a level that surpassed anything achieved in simpler societies. For example, a tax roll for Paris from the year 1313 lists 157 different trades, and tax records from two sections of Barcelona in 1385 indicate a hundred occupations (see Table 7.1).[58] The clothing industry alone contained such specialized occupations as wool comber, wool spinner, silk spinner (two kinds), girdle maker, and headdress maker (seven kinds, including specialists in felt, fur, wool and cotton, flowers, peacock feathers, gold embroidery and pearls, and silk). Though such specialization was found only in the largest cities, smaller cities often had forty or fifty different kinds of craftsmen, and even small towns had ten or twenty.[59] In addition to craft specialists, urban centers also had specialists in government, commerce, religion, education, the armed forces, and domestic service. The list should also include specialists engaged in illegal occupations (e.g., thieves), since they were a normal part of urban life in advanced agrarian societies.

Command Economies Because politics and economics were always highly interdependent in advanced agrarian societies, the people who dominated the

TABLE 7.1 Occupations of Householders in Two Sections of Barcelona in 1385 A.D.

Sailors	227	Longshoremen	50	Silversmiths	29
Merchants	151	Innkeepers	49	Curriers	29
Shoemakers	108	Brokers	45	Notaries	28
Tailors	96	Carpenters	43	Tavern-keepers	27
Fishermen	94	Bakers	40	Spicers	26
Seamen	73	Janitors	39	Bargemen	25
Wooldressers	70	Hucksters	36	76 other occupations	525
Weavers	63	Butchers	34		
Tanners	61	Scriveners	32	Total	2000

Source: Adapted from Josiah Cox Russell, *Medieval Regions and Their Cities* (Bloomington: Indiana University Press, 1972), p. 170.

political system also dominated the economic system. The leading officehold-ers in government were usually the chief landholders as well, and in these societies land was the most important economic resource. As one economic historian expressed it, ''In pre-market societies [among which he includes agrarian], wealth tends to follow power; not until the market society [does] power tend to follow wealth.''[60]

As this statement suggests, the answer to central economic questions—how resources should be used, what should be produced and in what quantities, and how the products should be distributed—were determined less by the market forces of supply and demand than by the arbitrary decisions of the political elite. These were *command economies*, not market economies.[61]

The economy of an advanced agrarian society consisted of two distinct parts: its rural-based agricultural sector and its urban-based commercial and industrial sector. These were not of equal economic importance, however: one historian has estimated that the Roman state derived approximately twenty times more tax revenue from agriculture than from trade and industry. He went on to say that ''this apportionment of the burden of taxation probably corresponded roughly to the economic structure of the empire. All the evidence goes to show that its wealth was derived almost entirely from agriculture, and to a very small extent from industry and trade.''[62] The same could be said of every agrarian society. This does not mean, of course, that the urban economy was of little interest to the governing class. On the contrary, it was of tremendous interest because it provided the luxuries they valued so highly. The urban economy, however, depended on the ability of the rural economy to produce a surplus that could support the urban population.

In many respects the economy of the typical agrarian society resembled a tree with roots spreading in every direction, constantly drawing in new resources. The pattern was rather like that shown in Figure 7.10. At the

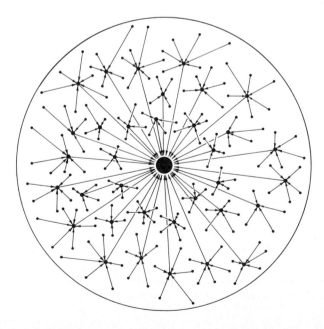

FIGURE 7.10 In agrarian societies, there was a steady flow of goods from villages to county seats and from there to regional and national capitals: graphic representation of the flow of goods in these societies.

economic center of the society was the national capital, controlled by the king or emperor and the leading members of the governing class. Surrounding it were various provincial or regional capitals controlled by royal governors and other members of the governing class. Each of these, in turn, was surrounded by smaller county seats and market towns controlled by lower-ranking members of the governing class. Finally, each of these towns was surrounded by scores of small villages. In the larger empires, there was often another layer interposed between the county seats and the regional capitals.

In this system, there was a steady flow of goods from smaller units to larger, or from villages to county seats and from there to regional and national capitals. Basically this flow was through taxation, but it was supplemented by rents, interest on debts, tithes, and profits, all of which helped transfer the economic surplus from the peasant producers to the urban-based governing class and their allies and dependents.

Some scholars have argued that this was actually a symbiotic relationship in which the villagers freely exchanged the goods they produced for goods and services produced in the urban centers. Although there is an element of truth in this, the historical record shows that basically the relationship was a one-sided one in which the peasants were forced to give far more than they received. The peasants greatly resented this, as indicated by the frequency of their protests and hopeless revolts.[63]

With what they retained of their surplus after paying taxes, rents, interest, and other obligations, peasants could go to the urban centers and trade for commodities that were not available in their villages (e.g., metal tools, salt, etc.). Many towns and cities were also religious centers, and the peasants often used these facilities. Finally, the peasants did benefit to some degree from the maintenance of law and order provided by urban-based governments, even though the law was used disproportionately to protect the rights of the governing class and keep the peasants in their place. The maintenance of order is extremely important in an agrarian society because so much depends on the success of each harvest, and each harvest depends on months of effort. Disruption at any point in the agricultural cycle can be disastrous for everyone.

The Rural Economy In most advanced agrarian societies, the governing elite (which included religious leaders) owned a grossly disproportionate share of the land. Although there are no precise figures for earlier times, the traditional pattern can still be seen in many parts of Latin America, the Middle East, and Southeast Asia. In recent years, a minority of 1 to 3 per cent of the population has owned from one-third to two-thirds of the arable land in these countries (see Table 7.2).

Not only did the governing class usually own most of the land, but it often owned most of the peasants who worked it. Systems of slavery and serfdom have been common in agrarian societies, with large landholdings and large numbers of slaves or serfs normally going hand in hand. Thus, one nineteenth-century Russian nobleman who owned 2 million acres of land also owned nearly 300,000 serfs.[64] Rulers, understandably, had the largest holdings. Prior to the emancipation of the serfs in Russia, the czar owned 27.4 million of them.[65]

TABLE 7.2 Landholdings of the Governing Class in Selected Nations in the Mid-Twentieth Century

Nation	Percentage of Population	Percentage of Arable Land Owned
Chile	1.4	63
Northeast Brazil	2.0	48
Portugal	0.3	39
Southern Spain	1.8	50+
Egypt	0.4	34
	3.0	56
Jordan	3.5	37
Lebanon	0.2	50
	1.4	65
Iraq	3.0	67
North-central India	1.5	39
	3.3	54
South Vietnam	2.5	50

Sources: Chile—Federico Gil, *The Political System of Chile* (Boston: Houghton Mifflin, 1966), p. 148; Northeast Brazil—Josue de Castro, *Death in the Northeast* (New York: Random House, 1966), p. 154; Portugal—Herminio Martins, "Portugal," in Margaret Archer and Salvador Giner (eds.), *Contemporary Europe* (New York: St. Martin's, 1972), p. 66; Spain—Salvador Giner, "Spain," in Archer and Giner, p. 134; the Middle Eastern nations—Morroe Berger, *The Arab World Today* (Garden City, N.Y.: Doubleday Anchor, 1964), pp. 196–199; North-central India—Baljit Singh and Shridhar Misra, *Land Reforms in Uttar Pradesh* (Honolulu: East-West Center Press, 1964), p. 28; South Vietnam—*The Washington Post*, October 17, 1965, p. A 8.

But even when the peasant owned his own land and was legally free, he usually found it difficult to make ends meet. A bad crop one year, and he had to borrow money at usurious rates, sometimes as high as 120 per cent a year.[66] In any event, there were always taxes, and these usually fell more heavily on the peasant landowner than on his wealthier neighbor, either because of special exemptions granted the latter or simply because of his greater ability to evade such obligations.[67] If a peasant did not own his land, he had to pay rent, which was always high. In addition, he was often subject to compulsory labor service, tithes, fines, and obligatory "gifts" to the governing class.[68]

Because the number and variety of obligations were so great, it is difficult to determine just how large the total was, but in most societies it appears to have been not less than half the total value of the goods the peasants produced.[69] The basic philosophy of the governing class seems to have been to tax peasants to the limit of their ability to pay.[70] This philosophy is illustrated by a story told of a leading Japanese official of the seventeenth century who, returning to one of his estates after an absence of ten years and finding the villagers in well-built houses instead of the hovels he remembered, exclaimed. "These people are too comfortable. They must be more heavily taxed."[71]

FIGURE 7.11　Peasant using traditional wooden plow in Iran.

Living conditions for most peasants were very primitive, and it is doubtful that they were as well off as hunters and gatherers. For example, the diet of the average peasant in medieval England consisted of little more than a hunk of bread and a mug of ale in the morning; a lump of cheese and bread with perhaps an onion or two to flavor it and more ale at noon; and a thick soup or pottage with bread and cheese in the evening.[72] Meat was rare and the ale usually thin. Household furniture consisted of a few stools, a table, and a chest to hold the best clothes and any other treasured possessions.[73] Beds were uncommon; most peasants simply slept on earthen floors covered with straw. And cooking utensils were apparently the only other household possessions.

In some cases, the lot of the peasant was worse than this. Conditions frequently became so oppressive that it was impossible to eke out a livelihood and the peasants were forced to abandon their farms.[74] In China, conditions were so wretched that female infanticide was widely practiced. One nineteenth-century scholar indicated that in some districts as many as a quarter of the female infants were killed at birth.[75] Sometimes signs were posted in these areas: ''Girls may not be drowned here.''

To compound the misery created by their economic situation, peasants were often subjected to further cruelties. Families were sometimes split up if it served their master's economic interests.[76] Peasants often found it difficult to defend their wives and daughters from the amorous attentions of the governing class, and in some areas the lord of the manor maintained the notorious *jus primae noctis* (i.e., literally the right of the first night, meaning the right to have sexual relations with a bride before her husband did).[77] Finally, peasants were subject at all times to the whims and tempers of their superiors, who could invoke severe punishments even for minor offenses. Petty thievery was often punished by death, frequently by cruel and frightful means.[78]

To the governing class, all this seemed only natural, since most of them,

TWO VIEWS OF PEASANT LIFE

The rural past often evokes nostalgia. People familiar with the ills of modern industrial societies sometimes covet the "quiet, happy, wholesome way of life" of an earlier era. To a large extent, this image of the past reflects a heritage bequeathed us by romantics who used their pens and paints to create a world that rarely existed. Oliver Goldsmith (1728–1774) was such a poet. Excerpts from his poem, "The Deserted Village," are followed by a few lines from Edwin Markham's remarkably prophetic poem, "The Man With the Hoe," written in 1899—eighteen years before the Russian Revolution and half a century before the Chinese and Cuban revolutions.

From "The Deserted Village," by Oliver Goldsmith

Sweet Auburn! loveliest village of the plain,
Where health and plenty cheered the laboring swain . . .
How often have I loitered o'er thy green,
Where humble happiness endeared each scene!
How often have I paused on every charm,
The sheltered cot, the cultivated farm,
The never-failing brook, the busy mill,
The decent church that topped the neighboring hill . . .
How often have I blest the coming day,
When toil remitting lent its turn to play,
And all the village train, from labor free
Led up their sports beneath the spreading tree . . .
A time there was, ere England's griefs began,
When every rood of ground maintained its man;
For him light labor spread her wholesome store,

like their predecessors in simple agrarian societies, viewed peasants as essentially subhuman. In legal documents in medieval England, a peasant's children were listed not as his *familia*, but as his *sequela*, meaning "brood" or "litter."[79] Estate records in Europe, Asia, and America often listed the peasants with the livestock.[80] Even so civilized a Roman as Cato the Elder argued that slaves, like livestock, should be disposed of when no longer productive.[81]

As shocking as these views seem today, they were not completely illogical, but simply one facet of the belief systems that emerged at this point in sociocultural evolution. These new beliefs and values reflected the cleavages within a society and the increasingly diverse experiences of its members. So divergent were the ways of life of the governing class and the peasantry, and so limited their contacts (normally a class of officials and retainers stood between them[82]), that it is perhaps more surprising that some members of the privileged class recognized their common humanity than that the majority did not.

Despite the heavy burdens laid on them, not all peasants were reduced to

Just gave what life required, but gave no more;
His best companions, innocence and health;
And his best riches, ignorance of wealth.

From "The Man with the Hoe," by Edwin Markham

Bowed by the weight of centuries he leans
Upon his hoe and gazes on the ground,
The emptiness of ages in his face,
And on his back the burden of the world.
Who made him dead to rapture and despair,
A thing that grieves not and that never hopes,
Stolid and stunned, a brother to the ox? . . .
Whose breath blew out the light within this brain? . . .

Through this dread shape the suffering ages look;
Time's tragedy is in that aching stoop;
Through this dread shape humanity betrayed,
Plundered, profaned and disinherited,
Cries protest to the Judges of the World,
A protest that is also prophecy . . .

O masters, lords and rulers of all lands,
How will the future reckon with this man?
How answer his brute question in that hour
When whirlwinds of rebellion shake all shores?
How will it be with kingdoms and with kings—
With those who shaped him to the thing he is—
When this dumb terror shall rise to judge the world,
After the silence of the centuries?

the subsistence level. By various devices, many contrived to hide part of their harvest and otherwise evade their obligations.[83] A small minority even managed, by rendering special services to the governing class or by other means, to rise a bit above their fellows, operating larger farms and generally living a bit more comfortably.[84]

For the majority, however, the one real hope for a substantial improvement in their lot lay, ironically, in the devastation wrought by plagues, famines, and wars. Only when death reduced their numbers to the point where good workers were scarce was the governing class forced to bid competitively for the peasants' services, raising their income above the subsistence level.[85] Normally, however, high birthrates kept this from happening or, when it did, soon brought about a return to the former situation.

The Urban Economy When we think of the famous societies of the past, most of us conjure up images of Rome, Constantinople, Alexandria, Jerusalem,

Damascus, Baghdad, Babylon, and the other great cities that loom so large in the historical record. Thus it is with a sense of shock that we discover that rarely if ever did all the urban communities of an advanced agrarian society contain as much as 10 per cent of its population, and in most cases they held far less.[86]

How can this be? The explanation is that history was recorded by literate men—men who nearly always lived in cities and towns and regarded the life of the rural villages as unworthy of their attention. Thus, the historical record is primarily a record of city life, particularly the life of the governing class.

The most striking feature of the cities and towns of these societies was the great diversity of people who lived in them. Urban residents ranged from the most illustrious members of the governing class to beggars and other destitute people who barely managed to stay alive. Unlike so many cities and towns in modern industrial societies, these were not primarily industrial centers. Though considerable industrial activity was carried on in them, their political and commercial functions, and frequently their religious ones, were more important.

Since the cities and towns were the centers of government, and social and cultural centers as well, most members of the governing class preferred to live in them.[87] As a result, urban populations included not only the necessary complement of civil and military officials, but the extensive households of the governing class as well. Servants were far more numerous in these societies

FIGURE 7.12   Peasant household in Colombia.

than in ours, both because of the absence of labor-saving devices and because the governing class viewed manual work of any kind as degrading. Furthermore, one of their chief forms of status competition was to see who could maintain the most luxurious household. The household staff of the head of one small kingdom, Edward IV of England, numbered 400.[88] A more important ruler, such as the Roman emperor at the height of empire, had thousands. As one historian put it, one "is dumbfounded by the extraordinary degree of specialization [and] the insensate luxury."[89] One group of servants was responsible only for the emperor's palace clothes, another for his city clothes, another for those he wore to the theater, yet another for his military uniforms. Other servants attended strictly to eating vessels, a different group to those used for drinking, another to silver vessels, and still others to gold vessels and those set with jewels. For entertainment, the emperor had his own choristers, an orchestra, dancing women, clowns, and dwarfs. Lesser members of the Roman governing class obviously could not maintain household staffs as elaborate as this, but many had staffs of hundreds, and some had a thousand or more.[90] All this was made possible by the labors of the peasantry.

Part of the peasants' surplus also went to support two important groups that were allied with the governing class yet separate from it. The first of these was the clergy, of whom more will be said shortly. The second was the merchant class. Merchants were a peculiar group in the structure of agrarian societies. Although some of them were extremely wealthy, they were rarely

FIGURE 7.13   Servants were far more numerous in advanced agrarian societies than in modern industrial, both because of the absence of mechanical labor-saving devices and because the governing class viewed manual work of any kind as degrading: slaves transporting wealthy Roman woman.

FIGURE 7.14 Like modern merchants, the merchants of agrarian societies often created the demand for their goods, especially luxury items: market scene in Morocco.

accepted as equals by members of the governing class—even by those less wealthy than they. For merchants worked to obtain their wealth, and this, by the values of the governing class, was unpardonable.[91] Nevertheless, the latter avidly sought the goods that the merchants sold and coveted their wealth, acquiring it whenever they could by taxes, marriage, or outright confiscation.[92] The attitude of the merchants toward the governing class was equally ambivalent: they both feared and envied them, but, given the chance, they emulated their way of life and sought to be accepted by them.

Like modern merchants, the merchants of agrarian societies often created the demand for their goods, thereby spurring productivity. And like modern advertisers, they were primarily interested in creating a demand for luxuries. One reason for this was the high cost of moving goods. With the primitive transportation available, only lightweight luxury items, such as silks, spices, and fine swords, could be moved very far without the costs becoming prohibitive. A report on China shortly after World War II indicates what an enormous difference there is between traditional and modern methods of transportation. To ship one ton of goods one mile, the costs were as follows (measured in United States cents):[93]

Steamboat	2.4	Animal-drawn cart	13.0	Pack donkey	24.0
Railroad	2.7	Pack mule	17.0	Pack horse	30.0
Junk	12.0	Wheelbarrow	20.0	Carrying by pole	48.0

Figures from Europe are strikingly similar: in 1900, for example, it cost ten times more to move goods by horse-drawn wagon than by rail.[94] In short, modern methods of transportation have slashed this cost by 80 to 95 per cent.

The prosperity of the merchant class was due in no small measure to the labors of another, humbler class with which they were closely affiliated—the artisans, who numbered approximately 3 to 5 per cent of the total population.[95] Except for the peasantry, this class was the most productive element in the economy. Most artisans lived in the urban centers and, like the rest of the urban population, were ultimately dependent on the surplus produced by the peasants. Craft specialization was rather highly developed in the larger urban centers, as we have seen.

The shops where artisans worked were small by modern standards and bore little resemblance to modern factories. In Rome in the first century B.C., a shop employing fifty men was considered very large.[96] A pewter business employing eighteen men was the largest mentioned in any of London's medieval craft records, and even this modest size was not attained until the middle of the fifteenth century.[97] Typically, the shop was also the residence of both the merchant and his workmen, and work was carried on either in the living quarters or in an adjoining room.[98]

The economic situation of the artisans, like that of the merchants, was variable. In Peking at the time of World War I, wages ranged from $2.50 a month for members of the Incense and Cosmetic Workers Guild to $36 a month for members of the Gold Foil Beaters Guild.[99] Those in highly skilled trades and some of the self-employed fared moderately well by agrarian standards. Apprentices and journeymen in less skilled trades, however, worked long hours for bare subsistence wages. In Peking, for example, a seven-day workweek and ten-hour workday were typical, and many artisans remained too poor ever to marry.

Merchants and artisans in the same trade were commonly organized into *guilds*. These organizations were an attempt to create, in an urban setting, a functional approximation of the extended kin groups of horticultural societies. Many guilds spoke of their members as brothers, for example, and functioned as mutual aid associations, restricting entry into the field, forbidding price cutting, and otherwise trying to protect the interests of their members.[100] But a guild included merchant employers as well as artisan employees, and the employers were naturally dominant, controlling key offices and formulating policies that benefited them more than the artisans.[101]

Beneath the artisans in the class structure of the cities were a variety of other kinds of people, including unskilled laborers who supplied much of the animal energy required by the system. The working conditions of these men were usually terrible, and injuries were common. As a result, their work life was short. For example, early in the present century, the average Peking rickshaw man was able to work only five years, after which he was good for little except begging.[102] The class of unskilled laborers shaded off into still more deprived groups—the unemployed, the beggars, and the criminals. The high birthrates of agrarian societies resulted in a perennial oversupply of unskilled labor, and such people drifted to the cities, hoping to find some kind of employment. As long as men were young and healthy, they could usually get work as day laborers. But after they were injured or lost their youth and strength, they were quickly replaced by fresh labor and left to fend for themselves, usually as beggars or thieves. No agrarian society ever found a solution to this problem. But then, the leading classes were not especially interested in finding one. The system served their needs quite well just as it was.

Many of the sisters of the men who made up the urban lower classes found their livelihood as prostitutes. Moralists have often condemned these women as though they elected this career in preference to a more honorable one. The record indicates, however, that most of them had little choice: their only alternative was a life of unrelieved drudgery and poverty as servants or unskilled laborers, and many could not even hope for that.[103] The men they might have married were too poor to afford wives, and the system of prostitution was often, in effect, a substitute for marriage forced on many men and women by society. To be sure, the poor were not the only ones to avail themselves of the services of prostitutes, nor were all girls in that "profession" because of poverty. But economic factors were clearly the chief cause of its high incidence.

The number of profitable working years for prostitutes was hardly longer than that for the rickshaw boys, porters, and others who sold their physical energy for a meager livelihood. As a result, the cities and towns in agrarian societies often swarmed with beggars of both sexes. Estimates by observers suggest that beggars comprised from a tenth to as high as a third of the total population of urban communities.[104] The proportion was not so high for the society as a whole, of course, since many of the rural poor migrated to the cities and towns in the hope of finding greater opportunities.

The Polity: Continuing Development of the State

In nearly all advanced agrarian societies, government was the basic integrating force. It was inevitable in any society created by conquest and run for the benefit of a tiny elite that coercive power was required to hold the society together. Not only did the natural antagonisms of the peasant masses have to be kept in check, but diverse groups of conquered people often had to be welded together politically. The scope of this problem is suggested by the geographical size of some of these societies. Whereas the largest simple agrarian society was probably Egypt, which controlled roughly 800,000 square miles, several advanced agrarian societies covered between 2 and 8 million square miles.

Nearly every advanced agrarian society was a monarchy: it had at its head a king or an emperor, a position that was usually hereditary. Republican government, in which power was divided among a small ruling elite, was an infrequent exception limited almost entirely to the least powerful and least developed societies and to those on the margins of the agrarian world.[105] The prevalence of monarchical government seems to have been the result of the militaristic and exploitative character of societies at this level. Governments were constantly threatening, or being threatened by, their neighbors. At the same time, they were in danger from internal enemies—dissatisfied and ambitious members of the governing class, eager to seize control for themselves, and restless, hostile members of the numerically dominant lower classes. Under such conditions, republican government was nearly impossible.[106]

Because of a tendency to romanticize the past, many people today are unaware of the frequency of both internal and external conflict in the great agrarian empires. In Rome, for example, thirty-one of the seventy-nine emperors were murdered, six were driven to suicide, four were forcibly deposed, and several more met unknown fates at the hands of internal enemies.[107] Though Rome's record was worse than most, internal struggles occurred in all advanced agrarian societies.[108]

Peasant uprisings were also indicators of internal stress. One expert states that "there were peasant rebellions almost every year in China," and an authority on Russia reports that in the short period from 1801 to 1861, there were no less than 1,467 peasant uprisings in various parts of that country.[109] Most of these disturbances remained local only because authorities acted swiftly and ruthlessly. Had they not, many would have spread as widely as the famous English revolt of 1381 or the German Peasants' War of 1524–1525.[110]

External threats were no less frequent or serious, and warfare was a chronic condition. As we noted in an earlier chapter, a survey of the incidence of war in eleven European countries in the preindustrial period found that, on the average, these countries were involved in some kind of conflict with neighboring societies nearly every second year.[111] Such conditions obviously required strong centralized authority. Societies without it were eliminated in the selective process, unless they happened to occupy a particularly remote and inaccessible territory.

Most members of the governing class considered political power a prize to be sought for the rewards it offered rather than an opportunity for public service, and the office of king or emperor was *the supreme prize*. This is the only interpretation one can put on the perennial struggle for power within agrarian states or the use made of it after it was won. Efforts to raise the living standards of the common people were rare, efforts at self-aggrandizement commonplace.[112] In many of these societies, government offices were bought and sold like pieces of property, which purchasers used to obtain the greatest possible profit. Officeholders demanded payment before they would act on any request, and justice was typically sold to the highest bidder. No wonder the common people of China developed the saying "To enter a court of justice is to enter a tiger's mouth."[113]

These practices reflected what is known as *the proprietary theory of the state*, which defines the state as a piece of property that its owners may use, within broad and ill-defined limits, for their personal advantage.[114] Guided by

SONG OF THE TROUBADOUR

I love the gay Eastertide, which brings forth leaves and flowers; and I love the joyous songs of the birds, re-echoing through the copse. But also I love to see, amidst the meadows, tents and pavilions spread; and it gives me great joy to see, drawn up on the field, knights and horses in battle array; and it delights me when the scouts scatter people and herds in their path; and I love to see them followed by a great body of men-at-arms; and my heart is filled with gladness when I see strong castles besieged . . . and the warriors . . . [with] maces, swords, helms of different hues, shields that will be riven and shattered as soon as the fight begins; and many vassals struck down together; and the horses of the dead and the wounded roving at random. And when battle is joined, let all men of good lineage think of naught but the breaking of heads and arms; for it is better to die than to be vanquished and live. I tell you, I find no such savour in food, or in wine, or in sleep, as in hearing the shout "On! On!" from both sides, and the neighing of steeds that have lost their riders, and the cries of "Help! Help!"; in seeing men great and small go down on the grass beyond the fosses; in seeing at last the dead, with pennoned stumps of lances still in their sides.

Attributed to Bertrand de Born, a petty nobleman and troubadour of the twelfth century. From Marc Bloch, *Feudal Society*, p. 293. By permission of The University of Chicago Press.

this theory, agrarian rulers and governing classes saw nothing immoral in the use of what we (not they) would call "public office" for private gain. To them, it was simply the legitimate use of what they commonly regarded as their "patrimony." It is said of the Ptolemies of Egypt, for example, that they showed the first emperors of Rome "how a country might be run on the lines of a profitable estate."[115] In the case of medieval Europe, we read:

> The proprietary conception of rulership created an inextricable confusion of public and private affairs. Rights of government were a form of private ownership. "Crown lands" and "the king's estate" were synonymous. There was no differentiation between the king in his private and public capacities. A kingdom, like any estate endowed with elements of governmental authority, was the private concern of its owner. Since *"state" and "estate" were identical,* "the State" was indistinguishable from the prince and his personal "patrimony."[116]

The proprietary theory of the state can be traced back to horticultural societies and, in a sense, even to hunting and gathering bands. In those simpler societies, no distinction was made between the private and public aspects of political leadership. When a surplus first began to be produced, at least part of it was turned over to the leader, who held it as trustee for the group. As long as the surplus was small and in the form of perishable commodities, there was little the leader could do with it except redistribute it, thereby winning status for his generosity. Eventually, however, as we saw in Chapter 6, it grew large enough to permit him to create a staff of dependent retainers who could be

FIGURE 7.15   One use of the economic surplus in an agrarian society: the Taj Mahal, a tomb erected by the Mogul emperor Shah Jahan in memory of his favorite wife.

used to enforce his wishes. At this point, the proprietary theory of the state was born. Later rulers merely applied it on an ever-expanding scale, as productivity and the economic surplus steadily increased.

Recent research provides a good picture of the extremes to which rulers and governing classes have carried the proprietary principle. In late nineteenth-century China, for example, the average income for families not in the governing class was approximately 20 to 25 taels per year. By contrast, the governing class averaged 450 taels per year, with some receiving as much as 200,000.[117] The emperor's income, of course, was considerably larger than even this. To cite another example, the English nobility at the end of the twelfth century and early in the thirteenth had an average income roughly 200 times that of ordinary field hands, and the king's equaled that of 24,000 field hands.[118] Putting together the evidence from many sources, it appears that the combined income of the ruler and the governing class in most advanced agrarian societies equaled not less than half of the total national income, even though they numbered 2 per cent or less of the population.[119]

Despite their many similarities, the political systems of advanced agrarian societies did vary in a number of ways, the most important being the *degree of political centralization*. In some societies the central government was very strong; in others its powers were severely limited. In the main, these differ-

FIGURE 7.16   Working equipment for a member of the governing class in sixteenth-century Europe.

ences reflected the current state of the perennial struggle between the ruler and the other members of the governing class. The king or emperor naturally wanted the greatest possible control over his subordinates, and the subordinates just as naturally wanted to minimize it. Since land (including the peasants who worked it) and political office were the most valuable resources in agrarian societies, most of the struggles between rulers and the governing class were over them. In a few instances, extremely powerful rulers managed to gain such control over these resources that both land and political offices were held solely at their pleasure and were subject to instant confiscation if an individual's services were judged unsatisfactory.[120] A Dutch traveler of the early seventeenth century left a vivid picture of the situation in the Mogul empire.

FIGURE 7.17   Armor of a Japanese nobleman of the sixteenth century.

> Immediately on the death of a lord who has enjoyed the King's [favor], be he great or small, without any exception—sometimes even before the breath is out of the body—the King's officers are ready on the spot and make an inventory of the entire estate, recording everything down to the value of a single piece, even to the dresses and jewels of the ladies, provided they have not concealed them. The King takes back the whole estate absolutely for himself, except in a case where the deceased has done good service in his lifetime, when the women and children are given enough to live on, but no more.[121]

And in Turkey under Suleiman, the chief officers of state were recruited from the ranks of specially trained slaves over whom the sultan held life-and-death power.[122]

At the other extreme, during much of the medieval period in Europe, the governing classes were virtually autonomous. Though their lands were typically royal grants given in exchange for pledges of service, monarchs usually lacked the power to enforce these pledges.[123] Although examples of both extremes can be found, the usual pattern was something in between, and in most cases the powers of the ruler and the governing class were fairly evenly balanced.

Religion: The Emergence of Universal Faiths

During the era in which advanced agrarian societies were dominant, there were a number of important changes in the religious sphere. The most important by far was the emergence and spread of three new religions, Buddhism, Christianity, and Islam. Each proclaimed a *supranational or universal faith*, and each succeeded in creating a community of believers that transcended societal boundaries. In all of the older religions, people's beliefs and loyalties were determined by the accident of birth. Where one lived determined the god or gods one worshiped, for the prevailing view was that there were many gods and that, like kings, each had his own people and territory.

The ancient Israelites were perhaps the first to reject this view and move toward a more universalistic outlook. Centuries before the birth of Christ, the prophets proclaimed that there was only one God and that He ruled over the entire world. For a time, Judaism was a missionary religion and won converts in many parts of the Roman world.[124] This phase ended, however, when the early Christian missionaries won most of these Gentile converts to their faith. From then on, implementation of the universalistic vision became the mission of Christians and Muslims, who eventually converted, at least nominally, most of the population of Europe, North Africa, and the Middle East, and some of the people of India, Central Asia, China, and Southeast Asia.

Buddhism, the other great universal faith, began in India as a heretical offshoot of Hinduism and spread through most of Southeast Asia, China, Korea, and Japan, though it later died out in the land of its origin. The older ethnic faiths, such as Hinduism, Confucianism, and Shintoism, still survived in much of Asia, but even they now incorporated some elements of universalism in their thought.

The emergence and spread of universal faiths reflected the broader social

FIGURE 7.18   Islam is one of the universal faiths that emerged in the agrarian era. Women worship in the same mosque, separated from the men by a curtain.

and intellectual horizons that came with improved transportation and the spreading web of trade relations. Empire building, by bringing diverse populations under a single government, also helped to weaken parochial or "tribal" views. As people's knowledge of other societies increased, and with it their awareness of the essential unity of all humanity, the basic postulate of the older ethnic faiths (i.e., the belief in tribal deities) was gradually undermined.

Another important development was the growing separation of religious and political institutions.[125] Compared with the situation in advanced horticultural and simple agrarian societies, the governments of advanced agrarian societies were decidedly more secular. Kings and emperors were, it is true, still said to rule "by the grace of God"; the divine right of kings was still generally accepted; and occasionally a ruler even claimed to be a god. But few rulers functioned as high priests, and theocracies (i.e., states in which a priesthood rules in the name of a god) were almost unknown. This separation of church and state was part of the more general trend toward institutional specialization that is so basic in the evolutionary process from the horticultural era on.

Despite the growing organizational separation of politics and religion, the two systems continued to work closely together, and *political and religious leaders were normally allied*. This was especially evident in struggles between the governing class and the common people. When rebellious voices challenged the right of the governing class to control the economic surplus

FIGURE 7.19   Religious procession in a Venezuelan village.

FIGURE 7.20 This eighteenth-century French cartoon attacked the clergy and the nobility for "riding on the back" of the peasantry.

produced by the peasants, the clergy usually defended the elite, asserting that their power had been given them by God and any challenge to it was a challenge to His authority.[126] By legitimizing the actions of the governing class in this way, the clergy reduced the need for costly coercive measures.

In appreciation for this, and also because of their own religious beliefs, agrarian rulers were often extremely generous with religious groups, giving them large grants of land and special tax exemptions. In effect, a symbiotic relationship was established, with a religious organization legitimizing the actions of the governing class in return for generous financial support. Modern research indicates that religious groups frequently owned as much as a quarter or a third of a nation's land.[127]

Despite such profitable alliances, most religions of the agrarian era fostered some concern for distributive justice. This is especially evident in Judaism and Christianity.[128] One historian captured the contradictory nature of medieval Christianity in this discerning characterization: "Democratic, yet aristocratic; charitable, yet exploitative; generous, yet mercenary; humanitarian, yet cruel; indulgent, yet severely repressive of some things; progressive, yet reactionary; radical, yet conservative—all these are qualities of the Church in the Middle Ages."[129]

Magic and Fatalism Two other aspects of the beliefs of agrarian societies deserve comment: (1) a widespread belief in magic and (2) an equally widespread attitude of fatalism.[130] Logically, these are contradictory. If magic really works, people do not need to be fatalistic, and if they are true fatalists, they should have no confidence in magic. But people are not always logical in their view of life. In their more optimistic moments they are inclined to hope for things they know are impossible. Considering the tremendous pressures operating on the masses of common people in agrarian societies, and their limited sources of information, it is hardly surprising that so many of them held these mutually contradictory views.

Fatalism and belief in magic both contributed to the slowdown in the rate of technological advance in agrarian societies. One encouraged people to look to supernatural forces for the answers to problems; the other convinced them that control was out of their hands. Neither attitude was likely to motivate people to strive to build better tools or devise better techniques for satisfying their needs.

Kinship: Declining Importance in Society

For individuals, kinship ties remained of great importance throughout the agrarian era. For societies, however, they ceased to be *the chief integrating force*. In most horticultural societies, the largest and most powerful clan in a society, aided perhaps by dependent retainers, could still provide enough people to staff the important political offices. But by the level of advanced agrarian societies, this was no longer possible. Civil and military offices were so numerous that not even the largest of extended families could fill them all.

The fact that kinship ties were no longer the chief integrating force in societies did not mean, however, that they were no longer politically significant. The royal office itself was, in most societies, inherited, as were numerous other powerful positions among the governing elite. Many of these, civil and military offices alike, were a family's patrimony, handed down, like any other family possession, from father to son (or, sometimes, daughter). Offices that were not actually owned might still be closed to anyone who was not a member of the nobility or who did not qualify as coming from one of the "right families."

Even in the allocation of offices to which such restrictions did not apply, families continued to play an important role. Family funds might be used to purchase an office, for example. And those who had it in their power to assign an office were naturally influenced by their own family's interests. Although similar practices still occur in modern industrial societies, they are usually a violation of the law and lack public approval. But in advanced agrarian societies, these practices were usually an accepted part of life, and there was little criticism, and still less punishment, of those who engaged in them.

During the agrarian era, the family remained very important in the economic sphere as well. It was usually *the basic unit of economic organization*, in both urban and rural areas. Businesses were almost always family enterprises; the corporate form of enterprise, owned jointly by unrelated persons, was virtually unheard of, even in the largest cities. And in rural areas the basic work unit was the family.

The family's economic significance can be demonstrated in many ways, but some of the best examples are associated with marriage practices. For instance, because of its economic implications, marriage was considered much too important to be decided by young people; even among the peasantry, marriages were usually arranged by the parents, often with the aid of marriage brokers.[131] Sometimes the young couple did not even meet until the ceremony itself. In selecting spouses for their children, parents were primarily concerned with the economic and status implications of the match and only secondarily with other matters. Marriage arrangements often involved an outright economic transaction. The husband would pay the parents for the bride, or her parents would provide her with a dowry.[132]

As one would suppose, marriages contracted in this way did not necessarily produce sexual or psychological compatibility between the spouses, but then, this was not seen as the primary purpose of marriage. Ties between man and wife usually endured because of the value that was placed on the relationship by their society, and because the economic arrangement was usually of critical importance to the individuals involved. Within the families thus established, male dominance was the rule, for obedience was generally held to be one of the prime virtues in women and children.[133] In this, the family simply reflected the general authoritarian pattern of life in agrarian societies.

Leisure and the Arts

Although the life of the peasant was hard, even harsh, there were occasional opportunities for leisure and recreation.[134] Weddings and religious festivals, for example, were important occasions for people to get together for a good time. Singing and dancing were the basic entertainment at such festivities, and, in most societies, alcoholic beverages added to the merriment. People also amused themselves with games and contests, courtship and lovemaking, gossiping and storytelling, and a host of other activities.

Class distinctions were evident in leisure activity as in any other, with falconry, jousting, and chess among the activities generally identified with the governing class. But some forms of entertainment, such as archery and dice, had a universal appeal. Gambling in particular was popular with every class.

The rise of professional entertainers was part of the general trend toward occupational specialization. Actors, minstrels, jesters, clowns, acrobats, jugglers, and geishas are a few of the more familiar. In general, the status of such people was extremely low, probably because of their economic insecurity and their excessive dependence on the favor of others. Yet entertainers who had a powerful patron might find their work quite lucrative.

Recreation was frequently raucous and crude. It could also be brutal and violent and, in this, the Romans were probably unsurpassed. In their so-called games, first in the Circus Maximus, later in the Colosseum, tens of thousands came to watch wild animals devour helpless victims, and armed gladiators

FIGURE 7.21 *Peasant Wedding* by Pieter Breughel the Elder (1520?–1569).

maim and kill one another. When the Colosseum was first opened in 80 A.D., the Emperor Titus promised the people of Rome 100 consecutive days of such games, with fights to the death between more than 10,000 prisoners and 5,000 wild animals (including lions, tigers, and elephants), and a naval battle between 3,000 men in an arena flooded for the occasion.[135]

In agrarian Europe, cockfights and dogfights were very popular, and public hangings often drew large and exuberant crowds. Wedding parties and other festivities frequently ended in drunken brawls. In fact, violence typically followed drinking. From what we know of life in agrarian societies, it would appear that alcohol simply removed a fragile overlay of inhibitions, revealing people's frustrations and bitterness.

But if the agrarian world at play was often unattractive, its artistic accomplishments were quite the opposite. In their sculpture, their painting, and their architecture, these societies left monuments of lasting beauty. Thousands of cathedrals, churches, mosques, pagodas, temples, and palaces, and all the treasures within them, testify to an impressive development of the arts during that era. Achievements in literature were probably no less impressive, though language barriers make it difficult for us to appreciate them as fully.* Developments in music during most of the agrarian era seem to have

---

*Robert Frost once said that "poetry is what gets lost in translation," and anyone who has ever seriously tried to translate a poem understands the complexity of the language problem.

FIGURE 7.22   Recreation was frequently brutal and violent in agrarian societies, and the Romans were probably unsurpassed. In their so-called games, tens of thousands came to watch wild animals devour helpless victims, and armed gladiators maim and kill one another.

been less spectacular than in the other arts. Toward the end of the era, however, the invention of new instruments and the genius of composers like Bach, Mozart, Beethoven, and Handel combined to produce an outburst of magnificent music that transcended societal boundaries in unprecedented fashion.

Most artists were subsidized by the governing class or the religious elite, drawing on the economic surplus extracted from the peasant masses. Thus, the artistic achievements of agrarian societies were a product of the harshly exploitative social system. Yet, if the peasants had been allowed to keep the surplus, the result would simply have been more poor people. Again, as with horticultural societies, this link between an exploitative class system and cultural achievements reminds us of the difficulty we face in passing ethical judgments on complex sociocultural systems.

Stratification: Increasing Complexity

The basic cleavages in advanced agrarian societies were much the same as they had been in simple agrarian societies, and, as a consequence, so were the basic patterns of inequality. The principal division in a society was still the one between the governing class and the great mass of peasants and other people of low status over which it exercised control both politically and economically. But the system of stratification had altered in one respect from that of simpler societal types: it had become much more complex.

This growing complexity can be seen in two areas. First, in advanced agrarian societies there were more people in occupations whose status fell somewhere between the two extremes. These people either were directly employed by the governing class (e.g., household servants, stewards, men-at-arms) or served them indirectly (e.g., merchants, artisans).

Second, advanced agrarian societies experienced a growing overlap in the status of different categories of people, especially in terms of wealth and property. Some merchants, for example, now had more wealth than some members of the governing class. In fact, even a tiny minority of peasants, by luck and hard work, amassed greater wealth than some impoverished members of the nobility. Although members of the governing class still had greater wealth *on the average* than merchants or any other group, this was no longer true of every member of the class. Similarly, although merchants were, *on average*, wealthier than peasants, there were exceptions.

Figure 7.23 depicts the status system of advanced agrarian societies. The ruler was invariably the most powerful, prestigious, and wealthy individual in society: he was, in fact, literally in a class by himself. For example, the English

FIGURE 7.23 The class structure of advanced agrarian societies.

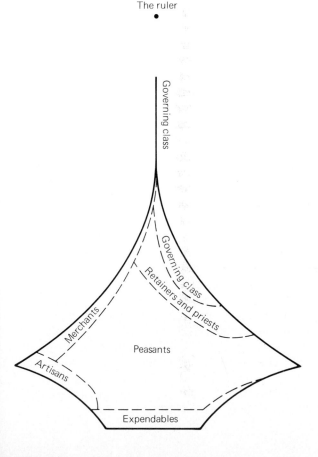

kings Richard I and John, who ruled in the last decade of the twelfth century and the first decade of the thirteenth, had incomes thirty times that of the wealthiest nobleman of the day.[136] By the reign of Richard II, at the end of the fourteenth century, the king's income had risen to forty times that of the wealthiest member of the governing class. In late fifteenth- and early sixteenth-century Spain, the king was reputed to enjoy one-third of all the revenues of the land (meaning, apparently, one-third of the economic surplus). Similar patterns are reported in virtually every advanced agrarian society.

At the opposite extreme in the system of stratification was a wretched class of individuals for whose labor the society had no need. These were mostly peasant sons and daughters who were unable to inherit land or to marry anyone who did, and were thus forced out on their own in a society that suffered a chronic labor surplus. As we have seen, these individuals could usually eke out a living while they were young and healthy, but most of them soon joined the ranks of the expendables and died at an early age.[137]

On the whole, the class divisions within advanced agrarian societies were more serious than those within simple agrarian societies. In particular, they were more likely to lead to violence. Earlier, we noted the frequency of peasant risings. Though most of these were local incidents involving small numbers of people, some spread to become large-scale insurrections. In either case, they were something new in history and a foreshadow of revolutions to come. Nor was it only the peasants who revolted against the governing class. The artisans followed suit on a number of occasions, as did the merchants,[138] and these groups, unlike the peasants, sometimes emerged victorious. In Europe, the merchants were so successful in their challenges to the governing class that eventually *they* became the governing class in many cities and towns. From the evolutionary perspective, this proved to be a very important development indeed, as we will see.

Variations on Agrarian Themes

In surveying societies at the same level of development, it is natural to emphasize those characteristics which are found in all of them, or are at least widespread, and to slight the differences. This may give an impression of greater uniformity than really exists. Obviously there were variations in every area of life in advanced agrarian societies, and we have noted many of them, or at least hinted at them in qualifying phrases, saying that a particular pattern was found in "most" or "many" of these societies.

To begin with, advanced agrarian societies varied technologically. The first to emerge resembled their simple agrarian predecessors more than the advanced agrarian societies of Europe on the eve of the Industrial Revolution. Furthermore, the size of societies in this category ranged all the way from tiny principalities to great empires. Most were monarchies, but a few were republics. Some were governed by enormously powerful autocratic rulers; in others power was diffused more widely among members of the governing elite. Similar variations occurred in almost every area of life.

Clearly, then, there is variation among societies at the advanced agrarian level—indeed, at *every* level of societal development. There is, however, one important difference. In the less advanced societal types (i.e., hunting and gathering, fishing, and simple horticultural), intratype variation results primarily from differences in the *biophysical environment*. We see this clearly when we compare the Eskimo with the Australian aborigines, or the Bushmen of the Kalahari Desert with the Pygmies of the rain forest. In advanced agrarian societies, on the other hand, differences in biophysical environment have been much less responsible for intratype variation. This is exactly what ecological-evolutionary theory would lead us to expect, since the further a society advances on the evolutionary scale, the greater its ability to overcome the limitations imposed by the biotic and physical world and the more likely it is, because of geographical expansion, to include within its borders a variety of environments, thereby making its own biophysical environment less distinctive.

In studying advanced agrarian societies, historians have often focused attention on religion as the chief source of the differences among them. Thus, they have contrasted Christian societies with Islamic societies, for example, or Buddhist societies with Hindu societies.

There is, of course, no doubt that each of these religions was responsible for social and cultural variations among advanced agrarian societies. Christianity and Islam, like Judaism, had a special day of worship each week, while the Oriental religions did not. Most of the religions encouraged monasticism, while Protestantism and Islam did not. Islam sanctioned the practice of polygyny, which Christianity forbade; Confucianism encouraged ancestor worship; Buddhism encouraged all families to send their sons to live in monasteries for a year or two before assuming adult responsibilities; and Hinduism had a hereditary priestly caste. Theologically, too, there were tremendous differences among the different religions, and members of advanced agrarian societies often fought and died in order to extend or defend their faith.

Without denying the importance of these and other religious influences, we cannot fail to note that neither the new universal faiths nor the older ethnic faiths proved capable of breaking the "agrarian mold" that shaped the basic patterns of life in these societies. For regardless of its dominant religion, every advanced agrarian society was essentially like the rest with respect to its fundamental characteristics. Class structure, social inequality, the division of labor, the distinctive role of urban populations in the larger society, the cleavage between urban and rural subcultures, the disdain of the governing class for both work and workers, the widespread belief in magic and fatalism, the use of the economic surplus for the benefit of the governing class and for the construction of monumental edifices, high birth and death rates—all these and other patterns were much the same in all advanced agrarian societies.

The greatest variations among advanced agrarian societies stemmed not from ideological differences, but from differences in their *social environments*. One set of differences involved proximity to trade routes; the other set involved frontier territories.

From the standpoint of trade, the most advantageous location for a society was at the point where several trade routes intersected.[139] Having such a location ensured continuing contact with large numbers of other societies and increased opportunities for acquiring useful information through diffusion. It also provided a society with a source of income and fostered its economic growth and development. Societies that were not so well situated were handicapped and tended to be less developed and less cosmopolitan, unless some compensating factor offset this handicap. Because of the importance of trade routes, societies in the Middle East, where routes from Europe, Asia, and Africa converged, remained at the forefront of social and cultural development for most of the agrarian era. Toward the end, however, when trade with the New World became important, the advantage shifted to western European societies.

A different kind of variation, the frontier society, developed when an agrarian society expanded into territories that were either uninhabited or inhabited by preagrarian societies. The first known instance of this occurred when the nation of Israel was established in the previously uninhabited hill country of Palestine in the thirteenth century, B.C.[140] More recently, this process was repeated in the settlement of North and South America by migrants from various European societies, in the British settlement of Australia and New Zealand, in the Norwegian-Irish settlement of Iceland, in the Dutch (or Boer) settlement of South Africa, and in the Cossack settlement of the Russian steppes.[141] In each instance, the social environment of the frontier territory was radically different from that of other agrarian societies, consisting entirely of small, technologically less advanced societies that could not adequately defend their territories. As a consequence, substantial quantities of new land became available to lesser members of agrarian societies who were willing to risk their lives and to endure the hardships of frontier life.

Frontier societies are of special interest to ecological-evolutionary theorists because they show the extent to which the agrarian way of life was shaped by an oversupply of labor and an undersupply of land. When these conditions were eliminated even temporarily, as they were in frontier regions and frontier societies, many deviations from the usual patterns of agrarian life developed.

To begin with, the settlers themselves tended to be people with little stake in the existing social order. Typically, they were the poor, the dispossessed, the noninheriting sons and daughters, the troublemakers, the misfits, and even criminals deported by the parent society. Frontier regions usually held little attraction for the rich and successful, who preferred to remain close to the traditional centers of power and influence. Thus, when migrants arrived in a frontier region, they usually found that established authority was weak or absent. Because societal life was not under the control of the governing class, traditional agrarian patterns tended to break down, and new patterns of life emerged.[142]

One of the most significant changes that occurred was the breakdown of the traditional class system. Except where the native population was enslaved or enserfed (as in much of Latin America) or where slaves were imported (as occurred in the Caribbean and the southern United States) a highly egalitarian system of small family farms was likely to develop. This is what happened in Canada, the United States outside the southern region, Australia, New Zealand, and South Africa. In such areas, there was always a serious shortage of labor; workers were much more valuable than they were in the older, settled areas with their usual labor surplus. On the frontier, there were neither enough farmers to cultivate the newly opened land nor enough fighters to defend it. It is not surprising, then, that frontier life produced a striking independence of spirit and a stubborn resistance to authority. Having risked their lives to establish themselves in a new territory, frontiersmen were not prepared to hand over their surplus to anyone. Thus, frontier conditions often broke down the sharp inequalities and exploitative patterns that characterized all traditional agrarian societies.

This condition was usually temporary, however. As the resistance of the native population came to an end and the population of settlers grew in number and density, as roads were built and governmental authority was established, there was a waning of the spirit of independence and individualism, opportunities for resistance declined, and the traditional system began to assert itself. To be sure, this never happened overnight. On the contrary, it usually took a century or more. But in the end, the typical agrarian pattern prevailed.

Only one thing ever prevented this from happening—the onset of industrialization. In a number of instances during the last century and a half, the Industrial Revolution generated a new demand for labor before the demands of the frontier had been satisfied and thus aborted the rebirth of the old system. This happened in the United States in the nineteenth century and subsequently in Canada, Australia, and New Zealand. All these societies were thus spared the agony of slowly sliding into the classic agrarian pattern in which a massive, impoverished peasantry is dominated and exploited by a small, hereditary aristocracy.

In the United States, this process had actually gotten well under way in much of the South with its system of slavery. But the Confederacy's defeat in the Civil War and the South's eventual industrialization halted the restoration of the old agrarian system. In other parts of the country, the process had not really developed very far before the forces of industrialization intervened.

Looking back, it seems clear that the frontier experience was excellent preparation for the Industrial Revolution. Above all, it established a tradition of innovation and a receptivity to change that were lacking in other agrarian societies. Also, by creating a more egalitarian class system, the frontier prepared the way for the more open and fluid class systems of modern industrial societies. These developments help explain the relative ease with which the overseas English-speaking democracies (i.e., the United States, Australia, Canada, and New Zealand) made the transition to the industrial era, and why they have so long been in the forefront with respect to productivity, standard of living, and political stability. It is interesting to speculate on what the situation in these societies might be today if they had been settled a thousand years sooner and a more typical agrarian social system had had time to take root.

Agrarian Societies in Theoretical Perspective

The most basic effect of the shift from horticulture to agriculture, as we saw at the beginning of this chapter, was the increase in food production. Societies that adopted the plow were able to produce substantially more food in a given area than those that relied on the hoe and the digging stick.

This increase in productivity could be used, as Figure 7.24 indicates, either to expand the economic surplus of the society or to expand its population. Actually, the historical record shows that in most agrarian societies both of these things happened. The expansion of the economic surplus was more significant than population growth, however, since it was prerequisite for so many social and cultural changes. Figure 7.24 makes no attempt to portray all of these changes, or all of their interrelationships, since that would require an exceedingly complex diagram. Instead, the figure focuses on the most critical developments.

The single most important consequence of the greater economic surplus was further growth in two closely related phenomena: the *state* and *the power of the governing class* that controlled it. This contributed, directly or indirectly, to virtually all of the other important social and cultural changes of the agrarian era. It lay behind the shift from militias to professional armies, the increase in wars of conquest, the growth of inequality and of the division of

FIGURE 7.24   Model of the primary effects of the shift from horticulture to agriculture.

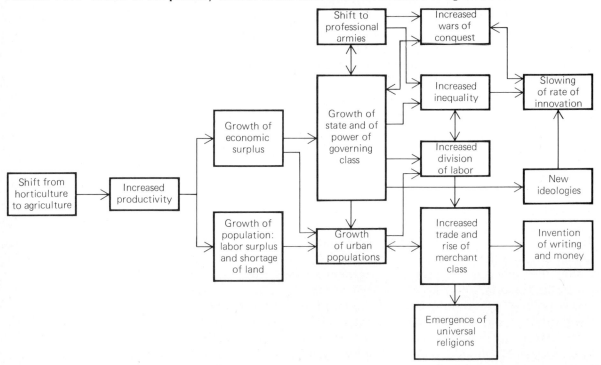

labor, the expansion of urban populations, the growth of trade and the rise of the merchant class, the invention of writing and of money, and the emergence of the new universal religions. And finally, it was responsible for the lagging rate of technological innovation.

Many of the changes in agrarian societies were essentially a continuation of trends that began in horticultural societies. But the shift to agriculture magnified those trends dramatically. To cite a single example, the largest societies ever constructed on a horticultural foundation appear to have been the Incan empire in the years immediately preceding the Spanish conquest of Peru, and Songhay, a west African empire of the sixteenth century. Both of these, at the peak of power, had populations of several million.[143] In contrast, mid-nineteenth-century China, before it began to industrialize, had a population of approximately 400 million, and the Roman and Russian empires each had at least 70 million.[144]

As great as they are, these differences in population size are probably no greater in degree than differences in many other basic features of these sociocultural systems. Their numbers, in other words, were but one reflection of the vastly different potentials inherent in the subsistence technologies on which horticultural societies and agrarian societies were built.

CHAPTER 8

Some Evolutionary Bypaths and a Brief Review

Specialized Societal Types

Up to this point in our survey of human societies, we have concentrated on those types which are in the mainstream of evolutionary history, those which developed their technologies around the resources of fields and forests. The types of societies to which we now turn have adapted to *more specialized, less typical environments*—two to aquatic conditions, the third to semidesert grasslands and other marginal environments. Though these specialized societies have contributed to sociocultural evolution in many important ways, their contributions have been more limited than those of the mainstream societies. This is chiefly because of the specialized nature of the problems with which they have dealt in their subsistence activities. Because of this, we will not examine them in the same detail as the others.

Fishing Societies

Actually, it is something of a misnomer to call any group a ''fishing'' society, for none ever depended exclusively on fishing for its food supply.[1] Except in the Arctic, nearly all fishing peoples obtain fruits and vegetables by foraging or cultivation. Many of them also supplement their diet by hunting, and occasionally by raising livestock. To call a society a fishing society, then, simply indicates that fishing is its most important subsistence activity.

In recent centuries, fishing societies have been found in many parts of the world, but the majority have been in the northwestern part of North America—Oregon, Washington, British Columbia, Alaska, and the arctic regions of Canada. There have also been some in northeastern Asia and among the islands of the Pacific (most of the Pacific peoples have been simple horticulturalists), in scattered parts of Africa and South America, and elsewhere.

Historically, fishing societies are probably the second oldest type, emerging about a thousand years before the first horticultural societies. The actual practice of fishing is, of course, even older and more widespread and has provided a supplementary source of subsistence in most societies for at least 12,000 years.

In some ways fishing societies might be regarded simply as hunting and gathering societies that have adapted to aquatic environments rather than terrestrial. One might argue that the chief difference is simply that fish, rather than land animals, are the object of the chase and that the technology of the group is modified accordingly. But there is a reason why fishing societies must be considered a separate societal type: a fishing economy has the potential for supporting a larger, more sedentary population than a hunting and gathering economy.

FIGURE 8.1   African fishing village, Benin.

This is a consequence of the fact that primitive fishing peoples are much less likely to deplete the food resources of their environment than hunters and gatherers are. For one thing, fish have much higher reproductive rates than most land animals do. In addition, because their simple boats keep them from going too far out into oceans, seas, or large lakes, most fishing peoples work only a small part of their food-gathering territory. Even if they catch all the fish in their immediate area, the supply is quickly replenished by the great surplus spawned in adjacent areas. This could not happen with land animals, at least not after hunting and gathering bands became numerous and occupied much of the habitable territory.

Thus, although fishing societies are only a bit more advanced technologically than hunting and gathering societies, we would expect them to be somewhat larger, more sedentary, and more complex.[2] This is, in fact, precisely what we find. With respect to size, they are half again as large: Murdock's data set shows that the average size of fishing communities is approximately 60, the average size of hunting and gathering groups only 40.[3] With respect to settlement patterns, only 10 per cent of the hunting and gathering societies live in permanent settlements, compared to 49 per cent of the fishing societies.

Their political systems also indicate the greater potential inherent in a fishing economy. Less than 10 per cent of hunting and gathering societies have two or more communities, in contrast to nearly a quarter of the fishing societies. Social inequality, too, is both more common and more pronounced. A system of hereditary nobility is found in 32 per cent of fishing societies and in only 2 per cent of hunting and gathering societies. And slavery occurs in slightly over 50 per cent of fishing societies, but in only 10 per cent of hunting and gathering. Finally, as another indication of their greater economic development and wealth, fishing peoples are much more likely to link marriage with some economic transaction. This happens in 77 per cent of these groups but in only 48 per cent of hunting and gathering societies.

In terms of structural development, fishing societies have about as much in common with simple horticultural societies as with hunting and gathering societies.[4] Depending on the criterion, they sometimes lean more toward one, sometimes the other. For example, in community size they more closely approximate hunting and gathering societies,[5] in permanence of settlements they are midway between hunting and gathering and simple horticultural,[6] and in frequency of multicommunity societies they are almost indistinguishable from simple horticultural.[7]

From an evolutionary standpoint, the line of development represented by fishing societies has been something of a blind alley in that they, unlike hunting and gathering societies, did not evolve into a more advanced type.[8] The reasons for this are quite simple. To begin with, the areas suited to a predominantly fishing economy are not only very limited; they are scattered and strung out along thin coastal strips, so that it has been virtually impossible to consolidate several groups into one large, defensible, political entity.[9] Instead, when neighboring horticultural societies became powerful enough, fishing societies were usually conquered and absorbed. Then, even though

FIGURE 8.2 The Shui-jen, or water people, of southern China are descended from fishing peoples of an earlier time. They still depend on fishing for their livelihood and remain largely separate from the mainland population.

fishing continued in the area, it was only a minor part of the economy of the larger society, and the leaders of the fishing groups were reduced to the status of minor officials, too weak to hold on to the local surplus. As a result, fishing communities in *agrarian* societies have often been socially and culturally less advanced (except in subsistence technology) than fishing communities in more primitive *fishing* societies. Typically, their situation was no better than that of peasant villages, and for the same reason—their surplus was confiscated by the more powerful elements in the society.[10]

Herding Societies

Herding societies, like fishing societies, represent an adaptation to specialized environmental conditions. Other than that, the two have little in common. Their environments are radically different, and their technologies are basically on different levels.

Herding groups cover the same range of technological development as horticultural and simple agrarian societies. Animals were first domesticated

221

about the same time plants were first cultivated, and the two practices typically went hand in hand in the horticultural and agrarian societies of the Old World.* In some areas, however, crops could not be cultivated because of insufficient rainfall, too short a growing season (in northern latitudes), or mountainous terrain. This was true of much of central Asia, the Arabian peninsula, and North Africa, and also of parts of Europe and sub-Saharan Africa. Because it was often possible to raise livestock in these areas, however, a new and different type of society emerged.†

A pastoral economy usually necessitates a nomadic or seminomadic way of life.[11] In fact, "nomad" comes from an early Greek word meaning a "herder of cattle."[12] In the sample of herding societies in Murdock's data set, more than 90 per cent are wholly or partially nomadic. In this respect they closely resemble hunters and gatherers.

Herders are also like hunters and gatherers in the size of their communities. On the average, they are a bit smaller than fishing communities and much smaller than simple horticultural, as the following population figures show:

Hunting and gathering communities	40
Herding communities	55
Fishing communities	60
Simple horticultural communities	95

The explanation for this is primarily environmental. Given the sparse resources of their territories, large and dense settlements are impossible.[13]

Despite the small size of their communities, herding *societies* are usually fairly large. Whereas the typical hunting and gathering, fishing, or simple horticultural society contains but a single community, the average herding society contains several dozen.[14] Thus the median population of herding societies far surpasses those of the other three types:

Hunting and gathering societies	40
Fishing societies	60
Simple horticultural societies	95
Herding societies	2,000

The size of herding societies results from the combined influence of environment and technology. Open grasslands, where the majority of herders live, present few natural barriers to movement and, therefore, to political expansion. Furthermore, since early in the second millennium B.C., many of the

---

*This was not true in most of the New World, where there were almost no large animals suitable for domestication.

†Most of these societies have also had some secondary means of subsistence, frequently horticulture or agriculture on a small scale.

FIGURE 8.3   Herding societies have adapted to environments where crop cultivation is not possible. Bedouin shepherd with his flock, near Jericho.

herding peoples have ridden horses or camels, which greatly facilitated military conquest and political expansion.

The basic resource in these societies is livestock, and the size of the herd is the measure of a man. Large herds signify not only wealth but power, for only a strong man or the head of a strong family can defend such vulnerable property against rivals and enemies. Thus, in most of these societies, and especially in the more advanced (i.e., those with horses or camels and herds of larger animals such as cattle), marked social inequality is the rule. Hereditary slavery, for example, is far more common in herding societies than in any other type.[15] Other kinds of inequality are also very common, especially inequality of wealth.[16]

With respect to kinship, herding societies are noteworthy on at least two counts. First, they are more likely than any other type of society to require the payment of a bride price or bride service.[17] Second, they are the most likely to require newly married couples to live with the husband's kinsmen.[18]

These strong patriarchal tendencies have several sources. To begin with, they reflect the mobile and often militant nature of pastoral life. Raiding and warfare are frequent activities, and as we have noted before, these activities stimulate the growth of political authority. Moreover, the basic economic activity in these societies is man's work. In this respect they stand in sharp contrast to horticultural societies, where women so often play the dominant role in subsistence activities. It is hardly coincidence that horticultural societies are noted for their frequent female-oriented kinship patterns, herding societies for the opposite.

Herding societies are extremely interesting from the religious standpoint. Their concept of God corresponds to the Jewish and Christian concept more closely than that of any other societal type. In forty of the fifty herding groups for which Murdock provides data, there is belief in a Supreme Diety who created the world and remains actively concerned with its affairs, especially with a people's moral conduct. This combination of beliefs is rare in other societies, except agrarian, where it occurs in two-thirds of the cases.[19] But even there, as Table 8.1 makes clear, its occurrence varies directly with the importance of herding activities to the particular group.

For those familiar with religious history, this relationship is not surprising. Herding was an important secondary activity in the life of the early Hebrews, who played such a critical role in the rise and spread of monotheism. And Islam, the most uncompromisingly monotheistic of faiths, enjoyed most of its early successes among the herding peoples of the Arabian peninsula.

Why this relationship developed is far from clear, but the relation itself is undeniable. One can find repeated evidence of the affinity between the pastoral way of life and these religious concepts in Biblical texts that describe God as a shepherd and his people as sheep (e.g., Psalm 23). The shepherd's simultaneous awareness of his flock's dependence on him and of humanity's dependence on forces beyond its control may have suggested answers to the perennial questions about the nature and destiny of humans, and the power that ultimately controls them. These answers have not been obvious to all herding peoples, however; a number of pastoral groups in Asia and Africa have come up with very different ones. The most we can say is that pastoral life seems to increase the probability that a society will develop this kind of explanation.

One of the most important technological advances made by herding peoples was the utilization of horses, and later camels, for transportation. This practice originated in the eighteenth century B.C., when certain herding groups in the Middle East began harnessing horses to chariots.[20] This gave them an important military advantage over their less mobile agrarian neighbors and enabled them to win control of much of the Middle East—at least until the new technology was adopted by the more numerous agrarian peoples. Herders later learned to *ride* their horses, which led to a new wave of conquests, beginning in the ninth century B.C.[21] During the next 2,500 years, a succession of herding

TABLE 8.1 Religious Beliefs of Agrarian Societies, by Percentage of Subsistence Derived from Herding

Percentage of Subsistence from Herding	Percentage Believing in Active, Moral Creator God	Number of Societies
36–45	92	13
26–35	82	28
16–25	40	20
6–15	20	5

Source: See note 12, page 454.

groups attacked agrarian societies from China to Europe, and frequently conquered them. The empires and dynasties they established include some of the largest and most famous in history—the great Mongol empire, for example, founded by Genghis Khan early in the thirteenth century A.D. and expanded by his successors. At the peak of its power, the Mongol empire stretched from eastern Europe to the shores of the Pacific and launched attacks against places as far apart as Austria and Japan. Other famous empires and dynasties founded by herding peoples include the Mogul empire, established in India by a branch of the Mongols, the Manchu dynasty in China, the Ottoman empire in the Middle East, and the early Islamic states established by followers of the prophet Muhammad.

Despite their frequent military victories, herding peoples were never able to destroy the agrarian social order. In the end, it was always they, not the agrarian peoples, who changed their mode of life. There were a number of reasons for this, but it was primarily because the economic surplus that could be produced by agricultural activities was so much greater than what could be produced by converting the land to herding activities. After a few early conquerors tried to turn fields into pastures, they realized they were, in effect, killing the goose that lays the golden eggs, and abandoned their preferred way of life for economic reasons. Thus, despite many impressive victories, the limits of the herding world were not permanently enlarged.

Although herding continued to be an important secondary source of subsistence in the agrarian world, it was the primary source only in areas not suited to cultivation. In recent centuries, even these areas have, in most cases, been brought under the control of agrarian or industrial societies, and herding societies, like other preindustrial types, are vanishing.

Maritime Societies

Maritime societies have been the rarest of all the major societal types. Never have there been more than a small number at a time, and not one survives today. Yet they once played an important role in the civilized world.

Technologically, maritime societies were very much like agrarian societies. What set them apart was the way they used their technology to take advantage of the opportunities afforded by their environmental situation. Located on large bodies of water in an era when it was cheaper to move goods by water than by land (see page 197), these peoples found trade and commerce far more profitable than either fishing or the cultivation of their limited land resources and gradually created societies in which overseas trade was the chief economic activity.

The first maritime society in history was probably developed by the Minoans on the island of Crete, late in the third millennium B.C. We are told that the wealth and power of the Minoan rulers "depended more upon foreign trade and religious prerogative than upon the land rents and forced services."[22] The island location of Minoan society was important not only because it afforded access to the sea, but also because it provided protection

FIGURE 8.4 Maritime societies usually developed on islands or peninsulas that were difficult to attack by land: aerial view of the Lebanese city of Tyre, once an important maritime society. When Tyre was a leading Phoenician city-state, no land bridge connected it to the mainland.

against more powerful agrarian societies. Maritime societies developed only in the absence of powerful neighboring societies, and for this reason they were usually found on islands or peninsulas that were difficult to attack by land (see Figure 8.4). Their only military advantage was in naval warfare.

During the next 1,500 years a number of other maritime societies were established in the Mediterranean world. These included the Mycenaeans, or pre-Hellenic Greeks of the second millennium B.C., the Phoenicians, the Carthaginians, and possibly some of the Greek city-states. The spread of the maritime pattern was largely, perhaps wholly, the result of diffusion and the migration of maritime peoples. Eventually, all of these societies were conquered by societies of other types and either destroyed or absorbed as subunits. This was not the end of overseas trade and commerce, of course, since these remained important activities in advanced agrarian societies. It was, however, a temporary end to societies in which they were the *dominant* economic activities.

Then, more than a thousand years later, there was a revival of maritime societies during the Middle Ages. Venice and Genoa are the best known, but there were others (e.g., Danzig and Luebeck in northern Europe). The last important maritime society was Holland, which in the seventeenth and eighteenth centuries apparently derived the major part of its income from overseas trade.[23] England moved far in this direction in the seventeenth, eighteenth, nineteenth, and early twentieth centuries but probably never quite reached the point where her dependence on overseas commerce exceeded her dependence on, first, agriculture and, later, industry. Nevertheless, because of the great growth of overseas commerce, she took on a number of the characteristics of maritime societies.

In many ways maritime societies resembled advanced agrarian societies, particularly their urban centers. But there were also important differences. To begin with, most maritime societies were much smaller, often containing only a single city and the area immediately around it. Only two maritime societies, Carthage and Holland, ever developed empires worthy of the name and, significantly, both of these were *overseas* empires.[24] In each case the empire was created more as an adjunct of commercial activity than as a militaristic venture.

This curious feature is linked with another, more basic peculiarity of maritime societies. In a largely agrarian world in which monarchy was the normal—almost universal—form of government, maritime societies were usually republics. There were some monarchies, but this pattern was most likely to occur early in a maritime society's history, suggesting a carry-over from a premaritime past.

FIGURE 8.5 A Venetian room reveals the wealth that commercial activities brought to the merchants and officials of maritime societies.

The explanation for the republican tendency in maritime societies seems to be that commerce, rather than warfare and the exploitation of peasant masses, was the chief interest of the governing class. Being less concerned than the typical agrarian state with conquest and the control of large peasant populations, these nations had less need for a strong, centralized, hierarchical government. An oligarchy of wealthy merchants could do the job, since their primary responsibilities would be to regulate commercial competition and to provide naval forces to defend their access to foreign ports.

Another peculiarity of maritime societies was their unusual system of values and incentives. As we saw in the last chapter, the governing class in agrarian societies typically viewed work of any kind as degrading. Since this was the class that all others looked up to and emulated, its view of economic activity rubbed off on the rest. This was especially evident in the case of merchants, who, when they became wealthy, usually gave up their commercial activities. As we noted, this antiwork ethic undoubtedly contributed to the slowdown in the rate of technological innovation and progress. In maritime societies, by contrast, the merchants were the dominant class, and a very different view of economic activity prevailed. Though much more research is needed on the subject, there is reason to believe that the rate of technological advance was greater in maritime societies than in agrarian, and that maritime societies made disproportionate technological and economic contributions to the emergence of modern industrial societies. Moreover, the rate of technological advance in *agrarian* societies seems to have been correlated with the social and political strength of their merchant class. In other words, the greater the social status and political influence of its merchants, the higher the rate of technological and economic innovation in a society tended to be.[25]

A Brief Review: Sociocultural Evolution to the Eve of the Industrial Revolution

Now that we have completed our survey of the various types of preindustrial societies, we need to pause and briefly review the ground we have covered. In particular, we should consider how well the evidence we have examined conforms to ecological-evolutionary theory.

As we saw in Chapter 3, the central thesis of this theory is that subsistence technology is the key to societal growth and development, both for individual societies and for the world system of societies. Technological advance expands the limits of what is possible for a society and thereby increases its advantage in the process of intersocietal selection. As a consequence, technological advance has also been the basic determinant of the patterns of sociocultural evolution in the world system.

Figure 3.7 on page 80 asserts that this evolutionary process has generated a number of trends in the world system. These trends provide us with an excellent means of checking the validity of ecological-evolutionary theory as it applies to the experience of human societies through most of human history. What exactly *had* happened with respect to those trends by the time the agrarian era was coming to a close?

Growth of human population: In the opinion of the experts, there were between 5 and 10 million people at the end of the hunting and gathering era. By the end of the agrarian era, there were more than 700 million.

Growth in average size of societies and communities: At the end of the hunting and gathering era, the average size of both societies and communities appears to have been somewhere between 25 and 50. Although it is impossible to obtain reliable estimates of average societal and community sizes for the entire world system at the end of the agrarian era, there is no doubt that both were substantially larger because by then there were so many horticultural, herding, maritime, and agrarian societies. We also know that, whereas the largest society prior to the horticultural era had no more than 400 to 600 members, at the end of the agrarian era there was one with 400 million, and a number with over 10 million.

Increased permanence of communities: Before the first fishing and horticultural societies appeared, nearly all human communities were nomadic. By the end of the agrarian era, only a small minority of them were nomadic.

Expansion of societies into new environments: Most of this trend occurred either before the end of the hunting and gathering era or during the industrial era. The horticultural and agrarian eras, however, did see greatly heightened activity in marine environments. By the end of the agrarian era, oceans, lakes, and rivers had become important both as sources of subsistence and as trade routes.

Increasing impact of societies on the biophysical environment: Prior to the horticultural era, the most notable impact of human societies on the biophysical environment seems to have been their apparent extermination of a number of species of large mammals. Societies of the horticultural and agrarian eras had a far more profound effect on the physical landscape, clearing vast forests, damming rivers and irrigating arid areas, and mining an increasing variety of minerals.

Invention of new symbol systems: During the horticultural era, the first primitive record-keeping systems were invented. These were followed, during the agrarian era, by prealphabetic and eventually alphabetic systems of writing, numeral systems, measurement systems, systems of musical notation, and monetary systems.

Increasing store of technological information: During the horticultural and agrarian eras, the store of technological information increased enormously, a fact amply documented by the great growth of human population. Striking technological advances occurred in plant cultivation, animal domestication, metallurgy, transportation, and communication. By the end of the agrarian era, societies could produce enormous quantities of foods, fibers, and other goods; move people and products over great distances; build monumental edifices of great durability; and inflict great damage on one another, to cite but four of the more significant consequences of the expanded store of technological information.

Increasing store of other kinds of information: During the horticultural and agrarian eras, there was a dramatic increase in the store of nontechnological information. By the close of the agrarian era, many societies had amassed great amounts of political, economic, philosophical, ideological, historical, aesthetic, scientific, and other kinds of information. Much of this new information emerged as a by-product of the growing size and complexity of societies, a process that both generated new factual information and led to the emergence of new norms, beliefs, and values.

Growth in the quantity, diversity, and complexity of material products: No brief statement can do justice to this trend, though there are many areas that provide dramatic illustrations. Compare, for example. the greatest structures created by advanced agrarian societies—cathedrals, temples, palaces—with the greatest created by the members of hunting and gathering societies— shelters created from rocks and branches to provide temporary housing for one or more families. More important, by the end of the agrarian era, human societies were providing the food and other material necessities required to sustain a population of 700 million people, or 70 to 140 times the population at the end of the hunting and gathering era. And by the end of the agrarian era the quantity, diversity, and complexity of *capital goods* (e.g., windmills, sailing ships, agricultural implements) far surpassed the stock of capital goods available to societies at the end of the hunting and gathering era.

Increasing complexity of social structures: In hunting and gathering societies, full-time occupational specialization was extremely rare, possibly nonexistent. The usual pattern was a division of labor by age and sex, with part-time specialization by a headman and/or a shaman. In agrarian and maritime societies, in contrast, occupational specialties numbered in the hundreds, and there was a complex division of labor that often involved specialization by communities and even regions. In hunting and gathering societies, the only organized groups were families, whereas in agrarian societies, there were numerous communities, often organized into provinces, plus a great variety of specialized associations, especially religious, political, economic, and educational. Political and religious associations, in particular, tended to be extremely complex.

Increasing inequality within and among societies: In hunting and gathering societies, there were only minor status distinctions among individuals. The members of agrarian and maritime societies, however, were usually born into one of a number of classes, which profoundly influenced their opportunities in life. Similarly, prior to the horticultural era, differences among societies were minimal; but by the end of the agrarian era, advanced agrarian and maritime societies were far wealthier and far more powerful than other societies in the world system (i.e., surviving hunting and gathering, horticultural, and fishing societies).

Accelerating rate of social and cultural change: During the last 9,000 years of the hunting and gathering era, the rate of social and cultural change was greater than it had previously been, yet the changes in those years could not compare with the changes that occurred in the next 9,000 years. Although there was a temporary slowing of the rate of *technological* innovation during the first part of the agrarian era, it accelerated again well before the end of the agrarian era, as shown in Figure 3.3 (page 68).

By 1800 A.D., near the close of the agrarian era, the patterns of human life had been dramatically altered for all but the relative handful of people who still lived in hunting and gathering societies in remote areas. The vast majority of humans were now living in either agrarian or advanced horticultural societies, with smaller numbers living in simple horticultural, herding, and fishing societies. This was not, of course, a stable world system: the deadly process of intersocietal selection that had begun thousands of years earlier was still working to the disadvantage of the technologically less advanced. And every time advanced agrarian societies took another step forward, they tilted the balance a bit more in their favor and against the rest.

This was the situation on the eve of the Industrial Revolution.

PART III

Industrial and Industrializing Societies

CHAPTER 9

The Industrial Revolution

Throughout most of the agrarian era, technological innovation in advanced agrarian societies was far less frequent than one would expect in view of their size, the amount of information available to them, and the extent of contact among them. As we have seen, the explanation of this lay in their highly exploitative social systems and in the ideologies that shaped economic attitudes and activities in these societies. Not surprisingly, these produced *negative feedback effects* on both technology and the economy.

Yet late in the agrarian era, the rate of innovation in western Europe increased substantially within a relatively short period of time, and by the latter part of the eighteenth century the Industrial Revolution was well under way. Not long thereafter, England became the first truly industrial society—that is, the first society to derive most of its income from productive activities involving machines powered by inanimate energy sources. With this, a new era of far more rapid and pervasive social and cultural change was launched.

What was responsible for this? Above all, what happened to break the agrarian mold and produce such a burst of technological innovation in societies that were notorious for their resistance to change? What happened, in other words, to turn the system of negative feedback into a *positive* one?

Causes of the Industrial Revolution: Prior Technological Advance and its Consequences

The Accumulation of Information in the Agrarian Era

Probably the least heralded of the major causes of the Industrial Revolution was the gradual accumulation of technological information during the agrarian era. For despite the slowdown in the rate of innovation, discoveries and inventions did not come to a halt. There is evidence of this in agriculture, mining, metallurgy, transportation, construction, and various other fields.[1] Advances in both construction and engineering, for example, can still be traced if one compares the churches and cathedrals built in western Europe in successive centuries. As a result of many such advances, the store of technological information available in the eighteenth century was far greater than in the thirteenth, just as it had been far greater in the thirteenth century than in the eighth. This enormous store of information held obvious potential for an increase in the rate of technological innovation when other conditions within societies became favorable.

Advances in Water Transport and the Discovery of the New World

Some innovations of the late agrarian era were more important for sociocultural evolution than others, and those with a potential for altering agrarian social structure and ideology were most important of all. In this respect, improvements in ships and navigation proved to be some of the most critical.

Prior to the introduction of the compass in Europe, late in the twelfth century, navigation beyond the sight of land was so hazardous that it was undertaken only for short distances or in familiar areas, as in crossing the English Channel or the Mediterranean. Acquisition of the compass was followed, over the next several centuries, by a series of important advances in the technology of shipbuilding. These included the invention of the stern rudder (which replaced steering oars attached to the sides of ships), the construction of larger ships with multiple masts, the substitution of several smaller sails for a single large sail on each mast, and a reduction in the width of ships relative to their length.[2] All of these innovations made ships more responsive and more manageable, and therefore safer on stormy seas.

With such ships at their command, and with the compass to guide them, western European sailors increasingly ventured out into the open seas for extended periods of time. During the fifteenth century, they began a series of voyages designed to open up new trade routes to India and China that would bypass the merchants of the Middle East. Instead, of course, they discovered, and quickly subdued, the New World. Less than fifty years after Columbus first set foot in America, Spain had already conquered both of its most powerful societies, the Incan empire in Peru and the Aztec empire in Mexico.

It is difficult to exaggerate the importance of the conquest of the New

FIGURE 9.1   The Santa Maria, flagship of Christopher Columbus's first voyage to the New World, illustrates advances in shipbuilding. Note the multiple masts and sails, the stern rudder, and the relatively narrow beam.

World for the subsequent growth and development of the societies of western Europe. Suddenly, they were endowed with material resources many times as great as those available in the biophysical environments of their homelands. *European societies thus had a unique opportunity to expand greatly their economic surplus.*

Almost immediately the new conquerors began to ship vast quantities of gold and silver back to Europe. This had a number of consequences, one of which was a tremendous growth in the money economy and a decline in the older barter system.[3] Although money had been used for more than 2,000 years, the supply of precious metals was so limited that many payments were still made in goods rather than in cash—especially in rural areas, but by no means only there. This situation had seriously hindered both economic and technological advance, because an economy that operates on the basis of barter is not flexible and the flow of resources from areas of oversupply to areas of short supply is sluggish. Furthermore, it is difficult to figure what is economically most advantageous in a barter system. The more widely money is used, however, the easier it is for people to calculate their costs and incomes and determine which of the alternatives open to them is likely to yield the greatest profit.

This is extremely important in breaking down barriers to technological innovation. In a society where technological progress has been halting and uncertain for centuries and where there is no efficient accounting system, people with money will generally invest only in long-established and proven kinds of enterprises. Also, where money is scarce, people tend to state obligations (e.g., wages, rents, debts) in relatively inflexible and traditional terms, which makes the economy less responsive to changing conditions and new opportunities. But all of this began to change in western Europe during the sixteenth and seventeenth centuries because of the flow of precious metals from the New World.

This influx of gold and silver had a second important effect: it produced inflation.[4] This was a natural consequence of the greatly increased supply of money together with the much more limited increase in the supply of goods. Prices doubled, tripled, even quadrupled within a century. As is always the case when this happens, some people prospered and others were hurt. In general, those with fixed incomes, especially the landed aristocracy, were hurt. But all sorts of entrepreneurs tended to benefit. This meant a marked improvement in the position of the merchants relative to the governing class. More of the economic resources of European societies began to wind up in the hands of people who were interested in, and knew something about, both economics and technology. More than that, *these were people oriented to rational profit making (a far from typical orientation in agrarian societies) and therefore motivated to provide financial support for technological innovations that would increase the efficiency of people or machines.* The rise in prices in the sixteenth century was simultaneously a stimulant to feverish enterprise and an acid dissolving traditional relationships.[5]

The benefits to Europe from the discovery of the New World were even greater in the eighteenth and nineteenth centuries than they had been earlier. As the population of European colonists increased, so did opportunities for trade. The colonists provided a growing market for manufactured goods, paying for them with a swelling flood of raw materials.[6] Between 1698 and 1775, Britain's trade with its colonies increased more than fivefold,[7] and that was only the beginning. As a result, *the center of world trade shifted for the first time in more than 5,000 years, as western Europe replaced the Middle East in the favored position.*

The Printing Press and the Spread of Information

The printing press was another technological innovation that played an important role in helping western European societies break out of the traditional agrarian mold. Printing sped the dissemination of both new technological and new ideological information, and was thus a major factor in overcoming the historic resistance to innovation and change.

Printing apparently originated in China about the fifth century A.D.[8] This early method of printing was extremely expensive, however, because it required a highly skilled craftsman to engrave the contents of every page on a separate block of wood. As a result, printed materials remained a luxury until Johann Gutenberg, a German goldsmith and engraver, invented a system of movable type in the middle of the fifteenth century.[9] With this method, the

**FIGURE 9.2   The earliest known picture of a
printing press, dating from 1499. The typesetter
is reading copy on the left, the press and
pressmen are on the right. The large figures in
the rear symbolize the constant presence of
death, a recurring theme in medieval art.**

expense of skilled engraving was eliminated from printing, except in the
manufacture of the type (i.e., letters and other symbols), which could be
combined in various ways and used over and over again.

Gutenberg's invention resulted in a tremendous increase in the quantity of
printed materials in western Europe. Among the materials that achieved wider
circulation were treatises on the new scientific theories of men like Copernicus
and Galileo in the sixteenth and seventeenth centuries and books on farming
that revolutionized English agriculture in the eighteenth. One of the most
significant applications of the printing press, however, occurred less than a
century after its invention, when it was used to spread the teachings of the
Protestant reformers. Historians today regard the printing press as a major
factor in the success of the Protestant movement.

As many scholars have observed, a number of the new Protestant doctrines
substantially altered the thinking of many members of agrarian societies in
ways that were conducive to economic and other kinds of change.[10] In the first
place, the reformers taught that work is a form of service to God. Martin
Luther, for example, insisted that all honest forms of work are just as truly
Christian callings as the ministry or priesthood. This challenged both the
medieval Christian view of work as a punishment for sin and the traditional
aristocratic view of work as degrading and beneath the dignity of a gentleman.
At the same time, it supported the merchants and craftsmen in their efforts to

upgrade their status. Second, the new Protestant faiths undermined fatalism and trust in magic and encouraged the growth of more rationalistic thought processes. Though the reformers dealt with these things only in the area of religion—and even there only imperfectly—they strengthened a trend that ultimately had broad ramifications. Some branches of Protestantism, for example, encouraged their adherents to plan their lives in rational terms rather than simply live from day to day, as the name "Methodism" reminds us. Third, many of the newer Protestant faiths emphasized the value of denying the pleasures of this world and living frugally, a practice that led those who were economically successful to accumulate capital.

To the extent that people followed these teachings, they developed a new outlook on life: they worked harder, acted more rationally, and lived more thriftily. In short, the Reformation remolded the attitudes, beliefs, and values of many people in ways that helped to undermine the traditional agrarian economy and stimulate economic and technological innovation. Related to this, certain branches of Protestantism, notably Calvinism, elevated the activities of merchants and other businessmen to a status they had not previously enjoyed in any agrarian society. As one scholar has noted, this was not surprising in a faith which had its headquarters in Geneva and its most influential adherents in leading business centers, such as London, Antwerp, and Amsterdam.[11]

In summary, it seems more than coincidence that the Industrial Revolution had its beginnings in predominantly Protestant nations. The new Protestant ideology, like the conquest of the New World, helped weaken belief systems and social structures that had been formidable barriers to innovation and change. Above all, it encouraged a new respect for work and rational planning and discouraged both fatalism and reliance on magic. But it is important to recognize that the success of the Reformation movement and its influence on the subsequent course of European history were due in no small measure to prior changes in technology and economics, and thus constituted, to a large extent, a form of positive feedback.

Advances in Agriculture

Throughout the agrarian era, the chief restraint on societal growth and development was the backward state of agricultural technology. The rural elite, so long as it managed to extract a surplus sufficient to maintain its customary lifestyle, was content to let things continue as they were. And the peasants, so long as they managed simply to survive, were content to follow the practices inherited from their forebears—or, if not content, at least not inspired to change them. Thus agriculture, on which the entire society depended for its survival and which was the basis of the economic surplus, remained largely the same from one century to the next.

In the sixteenth century, however, the situation began to change in much of western Europe.[12] The growth of trade, the increased use of money, and, above all, inflation began to undermine the traditional system. On the one hand, a growing number of large landowners found that, as transportation costs declined in the wake of advances in shipping, markets for certain farm commodities (e.g., wool, grain) were expanding. On the other hand, the effects of inflation were threatening the profitability of their farms, which depended on rents and other obligations established long before the rise in prices. Many landowners realized that if they hoped to maintain their traditional standard of living under the new economic conditions, they must try something new. Some of them subsequently brought new land under cultivation by draining swamps, or by enclosing land that had previously been "common pasture" and at the disposal of peasants and elite alike. Others turned to raising sheep in an effort to benefit from the growing trade in wool. Still others eliminated traditional modes of payment by which tenants fulfilled their obligations to their landlord through customary services or by furnishing him with goods or produce, and began to require instead payments of money, which had become more important in economic relationships and which could more easily be adjusted to take account of inflation. Thus, during the sixteenth and seventeenth centuries, agriculture in Europe, and particularly in England, gradually became a more rationalistic and less traditionalistic enterprise.

Then, in the eighteenth century, a new wave of inflation hit western Europe, and landowners were again faced with a choice between innovation and a declining standard of living.[13] In England, where the traditional system of agriculture had already been seriously weakened, a number of other important innovations were made. Early in the century, for example, one landowner devised a system of crop rotation that enabled farmers to keep all of their land continuously under cultivation; previously, farmers had to leave a quarter of their land always fallow, or uncultivated, in order to restore its fertility. A little later, another landowner discovered the principle of selective breeding, simultaneously making a fortune for himself from his stud farm and greatly improving the quality of British livestock. Other members of the rural elite invented a variety of simple machines that increased the efficiency of farm labor, while still others published books expounding the new techniques. The practice of land enclosures, meanwhile, continued.

By the end of the eighteenth century, the older system of agriculture was largely destroyed in England, and its place taken by a new system of larger, more efficient farms operated on rationalistic and capitalistic principles. But this new system meant the massive displacement of poor rural families whose labor was no longer needed and whose rights to use the land were no longer protected by tradition. Some of these people migrated to the new frontiers overseas. Many others, however, migrated to the cities and towns, where they became the primary source of cheap labor in the new mills and factories that were beginning to appear.

A Model of the Causes of the Industrial Revolution

Figure 9.3 provides a graphic model of the principal developments that led to the rapid increase in the rate of technological innovation and ultimately to the Industrial Revolution. As the model indicates, *the basic underlying cause was*

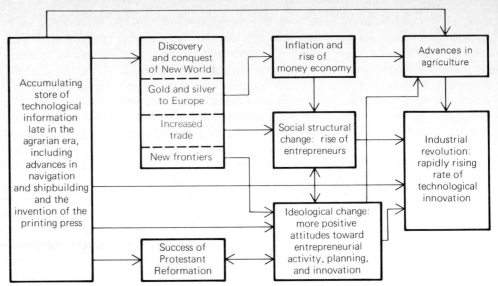

FIGURE 9.3   Model of the causes of the Industrial Revolution in western Europe.

the growing store of technological information in the latter part of the agrarian era.

Advances in navigation and shipbuilding were especially important because, without them, the societies of western Europe could not have gained control of the resources of two vast continents. This revolutionary development, abetted by the success of the Protestant Reformation, led to the changes in economics, social structure, and ideology that made it possible for these societies to break out of the historic agrarian mold. Above all, the pattern of negative feedback from social structure and ideology to technology was transformed into a positive one, thereby freeing creative forces that had been severely curbed for centuries.

It is interesting to note that England, the first society to become industrialized, experienced significant change in each of the factors we identified earlier as responsible for shaping a society's development (see Figure 3.5, page 73). Her environment was drastically altered through the discovery of the New World and her participation in its conquest, and her stores of both technological and ideological information underwent substantial change in the sixteenth, seventeenth, and eighteenth centuries. These developments produced major changes in the processes of innovation and selection. These facts will provide us with useful clues when, in a later chapter, we ponder the question of why societies trying to industrialize today find it so much more difficult than did the societies that industrialized a hundred years or more ago.

A Brief History of the Industrial Revolution

Before the end of the nineteenth century, economic historians were already beginning to use the term "Industrial Revolution" to refer to the series of dramatic technological and economic innovations that had occurred in England during the period from about 1760 to 1830. In their judgment, the mechanization of the textile industry, the technical advances in, and expansion of, the iron industry, the harnessing of steam power, the establishment of the factory system, and other, related developments of that period had revolutionized English society. What was still essentially an agrarian society (or agrarian-maritime hybrid) in the middle of the eighteenth century had become an industrial society by the middle of the nineteenth.

The time limits that early writers assigned the Industrial Revolution have subsequently been questioned. Many scholars today believe it is a mistake to put a terminal date (i.e., 1830) on a revolution that is still continuing.[14] Others argue that 1760 is too late a starting date, since the acceleration in industrial activity began not in the middle of the eighteenth century but in the middle of the sixteenth or earlier.[15]

There is some merit in both criticisms. The rate of technological advance did, in fact, begin to accelerate long before 1760, as we have seen. But it does not follow that we should treat those earlier developments as part of the Industrial Revolution. To be meaningful, this term must be reserved for *developments that led directly to a rapid and substantial increase in the economic importance of machine-based industry.* Refinements and improvements of older techniques do not qualify unless they significantly increased the proportion of the population dependent on industrial activity or the percentage of the gross national product obtained from this source.[16] Using these criteria, we cannot put the start of the Industrial Revolution much, if any, before the middle of the eighteenth century.[17] The earlier events, however, obviously contributed to the later ones, as we have seen.

The other criticism of the dates is sounder: the Industrial Revolution definitely was *not* over by 1830. Only its first phase ended at that time. Subsequently, there have been three other phases, and each has contributed substantially to the importance of industrial activity in the societies involved, and to their general transformation.

We cannot assign precise dates to these phases, since they are all rather arbitrary divisions in what has been essentially a continuous process of development. However, by organizing our review in terms of phases, we can see more clearly the progression of events. In the first phase, which began in mid-eighteenth-century England, the revolution was centered in the textile, iron, and coal industries, and the invention of the first true steam engine was probably the most important innovation. The second phase got its start in the middle of the nineteenth century and involved rapid growth in the railroad industry, the mass production of steel, the replacement of sailing ships by steamships, and use of the new technology in agriculture. Around the turn of the century, the Industrial Revolution entered its third phase, with rapid growth in the automobile, electrical, telephone, and petroleum industries. World War II marked the beginning of the fourth phase, distinguished by remarkable developments in aviation, aluminum, electronics, plastics, nuclear power, computers, and automation.

The four phases should not be thought of as stages that each society must pass through to become industrialized. On the contrary, many societies in recent decades have skipped over certain phases, or at least parts of them, and combined elements from different phases. For example, a Third World nation today will often develop its railways, highways, and air transportation system simultaneously. But a review of the way things happened *initially* enables us to "get inside" the process of technological advance and see how one innovation makes further innovations possible, even imperative.

First Phase

The first phase of the Industrial Revolution, as we just noted, began in the middle of the eighteenth century and lasted about a hundred years. Geographically, it was centered in England, where there was a great burst of technological innovation. Many of the best-known innovations occurred in the textile industry and were of two kinds: machines that increased the efficiency of human labor and machines that harnessed new sources of energy. The flying shuttle is a good example of the first—and a good example, too, of the way one invention stimulated others. Because it enabled one weaver to do the work formerly done by two, spinners could no longer keep up with the demand for yarn. This disruption of the traditional balance between spinning and weaving triggered a succession of additional inventions. First, the traditional spinning wheel was replaced by the spinning jenny, which enabled a worker to spin 4 threads simultaneously and, after a number of modifications, 120 threads. But although the spinning jenny was a tremendous improvement from the standpoint of speed, its yarn was so coarse and loose that flax had to be mixed in with the cotton to produce a satisfactory fiber. This was remedied with the water frame, a machine that could satisfactorily spin pure cotton, and later

FIGURE 9.4   James Hargreaves's spinning jenny.

with the spinning mule, whose cotton threads were stronger and finer. All these advances in spinning reversed the earlier situation: now weaving was the bottleneck in the industry—until a new series of innovations in weaving machines helped restore the balance.

By the end of the eighteenth century, the new looms had become so large and heavy that they were almost impossible to operate. To work the treadle even at a slow speed required two powerful men—and they had to be relieved after a short time.[18] This led to a search for alternative sources of power. One possibility was waterpower, which had already been used for a variety of purposes for many centuries. But England was poorly supplied with suitable streams and rivers, and the wheels and troughs used in water systems were extremely inefficient.[19] Eventually, James Watt developed the first true steam engine,[20] a source of power that could be employed anywhere, and by the end of the century it had been adapted for use in the textile industry.

The net effect of these innovations was such a rapid expansion of the British textile industry that between 1770 and 1845 its contribution to the national income increased more than fivefold.[21] Though unspectacular by more recent standards, this was a striking rate of growth by traditional agrarian standards. The actual increase in production was even larger, since per unit costs of production dropped considerably during this period.

One of the immediate consequences of advances in textile production was *the creation of the factory system*. Prior to the Industrial Revolution, and even

FIGURE 9.5 Prior to the Industrial Revolution, and even during its early years, entrepreneurs provided poor families with raw materials for spinning, weaving, and garment making in their own homes. Early 19th-century print of English family sewing uniforms for the British army under the domestic, or putting-out, system that preceded the factory system.

during its early years, spinning and weaving were cottage industries. Entrepreneurs provided the raw materials, and poorer families, using their own spinning wheels and looms and working in their own homes, provided the labor. But after heavier and more expensive machines were invented, this arrangement was impossible: families could neither afford the new equipment nor power it. Businessmen were forced to buy their own machines, construct buildings to house them, and provide engines to run them, thereby creating the factory system that is such a prominent feature of modern industrial societies.

Another industry that expanded greatly during the first phase of the Industrial Revolution was iron manufacturing. Despite increasing demand for iron by both the textile industry and the military, technical difficulties greatly restricted its manufacture until late in the eighteenth century. One problem was England's growing shortage of wood, which was needed to make charcoal for smelting and refining. This problem was partially solved earlier in the century, when someone found that coke could be substituted for charcoal, at least in the smelting process. But a serious bottleneck remained. Because it is hard and brittle, pig iron must be converted into wrought, or malleable, iron before it can be used for most purposes. Again, the process required charcoal, and it was very slow until the traditional forge was replaced by the newly invented coal-fired blast furnace. These innovations opened the way for rapid expansion: in 1788, England produced only 68,000 tons of iron; by 1845, twenty-four times that.[22] The new blast furnaces also made it possible to perform all the processes of iron making in the same establishment. Thus, the factory system spread from the textile industry to the iron industry.

Between them, the iron industry and the steam engine substantially increased the demand for coal. But the steam engine helped alleviate the ancient problem of flooding in coal mines, providing power to pump out the water that constantly seeped into shafts and tunnels. The growth of the coal industry, though not quite so dramatic as that of the iron industry, was still impressive: in 1760, Britain produced barely 5 million tons; by 1845, the figure had risen over ninefold.[23]

No discussion of developments in this period would be complete without mention of the machine-tool industry. Although never as large or as financially important as the textile, iron, and coal industries, it was crucial for technological progress because it produced the increasingly complex industrial machinery. This industry, which began undramatically with the invention of the first practical lathe, was soon producing machines capable of precision work to the thousandth of an inch.[24] For many years a single tool was used for drilling, boring, grinding, and milling; but special tools were gradually designed for each operation.

Another basic advance in the eighteenth century was the production of machines with interchangeable parts. This greatly facilitated industrial growth, since damage to one part of a complex machine no longer meant that the entire machine had to be discarded or a new part specially made. Spare parts could now be kept on hand and replacements made on the spot by mechanics with limited skills and equipment.

During this initial phase of the Industrial Revolution, shortly after 1800, Britain became the first nation in which machine-based industry replaced agriculture as the most important economic activity, and thus the first industrial society.[25] The United States would not reach this point until 1870.[26]

Second Phase

The second phase of the Industrial Revolution began in the middle decades of the nineteenth century. Expansion continued at a rapid pace in the textile, iron, and coal industries, but now there were breakthroughs in a number of others as well. By the end of the century industrialization had occurred in most segments of the British economy. Meanwhile, the Industrial Revolution began to make significant headway in some of the other countries of northwestern Europe and in the United States.

One of the most important developments during this phase was the application of the steam engine to transportation, something inventors had been trying to accomplish for decades. Finally, about 1850, most of England was linked together by a network of railroads.[27] The results were tremendous: the greatly reduced cost of moving goods by rail contributed to a significant reduction in the price of many heavy, bulk commodities, and this, in turn, led to greater demand. In addition, railroads helped break down local monopolies and oligopolies (i.e., markets with only a few sellers), which added to competition and further lowered prices. Thus, England gradually became a single giant market for an increasing number of commodities, a development destined to have far-reaching consequences.

Even before the steam engine was adapted to land transportation, it had been used on water. For many years, however, it was limited to coastal and river shipping, both because inefficient engines made it impossible to bunker enough wood or coal for long voyages and because paddle wheels worked poorly in high seas. Then, in only a few decades, efficient compound engines solved the problem of bunkering fuel; iron and steel began to replace wood in ship construction, permitting longer and larger ships with greater carrying capacity (the upper limit in length for wooden vessels was only about 300

FIGURE 9.6   Model of the DeWitt Clinton, built in New York in 1831. On its first run between Albany and Schenectady, it covered twelve miles in less than an hour.

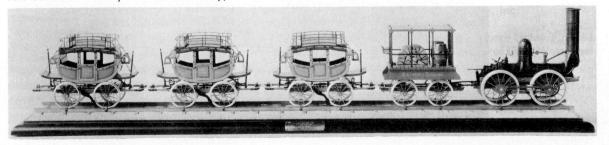

feet); and the screw propeller replaced the cumbersome and easily damaged paddle wheel.[28] After this, steamships increased so rapidly that by 1893 world steam tonnage exceeded sailing tonnage.

In the iron industry, meanwhile, a way was finally found to produce steel cheaply and in large quantities, making it available for many new purposes.[29] Between 1845 and the early 1880s, Britain's production of iron and steel increased more than fivefold.[30] This meant that in less than a century, the increase was 100-fold, and the quality of the product was vastly improved.

The tremendous growth in railroads and steamships and the expansion of the iron industry all combined to increase the demand for coal. Though there were no spectacular breakthroughs in mining techniques, improvements in engines and in the quality of steel tools pushed production up fivefold.[31]

A number of new industries emerged in addition to the railroads, none as important at the time, but some destined to surpass them later on. The rubber industry developed after Charles Goodyear discovered the technique of vulcanization, which prevented rubber goods from becoming sticky in hot weather, stiff and brittle in cold. About the same time, Samuel Morse and several others invented the telegraph, and this quickly became the basis of another new industry. A method for making dyes from coal tar helped establish the chemical industry. Then, in the 1860s, the electric dynamo was invented, and the door was opened to the use of electricity in industry. A second critical development in this field, the invention of the transformer, helped alleviate one of the greatest impediments to the use of electricity: the loss of energy during long-distance transmission. The petroleum industry also got its start in these years, chiefly by providing a substitute for whale oil in lighting homes.

The Industrial Revolution began to make an impact even on agriculture, through improved equipment (e.g., sturdier steel plows), new kinds of machines (e.g., threshing machines, mowers, reapers, steam plows), and synthetic fertilizers from the growing chemical industry. The result was a substantial increase in productivity. In Germany, for example, production per acre rose 50 per cent in only twenty-five years. In the United States, the number of man-hours required to produce its corn and wheat declined 45 and 57 per cent, respectively, between 1840 and 1900.[32]

Another significant development in this second phase of the Industrial Revolution was the formation of the *multidivisional enterprise with its hierarchy of salaried managers*.[33] This happened first in the new railroad, steamship, and telegraph industries, which required workers in widely scattered locations. No longer was it possible for a single family to fill all or even most of the managerial positions needed to supervise its employees and coordinate their activities: hired personnel had to assume this responsibility. This was an important step in the development of the modern *corporation*.

Another spur in this direction was the great quantity of new material products that had become available to the members of society. As advances in production and transportation continued to lower the cost of goods and increase the demand for them, the sheer volume of sales made it impossible for the owners of some businesses to oversee all of the transactions. For example, around the turn of the century, Sears, Roebuck was processing 100,000 orders a day, more than any merchant of an earlier generation would have handled in a lifetime.[34] As sales increased, so did the number of retail outlets in a wide variety of businesses, each requiring a local manager at first, and eventually intermediate layers of management.

All during this period, industrialization was spreading rapidly in northwest Europe and in North America. Before the century closed, Britain had lost her position of economic and technological leadership. The iron and steel industry illustrates the trend: although Britain nearly doubled her production of pig iron between 1865 and 1900, her share of the world market dropped from 54 to 23 per cent.[35] Her chief rivals were the United States and Germany, whose respective shares rose from 9 to 35 per cent and from 10 to 19 per cent.

As these figures indicate, though industrialization was spreading, it was still largely limited to a few countries. The United States, Britain, Germany, and France, for example, produced 84 per cent of the world's iron in 1900. A similar picture emerges when we look at national shares of all manufacturing activity. In 1888, the percentages are estimated to have been as follows:[36]

United States	32%
Britain	18%
Germany	13%
France	11%
All other countries	26%

The fact that "all other countries" contributed more to *all* types of manufacturing than they did to iron production reflects the fact that the new technology was spreading faster in light industries, such as textiles, than in heavy industries. This was because light industries required less capital and because the rate of innovation in them had already slowed considerably, reducing the need for highly skilled and innovative personnel.

The last factor points to a final characteristic of this phase of the Industrial Revolution: a growing dependence on science and engineering. Before 1850 most of the major advances were made by simple craftsmen or gentlemen amateurs. After that date, key inventions came primarily from people with formal technical or scientific training. This was especially true in the chemical industry, but it was evident in others as well.

Finally, near the end of the nineteenth century, the innovative process began to be institutionalized, and laboratories were built to enable teams of trained people to work together to solve technical problems.[37] The laboratories established by Thomas Edison are an excellent example of the new trend, and the successes he and others achieved led many to emulate them, especially in Germany and the United States. These developments also contributed to the growth of scientific study in universities, to the training of engineers, and to increasing cooperation between innovative industries and institutions of higher education. Most of these developments did not come to full flower, however, until the third and fourth phases of the Industrial Revolution.

Third Phase

Around the turn of the century, the Industrial Revolution entered a phase that lasted until the beginning of World War II and was characterized by major advances in *energy technology*. The foundation for some of the twentieth century's most distinctive innovations had been laid in the late nineteenth century with the invention of the internal combustion engine and of machines capable of generating and transmitting electricity in quantities great enough, and at prices cheap enough, to be industrially useful and commercially profitable.

One of the most dramatic developments was the tremendous expansion of the automobile industry. In 1900 no more than 20,000 cars were produced in the entire world, most of them in France.[38] By 1913 annual world production was 600,000, with the United States turning out over 80 per cent. By 1929, the total was over 6 million, 85 per cent of them made in the United States.[39]

Just as remarkable as the automobile industry's own rate of growth was its impact on other industries. In 1937, for example, the manufacture of cars in the United States consumed 20 per cent of the nation's steel, 54 per cent of its malleable iron, 73 per cent of its plate glass, and 80 per cent of its rubber.[40] What is more, 90 per cent of its gasoline went to run those vehicles.

FIGURE 9.7   Early automobile assembly line: dropping the engine into the Model T chassis, Highland Park, Michigan.

**TABLE 9.1   Percentage Distribution
of World Industrial Output
(Excluding Handicrafts), in 1888
and 1937, by Society**

Society	1888	1937
United States	32	34
United Kingdom	18	10
Germany	13	11
France	11	5
Russia	8	10
Japan	No data	4
All others	17	26

Source: Calculated from W. S. Woytinsky
and E. S. Woytinsky, *World Population
and Production: Trends and Outlook* (New
York: Twentieth Century Fund, 1953), pp.
1003–1004.

The electrical industry was another that mushroomed during the third phase as electricity came to be widely used for industrial purposes. This was also the period in which small electric motors began to be used widely to power household appliances. Between 1900 and 1940 the capacity of all the generating plants in the world increased 200-fold.[41] Again the United States led the way, producing 40 to 45 per cent of the world's electric power.

The proportional growth of the petroleum industry was less dramatic, because it had already grown substantially before 1900. Even so, production in 1940 was thirteen times larger than it was in 1900.[42]

The telephone industry also grew rapidly in this period. The number of telephones in the United States increased from 1.4 million in 1900 to 20.8 million in 1940, by which time the industry had investments valued at $5 billion.[43]

During this phase, as during the second, the Industrial Revolution was felt not only in new sectors of the economy but in new parts of the world as well, which meant some change in the relative ranking of nations. While the United States continued in the lead, Britain, Germany, and France all lost ground relatively (see Table 9.1) despite substantial growth in absolute terms. The chief gains were registered by nations that were just beginning to industrialize, especially Russia and Japan.

Fourth Phase

No previous war was as dependent on industrial activity as World War II, as every major nation made tremendous efforts to increase its output of military supplies. One of the long-term consequences was the great stimulus to the aviation industry. In the United States, the production of aircraft rose from 3,600 in 1938 to more than 96,000 in 1944.[44] Though the manufacture of new aircraft declined substantially at the end of the war, the air transportation industry expanded rapidly. Between 1940 and 1978, the number of passenger-miles flown by scheduled airlines rose from 1.2 billion to 227 billion, and the number of ton-miles flown in hauling freight and mail rose from 14 million to over 5.2 billion.[45] The year 1958 marked a significant shift in transportation patterns: for the first time, planes covered more passenger-miles in the United States than trains, and they also replaced steamships as the chief carriers of transatlantic passengers.

Just as automobiles spurred the petroleum industry, so aviation spurred aluminum. Though it was first manufactured in the nineteenth century, its production was quite limited until Germany and Italy began building their air forces in the 1930s. In just four decades (from 1938 to 1979), world production increased twenty-five times, and it is still increasing as new uses continue to be found.[46] As in most of the rapidly expanding industries of the third and fourth phases, American production has been a major share, varying from a third to a half of the world's aluminum output since World War II.

The plastics industry is another that came into its own during this fourth phase. Its origins go back to 1861, when nitrocellulose was plasticized with camphor to produce artificial ivory and used as a substitute for horn in frames for eyeglasses. Thanks to many subsequent developments, plastics have become the most versatile of modern materials: they can now be manufactured to almost any set of specifications. Not surprisingly, the industry has mushroomed: as recently as the late 1930s, world output was under 200,000 tons; by 1977, it was 47 million and growing, with American production a quarter of the total.[47]

The nuclear power industry has also grown tremendously since World War II. Although the Atomic Age began with Hiroshima, the world's first nuclear power facility did not begin operating until 1955, when the Soviet Union opened a small installation with a 5,000-kilowatt capacity.[48] By 1978, there were 200 or more reactors operative in at least twenty nations (data on the Soviet Union and some other nations was not available) with a capacity of 105 million kilowatts.[49]

Electronics is another industry with a spectacular rate of expansion, and its impact on daily life has been as dramatic as its growth. Its products include radio and television equipment, tape recorders, high-fidelity systems, computers, calculators, testing and measuring equipment, industrial control equipment, and microwave communications systems, to name a few of the more familiar. With the development of servomotors—small power units that respond instantly to signals of various kinds (e.g., a temperature change)—machines that not only act but *react* became possible, and the foundation was laid for automation.

The most revolutionary innovation of the fourth phase, however, has been the computer, which is the equivalent of a radical advance in certain capabilities of our species' most valuable tool, the human brain. The first electronic digital computer was built in 1946, less than forty years ago. A massive piece of equipment weighing thirty tons and occupying an entire room, it required 140,000 watts of electricity and had a memory of only 20 ten-digit numbers. Today, a far greater information-handling capacity resides in the circuits of a tiny quarter-inch silicon chip, while one of the newer

FIGURE 9.8 **The most revolutionary innovation of the
fourth phase of the Industrial Revolution has been the
computer, which is the functional equivalent of a
radical advance in certain of the capabilities of our
species' most valuable genetic resource, the human
brain.**

computers can perform more than 800 million information-processing operations per second.[50]

Such leaps in capability dwarf the other technological advances of the
fourth phase,* and carry with them a staggering potential for change in human
societies. One indication of this is the use of computerized robots in the
automobile industry, first in Japan and more recently in the United States.
Although early reports greatly exaggerated the impact of this innovation on the
size of the labor force in the plants where it has been adopted thus far,[51] some
experts believe that by the end of the century "smart robots" will be capable
of replacing from 50 to 75 per cent of all factory workers, and at significantly
lower costs.[52] Similar changes can be expected in other areas where labor
consists of relatively routine and repetitive operations. Meanwhile, computers
are already integral components in everything from children's toys to military
weapons systems.

Several of the rapid-growth industries of the third phase maintained their

---

*It is reported that if the automobile industry had made comparable advances, a
Rolls-Royce would now cost only $70.

high rate of growth in the fourth. Between 1940 and 1980, world output of electricity increased fifteenfold, world production of motor vehicles and petroleum tenfold.[53] The United States was still a major producer, but its contribution to total world production in these industries had declined considerably. For example, its share of world automobile production dropped from 85 per cent in 1929 to only 23 per cent in 1977.

A comparison of Tables 9.1 and 9.2 shows some of the important changes that have occurred in the last hundred years with respect to industrial development in the world system. The most striking fact revealed by this comparison is the precipitous decline of Britain, which in 1888 still ranked as the second leading industrial power. Japan and the Soviet Union, on the other hand, have made impressive advances. The dynamic nature of modern industrial technology means that no society is assured of continuing leadership simply because it enjoys that status during a particular phase of the continuing Industrial Revolution. It means, too, that it has become increasingly difficult for any nation or set of nations to dominate the industrial scene. In 1888, the five most highly industrialized societies were responsible for 83 per cent of the world's industrial output. But by 1937, the output of the top five was only 70 per cent, and by 1976 only 62 per cent, reflecting the continuing diffusion of industrial technology throughout the world system.

Until recently, the fourth phase of the Industrial Revolution has been a period of tremendous economic growth throughout the world. Between 1950 and 1977, for example, real gains in productivity (i.e., after adjusting for the effects of inflation) ranged from 146 per cent in east and southeast Asia (with Japan excluded) to 227 per cent in Latin America (see Table 13.3, page 370). These rapid gains were due largely to two factors: (1) the increasing availability of cheap energy sources up until 1973, and (2) the movement of millions of people out of agriculture into modern industries.

The sudden end of cheap energy, together with the appearance of several fundamental innovations, especially the computer, suggests that the world

TABLE 9.2   Percentage Distribution of Gross World Product, by Society, in 1976

Society	Percentage Share of Gross World Product
United States	26
Union of Soviet Socialist Republics	15
Japan	9
West Germany	7
France	5
China	5
United Kingdom	3
Canada	3
Italy	3
All others	24

Source: Adapted from *Statistical Abstract of the U.S., 1979*, table 1554.

system may be on the threshold of a new phase in the continuing Industrial Revolution—a phase characterized by a shift to new energy sources and more energy-efficient machines. Because of its great relevance for the future, we will return to this subject in the final chapter.

Levels of Industrialization in Contemporary Societies

Societies today differ enormously in the degree to which they have industrialized. Some have come to rely almost entirely on the newer energy sources (i.e., coal, petroleum, natural gas, hydroelectric power, and nuclear energy) and the machines powered by them, while others still depend primarily on the older energy sources (i.e., human and animal power, wind, water, and wood).

There is no single measure that enables us to gauge perfectly the degree of industrialization achieved by a society. One measure that might, at first glance, appear ideal for this purpose is the amount of energy societies consume each year. But even after figures on their consumption of the newer forms of energy have been adjusted to take account of the differences in their population size, serious distortions still occur. For one thing, societies in cold climates use more energy per person than societies at the same level of industrialization in warm climates. For another, societies with long distances between their towns and cities (e.g., Canada, Australia), or with a tradition of dependency on private ownership of automobiles (e.g., the United States), consume more energy than equally industrialized societies that are more densely populated and have a well-established system of public transportation (e.g., most European societies).

The best single measure of industrialization seems to be a society's gross national product, or GNP. This is highly correlated with the extent to which the members of a society depend on the newer forms of energy in their *productive* activities, and it is readily available for most contemporary societies. GNP is a measure of the value of all the goods and services produced by the members of a society in a given year. In order to make a meaningful comparison among societies with very different population sizes, it is necessary to modify the basic GNP figure by dividing it by the number of people in the society. This creates a measure known as *per capita GNP*. Societies that are highly industrialized have high per capita GNPs; societies with low per capita GNPs have not industrialized to a significant degree.*

Table 9.3 provides a portrait of industrialization in much of the world

---

*The only serious problem with per capita GNP as a measure of industrialization arises in the case of the smaller oil-producing societies, such as Kuwait. Currently, these nations have high per capita GNPs, yet they lack many of the other attributes of truly industrialized societies. For example, they have few scientists and engineers and no capacity for processing large quantities of different kinds of raw materials into manufactured products. In other words, although they have considerable wealth, it has not been converted into the kind of capital that characterizes industrialization: *capital that incorporates vast amounts of technological information*—both *human* capital (that is, a skilled labor force) and capital *goods* (machinery, factories, and so on).

TABLE 9.3 Per Capita Gross National Product, by Society, 1977.

Society	GNP	Society	GNP	Society	GNP
Sweden	$8,732	Greece	$2,559	Morocco	$501
Canada	8,391	Venezuela	2,486	Nigeria	479
United States	8,188	Bulgaria	2,372	Philippines	419
West Germany	7,469	Iran	1,846	Thailand	390
Australia	7,058	Portugal	1,816	China	360
France	6,728	Yugoslavia	1,797	Ghana	352
Netherlands	6,600	Iraq	1,437	Egypt	285
Japan	5,155	Argentina	1,351	Indonesia	274
East Germany	4,119	Brazil	1,260	Kenya	245
Czechoslovakia	3,993	South Africa	1,205	Uganda	237
United Kingdom	3,976	Turkey	1,069	Afghanistan	189
New Zealand	3,939	Mexico	1,055	Pakistan	180
U.S.S.R.	3,835	Algeria	1,036	Tanzania	173
Italy	3,074	Syria	862	India	141
Spain	2,925	Peru	810	Burma	131
Poland	2,742	South Korea	725	Zaire	109
Israel	2,708	Colombia	634	Ethiopia	95
Hungary	2,626	North Korea	581	Bangladesh	68

Source: U.S. Arms Control and Disarmament Agency, *World Military Expenditures and Arms Transfers 1968–1977,* table II.

system in the late 1970s. A number of societies that are absent in Table 9.2 rank at or near the top in Table 9.3. The reason for this striking difference is that a *per capita* measure makes allowance for population size and does not penalize relatively small societies.

With the exception of Japan and the overseas English-speaking democracies (i.e., Canada, the United States, Australia, and New Zealand), all the societies that are clearly industrialized are in Europe. The boundary between truly industrial societies and those that are best described as "industrializing" lies in the area of a per capita GNP of about $2,500. Whether societies like Greece, Venezuela, and Bulgaria are classified as industrial or industrializing is rather arbitrary. Societies below the level of these countries, however, clearly fall short of most current concepts of an industrial society.

For the remainder of this chapter, and in the three that follow, we will be primarily concerned with the minority of societies that have already industrialized. Our goal will be to see how the new technology has altered the conditions of life for their members and for the world system. We will then turn to those societies that are partly industrial and partly agrarian or horticultural, the hybrid societies that are often referred to as the Third World.

Consequences of the Industrial Revolution

From an early date it was clear that the Industrial Revolution meant far more than a change in techniques of production, that it had enormous implications for every aspect of life. Though our chief concern is with the long-run consequences of the revolution, we should not ignore its immediate effects on those who first experienced the new industrial way of life.

Immediate Consequences

The first indication of serious change came with the invention of the new spinning and weaving machines in the late eighteenth century. Because of their great size and weight, they required specially constructed buildings and steam engines or waterfalls to power them. In short, as we have seen, the new technology necessitated the creation of the factory system.

Factories, however, required a concentrated supply of dependable labor. A few of the early factories were built in open countryside, but their owners quickly found they could not hire enough workers unless they built adjoining tenements, which in effect created new urban settlements. Most factories were built in or near existing towns, and the cry that went out from them for workers coincided with the declining need for labor on the farms.

Although the ensuing migration into urban areas was not a new phenome-

FIGURE 9.9   Early English industrial town, Staffordshire.

non, its *magnitude* was, and most communities were unable to cope with the sudden influx. The migrants themselves were badly prepared for their new way of life. Sanitary practices that had been tolerable in sparsely settled rural areas, for example, became a threat to health, even to life, in crowded urban communities.

Equally critical problems resulted from the abrupt disruption of social relationships. Old ties of kinship and friendship were severed and could not easily be replaced, while local customs and institutions that had provided rural villagers with at least a measure of protection and support were lost for good. Thus, it was an uprooted, extremely vulnerable mass of people who streamed into the towns and were thrown into situations utterly foreign to them, and into a way of life that often culminated in injury, illness, or unemployment. A multitude of social ills—poverty, alcoholism, crime, vice, mental and physical illness, personal demoralization—were endemic.

Town magistrates and other local officials had neither the means nor the will to cope with rampant problems in housing, health, education, and crime. Cities and towns became more crowded, open space disappeared, and people accustomed to fields and woodlands found themselves trapped in a deteriorating environment of filthy, crowded streets and tenements, polluted air, and long workdays rarely relieved by experiences of either hope or beauty.[54]

FIGURE 9.10   Superintendent and spinner in North Carolina textile mill, 1909. One-quarter of the employees in this mill were this girl's age or younger.

The misery of the new urban dwellers was compounded by the harshness of the factory system, which often operated along quasi-penal lines.[55] Regardless of how hard life had been before, country folk had at least had some control over their own hour-to-hour movements; but now, work was, if anything, longer, more arduous, more confining. Women and children, though they had always worked extremely hard in their homes and fields, now worked in factories with dangerous, noisy machinery or in dark and dangerous mines. Minor infractions of complex rules, such as whistling on the job or leaving a lamp lit a few minutes too long after sunrise, led to fines, more serious infractions to floggings. One observer of the period wrote poignantly of hearing children, whose families could not, of course, afford clocks, running through the streets in the dark, long before time for the mills to open, so fearful were they of being late.[56]

The immediate effects of industrialization have been traumatic for vast numbers of people in virtually every society that has made the transition from agrarianism. The details vary, but the suffering was no less acute in the Soviet Union than in England. Whether life for the new urban working class was

---

CHILDREN AND THE FACTORY SYSTEM

The following testimony was given to a Parliamentary committee investigating working conditions in 1832 by Peter Smart. Similar testimony was provided by numerous others.

Q. Where do you reside?
A. At Dundee.
Q. Have you worked in a mill from your youth?
A. Yes, since I was 5 years of age.
Q. Had you a father and mother in the country at the time?
A. My mother stopped in Perth, about eleven miles from the mill, and my father was in the army.
Q. Were you hired for any length of time when you went?
A. Yes, my mother got 15 shillings for six years, I having my meat and clothes.
Q. What were your hours of labor, as you recollect, in the mill?
A. We began at 4 o'clock in the morning and worked till 10 or 11 at night; as long as we could stand on our feet.
Q. Were you kept on the premises constantly?
A. Constantly.
Q. Locked up?
A. Yes, locked up.
Q. Night and day?
A. Night and day; I never went home while I was at the mill.
Q. Do the children ever attempt to run away?
A. Very often.
Q. Were they pursued and brought back again?
A. Yes, the overseer pursued them and brought them back.
Q. Did you ever attempt to run away?
A. Yes, I ran away twice.
Q. And you were brought back?
A. Yes; and I was sent up to the master's loft, and thrashed with a whip for running away.
Q. Do you know whether the children were, in point of fact, compelled to stop during the whole time for which they were engaged?
A. Yes, they were.
Q. By law?
A. I cannot say by law; but they were compelled by the master; I never saw any law used there but the law of their own hands.

Source: *Parliamentary Papers, 1831–32,* vol. XV.

better or worse than it had been for the peasants and the urban lower classes of the old agrarian societies is still a matter of debate.[57] But one point is not debatable: the transition to an industrial economy has exacted a cruel price in terms of human suffering and demoralization for countless millions of people.

Long-Run Consequences

In subsequent chapters, we will examine in detail the new societies and the distinctive life patterns that have resulted from two centuries of industrialization. For the moment, however, we will note just a few of the most important and most striking consequences outside the realm of technology. Collectively, these changes in population, social structure, ideology, and language add up to a revolution without parallel in human history, from the standpoint of scope as well as speed.*

1. World population has multiplied nearly sixfold (from 725 million to 4.5 billion) just since 1750, a rate of growth more than fifteen times higher than the rate between the time of Christ and 1750.

2. The rural-urban balance in advanced industrial societies has been nearly reversed: agrarian societies were approximately 90 per cent rural; several advanced industrial societies are more than 80 per cent urban.

3. The largest communities of the industrial era are more than twelve times the size of the largest of the agrarian era.

4. Women in industrial societies give birth to only about a third as many children as women in preindustrial societies.

5. Life expectancy at birth is almost three times greater in advanced industrial societies than it was in agrarian.

6. The family, for the first time in history, is not a significant productive unit in the economy.

7. The role of women in the economy and in society at large has changed substantially.

8. The role of youth has also changed, and youth cultures have become a significant factor in the life of industrial societies.

9. The *per capita* production and consumption of goods and services in advanced industrial societies is at least ten times greater than in traditional agrarian societies.

10. The division of labor is vastly more complex.

11. Hereditary monarchical government has disappeared in industrial societies, except as a ceremonial survival.

---

*Documentation for these assertions will be found in Chapters 10 to 13.

12.   The functions of government have been greatly enlarged.

13.   Free public educational systems have been established and illiteracy
      largely eliminated in all industrial societies.

14.   New ideologies have spread widely (notably socialism and capitalism),
      while older ones inherited from the agrarian era either have been
      substantially modified or have declined.

15.   Worldwide communication and transportation networks have been creat-
      ed that have, for practical purposes, rendered our entire planet smaller
      than England in the agrarian era.

16.   A global culture has begun to emerge, as evidenced in styles of dress,
      music, language, technology, and organizational patterns (e.g., bureau-
      cratic organizations, small families).

17.   Global political institutions (e.g., the United Nations, the World Court)
      have been established for the first time.

18.   A number of societies have acquired the capacity to obliterate the entire
      human population.

All this in only 200 years!

Causes of the Continuing Industrial Revolution

The social and cultural revolution that first began to alter societal life over 200
years ago shows no signs of abating. This should not surprise us, since the
factors we identified as determinants of the rate of innovation in a society (see
pages 64–68) provide optimum conditions for continuing high rates of technological change—with all of the consequences that attend it in other areas. To
begin with, the *store of information* is now tremendous, and growing rapidly.
Population size, both of individual societies and of the world system, is far
greater than it ever was in the past. And *communication among societies,* as
well as within them, is at an extremely high level. The contribution of these
three factors to the continuing revolutionary rate of change is self-evident.
Several others, however, require comment.

Changing Attitude toward Innovation

The trend that began at the end of the agrarian era with western Europe's
changing attitudes toward innovation shows no signs of abating. Industrial
societies, and many other contemporary societies as well, no longer view
innovation as undesirable, even dangerous. Nor are they merely tolerant of
innovation: instead, they consciously promote and reward it.

This new orientation toward change is so fundamental and so pervasive in
industrial societies that sociologists often speak of *the institutionalization of*

innovation. As this suggests, not only have many of society's basic values, attitudes, and norms been reshaped, but many of its institutions—those systems noted for their resistance to change—have consciously and purposefully created mechanisms to promote innovation and enhance the rate of change. This is particularly evident in educational, political, and economic institutions.

In the educational sphere, the new attitude can be seen at every turn. Whereas in traditional agrarian societies the basic function of education was to transfer the cultural heritage of the past to the next generation, in industrial societies a major function is to stimulate and support the development of *new* cultural elements. Many educators now scorn rote learning, even in primary and secondary schools, and emphasize creativity instead, while in leading colleges and universities, creativity is one of the qualities most sought in students. And as increasing emphasis has been placed on science and engineering in institutions of higher learning, these have become more and more centers of research.

The institutionalization of innovation is equally evident in the economic and political spheres. Business groups and governmental agencies create research units within their own organizations and subsidize research in educational institutions as well. As a result, expenditures for research and development have risen enormously. In the United States, for example, the figures, even after adjustment for inflation, increased forty times between 1953 and 1979. Industrial societies are the first in history to search systematically and on a broad front for technological solutions to human problems.

The new attitude toward change in industrial societies sometimes assumes an extreme form known as *neophilia,* or the love of novelty. In the arts, for example, innovation is often praised simply for its own sake, without regard to aesthetic criteria. Many people are so prepared to applaud the individual who does something—anything—that no one has done before that entries submitted to contests as hoaxes have been known to win prizes. This tendency to value the new above the old, regardless of its merits by other standards, has affected even religion and family life.

As the new attitude toward innovation has permeated industrial societies, the consequences have been enormous in every area of life. Not least among them has been the rising flood of inventions and discoveries that extend and reinforce the revolutionary pace of technological change begun several hundred years ago. Ideology, which once slowed the rate of innovation, has now become a powerful stimulant.

Instability of the Social Environment

The world system of societies has been essentially unstable ever since horticultural societies first posed a threat to bands of hunters and gatherers. Intersocietal selection continues to favor those societies that are technologically most advanced, and their recognition of this fact is a powerful stimulus to

NEOPHILIC ART

Not long ago, the Associated Press reported that two pieces of sculpture by abstract expressionist John Chamberlain had been mistaken for junk and carted away by trash collectors. Walter Kelly, owner of the art gallery, valued them at $20,000. "I had them at the side of my warehouse to clean them up a little for a prospective buyer."

The pieces of art were the usual tangles of metal that have made Chamberlain famous. They were fashioned from car bumpers, sheet metal from old washing machines, and similar materials.

"I'm certain it wasn't a theft," Kelly said, "and that makes it worse, because whoever took them might destroy them. These are important works by a great artist. One of Chamberlain's works is on permanent display at the Art Institute of Chicago."

The Associated Press reported that it was difficult to describe the sculptures, but quoted Kelly as saying, "They are very powerful, dynamic, forceful and . . . you have to form your own opinion of what is represented."

Source: Associated Press wire service story published May 5, 1973.

---

innovation in areas ranging from communication satellites to space flight, and from improvements in food and energy production to weapons systems.

The changing nature of warfare in the last hundred years has been a particularly potent source of technological innovation.[59] Prior to the Industrial Revolution, military technology changed slowly. Among societies at *the same level of development,* victory was usually determined by the size of armies and the organizational and tactical skills of their commanders. Today, military technology becomes obsolete in a few years, and the sizes of armies and their commanders' skills are usually less important than the productive capacity of the nation's economy and the skills of its engineers and scientists. To maintain their relative military status, the leading nations invest increasing amounts in military research—biological, chemical, and space, as well as the more traditional kinds—and this has contributed greatly to the rate of social and cultural change.

Instability of the Biophysical Environment

For the first time in human history, the most significant changes in the biophysical environments of many societies are not the consequence of spontaneous natural forces but of their own technology. The biophysical environment of the world system of societies may well be less stable now than at any point in the past, both because it is called on to support the largest human population ever to inhabit the earth and because so many societies have such a tremendous capacity for extracting and consuming its raw materials and altering its ecology. Paradoxically, this is one of the greatest spurs to innovation in societies today, as they search for technological solutions to a wide range of problems they themselves have created, including air and water pollution, soil destruction, and the depletion of many nonrenewable resources.

Fundamental Innovations

A fundamental innovation, as we saw in Chapter 3, can increase the rate of innovation in one of two ways. It may involve a principle that is applicable to a great number of different areas. Or it may alter some facet of societal life so drastically that change in many other areas becomes either possible or essential. The Industrial Revolution has produced a tremendous number of fundamental innovations, probably far more than those of all the earlier historical eras combined. Some of those that occurred early in the industrial era, including innovations in energy production, transportation, and communications, continue to have an impact on the rate of change today. Technological breakthroughs in agriculture, sanitation, and preventive medicine (e.g., immunology) have also had drastic repercussions—these, in fact, are the fundamental innovations responsible for the current size of world population, and its pressures for further innovation. More recently, space technology has produced innovations with important applicability in many other areas. And nuclear technology has obvious and enormous potential for further change—a frightening one when applied to warfare, but hopefully a benign one in other areas (e.g., medicine and electric power).

Fundamental innovations in two very dissimilar areas are of particular concern to ecological-evolutionary theorists, however, because they have an enormous potential for influencing both the rate and the kind of innovation and change the world system will experience in the years ahead. One of these areas is birth control, the other is information handling.

Birth Control Few innovations of the industrial era have as great a potential for altering the conditions of human life as those in the area of birth control. After fundamental innovations in agriculture, sanitation, and medicine drastically lowered the death rate, not only in industrial societies but in many others throughout the world, population size took an enormous leap. As a consequence, the gains in living standards that could have accompanied technological advance have been largely eradicated in most societies by the sheer increase in their numbers. The result is a situation much like the one that prevailed in the agrarian era: masses of people who are hungry, ill, poorly housed, and illiterate. Life at this level is no more conducive to innovation and advance today than it was in the past.

The only contemporary societies in which the benefits of the new technology have significantly outrun growth in population size are those that have adopted the new methods of birth control. Although some drop in their birthrates would probably have been achieved by industrial societies with only traditional birth control techniques, their population growth would never have dropped to the present level without the new, safer, more dependable, and more widely accepted methods of contraception and abortion. The resulting high standards of living in such societies mean that far more people are healthy, educated, and highly motivated to participate fully in the life of society. And such individuals bring with them their own contributions to innovation and change.

Information Handling   As we noted in the discussion of the fourth phase of the Industrial Revolution, one of the most fundamental of all innovations involves humanity's burgeoning ability to handle information. The other major innovations in this area were the development of written symbol systems beginning in the fourth millennium B.C. and the printing press in the sixteenth century A.D.; both are still contributing to social and cultural change throughout the world system. The new computer and other electronic technologies will undoubtedly also have an impact on societal change and development for centuries, even millennia, to come.

For all the reasons we have identified, the revolutionary process of change that began in eighteenth-century Europe has not only continued but steadily gained momentum with every passing decade. It has so radically transformed some societies that they bear little resemblance to the agrarian societies from which they so recently evolved, and it has greatly altered numerous others.

In the next four chapters, we will examine in detail the long-term consequences of the continuing Industrial Revolution for these societies. Then, in the final chapter, we will consider what further changes seem likely in the decades ahead. For that revolution will continue into the future—unless, of course, humanity's remarkable new technological capabilities bring the great drama of sociocultural evolution to a premature and tragic conclusion.

CHAPTER 10

Industrial Societies: I

There are nearly thirty industrial societies in the world today. The majority of them are in Europe, where all societies are industrialized with the exception of Albania, Portugal, Yugoslavia, and possibly Bulgaria. The other industrial societies are the English-speaking democracies overseas (Australia, Canada, New Zealand, and the United States), Japan, Iceland, Israel, and possibly Venezuela. Some of these societies have barely crossed the threshold of industrialization and still have many of the characteristics of preindustrial societies. For this reason, our primary concern in the next three chapters will be with those societies that have moved well beyond this threshold and therefore provide the clearest picture of what industrialization means for a society.

The Informational Base

The same kinds of cultural information that are most important in shaping the patterns of life in other human societies are most important in industrial societies as well. First, there is technological information, which defines the "limits of the possible" for a society, and the costs of the various alternatives within those limits. Because the technological bases of all advanced industrial societies are fairly similar, these limits and cost calculations are much the same in all of them, leading to important similarities in various aspects of

Activity	Number of Man-Hours Required			Percentage Reduction in Man-Hour Requirements
	1800	1910–1917	1977	
Production of 100 bushels of wheat	373	106	9	97.6
Production of 100 bushels of corn	344	135	4	98.8
Production of a bale of cotton	601	276	10	98.3
Production of 1000 pounds of milk	n.a.*	38	4	89.5
Production of 1000 pounds of beef	n.a.*	46	14	69.6
Production of 1000 pounds of chickens	n.a.*	95	2	97.9

Sources: U.S. Department of Commerce, *Historical Statistics of the United States: Colonial Times to 1970*, pp. 500–501, and U.S. Department of Commerce, *Statistical Abstract of the United States, 1979*, table 1223.
* Not ascertained.

societal life. Second, there is ideological information, the basic system of beliefs and values that guides a society or its leaders in selecting from among the viable alternatives. Because there are certain fundamental differences in their ideologies, advanced industrial societies differ from one another in a number of important ways. Our discussions will cover both the similarities and the differences.

Technology

The best way to appreciate the dramatic difference between an agrarian society and an industrial one is to look at some of the measurable changes that have occurred as a result of the shift from the older technology to the new. There is no better place to begin than with *agricultural productivity,* on which everything else ultimately depends.

As Table 10.1 shows, the industrialization of agriculture has had a revolutionary impact on the production of foods and fibers, making it possible to produce a given quantity of grain, fiber, milk, or meat with only a tiny fraction of the workers required with agrarian technology.* The labor used to

---

*In this discussion, we will draw heavily on data from the United States because of the excellent statistical materials that make it possible to trace trends well back into the nineteenth century.

produce a given quantity of wheat, corn, cotton, and chicken has been cut approximately 98 per cent. In the case of milk and beef, the reductions have been somewhat less, but still dramatic. Because of these advances in agricultural technology, tens of millions of people who would otherwise be required on farms are free to engage in other kinds of economic activities. As a result, the percentage of farmers and farm workers in the American labor force dropped from 72 per cent in 1820 to less than 3 per cent today.[1]

The chief factor responsible for this remarkable trend has been the harnessing of new energy sources. In agrarian societies, people and work animals were the chief sources of the energy used in all forms of physical labor: pushing, pulling, digging, lifting, and cutting. Their efforts were supplemented to some extent by wind power and waterpower. As recently as 1850, these four sources still supplied over 87 per cent of the energy used in physical labor in the United States. Today, they account for less than 1 per cent.[2] In their stead, industrial societies use the energy of coal, petroleum, natural gas, hydroelectric power, and nuclear power. Except for coal, these sources were still

FIGURE 10.1   The key factor responsible for the revolutionary changes in modern industrial societies is their ability to harness enormous amounts of energy. Off-shore oil rig.

untapped in 1850, and even coal had not been used as a substitute for physical labor until the invention of the steam engine in the eighteenth century.

Not only have energy sources changed, but the quantities used have multiplied enormously. In 1850, all the prime movers in the United States (i.e., human bodies, work animals, steam engines in factories, sailing ships, etc.) had a capacity of less than 10 million horsepower; by 1980 this had risen to nearly 30 *billion*—a 300-fold increase in per capita terms in only a little more than a century.[3]

This remarkable jump in the production and consumption of energy was closely linked with increases in the production and consumption of a wide variety of other raw materials. Consider iron and steel, for example: British production rose nearly 7,000-fold between 1750 and 1970,[4] while American production increased 12,000-fold between 1820 and 1974.[5]

Equally dramatic growth is evident in the production and consumption of many other raw materials. In one recent year, the United States produced 4.9 tons of stone for every man, woman, and child in the population, 4.6 tons of sand and gravel, 3.2 tons of coal, 2.4 tons of crude petroleum, 900 pounds of iron ore, 780 pounds of cement, 575 pounds of clay, 440 pounds of salt, 430 pounds of phosphate rock, 220 pounds of uranium ore, 200 pounds of lime, 115 pounds of gypsum, and 85 pounds of sulfur, to cite but a few items.[6] Altogether, mineral production equals 17 tons per person per year.

Change in the gross national product of a society, corrected for the effects of inflation, is probably the best simple measure we have of the magnitude of

FIGURE 10.2 The Krupp steel works at Rheinhausen, Germany, operates twenty-four hours a day, producing 2 million tons of steel a year.

TABLE 10.2 Trends in the Subject Matter of Books Published in the United States, 1880–1975 (in percentages)

Subject Matter	1880	1975
Technology, natural science, and social science	10.5	28.5
Religion	11.5	4.5
All other areas, including fiction and poetry	78.0	67.0

Source: Adapted from Christopher Sterling and Timothy Haight, *The Mass Media: Aspen Institute Guide to Communication Industry Trends* (New York: Praeger, 1978), tables 510 A and B.

the technological advance brought about by industrialization.* It tells us the extent to which the changes in technology have enhanced the society's ability to produce goods and services.

When we compare American society's GNP in 1878 (the first year for which reliable data are available) with current figures, we find that there has been a *fortyfold* increase.[7] As striking as this figure is, it is considerably smaller than the British figure, which shows a *ninetyfold* increase since 1801.[8] As these figures demonstrate, the technologies of advanced industrial societies are far more powerful than the technologies of even the most advanced agrarian societies of the past. Small wonder that such a change has been accompanied by revolutionary changes throughout the sociocultural system!

Ideology

During the last five centuries, the bounds of human knowledge have expanded enormously. The voyages of exploration that began in the fifteenth century gave humans their first accurate picture of the earth as a whole. Astronomers of the sixteenth and seventeenth centuries did the same for the solar system. More recently, science has given us a vision of a universe of infinite complexity, whose age must be measured in billions of years and whose size can be expressed only in billions of light-years. Finally, in the last hundred years, the social sciences have begun the task of demythologizing the social order, challenging ancient theories about the nature of humanity and subjecting virtually every aspect of human life to systematic scrutiny.

Theistic Religions Not surprisingly, this flood of new information about ourselves and the world we live in has shaken and unsettled many traditional beliefs, and the institutional systems based on them. This is most evident in the

*Change in per capita GNP is the more appropriate measure when comparing societies that vary greatly in size, such as China and Uganda. This is why we used that measure in Table 9.3 (page 256). When comparing the same society at two different times, however, simple GNP may be preferable, especially when our concern is to identify the magnitude of change in its total capacity to produce goods and services.

area of theistic religion. The thought forms of all the great historic faiths—Judaism, Christianity, Islam, Hinduism, Buddhism, and Confucianism—bear the imprint of the agrarian era during which they evolved. But beliefs about the natural world and the social order that were "self-evident" to members of agrarian societies often appear alien and inadequate to members of industrial societies. This has created an acute theological crisis for all theistic faiths in industrial societies. Their intellectual leaders have, in many cases, tried to translate the most important elements of their traditions into modern terms, while steering a course between irrelevant orthodoxy and heretical innovation. The turmoil within the Roman Catholic Church since Vatican Council II is but the latest in a series of intellectual crises that began with the theories of Copernicus and the research of Galileo.

While the majority of people in most industrial societies still profess a belief in God, fewer of them accept the fundamental teachings of the historic faiths (e.g., belief in a life after death) or consider their religious beliefs to be an important part of their lives (see Table 10.3). As the traditional sources of religious authority have come more and more into question, religion has become more privatized and individualized. There has also been a great proliferation of new sects and cults of many kinds, reflecting the growing spirit of neophilia. One of the most important consequences of these trends has been the gradual elimination of ties between governments and state churches, religious groups that were supported by the elite during the agrarian era and that taught, in return, that the state and its officials should be obeyed as servants of God. While some industrial societies (e.g., Britain, Sweden) still have an officially recognized state church, their governments now provide minimal support for them, and it is probably only a matter of time until the relationship is dissolved.

The New Secular Ideologies Beginning in seventeenth- and eighteenth-century Europe, a number of new ideologies appeared in which the theistic element was substantially reduced or totally eliminated. While some of these

TABLE 10.3 Religious Beliefs in Fourteen Industrial Societies, in Percentages

Society	Belief in "God or Universal Spirit"	Belief in Life after Death	Religious Beliefs "Very Important"
United States	94	69	56
Canada	89	54	36
Italy	88	46	36
Australia	80	48	25
Belgium, Netherlands	78	48	26
United Kingdom	76	43	23
France	72	39	22
West Germany	72	33	17
Sweden, Norway, Denmark, Finland	65	35	17
Japan	38	18	12

Source: Gallup Poll report, Sept. 9, 1976.

newer ideologies quickly died out (e.g., Deism and various cults that arose in France at the time of the Revolution), several of them not only survived but went on to become the dominant faith of the political elite in one or more industrial societies. The most important of these new faiths are capitalism, democratic socialism, revolutionary socialism, democracy, and nationalism.

The intellectual father of modern capitalism was Adam Smith, a Scottish professor of moral philosophy who combined a keen analytical mind with a crusading nature.[9] In his most influential work, a book published in 1776 and entitled *An Inquiry into the Nature and Causes of the Wealth of Nations*, Smith made a powerful case for the thesis that the intervention of government into a society's economic life will only retard its growth and development. The only useful function of government in the economic sphere, according to Smith, is to enforce contracts that individuals enter into of their own free will. Anything more than this is harmful. Smith backed up his argument with an impressive analysis designed to show that the law of supply and demand, operating in a truly free market situation, would ensure that "the private interests and passions of men" are led in the direction "most agreeable to the interest of the whole society."[10] It would be a self-regulating system, but it would function, said Smith, as though an "invisible hand" were at work, ensuring the best possible outcome.

Smith's work laid the foundation for the emerging academic discipline of modern economics. More important than that, however, his basic beliefs

FIGURE 10.3   Adam Smith.

about the harm done by governmental intervention in the economy became the basis of a powerful new ideology that for 200 years has exercised a profound influence on societies around the globe. Above all, it has provided moral justification for governmental policies that minimize public control of businessmen and business enterprises. In societies where capitalism is the dominant ideology, the term "free enterprise" has become a sacred symbol that is often invoked with considerable success to manipulate public opinion. As we will see later, the realities of contemporary capitalism are strikingly different from the ideals proclaimed by the ideology, which is true, of course, of every ideology from Christianity to socialism.

The second important new ideology of the industrial era is socialism. While its underlying principle has been applied in many simpler societies for thousands of years, the modern concept dates from the nineteenth century and was an explicit response to, and reaction against, the realities of capitalism. Socialists argued that the basic economic resources of a society should be the common property of all its members, and used for the benefit of all. Where proponents of capitalism praised free enterprise for the growth in productivity it generated, socialists attacked it for its harsh working conditions, its low wages and economic inequality, its unemployment, its child labor, its boom and bust cycles, and its alienating and exploitative character. Where capitalists advocated the private ownership of the means of production, socialists favored public ownership. Where capitalists argued for economic inequality to provide incentives for people to work productively, socialists insisted that a more egalitarian distribution would achieve the same result.

Since early in its history, the socialist movement has been split into a variety of warring sects that have often fought more with one another than with the advocates of capitalism and other ideologies.[11] In the long run, however, the most important split has been the one between *democratic socialism* and *revolutionary socialism*.

Democratic socialism, as its name implies, believes that socialist principles have an inherent appeal to the vast majority of people. Its adherents therefore maintain that, in democratic societies, socialist governments should seek to achieve power through democratic means, and that, after coming to power, they should allow opposing political parties to compete freely for the support of the electorate and to return to power any time they can secure it. Democratic socialists believe that any other policy defeats one of socialism's fundamental aims: to maximize the freedom of individuals. They argue that the practice of political democracy is as essential to true socialism as public ownership of the means of production, and that failure to practice political democracy subverts the very nature of socialism.

During the twentieth century, parties adhering to these principles (e.g., the Labour Party in Britain, the Social Democratic Party in Germany, the Socialist Party in France) have developed large followings, and in many cases they have been successful in electing governments. Because of the continuing appeal of capitalist principles, however, none of them has attempted to carry out a thoroughgoing program of abolishing private ownership of the means of production. While these parties have taken some steps in that direction (i.e., they have nationalized some industries), the major thrust of their policies has become the creation of a *welfare state*. In other words, they have used the powers of government to tax the profits of privately owned enterprises in order to fund health, educational, and social service programs that benefit the masses of citizens who do not own any part of the means of production. This allows everyone to share in the benefits of the productive system without totally abolishing private ownership.

In contrast, the other major faction within the socialist movement has denied the possibility of achieving socialism through peaceful, democratic means, even in democratic societies. In their view, socialism can be established only by the forcible overthrow of the bourgeoisie (i.e., the capitalist class) and the expropriation of its properties.

The spiritual father of modern revolutionary socialism is Karl Marx, whose writings and political activities in the nineteenth century laid the foundation for the Communist parties of the twentieth. In contemporary societies controlled by his followers, he occupies an honored status not unlike that accorded the prophet Muhammad in Islamic societies. His writings are

FIGURE 10.4   Karl Marx.

constantly cited by the party elite to justify their policies, and pictures and statues of him are widespread in public places.*

Marxist socialism is a far more comprehensive ideology than either capitalism or democratic socialism. Where these other ideologies allow people to make their own choices in most areas of their lives, Marxism imposes standards on everything from politics and economics to art and religion. In this respect, Marxism is closer to medieval Catholicism than to capitalism or democratic socialism. Maurice Duverger, a French social scientist, summarized this aspect of Marxist socialism when he wrote:

> The party not only provides [the militant Communist] with organization for all his material activities, more important still it gives him a general organization of ideas, a systematic explanation of the universe. Marxism is not only a political doctrine, but a complete philosophy, a way of thinking, a spiritual cosmogony. All isolated facts in all spheres find their place in it and the reason for all their existence. It explains equally well the structure and evolution of the state, the changes in living creatures, the appearance of man on the earth, religious feelings, sexual behavior, and the development of the arts and sciences. And the explanation can be brought within the reach of the masses as well as being understood by the learned and by educated people. This philosophy can easily be made into a catechism without too serious a deformation. In this way the human spirit's need for fundamental unity can be satisfied.[12]

Revolutionary socialism makes broad claims on the lives not only of its adherents but of all who come under its power. Despite its professed aim of maximizing human freedom, it has become the most authoritarian of all the major current ideologies. The explanation of this paradox seems to lie in its adherents' belief that socialism can be established and sustained only by means of a quasi-military organization.

Marx believed that this kind of organization was required to overthrow capitalism, but he did not anticipate how difficult it would be for a society to free itself from authoritarian rule once that was accomplished. He wrote, in passing, that a "dictatorship of the proletariat" would be necessary after a successful revolution, but he thought of this as a brief period during the transition from capitalism to socialism.[13] Lenin, his most famous disciple, picked up this phrase and expanded on it, giving it a more precise meaning. For him, it meant, in effect, dictatorship by the Communist Party elite.[14] Today, more than sixty years after the Russian Revolution and more than twenty years after the Chinese and Cuban revolutions, authoritarian rule by the Party elite seems to have become as integral a part of revolutionary socialism as state ownership of the means of production.

Democracy, the fourth of the new ideologies, is closely linked to the first three. Democratic socialism, as we have seen, has an explicit commitment to a democratic polity. Revolutionary socialism, too, has a theoretical commitment to democracy, but qualifies it by belief in the need for a "dictatorship of

---

*Islamic societies do *not* display pictures or statues of the prophet, since public display of pictures or images portraying the human form are forbidden.

the proletariat" for an unspecified period of time. Capitalism, in its classical statement by Adam Smith in the eighteenth century, does not address the question of *where* political power should reside—which is the central concern of democratic ideology—but simply advocates the principle of *limited* government. Smith's lack of attention to the subject is hardly surprising, since democracy had not yet become a reality in any advanced society in his day. In the nineteenth and twentieth centuries, however, such a close affinity developed between capitalism and democracy that capitalist societies were generally the first to become democratic.

The central tenet of democratic ideology is the assertion that the powers of government are derived from the members of the society and the government is therefore answerable to them for its actions. This doctrine stands in sharp conflict with the older doctrine that the king or emperor is sovereign and accountable only to God for his actions. The concept of popular sovereignty is an old one, but it was not adopted as a constitutional principle in any advanced society until after the American and French revolutions late in the eighteenth century and, even then, the principle was by no means fully implemented. The great majority of the adult population of the United States, for example, was excluded from even such minimal participation as voting in elections. To vote, one had to be male and a property holder. This excluded not only all women and virtually all blacks, but the great majority of white men. Democracy as we think of it today is essentially a twentieth-century phenomenon.

Ideally, democracy implies the participation of all adults in all of the decisions made in their society that affect them. Most people, however, recognize the practical impossibility of this ideal in societies that have millions of members. Thus, modern advocates of democratic government generally support the concept of *representative democracy*, a system in which the larger population chooses individuals to represent them in the actual process of decision making.

Like capitalism and socialism, democracy has become not only a widely accepted ideology but a widely implemented one as well. Three-quarters of the nearly thirty industrial societies in the world today are representative democracies with contested, secret-ballot elections. Even the remaining quarter of industrial societies, the Marxist societies of Eastern Europe, claim to be democratic and maintain the outward forms of representative democracy.

The fifth important new ideology of the industrial era is nationalism.[15] As with socialism and capitalism, some of its elements existed long ago: group loyalty and tribalism are certainly not new. During the agrarian era, however, the peasant masses, who made up 80 per cent or more of the population, had little interest in politics beyond the village level. The rise and fall of empires were of no consequence to them—unless, of course, they were drawn into the struggle against their will. This was a natural consequence of the theory which viewed the state as the private property of the sovereign.

With industrialization, the situation gradually changed. Expanded educational systems and the mass media, combined with urbanization, shortened workweeks, and an improved standard of living, brought politics within the sphere of concern of the average citizen. With this came a heightened sense of personal identification with the nation-state, especially in times of international tensions and conflict. Nationalism has been an especially potent ideology in colonial territories ever since the American Revolution, and it is important today in many societies of the Third World that have recently escaped colonial control. It has also become a potent force among ethnic and religious minorities in many industrial societies, such as the French in Canada, the Irish in Ulster, the Lapps in Sweden, and the Basques in Spain. Black nationalism in the United States is a modified form of nationalist ideology: although it does not seek political autonomy, it stresses the importance of racial unity in political efforts and the maintenance of separate black organizations and institutions.

In many societies in recent decades, nationalism has been combined with other ideologies. The Nazi (literally, National Socialist) regime in Germany prior to World War II is a classic example. In American society, nationalism of a far more temperate variety is often linked to Christianity and capitalism to form what some have called this nation's "civil religion."[16]

Despite their many differences, the new ideologies of the industrial era all have one thing in common: *they are predicated on the belief that humans can, to a substantial degree, shape and control the development of their societies.* This is in sharp contrast to the ideologies that originated in preindustrial societies. They asserted that events in human life depended on forces beyond human control—fate, destiny, God, the gods—and taught that the best way to appease those forces was through magic, ritual, and adherence to tradition. Some ideologies held that every development in societal life, from the power wielded by its ruler to the debasement of his lowliest subject, was ordained by a higher power, and that mere mortals had no right to try to change conditions. This was as much the belief of the masses of common people as it was of those who ruled them.

The members of modern societies are not so passive. New information in areas from science to history have improved their understanding of their own nature and of the world they inhabit, while new technological information has broadened their capacity to adapt to that world. The result has been a new perception of humanity's potential for shaping its own future. This basic belief underlies all of the new ideologies of the industrial era, and the members of modern societies have come to rely increasingly on these ideologies, and less and less on traditional ones, in their efforts to shape their own lives and the life of society as a whole.

Despite this basic similarity, there are, as we have seen, some fundamental differences between these new ideologies. More important from the standpoint of ecological-evolutionary theory, ideological variations among societies at the same level of development are of greater significance today than at any time in human history. For as technology has expanded the limits of the possible and has increased the viable alternatives of industrial societies, *the ideologies that guide them in choosing among those alternatives have become a source of major intratype variation—and thus a significant factor in the process of intersocietal selection.*

Population

Growth in Size of Societies

Industrialization has led to a substantial increase in the size of most human societies since the beginning of the industrial era. Population growth in the most industrialized societies, however, has not been nearly as great as their technological advances and gains in productivity would lead one to expect. For example, England and Wales had a population of approximately nine million at the start of the nineteenth century, and their current population is about fifty million.[17] While this fivefold to sixfold increase is impressive when compared to rates of population growth in preindustrial eras, it falls far short of the ninetyfold increase in Britain's gross national product during that same period of time. The same thing is true of other societies that have industrialized, with the exception of the United States, Canada, Australia, and other former frontier societies that entered the industrial era with abnormally small populations for their geographical size.

Declining Birthrates and Death Rates: Shift to a New Equilibrium

The reason for the surprisingly low rate of population growth in industrial societies is their success in controlling their birthrates. Throughout most of human history, birthrates and death rates were nearly equal, partly as a result of the widespread practice of abortion and infanticide in societies of every type. Then, during the late agrarian era this historic balance began to break down in the advanced agrarian societies of Western Europe, because technological advances lowered the death rate *before* comparable improvements were made in birth control technology, and too rapidly to be offset by changing norms (e.g., greater practice of infanticide).[18]

The demographic equilibrium did not begin to be restored until technological advance had achieved two things. The first, of course, was a series of improvements in birth control technology. This began with the vulcanization of rubber in 1844 (permitting its use in condoms) and ultimately produced a wide variety of birth control methods that are far safer and more reliable than those of the past.

The second effect that technological advance had in this area was to alter dramatically the perception of the economic value of children. This change has been as important in lowering the birthrate as new contraceptive techniques and safer abortion, for without a change in attitudes and values, they would not have been widely accepted. The cause of this ideological shift was the rise of the new technologically advanced industries that developed during the last century, and which gradually eliminated the need for child labor. This meant that children had become an economic liability to their parents rather than an economic asset. This effect was intensified by the growing need in industrial societies for a better-educated labor force, which caused children to remain financially dependent for increasing longer periods of time, even into their adult years.

As a consequence of these developments in technology, birthrates have been drastically reduced in all industrial societies from the traditional rate of 40 or more per 1,000 population per year in the typical horticultural or agrarian society of the past. As Table 10.4 reveals, many of them now have rates of only 10 to 15. Modern techniques of birth control are now used by the majority of the members of virtually all industrial societies during potential childbearing years. For example, a recent survey of American married women between the ages of 15 and 44 revealed that 68 per cent were using some method of contraception.[19] Of this number, about one-third used the pill (most popular among younger women); over a quarter of the women or their husbands had been sterilized (more common among older couples); and the remainder used a variety of other methods. When contraceptive techniques fail, women in industrial societies increasingly turn to abortion. In the United States, for example, there were 400 legal abortions for every 1,000 live births in 1977, and similar patterns are reported in other industrial societies.[20]

From current evidence, it appears that modern industrial societies are moving toward a new equilibrium of births and deaths in the neighborhood of 12 to 13 of each per 1,000 population per year. Such an equilibrium is not, of course, inevitable. There is nothing to prevent the members of these societies from limiting births to the point where their populations actually become smaller. On the other hand, they may permit so much immigration from nonindustrial societies (a trend apparent not only in the United States but in much of Western Europe, Canada, and Australia) that growth will be unavoidable. Finally, either economic pressures (e.g., the need for a labor force capable of supporting a large population of retired people) or political considerations (e.g., the need for military manpower) could conceivably induce industrial societies to increase their birthrates again. Whatever the outcome, one of the striking demographic features of modern societies is their ability to control their rates of reproduction.

TABLE 10.4   Crude Birthrates for Selected Industrial Societies

Society	Crude Birthrate*	Society	Crude Birthrate*
West Germany	9	Japan	15
Austria	11	Australia	16
Sweden	11	Hungary	16
United Kingdom	12	New Zealand	17
Italy	13	Czechoslovakia	18
East Germany	14	U.S.S.R.	18
France	14	Poland	19
United States	15	Ireland	21
Canada	15	Israel	25

Source: United Nations, *Population and Vital Statistics Report*, series A, vol. 32, no. 1 (January 1980).
*Live births per 1,000 population per year.

TABLE 10.5   The World's Largest Cities, from 3000 B.C. to 1970 A.D.

Date	City	Population*	Date	City	Population*
3000 B.C.	Memphis	40,000	620 A.D.	Constantinople	500,000
2000 B.C.	Memphis	100,000	900 A.D.	Baghdad	900,000
1360 B.C.	Thebes	100,000	1300 A.D.	Hangchow	430,000
650 B.C.	Nineveh	120,000	1500 A.D.	Peking	670,000
430 B.C.	Babylon	250,000	1700 A.D.	Constantinople	700,000
200 B.C.	Patna	350,000	1800 A.D.	Peking	1,100,000
100 A.D.	Rome	650,000	1900 A.D.	London	6,480,000
360 A.D.	Constantinople	350,000	1970 A.D.	New York	16,200,000

Sources: Tertius Chandler and Gerald Fox, *300 Years of Urban Growth* (New York: Academic Press, 1974), pp. 300–341 and 362–363, and *World Almanac, 1978*, p. 602.
*Population includes suburbs.

Population Distribution: The Growth of Urban Populations

Another revolutionary demographic change has been the massive shift of population from rural areas to cities and towns. Even in the most advanced agrarian societies, the limitations of agricultural technology required that 90 to 95 per cent of the population live in rural areas, where the basic raw materials were produced. Since urban communities were almost totally dependent on the surplus that could be extracted from the peasantry, they could never grow beyond 5 to 10 per cent of the population.

The advances in agriculture that began in the eighteenth century and became far more rapid and potent in the nineteenth and twentieth destroyed this historic constraint on urban growth. Thanks to the new technology, farms required fewer workers. Simultaneously, the new system of industrial production, with its need for large concentrations of workers, stimulated the growth of cities and towns. Nearly 70 per cent of the populations of Britain and the

FIGURE 10.5   Cities in industrial societies are much larger than cities of the preindustrial era. The population of greater New York is approximately 16 million.

United States now live in cities of 100,000 or more, and in a number of societies, 80 per cent or more live in urban areas.

Not surprisingly, cities in industrial societies are much larger than cities of the past. In agrarian societies, the capitals of a few great empires appear to have had populations of about a million (see Table 10.5). Today, less than two centuries later, there are more than seventy urban areas with populations of 2 million or more, and the largest of them, New York and its urban satellites, has a total population of more than 16 million.[21]

The Economy

A society's economic system is, in effect, the set of answers it has developed to the basic questions of production and distribution. What kinds of goods and services will be produced? In what quantities? For whose benefit? And, above all, who makes the basic decisions about these matters?

The way these questions are answered by an industrial society reflects the ideology of its political elite, modified to some extent by past experience. Capitalism and socialism, both revolutionary and democratic, address themselves to the full range of economic questions: ownership and control of the means of production, use of the economic surplus, mechanisms to determine the quantities and prices of various goods and services, and more. Thus, as we examine the economic institutions of industrial societies, we will find that the most important differences among them are reflections of the differences in these new secular ideologies.

Before we consider the differences in the economies of Marxist and capitalist societies, however, we must see what they have in common. For a number of very basic economic characteristics are shared by *all* industrial societies, regardless of whether their political elites are capitalists, democratic socialists, or revolutionary socialists.

Rise in Productivity and the Standard of Living

The most striking characteristic of the economies of industrial societies is their remarkable productivity. As we noted earlier, Britain's gross national product has grown approximately ninetyfold since 1801, and that of the United States about fortyfold since 1878. All other fully industrialized societies have experienced comparable growth. Because this increase in productivity has not been consumed by population growth, there has also been an enormous increase in the size of the economic surplus in every industrial society.

In agrarian societies, this new surplus would have been absorbed almost entirely by a small minority of the population. In industrial societies, while it is by no means evenly distributed, the surplus is spread far more widely among the members.[22] In other words, the economic surplus has gone primarily to improve the standard of living for the great majority of people who live in these societies. Per capita income in Great Britain is approximately sixteen times

PRISON PROVES "BEST HOME"

HAGERSTOWN, Md.—Ramchandra Gnanu Malekar, Maryland Correctional Training Center inmate 130755, leaned back in his chair and raised both feet to display his shoes. "Look here," he said in wonder. "I have never seen shoes like this kind."

They were fairly ordinary two-tone shoes, but Malekar, who grew up in a village outside Bombay where sandals were considered something of a luxury, found them astonishing. "And I have undershirts," he said, unbuttoning far enough to show off a small patch of silky blue material. "Nylon, poplin, cotton. I have never in my whole life had such clothes in my house."

What Malekar refers to as "my house" now is a large Maryland jail facility, where the young Indian citizen is serving a six-year sentence for manslaughter. He was convicted in July, 1974, of strangling Lalita Khambadkone, the 45-year-old-woman who brought Malekar from Bombay to Potomac to work as a manservant.

Last Friday, almost two years to the day after the slaying, Malekar sat in the brightly lit visiting center of the Hagerstown jail and described it as the finest home he has ever known. He has a bed for the first time in his life, he said. He eats off the same plates as the other inmates. Though he had been "so emaciated that a child could have pushed him," as a woman who saw Malekar in January, 1974, described him, he has now developed into a robust young man with muscular upper arms that he boasts are 13 inches around.

"Fried chicken," he said delightedly, when asked what foods were new to him. "French toast, scrambled egg, pancake, Spanish rice, Chinese rice, chicken stew, macaroni, sweet potato, mashed potato."

It is all very different from the poverty-ridden village where Malekar grew up. Prison in the United States is far better than the life he knew in India.

Source: *The Washington Post*, January 19, 1976. Quoted by permission.

what it was in 1801, and in the United States, it is nine times greater than in 1878.

That these figures reflect real gains in the living standards of the masses becomes apparent when we consider some of the basic characteristics of the lifestyle of the average member of an industrial society today—keeping in mind the situations of the typical agrarian peasant (pages 189–193) and of the workers during the early stages of industrialization (pages 257–260). To begin with, the vast majority of the members of every industrial society have a food supply that is larger, far more dependable (i.e., less subject to acute shortages), and of higher quality and greater variety than in any agrarian society of the past. They live in superior housing, with an indoor water supply, plumbing, electricity, usually central heating, and often air conditioning in warmer climates. The majority of their homes and apartments are equipped with furnishings and appliances that are far more than adequate for health and comfort, and some of them would arouse envy in the elites of agrarian societies. Widespread educational opportunities are available to them, and so is vastly improved health care. Modern transportation and communication systems broaden and enrich their lives and provide them with entertainment and relief from boredom. And countless other goods and services too numerous to catalog, and unheard of in agrarian societies, are also available to the great majority of people in every industrial society.

This is not meant to suggest that such people have no problems or that life in industrial societies does not have its deficiencies and worse: we will discuss the negative aspect of industrial societies in Chapter 12. But it is not possible to deny that industrialization has meant a remarkable improvement in the standards of living for the average individual compared with his or her counterpart in agrarian or industrializing societies. Relative to the peasants of the agrarian era, modern industrial workers live a life of unbelievable affluence and abundance. And there are very few people in these societies whose conditions come near to approximating those of the expendables of agrarian societies. (See "Prison Proves 'Best Home'"). Even those who are forced to depend on public welfare do far better than that.

The Shift from Labor-Intensive to Capital-Intensive Industries

The ultimate basis of the enormous productivity and affluence of modern industrial societies is their fantastic store of technological information. But most of this information is useless until it has been *converted into capital goods*. Without the complex machines, factories, transportation facilities, power plants, and other capital goods that are central to production in an industrial society, the output of its workers would be little different from that of workers in agrarian societies.

We can begin to recognize the importance of capital goods when we compare two contemporary industries, one capital-intensive and the other labor-intensive. The petroleum industry is a classic example of the former, with expensive, highly automated machinery and a small labor force; the fast-food industry, utilizing simpler and less expensive machines, is far more labor-intensive. Standard Oil of California, for example, recently reported average annual sales of more than $750,000 *per employee,* while the sales of McDonald's hamburger chain amounted to only $17,400 per employee per year.[23]

One of the causes of the tremendous growth in per capita GNP in industrial societies has been the massive migration of workers out of traditional subsistence agriculture and into capital-intensive industry during the last 150 years. In traditional subsistence agriculture, farmers raised cash crops only to the extent required to pay taxes, rent, and interest on loans, and to enable them to buy the simple tools and other necessities they could not produce themselves. Thus, only a small fraction of their total productivity became a part of the larger economy. As these farmers abandoned their farms and entered the urban labor force, their economic contribution increased substantially. Since about 80 per cent of the population of the typical agrarian society were food producers, in contrast to a tiny minority—in some cases less than 5 per cent—in industrial societies, the impact of that shift is obvious.

FIGURE 10.6   Agriculture, like urban industry, has become capital-intensive: harvesting wheat in North Dakota.

Today, however, that flow has ended (and with it a major boost to economic growth). Few farmers still practice subsistence agriculture in most industrial societies, and the traditional family farm has been replaced by large agri-enterprises that, like urban industry, are capital-intensive.[24]

To appreciate the changes that have occurred in farming, one need only visit an enterprise like First Colony Farms, a 375,000-acre, $300 million business in northeastern North Carolina.[25] This highly mechanized, capital-intensive industry employs less than 1,000 workers and operates on the same principles that govern other large companies. Its production is primarily grain and livestock, which are sold in national and international markets.

Agricultural operations on this scale are still unusual in western societies, but they are already dominant in most of Eastern Europe. The new technology requires that farming be operated as a business in industrial societies today. A single tractor may cost $150,000, and in the United States it is estimated that the minimum investment in land and capital goods required for a profitable farm in many areas is half a million dollars.[26]

The Changing Labor Force

The Shift from Primary Industries   During the early stages of industrialization there is, as we have seen, an inevitable movement of workers out of the *primary industries*, which are those that produce raw materials. These include

TABLE 10.6 Changing Patterns of Employment in the American Labor Force, 1840 to 1978: Percentages Employed in Primary, Secondary, and Tertiary Industries

Year	Primary Industries	Secondary Industries	Tertiary Industries	Total
1840	69	15	16	100
1870	55	21	24	100
1900	40	28	32	100
1930	23	29	48	100
1960	8	30	62	100
1978	5	29	66	100

Sources: Calculations based on *Historical Statistics of the U.S.: Colonial Times to 1970*, series D152–166; *Statistical Abstract of the U.S., 1979*, table 668.

farming, fishing, mining, and similar activities, which in traditional agrarian societies usually comprised over 80 per cent of the labor force. With industrialization, these people move into *secondary industries*, such as mills and factories, which process the raw materials and turn them into finished products, and into *tertiary industries*, which provide the varied and growing kinds of services found in industrial societies: education, health care, police and fire protection, social services, government, retail trade, and so on. As industrialization proceeds, the initial rapid growth in secondary industries slows down considerably, and tertiary industries become the chief growth sector of the economy.

Table 10.6 shows how striking this process has been in the United States, completely transforming the labor force in 140 years. From a 70 per cent concentration of workers in primary industries, there are now 70 per cent in the tertiary sector, and growth in that area continues at the expense of the number of people in the other two areas. Similar trends are found in every industrial society, although growth of the tertiary sector has been less pronounced in the socialist societies of Eastern Europe.

Declining Self-Employment One by-product of the other economic changes in industrial societies is a decline in the proportion of workers who are self-employed. Throughout most of the advanced agrarian era, merchants, many artisans, and the majority of farmers were self-employed. In the Marxist societies of Eastern Europe, self-employment has been virtually eliminated as a matter of deliberate policy. Even in Poland, which has been more tolerant of private enterprise than most Marxist societies, self-employed workers outside of agriculture were only 1.7 per cent of the total work force in 1975.[27] In the Soviet Union, the percentage is almost certainly lower.

In capitalist societies, despite an official policy that is supportive of self-employment, economic forces have accomplished much the same thing as government actions in Marxist societies. Thus, in the United States only 6.9 per cent of the labor force outside of agriculture is currently self-employed, and this number is dropping steadily.[28]

Growth in Size of Organizations   As opportunities for self-employment have declined, workers in both socialist and capitalist societies find themselves increasingly in the employ of organizations of enormous size. Governments themselves have become the largest employers of all, even in nonsocialist societies. The federal government of the United States currently employs 4.8 million people,[29] while the governments of nine states or municipalities employ over 100,000 each (the largest, New York City, is the employer of more than 300,000).[30] A number of private enterprises have even larger work forces. American Telephone and Telegraph employs more than a million; General Motors, 850,000; Ford Motor Corporation, 500,000; Sears, Roebuck, 425,000; General Electric, 400,000; International Telephone and Telegraph, 370,000; and International Business Machines, 335,000.[31]

Growth in Specialization   Accompanying growth in the size of work organizations and the growing store of information is another trend: increasing specialization. Contemporary industrial societies have an astonishing number of highly specialized occupations. The United States Department of Labor currently lists more than 20,000 different kinds of jobs present in American society.[32] The meat-packing industry illustrates the extremes to which occupational specialization is often carried. Forty-hour-a-week jobs in that industry include:

aitchbone breaker	jowl trimmer
belly opener	leg skinner
bladder trimmer	lung splitter
brain picker	rump sawyer
gland man	side splitter
gut puller	skull grinder
gut sorter	snout puller
head splitter	toe puller

("What does your daddy do, little girl?" "Oh, he's a snout puller at the packing house.")

Greater specialization seems unlikely in most blue-collar occupations. The reason is that extreme specialization of the kind associated with the modern assembly line appears to be counterproductive: workers quickly become bored and this can lead to carelessness, hostility, and even sabotage. In many industries, management has responded by diversifying work activities, thus reversing the trend toward extreme specialization. Indiana Bell Telephone, for example, used to assemble its telephone books in twenty-one steps, each performed by a different clerk. Now, each clerk has responsibility for assembling an entire book, with the result that worker turnover (a sensitive measure of worker morale) has been reduced as much as 50 per cent.[33] Volvo,

FIGURE 10.7   Extreme occupational specialization is characteristic of industrial societies: women processing poultry.

the Swedish automobile manufacturer, developed two experiments to reduce boredom and improve morale: one is a system of job rotation involving work at a variety of highly specialized tasks; the other is a system of teamwork involving groups of three to nine workers who share a common responsibility, choose their own leader, and are paid on the basis of group output.[34] These changes reduced Volvo's annual worker turnover from 40 per cent to about 10 per cent. Other industries are responding to the problem of boredom by replacing increasing numbers of their workers with automated machines. Because this solution not only avoids labor problems but cuts costs, it may become industry's preferred solution in the future.

While the trend toward increasing occupational specialization is apparently waning in blue-collar occupations, it is still growing in many kinds of white-collar jobs. This is especially evident in professional and managerial occupations, where people often seem to derive greater satisfaction from their work when their areas of responsibility and expertise are more narrowly defined. This is because professional and managerial occupations usually involve such complex bodies of information that no one can entirely master them; as a result, frustration is more likely to occur from too little specialization than from too much. Thus, general practitioners in medicine have been largely replaced by a variety of medical specialists, just as general historians in the academic world have been replaced by specialists in such fields as medieval English history and modern German history. In addition, some of the traditional components of most professional and managerial jobs are now being partially performed by machines, and more effectively. This is true, for example, of some kinds of teaching (e.g., foreign-language instruction, elementary math) and medical diagnosis (e.g., CAT-scans, computerized laboratory tests).

The Economies of Non-Marxist Societies

The economic systems of non-Marxist societies differ in some very basic respects from those of Marxist societies. Where revolutionary socialists, or Marxists, are in firm political control, the state owns the means of production and there is a *command economy*.* In non-Marxist societies, in contrast, *private* ownership of the means of production is the dominant pattern, and this was traditionally accompanied by a *market economy*. Today, however, every non-Marxist industrial society has what is best described as a mixed *market-command economy*.

In a command economy, the basic decisions that govern the economic system are made by those who control the government. In a market economy, economic questions are resolved through the interaction of the forces of supply and demand, which reflect the values and desires of all the members of society, *but weighted in proportion to their wealth*. In a mixed market-command economy, both government and the forces of supply and demand have a substantial impact on basic economic decisions.

The Rise of Market Economies   The origins of the modern market system can be traced back to the simple barter systems of prehistoric societies. But the development of a true market economy (i.e., one in which market forces shape the great majority of economic decisions) could not occur until the use of money became widespread and most of the goods and services people value were assigned a monetary value. In addition, the basic economic resources of land, labor, and capital had to be freed from the traditional restraints on their use or transfer. People had to be free to sell ancestral lands when that was profitable; workers had to be free to leave their jobs and take new ones when they could get higher wages or better working conditions; and owners of businesses had to be free to use their capital however they wished. Restraints on economic activity based on family sentiments, religious taboos, social customs, or organizational restrictions (guild restrictions on output, for example, or legal restrictions on the migration of serfs and slaves) had to be substantially reduced. In short, individual economic advantage, as measured in monetary terms, had to become the decisive determinant of economic action.

As we saw in Chapter 9, the discovery of the New World gave a powerful

---

*Yugoslavia, which falls a bit short of our standard for an industrial society, has developed a unique type of economy which some describe as "market socialism," since it combines market economics with state-owned enterprise.

impetus to the first requirement: the great flow of gold and silver led to the emergence of a money economy in Western Europe. At the same time, a series of ideological changes weakened traditional social bonds that tended to immobilize both people and property. These same factors also sparked the Industrial Revolution, and once that was under way and the economy had changed further, the effect tended to be cumulative. Each change stimulated further change; the more resources that came under the control of Western Europe's entrepreneurial class, for example, the better they were able to promote further change.

By the end of the nineteenth century, it looked as if every industrial society would soon have a basically market economy. Industrial societies were coming increasingly under the control of political parties dominated by businessmen committed to the philosophy of laissez-faire capitalism or free enterprise. Following the teachings of Adam Smith, this new governing class argued that the most productive economy, and the most beneficial, was one that was free of governmental restrictions.

Shift toward a Mixed Economy   It was not long, however, before it became evident that the new market economy was not the unmitigated blessing its enthusiasts made it out to be. In the pursuit of profits, businessmen adopted practices that were obviously harmful to others. In an attempt to cut labor costs, many employers fired adult workers and replaced them with children, simultaneously creating adult unemployment and endangering the health and safety of children. Efforts to reduce costs also led to dangerous working conditions and the production of shoddy, even unsafe, merchandise.

Protests soon began to be raised, sometimes by social reformers like Robert Owen, sometimes by poets and novelists like Thomas Hood and Upton Sinclair. Even before the middle of the last century, the British Parliament began enacting legislation to protect society against the extremes of free enterprise. The Factory Acts of 1833 and 1844, the Mines Act of 1842, and the Ten Hour Law of 1847 prohibited the employment of children under the age of nine in textile factories, restricted children under thirteen to six and a half hours' work per day in factories, forbade the employment of women or of boys

FIGURE 10.8   Children working in a British mine in the 19th century: the Mines Act of 1842 prohibited the employment of boys under the age of ten in mines.

under ten in the mines, limited women and young people aged thirteen to eighteen to ten working hours per day, and provided for inspectors to enforce these laws.[35] By 1901, the minimum age for child labor in England was raised to twelve, and in 1908 limitations were finally imposed on the working hours of men. Other legislation forced employers to provide for the safety of their employees in dangerous industries and established the first minimum wage. In Germany, the Old Age and Security Law of 1889 provided for sick leave and for workmen's compensation in the case of injuries sustained on the job.

None of these reforms would have come about, however, without the efforts of workers themselves, which gave rise to *the labor movement*. By the latter part of the eighteenth century, small groups of workers had already begun banding together to negotiate with their employers on wages, hours, and working conditions. During the nineteenth century, this movement had many ups and downs, but by 1900, there were 2 million members of labor unions in Britain and nearly a million each in the United States and Germany.[36]

Before that date, however, another major defect in the market system had become evident. There was a tendency for it to lose its competitive character and evolve in the direction of monopoly. This danger was greatest in industries in which *fixed costs* were a significant part of the total costs. Fixed costs are production costs that do not increase in proportion to the quantity of goods produced. The costs of designing, tooling, and advertising a new model car, for example, are all fixed costs: they are essentially the same whether 5 million cars are produced, or only 1 million. As a result, the company that sells 5 million cars is in a better position to undersell its competitors, or to offer a better product for the same money. Either way, the larger company will tend to win its rivals' customers, further increasing its own advantage.

Table 10.7 illustrates how, in an industry in which fixed costs are

TABLE 10.7   Illustration of How Fixed Costs Contribute to the Growth of Monopoly in a Free Enterprise System

Time Period and Firm	Number of Units Sold	Variable Costs*	Fixed Costs*	Total Costs	Cost per Unit†
Time I:					
Company A	10,000	$10,000	$5,000	$15,000	$1.50
Company B	9,000	9,000	5,000	14,000	1.56
Company C	8,000	8,000	5,000	13,000	1.63
Time II:					
Company A	11,500	11,500	5,000	16,500	1.43
Company B	8,500	8,500	5,000	13,500	1.59
Company C	7,000	7,000	5,000	12,000	1.71
Time III:					
Company A	13,000	13,000	5,000	18,000	1.38
Company B	8,000	8,000	5,000	13,000	1.63
Company C	6,000	6,000	5,000	11,000	1.83

*Variable costs need not be exactly proportional to sales volume, and fixed costs need not be exactly identical for all firms, but they have been shown this way to make the essential principles clearer.
†Cost per unit equals total cost divided by number of units sold.

relatively great compared to variable costs, the company that has the highest volume of sales to begin with will have *a growing competitive advantage*. Note that all three companies spend the same amount, one dollar, for each unit they produce. But fixed costs are the same for every company—$5,000—regardless of how many units it produces. The differences in "cost per unit" are thus due entirely to the influence of fixed costs. Note also that the initial pricing advantage enjoyed by Company A because of its initial high volume of sales enables that company to acquire a growing share of the market, and, with it, a growing ability to undersell its competitors. It is clear from this example that if pure market forces were allowed to operate with no restrictions, smaller competitors would eventually be forced out of business in the many industries in which fixed costs are a significant part of total costs.

In an effort to prevent the growth of monopolies, the United States Congress passed the Sherman Antitrust Act in 1890. Although it has not been vigorously enforced, this Act has served as a deterrent. A number of industries might now be dominated by a single company had not the managers of the leading firms been fearful of the legal consequences. For example, economists have testified before Congress that economies of scale have long made it possible for General Motors to substantially undersell its American competitors. But rather than face antitrust action, GM's managers chose to price their cars competitively, offering, perhaps, a bit more for the money and taking advantage of the situation primarily through higher profits.

The situation in which an industry is dominated not by a single firm but by a very few of them is known as *oligopoly*. This has become common in capitalist societies. Table 10.8 provides some indication of the current situation in the United States. As a rough rule of thumb, economists consider an industry oligopolistic when as few as four companies control 50 per cent or more of production.[37] This standard can be deceptive, however, because degree of national concentration means different things in different industries, depending chiefly on whether the market is local, regional, or national. The

TABLE 10.8 Percentage of Production Accounted for by the Four Largest Companies in Selected Industries in the United States

Industry	Percentage	Industry	Percentage
Motor vehicles	92	Steel mills	48
Cereal preparation	88	Metal office furniture	38
Typewriters	81	Petroleum refining	33
Cigarettes	81	Meat packing	26
Home refrigerators	73	Pharmaceuticals	24
Tires	70	Frozen fruits and vegetables	24
Soap and detergents	70	Fluid milk	22
Aircraft	69	Paints	22
Synthetic rubber	61	Newspapers	16
Phonograph records	58	Soft drinks	13
Distilled liquor	54	Women's dresses	7
Roasted coffee	53	Fur goods	5

Source: U.S. Bureau of the Census, *Census of Manufacturing, 1967* (Washington: 1971), vol. 1, chap. 9, table 5.

newspaper industry in the United States, for example, might appear highly competitive, because according to government statistics the four largest companies produce only 16 per cent of the papers. But a moment's reflection reminds us that most newspapers produce for a local market, and in most communities, the paper or papers are owned by a single person or firm.[38] Thus Table 10.8 *understates* the extent of oligopoly.

Where oligopoly prevails, the law of supply and demand often stops functioning, primarily because collusion between firms is so easy. Collusion can take a variety of forms. A fairly common practice in the construction industry is the rigging of bids, whereby firms get together and decide among themselves who will take which job and then bid accordingly, with the "low" bid set as high as they dare. Price leading, a perfectly legal practice, appears to be standard procedure in several major industries: one firm, usually the largest, sets its prices at a level that ensures profits for all and maximum profits for the larger firms. In this situation, competition is largely restricted to such secondary matters as design and advertising.

Another development that has weakened the role of market forces has been the increase in what is known as *vertical integration*, the process by which a company gets control of companies in other industries that either supply it with materials or buy its products.[39] A furniture manufacturer, for example, buys up a number of lumber companies and sawmills to provide his raw materials and then buys into retail establishments that sell the furniture he produces. In this way, he eliminates a lot of the uncertainties of the market situation. Another device with a similar purpose is to establish interlocking directorates, which bring the top officials or directors of a company on which one depends for some essential commodity onto the controlling board of one's own company. This device is widely used to bring officers of banks onto the boards of firms that require ready access to large amounts of capital.[40]

Finally, the market system has been weakened by the nature of military technology. Modern warfare requires the mobilization of all of a nation's economic resources. Obviously this effort cannot begin with the outbreak of hostilities; it must be planned and implemented far in advance. In societies that wish to maintain a strong military position, this inevitably leads to the development of a military-industrial complex from which most of the elements of the market system are eliminated. For one thing, there is only one buyer for the product, the government. In addition, there is frequently only one producer, and seldom more than a handful, for a particular weapons system. The situation is prejudicial to an open market in yet another way: the military is not inclined to shop around for bargains, because this increases security risks, while truly competitive bidding might cause companies to cut corners and turn out defective products. So long as the military has the taxing power of the government behind it, it has little motivation to economize. Thus, there is a natural tendency for market forces to be replaced by the principles of command in the vast and important area of military procurement, even in societies whose leaders are committed to the principles of free enterprise.

We could summarize most of the foregoing by saying that the last two hundred years have revealed *three basic flaws in the market mechanism*. First,

not only does it fail to protect the weaker and more vulnerable members of
society, such as industrial workers and consumers, it compels the strong to act
ruthlessly if they wish to remain strong. Second, the market system has what
might be called a built-in self-destruct element, which causes most free
competitive markets to evolve into oligopolistic or monopolistic markets
unless checked by governmental intervention (see Table 10.9). Finally, the
market system cannot respond adequately to many or most of the needs of
society as a whole, as contrasted with the needs and desires of individuals.

This final weakness is particularly evident during societal crises, such as
wars, depressions, or environmental crises. As long as individuals and organizations are free to act according to what they perceive as their own best
interests, the more selfish ones tend to win out. A corporation that responded
voluntarily to the environmental problem by installing expensive anti-pollution
devices, for example, would find itself at a competitive disadvantage with firms
that did not.

For a variety of reasons, then, even those societies whose leaders and
members are ideologically most committed to free enterprise have been
edging away from the market system. Public rhetoric to the contrary, the
economies of these societies can now be described only as a *highly complex
mixture of market and command economies.*[41] One indication of this is the
steady growth of governmental expenditures as a percentage of GNP, which is
shown for the United States in Table 10.10. There seems little danger,
however, that the market component will disappear altogether: the experience
of the socialist societies of Eastern Europe suggests that a command economy
would not be a rewarding alternative.

Corporations   Although there are still many businesses owned and operated
as family enterprises in capitalist societies, this traditional form of economic
organization has been relegated to a secondary place in their economies.

TABLE 10.9   Oligopolistic Trends in the United States and Sweden

	Percentage Share of All Business Activity*	
United States	1947	1978
50 largest companies	17	25
200 largest companies	30	43
Sweden	1942	1964
50 largest companies	16	21
200 largest companies	25	32

Sources: *Statistical Abstract of the U.S., 1979,* table 953; Swedish
Finance Department, State Public Investigations (SOU), *Ägande och
inflytande inom det privata näringslivet: Koncentrationsultredningen, V.* [Ownership and influence in the private sector of the
economy] (Stockholm, 1968), p. 7.
*The measure of business activity used for the United States is total
value added; the measure used for Sweden is industrial employment.

TABLE 10.10 Federal, State, and Local Government Expenditures as a Percentage of Gross National Product in the United States, 1902–1977

Year	Expenditures as Percentage of GNP
1902	7.7
1927	11.8
1952	28.9
1977	36.8

Sources: Adapted from *Historical Statistics of the U.S.: Colonial Times to 1970*, series F-1 and Y-533, and *Statistical Abstract of the U.S.*, *1979*, table 472.

Family enterprises are usually not able to marshall the enormous sums of money necessary for huge, technologically advanced, capital-intensive industries, nor are they able to manage the affairs of far-flung industrial empires.

In socialist societies, these tasks are assigned to state enterprises, which have the financial resources of the state behind them. In capitalist societies, a new kind of economic organization, the corporation, has gradually evolved and is now the most important form of economic organization in these societies.

The origins of the corporation lie in the sixteenth century, when English and Dutch merchants, trading with remote areas, banded together in what came to be known as joint stock companies.[42] This form of organization had several advantages over family enterprises and partnerships. Above all, it permitted people to pool their capital and thereby spread their risks. This was extremely important in ventures where risks were great and large investments essential. In addition, a joint stock company, unlike a family enterprise or a partnership, was not disrupted by the death of one of the owners.*

During the next several centuries, the joint stock company, or corporation, gradually spread to new fields of enterprise, and a series of changes made this form of organization safer and more attractive to investors. The most important change was the adoption of the principle of *limited liability*. Prior to the nineteenth century, stockholders in most corporations had unlimited liability: in case of bankruptcy they could lose not only their investment in the company but all their personal property as well. This naturally made investors extremely cautious; unless they had firsthand knowledge of a business and those running it, they were taking a great risk. The passage of laws limiting the liability of stockholders to the investment itself greatly stimulated the flow of capital into this new form of enterprise.

In non-Marxist societies today, nearly all of the largest and most powerful

---

*The law requires, for example, that a partnership be dissolved on the death of any of the partners. This was not required of joint stock companies.

private enterprises are corporations. In the United States in recent years, for example, 86 per cent of all business was done by corporations, and among larger concerns (i.e., those with annual receipts of $1 million or more), they accounted for 96 per cent of the total.[43] The very largest concerns, those with annual profits in the hundreds of millions or billions of dollars, are all corporations.[44]

As corporations have grown, there has been a tremendous change in their character, especially with respect to their control. To begin with, the largest ones are rarely controlled by the people who own them (i.e., the stockholders); they are controlled by the employees who are hired to manage them.[45] This shift is a consequence of the fragmentation of stock ownership that has accompanied the enormous growth in size of these organizations. In AT&T, for example, not a single one of its 3 million stockholders owns as much as 1 per cent of the stock, and most own only a minute fraction of 1 per cent. Furthermore, the stockholders are scattered around the world. Mobilizing a majority of the voting stock to wrest control from the managers would be almost impossible.

The character of the modern corporation has also been altered during the twentieth century by increasing government control. As we have seen, this intervention of government into capitalist economies has been a response to the inherent weaknesses of an unregulated market system. Over the years, the scope of government involvement in corporations and other kinds of economic enterprises has steadily increased, creating some problems as it alleviates others. Many economic questions that were once resolved by the forces of supply and demand are now resolved by government officials, much as they are in socialist societies. Minimum wages, working hours and conditions, hiring and promotion practices, product quality, advertising practices—all this and much more is now subject to governmental regulation. In summary, the owners of the largest corporations have become, in most cases, merely investors: *the real power of decision making now lies in the hands of management and the government.* In smaller corporations and family enterprises, ownership and control are usually still combined. But even for them, the traditional market forces of the early industrial era have been severely weakened by governmental regulation and control.

State Enterprises   All non-Marxist societies have some state enterprises, but their importance in the economy varies considerably. These enterprises may be owned by government at any level—local, state, or federal. In the United States, government-owned and run enterprises include the postal system, many electric and water companies, some hospitals and other health facilities, many insurance programs (e.g., Medicare, veterans' insurance), most educational institutions, some housing facilities, quite a few recreational facilities, many transportation facilities (e.g., highways, ports, local transit systems, passenger trains), and many banking services.

The non-Marxist societies of Western Europe stand somewhere between the United States and the Marxist societies of Eastern Europe with respect to the scope of state enterprise. Their railroads, for example, are 90 to 100 per cent government-owned.[46] Of the scheduled airlines in Western Europe, only Swissair is less than half government-owned, and radio and television broadcasting are entirely government enterprises in every country except the United Kingdom and Luxembourg. The state also plays a major role in Europe's electric, gas, insurance, banking, mining, iron, and steel industries, and, in some countries, in the automobile, chemical, and machine-tool industries as well. In short, state enterprises are thriving and apparently increasing in non-Marxist societies.

The Economies of Marxist Societies

All of the fully industrialized Marxist societies are in Eastern Europe (the Soviet Union, East Germany, Czechoslovakia, Poland, Hungary, Rumania, and possibly Bulgaria). In each of them, market forces have been relegated to a very secondary position in the economy and private ownership of the means of production has been largely eliminated.[47] In their place are state enterprises and a command economy.

State Enterprises   In Marxist societies, not only are most of the organizations that produce *goods* state enterprises (i.e., factories, farms, mines), but so are most of those that provide *services*. For example, in Soviet society, state enterprises provide education, transportation (e.g., airlines, railways, local transit systems), medical care (e.g., clinics, hospitals), communications (e.g., newspapers, television, telephone), as well as retail services (e.g., department stores), eating facilities, entertainment, and much more. The only private enterprise in that society's economy appears to be the trade that goes on in farmers' markets, and moonlighting (i.e., working after a regular job) by people with marketable skills.

In recent years, state enterprise has accounted for 98 to 99 per cent of all nonagricultural production in the Soviet Union, and nearly half of its agricultural production (the rest of its agricultural production came largely from so-called "cooperative farms," which are actually more like state enterprises than like the cooperatives of western societies).[48] In Poland, state enterprises produce 78 per cent of the GNP.[49]

In some respects, the state enterprises of Marxist societies are remarkably like the large corporate enterprises of capitalist societies. Both of them are administered by a complex hierarchy of officials whose powers, responsibilities, and rewards vary according to level. Both of them have a highly complex division of labor, in which the duties of every specialist are carefully defined. And both of them require individuals in subordinate positions to follow the directives of their superiors.[50]

There are, of course, some important differences between corporations and these state enterprises. For one thing, Marxist societies place great emphasis on economic goals and central planning. The famous Five Year Plans of the U.S.S.R. are the classic example. Government officials in the national capitals set production goals for each enterprise, but these often prove

FIGURE 10.9   State-operated supermarket, Warsaw.

unrealistic. In an effort to meet their quotas, the managers of these organizations frequently strive to comply with the letter of the plan, while ignoring the spirit (e.g., they produce the required quantity, but cut corners on quality). Several years ago, *Pravda* published a poll of more than 1,000 industrial managers, and 80 per cent complained of interference in day-to-day operations by higher authorities, while 90 percent said they needed more flexibility in decision making to do a better job.[51]

Another way in which the state enterprises of Marxist societies differ from private enterprises is that their workers run little risk of being unemployed. As a result, work discipline is often slack, absenteeism high, and workmanship careless.[52] Job turnover also appears to be a problem in many state enterprises.[53] If workers become bored with their jobs, they usually feel free to quit, knowing other jobs are available. While this may be beneficial to the worker, it has not been beneficial for the economies of Marxist societies.

State enterprises in Marxist societies also differ from enterprises in other industrial societies because of the nature of trade unions in these societies. These unions are part of the central power structure of Marxist societies, but subordinate to the authority of the Party and political elite. From a functional standpoint, they are similar to the company unions that managers in capitalist enterprises established in an earlier period in response to the growing threat of worker-organized unions. The basic task of trade unions in Marxist societies is to maintain productivity. To achieve this, union leaders report labor problems to both the management and the Party, while providing a variety of social services to members (e.g., insurance, access to health and vacation facilities, counseling services). Strikes and collective bargaining are forbidden, but union leaders are supposed to bring workers' grievances to the attention of the management. The response to these grievances apparently varies a great deal and depends, to some extent at least, on the motives and the negotiating skills of union leaders. It is clear, however, that labor unions have far less power and influence in Marxist societies than labor unions do in non-Marxist societies. The Party's justification for this is that worker interests in these societies are basically protected by the Party itself.*

Prior to the Russian Revolution, many critics of socialism argued that it would be impossible to operate an economy successfully without private ownership and the operation of market forces. Today, however, this argument is no longer heard, since the Soviets and other Marxist societies have proved that there is nothing incompatible about a socialized economy and economic growth. In fact, compared to other societies that, like themselves, were not among the early industrializers, their record has been very good. The Soviet Union has now surpassed every nation except the United States in total productivity (see Table 9.2, page 254).

In addition, Marxist economies have overcome unemployment, one of the great scourges of capitalist economies. In part, this is achieved by the creation of "busywork" (e.g., women ride the escalators of the Moscow subway system, hour after hour, wiping the handrails with a rag), and often, as we have seen, at the expense of economic efficiency. Nevertheless, it is a significant accomplishment. Closely related to this, the command economies of Marxist societies have generally been successful in eradicating abject poverty, especially in urban areas (rural populations have been slower to benefit). Finally, Marxist societies have been quite successful in reducing the degree of economic inequality—partly by a reduction in wage inequalities, partly by the virtual elimination of the private ownership of the means of production.

We need to beware, however, of exaggerating the differences between Marxist and non-Marxist economies. Supermarkets in Warsaw, for example, function in a manner strikingly similar to those in Washington D.C.: visitors from capitalist societies are likely to have to remind themselves that the former are state enterprises. Even in factories, where we might expect greater differences, the similarities are striking. One of Poland's leading sociologists made this point when he wrote:

---

*During the summer of 1980, Polish workers challenged this claim in a nationwide series of strikes. A major objective of the strikes was the formation of independent unions (i.e., unions free of Party control). Eight million workers are reported to have joined the new unions, about three times the membership of the Communist Party. The long-term effects of this remain to be seen, but it is noteworthy that Hungary has recently taken steps to give its unions a somewhat greater degree of independence from Party control in the hope of averting conflict similar to that in Poland.

. . . the workers are still hired labor. The socialist revolution does not change the relation of the worker to the machine, nor does it change his position within the factory . . . His relation to the machine and the organizational system of work requires his subordination to the foreman and the management of the factory. He receives wages according to the quantity and quality of work performed, and he must obey the principles and regulations of work discipline.[54]

Inclusion of Market Elements   During the last twenty years, Communist Party leaders have become increasingly aware of the difficulties inherent in a completely planned command economy. Effective planning must take account not only of all the tens of thousands of items produced but also of *all the interrelations among them*, since the production of one thing is always contingent on the availability of others. The Soviet machine industry alone would require provision for more than 15 billion interrelations.[55] Because it is impossible to coordinate successfully such a fantastic number of relationships, shortages repeatedly develop in some goods, surpluses in others.

The great virtue of the market system is its automatic mechanism for balancing supply and demand. When the demand for a product goes up, so does the price, giving producers an incentive to increase production. Conversely, a slump in demand lowers prices and reduces incentives. All of this is accomplished without costly centralized planning and the growth of bureaucracy. But despite this attractive feature, the market system had always been so closely identified with capitalism that it was unthinkable for Soviet leaders.

During recent decades, however, a number of Marxist economists have been able to demonstrate that the market mechanism is not necessarily linked to private enterprise, and that its introduction into socialist economies need not stimulate a revival of capitalism. With this point clarified, and with the increasing pragmatism of Communist leaders, the way was cleared for experimentation. Elements of the market system have since been reintroduced into areas of the economy from which they had been excluded for years.[56]

The use of market mechanisms in Marxist economies suggests that in the future there may be somewhat less variation in the economies of industrial societies than there has been in the past. Marxist and non-Marxist societies alike appear to be moving toward a mixed type of economy, in which both market and command will play important roles. Market forces will be used to achieve greater efficiency, while command will be used to protect the corporate interests of society and to limit the degree of social inequality. This is not to say, of course, that differences between economic systems will be eliminated (East European Communist leaders seem determined to prevent the reestablishment of large privately owned enterprises, for one thing), but they will probably be reduced.[57]

The Increasing Economic Integration of the World System

To be complete, our survey of the economies of modern industrial societies must take note of one further development: the growing web of economic ties among societies, industrial and nonindustrial, throughout the world.

Human societies have exchanged goods with one another since prehistoric times, but the volume of trade was small because of the limitations of technology. Since the cost of transporting goods was often greater than the cost of producing them, intersocietal trade was largely restricted, for thousands of years, to small items of substantial value, especially luxury goods for the elite.

With advances in ship construction and navigational technology in the thirteenth, fourteenth, and fifteenth centuries, the volume of international trade began to increase. By 1850, the volume of goods exchanged was six times what it had been in 1750, and in 1950, twenty times what it was in 1850.[58] And for the last forty years, the volume of international trade (corrected for inflation) has increased at a rate equivalent to a 400-fold increase over a 100-year period.[59]

The net effect of this trend has been a substantial increase in the division of labor among societies, and the growing economic integration of the world system. The other side of the same coin, of course, is that societies are steadily declining in economic self-sufficiency. As Table 10.11 shows, most of the industrial societies of the world today import goods that are the equivalent of 20 to 50 per cent of their gross domestic product (see Glossary).

The societies of Western Europe have moved further in this direction than other industrial societies and have formed the European Economic Community, whose goal is the complete integration of the economies of the nine member societies. This development could be the prelude to political unification and the formation of a new multinational society embracing much of Western Europe.

In the world system as a whole, movement toward economic and political unification is far less advanced, but a number of international organizations—

TABLE 10.11 Imports as a Percentage of Gross Domestic Product in Selected Industrial Societies

Society	Imports as Percentage of Gross Domestic Product
Netherlands	49
Belgium	48
Austria	39
Switzerland	34
Denmark	33
Sweden	30
United Kingdom	30
Italy	28
Canada	24
West Germany	23
France	22
Australia	16
Japan	13
United States	10

Source: *Statistical Abstract of the United States, 1979*, table 1555.

economic and political—have emerged. These include the International Monetary Fund, the Food and Agriculture Organization, the World Bank, the International Labor Organization, the World Health Organization, the International Court of Justice, and the United Nations. While the powers of these bodies are far more limited than those of the European Economic Community, they reflect the growing web of relations that binds all human societies together as a consequence of the technological advances of the industrial era.

CHAPTER 11

Industrial Societies: II

The Polity

As recently as 1750, the idea that the powers of government are derived from the members of a society was still only an abstract philosophical concept. Today, just a little more than two hundred years later, this concept has become the foundation on which the governments of all industrial societies, and many industrializing societies, are based. As we noted earlier, three-quarters of contemporary industrial societies are representative democracies. In the remaining quarter, the Marxist societies of Eastern Europe, the principle of popular sovereignty is also accepted as the basis of the political system, but it is implemented in quite a different way, as we will see.

This shift from the older idea that a tiny group of people had been given a divine mandate to rule the rest has had far-reaching consequences. Perhaps they are best symbolized by the way a society's legal codes refer to its rank and file members. In the agrarian era, they were called "subjects"; in modern legal codes, they are "citizens." The new concept of government is also reflected in a new kind of association: the mass political party that seeks to mobilize the citizenry. But most important of all, the shift to democracy is reflected in the degree to which the powers of government in every industrial society are used to benefit ordinary people.

People who are sensitive to the many undemocratic elements in the political system of every industrial society sometimes find it difficult to appreciate the degree of democratization that has occurred. Critics of the Marxist regimes of Eastern Europe in particular often fail to recognize that even in these societies there is very real evidence of a democratic trend since the agrarian era. But those who are critical of the representative democracies of Western Europe, Canada, the United States, Australia, New Zealand, and Japan often seem to have just as little historical perspective.

Yet when we compare these societies with the monarchical societies of the agrarian era, the differences are striking.* Access to high political office is no longer restricted to individuals who are born into a small, hereditary elite, nor is political decision making the exclusive prerogative of a tiny handful of individuals. Even in Eastern European societies, where participation in political decision making is far more restricted than in other industrial societies, a number of groups have some influence on decisions that affect their interests, or can make their voices heard in areas where their skills are relevant.

Democracy as a Variable   In discussing political systems, we have to resist treating democracy in categorical, rather than variable, terms. To divide governmental systems into those which are democracies and those which are not, greatly oversimplifies matters and leads to an unrealistic view of the world.

To begin with, no society is a pure democracy; this is impossible in any group with millions of members. Pure democracy would require, in effect, that every citizen participate equally in every political decision. This is hardly possible even in the smallest and simplest of hunting and gathering societies. To attempt it in a large, complex industrial society would require a drastic reversal (were that possible) of one of the basic trends of sociocultural evolution: increasing specialization and division of labor in every area of societal life, including government. Even approximately equal involvement in political decision making by all of the members would mean chaos and the abandonment of most other activities. Further technological advance could alter this, it is true: electronic devices in every home, for example, might enable citizens to register their views on a wide variety of subjects. But for the present, even the most democratic industrial society has achieved no more than representative democracy.

Representative democracy, as we noted in Chapter 10, is a system in which the adult population is permitted, at infrequent intervals, to choose among a limited number of candidates for public office and to voice their

---

*A number of democracies—Britain, Japan, The Low Countries, and the Scandinavian societies—still retain certain monarchical trappings, but kings and queens are now little more than ceremonial heads of state. Real power in all of these nations lies in the hands of elected officials.

opinions of official policy between elections.* Without denying its democratic elements, it is clear that, even in this system, a small political elite actually determines most political decisions. This elite consists of varying mixtures of professional politicians, civil servants, news media personnel, business leaders, leaders of labor unions, and leaders of other organized interests from gun lobbyists to racial and ethnic groups. In addition, wealthy individuals and groups often play a political role simply by helping finance elections and otherwise subsidizing and influencing public officials. As a consequence, by the time the majority of citizens play their political role—that is, go to the polls to cast their ballots—the real choices may already have been made and they may be confronted by alternatives that are either very similar or equally unattractive.

Despite this limitation, however, there is a basic characteristic of democratic political institutions that substantially improves the potential for political influence of virtually every citizen. Because the political elite of a democracy is large and represents a wide range of interests, individuals can penetrate its ranks through many different career paths or through activity in a great variety of organizations. In Marxist societies, in contrast, almost the only route to this elite is through the Communist Party.†

Once we recognize that pure democracy is an impossibility in any industrial society, it is easier to distinguish the varying degrees of democracy attained by different societies, or by a particular society at different times. The United States, for example, enjoys a much greater degree of democracy today than it did at the beginning of the nineteenth century. In the presidential election of 1824, the first for which figures are available, only 350,000 votes were cast, representing just 7 per cent of the adult population. Since then, the elimination of property restrictions on the franchise and on the right to hold office, the direct election of senators, women's suffrage, the voting provisions in recent civil rights legislation, the "one man, one vote" decisions of the Supreme Court, and the vote for eighteen-year-olds have all increased the percentage of Americans allowed to participate in the electoral process and the effectiveness of their participation in the political process as a whole. Similar trends can be observed in the recent history of other highly democratic nations, such as Britain and Sweden (see Table 11.1).[1]

When we think of democracy as a variable, we are able to recognize a surprising fact: of all the industrialized societies in the world system, from the time the first emerged early in the nineteenth century, there have been *only a handful of instances in which the trend toward a greater degree of democracy was reversed.* The chief examples of this were Germany in the 1930s, Hungary in the middle 1950s, and Czechoslovakia in the late 1960s. In the first instance, Germany was a society confronted with an unusually severe set of problems, while in Hungary and Czechoslovakia, the reversal was due to the

---

*In some societies the electorate may also vote on a small number of issues through referenda.
†A few non-Party people seem to have achieved this status in Poland, and in Czechoslovakia under Dubček.

TABLE 11.1 Percentage of the British Population Age Twenty-One and Over Eligible to Vote

1831	5.0
After First Reform Act, 1832	7.1
After Second Reform Act, 1867	16.4
After Third Reform Act, 1884	28.5
After 1918	74.0
After Equal Franchise Act, 1928	96.9

Source: Judith Ryder and Harold Silver. *Modern English Society: History and Structure, 1850–1970* (London: Methuen, 1970). p. 74.

military intervention of the Soviet Union. Although such cases serve to warn us that a reversal of the democratic trend in industrial societies is possible, they indicate that it is likely to happen only under exceptional circumstances.

Democratic Tendencies in Marxist Polities Compared with the representative democracies of other industrial societies, the polities of the Marxist societies appear extremely authoritarian, as in fact they are. In these societies, the traditional symbols of democratic government are widely used, but they are stripped of their significance. For example, elections are held at regular intervals, but the restrictions on both voters and would-be candidates rob them of the significance of elections even in the imperfectly democratic, multiparty politics of other industrial societies. Some Marxist societies (e.g., East Germany, Poland) actually have multiple parties, but the non-Marxist parties are assigned quotas for seats in parliaments and local councils and are severely limited in their activities and influence.

Similarly, although parliamentary groups such as the Supreme Soviet meet regularly to enact legislation, just as their counterparts do in democratic societies, the actions they take in these sessions have already been largely determined by the Communist Party elite.[2] Where the real power lies in Marxist societies is revealed by the individuals who represent them in truly important international meetings. On such occasions, the Soviet Union and other Eastern European nations are always represented by the First Secretary of the Communist Party, not by the president or head of state (except when the same person holds both offices).

Influence on decision making by individuals and groups outside the ranks of the Party elite is not great, but it does exist and can sometimes be important on certain kinds of issues. Economists, scientists, educators, managers of industrial enterprises, and military leaders have all made their influence felt from time to time. On rare occasions, their influence has even reversed an action planned by Party leaders. This happened, for example, when Khrushchev, while at the height of his power in the Soviet Union, attempted to reform the educational system by increasing admissions to the universities of children of peasants and workers who could not be admitted on strictly academic grounds. After some initial success, Khrushchev's plan was rejected by educational leaders who were supported by other segments of the Soviet populace.[3]

Despite the relatively closed nature and lack of democratic procedures in Marxist political systems, their economic policies have benefited broad segments of the population outside the ranks of the political elite. Unemployment has been largely eliminated, as we noted in the last chapter, and economic differences between manual workers and nonmanual workers are generally smaller than in other industrial societies.[4] Compared with those of agrarian elites of the past, the economic policies of Marxist elites are very democratic.

Even in the area of political procedures, there are signs of a gradual shift in a more democratic direction. In the Soviet Union, for example, the treatment of political dissidents, though still extremely harsh by the standards of non-Marxist industrial societies, is less extreme than in the Stalinist era. In addition, parliamentary bodies have begun to play a more active role in recent years in the formulation of public policy. Within committees of the Supreme Soviet, and its counterparts in other Eastern European societies, genuine debates now occur periodically.[5] In referring to the Polish parliament, one western specialist reports that "it has come alive in the last six or seven years."[6] In some of the committees of the parliament, members of the United Workers Party (i.e., Communist Party) are now in the minority; and committees have occasionally blocked social legislative proposals initiated by the Party, and have amended other proposals. In Hungary and Poland, the law now requires that at least 50 per cent more candidates must stand for parliamentary positions than there are positions to be filled. In Hungary, this has led to openly contested elections, while in Poland it has led to active bargaining between representatives of the United Workers Party, the United Peasants Party, and the Democratic Party to compose a slate which they then jointly endorse. Finally, in some of the Eastern European Marxist societies, Party leaders now use public opinion polling to learn the views of the population on a wide range of political issues. The influence of polling on policy decisions is not clear, but it seems unlikely that Party leaders would go to the expense of conducting such polls if they intended to ignore them. In short, while the degree of political democratization so far achieved in Marxist industrial societies leaves much to be desired, the direction of the trends has, for some years, been toward wider participation in, and greater popular influence on, political decision making.

Causes of the Democratic Trend

Many factors contributed to the emergence, spread, and influence of the democratic ideology. Basically, they are the same forces that gave rise to the other new ideologies of the industrial era—the Protestant Reformation, the conquest of the New World, and, most important of all, the Industrial Revolution.

Protestantism appears to have been especially significant in the early rise and spread of democratic beliefs and values.[7] If it did nothing else, the Protestant Reformation proved that established authority *could* be challenged and overthrown. But even more important, the Protestant doctrine of the priesthood of all believers—that all believers are equal in God's sight and can relate directly to Him without the mediation of the clergy—had *political implications of a revolutionary nature*. Though Luther and Calvin did not recognize that fact, others soon did, and the bitter German Peasants' Revolt of 1524–1525 and the Leveler movement a century later in England were both stimulated by it.

FIGURE 11.1   Luther nailing his famous 95 Theses to the door of the castle church, Wittenberg, Germany, 1517. Luther's doctrine of the priesthood of all believers had revolutionary political implications; though Luther did not recognize this, others soon did.

This new doctrine also led to the adoption of democratic or semidemocratic polities by many of the more radical Protestant groups, such as the Anabaptists, Mennonites, Baptists, Quakers, Puritans, and Presbyterians. It is no coincidence that democratization began in ecclesiastical (i.e., church) governments some generations before it began in civil governments. Nor is it just a coincidence that when it did begin in civil government, its early successes were chiefly in countries where ecclesiastical democratization had already made considerable headway. The first major and enduring victory of the democratic movement was in the United States, a country which since colonial days had been a refuge for the more radical and more democratic Protestant groups.

The conquest of the New World was another major factor in the spread of democratic government. Conditions in the frontier regions of the United States, Canada, Australia, and New Zealand were far more favorable to this ideology than conditions in the older, heavily settled societies of Europe. It is no coincidence that the Jacksonian movement, which did so much to broaden the base of political participation in American society, had its greatest strength in what was then the western part of the country, where frontier conditions were most pronounced. The conquest of the New World was also important because, as we noted in Chapter 9, it weakened the power of the traditional governing classes in European societies and strengthened the influence of the merchant class, which had long been noted for its republican tendencies.

As important as these influences were, the democratic movement could not have succeeded as it did without the Industrial Revolution. To begin with, industrialization eliminated the traditional need for large numbers of unskilled and uneducated workers living at or near the subsistence level, and as new sources of energy were tapped and new machines invented, societies had to produce more skilled and educated workers. Such people, however, are much less likely to be politically apathetic and servile. On the contrary, they tend to be self-assertive, jealous of their rights, and politically demanding.[8] Such characteristics are essential in a democracy, for they counterbalance and hold in check the powerful oligarchical tendencies present in any large and complex organization.

Industrialization also made possible the remarkable development of the *mass media*. To a great extent, this has been a response to the spread of literacy and to the increased demand for information generated by the rising level of education. Through newspapers, magazines, radio, and television, the average citizen of a modern industrial society is vastly more aware of political events than his or her counterpart in agrarian societies. Although much of the information received is extremely superficial and distorted, it nevertheless generates interest and concern. Thus the media not only satisfy a need, they also stimulate it.[9]

Finally, industrialization, by stimulating the growth of urban communities, further strengthened democratic tendencies. Isolated rural communities have long been noted for their lack of political sophistication and for their patriarchal, paternalistic political patterns. Urban populations, in contrast, have always been better informed and more willing to challenge established authority. Thus, merely by increasing the size of urban populations, industrialization contributed to the democratic trend.

Political Parties

The growth of democracy and the rise of industrial societies have produced a totally new kind of political organization, the mass political party, which serves to mobilize public opinion in support of political programs and candidates. Wherever there are more candidates than offices, there is a process of selection, and the candidates that are supported by parties are usually the ones who survive.

At the present time, party organizations differ in several respects. Some, including the Republican and Democratic parties in the United States, are largely pragmatic, *brokerage-type parties*. They have no strong ideological commitments and no well-defined political programs. Their chief goal is to gain control of public offices in order to trade favors with special-interest

FIGURE 11.2   The rise of industrial societies has produced a totally new kind of political organization, the mass political party: British Labour Party assembled in convention.

groups, giving preferential legislative treatment in exchange for electoral and financial support. This cannot be said publicly, of course, and so party rhetoric takes the form of glittering generalities about service to the nation. In this type of party, discipline is weak or nonexistent, since each elected official is a free agent, permitted to work out his or her own "deals." Some degree of party unity is maintained, however, because once an interest group establishes close ties with the officials of a certain party, it usually prefers to continue working with them. This is reinforced by the tendency of the more ideologically inclined to separate into opposing camps, liberals gravitating toward one party, conservatives toward the other. Sometimes the more ideologically inclined win control of the party machinery, as did the Goldwaterites in 1964 and the McGovernites in 1972, but this is usually short-lived.

In contrast to brokerage-type parties, most of which were formed in the nineteenth century, political parties formed in the twentieth century have had strong ideological commitments. Such parties, including both the fascist parties of the right and the democratic socialist and revolutionary socialist parties of the left, have usually had well-developed programs for what they regarded as the rehabilitation of society; in most instances, they were willing to be defeated again and again rather than compromise with principles they held sacred. Since World War II, however, many of these parties have become less ideological and more pragmatic.[10]

Nationalist ideologies have also given rise to political parties in several industrial societies. The most famous of these was the German National Socialist (Nazi) Party organized by Adolph Hitler following Germany's defeat in World War I. Nationalist ideologies are more likely, however, to be simply one of the elements in the overall program of the major conservative parties in democratic societies. Thus, the Republicans in the United States, the Conservatives in Britain and Canada, and the Gaullists in France usually place more emphasis on national defense and other policies relevant to nationalist ideals than do their opponents.

In ethnically divided societies, minorities sometimes form nationalist parties to protect or promote their own group's special interests. This has happened among the French in Canada, the Scotch and Welsh in Britain, and the Basques in Spain. Such parties often advocate radical policies, especially political autonomy for their own group.

Finally, religious groups in Western Europe and Japan have formed a number of political parties. The most successful of these have been the Christian-Democratic parties formed by Catholics in Italy, Germany, Austria, and several other countries. While the original aim of these parties was to defend the church's position on such issues as birth control, abortion, and tax support for church schools, they have often become the conservative opposition to social democratic and Communist parties. Like most political parties, religious parties tend to combine elements from differing ideological traditions in order to maximize their support among the voters.

Experience has taught professional politicians that parties that remain ideologically pure are likely to remain numerically small and politically weak, except in times of national crisis. Thus, even the more successful Communist parties of Western Europe have softened their stance on many issues in recent years. The Italian party, in fact, has gone so far as to support the continued participation of Italy in the NATO alliance and to pledge its support to the principle of western-style democracy.

Political Conflict and Stability

Every social system generates internal conflict, and industrial societies are no exception. Nevertheless, they are remarkable for their success in channeling it into nonviolent forms. Compared with agrarian societies in particular, they are much less prone to revolution and serious political upheavals. This is especially true of those societies which are past the transitional or early phase of industrialization. One study of sixty-two nations found a strong, positive correlation of 0.965 (see Glossary) between level of political stability and level of economic development.[11]

There are a number of reasons for this. First, the greater productivity of industrial societies and the resultant higher standard of living give the majority of the population a vested interest in political stability. Revolution and anarchy would be very costly for most members of advanced industrial societies. Second, a democratic ideology strengthens the allegiance of most segments of the population to their government and weakens support for revolutionary movements. Especially noteworthy in this connection is the loyalty shown the government by the military and the absence of military coups in the more advanced industrial societies. Finally, the very complexity of the structure of industrial societies seems to generate a readiness to compromise controversial issues. This is partly because *there are so many people in intermediate positions between the contending groups*. Most of the population, for example, has modest property holdings. Such people are likely to benefit from peaceful compromise and to shy away from extreme or violent solutions. Contrary to Marxian expectations, this is true of the great majority of blue-collar workers. Moreover, since the complexity of industrial societies means that each individual simultaneously fills a number of different roles and often belongs to a variety of groups, people who are opponents in one controversy are likely to be allies in the next. For example, middle- and working-class blacks who are divided over labor-management controversies find themselves allies on racial issues. This, too, has a moderating effect.

Although political conflicts are restrained in industrial societies, they are still present in a variety of forms and involve a wide range of issues. The most common type of conflict is between economic classes, and, in most democratic nations, this conflict is the most important factor defining the basic framework for partisan politics. Typically, some parties appeal to the working class and other disadvantaged elements in the population, promising improved conditions if they are elected. Opposing parties rely for support on the more privileged elements in the population, though they usually avoid stressing this in their campaign rhetoric. Nevertheless, the relationship is recognized by most people.

TABLE 11.2 Party Preferences of the British Population by Economic Class, in Percentages (average of four surveys)

Class	Labour	Liberals and Conservatives	Total
Upper and middle classes	27	73	100
Working class	61	39	100

Sources: Adapted from Robert Alford, *Party and Society* (Chicago: Rand McNally, 1963), p. 136; and Richard Rose, "Class and Party Divisions: Britain as a Test Case," *Sociology*, 2, (1968), pp. 129–162.

Britain provides a good example of the typical relationship between economic class and party preference. As Table 11.2 shows, support for the Labour Party is more than twice as strong in the working class as in the middle and upper classes. The strength of the relationship between party preference and economic class varies greatly in industrial societies, and Britain's position is intermediate. The relationship is most pronounced in Scandinavian societies, least pronounced in those of North America, as Table 11.3 shows. The limited relation between class and party preference in the United States and Canada is due in part to the absence of major working-class parties with strong ideological commitments. All of their major parties are pragmatic, brokerage

TABLE 11.3 Strength of Relationship between Occupational Class and Party Preference in Eleven Industrial Societies

Society	Percentage Point Difference*
Finland (average of 3 surveys)	50
Norway (average of 3 surveys)	46
Denmark (1 survey)	44
Italy (1 survey)	37
Sweden (average of 5 surveys)	35
Australia (average of 7 surveys)	35
Britain (average of 4 surveys)	34
West Germany (average of 2 surveys)	26
France (average of 2 surveys)	22
United States (average of 9 surveys)	17
Canada (average of 10 surveys)	7

Sources: See note 12, page 476.

*Specifically, the figures are the difference between the percentage of urban upper- and middle-class people who support Labor, Socialist, and Communist parties and the percentage of urban working-class people who do so. Canada's Liberal Party and the Democratic Party in the United States are also included, since there are no mass socialist parties in those societies.

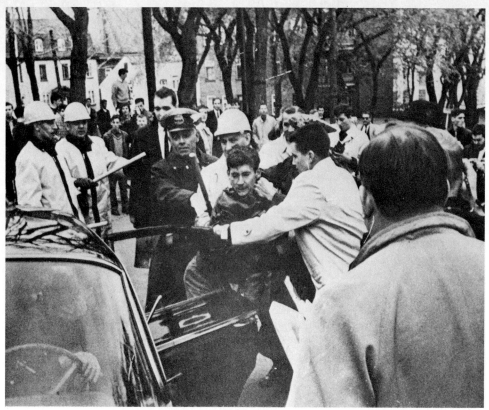

**FIGURE 11.3   Canada has for years been torn by struggles between an
English-speaking Protestant majority and a very large French Catholic minority:
French separatists demonstrating in Montreal.**

types, which tend to play down class-related issues rather than emphasize
them.*

Another factor that influences the relation between economic class and
party preference is the presence of important ethnic and religious divisions
within the population. It is probably no coincidence that the countries in Table
11.3 with the strongest relation between class and party preference are also
generally the most homogeneous from an ethnic and religious standpoint. By
contrast, Canada has for years been torn by struggles between an English-
speaking Protestant majority and a very large French Catholic minority. In both
Canada and the United States, religion and ethnicity are at least as powerful as
economic class in determining party preference.

Modern industrial democracies differ dramatically from traditional agrarian societies by virtue of their willingness to permit ethnic and religious

---

*The New Democratic Party in Canada is a democratic socialist party, but it has not yet
achieved the stature of a major national party. Its growth in recent years suggests,
however, that this is a distinct possibility, especially if Quebec, the long-time bastion
of support for the Liberal Party, should secede from Canada.

minorities and the economically disadvantaged to participate in the political process. In agrarian societies, such groups had little or no political power. In industrial societies in contrast, these groups have sometimes won control of the machinery of government, or at least a share in it, as the social democrats have done in Scandinavia and Britain, the French in Canada, and the Catholics in the Netherlands.

The Growth of Government

Apart from the rise of democracy, the most important political change associated with industrialization has been the great growth of government. The range of the activities and the diversity of the functions performed by government are far greater in modern industrial societies than in any other type of society. In a traditional agrarian society, the government's chief functions were the preservation of law and order, defense, taxation, and the support of religion. In modern industrial societies the last has usually been dropped, but dozens of new ones have been added.

The broader scope of government in industrial societies is closely linked with their increasing democratization. As the masses of common people gain a voice in government, they demand services seldom, if ever, provided in agrarian societies. They want educational opportunities, job training, assistance when they are old or sick or unemployed, protection against dishonest businessmen, recreational facilities, and many other things. The provision of such services further strengthens democratic tendencies, since an educated, economically secure population usually participates more intelligently and effectively in the democratic process and is less likely to be attracted to anti-democratic programs than an illiterate and economically insecure population.[13]

Another factor contributing to the growth of government in an industrial society is the greater interdependence of its population. Occupational specialization has progressed to the point where virtually everyone is engaged in specialized work. Everyone, therefore, is dependent on the labors of others, and on the maintenance of the complex system of exchange by which goods and services reach their ultimate consumers. In a society like this, a disruption at any point in the economy has serious adverse consequences for almost everyone.

Similarly, in a society geared to a high degree of interaction among its members, dependable systems of transportation and communication are essential. And in its urban centers, where people live close together, well-organized fire, police, and health services are imperative. Private individuals and organizations are unable to assume these responsibilities: only government can commandeer the resources and exercise the authority needed to deal with such fundamental problems.

The Growth and Transformation of Government Bureaucracies One of the best measures of the growth of a government's activity is the size of its bureaucracy. In the United States, for example, the number of civilian employees of the federal government has risen steadily for the last century and a half.[14]

1821	7,000
1861	37,000
1901	239,000
1941	1,438,000
1978	2,875,000

This increase far outdistanced the growth of the population as a whole. While the latter increased 20–fold, the number of federal employees shot up 400–fold. Contrary to what many people think, it is not only the federal bureaucracy that has been growing: between 1929 (the earliest year for which national totals are available) and 1978, the number of employees in state and local government increased more than 400 per cent, while the general population grew only about 80 per cent.[15]

The great growth in the powers of governments and in the size of their bureaucracies has made top administrative officials (i.e., civil servants) extremely powerful figures in every industrial society. Although this might be interpreted as simply a perpetuation of the old agrarian pattern with its dominance by a hereditary governing class, it is not. Government offices are no longer private property to be bought and sold and transferred to one's children. Rather, they are usually assigned on the basis of competitions in which technical competence, education, and experience are the chief criteria. Furthermore, in the exercise of office, officials are expected to act on

FIGURE 11.4 "Now that the elections are over we can get back to the real business of government . . . Growing bigger!"

the basis of the public interest rather than of private advantage. Although reality falls far short of these ideals, there is still a marked contrast between the practices of officials in most modern industrial societies and the practices of those in traditional agrarian societies. The United States has discovered this repeatedly in dealing with the officials of many of the governments of Southeast Asia, the Middle East, Africa, and Latin America.

In large measure, the explanation for this change lies in the new democratic ideology, which asserts that the powers of government are derived from the people and should therefore be used for their benefit. This is in sharp contrast to the traditional ideology of agrarian societies, which defined the state as the property of the ruler. When modern officials use public office for private advantage, they are subject to a variety of official sanctions, including criminal prosecution. Such restraints were largely lacking in agrarian societies.

Despite the less venal behavior of public officials in industrial societies, the growing size and power of government bureaucracies has become a matter of serious concern. This is especially true in Marxist societies, because the system of centralized planning has led to a tremendous multiplication of rules and regulations that must then be interpreted and applied by a huge and often unresponsive bureaucratic apparatus.[16] Both supporters and critics of these societies, in fact, consider the unsatisfactory performance of their bureaucracies to be one of their most serious defects.[17]

One of the chief problems of bureaucracies everywhere is maintaining a sense of public responsibility in their personnel. Officials in welfare agencies, for example, often become more concerned with enlarging their staffs, and hence raising their own rank and salary, than with delivering services to those whom the agency was created to serve. In most governmental bureaucracies it it also difficult to get individuals to accept responsibility for any decisions other than the purely routine. Buck-passing, paper-shuffling, and endless delays become standard operating procedures. Because of the tremendous division of labor, and of responsibility, within these organizations, it is frequently impossible to establish accountability, with the result that these patterns persist year after year, and even generation after generation. To compound the problem, the larger a bureaucracy becomes, and the longer these patterns persist, the more difficult it is to eliminate them.

So far, critics of bureaucratic power have not come up with any feasible alternative. The sheer size and complexity of government in a modern industrial society makes mass participation in decision making impossible. A substantial delegation of power, therefore, is inevitable, and those to whom the power is delegated will generally do what they deem appropriate. As we have seen, there are decided limitations to the applicability of democratic principles in any large-scale organization.

Warfare

Compared to some of the wars of the agrarian era (e.g., the Thirty Years' War), wars among industrial societies have been of rather short duration. This is an indication not of pacifism, but of the awesome power of industrial technology. World Wars I and II alone caused over 23 million military deaths, maimed and killed many millions of civilians, and destroyed so much property that a reliable estimate is virtually impossible.[18]

Since the second World War, weapons technology has advanced at a startling pace. The atomic bomb that fell on Hiroshima was the equivalent of 13,000 tons of TNT, while a single hydrogen bomb today may be the equivalent of 59 *million* tons.[19] Any future conflagration involving the major military powers would cause vastly more suffering and devastation than wars of the past. In fact, many experts believe that full-scale war between the United States and the Soviet Union would, at a minimum, cause industrial societies to regress permanently to a preindustrial state.

The tremendous destructive power of the modern military machine is simply a corollary of the tremendous power of modern industrial technology. The invention of the automobile led inevitably to the tank, the invention of the

FIGURE 11.5   The tremendous destructive power of the modern military machine is a corollary of the tremendous productive power of the modern industrial economy: center of Hiroshima, one year after the bomb.

airplane to fighter planes and bombers. While the relationship is sometimes reversed, with advances in weapons technology leading to important civilian innovations (as was the case with radar, for example), the point is the same: industrial societies, like societies before them, are unable to segregate or separate the military and nonmilitary components of their technology. As a consequence, technological advance carries with it the potential for greater destruction.

Unfortunately, industrial societies, again like their predecessors, have failed to develop nonmilitary means of settling their really serious disputes. Some kind of world government appears to be the only solution, but this raises difficult problems of its own, as we will see in Chapter 14. For the present, none of the major industrial societies seem at all inclined to move in this direction, and the arms race, with all its hazards, continues.

Social Stratification

Prior to the Industrial Revolution, every major technological advance led to an increase in the degree of social inequality within societies. This was true of the horticultural revolution, and it was true of the agrarian. During the early stages of the Industrial Revolution, it seemed that the historic pattern would be repeated once again and that industrial societies would prove to be the least egalitarian in history.

More recently, however, as a number of societies have reached a more advanced stage of industrialization, this 9,000–year trend toward greater inequality has begun to falter, even to show signs of a reversal. This has not meant a return to the highly egalitarian patterns of hunting and gathering societies. Far from it. But it has meant a somewhat less unequal distribution of power, privilege, and prestige within advanced industrial societies than was characteristic of either early industrial or advanced agrarian societies.

As we saw in Chapter 2, the basic function of any society's system of stratification is to distribute the things of value that people produce in their life together in society. These include not only material goods, but power and prestige as well. In both Marxist and non-Marxist societies, an individual's access to these things depends to a great degree upon his own or his family's status with respect to such key resources as occupation, education, wealth, ethnicity, political status, age, and sex. We cannot hope to understand the distributive process in advanced industrial societies without taking into account all these separate but interrelated resources and the class systems based on them.

It is important to note at the outset that the distributive process in an industrial society is affected, to a significant degree, by the ideological commitments of its politically dominant group. In Eastern European societies, the dominant class consists of people who occupy key positions in the Communist Party. In most other industrial societies, the dominant class is made up of people who manage giant private corporations or own great fortunes and who are committed to a capitalist ideology. But as important as the differences are, they should not be allowed to obscure basic underlying similarities. In every industrial society, for example, people with advanced education are highly rewarded, as are those in key managerial and political offices. Similarly, power is concentrated in older male hands, and minority ethnic groups tend to be disadvantaged.

Occupational Stratification

For the vast majority of people in any industrial society, the most obvious determinant of their access to society's rewards is their position in the occupational system of stratification. The financial rewards attached to this resource can vary greatly. For example, in the United States today, there are a number of persons, chiefly business executives, athletes, and entertainers, who hold positions that pay a million dollars or more a year in salary, bonuses, and fringe benefits. Meanwhile, others are unable to find employment of any kind. Between these extremes, the great majority have jobs that provide anything from bare subsistence to substantial affluence.

In the Marxist societies of Eastern Europe, occupational inequality is generally not as great as in non-Marxist societies, but it is still substantial. At the lower extreme, workers on poor collective farms and many pensioners barely eke out an existence, while at the upper extreme, high Party and government officials, scientists, writers, and entertainers enjoy great affluence, including multiple homes, servants, vacations in exclusive resorts, and so forth.[20] A Soviet writer recently reported that in the last years of Stalin's reign, the incomes of some high-ranking officials, though not the very highest, were a hundred times the average worker's and several hundred times the most poorly paid worker's.[21] Since then, there has been a deliberate effort to reduce these differences, however, and in recent years differentials in wages have been no more than 50 to 1.[22]

The basic structure of the occupational system of stratification is remarkably similar in Marxist and non-Marxist societies. In both, managerial and professional occupations are the most highly rewarded, skilled technicians and skilled manual workers come next, then the lower echelons of nonmanual workers (such as clerks) and semiskilled manual workers. And—again in both types of societies—unskilled manual laborers, small farmers, and farm laborers have the lowest incomes and the least power and prestige. The chief difference between the two systems is the position of self-employed businessmen. In non-Marxist societies their status depends on the amount of capital they control, but generally they rank high (usually on a par with managers and professionals). In Marxist societies their position is very ambiguous: they sometimes enjoy large incomes, but they also run the risk of imprisonment and are viewed by much of the public as engaged in morally questionable activities.[23] Their extreme status inconsistency resembles that of racketeers and other wealthy people who are involved in illegal or immoral activities in non-Marxist societies.

One of the most basic divisions in the occupational hierarchy of all industrial societies is the one that separates manual from nonmanual workers. This, of course, is the basis for the popular distinction between the working and middle classes: people in families headed by manual workers usually think of themselves, and are thought of by others, as members of the working class, while people who belong to families headed by nonmanual, or white-collar, workers are thought of as middle class. Nonmanual jobs tend to be more rewarding not only in terms of income, but in terms of working conditions, job security, chances for promotion, and prestige as well.

Neither of these classes is a homogeneous entity: each has significant internal divisions. In non-Marxist societies there is an upper-middle class composed of proprietors, managers, officials, and professionals, and a lower-middle class consisting of clerks, salespeople, secretaries, and similar workers. The division in Marxist societies is similar, except for businessmen, as we noted. But what we will call the upper-middle class is usually referred to in these societies as the intelligentsia (a reflection of historic educational prerequisites for entry into the class).[24]

In both types of societies, the working class has at least three fairly distinct skill levels. Its elite are highly skilled and well-paid workers who have usually

FIGURE 11.6   One of the basic divisions in the occupational structure of industrial societies is that which separates manual from nonmanual workers.

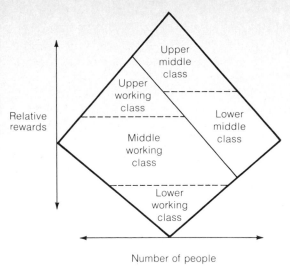

Relative rewards

Number of people

FIGURE 11.7 Many skilled manual workers are more highly rewarded than many clerks and other members of the lower-middle class in industrial societies. This is especially common in Marxist societies.

served long apprenticeships to master their trades. Included are such people as tool-and-die makers, electricians, plumbers, and miners. Beneath them is a stratum of semiskilled workers of the kind found on assembly lines, and on the bottom are day laborers, domestic servants, and other workers with minimal skills or training.

But the occupational system of stratification is more complex than this breakdown reveals. For example, as Figure 11.7 illustrates, many skilled members of the upper stratum of the working class are more highly rewarded than many clerks and other members of the lower-middle class. For Marxist societies, the line dividing the middle and working classes would be tilted a bit more toward the vertical to reflect the more favored position of the upper working class; for non-Marxist societies it might be tipped a bit more toward the horizontal. Fifty or seventy-five years ago, that line would have been even closer to the horizontal for *all* industrial societies. Since then, however, the middle and upper segments of the working class, through the efforts of labor unions and working-class parties, have substantially improved their position, while the largely unorganized lower-middle class has lost ground relative to the rest.

An even more significant change in the occupational system of stratification has been the great proportional increase of higher-status occupations. As Table 11.4 shows, in the United States, white-collar workers, who comprised only 17 per cent of the labor force at the turn of the century, constitute more than half the total. These gains have been accomplished by a reduction in unskilled manual work and farming. Industrialization and technological advance have thus effected a drastic restructuring of the occupational hierarchy, eliminating many low-status occupations, which are physically so demanding, and replacing them with higher-status, nonmanual forms of work.

It is no longer valid, as it was in agrarian societies, to depict the occupational hierarchy as more-or-less a pyramid, with the masses of people

TABLE 11.4 Frequency Distribution of Adult Population among Occupational Classes in the United States, 1900 and 1979 (in percentages)

Occupational Class	1900	1979
Upper white-collar	10	27
Lower white-collar	7	25
Upper blue-collar	11	13
Middle blue-collar*	17	22
Lower blue-collar*	17	10
Farmer and farm laborer	38	3
	100	100

Sources: Figures based on data in U.S. Bureau of the Census, *Historical Statistics of the United States: Colonial Times to 1970*, series D182–232, and U.S. Bureau of the Census, *Statistical Abstract of the United States, 1979*, table 685.
*Includes half of service workers.

concentrated at or near the bottom. In advanced industrial societies, the structure more nearly approximates a diamond, with the largest concentrations in the middle levels (see Figure 11.7).

Property Stratification

The most basic difference between the stratification systems of Marxist and non-Marxist societies involves the locus of power. In the Marxist nations of Eastern Europe, power is concentrated in the hands of those who dominate the *political* system of stratification, the leaders and key officials of the Communist Party. In non-Marxist societies, power tends to be concentrated, though not nearly to the same degree, in the hands of those who dominate the *property* system of stratification, the wealthy, propertied elite.

In all industrial societies, both Marxist and non-Marxist, virtually every individual or family unit owns some property. There are limits on what may be owned in the former, however. In Eastern Europe's Marxist societies, few of the means of production are the property of individuals, although there are some privately owned farms and businesses (e.g., restaurants) in some of these societies. But people may own a home or an apartment, an automobile (though this is uncommon), and personal property, including interest-bearing bank accounts and household furnishings. Privately owned vacation homes are not unusual in some of the Eastern European societies. The amount of wealth individuals accumulate is, of course, limited by the fact that all major businesses are state enterprises. On the other hand, many services for which the members of capitalist societies pay dearly are free, or available for a minimal fee (for example, medical care, higher education, and public transportation).

In non-Marxist societies, in contrast, the means of production are still largely in private hands. For this reason, property is much less evenly distributed among individuals and families. Unfortunately, it is impossible to obtain reliable data on the distribution of wealth in most societies. In the United States, for example, the only data on the subject is what the federal government gathers from estate (i.e., inheritance) tax returns, and these provide information only on individuals. Families, not individuals, however, are the more meaningful unit of analysis, because wealth tends to be shared within a family, or at least made available for the benefit of all the members. Furthermore, the data are gathered only at the time of death, when wealth is usually greater than earlier in life; and this, too, exaggerates the degree to which wealth is concentrated. Finally, as of 1981, no tax return was even required from the estates of individuals whose net worth at the time of death was less than $175,000, thereby excluding the majority of the population from the data.

After the best possible corrections have been made for some of these deficiencies, it appears that in the early 1970s the wealthiest 6 per cent of the American population owned about 43 per cent of the wealth of that society, while the wealthiest 1 per cent owned about 21 per cent.[25] If we go on to make adjustments for the fact that families—spouses, children, and grandchildren— usually share in the benefits of this individually owned wealth, and will eventually inherit most of it, the ratios would be somewhat less, but still substantial.

Recent research by a specially appointed Royal Commission on the Distribution of Income and Wealth yields a similar picture for Britain, though their more thorough examination of the subject identified additional difficulties involved in efforts to obtain reliable measures of the distribution of wealth. For example, as Table 11.5 indicates, when one takes into account the accumulated equity which workers have built up in governmental and private pension systems, the concentration of wealth is not nearly as great as it appears when this is ignored (as in American data).[26] Nevertheless, it is still considerable.

If the power of the very wealthy were confined to the economy, it would be impressive; but when it spills over into the polity, as it commonly does in capitalist societies, it becomes awesome. This situation arises in part because of the tremendous costs of modern election campaigns. An analysis of the 1972

TABLE 11.5 Distribution of Wealth in Britain

	Percentage of Wealth Owned	
Percentage of Population	Excluding Pension Rights	Including Pension Rights
Top 1 per cent	28	17
Top 5 per cent	54	35
Top 10 per cent	67	46
Top 20 per cent	82	59
Bottom 80 per cent	18	41

Source: Royal Commission on the Distribution of Income and Wealth. Report No. 1. *Initial Report on the Standing Reference* (London: H. M. Stationery Office, 1975), tables 36 and 39.

elections in the United States found that they cost $425 million. The more powerful the office, the greater the costs: candidates for the office of the presidency alone spent $138 million. In Japan, political parties collected $443 million in 1979.[27] As a consequence, candidates for important public office tend to be either very wealthy individuals themselves or indebted to such individuals. The only alternative is financial support of candidates by broadly based mass organizations, such as labor unions, public interest groups, or political parties (though the latter often become financially dependent on a limited number of wealthy donors).

Because of their great political power in capitalist societies, the propertied elite are able to secure many striking financial advantages. In the United States, for example, many provisions of the tax laws have been written for their special benefit. For one thing, while large salaries can be taxed at rates up to a maximum of 50 per cent, capital gains can be taxed only to a limit of 28 per cent, and even this can be avoided if the individual does not sell the property, but passes it on to his or her heirs. In addition, many members of the propertied elite are legally able to avoid income tax payments *entirely*. In 1970, for example, Ronald Reagan and Nelson Rockefeller, both multimillion-aires, managed to find sufficient loopholes in the federal tax laws to avoid any income tax obligations at all—despite the fact that people with incomes of less than $5,000 per year were being taxed an average of 9 per cent. And Reagan and Rockefeller had a lot of company. Reports from the Department of the Treasury show that every year hundreds of people in the upper brackets manage to do the same thing. The late J. Paul Getty, reputed to have a net worth of $2 billion, paid only $500 in federal income tax in 1962—and did this quite legally because of class-biased tax legislation.[28]

The dominance of the propertied elite is not reflected only in tax benefits, of course. In countless ways, subtle and not so subtle, their influence pervades the life of society. Government policies on education, health care, environmental pollution, and even relations with other nations are affected by the fact that so many of those who make the decisions are members of the propertied elite or obligated to it. Thus, government officials do not determine defense appropriations simply on the grounds of national security; they also take into account the implications for giant corporations whose profits depend on a continuing flow of government contracts. And in finding solutions to the health needs of the nation, they must consider the special interests of the American Medical Association and the drug industry. The United States is not unique in all of this: the situation in France, Italy, Japan, Canada, West Germany, and other capitalist societies is similar in many respects.[29]

Yet for all their immense power, the propertied elites of non-Marxist societies do not have anything approaching the degree of power Marxist elites enjoy. The democratic political system ensures a substantial degree of influence for the more numerous, but less wealthy, segments of the population, provided they organize effectively. Groups as dissimilar as Common Cause and the United Auto Workers Union and techniques as disparate as running candidates for office and organizing protest rallies are used successfully by the less powerful members of these societies to fight the propertied elite and protect their own interests.

TABLE 11.6   Distribution of Wealth in the United States and in Sweden Compared

Wealth Category	Percentage of Wealth Held	
	United States	Sweden
Top 2 per cent	39	20
Top 10 per cent	61	39
Top 25 per cent	80	56
Top 50 per cent	96	75
Bottom 50 per cent	4	25

Sources: *Federal Reserve Bulletin* (March 1964), pp. 285–293; and Swedish Finance Department, State Public Investigations (SOU). *Ägande och inflytande inom det privata näringslivet; Koncentrationsultredningen, V* [Ownership and influence in the private sector of the economy] (Stockholm, 1968), 7, table 6/4b. Minor corrections were required in United States data to make them comparable to the Swedish data.

The most effective opposition to the power of the propertied class, however, has come from the working-class parties. In some countries, such as Sweden, Norway, and Denmark, these parties have held office most of the time since the 1930s.[30] In other countries, such as the United States, there is no real working-class party, and both major parties are substantially influenced by the propertied elite. Table 11.6 provides some indication of the difference this can make in the distribution of wealth within societies.

Political Stratification

According to democratic theory as taught in public schools and extolled by politicians, the members of a society are all made politically equal by giving each of them a single vote. But most people soon learn that the system does not work this way. In George Orwell's often-quoted phrase, some people are more equal than others. There is, in other words, a political hierarchy, just as there are hierarchies of wealth and occupation, and an individual's status in this hierarchy also affects his access to rewards. This is especially true in one-party societies.

The system of political stratification so important in the Marxist societies of Eastern Europe has a structure both simpler and more sharply defined than that of other industrial societies. The top stratum in the political hierarchy, and the dominant class in these societies, consists of full-time Party professionals, or functionaries, and their families. In the Soviet Union they are known as the *apparatchiki* (literally, "members of the apparatus or machine"; in effect, organization men). Milovan Djilas, the outspoken Marxist heretic, denounced this group, calling it "the new class" to direct attention to its striking similarity to the power-wielding, privilege-seeking, exploitative classes of other societies.[31]

Numerically, the *apparatchiki* and their immediate families are only a fraction of 1 per cent of the population,[32] but their near monopoly of political and economic power gives them a strength far out of proportion to their numbers. When the class first came to power, idealists and political zealots dominated it; but once its position was secure, careerists began to infiltrate, and the class became increasingly concerned with its own special interests, as Djilas noted.

Beneath the Party functionaries is the much larger class of ordinary Party members. In the Soviet Union, it includes about 9 per cent of the adult population. A minority of these members are volunteer activists who provide leadership in the lower echelons of the Party. The majority play a much more limited role.

Still lower in the political class system of a one-party state are those who, though outside the Party, are not regarded as hostile to it. In this group are people who would like to join the Party but lack relevant qualifications, others who are covertly hostile to the Party and stay outside as a matter of principle, and still others who are politically apathetic. This class includes the vast majority of the population. Finally, at the bottom of the system are people who are regarded as hostile to the Party. The size of this class varies considerably from time to time, and from country to country.

Status in the political class system in Marxist societies affects the lives of individuals in many ways. Its consequences for participation in the process of political decision making is obvious. But even outside the political arena, an individual's political status may be critical. For example, party membership is extremely important if an individual hopes to rise to managerial or administrative rank in the occupational system. The Party maintains a list of all important or sensitive jobs in the society, and a list of individuals judged to be politically and otherwise qualified to hold such positions.[33] While Party membership is not essential for appointment to one of these positions, it is a tremendous asset. As one writer puts it, "Although there are a few exceptions, managers [in industrial enterprises] generally cannot move up even to the plant-director level without first becoming Communist Party members."[34] This is equally true of administrative positions in government, education, health, and elsewhere. Party membership is, in fact, an asset in advancement at all levels in the occupational system.[35]

A second important advantage of Party membership is an improvement of living standards.[36] This is not merely a matter of income. In societies in which good housing is scarce, Party membership can facilitate access to a better apartment. It can also provide access to stores that are closed to the general public and specialize in products that are in short supply (e.g., imported goods, luxury foods). Finally, Party membership can facilitate travel abroad, which is highly valued in all Marxist societies.

At the opposite extreme in the hierarchy, the status of dissenters and others who are judged to be hostile to the regime carries a variety of unpleasant consequences. Depending upon the time, place, and circumstances, these may involve anything from occasional police surveillance to psychiatric commitment, imprisonment, or execution. The more severe consequences are far less common today than in the past, even rare in some Marxist societies.[37]

Democratic multiparty societies also have political hierarchies, but they are not associated with such extremes of reward and punishment. Nor are they as important in the life of the nation. Structurally, however, they resemble the political class system of Marxist societies. At the top is a class of people for whom politics is a vocation. Although many of these professionals depend on politics for their livelihood, others, like the Kennedys, are people of wealth who have become involved for other reasons. In a number of countries, including the United States, party activity can be extremely lucrative. For example, in 1964 President Johnson's family had a fortune valued at $9 to $14 million, "amassed almost entirely while Mr. Johnson was in public office; mainly [after] he entered the Senate and began his rise to national power in 1948."[38] His is not an isolated case, at least not among politicians in brokerage-type parties. Typically, these men seem to feel they are entitled to use their public offices for private gain and regard the income as a kind of "broker's fee" paid for their services.[39] Though the ethics of such practices are dubious, to say the least, most political leaders stay carefully within the law (as interpreted by fellow members of the political class).

In ideologically oriented democratic parties, such as the Social Democrats in Scandinavia or the Labour Party in Britain, leaders are much less likely to use their positions for private financial advantage. Their rewards are chiefly power, fame, and the satisfaction of implementing their beliefs.

A second important political class in most multiparty nations is composed of wealthy individuals and business leaders who take an active interest in politics but do not make it their vocation. These people, the so-called "fat cats," provide political organizations with one of their most essential ingredients—money. Some of them seem to want only the excitement of political participation and other psychic benefits, but most are interested in more substantial rewards, such as special tax advantages or lucrative government contracts.

Beneath the professional politicians and wealthy contributors is a class of volunteer workers. This is a diverse group and includes people motivated by political ideals, by private ambition (such as the hope of joining the ranks of the professionals), or by a combination of both. This class is always small, seldom more than a few per cent of the population, and it has a high rate of turnover.[40]

The lowest rung in the political system in democratic societies is occupied by the great majority of citizens whose political activity is limited to voting and a vague identification with one or another of the parties. As records show, many people do not take even this much interest in the political process: half of the adult population does not bother to vote even in presidential elections in the United States.[41]

In the political class system, as in some of the others, an individual tends to benefit in proportion to his investment of time and money. For this reason, a disproportionate share of the benefits accrues to the professional politicians and their wealthy allies. Fortunately, their opportunities for self-aggrandizement are somewhat limited by the widespread right of suffrage, which serves as a check on their self-seeking tendencies: they know that if they push their private interests too far, they can be voted out of office.

Educational Stratification

The roots of educational stratification go far back in history. Even in hunting and gathering societies, shamans enjoyed power and prestige because of their special knowledge. After the invention of writing and the formation of schools early in the agrarian era, educational stratification became increasingly important. As we saw in Chapter 7, only a minority learned to read and write, because the costs of education were prohibitive for peasants. The literate were primarily children of the middle and upper classes, and their skills helped to ensure that they would remain at that level. For the top positions in society, education was seldom of crucial importance; at most, literacy was required, sometimes not even that. Because these positions were usually filled by inheritance, the best-educated men tended to occupy the middle levels of the governmental and religious establishments and used their abilities in the service of the elite.

Some elements of this older system have carried over into modern industrial societies. Most important, an individual's educational opportunities and attainments are still linked with the class position of his or her parents, so that the children of the powerful and wealthy stand a better chance of obtaining a university education, especially at the best institutions, than the children of the poor. This is true even in Marxist societies.[42] But it is easy to exaggerate the similarity between the old system and the present one. Both the new technology and the new democratic ideology have created a need for a populace that is at least literate. Literacy is necessary for effective participation in a modern bureaucratized economy, and it is equally important for the effective operation of a democratic political system. And as technology and ideology have created this need, they have provided the means and the motivation for meeting it: technology has become so productive that child labor is no longer needed, and the newer ideologies have made education a basic right of every child.

As a result, there is no longer the traditional cleavage between a literate minority and an illiterate majority. Illiteracy has largely disappeared in advanced industrial societies. At the same time, other educational distinctions have become important, particularly those based on amount of education. In the United States, individuals are often categorized according to whether they have less than a high school education, a high school diploma, a college diploma, or an advanced degree. As a result of the bureaucratization of both government and industry, the great majority of jobs in the United States, and increasingly in other industrial societies as well, have educational prerequisites, and the individual who lacks them is automatically ineligible. This affects not only one's chances of being hired, but one's chances for promotion as well.[43] In this respect, modern bureaucratic personnel practices have created a civilian counterpart of the military caste system, with its sharp cleavage between officers and enlisted men. Just as the ceiling for the promotion of privates is normally the rank of sergeant, so the ceiling for production workers tends to be the rank of foreman or possibly plant superintendent. Higher ranks are reserved for people with more education, and they are recruited outside the organization. Figure 11.8 illustrates this pattern.

A good measure of the importance of education today is found in recent

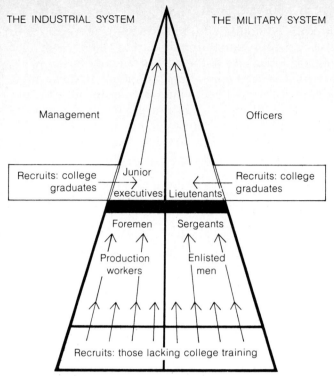

Management   Officers

Recruits: college graduates   Junior executives / Lieutenants   Recruits: college graduates

Foremen   Sergeants

Production workers   Enlisted men

Recruits: those lacking college training

FIGURE 11.8   Recruitment and promotional patterns in modern industry compared with those in the military.

census data on the relationship between education and income. As of 1972, lifetime incomes of American males, classified by years of formal education, were calculated to be as follows.[44]

0–7 years of education	$280,000
8 years of education	$344,000
1–3 years of high school	$389,000
4 years of high school	$479,000
1–3 years of college	$543,000
4 years or more of college	$758,000

The educational elite today appear to have more influence on public policy than their counterparts in the past. This is not to suggest that they have become politically dominant or that advanced academic degrees are necessary for top political office. However, college or university training has become almost a prerequisite for top office. Moreover, political leaders are increasingly forced to rely on the educational elite for counsel in making major decisions.[45] The role of physical scientists and engineers in planning military and space programs, and of social scientists in economic and social policies, is taken for granted today. This pattern is by no means limited to the United States. In the Soviet Union, for example, the reintroduction of market mechanisms into the economy was due in no small measure to the efforts of economists, while physical and medical scientists have had comparable influence in other areas of public policy.[46] Although the political elite are interested only in the factual information these experts can provide, this is hard to get in pure form. The personal values of the experts often intrude, but so subtly as to be unrecognized even by the experts themselves. Because of this, today's educational elite have a much greater impact on high-level decision making than their predecessors in agrarian societies.

Racial and Ethnic Stratification

Many industrial societies have racial or ethnic cleavages. Canada, for example, has the serious cleavage between its French- and English-speaking groups; Belgium between Flemings and Walloons, and the United States between blacks and whites—to name but a few of the more serious ones. As long as groups like these have no effect on how the benefits of a society are distributed, they are not a part of the system of social stratification. But when membership in such a group has an appreciable influence on an individual's access to those benefits, the group becomes a part of the system. The group becomes, in effect, a class: it is an aggregation of people who stand in a similar position with respect to a resource that influences their access to power, privilege, or prestige.

Classes of this kind, however, are different from most others in several respects. For one thing, the resource that is involved in ethnic and racial stratification systems is *an ascribed characteristic*. Unlike such characteristics as occupation, political affiliation, and wealth, an individual cannot alter his or her racial or ethnic background. For another thing, such classes usually have a greater degree of group or class consciousness than most others, more, say, than the educational class of people with high school diplomas, more even than the class of manual workers as a whole. Finally, because physical traits (e.g., racial traits, coloring) and primary relationships (i.e., with family and close friends) are often involved, it is more difficult for an individual to move into or out of an ethnic or racial class.

The most striking example of this type of stratification in the United States involves the two major racial groups. Since early in this country's history, blacks have been a subordinated group. Before the Civil War this was underlined by the legal position of the majority of blacks, who were slaves and the property of members of the white group. Even before the Emancipation Proclamation, some blacks achieved considerable success in the occupational, educational, and property systems of stratification; but despite this they continued to suffer from handicaps imposed because of race. Their access to clubs, churches, housing, and services of almost every kind was much more limited than that of whites with comparable status in other aspects of the system of stratification.

FIGURE 11.9   Much basic learning occurs while a child is small: learning opportunities in Spanish Harlem.

Today, many of these limitations have been removed. Civil rights legislation ensures blacks equal treatment in stores, hotels, restaurants, and other business establishments. But discrimination often continues in housing, club membership, and some other areas. Even more important, the general cultural and economic deprivation of recent centuries has left many blacks unable to take full advantage of the new opportunities. So much basic learning occurs while a child is small that large numbers of black children with poorly educated, low-income parents are already badly handicapped when they begin school. These youngsters generally make slow progress and leave school poorly equipped to compete in the occupational system.

These problems are frequently aggravated by family situations in which the father is absent because of divorce, desertion, illegitimacy, or other reasons. In 1977, this was true of 39 per cent of black families compared with less than 12 per cent of white.[47] Such children are deprived not only of a father's contribution to socialization but of an important source of income as well. The average income of these families in 1977 was $6,959, compared with $15,190 for black families in which both parents were present.[48] Whatever the underlying causes of the high proportion of broken families among blacks (the subject of a lively controversy), its impact on black children is undeniable.

Although the white population is sometimes thought of as a unit, it is, of course, divided along ethnic lines. People of British extraction enjoy the highest status, then those of other northwestern European ancestry, followed by those of southern and eastern European ancestry.[49] This reflects the historic dominance of those who first settled this country. Until about 1830, most of the white population was of British extraction, and these people naturally occupied the dominant positions in all the major institutions. Since most of the later immigrants were poor, had little education, and were unable to speak English, they tended to fill the more menial positions. The more they had in common with the older stock, the more readily they were accepted in marriage and in the better jobs, clubs, and neighborhoods. Northwestern European Protestants were thus accepted more readily than southern and eastern European Catholics and Jews.

In Canada, the most serious cleavage is along ethnic lines and divides French-speaking Canadians from English-speaking ones. Although the French settled the country first, they were conquered by the British, who dominated the political system from the eighteenth century on. The problem was further aggravated because the English industrialized while the French clung to the agrarian way of life. As a consequence, the English also dominated the economy, even in Quebec, the home province of the French.[50] In recent years the French have succeeded in eliminating many discriminatory practices through political action, but many of them still favor political independence for Quebec.

Age and Sex Stratification

Like racial and ethnic stratification, age and sex stratification are also based on ascribed characteristics. Unlike the situation with race and ethnicity, however, age and sex have been bases of status differentiation in every known society. The reason for this is clear. Racial and ethnic status systems have a purely *cultural* basis; that is, they reflect the differing experiences of different human societies. Age and sex status systems, however, have their ultimate basis in *human biology;* that is, they are at least partially the consequence of our common genetic heritage.

But biology is not the only factor that operates on age and sex distinctions. There have always been cultural influences as well, sometimes tremendous ones. As a result, the roles of children, adults, and the aged have varied both within and among societies, and the same is true of the roles of men and women. And in almost every instance, these role differences have been linked to differences in power, privilege, and prestige.

The basis of age differentiation is obvious. Children are both physically and intellectually less developed than adults. Having had fewer chances to acquire experience and information, they are at a competitive disadvantage. For women, the primary handicap has been quite different. Throughout most of human history, the limitations imposed by frequent pregnancy and lactation prevented women from competing with men in political and military activities and hunting, which were the basic determinants of power and prestige.

Although the systems of age and sex stratification in industrial societies have changed in some respects, there is also continuity with the past. Thus middle-aged and older people continue to be dominant in the political, property, and occupational systems. In recent years, for example, the median age of United States Senators has been fifty-six, and, with the Senate's system of seniority, committee chairmen have been even older.[51] One national study of business leaders indicated a median age of fifty-four; another, limited to the managerial elite, showed a median of sixty-one.[52] A study of American military leaders found their average age was fifty-four; and a study of the very wealthy showed that the average age of men with estates valued at $5 million or more was sixty-nine.[53] In Marxist societies, top political elites are often in their seventies. On the other hand, younger people now challenge the authority of their elders to a degree that was unthinkable in agrarian societies.

With respect to sex stratification, although men are still dominant both politically and occupationally, women have made substantial gains in the property and educational systems. Laws that restricted their right to own property have been eliminated in industrial societies, and women now own much of the wealth.[54] Similarly, barriers to higher education have been largely eliminated. Even in the political arena, women have made substantial gains. As recently as 1900, women were permitted to vote only in New Zealand and four American states.[55] Today they enjoy this right in every advanced industrial society. And women have served as prime ministers of both Britain and Israel.

Women are still far from achieving equality in the occupational world, however, and most experts agree that the underlying reason is their historic role in the family. In Chapter 12 we will discuss in some detail the changes that have occurred in that role and the reasons for them. What is relevant here is that, because of large families and heavy domestic responsibilities, most women who worked outside the home prior to the last several decades did so only when economic pressures required it (e.g., unmarried women without other means of support, women whose husbands died or were ill). As a result, women were frequently in the labor force only for brief periods before they returned to their domestic duties.

Because of their relative lack of experience in work outside the home, and because of society's perception of what constituted suitable work for their sex, women were, for a long time, encouraged to enter only those fields that were closely identified with their domestic roles: food service, teaching, nursing, domestic service, certain jobs in the textile and garment industries. When they were admitted to occupations that also employed men, they were not only conditioned to play a subservient role, but their sporadic work patterns usually prevented the accumulation of experience or seniority equivalent to male workers. For these reasons, and also because they were often perceived as being only "secondary" breadwinners, women were generally paid less than men for the same work. What is more, women were concentrated in fields where the pay scales, even for men, tended to be depressed.

Today, much of the historic basis for sex differentiation in employment has been eroded. Technology has eased women's domestic burdens and altered most work activities outside the home as well, making them as suitable for females as for males. Meanwhile, there have been ideological changes, resulting in the provision of education and training for women, and the opening of doors for them in virtually every area of work. In some societies women now enter the labor force in almost the same numbers as men. In one recent year, women constituted 51 per cent of the labor force in the Soviet Union.[56] This figure was inflated somewhat as a result of the heavy death toll among Soviet men in World War II; but even if there had been equal numbers of both sexes in the population, women would still have made up 43 per cent of the labor force. In the United States, too, the percentage of gainfully employed women has steadily risen. In 1890 only 14 per cent of women between twenty-five and sixty-four years of age worked outside the home.[57] Today, more than half of the women in this age category are employed outside the home, and 42 per cent of the labor force is female.[58]

Yet despite this increased involvement in the labor force, women are still disproportionately concentrated in a relatively small number of poorly paid occupations. In the United States, for example, two-thirds of all employed women are in secretarial and clerical work, retail sales, public school teaching, nursing and health care, social work, food service, personal service, and domestic service.[59] In the Soviet Union, nearly one-third of all female

FIGURE 11.10   Female locomotive engineer, U.S.S.R.

employees are in occupations that are 85 per cent or more female, up from only one-fifth in such occupations in 1959.[60]

The occupations in which women are concentrated vary somewhat from one society to another. In the Scandinavian societies, many dentists are women; in Finland, for example, they are 70 per cent of the total.[61] In the Soviet Union, nearly 70 per cent of the doctors are women. But the skill level of most Soviet doctors is closer to that of the nurse-practitioner in the United States, with the result that the occupation is poorly paid and has a relatively low status. Among the most highly skilled physicians, women are a small minority: only 10 per cent of the members of the Soviet Academy of Medicine are female.[62] The pattern is much the same in politics and economics, where women are well represented in the lower echelons, but conspicuously absent at the top. Thus, while 25 per cent of the members of the Communist Party in the Soviet Union are female, they comprise less than 3 per cent of the full members of the Central Committee, and are not represented at all in the Politbureau.[63] One specialist on Soviet society recently summarized the situation by saying, "The position of Soviet women does not differ in principle from that of their counterparts in capitalist society."[64] This conclusion is borne out by a recent survey of the causes of income inequality in Poland, which found that sex explained more of the income variance in that society than any other single factor, including education, Party membership, or type of industry.[65]

In short, sex-segregated employment is still a prominent feature of the world of work in industrial societies. Although this is reflected in the degree of power, privilege, and prestige enjoyed by women, perhaps it can best be demonstrated with reference to income. In the United States, France, Britain, West Germany, and the Soviet Union, women's incomes average between 61 and 68 per cent of those of men.[66]

Consequences of Social Stratification

The unequal distribution of power, privilege, and prestige divides the members of industrial societies as surely as it did the members of agrarian societies. Those who have similar resources and backgrounds tend to associate with one another and to stand apart from the rest. This inevitably leads to the formation of class-based subcultures and class-based communities.

The differences that divide the classes are partly economic. The poor obviously cannot afford many of the things that are an integral part of the middle-class way of life, and the middle classes cannot afford many of the things that are essential to the upper-class way of life. But it is not only material differences that are divisive. Because their experiences have been different, the members of these classes have different information on a wide variety of subjects, and thus different values and beliefs, social norms, and even speech patterns. These can be even more potent than economic differences in separating the members of a society.

It would be impossible to describe here all the differences that sociologists have found between the classes in modern industrial societies. The subject fills volumes.[67] Suffice it to say that hardly any aspect of life is untouched. Even one's chances for survival are influenced by class membership. For example, white babies born in the United States today can expect to live five years longer than nonwhite babies (the difference was 9.6 years in 1920).[68] Class also affects many personality traits, since its influences begin to operate immediately after birth. To a large degree, a person's needs and desires, goals and ambitions, and even self-image are molded by the system of stratification. And not least of all, class affects an individual's chance of success both in school and in the world of work, Sometimes these influences are extremely subtle: children of the poor, for example, may suffer permanent mental impairment because their mothers' diet during pregnancy, or their own early diet, was deficient in protein.

Despite our physical proximity to people of other classes, most of us never have the opportunity to see their lives "from the inside." At best, we are spectators who watch from a distance—and often misunderstand what we see. (This is what black militants mean when they say that whites are unable to "think black.") Talented novelists and other writers help to bridge this gap by sharing insights of their own experiences, and sociologists and anthropologists can also add to our understanding of what it means to live in other classes.[69] But it is important to remember that vicarious experiences are no substitute for direct, personal, lifelong experience.

From the standpoint of society, one of the most important consequences of stratification is the dissension it generates between individuals and between classes. Where there is opportunity for upward mobility, there will be competition. But where status is primarily ascribed, there will probably be class conflict. People born into classes to which many of the good things of life are denied are likely to join others in the same situation and try to force society to make more rewards available to them, while those in the favored classes usually resist these efforts. We see this in struggles between workers and employers, in racial conflicts, and in student efforts to get more power in the affairs of universities and colleges.

The stakes in struggles like these can be extremely high. In industrial societies, the outcome, more often than not, has favored the *less* advantaged class, resulting in a gradual reduction in social, economic, and political inequality. Even if this is not always evident in short-run comparisons, it becomes clear whenever we compare advanced industrial societies of the modern world with agrarian societies of the past.

Vertical Mobility

Compared with agrarian societies, industrial societies offer tremendous opportunities for individuals to better themselves. In the agrarian era, birthrates ensured an oversupply of labor in almost every generation. At every social level, a certain percentage of the children were forced to work in occupations less rewarding than their fathers' or to join the ranks of the beggars, outlaws, prostitutes, and vagabonds. Though some did improve their situations, far more were downwardly mobile.

In industrial societies, conditions are strikingly different. While birthrates have been falling, technology has been increasing the proportion of high-status occupations (see Table 11.4). As a result, the situation has been reversed: there is now more upward than downward mobility. A survey by the United States Bureau of the Census compared the occupations of men today with those of their fathers and found that two and a half times as many had risen from blue-collar occupations to white-collar as had dropped from white-collar to blue-collar.[70] Even if we divide the urban occupational hierarchy into three or four levels, the ratio of upward to downward mobility is about the same. This ratio is higher than in most other industrial societies, owing, apparently, to a more rapid expansion of higher-status occupations in the United States. But nearly every industrial society has eliminated the excess of downward mobility.[71]

This has undoubtedly been a factor in reducing the threat of the working-class revolution predicted by Marx and Engels. If, in every generation, a quarter or more of the children of workingmen are able to rise into the ranks of the middle class, resentment against the system is almost certain to be less than if only a few per cent move up the ladder, as Marx and Engels expected. Furthermore, since those who rise are generally some of the most talented and ambitious members of their generation, a lot of potential leadership for protest movements is permanently lost to the working class.

It is probably no coincidence that a great deal of the leadership and support for protest movements in advanced industrial societies has come from members of racial and ethnic minorities. Upward mobility for such people is more difficult, sometimes impossible. Unable to escape the limitations society imposes on them, many turn their energies to social protest, especially programs designed to eliminate the differential between their own group and more favored ones.

Social Inequality: Two Trends

When we began our examination of stratification in industrial societies, we noted the trend toward increasing social inequality that started with the horticultural revolution 10,000 years ago and continued into the early stages of the Industrial Revolution. We also noted that with further industrialization this trend was halted, even reversed. Before concluding our review of stratification, we need to take a closer look at this important development, and at another critical trend as well.

In advanced agrarian societies of the past, systems of inequality were often built into the legal codes. There was no pretense that people were equal. Some were legally classified as privileged nobility, some as commoners, others as slaves or serfs, and legal rights and privileges varied accordingly. Democracy as we understand it was unknown in these societies. Political decisions were the God-given prerogative of a tiny elite; the rest of the population had no influence. The only thing that set limits on the actions of the elite was the knowledge that, if conditions became too oppressive, the masses would revolt. The ruler and the governing class usually received not less than half of the national income, sometimes as much as two-thirds.[72]

In advanced industrial societies, legally based hereditary statuses have been virtually eliminated. In Britain and a few other societies, titles of nobility remain, but the special rights that were once attached to them have been largely stripped away. It is true, of course, that people still receive unequal treatment in courts of law, in both Marxist and non-Marxist societies,[73] but the situation has improved greatly since the time when the poor were often hanged for the theft of an egg or a loaf of bread.

Except in the one-party states of Eastern Europe, opportunities for participation in the political decision-making process have been substantially increased. The right of franchise has gradually been enlarged until virtually the entire population is able to vote (see Table 11.1, page 305). Though the value of such limited participation may seem questionable at times, the record of the Scandinavian democracies shows what is possible; and even in countries like the United States and Canada, much of the newer legislation reflects the increased political influence of less advantaged segments of the population.

While Marxist societies lag in terms of political equality, they are ahead in terms of economic equality. Substantial differences in income still exist, but they are, as we have seen, less than in non-Marxist societies, and far less than in traditional agrarian. Even in non-Marxist societies, the upper 2 per cent of the population does not appear to receive more than 25 per cent of the national income, and usually less than that.[74] Though far more than their proportionate share, it represents a significant reduction in inequality. But far more important than this is the fact that, in all advanced industrial societies, the majority of people live somewhere *between* wealth and poverty, and their living standards, though greatly varied, would be judged enviable by traditional agrarian standards.

The factors responsible for the egalitarian trend are essentially the same as those that have produced the democratic trend. The entire movement away from the extreme social inequality that developed in agrarian and early industrial societies is intimately related to the speed and magnitude of the increase in productivity in industrial societies.[75] When national income is rising rapidly and promises to continue to rise as long as political and economic stability are maintained, the dominant classes find it in their interest to make concessions to the lower classes to prevent costly strikes, riots, and revolutions. Even though they give ground in *relative* terms, they come out far ahead in *absolute* terms in an expanding economy. For example, an elite would enjoy a substantially greater income if it settled for "only" 25 per cent of the national income in a $500 billion economy than if it stubbornly fought to preserve a 50 per cent share and, in the process, provoked so much internal strife that the economy stalled at the $100 billion level. In short, the new technology has provided the elites of industrial societies with an option undreamed of in agrarian societies; and judging by the results, it has proved highly attractive.

FIGURE 11.11   Public housing project for low-income families, Denmark.

But as the new technology has helped to reduce the level of inequality within industrial societies, it has had the opposite effect for the world system. The gap between rich and poor nations has been widening ever since the start of the industrial era. One expert estimates that in the 100 years between 1860 and 1960, the wealthiest quarter of the nations increased their share of the world's income from 58 to 72 per cent, while the share of the bottom quarter fell from 12.5 to 3.2 per cent.[76] With the new technology gradually eroding the barriers between societies, this trend is bound to grow in relevance for everyone. We will return to this subject in Chapter 13, when we examine the complex problems of societies that are struggling to industrialize in the shadow of far wealthier and more powerful societies.

CHAPTER 12

Industrial Societies: III

The Family

The impact of industrialization on kinship has been no less dramatic than its impact on population, the economy, the polity, and stratification. The consequences for kinship, the oldest institution in human societies, can be seen in its declining functions, in the smaller size of nuclear families, in the high incidence of divorce, and in the changing roles of women and young people.

Declining Functions of the Family

In the simplest human societies, the basic integrative force in societal life was the kin group, an all-purpose organization that provided for the political, economic, educational, religious, and psychic needs of all of its members. As societies grew in size and complexity, this had to change. No longer could an individual's relationships with other people always be defined in terms of kinship. Rather, new roles and organizations began to take shape, and, in the process, some of the functions of the kin group were eroded.

Although this process began thousands of years ago, kin groups still remained central to the life of society even into the late agrarian era. For one thing, the nuclear family (i.e., mother, father, and children) was still the basic productive unit in the economy. The peasant family was almost invariably a work unit, but this was typical of artisans as well. Place of work and place of residence were normally the same, and all of the members of a family, including the children, shared in the work.

The political system, too, was still a family matter. The elite usually inherited their status, while the royal family considered the state to be its personal property. Education remained primarily a family responsibility: boys learned the male role and their productive skills from their fathers and other male relatives; girls learned theirs from older females in the family. Due to the growth of urban communities, the kinship system was not always as strong or pervasive as it had been in simpler societies. But family ties remained critical in the lives of most individuals and provided the basic framework for societal life.

In industrial societies, many of the family's traditional functions have been removed or greatly altered. The family is an economic unit only in terms of consumption, not of production. Families do not control the political system; nepotism may still occur, but it is not accepted as normal or legitimate. Schools, religious groups, and other organizations have assumed much of the responsibility for the education, socialization, and supervision of children, and a wide variety of organizations from 4-H clubs to summer camps and from beauty colleges to universities have taken over the task of training young people in the skills they will use in their adult lives.

But the family has by no means been stripped of its historic functions by industrialization. Some of the most critical ones, including reproduction and the early socialization of new members, still fall to the nuclear family. And as the larger kin system, or extended family, has diminished in importance, and as societal life has become increasingly complex and depersonalized, the nuclear family's responsibilities have in some ways become more important. For one thing, it bears the primary burden for fulfilling the psychic and emotional needs of its members. With respect to its children, the nuclear family is still expected to be the major factor in personality development, instilling basic values, providing affection, providing guidance and encouragement in school and career decisions, training in the use of money, and much more. And all of this must be accomplished in a social environment that is far less homogeneous, and therefore far more difficult, than the one in which agrarian families raised their children.

The altered functions of the nuclear family are reflected in courtship and marriage. Marriage has become more individualized, and it is undertaken for more personal reasons than in the past. Because most horticultural and agrarian societies viewed marriage largely in economic terms, marriages were arranged by parents with this function in mind. The individuals most intimately involved were often denied even veto power. Sexual attraction and affection were not considered important factors: everyone knew that these might grow or they might wane, but the need for a firm economic base would persist.

In industrial societies, in contrast, an individual's role in the economy is not directly related to his or her situation with respect to family. As a consequence, marriage has become an arrangement that is undertaken primarily to enhance personal happiness and to permit one to fulfill personal goals, such as establishing a home or having children. Most people view marriage as the union of a man and a woman who are attracted to one another both physically and psychologically and who hope to find pleasure, comfort, convenience, and companionship by sharing their lives with one another, hopefully until death. In short, personal satisfaction, as opposed to basic survival needs, is the underlying reason for most marriages in contemporary industrial societies.

Causes of Change in the Family

Change in the family, like change in every other institution, is essentially the result of technological advance and the trends that accompany it. One of the most fundamental and pervasive trends accompanying industrialization has been an enormous increase in specialization. As a result, specialized organizations, institutions, and businesses have steadily removed from the home and family much of the responsibility for performing a wide range of service functions. These include not only educating and caring for the young, but caring for the ill and the aged, building both home and furnishings, processing food and preparing meals, making and caring for wearing apparel, and much more. As a result, the nuclear family, too, has steadily become a more specialized institution.

Specific elements of the new technology have also had a great impact on the nuclear family, especially those that have given people control over their fertility. Nothing better illustrates how technological advance expands the "range of the possible," for individuals and families as well as for societies, than advances in methods of birth control. Because of these advances, most couples today have a much wider range of options available to them in almost every aspect of their lives than couples had in societies of the past.

Industrialization has also served to undermine the traditional structure of the family with respect to authority. The father is no longer the head of the family in the way he was in agrarian societies, and parents do not have as much control over their children's conduct as they had either in agrarian societies or earlier in the industrial era. Peer group influence has become more powerful than family influences for many teenagers, and serious family conflict often results.

In large measure, this drastic decline in authority of parents is simply the inevitable consequence of the technological and other societal changes that have destroyed the family's role as a productive unit, which once had to work together for the mutual benefit, even the survival, of its members. Related to this, industrialization has had the effect of drawing families apart both physically and psychologically. Most fathers and a large number of mothers are away from the home all day, while schools and other organizations draw children out of the family and into a different environment. Children in the lower grades may spend far more time with their teachers than with their mothers, and teenagers often spend more time with their friends than with parents or siblings. Similarly, husbands and wives see less of one another or of their children than of their co-workers. One study of the fathers of one-year-olds in the United States found that they spent an average of only twenty minutes a day with their infants.[1]

Another important influence on the decline of authority within the home has been the new democratic ideology which has permeated almost every area of industrial societies, and which carries with it an individualistic bias that puts more emphasis on the rights of individuals than it does on their responsibilities to the groups of which they are part. Just as the democratic trend has altered the roles within other institutions (e.g., political, economic, and educational), it has altered the roles of individuals within the family. A final factor contributing to this trend is the greater number of options available to individuals in modern societies who want to break family ties. Divorce is easier (see below), and so is economic independence for women, while such options as food stamps, welfare, and refuge centers are available to both women and children departing the nuclear family. As a result of all of these factors—specialization, new ideologies, and new technologies—the nuclear family today is less cohesive than its agrarian predecessor.

Finally, the extended family has been substantially weakened by technological advances that make the populations of industrial societies more mobile. Although the lower cost and greater ease of transportation and communication make it possible for individuals to maintain contact with relatives across greater distances, the relationships are not the same as when these relatives lived within the same community.

The Nuclear Family in Industrial Societies

Size and Composition   The most drastic change in the nuclear family is in the number of children, as Table 12.1 indicates. British marriages contracted around 1860 produced a median of six children. Only two generations later, the median had dropped to two. Families with eight or more children declined from 33 per cent of the total to only 2 per cent. Although the decline was more rapid in Britain than in most industrial societies, the general pattern has been quite similar.[2]

Comparisons like the one in Table 12.1 are misleading if we assume that they reflect differences in the number of children actually living within a family at the same time. For one thing, in the earlier period the death rate among children was so much higher than it is today that there were considerably fewer children living in an agrarian family than were born into it. Another factor that reduced the number of children living with their parents at any given time was the long duration of the childbearing period. Women who had eight, ten, or more children often bore them over a twenty-year period or longer. By the time the youngest children were five or ten, many of their older brothers and sisters had left home or died. Thus, although the nuclear family was certainly larger in agrarian societies, the number of its members who actually lived together at one time was not as different as the birthrates suggest.

**TABLE 12.1   Number of Children Born to
British Couples Married Around 1860 and
Around 1925**

Number of Children Born	Percentage of Marriages	
	Marriages Around 1860	Marriages Around 1925
None	9	17
One	5	24
Two	6	25
Three	8	14
Four	9	8
Five	10	5
Six	10	3
Seven	10	2
Eight	9	1
Nine	8	0.6
Ten	6	0.4
Over Ten	10	0.3
Total	100	100.3

Source: Royal Commission on Population, *Report*
(London: H. M. Stationery Office, 1949), p. 26.

A second noteworthy change in the composition of the family is the elimination of the last vestiges of polygyny. Industrial societies are the only major type in which polygyny has never been socially approved. Among preagrarian societies, only a minority, around 13 per cent, insist on monogamy.[3] In agrarian societies, monogamy is more common, though still far from universal. Until recently, polygyny was practiced throughout the whole of the Islamic world extending from the East Indies to Morocco. The shift in industrial societies reflects the changing character of the family, especially the growing importance of affective ties between husband and wife and the declining importance of economic functions. Monogamy in industrial societies is also an expression of democratic, egalitarian values and a reaction against inequalities inherent in polygynous marital systems.

The modern nuclear family also has fewer relatives living with it. Their households less frequently accommodate aged grandparents, unmarried aunts and uncles, or even grown children. This is no longer as necessary because modern urban communities provide so many alternative facilities for the individual—apartments, nursing homes, restaurants, laundries, and so on. Moreover, as these facilities have developed, changes have occurred in societal values: most members of industrial societies are extremely jealous of their privacy and regard it more highly than they do the advantages that go with more inclusive households.

Disrupted Nuclear Families   During the last hundred years, the divorce rate in virtually every industrial society has risen substantially. In the United States in 1890 it was only 0.5 per 1,000 population; by 1978 it had risen tenfold to 5.1.[4] In large measure, this trend is an inevitable result of the altered functions of the family, the changed perception of marriage that has accompanied it, the new options available to women, and the newer attitudes of society toward divorce. Half or more of all divorced people eventually remarry, however, which suggests that marriage is still considered a meaningful and valuable institution.

Despite the great increase in divorce, its impact on the nuclear family has not been as dramatic as one might suppose. This is because marriages during the agrarian era, and early in the industrial era, were disrupted about as often as they are today, but for a different reason: *the death of one or both parents*. In eighteenth-century Sweden, approximately 50 per cent of nuclear families were broken in this way before all of the children had reached adulthood; in late eighteenth-century France, the figure was 60 per cent, and in early twentieth-century India it was 70 per cent.[5] Thus, despite the rising divorce rate, the percentage of ever-married women between the ages of forty-five and sixty-four who were still living with their first husband remained virtually unchanged in the United States from 1910 to 1970.[6]

More recently, however, as the divorce rate has continued to rise and the death rate has leveled off, the picture has begun to change for the nuclear family. Most important, the proportion of children living with *both* of their natural or adoptive parents has begun to fall. In 1968, 12 per cent of American

FIGURE 12.1   Prior to industrialization, many marriages were broken during the child-rearing years by the death of one or both parents.

children under eighteen years of age were living with only one of their parents; a decade later, the figure had risen to 18 per cent.[7] This pattern is especially common among blacks: 44 per cent of black children under eighteen live in one-parent households.[8] And on the basis of recent trends, projections indicate that nearly 40 per cent of *all* American children born around 1970 will live in a one-parent family for some part of their first eighteen years.

Changing Role of Women

Nowhere can the effects of industrialization on society's norms, values, and sanctions be seen more clearly than in the changing role of women.[9] Throughout recorded history most women were destined to spend the prime years of their lives bearing children, nursing them, caring for them when they were sick and dying, and rearing them if they survived; doing domestic chores; tending a garden; and often helping in the fields. It is hardly surprising, therefore, that women seldom played significant roles outside the home or made outstanding contributions to the arts.

The first signs of change came early in the Industrial Revolution, when the new economic conditions caused children to be perceived less as economic assets and more as liabilities. Efforts to reduce fertility were soon aided by innovations in the area of birth control. During the nineteenth century, however, the average woman still produced a large family, still had babies for whom there was no real alternative but prolonged breast feeding, still carried

FIGURE 12.2   During the nineteenth century, large families were still the rule.

THE YOUNG HOUSEKEEPER'S FRIEND

Women's liberation owes more to technological advance than many people appreciate. Cookbooks and other guides for nineteenth-century housewives are interesting reminders of the revolutionary transformation that has occurred in the care of a home and family.

Baking, for example, was a very time-consuming job in a day when homes had either a reflecting oven beside an open fire or a brick oven built into a chimney. Books written for young housewives often advised them to set aside a day or two each week for baking, and *The Young Housekeeper's Friend*, published in 1859, stressed the importance of careful planning. As Mrs. Cornelius, the author, advised, "The bread first—then the puddings—afterward pastry—then cake and gingerbread—lastly, custards." With respect to bread, Mrs. Cornelius wrote that "A half hour is the least time to be given to kneading the bread . . . and an hour's kneading is not too much."

Laundry was another time-consuming task, and an exhausting one as well. Water had to be carried from the well or cistern to the stove to be heated, and then carried to the washtubs. White items required boiling. Most items required scrubbing by hand while bending over a washboard. After washing, rinsing, boiling, blueing, and starching, everything had to be carried outside and spread on bushes or hung on a line to dry, and collected later. Ironing for a large family could easily consume most of a day. And from time to time the housewife had to prepare her own soap from wood ashes, fat, and grease.

Today, with a single twist of the dial on a modern gas or electric oven, an individual accomplishes the equivalent of cutting and splitting the firewood, hauling it in from the yard, and building and maintaining the fires, and "brown and serve" rolls are more likely to go into the oven than bread kneaded for half an hour. Similarly, automatic washers and driers and no-iron fabrics have reduced the expenditure of time and energy required by a family's laundry by 95 per cent, even as standards of personal care and cleanliness have risen.

the full burden of child care and housework, and sometimes was obliged to work outside the home.

Because women were usually supplementary wage earners for their families, they were not trained for skilled jobs and were relegated to those that paid the least. Their availability for work at low wages posed a threat to the emerging labor movement and, as a consequence, women were virtually excluded from it. That was, in effect, a working*man's* movement, and its goal was to wrest a greater share of the new economic surplus from the upper classes.

In contrast, the early women's movements were dominated by the better educated, more leisured, and economically more secure women of the upper classes, and their goals were primarily to obtain for women some of the legal and civil rights that already belonged to upper- and middle-class men: the right to vote, to hold public office, to own property, and to enter universities. Late in the nineteenth century, they also became concerned with the situation of the

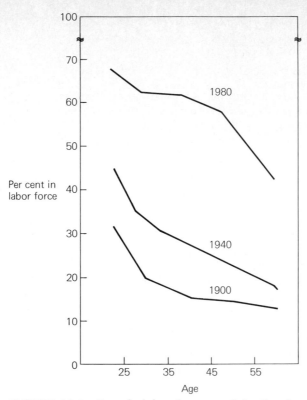

FIGURE 12.3   Female labor force participation in the United States by age: 1900–1980.

working mother and sought to have her working hours shortened and night work eliminated.

By the early years of the twentieth century, these initial goals had been accomplished and the movement virtually died out. Changes continued in women's role, however, and these, too, were consequences of continuing technological and economic change. One of the most significant was the development of an alternative to breast feeding, which freed the mothers of infants from the need to remain in the home.

Women's educational levels, meanwhile, continued to rise, and the growing needs of industrial societies for people in service industries (e.g., nursing, social work, teaching) and the growth of organizations requiring large numbers of secretarial and clerical workers (business and government) opened up new occupational possibilities for women from every social class. By the middle of the century, not only were more women in the labor force, but more of them were married women, a trend that still continues. This trend would not have developed, however, without lower fertility rates. American women with two children now spend an average of only 8.5 years—or less than 20 per cent of their adult years—with children under six years of age. Women in agrarian societies, in contrast, often had children this young until they were nearly 50—or dead.

The newer women's movement that got under way in the 1960s has a

**TABLE 12.2 Average Hours Urban Americans
Devoted Each Week to Work for Pay and to Care
of Home and Family, in 1975, by Employment
Status, Marital Status, and Sex**

Employment Status, Marital Status, and Sex	Work for Pay	Home and Family Care
Employed married men	47.4	9.7
Employed married women	30.1	24.9
Full-time housewives	1.1	44.3

Source: U.S. Department of Commerce, Bureau of the
Census, *Social Indicators, 1976,* table 10/1.

diversity of goals, but one underlying objective: to break the restrictive molds
in which societies have cast women. This goal is based on the premise that
with a single exception—women's capacity for childbearing—the differences
between the sexes no longer provide a valid basis for the division of labor.
Modern technology largely compensates for those differences that are physical
(e.g., strength, lactation), while those differences that are psychological (e.g.,
emotional responses, competitiveness) are to an indeterminate degree the
result of socialization rather than genetics.

The women's movement also emphasizes the fact that power and prestige
in modern societies derive from activities outside the family and that if women
are to have equal access to these rewards and share equally in shaping
society's institutions, they must participate fully in the occupational system.
But women cannot have equal access to the more interesting and demanding
jobs, promotions, higher pay, political offices, or other opportunities outside
the home unless the burden of responsibilities *within* the home is divided more
evenly. Thus, the women's movement in the United States and other societies
is seeking both to increase men's participation in household responsibilities
and child care and to spread the burden of child care by tax rebates for working
parents and by the creation of tax-supported child care centers.

As Table 12.2 indicates, married men and women in the United States
spend approximately equal amounts of time working (57 hours per week for
men, 55 hours per week for women), but men spend a much higher percentage
of time working for pay, while women spend proportionately more on family
responsibilities. Similar patterns are reported in the Soviet Union and elsewhere.[10] This is, of course, a major reason for both the differences in earnings
between the sexes and the lower proportion of women who rise to supervisory
and managerial positions. One interesting response to the problem has been
the Swedish decision to provide the parents of a newborn child with nine
months leave at 90 per cent pay, with the parents free to divide the leave
between them as they see fit.[11]

In some of the Marxist societies of Eastern Europe, the employment rate of
women is nearly that of men. In East Germany, 81 per cent of all women are in
the labor force, and in the Soviet Union the figure is reported to be close to 85
per cent.[12] These high rates reflect a mixture of governmental pressures that
stigmatize the role of housewife, economic pressures within the family,

changing attitudes and values, and the availability of child care facilities. The latter are not nearly as good in the Soviet Union as in East Germany, however, where it is reported that 60 per cent of all children under three are now provided for.[13] Children as young as ten weeks can be brought to these centers, where the personnel and facilities are reported to be excellent and the cost as low as 60 cents a day. East German authorities are reported to be somewhat cautious, however, about the long-run effects of this early separation of children from their mothers. As the head of one district hospital stated, ''So far the children have not shown any damage, but how it turns out historically with a large number of people we cannot say.''[14]

For women themselves, the consequences of changes in their role are becoming increasingly evident. Not surprisingly, they indicate the erosion of many traditional differences between the sexes in areas beyond employment and family life. This is evident in everything from clothing to mental and physical health, and from tobacco and alcohol consumption to frequency of crime, automobile accidents, and suicide.[15] Betty Friedan has argued that middle-aged women suffer less from depression and insomnia today than fifteen or twenty years ago, and others report a decline in the use of tranquilizers by women. The once-large differences between the sexes in smoking habits has been all but eliminated, and among teenagers, more girls than boys now smoke. Similarly, differences in the incidence of heart disease between men and women are declining, and one recent study found that heart disease among middle-aged mothers employed in clerical and sales jobs was twice as frequent as among housewives.[16] And, in 1977, one in three Americans arrested for larceny and theft was a woman, compared with one in six in 1960.

Changing Role of Youth

In preindustrial societies, the transition from childhood to adulthood occurred rather swiftly and at an early age. Children were typically given chores to do while they were still quite young, and their responsibilities gradually increased. By the time they were in their middle teens, sometimes earlier, they were doing much the same work as their parents and other adults. Traces of this older pattern still survive in the rites of passage of certain religious groups (e.g., confirmation rites and bar mitzvahs), which occur around the age of thirteen. In an earlier era, these commonly signaled the end of childhood and the beginning of adulthood, a period in which the individual would be obliged to earn his or her own way and contribute to the support of others.

With the rise of industrialization, the need for human labor was reduced to such an extent that children came to be viewed as a threat on the job market, and labor unions fought to make child labor illegal. Their efforts were reinforced by the passage of legislation to make school attendance compulsory, and young people were gradually edged out of the labor force or into marginal, part-time jobs. In the home, there were fewer siblings for older children to care for, and fewer chores to perform. In short, opportunities for participation in the adult world were drastically curtailed. As a consequence, a new age role was, in effect, created. Whereas most people in their teens, and certainly those in their early twenties, had previously been viewed as young adults, they increasingly came to be seen as occupying an intermediate role, a role that is neither that of adult nor that of child.

Most of the individuals in this new age role are students. Table 12.3 shows how rapidly the school population in the United States increased during the last hundred years. By 1978, 94 per cent of Americans aged fourteen to seventeen were enrolled in school, and 29 per cent of those aged eighteen to twenty-four.[17] As this suggests, advanced industrial societies have expanded their educational institutions far beyond what is required to equip their members for roles in the economy, or even for roles as citizens in a democratic society.[18]

Unfortunately, many of these societies have failed to take account of the fact that all individuals are not equally disposed to be students for such a protracted period. Many young people have little interest in the intellectual aspect of education, or even in its vocational relevance, but would rather move on into adult roles. They frequently discover, however, that there are no viable alternatives. Many who drop out of secondary school, or even out of college, have trouble finding work and often drift into street gangs and other groups whose members are recruited almost entirely from this age stratum.

As always happens when one segment of a population is cut off for an extended period from full participation in the life of the larger society, young people have developed their own subculture. Many of its more distinctive features (e.g., music, sports, experimentation with sex and drugs, etc.) are a natural consequence of some of the distinctive attributes of youth, such as great vitality, curiosity about life, the desire for fun and excitement, and resistance to adult authority. The high rate of innovation that occurs in areas like music, language, and dance is also, to some extent, the result of deliberate efforts to create a barrier between the youth community and the adult community. The faster such things change, the harder it is for outsiders to keep up with them, thereby forcing adults to keep their distance and preventing them from moving in and dominating the youth scene.

At a more fundamental level, though, youth culture simply reflects some of the most distinctive characteristics of industrial societies themselves: their high

TABLE 12.3   Growth of the Student Population in the United States, 1880–1980

Date	Enrollment in Public Schools, Grades 9–12	Enrollment in Colleges and Universities	Total	Percentage of American Population Enrolled
1880	100,000	100,000	200,000	0.4
1930	4,400,000	1,100,000	5,500,000	4.4
1980	14,600,000	11,600,000	26,200,000	11.8

Sources: U.S. Department of Commerce, Bureau of the Census, *Historical Statistics of the United States: Colonial Times to 1970* (1975), series H 424 and H 706, and *Statistical Abstract of the U. S. 1979*, table 219.

rate of innovation, their affluence, their increased leisure, their emphasis on individuality, and their tendency to specialize. The preoccupation of young people with changing fads and fashions, for example, is just one more expression of their society's enormous economic surplus and its attitude toward the new and the different.

The differences between the norms and values of the youth culture and those of the larger society can cause serious problems, however, especially when they involve decisions with long-term implications for young people and for others. Teenage pregnancy is a compelling example of this. Every year in the United States alone, several hundred thousand unmarried girls in their teens become pregnant,[19] usually because they begin sexual activity without adequate information on reproduction and contraception. These individuals are thus forced to make decisions that neither experience nor the norms and values of the youth culture have equipped them to make. Should the girl have an abortion or have the child? Marry the father or remain single? Put the child up for adoption or struggle to raise it alone? One consequence of young women's answers to these questions has been a dramatic increase in the United States in the number of very small children raised by only one parent— 13 per cent of all babies under three in 1974.[20]

Even when the decision to marry is made without the complications of an unexpected pregnancy, teenaged marriages are an especially high risk, largely because the qualities that the youth culture values most highly may have little to do with the qualities an adult finds most desirable in a marriage partner. Similarly, because their peer group values success in sports more highly than success in academics, many boys make a heavy investment in athletics at the expense of their studies, only to find their skills are no longer in demand once they are through high school or college. As Table 12.4 shows, no more than one-tenth of 1 per cent of high school varsity athletes make it into the ranks of the professionals.

In most industrial societies, youth culture has flourished to the extent that great numbers of specialized youth groups have developed, each with its own distinct subculture. In the United States, these have included a wide variety of religious cults, counterculture groups, black separatists, ghetto gangs, motorcycle gangs, homosexual groups, and political groups of various persuasions.

Youth culture is now as much a part of the Marxist societies of Eastern

TABLE 12.4   Number of Men and Boys Playing Basketball and Football in High School, College, and Professional Sports

Level of Competition	Basketball	Football
High School	700,000	1,100,000
College	18,000	43,000
Professional	264	1,194

Source: Adapted from Leonard Shapiro and Donald Huff, "The Games Always End," *Washington Post*, Mar. 20, 1977, p. D4.

FIGURE 12.4   Great numbers of specialized youth groups have developed in most industrial societies, each with its own distinct subculture: Hare Krishna festival, San Francisco.

Europe as it is of other industrial societies. After trying for years to prevent the intrusion of what were viewed as degenerate products of decaying capitalist societies, Communist Party officials appear to have adopted the philosophy that "if you can't beat them, join them." Thus, the Komsomol (the party youth organization) now operates, in Moscow alone, more than 260 clubs where disco dancing and punk rock are featured.[21] State factories, meanwhile, produce great quantities of blue jeans. Despite this, a growing number of Soviet youth still seem determined to flout authority, turning to such unacceptable alternatives as church attendance on the one hand and crime on the other.

Crimes of violence have come to be associated with youth in both Marxist and non-Marxist societies. In Soviet society, for example, 80 per cent of those convicted for assault with intent to rob are under twenty-five years of age.[22] In the United States, 75 per cent of those arrested for robbery, the legal definition of which involves the threat or use of violence, are under twenty-five years of age, and so are 72 per cent of those arrested for all crimes classified as "serious."[23] What is more, political violence is largely the work of younger people, as evidenced by such groups as the IRA in Northern Ireland and the Red Brigades in Italy.

Many attempts have been made to explain the tendency toward violence among younger people, especially younger males, in industrial societies. In American society, currently favored explanations place the blame primarily on society (e.g., widespread unemployment among youth, racism).[24] In Soviet society, in contrast, blame is usually placed on individuals (e.g., the parents of the criminal, the criminal himself).[25] Soviet scholars also explain the problem as an inevitable by-product of the difficult transition from the submissiveness and obedience of childhood to the self-assertiveness and relative autonomy of adulthood.[26]

In trying to understand this phenomenon, it is important to keep in mind what many experts seem not to realize: young men were often involved in crimes of violence in agrarian societies, and most hunting and gathering and horticultural societies provided socially approved opportunities for violence in hunting or warfare. While there can be no definitive explanation of violence in younger men, it is certain that the causes are many and complex. In most instances, they probably include the biological influences of age and sex, the characteristics of the individual, and a number of characteristics not only of his nuclear family and other close associates but of his society as well.

Leisure, the Arts, and the Mass Media

Leisure and the Arts

No preindustrial society ever offered such varied opportunities for filling leisure hours as modern industrial societies provide. With electronic aids, one can vicariously explore the moon, follow sports events in distant places, or enjoy "command" performances by the world's greatest artists, dead as well as living, all in the privacy of one's own living room. If one is inclined to physical activity, the affluent society offers everything from miniature golf to skydiving.

Industrial societies are also unique with respect to the commercialization of their recreation, the vicarious nature of so much of their leisure-time activities, and their dependence on manufactured aids in the search for pleasure. Both entertainment and the production of equipment for leisure activities are major industries. Ironically, even when members of industrial societies "return to nature," they often take along every conceivable substitute for the conveniences of urban life they can cram into their trailers and campers.

One of the happier features of leisure in modern societies is its relative democracy. Many of the gross inequalities of agrarian societies have been drastically reduced. For one thing, the working hours of the average adult in an industrial society are shorter than those of many children in agrarian or industrializing societies. Table 12.5 shows some of the consequences of this for their daily lives. Most people now have the time and the means for participation in a wide variety of sports, hobbies, and other activities. Unattractive as it is in many respects, the commercialization of entertainment has expanded opportunities for new kinds of careers, thus enabling far more people to develop their abilities more fully.

Although the influence of the new technology is most obvious in things like waterskiing and photography, its impact on the fine arts has also been substantial. The modern symphony orchestra is a triumph of modern technology, and trends in painting reflect the influence of materials and processes not

FIGURE 12.5   The modern symphony orchestra is a triumph of technology as well as of art: the New York Philharmonic at Avery Fisher Hall.

available to artists of an earlier era. But perhaps the most important consequence of the new technology in this area is an indirect one: traditional standards have given way to the belief that "newer is better." This could not occur except in societies inured to, and favorably disposed toward, change in other areas.

TABLE 12.5   Average Hours Urban Americans Spent per Week on Leisure Activities and Personal Care, in 1965 and 1975, by Marital Status, Employment Status, and Sex

Marital Status, Employment Status, and Sex	Hours per Week of Leisure and Personal Care	
	1965	1975
Single individuals:		
Employed men	58.1	64.0
Employed women	55.0	58.3
Married individuals:		
Employed men	54.6	57.5
Employed women	57.0	57.9
Housewives	63.6	65.8

Source: Adapted from U.S. Department of Commerce, Bureau of the Census, *Social Indicators, 1976,* table 10/1.

The Mass Media

When historians of the future look back on industrial societies, they may call this the era of the mass media. Ever since daily newspapers and weekly and monthly magazines first hit the streets in the nineteenth century, the outreach, the scope, and the impact of the media have steadily expanded. Early in the twentieth century, motion pictures became technologically and commercially feasible, followed by radio, talking pictures and, in the late 1940s, television.

The mass media have had a powerful influence on industrial societies. To begin with, they have been an important unifying force, helping to overcome regional and local prejudices and steadily eroding local subcultures. As a result, industrial societies are culturally and linguistically more homogeneous than societies of the past. The media have also served as a vital means of informing the members of society on a wide variety of matters, increasing their awareness of, and involvement in, economic and political activities. This has had the effect of promoting democratization and greater equality.

The lives of countless millions of people, including those whose other contacts are limited by such factors as illness or poverty, have been enriched and broadened by the mass media. Because printed materials, movies, radio, and TV have given the members of industrial societies a view of the world beyond their own neighborhood or town, people have a heightened awareness of the problems of other classes and societies and of the common threads of human experience. Educational TV, a medium whose enormous potential for use in the schools as well as the home is poorly utilized, offers, among other experiences, a chance for the ordinary citizen to visit the very frontiers of scientific inquiry.

Studies show that the leisure hours of the members of industrial societies have been increasingly consumed by the mass media, especially television. A 1975 study of urban American adults, for example, found that TV viewing filled nearly half of their leisure (i.e., time not spent working, sleeping, or on personal care).[27] Even more striking, 95 per cent of their *gain* in leisure time between 1965 and 1975 was given to this medium.*

The impact of TV on younger Americans is evident in reports by the Nielsen Company, which monitors television viewing for the networks and for commercial advertisers. The average weekly hours of television use per American *household* in 1975 was 45 hours, but in households with children under eighteen, the average was over 53 hours.[28] For young children, TV has become a new kind of child care arrangement; the average preschooler is estimated by different experts to watch it an average of 33 to 50 hours every week![29]

The appeal of television is due to several factors. First, it combines the most attractive features of the other media: like printed matter and the radio, it can be enjoyed in the home; like the movies, it presents material vividly. Second, it can inform or entertain people at relatively little cost, while requiring little expenditure of energy, physical or mental. As a consequence,

---

*Recent studies suggest that the saturation point for this activity may at last have been reached in the United States.

TV has the greatest potential of all the media for shaping the attitudes and values of a society.

A leading historian of the broadcasting industry has likened television to the central nervous system, noting that it "sorts and distributes information, igniting memories. It can speed or slow the pulse of a society [and] the impulses it transmits can stir the juices of emotion and can trigger action." He concluded by saying that "as in the case of the central nervous system, aberrations can deeply disturb the body politic."[30]

A recently completed study of the role of the mass media in the 1976 presidential election in the United States confirms that view.[31] This study found that the media, by the biases in their coverage, create a bandwagon effect that tends to throw elections to those who win the earliest primaries.* For example, Jimmy Carter won a very modest plurality in New Hampshire, where the first Democratic primary was held; he received only 28 per cent of the vote, compared to 23 per cent for the candidate who ran second. But he won an overwhelming victory in the media. *Time* and *Newsweek* both featured him on their covers and devoted 90 per cent of their reports on the primary to him, dividing the remaining 10 per cent among all of the other Democratic candidates. During the week that followed, television and the daily press gave Carter four times as much coverage as the average of his rivals. This proved to be a tremendous advantage, since a study of those who voted in the Democratic Party primaries showed that 95 per cent voted for the candidate they felt they knew best—and, thanks to media coverage, this was Carter.

This bias in the allocation of media coverage was reinforced by bias in its content. A national sample of Democratic Party members interviewed prior to the primaries indicated that the two things they most wanted to learn about the candidates were their stands on policy questions and their leadership capabilities. Instead, the majority of the material offered by the media, and by television in particular, concerned the candidates' campaign tactics and styles and reports on who was leading in the latest polls. It is hardly surprising that, when the primaries were over and these same voters were interviewed again, 65 per cent of the new information they had assimilated was about tactics and styles and only 35 per cent involved policy issues and leadership ability. The deficiencies of campaign coverage by American television were especially evident to anyone who had an opportunity to compare it to Britain's: BBC's television reporters asked American presidential candidates exactly the kinds of questions American voters wanted answered, but which their own society's networks were not asking.

The political impact of the media on democratic societies is evident in other areas, too. Both community activists and political terrorists have learned that TV news programmers cannot resist dramatic confrontations, with the result that tiny groups who are willing to create such events receive far more coverage than vastly larger groups that confine themselves to more conventional activities.[32]

---

*Thus, the "momentum" in election campaigns that TV newscasters are so fond of talking about is essentially the product of their own activities.

The news media have also created problems in the administration of justice, by pretrial reporting of information that prejudices potential jurors. (In a number of societies, including Britain, this type of coverage is forbidden by law.) Recently, another kind of problem has surfaced, but this one has its origins in the entertainment sector of the media. Many viewers are apparently so steeped in fictional presentations of social phenomena that they are unable to discriminate between them and the real thing. In illustration, a dismayed district attorney reported that, after he had lost a rape case despite compelling evidence, one of the jurors explained to him that she had voted for acquittal because the defendant had not confessed on the stand. "I've never seen that happen," said the astonished DA. The juror replied, "You must not be very experienced; it happens all the time." The DA, who had eleven years of trial experience, finally learned that the juror's image of courtroom reality was based on years of watching fictional trials on television.[33] Defense lawyers, meanwhile, complain that many jurors expect them not only to defend their client, but to prove who is really guilty, as Perry Mason would do.

Only the naive and unreflective can fail to appreciate the tremendous power inherent in a machine that is able to shape perceptions of reality for tens of millions of viewers. It is no accident that the editors of *Webster's Third New International Dictionary* have come to define the mass media as communications media "designed to reach the mass of people *and that tend to set the standards, ideals, and aims of the masses.*"[34]

Intratype Variation: Trends and Prospects

In recent decades there has been a great deal of variation among industrial societies. As we have seen, the differences have been especially pronounced between the one-party Marxist societies of Eastern Europe with their command economies on the one hand, and the multiparty, democratic societies of the West and Japan with their mixed market-command economies on the other. Thirty years ago it seemed that these were fundamentally different kinds of industrial societies, both stable and durable, both with excellent chances of surviving for the indefinite future.

For a number of years, however, there have been increasing signs of some convergence. Since Stalin's death in 1953, and even more since the Twentieth Party Congress in 1956, there has been a definite, though slow and halting, movement away from the extremes of totalitarianism and political repression in the U.S.S.R. Compared with the Stalin years, the present system seems almost liberal, even though political dissent is still likely to lead to prison sentences, exile, or commitment to a mental institution. In the economic area, there has been a clearly discernible shift away from more extreme forms of the command economy. For a number of years, market forces have been permitted to operate in certain areas of the economy, and the role of centralized planning has been somewhat curtailed. These trends, as we have noted, are not limited to the Soviet Union, but extend throughout most of Eastern Europe.*

Meanwhile, non-Marxist industrial societies have taken steps to increase governmental intervention in their economies and to restrict the free play of market forces. Even as conservative a President as Richard Nixon found it necessary to introduce wage and price controls of a sort, as did the British Prime Minister, Edward Heath, a Conservative. These are only two minor developments in the trend toward a mixed market-command economy that began decades ago and is expressed in expanded programs in health, education, and welfare, and in increasing governmental regulation of private enterprise. Politically, revelations of the activities of the FBI and CIA during the Kennedy-Johnson-Nixon years warn us of the dangers of assuming that multiparty democracies are necessarily free of police-state tactics or that criticism of a democratic government is always safe.

Signs of convergence between Marxist and non-Marxist societies are not restricted to the political and economic areas. A declining birthrate, the movement of women into the labor force, the growth of urban populations, the growing importance of education, the growth of tertiary industries, the generation gap, the emergence of a distinctive youth culture—these trends and many more are found in *all* industrial societies.

These societies are not, of course, moving toward a single, uniform pattern. Differences will certainly remain; but they will probably be less marked than those which separated Hitler's Germany or Stalin's Russia from the still largely laissez-faire, capitalistic western democracies of the 1930s. The reason for this seems to be that *the social, psychological, economic, and political costs inherent in these more extreme systems are more than most citizens are willing to pay.* Public pressure thus led to the gradual erosion of both laissez-faire capitalism in the West and totalitarian rule in Marxist societies. Although future crises may cause some industrial societies to return to the extremes of totalitarianism, this does not seem likely at present, and a return to the older forms of capitalism seems even less likely.

Problems and Progress

The members of contemporary industrial societies are in a paradoxical situation. They are, on average, far healthier, wealthier, and freer to choose among alternative lifestyles than were the vast majority of their ancestors of at least the last 5,000 years, and they are probably happier as well (see pages 413–415). Yet they are far more vocal concerning the shortcomings and problems of their societies.

Like so many other changes, this is essentially a consequence of industrialization. The mass media and, in most industrial societies, multiparty political systems serve to keep social problems before the attention of the general

---

*Czechoslovakia is clearly a special case, though it should be noted that its difficulties since 1968 were the result of an effort by Communists and others to push political and economic liberalization much more rapidly than the more cautious Soviet leaders would tolerate. Thus, there has been no lack of liberalizing forces within Czech society.

public. Better education and new ideologies, meanwhile, provide people with an enhanced capacity for envisioning superior alternatives to the status quo. Finally, affluence gives people the means and leisure, and democratic polities give them the opportunity, to express themselves on societal defects.

In addition, there are good substantive grounds for the members of industrial societies to be concerned, and to express their concern. For the new high-information, high-energy technologies of industrial societies have a potential for creating problems far more serious than those that confronted societies of the past.

Warfare and Environmental Problems

War, like many other problems confronting industrial societies, is an old problem. But the nature of the problem has been altered by the power of the new technology. War can now be carried on by societies on opposite sides of the globe, with all that implies for the involvement of other societies. More important, some industrial societies have amassed military arsenals that are capable of obliterating not only an entire enemy nation, but humanity as well. This is a new and frightening situation, and it is one that present political institutions are not equipped to handle. In the final chapter, we will return to this critical problem, in the context of an analysis of the future.

The impact of modern technology on the biophysical environment is another major problem confronting industrial societies today. They are able to level mountains, redirect rivers, erase forests, and remove fossil fuels and other minerals from deep below the surface of both land and sea. Their unprecedented manipulation of the environment and consumption of its resources, which are at the very heart of the Industrial Revolution, have had two major negative consequences: environmental pollution and the depletion of resources. Rivers have been converted into sewers, giant lakes have become incapable of supporting life, the oceans are beginning to send out distress signals, and even the air and upper atmosphere are life-threatening in some areas. Many societies have allowed chemical wastes to be dumped into rivers or buried in the ground where they subsequently contaminate water supplies. Many forms of plant and animal life have been destroyed, and shortages are developing in a growing number of important and nonrenewable resources.

Finally, in their efforts to solve the problems created by vanishing fossil fuels, industrial societies have created a new environmental threat: nuclear pollution. No society has yet found a fully satisfactory method of disposing of the wastes from nuclear power plants. And no society has yet devised a really foolproof means of preventing disastrous accidents—nor are they likely to do so. While it is true that improvements in technology, better training of nuclear engineers and other workers, and greater care in the location of these plants (e.g., not building them on top of geological faults) will eventually make their operation much safer, it is difficult to see how societies can fully protect themselves against such things as terrorist bombings or the emotional instability of workers.

It is impossible at the present time to assess accurately the damage done by environmental pollution in industrial societies, or to gauge the true magnitude of the threat it poses to health in the future. There is no doubt, however, that both this problem and the problem of material shortages are very real, with enormous potential for affecting human life and the development of human societies.

Other Major Problems of Industrial Societies

The problems of *political and economic injustice*, which date back to the horticultural era, are still problems for industrial societies today. In Marxist societies, as we have seen, the problems are more severe in the political sphere; in non-Marxist ones, in the economic. In both instances, however, the problems have taken on new dimensions with industrialization.

Crime is another ancient problem that persists in modern industrial societies, but it often assumes new forms. Economic crimes are no longer limited to such activities as embezzlement and theft, but include stock market fraud and bank robbery via computers, while crimes of violence include terrorist activities and airplane hijacking as well as murder, robbery, and rape. Marxists once believed that public ownership of the means of production would eliminate economic crimes and substantially reduce crimes of violence, but these hopes have been dashed by the experiences of Eastern European societies. The problem is even more acute in many non-Marxist societies, particularly in the United States.

A number of the problems facing most industrial societies today stem from *excess population*, people who are not actually required in the labor force. With industrialization and continued technological advance, fewer and fewer people are needed to produce a given quantity of goods and services. Most people continue to be employed, of course, because the quantity and variety of goods and services have steadily increased. But as population growth has continued, even though its rate has been modest, a labor surplus has inevitably developed.

Industrial societies have responded to this problem in two basic ways. Marxist societies, and to a lesser degree certain non-Marxist societies (e.g., Britain), have created "make-work" positions or have kept workers employed in unprofitable industries, thus absorbing part or all of their excess populations into the labor force. This is done, however, at the cost of lower rates of productivity and less rapid improvements in standards of living. In contrast, most non-Marxist societies (including some, like Britain, that also employ the first solution) have developed extensive welfare systems that support the unemployed. It is becoming increasingly evident that, in some societies, these systems are poorly planned and executed and tend to become self-perpetuating, with second- and third-generation members of the same family often caught in the same trap.[35] Not surprisingly, this class contributes disproportionately to many of the problems in these societies, especially in such areas as education, health care, and crime.

With many of the problems of industrial societies, it is difficult to assess their extent or severity, or even to determine whether or not they have increased with industrialization. This is true of crime, and it is also true of many problems of the family. For example, no statistics were kept in agrarian societies that would permit comparisons of the relative frequency of child and wife abuse or incest in those societies and in industrial societies. Whether these things have actually increased, or whether they are simply more widely reported, is impossible to say. It is equally difficult to gauge the consequences for the next generation of such things as the growing number of one-parent families or the longer periods young children spend away from their mothers, or to pin down the precise causes of the declining levels of academic performance in some societies, or the rising rates of teenage suicide. Interesting research is being done on these subjects, but it is usually difficult to isolate the causes, since so many things have changed so rapidly in industrial societies.

Although there is a great deal of controversy on the subject of how much progress industrial societies have actually made in solving humanity's problems, there is generally agreement on several points. First, despite significant elements of continuity, the problems facing industrial societies are, in many major respects, new problems. Second, these new problems are largely by-products or consequences of technological advance. Third, although many of these problems are distressingly complex, they can all be substantially alleviated by rational human effort—another point we will address in our discussion of the future. Finally, a truly problem-free society is unlikely to be realized in the course of sociocultural evolution, since the process of problem solving so often generates new needs and new problems.

Industrial Societies in Theoretical Perspective

When we compare industrial societies with societies of the past, it is clear that they are a radically new type of sociocultural system. This is evident in everything from the family to the polity, and from ideology to technology. The foundation for these societies is, of course, their rich store of information, especially the technological information that enables them to harness vast amounts of energy to enormously productive machines.

If human societies had never created that technology, we would still be in the agrarian era. The vast majority of people would be illiterate peasant farmers eking out a marginal existence, women's lives would be dominated by the cycle of reproduction and child care, and authoritarian elites that knew little and cared less about the lives of the masses would regard the economic surplus as their rightful property. If we imagine a different sequence of events—one in which industrial societies evolved, but subsequently, in the 1980s, were forced to return to agrarian life—we must add a further note: 75 per cent or more of the world's current population would die. For an agrarian technology could probably sustain no more than one-third to two-thirds more people than were alive when the agrarian era ended.

We will not try to trace here all of the consequences of the shift from an agrarian to an industrial technology, or to detail all of the causal linkages, as we did at the ends of earlier chapters. These consequences are so numerous, and the linkages so complex, that a single diagram could not do justice to them. Instead, we will simply state the basic points that emerge from our analysis.

First, in industrial societies, as in their predecessors, *technological innovation continues to be the basic underlying force responsible for societal change and development*. Although other kinds of innovations also affect the process of social and cultural change, they are largely dependent on prior technological change. We have seen numerous examples of this, especially in the new beliefs and values that shape these societies' institutions, beliefs and values that, without industrialization, would have had little or no impact.

Second, *many of the trends of the industrial era are continuations of trends that began in earlier eras*. Although industrialization intensified them, each of the following was initiated by technological advance in the distant past:

The growing store of information

The use of increasingly powerful energy sources

The growing productivity of societies and the enlarging economic surplus

The growth of world population

The growth in size of societies and communities

The increasing diversity of material products

The growth of capital goods

The increasing division of labor within societies

The growing complexity of associations and communities

The increasing division of labor among societies, and their growing economic interdependence

The relative decline in importance of kinship systems

The increasing number of symbol systems

The increasing impact of human activities on the biophysical environment

The growing destructive potential of military technology

Third, *a number of trends in industrial societies are new and represent a break with trends of the past*. The most significant of these involves inequality. During the long period between the close of the hunting and gathering era and the early stages of the industrial, technological advance was accompanied by a steady decline in both political and economic equality. As a result, either advanced agrarian or early industrial societies achieved the dubious distinction of having the greatest degree of inequality of any type of society in history.

Advanced industrial societies have appreciably reversed this trend in both the economic and political spheres, Marxist societies being more successful in the former, non-Marxist in the latter. Other new developments that are evident in all industrial societies include greater democratization, greatly improved opportunities for education, more upward mobility, movement toward an equilibrium of birth and death rates at a level far below that of any other type of society, and the institutionalization of innovation.

Fourth, *industrial societies are the first in human history in which the greatest threats posed by the biophysical environment are the results of human activity.* Prior to the Industrial Revolution, famine and disease were two of the greatest threats to a society. Technology and science have succeeded in removing the first of these scourges in industrial societies, and they have reduced the second to tolerable proportions: the members of industrial societies now die primarily from degenerative diseases that reflect the natural limits of our species' life-span. Societies are, instead, increasingly threatened by the *feedback effects of their own technology* on the biophysical environment. Since this and the other unsolved problems of contemporary societies make up an agenda for the future, however, we will postpone further discussion of them until the final chapter.

Fifth, and finally, *the role of ideology in generating intratype variation among societies has increased significantly as a result of industrialization.* This is due to the fact that, for the first time in history, societies have a large number of options available to them in a fairly wide variety of areas. And this, of course, is due to the new technology and to the enormous economic surplus and other consequences of that technology.

To appreciate how the role of ideology has changed, we need to look again at the other major societal types. Ideological differences among hunting and gathering societies gave rise to no important intratype variations among them, because their technology could not provide a sustained economic surplus. Without that, no society could become significantly larger than the rest, develop a greater division of labor, or become appreciably different with respect to other basic societal characteristics. The "range of the possible" in these societies was extremely narrow and provided little latitude for choices based on ideology.

During the horticultural era, ideology first began to play a significant role in producing intratype variation by enabling some societies to develop an economic surplus. Because religious beliefs and values motivated their members to turn over a part of their harvest and other resources to their leaders, population growth did not consume all of the potential surplus. And because of the stable surplus, these societies became more specialized, developed greater inequality, and changed in other important ways. Thus they were differentiated from other horticultural societies that, lacking such ideologies, never developed a stable surplus and remained less complex.

Although agrarian societies had a larger economic surplus than any horticultural society, the main effect of their ideologies was a negative one insofar as intratype variations are concerned. For they all had beliefs and values that tended to impede technological advance and to inhibit change in the important characteristics they all shared. Although there were differences in their dominant ideologies (e.g., Christianity, Islam, Buddhism), these did not produce many important differences in their economic, political, or kinship institutions, or have great consequence for altering their technology, stratification systems, population size, degree of urbanization, or other basic characteristics. In fact, differences in the social environments of agrarian societies (such as proximity to trade routes and frontier locations) were much more important in generating intratype variations than were differences in their beliefs and values.

In industrial societies, in contrast, *ideology has helped to shape their political and economic institutions*, creating such important intratype variations as multiparty democracy versus one-party rule, and state versus private ownership of the means of production. These basic variations, and the consequences for *other* social institutions of policy decisions based on ideological considerations, are most apparent in a comparison of Marxist and non-Marxist societies. But there are also important variations within each of these two basic subtypes, as the differences between Poland and the Soviet Union, and between Sweden and the United States, make clear.

There can be no doubt that ideology has become a much greater force for change during the industrial era than it ever was in the past. Because the economic surplus not only is so large but has *increased so rapidly*, the leaders of contemporary industrial societies have had access to enormous "free resources"—resources not committed by precedent to some particular use. This has given them wide latitude in choosing from among the broad range of the possible that modern industrial technology has spread before them.

CHAPTER 13

Industrializing Societies

Despite the rapid spread of industrialization during the last two centuries, less than a third of the world's population live in societies that can be called "industrial" as we have defined the term. The great majority, however, do live in societies that have been substantially altered as a consequence of the diffusion of modern industrial technology. These hybrid societies are best described as *industrializing agrarian* and *industrializing horticultural* societies —the ones we commonly refer to as the underdeveloped, or developing, nations of the Third World.

These nations are in a transitional phase, moving from the older agrarian or horticultural way of life to the modern industrial. Social scientists usually refer to this as the *modernization* process, a process that involves all aspects of the life of society, not just the technological. Unfortunately, the transitional period is proving to be longer and more difficult than most scholars had expected. For both theoretical and practical reasons, then, these societies merit careful study.

In most analyses, industrializing agrarian and industrializing horticultural societies (all of which are *advanced* horticultural) are lumped together indiscriminately. This is a serious mistake, since the two types differ in a number of important respects. In this chapter, therefore, we will deal with them separately.

Although quite a number of hunting and gathering, fishing, and simple horticultural societies also survived into the modern era in remote and isolated areas, recent advances in transportation have opened up most of these areas and removed this source of protection. As a result, most of these groups have either been destroyed or herded onto reservations where they live as wards of their conquerors, usually under conditions that make their traditional ways of life impossible. Even the few groups that still preserve a fair degree of autonomy have usually adopted tools and other elements from more advanced societies and thus are no longer pure types. This does not make them *industrializing* societies, of course; that implies something utterly beyond their adaptive capacities. Groups with such a primitive subsistence base can not possibly evolve into anything so advanced in the little time that is still available to them. They are, at best, unusual hybrids with a very limited future.

Industrializing Agrarian Societies

Today, industrializing agrarian societies comprise most of Latin America, southern and eastern Asia, the Middle East, and North Africa, and are also found in parts of southern Europe. When we talk about industrializing agrarian societies, we are talking about China, India, Egypt, Yugoslavia, Portugal, Brazil, Cuba, Mexico, and several dozen other nations as well.

Naturally, these societies differ from one another in many ways, reflecting differences in their histories, in the social and biophysical environments to which they must adapt today, and in their precise level of technological advance. Yet despite their differences, they share a number of important characteristics, because they all combine elements of the agrarian past and the industrial present. Recognition of this fact can be enormously helpful to us as we try to understand them and their problems.

By one criterion, at least, industrializing agrarian societies are the most important type in the world today: more people live in them than in any other type of society. But this is not the only reason for their importance. These societies have, for decades, been struggling with problems that constantly threaten to overwhelm them. Despite a measure of industrialization, many of their citizens, a majority in some societies, are as poor as the common people ever were in traditional agrarian societies (see Table 13.1). At the same time, improved education and the mass media have raised their hopes and expectations and given them an awareness of a better kind of life. This contradiction has created a revolutionary situation that threatens to involve the entire world.

Sometimes it is suggested that the problem of the underdeveloped countries is simply their technological and economic backwardness. The problem is, of course, much more complex than that, for it involves all of their major social institutions—polity, economy, family, religion, and education—as well as the attitudes and values of their people. In short, the problem involves every area for which industrialization has major consequences. In addition, their position in the world system creates further problems, as will become clear later in this chapter.

**TABLE 13.1 An Industrial and an Industrializing Society Compared:
The United States and India**

	U.S.	India
Population (in millions)	217	643
Area (in millions of square miles)	3.6	1.2
Population density (population per square mile)	60	523
Birthrate per 100 population	15	37
Death rate per 100 population	9	15
Rate of natural increase (per cent per year)	0.6	2.2
Infant mortality per 1,000 live births	15	134
Life expectancy at birth	72	47
Hospital beds per 10,000 population	65	7
Doctors per 10,000 population	17	3
Secondary school students per 10,000 population	939	40
Percentage of adult population illiterate	1	67
GNP per capita, in dollars	8,188	141
Percentage growth in GNP, 1970–1977	23	22
Percentage growth in GNP per capita, 1970–1977	16	5
Percentage of population in manufacturing	10	1
Hundreds of kilograms of energy consumed per capita per year	115	2
Petroleum production per capita, in pounds annually	4,092	35
Coal production per capita, in pounds annually	6,138	343
Steel production per capita, in pounds annually	1,156	34
Wheat, rice, and corn production in pounds per capita per year	2,390	397
Meat and fish production in pounds per capita per year	179	2
Milk production in pounds per capita per year	550	88
Fiber production in pounds per capita per year	31	4
Passenger cars per 1,000 population	623	2
Telephones per 1,000 population	744	3
Newspaper circulation per 1,000 population	287	16
Radios per 1,000 population	1,882	24
Televisions per 1,000 population	571	1

Source: Calculations based on data in *Statistical Abstract of the U.S.*, *1979*, sec. 33, and
1975, sec. 32.

Technology and Productivity

Technologically, an industrializing agrarian society is a bewildering mixture of
the ancient and the modern. Peasant farmers using techniques and tools very
much like those their forefathers used 2,000 years ago work in sight of such
marvels of modern technology as the Aswan Dam in Egypt or the Tata Iron and
Steel Works in India.

The old technology is much more common, however, especially in the
agricultural sector of these economies. In one recent year, an average of 55 per
cent of the labor force of forty-six industrializing agrarian nations were
engaged in agriculture, and yet they produced only 26 per cent of the gross
domestic product.[1] The difference would have been even greater if many of
these countries did not have incomes from relatively modern plantations (tea,
rubber, etc.) operated by foreigners from industrial societies.

There is great variation in the level of technological and economic
development in industrializing agrarian societies. Their per capita GNPs range

FIGURE 13.1 The old and the new: Indian farmer plowing with oxen under high-power electrical transmission lines.

from only $68 per year in Bangladesh to $2,486 in Venezuela. Unfortunately, the average for all industrializing agrarian societies is closer to Bangladesh's: in 1977 the median for thirty-six of them was only $680.

Many discussions of the underdeveloped countries give the impression that they are technologically and economically stagnant or, at the very least, developing less rapidly than industrial societies. But the fact is that the productivity of industrializing agrarian societies has actually increased at essentially the same rate as that of industrial societies. Unfortunately, however, because they have far surpassed industrial societies in population growth, their gains in per capita income have often been small, as we will see.

Population Growth and Its Consequences

With the introduction of modern medicine and sanitation, death rates have been cut drastically in almost every industrializing agrarian society. But except

TABLE 13.2   Crude Birthrates, Death Rates, and Rates of Natural Increase for Seventeen Industrializing Agrarian Societies

Society	Crude Birthrate*	Crude Death Rate†	Rate of Natural Increase
Nicaragua	48	14	34
Bangladesh	47	21	26
Iran	43	12	31
Mexico	42	6	36
Indonesia	42	17	25
Philippines	41	10	31
Peru	41	14	27
Turkey	40	15	25
Thailand	40	11	29
Egypt	38	11	27
Brazil	37	9	28
India	34	15	19
Colombia	34	9	25
Sri Lanka	29	7	22
China	26	9	17
Argentina	26	9	17
Portugal	17	10	7

Source: United Nations, *Population and Vital Statistics Report*, Series A, vol. 32 (January 1980).
*Live births per 1,000 population per year.
†Deaths per 1,000 population per year.

in a few cases, birthrates have remained high, often over 40 per 1,000 population annually (see Table 13.2). Year in, year out, the populations of the underdeveloped nations continue to swell, consuming most of their hard-won gains in productivity.

Table 13.3 shows the cost of uncontrolled population growth for the industrializing agrarian societies of southern and eastern Asia and Latin America. Had they been able to maintain a balance between births and deaths from 1950–1977, their per capita income would have grown at a much faster

TABLE 13.3   Increases in Gross Domestic Product and in Per Capita Gross Domestic Product for Four Sets of Societies, 1950–1977

Set of Societies	Percentage Increase in GDP, 1950–1977	Percentage Increase in *Per Capita* GDP, 1950–1977
Non-Marxist industrial societies	178	86
Marxist industrial societies	197	85
Industrializing agrarian societies:		
East and Southeast Asia	146	41
Latin American and Caribbean	227	64

Source: Adapted from United Nations, *Statistical Yearbook, 1970*, table 4, and United Nations, *Statistical Yearbook, 1978*, table 4.

rate than industrial societies experienced. Instead, they fell further behind, even in Latin America, where the average annual increase in gross domestic product (see Glossary) was actually greater than in industrial societies.

The experience of the tropical island of Java in Indonesia is illustrative of the general trend. In 1800, this island had a population of just 2.5 million; today, its population is approaching 100 million and, if the present rate of growth continues, it will reach 300 million by the year 2000. Experts estimate that at the present time approximately two-thirds of the population is malnourished,[2] a figure that is not likely to get any smaller if population continues to grow 2 per cent or more every year.

Uncontrolled population growth is a serious problem for industrializing societies not only because it means so many more mouths to feed, but because of its implications for the entire process of economic development. For example, the high birthrate makes public education prohibitively expensive in these nations, and yet without education, the population is not equipped for most jobs in modern industry. This forces large numbers of people to find employment in traditional industries, especially farming. But even there they cannot be accommodated except by subdividing already small farms to the point where they are hopelessly inefficient and the introduction of modern machinery is impossible. In Egypt, for example, 70 per cent of the farm owners had less than half an acre in 1950.[3] As one observer wrote, "Most of those who are working the land work not because the land requires their labor but because they require the work."[4] He went on to say that as early as 1939 it was estimated that 10 per cent of Egypt's farmers could have supplied all the necessary labor if Egypt's farms had been even half as mechanized as America's were. The story is much the same in other industrializing agrarian societies.

Another factor retarding economic development is the poverty of the excess population. Because they are unable to buy anything but the most basic traditional commodities, they do not generate a demand for the kinds of products that are an essential component of the economy of every industrial society. Finally, this surplus population compounds all the other problems by its own productive achievements: an abundance of children. The society is thus trapped in a vicious circle.

In view of all this, it is hardly surprising to learn that there is a correlation of -0.49 (see page 92) between the birthrate and the annual growth of per capita productivity. This indicates a strong relationship between high birthrates and low rates of economic progress.[5]

In recent years the leaders of a few industrializing agrarian societies have finally begun to grasp the seriousness of the population problem and its relation to economic growth, and have encouraged the use of modern methods of birth control. In most cases, however, their efforts have not been very successful, largely because children are still perceived as an economic asset by the average peasant farmer. While they are growing up, they are cheap labor, and when their parents become too old to work, the children can support them. If too many children survive to adulthood, they can be sent to

**FIGURE 13.2   According to a recent United Nations' study, one-fourth to
two-thirds of the populations of most Third World metropolises live in squatter
settlements and shantytowns, such as this one in Lima, Peru.**

the cities to work. Unfortunately, modern sanitation and medicine are now
keeping so many children alive that an increasing proportion of them migrate
to the cities in search of jobs that do not exist, or jobs they can fill only while
they are young and vigorous. After that, they drift into the growing ranks of the
underemployed and the unemployed and become a further drain on the
economy. According to a recent United Nations study, people like these
largely comprise the squatter settlements and shantytowns that contain from
one-fourth to two-thirds of the populations of most Third World metropolises.[6]
Moreover, these settlements are growing at an annual rate of 12 per cent a
year, which means they double in size in less than seven years.

By the middle 1970s, there began to be an increasing concern for the
problems caused by unchecked population growth in a number of industrializing agrarian societies. In 1976, the Indian state of Maharashtra, which has a
population of 55 million, adopted a law that provided jail sentences and fines
for couples of childbearing age who had three or more children and refused
sterilization.[7] Introducing the legislation, the state's minister of health said, ''If
the alarming rate of growth is not checked it will be impossible to remove
poverty and realize the fruits of economic development.'' India's Minister of
Health and Family Planning announced that this law was soon to be adopted
nationwide, but plans for this were shelved as the result of a widespread
reaction against the government's quota system for male sterilization. This
public outcry led to the downfall of Indira Gandhi's government. Under the
government that succeeded her, the number of sterilizations performed

annually dropped by 90 per cent, and the birthrate edged up from 33 per 1,000 population per year to 35 and could soon reach 40 again.[8] Now that Mrs. Gandhi has returned to power, it is difficult to predict what India's population policy will be.

Meanwhile, the People's Republic of China, under its post-Mao leadership, has moved vigorously to check population growth. The government recently reported that if every woman of childbearing age had only three children, by the year 2080, China's population would rise to 4.3 billion, the equivalent of the present *world* population![9] To avert this, the government has created a complex structure of sanctions that encourage small families and discourage large. Contraceptives, abortions, and sterilizations are available at no cost. In most areas, women cannot register to marry until age twenty-three, and men until age twenty-five in rural areas and twenty-six in urban.[10] When women check into hospitals to have their first child, they are offered bonuses if they will permit postnatal sterilization, and a national campaign has been mounted to pressure young couples into signing a "one family, one child" pledge. Couples that marry late and those that have only one child are given top priority in housing assignments, while physicians, nurseries, and schools are instructed to give preference to children who have no siblings. There are punishments as well as rewards. Couples who have three children, for

---

SHUAI XIU RONG FINED $200

Chengdu, China—Shuai Xiu Rong was fined $200 yesterday because she became pregnant without permission and then refused to have an abortion. The No. 1 Brigade of the Golden Horse Commune, where Mrs. Shuai, her husband, and their 4-year-old daughter live, has a population of 1,200 and is allowed only 9 births per year. Mrs. Shuai was one of five women who became pregnant last year without permission, but the other four chose to have abortions.

In addition to the fine, Mrs. Shuai was subjected to public scolding for selfish thinking and wrote a public self-criticism. Authorities have decided that her son will not be registered for some years. This denial of a registration card means his family will have to stretch its present grain ration to provide for his needs or buy grain in the open market at higher prices. Also, until authorities issue such registration, he will not be eligible to attend school. It is expected that the boy will be registered in a few years, but that authorities have determined to make an example of Mrs. Shuai to discourage other women from following her example.

Sichuan Province, where the Shuai family lives, is home to nearly 100 million Chinese, or nearly the population of Britain and France combined. Family planning authorities report that, by a system of incentives and penalties, the province's annual growth rate has been reduced from 3.1 per cent per year in 1970 to 0.7 per cent in 1980.

Adapted from Associated Press wire service report, August 4, 1980.

example, are fined 10 per cent of their pay for fourteen years, the time it takes for most children to join the labor force. It is too early to say how successful China's effort to control population size will be. But it is clear that her leaders recognize the relationship between population growth and living standards, and that they are committed to improving those standards for their people.

Taiwan is another industrializing society whose leaders have recognized the need for vigorous action. They have created a system whereby couples with two children receive a credit of $25 a year for a period of ten years, with the accumulated funds plus interest later made available for the children's education. If a third child is born, the annual payments are cut in half, and a fourth child disqualifies the family.[11] The most recent figures on the birthrate in Taiwan indicate striking success: births are down to 26 per 1,000 population per year, a figure midway between those in advanced industrial societies and those in traditional agrarian societies. If other Third World nations are willing to initiate measures comparable to China's and Taiwan's, there is reason to hope that the era of runaway population growth is drawing to a close and that standards of living in these nations may soon begin to improve.

The Economy

The economies of industrializing societies consist of two basic components. The traditional component is very similar to the economy of the typical agrarian society of the last 2,000 years. The tools and techniques are much the same, and so is the level of productivity. The modern—or at least modernizing—component has tools, techniques, and patterns of economic organization that have, for the most part, been borrowed from advanced industrial societies.

Obviously, such a division results in tremendous internal variation within a society. The people in some areas are living just about the way their forebears did centuries ago, while in other areas, people are living very much like the residents of Washington, London, or Moscow. Table 13.4 illustrates the kind and degree of differences that can separate the members of industri-

TABLE 13.4   Some Indicators of Regional Differences in Greece in 1965

Indicators	Attica or Greater Athens	Thrace
Per capita consumption of electric energy in kilowatt-hours	833	34
Private cars per 10,000 inhabitants	168	8
Percentage of households with inside baths or showers	30	2
Percentage of households with drinking water installation	72	21
Number of doctors per 10,000 inhabitants	33	3
Number of hospital beds per 10,000 inhabitants	142	17

Source: Centre of Planning and Economic Research, *Draft of the Five Year Economic Development Plan for Greece* (Athens, 1965), p. 147, cited by Nikos Mouzelis and Michael Attalides, "Greece," in Margaret Archer and Salvador Giner (eds.), *Contemporary Europe* (New York: St. Martin's, 1972), p. 187.

alizing agrarian societies. A similar cleavage exists in most industrializing agrarian societies today.

But the modernizing sector of the economy in such societies is by no means simply a scaled-down version of the economy in the typical industrial

FIGURE 13.3 Two views of an industrializing society: *(a)* peasants plowing with oxen near Karlovac; *(b)* city scene in Belgrade, Yugoslavia.

society. In other words, it is not likely to contain a representative sample of industries, such as a few small steel mills, a small automobile plant or two, some textile mills, a number of wholesale and retail distributors, and so on. Rather, this sector of the economy will probably be very specialized and one-sided in its development as compared with the economy of a fully industrialized society.

To understand why this is so, we have to keep in mind the tremendous difference between the circumstances under which these nations are industrializing and those under which Western Europe and the United States industrialized. Today's developing societies have to make the transition in a world dominated politically and economically by *already industrialized* societies that have well-established home markets with high volumes of sales, and that are the builders of industrial machinery for the rest of the world. Add to this the relatively low cost of moving goods, even around the globe, and the industrializing countries are left without much of a competitive advantage *even in their home markets*. European, American, and Japanese firms can easily undersell Latin American and Asian manufacturers in a wide variety of fields, especially in high-technology, capital-intensive industries.

As a result, many of the industrializing societies have been forced into a peculiar ecological niche: they have become the producers of raw materials for the world economy. Furthermore, because of pressures generated by world markets and by their own desire to maximize income, they often become dangerously specialized (see Table 13.5).

A society that depends so heavily on just one commodity is highly vulnerable to any shift in the world economy that affects its specialty. Technological innovations (e.g., synthetic fibers, synfuels, coffee or sugar substitutes) may permanently reduce, or even eliminate, demand for the product. This sensitivity to change creates an unstable "boom or bust" atmosphere that is not conducive to rational economic planning and development by

TABLE 13.5 Leading Exports of Selected Industrializing Agrarian Societies and Their Percentage Dependence on These Commodities for Foreign Exchange

Society	Commodity	Percentage Dependence
Iraq	Petroleum	99
Cuba	Sugar	86
Chile	Copper	72
Indonesia	Petroleum	67
Colombia	Coffee	62
Pakistan	Textiles	39
Bolivia	Tin	38
Malaysia	Rubber	37
Honduras	Bananas	25
Thailand	Rice	19

Source: Adapted from United Nations, *Yearbook of International Trade Statistics*, 1978.

either businesses or the government. Instead, it encourages a speculative attitude whose goal is to make quick profits and then transfer capital to safer investments abroad.

Despite their drawbacks, these specialized industries can help developing societies industrialize more rapidly. For one thing, they make it possible for more people to shift from traditional subsistence agriculture into jobs in the modern sector. Such people are thus introduced to the new world of machine technology, to new skills, and to new attitudes and values.[12]

Equally important, these industries can serve as a source of capital to finance further industrial development. Some of the Middle Eastern oil states have begun to use their money for this purpose and appear to be well on the way to becoming industrialized societies, with their own steel mills, petro-chemical plants, aluminum smelters, fertilizer plants, and other kinds of industrial establishments.[13] One result is that, whereas industrializing societies were obliged to import 30 per cent of the steel they consumed as recently as 1970, they are now *net exporters* by a small margin.

It is still too early to say whether the benefits of specialized export industries will, in the long run, outweigh their costs. This will depend to a large extent on the product involved. In the case of products like petroleum and natural gas, which now command extremely high prices relative to the cost of producing them and whose prices will probably remain stable or even rise, the prospects seem excellent. The ultimate outcome, however, will depend on the ability of the leaders of these societies to make intelligent investments and to avoid the temptation to siphon off profits for their own personal use.

In contrast, societies that produce commodities that are not essential or for which substitutes can easily be found, or commodities whose prices are highly

FIGURE 13.4   State-operated department store in Beijing, China.

unstable, will probably be unable to industrialize rapidly. The experience of Cuba under Castro is a classic case. Despite the conversion of the economy to a model of Marxist socialism, Cuba's standard of living has deteriorated,[14] and the society must depend on a large and apparently permanent Soviet subsidy.

As the case of Cuba reminds us, a number of industrializing agrarian societies are controlled by revolutionary socialist regimes. In addition to Cuba, they include Yugoslavia, Albania, China, North Korea, Vietnam, Cambodia, Laos, Afghanistan, and Ethiopia. Several others, such as Guyana and Nicaragua, are under the control of elites who apparently favor a modified version of revolutionary socialism. These societies have developed such a diversity of economic programs that it is difficult to find any common denominator, other than state ownership of the means of production. Even the system of central planning, such a prominent feature of the economies of most Marxist industrial societies, is not a common economic feature. Yugoslavia has developed a strikingly innovative system of "market socialism," and China and Cuba give indications that they are edging in that direction.[15] In Cambodia, Afghanistan, and Ethiopia, conditions are in such turmoil that neither a market nor a command economy can function properly. And in Guyana and Nicaragua, the leaders seem content, at present, to combine elements of capitalism and socialism in a more or less pragmatic fashion.

The Polity

In industrializing agrarian societies, one of the greatest hindrances to modernization and industrialization has been the kind of governing class they inherited from the past. This class had a good thing going for centuries, and its members usually see no need to change in the twentieth century. Their ideal is the kind of society that flourished before intellectuals, students, and the common people ever heard of liberty, equality, democracy, socialism, and communism. From their perspective, change is something to be resisted, or, when possible, exploited for their private benefit.

In the last hundred years, a growing number of voices have been raised against this backward-looking, exploitative class. In some instances proponents of modernization have seized control of the government, with the idea of using the power of the state as a force for political, economic, and social change. These modernizers have been a heterogeneous lot. Some have been military men with a strong spirit of nationalism, like Egypt's Nasser; some have been civilians and democratic socialists, like India's Nehru. A number have been Marxists, like Tito, Mao, and Castro, while in at least one case—Iran—the monarch himself played this role.

Would-be modernizers have usually found, however, that it is not enough simply to win control of the government. To implement their plans, they must have the support of thousands of lower- and middle-level officials who are both efficient and honest. Unfortunately, such people are hard to find in societies that for centuries provided education for only a few, and that viewed government office as a means for self-aggrandizement. As a result, the efforts of the top leaders are often frustrated by the incompetence and corruption of lesser officials.[16]

One of the most basic questions confronting the leaders of industrializing societies today concerns what role the state should play in the industrializing and modernizing process. In recent decades there have been two radically different models for them to choose from, one provided by the western democracies, especially Britain, France, and the United States, the other by Marxist societies. Until World War II, most would-be modernizers chose the western democracies for their model. Parliamentary government and free elections looked as if they were the key to progress. The adoption of democracy by underdeveloped nations, however, seldom produced the results expected. Political elites found it easy to get bogged down in unproductive party rivalries, corruption was often widespread, and economic growth and development usually fell far short of what had been expected. In a number of societies, military elites ousted the ineffectual democratic leaders and took control of the government.

With the widespread failures of regimes modeled on the western democracies, Marxist movements began to gain more support in the years following World War II, and Marxist elites eventually led successful revolutions in China, North Vietnam, and Cuba.* Under these revolutionary socialist elites, Marxist ideology became the official dogma and the Soviet Union the model for development.

For a number of years it looked as if Marxism was providing the long-sought answers to the basic problems of industrializing societies. By restricting access to information about economic growth and development in their societies, the new Marxist elites projected an image of success that led others to imitate them. More recently, however, Mao's successors in China, as well as Castro in Cuba, have acknowledged major failures and made important shifts toward more pragmatic economic policies, including some limited reintroduction of market mechanisms.[17] Meanwhile, in Vietnam, where the leadership has adhered more rigidly to earlier policies, the economic situation has been deteriorating since the reunification of the North and the South, and visitors to Hanoi and the North report being stunned by the "grinding poverty." As one observer recently wrote, "The frail bodies, the tattered clothing, the dilapidated buildings, and the scarcity of everything from meat to medicine is not what one expects in the capital of a legendary military power and the third largest Communist country."[18]

Despite the problems of many of the developing societies that have embraced Marxism, there seems little likelihood of a widespread return to western-type democratic governments. Even western experts now generally agree that truly democratic regimes find it extremely difficult to withstand the terrible political stresses found in developing societies and at the same time provide the rate of economic growth that the members of these societies increasingly demand.[19] Authoritarian governments are better equipped to carry out necessary, but unpopular, programs, such as capital accumulation and compulsory population control. In addition, the record of the last thirty

---

*Castro did not declare himself to be a Marxist until the revolution was over, but some of his closest collaborators were already Marxists at the time of the revolution.

TABLE 13.6 A Comparison of the Median Annual Growth Rates of Per Capita Real Gross Domestic Product in Democratic and Nondemocratic Industrializing Agrarian Societies, 1950–1977 (in percentages)*

Time Period	Democratic Societies	Nondemocratic Societies	Difference
1950–1959	1.4†	2.4	1.0
1960–1964	0.9‡	2.3	1.4
1965–1969	1.4§	3.8	2.4
1970–1977	2.6¶	3.9	1.3

Sources: United Nations, *Statistical Yearbook, 1965*, tables 183 and 184; and United Nations, *Statistical Yearbook, 1970*, table 178; and *Statistical Abstract of the U.S., 1979*, table 1554.
*"Real" indicates the amounts are measured in constant dollars (i.e., the effects of inflation are controlled).
†The democratic societies in this period were Brazil, Chile, India, Pakistan, the Philippines, Sri Lanka, and Uruguay.
‡The democratic societies in this period were Brazil, Chile, Greece, India, Jamaica, the Philippines, Sri Lanka, and Uruguay.
§The democratic societies in this period were Chile, Colombia, India, Jamaica, the Philippines, Sri Lanka, and Uruguay.
¶The democratic societies in this period were Colombia, India, Sri Lanka, and Turkey.

years indicates that nondemocratic governments, both left-wing and right-wing, have been more successful than democratic governments in raising per capita income. As Table 13.6 shows, the average rate of growth for democratic societies was about 1.6 per cent per year, compared to 3.0 per cent for nondemocratic. This may look like a small difference to members of affluent industrial societies, but it is, in fact, the difference between doubling a nation's per capita income in more than forty-four years as opposed to only twenty-four. For people who no longer accept poverty as inevitable, that extra twenty years makes democratic government an insupportable luxury.

Social Stratification

Systems of stratification in industrializing agrarian societies are as varied as the polities and economies to which they are linked. In a number of them, the class structure is still very much as it was in agrarian societies of the past, though modified in varying degrees by the influences of industrialization. In others, the traditional class structure has been modified not only by industrialization but by socialism as well.

In societies of the first variety, the upper class is still largely an aristocracy of long-established, wealthy, landowning families that dominate the government, the army, the church, and other basic social institutions. The middle class is relatively small and made up of merchants, lesser officials, lesser members of the clergy, and a few prosperous peasants. In addition, it includes increasing numbers of business and professional people with modern education and skills, members of the civil service with modern educational qualifications, and teachers trained in the newer disciplines (e.g., science and engineering). As industrialization and modernization progress, some members of the new middle class may penetrate into the upper class by virtue of their wealth or political success. In effect, there tend to be two separate systems of stratification in these societies. One is dominant in rural areas and reflects the old order; the other is dominant in urban areas and reflects the new. With the passage of time, the newer system of stratification, which is based on the industrial economy, tends to become dominant throughout the country as a whole.

In societies with Marxist regimes, the transformation of the system of stratification is quicker and more ruthless. Often, many members of the old upper class are killed and the remainder dispossessed. They are replaced by a new elite made up largely of leading Party cadres (many of whom, ironically, are the children of members of the old upper and middle classes). Merchants and private entrepreneurs are also eliminated from the system of stratification and replaced by the managers of state enterprises, who make up a significant portion of the new middle and upper strata. Overall, the system of stratification in these societies closely resembles that in Marxist industrial societies, except that the proportion of peasants is much greater.

The value of modern education, especially training in engineering and science, is great in almost all industrializing societies. This has had one

FIGURE 13.5 Life is grim for large numbers in the lower classes in many industrializing agrarian societies: lower-class housing in Rio de Janeiro.

FIGURE 13.6 Large numbers of Calcutta's poor have no place of residence and are compelled to cook, eat, and sleep on the sidewalks.

interesting, though almost certainly temporary, consequence: it places the younger generation in a relatively advantageous position since they tend to be better educated. This advantage is often reinforced by the effects of political revolutions. Because they are usually the work of young people who distrust the older generation and prefer to surround themselves with their age peers, revolutions are usually followed by a period in which youth is an asset and young people are promoted much faster than they would be otherwise. As the Chinese, Russian, and Cuban revolutions demonstrate, however, this is a temporary phenomenon, and revolutionary elites tend to become gerontocracies.

The major variations in the composition of the lower classes in industrializing agrarian societies are the result of differences in level of economic development. The less development there is, the larger the peasant class and the smaller the urban working class, especially the number working in factories and other modern industries. Conversely, the more development, the fewer peasants there are and the more urban workers. At one extreme, 80 to 95 per cent of the labor force in Nepal, Afghanistan, and Ethiopia are still engaged in agriculture, and only a small percentage in industry. At the opposite extreme, countries like Mexico, Chile, and Portugal have less than half of their workers in agriculture and 15 to 25 per cent in manufacturing.[20]

Life is grim for large numbers of the lower classes in many industrializing agrarian societies. High birthrates, low death rates, and inadequate educational systems combine to ensure a constant oversupply of unskilled labor, a situation that is made much worse by the economy's shift from human labor to machines. The excess population typically migrates from rural areas to the cities, where there are at least some employment opportunities for the young and able-bodied. But, as in agrarian societies of the past, aging, accidents, and illness soon deprive them of their economic value, especially when there is a steady stream of fresh labor continually moving into the cities. The only industrializing agrarian societies that seem to have made much progress toward solving this problem are some of the Marxist societies, where, according to almost all reports, beggary, prostitution, and widespread unemployment and underemployment have been greatly reduced by drastic authoritarian measures.

Cleavages and Conflicts

Few societies in history have had such serious internal divisions as the majority of those now undergoing industrialization. Most of them are torn not only by the ancient cleavages that have always existed in agrarian and advanced horticultural societies, but by some that are peculiar to societies industrializing at this particular time.

Most basic of the older cleavages in industrializing agrarian societies is that between the few who control the nation's resources and the vast majority who supply the labor and get little more than the barest necessities in return. The traditional cleavages between urban and rural populations and between

FIGURE 13.7   Few societies have had such serious internal divisions as the majority of those now undergoing industrialization: supporters of Chairman Hua demonstrating against Maoists following Mao's death.

SATAHU SAHNI: RICKSHAW MAN

Modern Calcutta is a city of outrageous paradoxes: a hell hole of filth and disease, whose poor curse it and their bad luck in living there; a city of matchless fascination for its richest citizens, who would not live anywhere else, and for prosperous foreign visitors.

Satahu Sahni, one of its poorer citizens, pulls a rickshaw for a living. He works from 6 A.M. to midnight, earning a dollar a day. He lives in a one-room hut with his wife and two children. They spend about 80 cents a day for food alone, which provides tea and cookies for breakfast, a wheat cake for lunch, and rice and dried peas for supper. Satahu says of his work, "This job shouldn't be done by any human being, but I couldn't find any other thing to do."

Up and down hills, through broiling molten tar, across rough cobblestones, hauling heavy carts often loaded with more than one passenger as well as freight, Satahu and his fellow rickshaw men run day after day. Summer temperatures that are often above 100, and high humidity, cause a few each day to simply slip from between the shafts of their carts and drop dead. "It's really quite awful lately," said a British-educated Calcuttan, who has his own air-conditioned Mercedes and never rides in a rickshaw. "Not only do the poor runners die, but many passengers are injured when the rickshaws tip over backwards. Quite awful." But Satahu is fortunate compared to the hundreds of thousands of jobless persons and beggars in Calcutta who have no home at all and are forced to sleep on the open sidewalks at night and beg for a little food each day.

Adapted from a copyrighted story by Myron Belkind of the Associated Press by permission.

---

the literate minority and the illiterate majority are also still present, though they may be less pronounced now that advances in transportation and communication have reduced the isolation, and hence the ignorance, of the rural and the illiterate.

As we have already seen, the struggle to industrialize and modernize creates its own cleavages and conflicts. There is a split within the more favored classes, for example, between those educated along traditional lines and those with modern scientific and technical training. These groups have difficulty understanding one another and are mutually prejudiced. Another new cleavage separates the old landowning aristocracy and the new industrial entrepreneurs, who frequently surpass the former in wealth.

As the monarchical political system found in most agrarian societies breaks down, many new groups become politically active and many new issues become politically relevant. For example, the political unrest and other changes associated with industrialization often exacerbate historic tensions between religious and ethnic groups. One can see this in such widely scattered countries as Vietnam, Indonesia, India, Lebanon, Iraq, Iran, and Guyana, to name but a few whose interethnic or interreligious conflicts have been especially serious. The breakdown of the older political system and efforts to establish a modern regime can also produce serious tensions between civilian leaders and the military. Struggles between these groups have often caused crises in Latin American, Middle Eastern, and Asian nations. In more democratic countries, mass political parties have introduced yet another cleavage. Although support for the various parties tends to follow other lines of cleavage, it is seldom a perfect reflection of them. Therefore, it creates further divisions within an already badly divided population.[21]

Finally, the rapid rate of change characteristic of industrializing societies invariably creates a cleavage between the generations. Though there are no reliable measures, this gap appears to be more serious than the generation gap in societies that have already industrialized. This conclusion is suggested both by the frequency and bitterness of the conflicts between students and political authorities in these nations and by the frequency of revolutionary activity by "young Turks" (e.g., the Kemalists in Turkey after World War I, Nasser's associates in Egypt, and Castro's associates in Cuba). We would expect such a split, of course, in societies changing so rapidly. The experiences of the different generations are so dissimilar that conflict is almost inevitable. Universities are often the centers of discontent, because they bring together large numbers of people who have maximum exposure to new ideas but little power to implement them. The result, not surprisingly, is often explosive.

Authoritarian governments of both the right and left generally manage to suppress these conflicts so they are not visible to the outside world. Yet as the Chinese experience indicates, suppressing them is not the same as eliminating them. When Mao mistakenly assumed in the 1950s that the masses were solidly behind his revolution and announced a new policy of greater political freedom ("Let a hundred flowers bloom, let a hundred schools contend"), the situation quickly threatened to get out of hand. Cleavages within the People's Republic were again revealed during and after the Great Cultural Revolution of the middle 1960s, with violent conflicts between students and Party cadres, workers and managers, soldiers and civilians, young and old. Then, following Mao's death in 1976, dissension surfaced once more. The fact of the matter is that industrialization and modernization are extremely stressful processes and when the cleavages they generate are added to the historic cleavages inherent in an agrarian social order, the choice is between harsh repression and chronic and endemic conflict.

Education

The importance of education for economic growth is abundantly clear: the most prosperous nations are those that have invested heavily in education. In the United States, Japan, and the Soviet Union—three of the most striking examples of economic growth—high levels of national expenditure on education preceded industrialization.[22] In czarist Russia as early as the end of the last century, 44 per cent of the men between thirty and thirty-nine were literate, and in urban areas the figure was as high as 69 per cent. In Japan, half the male population was literate a generation before that; and in the United States, 90 per cent of white adults were literate as early as 1840.

Recent studies of the relation between education and economic growth reinforce this conclusion. They indicate that expansion of primary and secondary school enrollments, especially the latter, have been linked to increases in per capita GNP since World War II.[23] However, these same studies found this relation did not exist in the case of the expansion of enrollments in *higher* education. The reasons for this are not clear, but it may reflect the fact that many industrializing societies have overemphasized training in the humanities and neglected training in fields required by industrialization. In both Eastern and Western Europe, for example, from one-third to one-half of university students study science or engineering, compared to only 23 per cent of those in Asia and 16 per cent in Latin America.[24]

These figures are important not only because industrializing societies so urgently need technical and engineering skills but because they have so much trouble absorbing the nontechnical professionals their universities turn out. In India, for example, 58 per cent of the students were recently enrolled in the humanities, fine arts, and law.[25] But many graduates simply cannot find jobs that utilize these skills. Unwilling to accept lesser employment (a reflection of the traditional value system of agrarian elites and would-be elites), they become a kind of intellectual proletariat with deep-seated hostilities toward the existing social order. Because such people are easily attracted to revolutionary movements, this leads to more political instability, and this in turn hampers economic progress. In short, far from aiding economic growth, an oversupply of nontechnically trained students in a society can actually hinder it.

One might ask why the leaders of these societies allow this kind of educational imbalance to develop. There are several reasons. First, in allowing the humanities to dominate their educational systems, they are following the example of the oldest and most prestigious educational institutions in the world—Oxford, Cambridge, and the famous Continental universities—as well as their own native traditions. Second, it costs much more to provide technical education, and these nations have very limited resources. Finally, it has not been very long since the nature of this problem first became evident. Perhaps in the light of experience these nations will begin to revise their educational programs.

Ideologies: Old and New

Most leaders of modernizing movements are convinced that social and economic progress requires more than increased capital and improved techniques of production. New creeds and new gods are needed to arouse and mobilize the common people, who, after centuries of frustration, are often apathetic and take a fatalistic view of life. Ironically, even so dedicated a

Marxist as Mao Tse-tung came to place the spiritual struggle for people's minds and hearts ahead of the struggle to transform the economy.

Today, in all but the most backward parts of the industrializing agrarian world, there is an intellectual ferment and a clash of ideas between the advocates of traditional belief systems and the proponents of newer ones. The situation is often extremely complicated, because both traditionalists and modernizers are themselves divided on many points, while others favor various blends of the old and the new.

A lot of the intellectual and ideological resistance to modernization has come from advocates of the traditional faiths. In southern and eastern Asia, this means Buddhism, Hinduism, and sometimes Islam; in the Middle East, Islam; in Latin America, Spain, and Portugal, Roman Catholicism. In all these areas, religious leaders have often been the leaders of conservative and traditionalist movements. This is hardly surprising, considering the historical role of these groups in agrarian societies and the nature of their beliefs. In general, they believe that the quest for truth is essentially complete: what people need to know has already been revealed—in the Vedas, or in the Koran, or to the Sangha, or to the Catholic Church. True wisdom, in their opinion, lies in turning to religious authorities for guidance and following their directions. In describing the traditionalist approach to education in the Middle East, one writer has said, "Education, as far as it is under the control of the ulema [the spiritual leaders of the Muslim community], is still bound up with authoritarianism, rote learning, and a rigid devotion to ancient authorities—providing only already known solutions to already formulated problems."[26] Traditionalist education in Latin America and southern and eastern Asia is very similar. This approach sees little need for change, unless it is to root out whatever modernizing influences have crept in.

In the late nineteenth and early twentieth centuries, many western intellectuals thought these older faiths would simply die out as their adherents came to recognize the "obvious" superiority of western creeds such as Protestantism, humanism, and socialism. All three of these newer faiths were then winning converts, especially among the better educated, and it looked as if it were only a matter of time until the older faiths would vanish altogether.

Since World War I, however, and even more since World War II, the situation has changed drastically in many areas. With the development of nationalist movements and a growing resistance to colonialism of every kind, many of the traditional faiths have experienced a remarkable reinvigoration. After Sri Lanka won its independence, for example, a significant number of Christian converts there reconverted to Buddhism. In India, Hindu traditionalist forces became strong enough to pass laws forbidding the entry of foreign missionaries. In Egypt, Nasser imprisoned or executed most of the leaders of the Communist Party. In Iran, Khomeini led an Islamic revolution that overthrew the Shah and his program of modernization.

Although religious leaders have often been among the most conspicuous proponents of traditionalism, they have usually had strong support from the old governing class, especially the large landowners.[27] In fact, the rural population as a whole, emotionally involved in its traditional religion and unfamiliar with alternatives, has generally supported them. Members of such old "professions" as herbalists and practitioners of traditional medicine have also been strong supporters of traditionalist ideologies and belief systems, because they know their skills are rendered obsolete by newer technologies.

Ranged against traditionalists like these are individuals and groups who by virtue of educational, occupational, or other experience have been converted to the newer faiths. Early in a modernization movement, a disproportionate number of the leaders are people who were won over to the new outlook during visits to industrialized societies, either as students or as workers (this was true, for example, of India's Nehru and of Vietnam's Ho Chi Minh).[28] Later, however, most of the leaders are people who were converted by experiences in their own countries. Frequently they are children of members of the old governing class, who after conversion rose to positions of leadership because of their superior training and other resources.

As we noted earlier, there are usually competing movements within the camp of modernizers, some advocating western-style democracy, others the authoritarian Marxist model, still others some kind of hybrid political system. The liberal democratic model was the first to be tried in most industrializing agrarian nations, as we also noted. It has had its greatest support from the more prosperous segments of the new middle class—professional people, managers in new industries, and others with modern education. Socialist movements were usually introduced next. Their support has been greatest among intellectuals, students, and the economically insecure—landless peasants, unemployed urban workers, and the like.

The most recent approach to modernization is nationalism, which reflects the dissatisfaction of many of the current generation of leaders with both of the other models. Their idea is to synthesize not only capitalism and socialism but modernism and traditionalism as well. Most of the nationalist ideologies that have flourished in the industrializing agrarian world since World War II have had an especially strong element of traditionalism (e.g., Khomeini's Iran). To some extent, nationalism represents a reaction against colonialism, and this is crucial in the process of nationbuilding, especially in countries that were under foreign control until very recently.

There is more to modern nationalism than this, however: it is also an effort to reaffirm the importance of the cultural traditions of non-European peoples (in the case of Latin America, of peoples not in the Anglo-American tradition). This helps heal the breach between traditionalists and modernists by providing a position that is acceptable to both. Moreover, it gives dignity to a nation's leaders in their relations with European (or Anglo-American) peoples.

Unfortunately, the deliberate cultivation of nationalist sentiments can easily lead to the hatred of other nations. Even when this is not a spontaneous development, leaders of industrializing nations may encourage it solely to divert criticism from themselves and their policies. It can be very useful to blame foreigners for all the defects and shortcomings, inevitable and otherwise, of one's own policies.

Industrializing Horticultural Societies

During recent centuries, advanced horticultural societies flourished both in southeast Asia (from India to Vietnam) and in Africa south of the Sahara. In southeast Asia, however, all of these societies have been either conquered or assimilated by neighboring agrarian societies.[29]

In Africa south of the Sahara things have been different. There, much of the traditional horticultural way of life has survived into the second half of the twentieth century, apparently because the period of European colonial rule was so brief and its impact on most of these societies relatively limited. It is easy to forget that the period of European rule in most of sub-Saharan Africa did not begin until the last decades of the nineteenth century and ended early in the second half of the twentieth. Since the process of institutional disintegration and transformation was just beginning in these societies when colonialism ended, the concept of industrializing horticultural societies is applicable to them.

The problems of these societies are similar in a number of respects to those of industrializing agrarian societies. Both are confronted with a variety of radically new social and cultural elements introduced by diffusion from technologically more advanced societies. Both find that these new elements throw their traditional relationships out of kilter and create serious tensions. Furthermore, both experience an almost continuous state of crisis because things are changing so fast and because they lack the institutional and other resources to cope.

At the same time, there are a number of important differences between them that reflect their horticultural and agrarian backgrounds and often cause them to react differently to the impact of industrialization. To avoid unnecessary repetition, we will focus mainly on these differences, referring only briefly to the points of similarity. Unless these are kept in mind, the differences between industrializing agrarian and industrializing horticultural societies may appear to be greater than they actually are.

Technology and Productivity

Technologically, industrializing horticultural societies are much less advanced than industrializing agrarian, especially in their indigenous, or native, technology. This is revealed in a number of ways. For one thing, they are much less urbanized: in one recent year, industrializing agrarian societies had an average of 27 per cent of their populations in cities of 20,000 or more, while industrializing horticultural societies had only 9 per cent in cities that large.[30] This is important, because the size of the urban population is a good measure both of the size of the economic surplus and of the growth of specialized crafts and trade and commerce.

Per capita GNP is a useful summary measure of the level of both technological advance and productivity in the two types of industrializing societies. In the middle 1970s, the median per capita GNP for 39 industrializing horticultural societies was slightly over $200; for 58 industrializing agrarian societies, it was slightly over $500.[31]

One of the most disturbing features of industrializing horticultural societies is their inability to improve living standards. In a number of cases, per capita GNP has actually been declining in recent years, after allowance is made for the effects of inflation. In Ghana and Zaire, for example, it dropped more than 10 per cent between 1975 and 1977.[32] In both instances, this was due to a combination of runaway population growth and corrupt political leadership.[33] In Tanzania, in contrast, where the latter problem does not exist, small gains have been achieved. Even these have been disappointing, however, since far more rapid improvements were expected there after colonial rule ended (see below).[34] The chief exceptions to the generally bleak picture provided by the industrializing horticultural societies of sub-Saharan Africa are the handful of oil-producing states (Gabon, Nigeria, Angola), where the new revenues from oil exports have been sufficient to offset other factors.

Population

Industrializing horticultural societies have the highest birthrates and the highest rates of population growth of any set of societies in the world system. As Table 13.7 indicates, their birthrates are between 40 and 50 per 1,000 population per year, roughly one-third higher than industrializing agrarian

TABLE 13.7 Crude Birthrates, Death Rates, and Rates of Natural Increase in Selected Industrializing Horticultural Societies

Society	Crude Birthrate*	Crude Death Rate†	Rate of Natural Increase
Kenya	51	14	37
Nigeria	50	20	30
Zambia	50	19	31
Ivory Coast	49	20	29
Ghana	49	19	30
Zimbabwe	48	15	33
Angola	48	25	23
Tanzania	47	22	25
Zaire	47	21	26
Mozambique	46	21	25
Uganda	45	16	29
Cameroon	42	21	21
Guinea-Bissau	40	25	15
Gabon	31	23	8

Source: United Nations, *Population and Vital Statistics Report*, series A, vol. 32, no. 1 (January 1980).
*Live births per 1,000 population per year.
†Deaths per 1,000 population per year.

societies and three times higher than industrial societies. As a result, their populations are growing at rates ranging from 2.0 to 3.5 per cent per year.[35] This means they will double in size every twenty to thirty-five years and increase as much as *thirty-fold* in one century.

These growth rates result, of course, from the fact that technology borrowed from industrial societies has brought death rates far below tradition-al levels, while birthrates remain at traditional levels—or even somewhat higher because of the disproportionate number of young adults in these societies. Needless to say, many of the most serious problems confronting them stem from their failure to control population growth. Yet there is little evidence that any of their governments have plans to deal with the problem.

The Economy

The economies of industrializing horticultural societies resemble those of industrializing agrarian societies in some important ways. For one thing, they, too, are a mixture of both traditional and modern elements, with the result that there may be little resemblance between the economic patterns in a nation's outlying villages and those in its largest cities. In addition, like many or most industrializing agrarian societies, the societies of sub-Saharan Africa are unable to compete in world markets with industrial societies in the production of most manufactured goods. Thus they, too, tend to become highly special-ized and to be suppliers of raw materials in these markets.

Since their independence, many industrializing horticultural societies have proclaimed themselves socialist, or even Marxist, societies. But African socialism is very different from European or Asian socialism. It is, in fact, as variable as the societies that have adopted it. President Senghor of Senegal, in a book entitled *African Socialism,* wrote, "We have rejected prefabricated models," and the economy of Senegal combines a communal system of agriculture with mixed public-private utilities, and private ownership of banks, commerce, and industry.[36] Although the details vary from society to society, this blending of public and private ownership of the means of production is widespread. There are a few societies, such as Kenya, which lean heavily toward private ownership, and a somewhat larger number, including Tanza-nia, Angola, and Mozambique, that lean heavily toward state ownership, but the majority mix capitalist and socialist principles, together with a generous component of traditional African economic patterns.

The economic development programs of the more idealistic African leaders, such as President Julius Nyerere of Tanzania, have emphasized the need to improve the conditions of life for the common people and to reduce economic inequalities. According to many western experts, on whom he relied, this would lead to a burst of economic growth and prosperity. However, this has not happened. Despite the creation of an extensive educational system and greatly improved health and sanitary facilities in 8,000 villages, the production of cash crops for export (which is essential to the economy) has declined since 1965. Were it not for the infusion of huge

FIGURE 13.8   Many industrializing societies have been forced into a peculiar
ecological niche: they have become the producers of raw materials for the world
economy. In recent years, as much as 54 per cent of Ghana's foreign exchange has
come from the sale of cocoa, which is shown above being collected at a
cooperative marketing society.

amounts of foreign aid ($450–$500 million in 1978, or $30 for every Tan-
zanian), the economy would be in desperate shape, since this aid provides 60
to 70 per cent of the cost of the government's program of economic development.[37]

Because the urban sector of the economy in horticultural societies is so
much less developed than in agrarian societies, the urban population has had
even less experience with such fundamentals of modern life as money, trade
and commerce, markets, occupational specialization, literacy, and bureaucracy. This makes it very difficult for modernizing governments and businesses to
find skilled personnel to staff their organizations. The problem is especially
serious in an era of nationalism, because national pride often demands that
businesses and government be staffed with local personnel, regardless of the
cost in terms of organizational efficiency.[38]

Data on literacy give some idea of the relative magnitude of this problem
for the two types of industrializing societies. The most recent data available
show that 63 per cent of the adult population in the average (median)
industrializing agrarian society was literate, while in industrializing horticultural societies the comparable figure was only 15 per cent.[39] Assuming literacy
as a minimum requirement for effective participation in modern economic life,

and assuming also that these societies will not be able to increase their rate of literacy any faster than others have, it will take industrializing horticultural societies at least eighty years to develop a fully qualified labor force.[40]

Horticultural societies face still other problems in economic development. We can see why when we consider the traditional nature and meaning of work in these societies. Not long ago, the Inter-African Labour Institute character-ized work traditions in horticultural Africa this way:

1. Work is viewed in its relation to the basic institution of family or clan; within the family, it is divided on the basis of age and sex.

2. Work is linked with religious rites.

3. Work activities are considered and evaluated in the light of a subsistence economy rather than a profit economy (i.e., one oriented to the production of the necessities of life rather than to the maximization of profits in a market economy).

4. Work requires neither foresight nor planning.

5. Time is largely irrelevant in work activities; no time limits are set for most tasks.

6. There is little specialization.

7. For men, work is episodic; when a task has to be done, men often do it without a break, but intervals of inactivity are long and frequent.

8. Men hardly ever work alone; work activities (e.g., hunting parties and work parties) often resemble a collective leisure activity in modern industrial society.[41]

These traditions do little to prepare the members of these societies, especially the men, for work in a modern industrial society. A parallel list of the characteristics of work in industrial societies would, in fact, be an almost perfect contradiction.

One of the biggest problems is suggested by item 7. In analyzing horticultural societies in Chapter 6, we saw how often farming is primarily women's work. Men's responsibility is often limited to the occasional clearing of new fields. While women do the sustained, tedious chores—planting, cultivating, and harvesting crops—men are free to do more interesting and exciting things—hunting, fighting, politicking, socializing, and participating in ceremonial activities. The disciplined, routinized forms of work so typical of an industrial economy are seldom encountered by men in these societies. In this respect, the peasant farmers of agrarian societies are far better prepared for industrialization. Yet even they have found the transition difficult.[42]

There is tremendous economic and social variation within every industri-alizing horticultural society in sub-Saharan Africa. A few of its tribes and villages may remain virtually untouched by the influences of industrialization, while in some of its cities the older patterns have been largely destroyed.[43] In addition, there is every conceivable combination of the old and the new—such as the woman in Nairobi who practiced witchcraft in order to earn the down payment on a truck so she could go into the trucking business.[44] A more common practice is to work part-time in a factory while continuing to practice traditional horticulture.

One observer reports that there have been four basic economic patterns in Africa in recent years.[45] The first, which has become extremely rare, is a pure subsistence economy in which the local village consumes only what it produces or obtains through barter with its neighbors. The second pattern he calls "taxed subsistence," which means that a village raises a cash crop or sends its young men out to work for cash so it can pay the taxes levied by the government. The third might be called a mixed economy: villagers still rely on a subsistence economy for their basic necessities, but they simultaneously work for cash—not only because of taxes but so they can buy modern consumer goods. The fourth pattern is a predominantly cash economy in which even food is bought and laborers are hired to work on the farms.

These patterns, which typically follow one another in sequence in a particular area, show how internal and external forces combine to transform a society's economy. On one side, there are the values, preferences, and desires of the villagers themselves; on the other, are the demands made, and the attractions offered, by alien groups and institutions. It is easy to underestimate the power of the internal forces and interpret economic development as a process that is simply forced on reluctant villagers who prefer to be left alone to live as their forefathers did. But the problem is far more complex than this. Given a choice, most of the members of horticultural societies choose the industrial way of life—not knowing, it is true, all the implications and ramifications of their choice. Sometimes they adopt it *in toto*, like the family that migrates to the city. In other cases, they adopt only part of it, like the couple who stay in the village but earn all the cash they can to buy modern tools, cloth, soap, a sewing machine, a radio, a bicycle, and the other products of an industrial economy.

The Polity

One of the striking features of sub-Saharan Africa is how new most of its societies are: almost without exception, they were established in the late nineteenth or the twentieth century. Most of them are the products of European colonialism, and their boundaries are largely the result of the rivalries of colonial governments or missions, the outcomes of battles, the location of rivers, and other things that had little to do with the boundaries of the older societies they replaced. Actually, the process was not too different from the one that produced most of the modern nations of Europe, Asia, and the New World.

Because of their newness, most African societies suffer from serious internal divisions rooted in traditional tribal loyalties. Colonial powers seldom destroyed the older tribal groups. On the contrary, they usually preserved such groups in order to use them as instruments of administrative control, allowing tribal rulers to serve as lower-echelon officials in the new colonial societies. Colonial governments often pretended such tribal groups were autonomous, because that enabled them to put the burden, and the onus, of political control on their leaders. They also encouraged tribal rivalries, applying the ancient principle "Divide and rule." As a result, even after independence was won, there was a fundamental tension between tribal loyalties and national loyalties in most parts of Africa. This is a problem that few industrializing agrarian societies have had to contend with.

The consequences have been serious for sub-Saharan societies, however.

TRIBAL LAW VERSUS NATIONAL LAW: THE CASE OF THE MARAKAWET ELDERS

On March 17 Kap sirir rap Koech, better known as Chelimo, a member of the Marakawet tribe in Kenya, had a quarrel with his wife and beat her to death. He then fled into the bush, but his brothers, following tribal custom, hunted him down and brought him before village elders, who, after deliberation, rendered the verdict of death, a judgment that was accepted by both of the families involved. Chelimo was then tied face down on the ground, and his older brother and the father of his murdered wife together brought large stones and smashed the back of his head. Word of their action came to government authorities, and Kibor, the brother, and Kirop, the father, were brought to trial under national law, which is based on English law, and were themselves condemned to death for murder.

In discussing the case, a reporter for the *Los Angeles Times* wrote, "In more developed countries, like Britain and the United States, the law has evolved naturally, coming out of the folkways of the people. But in Africa, the law has been imported from an alien country and imposed upon a host of traditional laws of many different tribes.

"At independence, the new African leaders could have thrown out the colonial law and reverted to the old tribal laws. But they did not. Mainly because they feared chaos. The leaders want to create unified states, and unity would be held back if each small tribe practiced a law of its own.

"Selecting one tribal law and imposing it on all the others might even be more divisive. So the leaders decided to retain the foreign law that had become common to all tribes during colonial days.

"There was another reason. The new leaders consider themselves modern, educated men, and in their view much of traditional tribal law was not 'civilized.' They did not want justice governed by such law.

"But the use of European law has not been absolute. There has been an attempt, both in colonial days and now, to bend the European law to accommodate some of the traditional tribal law. In some cases, in fact, tribal law or, as it is called in the courts, 'customary law,' guides the decision of judges. If this were not the case, the legal system would be so alien that the people would attempt to ignore it."

Excerpted from a story copyrighted by the *Los Angeles Times*. Reprinted by permission.

Tribal divisions nearly destroyed the new nations of Zaire and Angola after they gained their independence. In Nigeria, Burundi, and Chad, the fuse burned more slowly, but the results were even worse. In most other countries, tribalism remains an important divisive force, sometimes with the potential for civil war.[46] When they were fighting for independence, many African leaders (as well as their friends in industrial societies) ignored or minimized the importance of these tribal loyalties, thinking that their compatriots valued them as little as they did and that the old ties were rapidly losing their vitality. Although this may be true in a few countries, it has proved a serious misjudgment in most.[47] Even in cities and towns, tribal loyalties are still meaningful to some degree.[48] In view of American experience with ethnic loyalties, and considering the virtual absence of any national institutions in these African societies until recently, this is hardly surprising. With increasing urbanization, with the establishment of schools that indoctrinate children in a nationalistic outlook, and with the growth of the mass media to reinforce these early lessons, tribal loyalties will eventually disappear. But this will probably take decades, and in the meantime these allegiances will produce bitter and often costly conflicts.

FIGURE 13.9   Tribal chief on visit to Monrovia, capital of Liberia.

Except for the influence of tribal loyalties, the polities of industrializing horticultural societies have a lot in common with those of industrializing agrarian societies. The majority of them profess socialist ideals, although their planning efforts, even basic administrative activities, are often hamstrung by the lack of trained personnel and by commitments to rapid Africanization of the civil service. This is especially serious because most of these governments, like those of most industrializing agrarian societies, are committed to programs of economic planning and development, a notoriously difficult and complex business.[49]

Another important similarity is the trend that one writer has referred to as "the erosion of democracy."[50] Prior to independence, most of the native political leaders in these countries professed to be democrats and to believe in parliamentary government, a multiparty system, and free elections. Subsequently, however, when the hostility that had previously been focused on the colonial regime was directed at them and their new governments and opposition forces threatened to turn them out of office, most leaders became advocates of a one-party state with control in the hands of a strong executive (i.e., themselves). Subsequently, in about half of these societies, the government was taken over by the military. Only two industrializing horticultural societies—Botswana and Gambia—have maintained stable democratic governments. Tanzanian President Julius Nyerere commented not long ago, "We spoke and acted as if, given the opportunity for self-government, we would quickly create utopias. Instead, injustice, even tyranny, is rampant."[51]

Related to this is the fact that the governments of many of the industrializing horticultural societies of Africa have had a major problem with corruption. In Zaire, for example, an international grant of $1.8 million to repair Kinshasa's broken-down city buses was reportedly "swindled down" to $200,000 by the time it reached the Transportation Ministry, while in Gabon the president built himself a $650 million marble palace with revolving rooms and walls that disappear at the touch of a button. For a number of years, oil-producing Arab nations were generous providers of foreign aid to sub-Saharan African societies, but they have now cut back on such aid after a series of bad experiences. A leading Arab publication recently reported, "In some cases now coming to light, for every $1 million of aid, less than $100,000 finds effective applications in African countries like Zambia and Zaire."[52]

Social Stratification

Although most industrializing horticultural societies profess socialist ideals, there has been relatively little concern about social inequality, probably because the level of inequality, until recently at least, was low compared to that found in industrializing agrarian and industrial societies.[53] Also, there was not the grinding poverty for millions that has been characteristic of agrarian and early industrial societies.

Since the elimination of the colonial powers, the composition of the upper class has been altered. In some areas, such as northern Nigeria, the rulers of the old society—the chiefs, kings, or emirs, together with their ministers and retainers—still constitute this class. Where modernizers are in control, the more typical situation, the upper class is largely composed of the new political and intellectual elite and, in many societies, the new entrepreneurial and military elites as well.

Beneath this politically and economically dominant class, there are two fairly distinct systems of stratification. In the rural areas, where traditional patterns prevail, an individual's status is largely a function of his own and his family's relation to traditional authorities (especially the village headman and the tribal chief). In urban areas, where industrialization is a greater force, the crucial criteria are education, occupation, income, and connections with the new political elite.

Religion and Ideology

The traditional religions of sub-Saharan Africa were relatively undeveloped, both organizationally and intellectually. There were no complex organizations of priests or monks, as in the major religions of the agrarian world, no body of sacred writings to serve as the core of a common faith, no tradition of religio-philosophical speculation, and, most important of all, no universal faith to provide a bond between members of different societies. As a result, these faiths could not easily defend themselves against the inroads of Islam and Christianity, especially when these were being introduced by peoples who were politically and economically stronger and whose way of life, therefore, seemed so obviously worthy of emulation.

Africans who still cling to the older tribal faiths are usually residents of the more isolated rural areas or the less educated residents of the towns. Since this describes the majority of people in these societies, however, adherents of the older faiths are obviously still numerous. In Benin, for example, only 28 per cent of the people are even nominally Christian or Muslim, in Zambia and Botswana, 15 per cent.[54] In the cities, however, the picture is very different. In Dar es Salaam, a city of 500,000 in Tanzania, 99.8 per cent of the population claim to be either Muslim or Christian—and this in a country 40 per cent non-Muslim and non-Christian.[55] Similarly, in Monrovia, the capital of Liberia, 72 per cent regard themselves as either Christian or Muslim, although in the country as a whole, only 25 per cent do so.[56]

Conversions to Islam and Christianity are frequently for nonreligious reasons. For many people, it is a status symbol, an effort to identify with modern ways and avoid being regarded as ignorant, backward country folk. In Dar es Salaam, for example, many pagan tribesmen "on arrival in town call themselves Muslims—some few call themselves Christians—in order to conform, not to be conspicuous in a [community] where Islam is supreme and where to 'have no religion,' as people put it, is the mark of the uncivilized. Some go so far as to be circumcised and to be formally admitted to Islam: most merely use a Muslim name instead of a tribal one; some have two names, a Christian and a Muslim, to cover all eventualities."[57] Under the circumstances, it is hardly surprising to find that "the outward observances of religion are strikingly absent in Dar es Salaam: it is rare to see an African Muslim praying his daily prayers [and] in Ramadhan [the Muslim month of fasting] people may be seen anywhere eating and drinking publicly during the daily hours [a forbidden practice]," and the consumption of alcohol, also forbidden, is almost universal.[58] In Monrovia, where Christianity is dominant, the pattern is not quite so pronounced, but even here "the professing of Christianity remains a basic requirement of 'civilized' status," and "for a great many of the civilized, church membership has become largely a question of social status."[59] In many areas, both urban and rural, those who have adopted Christianity or Islam continue to practice traditional tribal religions.[60]

In the early years of colonial rule, Christian missions were an important force for modernization. This was primarily due to the mission schools, which introduced literacy and elements of western culture and, most important of all, opened up channels of communication with the larger world. As a result, the areas that came under Christian influence advanced more rapidly than those where paganism or Islam prevailed. In discussing Tanzania, one writer asserts:

> Mission schools and mission hospitals have been very important factors in changing tribal society, although their influence has been felt much more strongly in some areas than others. Very nearly a one-to-one correlation exists between mission influence, the cash-crop economy, fertile land, education, and the general desire for progress.[61]

Similarly, many people have commented on the singular economic success of the Christian Ibo of southeastern Nigeria compared with the Muslim and pagan tribes to the north.

With the rise of the independence movement after World War II, identification with Christianity became a somewhat ambiguous social attribute. Christianity was linked with colonialism, and colonialism was, by definition, a force detrimental to Africa. Missionaries came under heavy attack for dominating the churches and refusing to let native Christians assume positions of leadership. Furthermore, in an era of great social change and uncertainty, mission-brand Christianity often seemed too tame and too western. In many areas, new sects were founded, some basically Christian, others largely pagan, many a mixture of the two.[62] These sects have their greatest appeal for individuals who are in mid passage in the difficult transition from traditional culture to modern. Such people are subject to great insecurity, both economically and intellectually, and the sects often provide a link to the past. They also are popular because they permit polygyny and other traditional practices condemned by the missionaries.

There are also new nontheistic ideologies in sub-Saharan Africa, and the most important is nationalism. In many cases, nationalism functions simply as a secular ideology. But sometimes, when it demands supreme loyalty, it assumes a truly religious character. In Ghana, for example, President Nkrumah assumed messianic titles, and his political party took on quasi-religious functions.[63] This tendency is so marked that some students of the modernization process now speak of *political* religion in contrast to *church* religion.[64] Whether nationalism will survive in this extreme form no one can say. Its chances are probably linked to the experience these new societies have with the modernization process. The quicker and easier it is, the poorer the chances for an extreme nationalism.

Kinship

In the horticultural societies of precolonial Africa, kin groups were extremely important. As one writer put it, in Africa "the [kin group] was the basic building block of society."[65] More than that, it was psychologically the center of the individual's world, establishing his identity and defining most of his basic rights and responsibilities.

Now the historic bases of power of the kin group are being destroyed in these societies. In the modern sector of the economy, the kin group no longer controls its members' access to the means of livelihood, which it traditionally did through its control of the land. Similarly, the family plays a smaller role in the political system. And the once-important cult of the ancestors, centered in the kin group, has declined in importance as Christianity and Islam have grown.

In the past, most of the advantages of the kin group were enjoyed by the older generation, while the disadvantages fell disproportionately on the younger. Before the growth of cities and towns, young people had no choice but to accept the burdens and patiently await the day when they would become the privileged elders. Industrialization changed all this: at the very least, it offered youth a way to escape the authority of the elders, at best, a rise to fame and fortune beyond the wildest dreams of those who stayed in the villages.

We get some idea of this change from the following excerpt from a document written by an African townsman explaining to a European why Africans leave the villages. In it, he describes a typical conversation between two young villagers, one of whom says:

> Lucas, old boy, we have a very hard life here in the country; the authorities—I don't know if it is the chief or his assistants—have their knives into us. And as for Father and even Mother! . . . Listen, it was only the other day, you've seen the maize, cucumbers, and vegetables, all ripe? Well, this day hunger followed me around all day, I ran away from it but my feet wouldn't get me away, so I thought it best to go to our field and help myself to some cucumber. I admit I took one and swallowed it down without chewing. Then I got a mad desire to eat some maize and broke off three and went home to roast them. Presto, as the first was ready I began to eat it, then the second, when in come my parents from visiting. They see me and start straight in to abuse me, tell me never to darken their door again. That evening there was a big storm with lightning, one bolt of which struck a tree in that field and it fell and ruined a stretch of crops: then in the morning everyone said: Ah, yes, Juma ate unblessed food before we had sacrificed, that's why their field was destroyed. So the news spread and they sent me to expiate it, and when I got there the omens were against me and I was an outcast to the whole village. My father is an old man but he has no gratitude; since he was exempted from tax he has been to work for the chief only five times, every time it is his turn it's me that goes . . . .

FIGURE 13.10   The lure of the city: Lagos, capital of Nigeria.

I hate it here, better get a change of air—town air—even if it kills me. I am lucky enough to have borrowed the fare down, though I haven't enough to come back. But every day they sit on me, and now there is nothing for it but to disappear and give myself a break; in the town there are many people and many jobs, but here what job can a chap get? It's just the messenger coming in the morning, early, with a little bit of paper summoning me to the court; you get there and they tell you, you are charged by the agricultural inspector for not having a cassava field; if you ask who the inspector himself is, you're told, "That child over there." If you ask who is prosecuting and where he is they'll say, "So you are one of these bush lawyers are you? Do you suppose a full agricultural inspector will tell lies?"

Elders like this are not to be borne, in the end you may be had up for murder. Better go to town where nobody knows me, and nobody will say what's that you're eating, what's that you're wearing, every man for himself and mind his own business: but here! You've only to cough and somebody ticks you off for getting your feet wet.

Last week I returned from safari with the dresser, carrying his loads, and only a little later they volunteered me again to carry the [District Commissioner's] loads, nothing but work, any time there's loads to be carried it's always me . . . Well now, the rains are starting and lorries won't pass, off I go again. Soon I'll develop wheels and be a public service vehicle. Go to town any day.[66]

Actually, the break with family and kin is seldom as sharp as Juma's musings suggest. When they get to town, young people usually search out their relatives, who help them find employment and get settled. But in the long run, ties with family and kin are seriously weakened, and industrializing societies of today, like those of the past, have not developed any substitute for them.[67] This is a fairly serious source of social instability.

Another problem confronting these societies is the shift from polygyny to monogamy. Polygyny was practiced in almost all of the traditional horticultural societies of sub-Saharan Africa, while monogamy, as we have seen, is the rule in all modern industrial societies. Although the Christian missions fought polygyny vigorously, they had only limited success. Their opposition to it is, in fact, reputed to be one of the major reasons many Africans have been reluctant to be baptized. Eventually, however, the same forces responsible for monogamy in other industrial and industrializing societies will probably prevail here.

Considering the historic importance of kinship in horticultural Africa, such revolutionary changes are bound to be unsettling. Their effects will be felt at both the individual and the societal levels for a long time to come.

Industrializing Societies in Theoretical Perspective

Not too many years ago, the prospects for industrializing societies looked bright. All they had to do, apparently, was follow in the path blazed by the industrial societies of Western Europe and North America. In fact, some people believed that because these societies had the experience of the others to go on, they would be able to avoid many of their problems and speed up the process of modernization.

A quarter of a century later, that prediction seems naive. With the exception of the oil-rich Middle Eastern societies and a small number of others that were already well on the way toward industrialization twenty-five years ago, their development has been disappointingly slow. Improvements in the standard of living of the masses of citizens in the majority of these societies have been especially disappointing. Hundreds of millions of people continue to live in poverty, and near starvation, with little prospect of any significant improvement in their situation.

Why were those earlier predictions so inaccurate? Why have the majority of societies of the Third World not been able to take greater advantage of the vastly expanded store of technological information available to them?

One answer, originally developed by a group of Latin American scholars in the 1960s and known as "dependency theory," is that the problems of underdeveloped societies are due to external forces, especially to forces in their social environment.[68] Specifically, their problems are the result of influences exerted by industrial societies. The backwardness and problems of the underdeveloped societies, they argued, are an inevitable consequence of the economic growth and prosperity of industrial societies. Dependency theory is, in effect, a revision of Marx's theory that the growth of an increasingly impoverished proletariat is a necessary consequence of the growing wealth and power of the bourgeoisie or capitalist class.

There are currently a number of versions of dependency theory, each providing a somewhat different explanation of the Third World's problems, but all locating the source outside industrializing societies themselves.[69] Some blame multinational corporations, some the governments of industrial societies, and others a capitalist world economy that has led so many of these nations to concentrate their production of exports in raw materials or in low technology industries. Whatever the cause, dependency theorists assign responsibility for the dilemma of the Third World to western industrial societies that drain away their economic surplus.

Another group of scholars, mostly American, has developed an alternative explanation of the Third World's problems. "Modernization theory" finds the source of these problems within the industrializing societies themselves.[70] As with dependency theory, there are a number of versions of modernization theory, but most of them focus on the attitudes and values of the members of societies as the chief deterrent to industrialization. Thus, the difficulties of Third World societies, in their opinion, are due to the persistence of ideologies and institutional systems that were inherited from the preindustrial past and that are incompatible with the needs and requirements of industrialization. They point out, for example, the persistence of fatalism, trust in magic, resistance to innovation and change, and the conflict between traditional patterns of work (see page 393) and the requirements of modern industrial enterprises. They emphasize the consequences of illiteracy and the lack of information and skills of many kinds that are essential in the modern world. In short, modernization theory locates the causes of underdevelopment within the underdeveloped societies themselves, rather than in their social environments.

In any attempt to evaluate the relative merits of dependency theory and modernization theory, it is important to keep two things in mind. First, there is little evidence to support the claim of some dependency theorists that life was better in most Third World societies before the industrial era. Such a view cannot be supported by the historical record of the last 5,000 years. It is not legitimate, therefore, to ask, What has caused these societies to regress? Rather, the question must be, Why have the conditions in most of them improved so slowly?

The second point to remember is that there is no reason to assume that the source of the problems in the Third World is primarily internal *or* primarily external. On the contrary, ecological-evolutionary theory holds that the process of development in *any* human society is the result of three basic factors: its environment, social as well as biophysical; its store of information, both technological and ideological; and the process of selection within the society. (See Figure 3.5, page 73.) Thus, the process of development in an industrializing society is the consequence of *both* internal and external factors. The characteristics of Third World societies, the characteristics of other contemporary societies, and the characteristics of the present world system all play a role.

The inadequacy of focusing on external factors as much as dependency theory does is indicated by the argument of many of its proponents that the solution to the ills of the Third World lies in a massive transfer of wealth from western industrial societies to industrializing societies. Unfortunately, the past use of more limited transfers of capital leads one to doubt whether most of these societies yet have the internal resources to put more massive transfers to constructive use. This requires large administrative staffs with modern technical skills, plus honest elites capable of organizing vast and complex programs. The experience of Tanzania, which has at least some of these internal resources, illustrates the inadequacy of capital transfers alone.

The greatest deficiency of both modernization theory and dependency theory, however, is their failure to focus more closely on the distinctive demographic features of Third World societies. For the fact is that *no society has ever successfully industrialized while burdened with anything approaching the rate of population growth existing in most of these societies today.* Even impressive economic gains can be completely consumed by runaway population growth.

From the perspective of ecological-evolutionary theory, it is clear that the demographic peculiarities of Third World societies, as well as those characteristics of ideology and social structure that work against the resolution of their problems, all stem from a more basic underlying source. In most societies throughout human history, all of the basic components of their sociocultural systems—population, technology, ideology, social structure, and material products—evolved more or less in concert with one another. *In industrializing Third World societies today, in contrast, selected elements of an enormously powerful industrial technology have been introduced into sociocultural systems that are still geared to much less potent agrarian or advanced horticultural technologies.*

Not surprisingly, these societies have had enormous difficulty in coordinating technological advance with changes in other areas of life. Even the western industrial democracies, in which the new technology evolved largely in concert with changes in population, ideology, social structure, and material products, have encountered difficulties in adjusting to the new industrial technology. In fact, most of their major problems reflect the failure of political ideologies, religious beliefs and values, legal norms, organizational principles, and other cultural and structural elements to respond quickly enough to the new conditions created by ongoing changes in their technology.

Considering the problems an industrial technology can create even in those societies in which it evolved, it is hardly surprising that an industrial technology creates far greater ones when it is introduced as an alien force in societies still geared to simpler technologies. And when only selected elements of the new technology are introduced, the results can be disastrous.

India provides an excellent example of this. Over the last hundred years, improvements in transportation (especially railroads) and food production steadily reduced the number of deaths from famine, and programs of mass immunization and other health measures reduced deaths from disease. While this drastic reduction in the death rate was occurring, the vast majority of Indians, unlike the members of earlier industrializing societies, were not really involved in the industrialization process as a whole. Most of them continued to live as peasant farmers in relatively isolated villages, eking out a marginal existence on tiny farms, using traditional tools and techniques. As a result, their beliefs, values, and customs remained much as they had been for centuries, with large families highly valued and change viewed with profound skepticism. Not only the family but all of India's institutions (e.g., its educational system and the polity) were little altered by this *partial and selective diffusion* of industrial technology. The experience of most Third World societies, especially those with the greatest problems, has been similar to India's.

In the past, such imbalances in a sociocultural system would have been corrected through the play of natural forces. We saw earlier (page 136) how population pressures during the late hunting and gathering era led to the overkill of large game animals and, eventually, to the emergence of a more advanced technology and a new way of life. And we have seen how plagues and famines of the past periodically decimated the populations of agrarian societies, restoring their demographic equilibrium. In the case of India and other societies industrializing today, however, more advanced societies have repeatedly averted this resolution of the problem by shipping in large amounts of food. In doing so, they have simply laid the foundation for more serious crises and greater problems in the future.

It is clear from this that the solution to the major problems of the Third World lies in correcting this basic imbalance as quickly as possible. If new cultural mechanisms, in the form of new beliefs, values, and sanctions to implement birth control technology, fail to alleviate this problem, the future role of such natural forces as famine and disease will increase. And the longer it takes for the leaders of Third World societies to devise the necessary cultural solutions, the greater the chance that other factors, including war, will also play a role.

Thus, from both the selfish and the altruistic points of view, it would appear that industrial societies should begin shifting the focus of their efforts to help the Third World. Instead of trying primarily to alleviate symptoms, such as hunger, malnutrition, and disease, they should be directing their attention toward eliminating the problem that produces those symptoms. They will have to recognize that it is irresponsible to provide aid programs that seek to increase food production or improve infant health, without simultaneously addressing demographic problems and providing powerful incentives for lowering birthrates. Aid programs, in short, must become far more selective than they have been in the past, focusing always on underlying problems, not only in the area of population but also in such areas as education and energy.

The importance of both education and energy are fairly obvious. In the case of energy, however, the members of industrial societies have a special responsibility toward societies that are currently trying to industrialize. Not because of evil motives but simply because they were the first to industrialize, advanced societies have been the major cause of the energy crisis and its spiraling prices. Yet we have seen that the availability of cheap energy was an essential ingredient in their own industrialization and a major factor in their rapid climb to affluence. Without assistance, either in the form of financial subsidies to reduce the cost of energy in key industries or in the form of new and inexpensive energy technologies, Third World societies could well be condemned to a kind of international ghetto. In this area too, however, industrial societies would probably be well advised to make rigorous population policies a precondition for aid.

One thing that the industrial democracies will probably have to learn to live with in the years ahead is authoritarian Third World regimes. Democratic governments are ill equipped to handle the critical problems facing these societies. In fact, there is good reason to believe that one-party socialist or communist governments are best adapted organizationally and ideologically to the needs of these societies, at least once they acknowledge the critical importance of the population problem.

Of one thing we can be sure: the problems of the Third World are not going to be solved quickly. The basic reason is that the population of most Third World societies would increase 50 per cent even if no couple ever again had more than two children. This is, in effect, a heavily mortgaged future: a 50 per cent gain in GNP under these circumstances would translate into no gain at all in *per capita* GNP. Thus, a quick fix seems out of the question.

Industrializing societies provide a fascinating means of testing ecological-evolutionary theory, and other sociological theories as well. Their problems are so complex that they compel us to consider all the components of sociocultural systems, as well as the relations among them. They also compel us to consider the relations of each sociocultural system with the larger world system, which is good preparation for an analysis of the future, our primary concern in the final chapter.

CHAPTER 14

Retrospect and Prospect

When we study something as complex as sociocultural evolution, it is easy to become so immersed in details that we lose sight of the larger picture. For this reason, we will begin this final chapter with a brief look back over the long sweep of human history. Then we will go on to consider an important question that we could not really address until this point: What has sociocultural evolution really meant for humanity? Has technological progress contributed to the betterment of human life, bringing greater freedom, justice, and happiness? Or have these qualities been unaffected by this progress, or even declined?

After considering this question, we must turn our attention to *the future*. What lies ahead for human societies? Can ecological-evolutionary theory help us anticipate the problems and prospects they will face ten, twenty, even thirty years from now? This is an important question, and a practical one as well. For most of us will live in that world, and it could be very different from the world we are living in today.

Looking Back

When we look back over the long course of hominid history, we see that our species' development has always been part of the same grand process of biological evolution that shapes all life on this planet, and that we and our societies are an integral part of the global ecosystem. Yet it is equally clear that our species' experience has been different from that of the rest of the biological world in some fundamental ways. If we can understand just where, and how, our path diverged, we can better understand our own problems and those of our societies, and perhaps discern a better, happier future.

The Divergent Path

For millions of years, there was little to suggest that our early ancestors were destined to be anything more than just another variety of primate. But genetic changes gradually provided our line with the ability to create symbol systems, a trait as much the product of natural selection as wings, gills, social instincts, and other adaptive mechanisms of the biotic world.

With symbol systems, hominids could use their primate capacity for individual learning to far greater advantage. They could now create and share vast amounts of cultural information gleaned directly from individual experience. Eventually, hominid societies came to depend far more on new cultural information than on new genetic information in their adaptive efforts. Thus, for the past 35,000 years, *humanity's evolution has been shaped primarily by the processes of cultural innovation and selection*, rather than by the processes of biological evolution.

The explanation of the adaptive capacity of cultural information is its potential for creating diversity. In this respect, it is like genetic information, which underlies the striking diversity in the biotic world. In the case of cultural information, however, *all of the diversity is concentrated within a single species*. As a result, despite their common genetic heritage, human individuals become, with culture, far more unlike one another than is true of the members of any other species. Human societies, too, are very dissimilar, again unlike the situation in other social species. Though such diversity enhances our species' survival potential, it is also a major source of problems, both within and among societies.

Another manifestation of culture's capacity for creating diversity is the great variety of needs and desires that humans have developed, *needs and desires not related to the survival of either individuals or our species*. To satisfy these culturally triggered or intensified needs, societies have depended primarily on the kind of information—technological—that helps people utilize environmental resources in new ways and for new purposes. As technology advanced, however, it altered the conditions of life, and as that happened, further needs emerged. Efforts to satisfy these needs created further change, which led in turn to new needs, a process of feedback that has continued at an accelerating pace for the last 10,000 years.

Through this process, *humanity established a new and unique relationship with the biophysical environment*. Since every other species of plant or of animal uses the resources of its environment to satisfy only a set of limited,

genetically programmed needs, this characteristic is perhaps the most fundamental divergence of them all.

The Question of Progress

Despite the problems that have attended our species' reliance on culture, one
thing is clear: *culture has been a highly successful adaptive mechanism.*
Humanity has not only survived, it has flourished by biological standards:
there are far more of us alive today than at any time in the past, and our
numbers are growing rapidly.

But mere numbers is too narrow a concept on which to base an assessment
of *human* evolution. Rather, we must ask whether or not the process of
sociocultural evolution has meant progress in terms of more fundamental
human goals, such as freedom, justice, and happiness.

It is not easy, however, to assess progress in terms like these. For one
thing, these concepts are so broad that they apply to many aspects of human
life. For another, the way we define such terms is the product of past
experience, and this, as we have seen, varies greatly among individuals,
groups, and societies. Nevertheless, because the subject is far too important
simply to ignore, we must at least make the effort to evaluate humanity's
progress in terms of these goals and determine whether our species' growing
store of cultural information has had the effect of advancing or hindering them.

Freedom   The high value that the members of modern industrial societies
attach to freedom is revealed in the growing challenge to all forms of authority,
not only in the liberal democracies of the West but in the authoritarian nations
of Eastern Europe as well. Even those who are not in the forefront of the
libertarian movement are likely to consider the degree of freedom accorded
the individual one of the basic measures of the attractiveness, and hence the
progress, of a society, and they would deny that a technologically advanced,
politically repressive society is truly progressive.

But human freedom is more than the absence of repressive social controls;
it is also freedom from the restraints imposed by nature. People who must
spend most of their waking hours in an exhausting struggle to produce the
necessities of life are not truly "free"—even if there are few social restraints on
them. A woman whose life is one long succession of unwanted pregnancies is
not "free"—regardless of the kind of society she lives in. Disease, physical and
mental handicaps, geographical barriers, and all the laws of nature restrict
people and deny them freedom. For freedom does not exist where there is no
alternative; and freedom can be measured only by the range of choices that are
available. The fewer the viable choices, the less freedom there is—and it
matters little, from the standpoint of freedom, whether the restrictions are
imposed by nature or by other people.

Once we recognize this, it becomes clear that humanity's long struggle to
advance technologically is not irrelevant to the desire for freedom. Every

technological innovation reflects the desire to overcome natural limitations on human actions. Thanks to this struggle, some of us are now free to talk across oceans, free to travel faster than sound, free to live longer lives in better health while enjoying a range of experiences that far surpass in richness and variety what was available to the greatest kings and emperors of the past.

There has been a price to pay, of course: technological progress has necessitated larger and more complex social systems. If we want the option of flying to another part of the country instead of walking there, or of watching the day's events on a screen in our home instead of hearing about them weeks later, we have to accept certain social controls. The goods and services essential for those options can be produced only where there are organizations with rules and with sanctions to enforce the rules, and individuals with authority to exercise the sanctions. And these organizations can function efficiently only within the context of a society with rules to govern the relationships between them, and an authority system to enforce the rules. The only alternative is anarchy—and the loss of all the freedoms that modern technology affords.

Critics of modern society often say that the price has been too high, that the increased social restrictions outweigh the gains in freedom we derive from modern technology.[1] They may be right—this is a matter each of us must decide for himself. In doing so, however, we need to beware of romanticizing the past. Before deciding that people are less free than they used to be, we should read the records of peasant life in agrarian societies and of the life of horticultural and hunting and gathering peoples. In doing this, we must resist the temptation to abstract the attractive features and ignore the appalling ones. We must remember that slavery and serfdom were not accidental characteristics of agrarian societies but reflections of basic, inescapable conditions of that way of life, as were the high mortality rate and short life-span of many hunting and gathering peoples. Finally, we must keep in mind that the restraints in those societies were not all physical ones; there were often powerful social restrictions operating too.

Once we recognize the danger of comparing some rosy version of life in less advanced societies with the negative side of life in industrial societies, we are in a better position to consider whether freedom is a correlate of technological advance. We can say, first of all, that technological progress has clearly raised the *upper* level of freedom in human societies. People with the greatest measure of freedom in modern nations—that is, members of the upper classes—have a far wider range of choice than people with the greatest measure of freedom in agrarian societies, and the elites of agrarian societies had more freedom than the elites of less advanced societies. This has been true with respect to everything from the individual's use of a leisure hour to the use of a lifetime. In this sense, then, there is a high positive correlation between technological advance and gains in human freedom.

The relation between technological advance and freedom for the *average* member of society is more complicated. If we compare the typical peasant in an agrarian society with a typical hunter and gatherer, it is not at all clear that there were any gains. In fact, the peasant had to live with a lot of new social

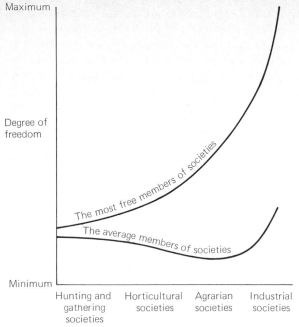

FIGURE 14.1   **Trends in freedom for various categories of people in four types of societies.**

controls, while gaining very little freedom from natural controls. Thus, during much of the course of evolutionary history—especially after the formation of the state—the average person probably experienced a decline in freedom. With industrialization, however, the pattern changed: once the difficult period of transition is past, technological progress and freedom for the average person *do* begin to be positively related, as Figure 14.1 illustrates. Whether people in industrial societies have more freedom than hunters and gatherers is a moot point. Clearly they have more social restraints, but far fewer physical and biological ones.

Before leaving the subject of freedom, we should take note of the popular misconception that governmental activity necessarily results in a loss of freedom for the members of society. This is at best a half-truth. Laws do, of course, place restrictions on people, but often this is done in order to increase freedom, not reduce it. The Pure Food and Drug Act, for example, was designed to restrict the freedom of businessmen who were willing to sell spoiled food and dangerous drugs for profit, but it increased the freedom of the rest of the population. Sometimes laws restrict everyone's freedom in one area—the freedom to proceed at will through a busy intersection, for example —in order to preserve it in others. In short, most legal norms *redistribute* freedom.

Justice   Justice has to do with the *fairness* of a society in its treatment of its members. Although no one would quarrel with the idea that a society should be "fair," we run into trouble when we try to define what this means. Is a society fair when it rewards people on the basis of their contributions to the common good, or is it more equitable to allocate rewards on the basis of people's individual needs? Should handicapped individuals, for example, be paid the same as those who are able to outproduce them with less effort? And how does one arrive at a fair evaluation of the relative contributions of people in highly dissimilar activities—a symphony conductor, a bricklayer, a mother, a garbage collector, a student?

And what about punishments? Does a "fair" society punish its members strictly in accordance with the letter of the law, or is it more just to take individual circumstances and intent into account? What of a parent's theft to feed a hungry child, for example, or a mercy killing? And should a society deal more severely with those in positions of power than with lesser members of society when a crime is committed, or should everyone be treated equally? Most important, perhaps, should a society seek to exact "an eye for an eye," or should it set a higher standard? Questions like these point up the difficulty of measuring progress with respect to justice. Since an adequate treatment of the subject would require volumes, all we will try to do here is call attention to basic trends and offer some tentative conclusions.

To begin with, as we observed in earlier chapters, social inequality became more pronounced as societies advanced technologically and status became increasingly dependent on the family into which one was born. The result was a weakening of the relationship between a person's *efforts* and a person's rewards. Whereas every boy in a hunting and gathering group had a chance of becoming the best hunter (and hence the most important man) in his society, a peasant's son had little hope of advancing even a notch above his father's social level, no matter how hard he tried.

The relationship between a person's *natural ability* and a person's rewards also declined with societal advance. For one thing, societies beyond the level of simple horticultural frequently excluded many of their members from access to rewards on the basis of religion or ethnicity, thereby denying them the chance to use many of their abilities. In addition, increasingly rigid stratification systems locked people into roles and situations where they could neither develop nor use their gifts, while those with few or none to use might occupy positions for which they were grossly unsuited.

The trend in punishment, meanwhile, was toward increasingly harsh and discriminatory treatment. In most agrarian societies, the privileged were free to abuse members of the lower class without fear of reproof; if the reverse occurred, however, an individual would be swiftly and speedily punished. A master involved in conflicts with slaves or serfs was often both judge and prosecutor; he could beat them with impunity and, in many societies, kill them if he wished. Nor were there legal sanctions against the beating of children by parents, employers, or schoolmasters.

Courts of law were equally harsh. In eighteenth-century England, 222 different offenses could draw the death penalty, including such minor infractions as the theft of a handkerchief, the shooting of a rabbit, or the forgery of a birth certificate.[2] Nor was execution always a humane process: we are told that the hangman in Elizabethan England was "an artist, and the knife was his chief instrument; the art consisting in tossing his man off the ladder, hanging him, but cutting him down before he breaks his neck, so that he may be dismembered and disemboweled while still alive."[3]

In general, societies seem to have become less fair and less just as they advanced technologically. Since the Industrial Revolution, however, there are clear signs of a reversal in this trend. With respect to economic rewards, industrialization has resulted in some decline in the level of social inequality among the members of a society. Public education now provides at least some chance for almost all children to develop their abilities, and women and minorities have gained numerous legal and economic opportunities long denied them. Industrial societies are also more solicitous of their poor and their handicapped, and provide a far broader range of legal rights and protections for their members, whatever their social status. Criminal justice is far less harsh. Industrial societies today rarely execute their members, and never for minor infractions, nor do they maim them, as was common in the agrarian era. In short, after a long period of declining justice with respect to both rewards and punishments, there is finally movement in the other direction.

Happiness   Of all the possible measures of progress, happiness is the most elusive, for it depends so much—perhaps primarily—on the quality of interpersonal relations, whether there is love, mutual respect, cooperation, and so forth. And these things do not seem to depend on the level of technological development. Studies of modern hunting and gathering groups indicate that the most primitive peoples develop these qualities as surely as members of modern industrial societies do.[4]

There are several respects, however, in which technological progress is relevant to this kind of happiness. To begin with, some of life's greatest tragedies involve the premature death of a loved one—a cherished child, a father or mother, or a partner in a happy conjugal relation. We saw how common this was in most societies prior to the Industrial Revolution and can therefore appreciate how the recently expanded life-span has contributed to human happiness.

Health, too, contributes to happiness. When we are seriously ill, life may not seem worth living. Disease was very poorly understood through most of human history, and it would be hard to argue that technological advance prior to the Industrial Revolution had any real impact in this area. More recently, however, advances in sanitation and medicine have dramatically improved the physical well-being of the members of many societies. Unfortunately, modern medical technology has also had a negative effect: it has been used to keep alive individuals who, in simpler societies, would mercifully be allowed to die. Still, the net result has undeniably been positive.

Hunger, another cause of enormous human misery over the centuries, has been drastically reduced in many societies as a result of industrialization. As recently as the eighteenth century, local crop failures in most parts of Europe could still result in starvation, because of an inadequate transportation network. Today, thanks to advances in technology, food supplies can be safely stored for long periods, or moved to areas of scarcity, in every industrial society and in an increasing number of industrializing ones.

The industrialization of agriculture has also meant a substantially improved food supply, with respect to quality, quantity, and diversity, for most members of industrial societies. During the winter, for example, people can enjoy fresh fruits and vegetables shipped in from areas with different growing seasons. Nor do the members of industrial societies have to subsist on short rations in the months prior to harvest, as the members of traditional agrarian societies had to do. As with improvements in health, it is easy to take such benefits for granted and to lose sight of the numerous links between technological advance and human happiness.

The increased production of other kinds of goods and services, especially nonessential ones, has probably had much less effect on happiness. The absolute quantity of luxuries we enjoy is certainly not as important in this regard as how they compare with what people around us have. Thus the headman in a simple horticultural society may be quite content with his few special possessions, because they are more than his neighbors own and as good as anything he knows about, while middle-class Americans, surrounded with goods and services the headman never dreamed of, may feel terribly deprived when they compare themselves with more prosperous neighbors. In other words, insofar as happiness depends on material possessions, the *degree* of inequality is probably more important than anything else.

When we take into account the advances in health, the greater abundance and improved quality of food, and the drastic reduction in premature deaths, it is clear that the Industrial Revolution has eliminated the sources of much of the misery of earlier eras. Putting it all together, we are again led to the tentative conclusion that the long-term trend for the average individual has been curvilinear. Conditions seem to have been more conducive to human happiness for the average individual in hunting and gathering societies than in horticultural, and better in horticultural than in agrarian, or even in early industrial. But with further advances in industrialization, the situation of the average individual seems to have improved considerably, reversing the long-term trend.

Recently published evidence, the first of its kind, tends to support this conclusion. In a study of almost seventy nations, containing two-thirds of the world's population, the Gallup Poll and its associates abroad found a striking relationship between the level of happiness expressed by the people they interviewed and the level of technological advance of the societies in which they lived (see Table 14.1). The same relationship was found between societal development and people's satisfaction with specific aspects of their lives (e.g., family life, health, housing, work). The results of this survey led George Gallup to comment: ''For centuries, romantics and philosophers have beguiled us with tales of societies that were 'poor but happy.' If any such exist, the survey failed to discover them.''

TABLE 14.1 Degree of Happiness and Satisfaction with Life Expressed by Members of Societies around the World

	Per Cent Very Happy or Fairly Happy	Per Cent Highly Satisfied with Their Lives*
North America	91	50
Western Europe	80	41
Latin America	70	40
Africa	68	15
Far East	48†	11

Source: Adapted from George H. Gallup, "Human Needs and Satisfactions: A Global Survey," *Public Opinion Quarterly*, 40 (Winter, 1976–1977), tables 2 and 6, pp. 465 and 467.
*The values shown in this column are the arithmetic means of responses to questions about satisfaction with ten specific areas of life (see Table 6 of Gallup's article).
†The Far East includes both Japan and India, and Gallup notes that "the differences between Japan [an advanced industrial society] and India [an industrializing agrarian society] with respect to personal happiness are very large."

Concluding Thoughts It is now clear that there is no simple one-to-one correspondence between technological advance and progress in terms of freedom, justice, and happiness. In fact, one may well ask whether technological advance has not proved to be a bitch goddess, luring societies into evolutionary paths where the costs often outweigh the benefits. Had human history come to an end several hundred years ago, one would have been forced to answer affirmatively. But during the last hundred years, technological advance has begun to make a positive contribution to the attainment of humanity's higher goals. Whether or not this will continue to be true in the future is another question. We can say this, however: technology has at last brought into the realm of *the possible* a social order with greater freedom, justice, and happiness than any society has yet known.

Whatever our judgment about the wisdom of our species' pursuit of technological advance, one thing is clear: *sociocultural evolution can be equated with progress only in the restricted sense of growth in the store of cultural information, and the consequences of its use.*

Looking Ahead

For thousands of years, hoping for a glimpse into the future, people turned to shamans and oracles, prophets and astrologers. Despite the sorry record of predictions made by such people, interest in the subject has not abated. Never, in fact, has it been greater than in modern industrial societies, as evidenced not only by the many serious books and articles produced on the subject but by the revival of interest in astrology.

The reason for this concern is clear: culture makes us aware of the relation between events of the present and those of the future, and the increased pace of social change in recent decades has heightened our perception of that relationship. But despite our desire to see into the future, and our need to do so, prediction remains a hazardous business. Only a hundred years ago, for example, Friedrich Engels wrote that warfare had reached the point where no significant advances in weapons could be expected. As he put it, "The era of evolution is therefore, in essentials, closed in this direction."[5]

There have been so many unsuccessful attempts to forecast the future that prediction might appear to be entirely a matter of luck. Successful prediction does, in fact, always involve an element of luck, for the future depends on the interaction of so many factors that no one can possibly assess them all correctly. Besides, the most critical factor in a situation may be so poorly understood that it upsets the most carefully reasoned analysis of the others. This is the case, for example, with certain aspects of the biophysical environment, on which all life depends. We simply do not have the ability to predict such things as major shifts in climate or the appearance of new and deadly strains of bacteria.

As we attempt to see what lies ahead for human societies, we need to keep three basic guidelines in mind. First, the shorter the time interval involved, the greater the chance of success. Predicting events far in the future greatly increases the probability that some important but unforeseeable factor will intervene and completely upset one's calculations. It also increases the chance that minor errors will be compounded, through repetition, into major ones. The safest predictions, therefore, concern the very near future. But these are also the least interesting and the least valuable. Because of this inverse relationship between accuracy and value, it makes sense to concentrate on predictions geared to an intermediate time span.

Second, the subject on which we can usually speak with the greatest confidence when discussing the future, especially the next twenty-five to fifty years, concerns *the problems societies will face*. The serious, unsolved problems of the world system today will necessarily continue to be problems in the years ahead. The energy crisis, for example, will remain a matter of grave concern until new technologies can be devised to provide substitutes for the world's dwindling supply of petroleum and natural gas. Such current problems provide us with some of our best clues to the future, and to the kinds of changes that are most likely to occur.

Third, and finally, the more thoroughly a prediction is grounded in an analysis of the past and present, the better its chance of success. This means we cannot simply extrapolate current trends into the future. Rather, we must know what conditions gave rise to each trend and what forces sustained it—or caused it to waver or accelerate—so that we can anticipate reversals and other shifts. For example, the birthrate in the United States dropped 40 per cent during a twenty-year period, beginning in the late 1950s; but it would be as irresponsible simply to project that trend to the end of the century as it would be to ignore it.

Applying the first of these guidelines, we will focus our analysis of the future on the next quarter century. This takes us beyond the point where we can simply say, "Things will still be pretty much the way they are today," yet it does not get us into the realm of science fiction or pure speculation. Applying the second guideline, we will devote much of our attention to the most serious problems facing the world system of societies today: the threat of nuclear war, uncontrolled population growth, energy needs, and environmental abuse. Finally, applying our third guideline, we will base our predictions of societal change on our analysis of sociocultural evolution up to the present, giving special attention to changes in technology, ideology, the biophysical environment, population, political and economic institutions, and the social environment.

This approach does not allow us to make flat, unqualified predictions, the kind everyone would prefer. Rather, it results in statements which say that, under conditions X, Y, and Z, outcome A is likelier than B, which in turn is likelier than C. The virtue of discussing the future this way is that it puts the assumptions on which predictions are based out in the open where other people can examine them, and challenge or modify them as new information or insights become available. This should, in time, lead to progressively better predictions about human societies.

Prospects: Technology

Technological advance has been the most important factor in shaping the evolution of the world system in the past, and there is little reason to doubt that it will continue to be of major, perhaps paramount, importance in the coming decades. Many of the most pressing problems of societies today provide tremendous stimulus for technological innovation, and any new technologies that result will almost certainly have great potential for effecting change throughout the world system.

Rate of Change Benjamin Franklin once said that nothing is certain in this world but death and taxes. Were he alive today, he might add technological advance. A prediction of continuing advance at an accelerating rate does not depend simply on an extrapolation of the current trend. The basic factors responsible for the trend—the magnitude of the existing store of information, the great size of societal populations, and the amount of communication between societies—are still operative, and they give every indication of providing even stronger impetus in the near future than they do today. Furthermore, advanced industrial societies are engaging, for the first time in history, in a systematic, large-scale pursuit of new information. Investments in scientific and technological research and development have grown immensely, while computers and other devices that increase our ability to acquire and analyze data add their own boost to the rate of change.

The only thing that seems likely to slow the rate of technological innovation during the next several decades is a nuclear holocaust. War between the United States and the Soviet Union could easily mean the end of industrial societies, and even of human life itself. The rate of innovation could conceivably be slowed by an acute energy shortage, since most of the more complex and productive activities on which modern technological innovation depends require large quantities of relatively cheap energy. But although energy shortages are likely in the years immediately ahead, they will probably not be so acute that resources cannot be found for essential activities, including technological research and development (see below).

Content of Change   The development of new energy sources is an area in which most contemporary societies have an enormous stake. Industrial societies, as we have seen, enjoyed an unprecedented rate of growth during the first three-quarters of this century, due in large measure to the availability of increasing quantities of petroleum and natural gas at very low prices. The loss of that kind of resource poses serious problems for those societies, and it has greatly increased the difficulties faced by societies that are trying to industrialize today. Although huge supplies of petroleum and natural gas are still available, they are no longer cheap. Furthermore, the limits of those supplies are becoming increasingly apparent—which is, of course, the reason it has been possible for the OPEC nations to raise prices so drastically.

As a result, industrial societies are investing enormous resources in a search for new sources of energy that are abundant, reasonably inexpensive, and safe. For a time, it seemed that nuclear fission would be the answer, and many Western European nations, as well as Japan, have already come to rely on it for a major portion of their energy needs. In recent years, however, serious questions have been raised about the safety of nuclear plants (including safety from terrorist attacks and earth tremors) and about the true cost involved in the safe disposal of nuclear wastes and the eventual disposal of the plants themselves. As a result, it now appears that this will not be the preferred solution of the future, as was so widely believed only a few years ago.

The increased use of coal is one possibility in the years ahead. The supply of coal is far larger than the supply of petroleum and natural gas, and conservative estimates indicate there are sufficient reserves to supply the entire world system for 200 to 300 years.[6] Converting power plants and transportation systems from petroleum and natural gas to coal would be expensive, but not prohibitively so. A shift to coal would also increase air pollution, especially in industrial centers, but technological advances can probably handle, or at least alleviate, this problem. But there is another consequence of greater reliance on coal for which no technological solution is in sight: the buildup of carbon dioxide in the earth's atmosphere. This is viewed as an extremely serious problem, because it could alter the earth's climate in a dangerous way (see Prospects: The Biophysical Environment below). The burning of fossil fuels of all kinds has increased the level of carbon dioxide in the atmosphere by 15 per cent in the last half century alone, and the rate of increase would rise even faster with a shift to coal, since it emits 25 per cent more carbon dioxide per unit of energy consumed than petroleum, 50 per cent more than natural gas.[7] This suggests that, while coal may be extremely valuable in the transition from petroleum and natural gas to new energy sources in the next few decades, it will not be a major long-term solution to the energy problem.

A variety of other energy sources are currently being investigated, including solar energy, geothermal energy (i.e., energy derived by tapping the heat of molten rock beneath the earth's surface), liquid hydrogen derived from water, nuclear fusion, wave power, wind power, shale oil, coal gasification, euphorbia lathyrus (an oil-producing plant), manure and garbage (which produce methane gas), gasohol, and the use of just plain trash for heat energy. Although none of these technologies is yet available at competitive costs for mass use, and while some of them will probably never prove practical or economical, it will be surprising if one or more of them, or others yet to be invented, do not contribute significantly to energy needs in the years ahead.

A growing number of experts are especially optimistic about the prospects of solar power and nuclear fusion. As recently as 1976, the cost of electricity generated by solar cells was still an impossible $50 per peak watt. By 1980, this had been reduced to $6, still well above the figure of 70 cents required to make it economically competitive for residential use.[8] Many experts insist, however, that both the cost and efficiency of these cells can be increased considerably, and that solar energy will become economically attractive for residential use by the end of the decade. Nuclear fusion will require more time, but it could conceivably make a significant contribution to energy needs by the end of the first third of the twenty-first century.[9]

A second major technological thrust in the next two decades will be the development of machines that use energy more efficiently. At present, the average *energy end-use efficiency* of the various technologies in use in industrial societies is estimated to be only 10 per cent.[10] While anything approaching 100 per cent efficiency will never be possible, even small improvements would be significant. If the efficiency of energy-using machines in the United States could be raised from the current 10 per cent to just 11 per cent, for example, this would be almost the equivalent of the energy required today to power all American automobiles.[11] And if such improvements were adopted by other societies throughout the world, it would be the equivalent of the discovery of a major new energy source.

A recent study of energy use concluded that one-fourth of the energy currently consumed in manufacturing processes in the United States, or one-tenth of the nation's total energy consumption, could be saved by applying technologies that are already available, and at costs no greater than would be offset by the energy savings. For example, many of the heating processes required for the manufacture of metals, ceramics, glass, and cement are carried out in furnaces at very high temperatures. Exhaust gases from these furnaces, which currently go unused, could be employed to generate electricity. The history of modern technology provides us with ample grounds for optimism about the prospect for increasing the energy efficiency of existing technologies. Figure 14.2 shows the steady improvement that has been achieved in the efficiency of both steam engines and forms of lighting, and the same could be demonstrated for other technologies as well.

Pollution of the environment, like the depletion of some of its resources,

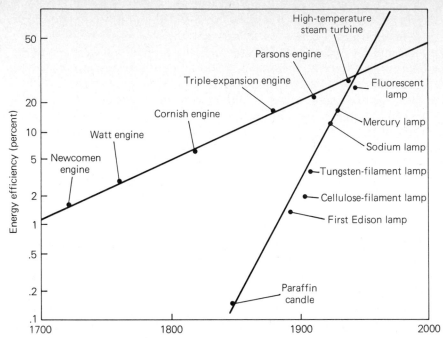

FIGURE 14.2   Increasing energy efficiency in two areas of modern technology: steam engines and illumination. Note that a logistic scale is used to plot energy efficiency in this diagram; if an ordinary linear scale were used, the trend lines would curve upward more sharply.

will also provide a spur for technological innovation during the next twenty-five years. Some of these efforts will be directed toward the development of devices that more effectively control undesirable emissions from industry and other sources into the air, water, and soil. Other efforts will be aimed at developing more economical solutions for recycling the refuse of societies that produce so many goods which so quickly become obsolete. It should be possible during the next few decades to build plants that not only burn waste to generate energy but also recover recyclable resources: iron, aluminum, glass, rubber, paper. Heat, too, is a pollutant, and new technological solutions for its recycling will not only save energy but benefit the environment.

Safer disposal of toxic substances will be another focus of research. Untold millions of containers of radioactive water, nerve gas, and other lethal materials are already buried or stored in unsafe containers. Scientists have recently made a breakthrough with respect to one of these problems: the disposal of plutonium, an extremely hazardous waste product of nuclear reactors that remains radioactive for thousands of years.[12] By slightly altering a molecule that occurs naturally in living organisms, they have devised a chemical means for removing plutonium from the wastewater in which it is stored, rendering it far more compact and thus much easier to dispose of. Similar techniques can probably be devised to aid in the safer handling of other hazardous wastes.

Another area in which there may be important technological innovations in the next quarter century is *population control*. Although the technology to limit population growth is already available, the members of many societies have been slow to accept it, as we have seen. It is clear that ideological changes will have to occur before the severity of this problem lessens appreciably, but the development of cheaper, safer, simpler, and more reliable methods of contraception, sterilization, and abortion would help to speed the process. For example, one new technique currently being tested is the administration of ovulation-controlling hormones by injection. Some women in Third World nations appear to be much more receptive to shots administered by medical personnel than to pills or devices they use at home.

The current effort to find technological solutions for *hunger*, which is so widespread in the Third World, will continue unabated in the years ahead. Although this problem is primarily the result of uncontrolled population growth in these societies, it is aggravated by dietary trends in industrial societies. The increasing consumption of meat by the members of advanced societies has necessitated increased production of grain for livestock feed. Since one calorie of food energy derived from meat requires approximately seven calories of grain to produce,[13] the average American today effectively consumes about 2,000 pounds of grain per year, compared to the 400 pounds consumed by the average person in a society with a predominantly cereal diet.[14]

At the present time, there are a number of new technologies at various stages of development that promise to increase the world's food supply. One of these, fish farming, is already in operation in Japan and promises to provide an increased supply of high-quality protein at relatively low cost.[15] Another promising innovation is soilless cultivation, which involves a recycled mixture of water and nutrients that is sprayed on the roots of plants suspended in frames. Developed in Israel, this technique should greatly increase food production in arid and semiarid areas. A bit further down the road, the new technology of recombinant DNA (see page 422), will probably provide new and improved strains of plants and animals.

As important as advances such as these may be, most agricultural experts believe that increases in the world's food supply during the next quarter century will come primarily from the diffusion of technologies already available. During the period from 1961 to 1974, 40 per cent of the increase in food production in ninety industrializing societies came solely from the increased use of fertilizers, and much of the rest came from the diffusion of other older technologies.[16] This pattern seems likely to continue during the next quarter century, since none of the areas of current agricultural research are likely to produce any major breakthough in this time period.

The most depressing aspect of technological innovation is the amount of money and effort that will be invested in *weapons* research and development in the years ahead. The leaders of some advanced societies argue that this is necessary for their defense; and it is true, of course, that military technology has been the major determinant of societal survival in the past. The situation today, however, is one in which the two nations already most advanced in this technology are in a race to keep ahead of one another, with the result that there is a relentless growth in the potential for mutual extermination—or even extinction of the entire human population.

Unless there is a major breakthrough in arms control negotiations in the years immediately ahead, we can continue to expect that any significant innovation by either the United States or the Soviet Union will serve to enhance the sense of urgency on the other's part to invent something to keep the first from gaining a "decisive advantage." The areas in which these innovative efforts of the major powers will probably be concentrated include the development of planes and missiles capable of eluding detection (e.g., by radar); the development of satellites and other monitors better able to detect planes and missiles; improvements in nuclear weapons that make their limited use more feasible (e.g., the neutron bomb that harms only people but leaves things intact); the development of new biochemical weapons, such as new nerve gases, as well as better equipment for protecting military personnel from them; and the development of anti-missile weapons, such as laser beams and killer satellites. Nor will military technology be advanced only by the major powers. Other societies are also active in devising improved weapons.

Another area in which we can expect technological innovations of major significance is in *the application of the computer and microcircuitry (i.e., the silicon chip) to new industrial tasks.* As we mentioned in Chapter 9, computers have already been devised to guide "smart robots" in spot-welding and other tasks in automobile assembly plants. Like other fundamental innovations, this one will undoubtedly be adapted for use in thousands of similar operations in a variety of industries, although the time frame for the widespread adoption of a technology that replaces so much human labor will probably be affected by such factors as the amount of unemployment in a society and the attitudes of its labor leaders and other elites.

Microcircuitry's potential for a wide variety of industrial applications is equally clear. By substituting microcircuitry for mechanical parts, a manufacturer of cash registers reduced the number of parts in its product from about 5,000 to several hundred. This, in turn, led to a reduction in the number of workers on its assembly line from about 400 to 15 or 20—an even more drastic reduction in labor than achieved by the automobile industry's use of "smart robots."[17]

Yet another fundamental innovation with revolutionary potential for human societies in the next quarter century is the new technology of *recombinant DNA*. In the last few years, geneticists have learned how to remove bits of genetic material from the cells of one kind of organism and implant it in the cells of another species. This emergent technology is particularly fascinating from the perspective of ecological-evolutionary theory, for it marks a new stage in our species' capacity for handling information. Until recently, the only information we could manipulate and recombine was cultural information. Now we can, in effect, use the genetic alphabet in this way (although only to a very limited extent so far) to create combinations of genetic information that do not exist in nature and that can serve as tools for accomplishing human purposes.

So far, most applications of recombinant DNA technology involve the removal of genes that govern the production of rare proteins from the cells of slower-breeding animals, including humans, and transplanting them into bacteria. These organisms grow and divide so rapidly that a single bacterium can produce 100 trillion identical cells in 24 hours, each one containing at least 100 molecules of the desired protein.[18] In this way, large quantities of rare and valuable chemicals can be produced at minimal cost.

The potential applications of recombinant DNA technology appear to be vast, but it is important at this time primarily in medicine. Diabetics, for example, do not produce enough insulin in their own pancreases and must rely on insulin derived from the glands of slaughtered cows and pigs. But it requires approximately 8,000 pounds of these pancreases to produce a single pound of insulin, and there has been grave concern that future supplies will prove inadequate to meet the needs of the growing number of diabetics in the world population. Now, bacteria-produced insulin is being tested on human subjects and will probably be produced commercially in the near future.[19]

Interferon is another chemical produced in the human body, but in minute amounts. Its function is to protect cells from the invasion of viruses, and it appears to have the potential for treating the entire range of viral diseases, as well as some forms of cancer. It also enables the body to withstand larger and more effective doses of other anti-cancer drugs. Currently, interferon is produced by extracting it from human cells grown in the laboratory, with the result that it is enormously expensive (the amount required to treat a single cancer patient costs well over $10,000) and research is severely limited.[20] With recombinant DNA, the supply will become plentiful, the cost will plummet, and large-scale testing of this potential new wonder drug can proceed.

No one can say with any certainty just how the revolutionary new technology of recombinant DNA will develop, or where it will ultimately lead. In 1980, patents were already pending for new forms of bacteria that can metabolize ethylene into ethylene glycol (antifreeze) and ethylene oxide (the basic component of plastics); for two new forms of wheat, one requiring only 10 per cent of the water that wheat normally requires, the other providing twice the protein of ordinary wheat; for "bugs" that convert oil spills into harmless biodegradable materials; and for bacteria that produce an enzyme that eats away the salts in low-grade copper ore, leaving behind almost pure copper.[21] As the final example suggests, this new technology has a potential for saving fuel by replacing traditional industrial operations that consume fuels with processes that depend largely on biochemical processes.

Many other kinds of technological innovations can also be expected during the next quarter century. Substantial resources are being invested in medical research of various kinds, including efforts to cure genetic diseases. Automobile manufacturers promise that electrical vehicles for short-distance travel will be in production by the mid-1980s. Striking advances have recently been made in communications, data processing, and office automation, and further advances in these areas should be only a matter of time. In addition, it is very possible that some unanticipated breakthrough comparable to the computer, the silicon chip, or recombinant DNA will lay the foundation, as all fundamental innovations do, for a host of new applications.

Prospects: Ideology

Ideological change during the next quarter century could play an even greater role in shaping the future of the world system than technological change. Although this may at first seem surprising, it is difficult to imagine any technological innovations likely to occur during that time that could have any greater consequences for human societies than changes in the beliefs, values, and norms that guide them in using the technological information they already have, or will acquire, during that period.

This larger role of ideology is, of course, a consequence of the fact that technological advance has provided societies today with a far wider range of options that they had in the past. Now, thanks to advances made only during the last several decades, the "range of the possible" has come to include, along with greater freedom and happiness, basic and irreversible damage to the global ecosystem, the devastation of dozens of human societies with highly developed cultures in a matter of days, and the destruction of humanity itself. It is obvious that when one kind of cultural information makes such a tremendous range of things possible for our species, the kind of information that guides us in using it becomes a critical factor in the process of sociocultural evolution.

To say that ideology is becoming a more important factor in sociocultural evolution does not mean there will be drastic or dramatic changes in the next several decades. In ideology, as in technology, change does not come about in a society through the abandonment of the total store of information, but by the addition of new elements and the gradual replacement of some older ones. Thus, except in societies that experience serious social upheaval or revolution during the next quarter century, we can expect more ideological continuity than ideological change. Most of the belief systems that are dominant in societies today, together with most of their related norms and values, will probably continue to be dominant. Certainly, Christianity, Islam, Buddhism, capitalism, democracy, democratic socialism, revolutionary socialism, and nationalism will retain the loyalties of tens of millions of people and influence the actions of those in positions of power.

Along with this fundamental continuity, however, we can also expect a high rate of change in ideology, higher for the world as a whole than at any previous time in human history. This prediction is based on trends that are already in progress, and on the fact that ideology has lost much of the aura of "the sacred" that tends to distinguish it from other kinds of cultural information and make it less amenable to change. Ideological innovation and selection are increasingly becoming less a matter of blind chance and more a matter of *purposive creation and conscious choice*.

Although this trend is evident even in theistic ideologies,* it is most pronounced in secular ones. As we have seen, the political and economic ideologies that are dominant in industrial societies today were consciously formulated to enable the members of societies, and especially their elites, to assume greater control over their futures. And although capitalism and Marxism emerged only in the eighteenth and nineteenth centuries, they have already been drastically altered by the elites of these societies to provide guidelines more useful to policymakers of the late twentieth century. The aura of the sacred, however, sometimes leads these elites to refer to their ideologies as though they were still the classic doctrines of Smith and Marx.

This movement from classical ideology to greater pragmatism is also evident in many industrializing societies. In China, for example, much of classic revolutionary socialism has been repudiated and replaced with more pragmatic programs designed to achieve specific goals in the decades immediately ahead. Today, one of the chief goals of China's elite is to achieve economic growth through the introduction of modern technology and by providing material incentives, such as higher pay for skilled work, as opposed to Marxism's prescribed moral incentives; by permitting greater social inequality (diametrically opposed to classical Marxist teachings); and by instigating a rigorous program of population control, which classical Marxist theory rejects. In a number of other countries, including Yugoslavia, Cuba, Mozambique, and Zimbabwe, economic pressures are also forcing revolutionary socialist elites to abandon basic elements of their ideology and to adopt programs especially tailored to help them solve specific problems.[22]

The political and economic ideologies of the Third World will almost certainly become increasingly pragmatic during the next few decades. The societies that are most successful in dealing with the severe problems facing them will be those whose elites create the most useful ideologies, including incentives and sanctions designed to instill new values and norms in their populations so they can achieve new goals.

One ideology that will continue to be important in many of these societies is neo-Marxist dependency theory, which, as we saw in the last chapter, blames the Third World's problems on industrial societies. This ideology has proved extremely useful to the leaders of many industrializing societies. At home, it deflects criticism from their leaders. Abroad, it stimulates guilt feelings and thereby increases the availability of loans and gifts. It has also helped to create a sense of solidarity among industrializing societies, whose interests are so diverse, and so often in conflict, that there is little else to unite

---

*In advanced societies, change and innovation in theistic ideologies are occurring at an unprecedented pace. How much the traditional religions of Buddhism, Islam, and Roman Catholicism change in the next few decades, and how great their influence will be in societal life, will depend in large part on the extent to which societies of the Third World in which these religions are still dominant are able to industrialize. But it is certain that, as modernization proceeds and greater educational opportunities are available to their members, the hold of passive, fatalistic belief systems will be weakened.

them. In view of its success to date, it would be surprising if this ideology did not continue to play an important role in the world system in the next quarter century.

Further evidence of the trend toward more conscious, purposive development of systems of belief is the enormous ideological diversity that has emerged within many societies in recent years, largely in response to culturally activated and intensified needs. In the United States, for example, these newer ideologies include everything from neo-Nazism to various versions of revolutionary socialism, from transcendental meditation to Protestant fundamentalism, from pro- to anti-abortionism, and a host of others. These systems of beliefs, values, and norms reflect the great surplus of resources and the broad range of options that are available to the members of advanced societies today, especially to members of the industrial democracies.

There is little reason to expect that ideological diversity will decline in these societies in the next several decades, particularly in those that place the greatest value on individualism and freedom of expression. But it will undoubtedly continue to be a source of social problems, as it is today. Problems are inevitable when so many diverse, and often contradictory, beliefs are expressed, and norms practiced, within a single society. Perhaps the most serious problem of all, however, is that it is becoming increasingly difficult for the leaders of democratic societies to establish broadly acceptable goals and policies when their members have such different motivations, and when so many of the newer ideologies place great emphasis on the rights and needs of individuals while ignoring their responsibility to the society of which they are part.

In the years ahead, ideological diversity will pose an even greater threat to societies that are trying to industrialize, because they must cope with so many other problems. It will be especially serious in societies that must contend not only with divisive new ideologies (e.g., those of political and economic movements and women's movements) but with major ethnic or religious differences inherited from the past. Unless an authoritarian regime is able to impose a dominant "unifying" ideology on the entire population, as the Communist Party has done in China, for example, the prospects for industrialization by societies so divided internally (e.g., Turkey, India) seem poor indeed.

Prospects: The Biophysical Environment

During the next twenty-five years, there are almost certain to be changes in the biophysical environment that will be of great significance to human societies. Some of these will be the result of unpredictable natural forces (e.g., volcanic activity, violent storms). But we can expect the majority to be the result of feedback effects from human technology.

Such a prediction would not have been possible, of course, until very recently. For millions of years, human societies simply adapted to environmental conditions; they could do nothing to alter them. Then, late in the hunting and gathering era, advances in weapons technology enabled societies to make their first irreversible alteration in the biophysical environment, when hunters apparently destroyed a considerable number of species of large animals.

Following the horticultural revolution, societies gradually began making changes on the earth's surface, clearing forests and planting gardens in their place. Although the balance of nature was affected wherever this happened, the impact was not great, because horticulturists usually had to move every few years and their abandoned gardens reverted to wilderness. The agrarian revolution, however, changed this. Fields became permanent and land no longer reverted to forests, while larger populations used increasing amounts of minerals and other natural resources. Even so, the impact of human societies on the environment was still limited.

Industrial technology, in contrast, has enabled human societies to change the biophysical environment in unprecedented ways. The landscape has been so drastically rearranged that large areas that once teemed with life have been destroyed. Complex ecosystems that required tens of millions of years to evolve have been damaged beyond repair in a matter of years, even months. The earth has been plundered of many of its resources, a number of them seriously depleted. Vast quantities of toxic matter have been poured into the earth's atmosphere and its great bodies of water. And some experts now predict that between 15 and 20 per cent of all the species alive in 1980—some 500,000 to 2 million of them—may be extinct by the year 2000 as a consequence of pollution and loss of habitat.[23]

Environmentalists have been warning for years that our biophysical environment is vulnerable, that it does not have an unlimited capacity for renewing itself. Yet even as we have heard the warnings, our demands on the environment have risen at a fantastic rate. Between 1950 and 1980, an infinitesimal period of time by geological standards, the gross world product rose from approximately $1.5 trillion to $8 trillion. If we consider what this means in terms of our impact on the environment, no future crises will surprise us. For the simple fact is that the biophysical environment can sustain neither an infinite growth of the human population nor the endless demands of an advancing technology.

This is precisely why it is difficult to be optimistic about the state of the environment during the decades immediately ahead. Barring a nuclear holocaust, the human population will increase by a minimum of 1.6 billion during the next twenty years alone,[24] while the technology of the world system will become increasingly industrialized. Merely providing for the survival needs of that many more people would put a formidable strain on an already over-worked environment. But at the same time, the factories of industrializing societies will be demanding greater quantities of raw materials, and their members more material products. Nor is it reasonable to expect that the governments of those hard-pressed societies will rank environmental protection as a high priority.

What we *can* expect during the next quarter century is that there will be new abuses of the environment by societies whose impact in the past has been relatively minor, and that those abuses will serve to aggravate the serious problems that already exist. We can see how this will happen by considering a problem that is currently of great concern to scientists: the buildup of carbon dioxide in the earth's atmosphere. Too great a concentration of this gas would trap so much of the sun's heat that the so-called "greenhouse effect" would result, causing a warming trend on the earth's surface. Many experts now predict an increase in average global temperature of 2 to 6 degrees Fahrenheit by the early to middle decades of the next century.[25] What is more, some believe this increase will have devastating consequences for agriculture in some regions and that it will melt the polar icecaps, causing the flooding of many major cities and coastal regions.

The reason for the growing amount of carbon dioxide in the atmosphere is that more of it is being released than can be handled by natural mechanisms—the leaves of green plants and the oceans and lakes that absorb it. Societies are currently producing 20 billion tons of carbon dioxide every year, and, as they turn to greater use of coal, the problem can only grow worse.[26] What is more, lakes, oceans, and forests are themselves vulnerable and will apparently be able to handle even less carbon dioxide in the future than they do now. Although forests have been leveled in the past, it is now happening at an unprecedented rate. In their search for affordable energy, many Third World societies have been destroying vast forest regions, leaving many of them unfit either for cultivation or for reforestation. It is now expected that 40 per cent of the forests that still remain in the poorer nations will no longer exist in the year 2000, and that virtually all of their physically accessible forests will have been harvested by 2020.[27]

The loss of these forests will have consequences even beyond the greater pollution of the atmosphere that will result, or the loss of species we noted earlier. It will also contribute to the accelerating deterioration and loss of the resources that developing societies so desperately need, both for agriculture and for industrialization. The depletion of forests will aggravate problems of flooding, cause siltation in their streams and rivers, deplete groundwater, and create water shortages. It is estimated that the worldwide use of fresh (i.e., not sea) water will increase at least 200 to 300 per cent by 2000, with the majority of this increase needed for irrigation.[28] Almost half of the societies in the world will need twice what they required in 1975 simply to support population growth, without any allowance for growing use in industry. Meanwhile, an area the size of the state of Maine becomes desert, and unsuitable for agriculture, every year. If this trend continues until 2000, there will be almost 20 per cent more desert than there was in 1975.

Growing world population, increasing industrialization, and energy needs are not the only reasons for predicting growing problems with the environment. Another cause for concern is that so many elements of industrial technology are widely used before their full potential for harm can be determined. Just as societies of the past could not predict that the burning of fossil fuels would lead to a potentially dangerous buildup of carbon dioxide in the atmosphere, so contemporary societies are adopting practices that could produce serious, but still largely unsuspected, problems. No one can predict, for example, what the ecological consequences will be if higher levels of radiation are produced through continued nuclear weapons testing, or by a major accident in one or more of the world's 200 nuclear power plants—to say nothing of the fallout from nuclear warfare. Toxic chemicals are another unknown quantity. Because they are of such diverse kinds, have been so widely used, and are so often poorly stored or disposed of, chemical pollution could do far greater environmental and ecological damage in the near future than it has in the past. Among those substances, for example, are vast quantities of lethal nerve gases that are stored in containers vulnerable to decay, earth tremors, and accidents. In short, a big question mark must be inserted into any predictions about the biophysical environment, since it could even now contain the seeds of a major disaster.

Another thing that makes it difficult to be optimistic about the state of the environment during the next twenty-five years is the response of advanced societies during the last twenty-five. Industrial societies are the ones that can best afford to develop and adopt new technologies to protect the soil, water, and air and help safeguard the finite store of resources on which they depend. Yet their responses have been fairly limited, and often dictated solely by short-term economic considerations.

Industrial societies will almost certainly become more active in this area in the years ahead, however. As the full impact of modern technology on the environment and the dynamics of the process become increasingly clear, so will the true costs of continued neglect of the problem. Thus, we can expect that these societies will begin to weigh more carefully the hidden costs (e.g., illness, genetic damage, loss of farmland) and that they will also recognize that it is far more costly to attempt to rectify environmental damage than to prevent it in the first place.

Another reason industrial societies will probably become more environmentally concerned in the next quarter century is that growing scarcity in a number of natural resources will serve to make them more valuable economically. This should lead to greater conservation efforts—not only of energy and minerals but of wood and water as well. Conservation will involve far greater emphasis on *recycling*—of heat, of water, of wood, of minerals. Recycling often produces multiple benefits. Not only does it reduce the quantity of materials that must be taken from the environment, it often saves energy as well (e.g., it takes only 4 per cent as much energy to produce recycled aluminum as to produce "new" aluminum from bauxite ore) and reduces air and water pollution (e.g., the recycling of steel is estimated to cut air pollution 86 per cent, and water pollution 76 per cent).[29]

Recycling and other techniques for reducing the harmful impact of human societies on the environment will require substantial capital expenditures, and it is therefore unlikely that they will be widely adopted in industrializing societies. Although there have been some encouraging signs (China, for example, recently closed several plants causing pollution, and heavily fined another[30]), pollution and a host of other environmental problems are certain to become far worse in the Third World during the years ahead. With respect to industrial societies, there is no reason to believe that they, even with their new technologies, will *remove* more pollutants, contaminants, and hazardous materials from the biophysical environment during the next quarter century than they put into it. Thus, we can predict that, even without a nuclear disaster, the environment will deteriorate seriously before societies can effect a reversal of that trend.

Prospects: Population

As our discussion of the environment makes plain, population growth during the decades ahead poses an ominous threat to the entire world system of societies. If our numbers continue to swell at the current rate, there will be 6.4 billion people by the year 2000. Even if we base our prediction on the admittedly optimistic assumption that there will be worldwide shifts in public policy that significantly increase access to family planning and lead to a 20 per cent decline in fertility by 2000, there will still be 6.1 billion of us by then. If we look a little further into the future (again being optimistic in our assumptions), we see a global population of nearly 10 billion by 2030, and 28.5 billion by the end of the twenty-first century![31] The year 2030 is within the expected life-span of the majority of today's college students, so it is interesting to note that a National Academy of Science group believes that a population of 10 billion is "close to (if not above) the maximum that an *intensively managed* world might *hope* to support with *some* degree of comfort and *individual choice.*"[32] The italics have been added to emphasize some of the problems and limitations that would be inherent in a world so full of people.

What will it mean to see the population climb from 4.5 to 6.1 billion in less than two decades? For one thing, it will mean that, by the end of the century, there will be almost 100 million more people alive *every year* than there were in the year preceding it. It will mean that the world system will have to find enough new resources to support another China, another India, and another United States, nearly one-third of the world's population today, in less than twenty years' time. It will mean that these people must be fed with an estimated increase in arable land of only 4 per cent, which will necessitate much greater use of fertilizers, insecticides, and water.[33] It means that, in addition to the added strain this will place on the environment, the cost of food worldwide will be double what it was in 1980, *after correcting* for inflation. It may very well mean an enormous increase in the number of hungry and malnourished individuals, because, despite predictions that technological advances will provide 15 per cent more food per capita by 2000, it does not follow that food will be more equally distributed than it is today. The World Bank predicts the number of malnourished people in the Third World (where 92 per cent of the population growth will occur) could rise from the estimated 500 million of the mid-1970s to 1.3 billion in 2000.[34]

But human life is more than mere survival, and uncontrolled population growth means more than hunger. Because of advanced agricultural technology in industrial societies and rural overcrowding and small farms in most developing ones, most of the additional 1.7 to 2 billion people will be forced to live in cities. Overcrowding of urban areas, especially in the Third World but not only there, will thus become far worse during the next 20 years, and so will the attendant problems of poverty, disease, crime, and social unrest. Calcutta's population, for example, is expected to increase from its current 8.1 million to 19.7 million by 2000, and Mexico City's from 10.9 to 31.6 million.[35] And most of this growth will occur in their already enormous slums.

It is absolutely clear that our species' population growth must be halted at some point, and it is equally clear that for every year that passes before this happens, the more serious the consequences will be. Even if every couple in the world from now on had no more than two children, world population would continue to climb for years, simply because the combination of high birthrates and low death rates in the last two decades has given us today a world population with a disproportionate number of young people. In the case of Mexico, for example, more than half of its population was still under twenty years of age in 1980. If we suppose (purely for illustrative purposes) that 15 per cent of the individuals in that age group will have no children and that the rest will produce only two per couple, Mexico's population will still rise from its present 66 million to 99 million before it levels off—assuming there is no increase in life expectancy. If life expectancy also increases, as it almost certainly will, then the predicted ceiling will be higher than 99 million.[36] And for every year that elapses before Mexico adopts such a stringent population policy, which is very unlikely in the near future, the higher that figure will go.

The most critical question for human societies today may well be, When will the nations of the Third World take steps to bring their population growth under control? Although this is impossible to predict, there are reasons to believe that a growing number of societies will take serious steps to that end during the next quarter century. For one thing, there has been a significant shift in the attitudes of the leaders of industrializing societies on the subject of birth control, from nearly universal indifference or condemnation of it only two decades ago to almost universal approval today. In 1960, only two societies, India and Pakistan, gave their official support to family planning.[37] The desire to industrialize subsequently helped to moderate the views of other leaders until, by 1977, sixty-three societies with 92 per cent of the Third World's population had either launched their own family planning programs or lent official support to private groups.[38] What is more, it is becoming increasingly apparent that most of the leaders of underdeveloped societies now recognize the futility of trying to improve living standards for their members when their numbers daily grow greater.

Their changing perception of the population problem has obviously done little to halt growth, however, because Third World leaders have taken so few official actions to implement it. Some are apparently reluctant, for ideological reasons, to intrude on this traditionally private area of their members' lives and place sanctions of any kind on their reproductive activities. Their hope is that increased education and gradually changing beliefs and values of their members will be enough to halt population growth before the consequences are too severe, even though this approach will hinder their efforts to industrialize. Other Third World leaders are undoubtedly more realistic—and pessimistic—in their assessment of the situation, but avoid imposing sanctions on their members because they fear the consequences of doing so. They have not forgotten that, after Indira Gandhi's government mandated forcible sterilization on a limited scale, she was swept from office and population control efforts in India were seriously disrupted.[39] So far, China has been the only major Third World nation to develop a program of population control that shows promise of eventually halting growth (see page 373).

It is difficult to believe that other Third World governments will not also begin to instigate more rigorous programs in the next two decades, but how many do so, and how effective their efforts will be, will depend on a variety of factors whose relative strength is often difficult to assess. They include ideological factors, such as the extent to which the elite is influenced by either Marxism or Catholicism (both of them traditionally opposed to population control), or the extent of the elite's commitment to planning. They also include such factors as the extent of hunger and poverty within the society, the degree of political unrest and the strength of the position of the elite, and, last, but not least, the amount of pressure applied by outside forces. The latter, as we noted earlier, might be in the form of offers of financial aid made conditional on the development of a serious program of population control. Until now, most aid has been given with the sole purpose of keeping people alive—and able to reproduce. It is difficult to believe that well-intentioned donors will not soon perceive that such aid does no lasting good unless it is linked to some program designed to check runaway population growth.

Another demographic trend we can anticipate is increasing migration from the Third World to industrial societies. This trend is already well under way, as evidenced by the growing numbers of Mexicans, Haitians, other Latin Americans, and Vietnamese who enter the United States, often illegally, every year. There is a similar migration of Turks and Yugoslavs into West Germany (Berlin now has the second largest Turkish population of any city in the world, including those in Turkey); of Algerians into France; and of Indians, Pakistanis, and Jamaicans into Britain. It is even possible to envision the day when the indigenous populations of some industrial societies will be minorities in their own territories, a circumstance that would almost certainly have explosive political potential.

Prospects: The Economy

Barring a nuclear holocaust, there will probably be continuing economic growth for the world system as a whole during the next quarter century. The wider application of techniques that are already known could so improve energy efficiency that increased productivity will be ensured, even in the face of rising energy costs. In addition, there could well be further advances in this area, which would have the effect of boosting world production higher still.

It is important to note that this prediction is for a rising GWP (i.e., gross world product), not for a rising standard of living for the world's people. Whether living standards also rise will depend on the number of people who must share the fruits of that increased productivity. The projected rates of population growth combined with rising energy costs could very well mean that there will be no rise in *per capita* GWP, and thus no improvement in living standards for the world as a whole. And even if per capita GWP rises, it will not necessarily follow that per capita GNPs (gross national products) will rise in every society. This is particularly unlikely in a number of African societies, where runaway population growth threatens economic disaster and widespread starvation. Although the situation may be temporarily alleviated by international aid programs, the basic problems in these societies will persist until their governments face up to the true nature of the difficulties confronting them. Unfortunately, there is little sign of this in Africa in the early 1980s.

Because so many societies with the least economic development have the greatest population growth, while societies with the greatest economic development have relatively little population growth, we have to expect that current inequalities in per capita GNPs are going to grow even larger in the years immediately ahead. Although this is regrettable, it is also inevitable, a consequence of immutable differences between industrializing in the late twentieth century and industrializing in the past. Industrial societies never had excess populations that even approached the size of those that are typical of much of the Third World today. Rather, as they became increasingly industrialized (largely because of plentiful, cheap energy sources), there was a massive and continuing migration of their members out of subsistence farming and into industry. This meant that a growing number of people were making a steadily larger contribution to their society's GNP. This is not happening in the Third World today, and it is not *going* to happen this way in the years ahead. The experience of advanced societies cannot be repeated, since it happened in *a different environment*—both social and biophysical—than the one that exists today.

Before the next quarter century comes to a close, we will probably see more industrializing societies headed by governments that accept this fact and that turn from dwelling on what they cannot change to the things they can. If there is responsible new leadership in societies with the lowest GNPs, they will try first of all to put a limit on the number of people their developing economies have to support. How much change there is in this area may well depend on current efforts by the Chinese elite to bring population growth in their society under control. If they are successful, and if it becomes evident that population control significantly improves living standards for the Chinese people, the impact will be felt throughout the Third World.

Increasing productivity in industrial societies during the next few decades could prove of limited benefit to them as well, though not because of population growth. Rather, the new technologies that will be responsible for much of their economic growth (e.g., automation, computerization) will reduce the need for labor at a time when the number of people of working age in these societies will be increasing. The United States, for example, will have 30 million more individuals between the ages of 22 and 65 in the year 2000 than it had in 1980.

Unless steps are taken in this and other non-Marxist industrial societies to spread work among more people, unemployment rates will rise substantially. This could lead to growing political unrest and a variety of other problems, regardless of whether the unemployed in these societies are left to shift for themselves or become part of an hereditary welfare class dependent on a working population that feels ill-used. The rational solution would be to shorten the workweek, which has been done in the past: in 1890, the average workweek in manufacturing in the United States was 60 hours, today it is only 40. To reduce it still further could mean regular employment for millions of people who would otherwise be chronically unemployed. This solution seems more attractive than the Soviet arrangement of employing more full-time workers than are actually needed. In any case, failure to address this economic problem will undoubtedly create widespread social discontent in many industrial societies.

Another economic trend, which seems almost certain to continue, is the increasing division of labor in the world economy. Since 1750, the volume of international trade has increased 1,000-fold, which reflects the extent to which economic specialization at the societal level has grown during that time. This trend, a consequence of technological advances that have drastically reduced the costs of moving goods, has been highly beneficial for the most part. Societies now export what they can produce more cheaply than other societies and import what they find more costly to produce.

This world economic system, which is essentially a *capitalistic* economy, has not been without its disadvantages, especially for societies like Cuba and Chile that specialize in products whose value on the world market tends to fluctuate sharply. Yet even these societies have found this system more rewarding than trying to produce everything they need at home. For a few societies, the oil producers in particular, the system has worked enormously to their advantage, greatly enhancing their position in the world economy. They will probably retain this position until at least the close of the century. At some point, however, they will no longer be able to rely exclusively on their single, extremely valuable product, and their future in the world economy will depend on the extent to which they have used their oil profits to build a modern industrial economy.

During the next quarter century, economic ties among societies will probably grow even stronger than they are today. As this happens, societies will gradually lose more and more of their economic independence. At some point, many of the societies in the world system, perhaps most of them, will find that these economic ties have become vital to them and must not be left vulnerable to disruption by international disputes or war. When this point is reached, it will provide an enormous boost for the creation of a true world polity, whether it is under the guise of the present United Nations or some other body. There is little likelihood of this happening in the next several decades, but it could well occur sometime during the twenty-first century.

Prospects: The Polity

During the next quarter century, the political elites of human societies will play a crucial role in the process of sociocultural evolution. We can predict this, of course, because we know that most human societies will be confronted with a number of critical problems during the period in question, and that their political systems will be obliged to respond to them. Some of the most difficult decisions will be made by leaders of the Third World, as they try to industrialize while simultaneously coping with growing populations, rising costs, and shortages of key resources. The polities of industrial societies will be facing new and unfamiliar problems created by declining rates of economic growth, rising energy costs, chronic inflation, and environmental pollution. Meanwhile, looming over the entire world system will be the gravest problem of them all: the threat of a nuclear holocaust.

In societies of the Third World, especially in those that suffer from widespread poverty and chronic economic crises, democratic polities are unlikely to survive the stresses of the years ahead. Judging from the experience of the last thirty years, we can expect to see a further increase in the number of revolutionary socialist governments, in both industrializing agrarian and industrializing horticultural societies. Governments that proclaim socialist ideals while firmly suppressing political dissent seem better able to survive in developing societies than either democratic or right-wing authoritarian regimes.

Despite the likely increase in the number of Marxist regimes, they will probably not form a cohesive bloc. It is clear by now that Marxism is like sixteenth-century Protestantism in this respect. Just as Protestantism divided along national lines in the sixteenth century, so Marxism has divided in the twentieth, with each national party organization jealous of its autonomy. Although the Soviet Union, by virtue of its military power, maintains a substantial degree of control over most of the parties of Eastern Europe, and maintains more limited control over party organizations in some other societies through financial subsidies, the basic trend has been one of increasing fragmentation. This has happened not only to the party structure but to its ideology, and we can expect this trend to continue. During the next quarter century, the political and economic alliances formed between societies will probably more and more often cut across the old cold war division between Communists and anti-Communists.

It is harder to predict political changes for industrial societies than for those of the Third World, because in politics, as in other areas of societal life, so many things are possible for societies with advanced technologies and enormous economic surpluses. New computer and electronic technologies, for example, have the potential for being used for wholly different political ends. Used one way, they could improve a population's access to information, increase its leisure, and provide it with the means to have greater input in the political process (see page 303), all of which would enhance democratic trends. Or, they could as easily be used for electronic surveillance equipment and police data banks that encroach on individual freedom and thus move a society in a more authoritarian direction.

Which direction non-Marxist industrial societies move in the next few decades will depend to a great extent on the severity of their problems and the effectiveness of their leaders in coping with them. If a democratic regime is unable to resolve the problems that are of the greatest concern to the majority of its citizens, or if the problems confronting the society become unexpectedly severe (e.g., as the result of an environmental disaster or serious civil strife), its members may become more willing to exchange some of their rights for a polity with stronger leaders.

For Marxist industrial societies, the probabilities seem to favor a gradual increase in democracy. This will depend, however, on the ability of these societies to avoid major economic or political crises, and on a relaxation in political tensions between the United States and the Soviet Union. Under these circumstances, a new generation of Soviet leaders may feel greater confidence in themselves and in their system and become less resistant to democratic tendencies within their society. If this occurs in the Soviet Union, it will probably occur in other Eastern European Marxist societies as well.

Prospects: The Social Environment

Discussion of this, the final factor responsible for producing change in sociocultural systems, had to be left until last. For when we ask, "What changes are most likely to occur in the social environments of human societies during the next few decades?" we are really asking, "How will the world system as a whole be different from what it is today?" In summarizing the prospects for the world system of societies, we will draw on all we have said earlier in this chapter, and once again our predictions apply only if widespread nuclear warfare can be avoided.

First, there will probably be somewhat fewer societies in the world system in the year 2000 or 2010 than there are today. This is less likely to be the result of military conquest than of the consolidation of some smaller societies for economic reasons and the elimination of most of the small, primitive societies that still survive. Second, we can expect the world system as a whole to become more advanced technologically during the time in question.

Third, the average size of societies will be larger than it is today. This will be primarily the consequence of demographic trends now in progress in industrializing societies, but it will also reflect the demise of primitive societies. Fourth, the societies of the world system will be even more economically interdependent than they are today. Fifth, the world system will be, for all practical purposes, a smaller system than it is now, since continuing advances in transportation and communication will further shrink the effective size of our planet.

Sixth, the level of intersocietal tensions will almost certainly rise during the decades ahead. Even if relationships among the major powers improve, resource shortages and population pressures will probably lead to deteriorating relations among many other industrial and industrializing societies. For example, in an era of growing water shortages and rising water requirements, 200 of the world's major river basins are shared by at least two different societies.

Seventh, and finally, the years immediately ahead will find increasing numbers of societies capable of initiating, or becoming active participants in, a nuclear war. In summary, when we try to envision the social environment of virtually any human society in the years ahead, we find it consists of a set of societies that are *more advanced technologically, more populous, more interdependent, less stable, more threatened and more threatening*, and *closer* than the societies that constitute its social environment today.

It is abundantly clear that any system with the potential for disaster that is inherent in the developing world system of the 1980s *requires some kind of regulation if chaos and collapse are to be avoided*. Yet there is still no mechanism to effect such regulation, because there is no world government. Anarchy (i.e., the absence of an effective government) has, of course, always prevailed at the level of the world system. But this was unavoidable in the technologically less advanced world of the past. More important, anarchy mattered less in a world system in which the range of the possible, for good and for ill, was so much more limited than it is today.

Nowhere are the new possibilities for ill more evident than in the area of warfare. As we saw in Chapter 3, military superiority has been the single most important determinant of societal survival and extinction during the last 10,000 years and, through its gradual elimination of the least advanced societies, has largely shaped the basic trends we detailed first on page 80. But future warfare could have *very different* consequences for sociocultural evolution than conflicts of the past.

No one can say with any assurance what the effect of a major nuclear war between the superpowers would be; the new weapons are so revolutionary that they render obsolete most of what we have learned of war from conflicts of the past. Experts have estimated, however, that even a very limited exchange of nuclear missiles between the United States and the Soviet Union, an exchange confined entirely to attacks on one another's missile installations, would result in between 3.4 and 21.7 million fatalities in the United States alone.*[40] In addition, many millions more would be crippled, burned, and incapacitated by radiation sickness, and large numbers of these would succumb later.

---

*The variation in this estimate depended on the size of the warheads used, whether they were exploded in the air or on the ground, and how the winds were blowing.

If a Soviet attack were directed at America's industrial facilities and population centers, the number of casualties would be far greater. For example, a 20-megaton attack on Boston could be expected to kill at least 2.2 million people from the initial blast and the subsequent firestorm.[41] People would be burned to death over a radius of twenty miles or more.[42] Not a single building would be left standing within four miles of the blast, and only the strongest reinforced concrete buildings would survive within the next two miles.[43] Bomb shelters would simply become ovens and pressure cookers. If comparable attacks were launched against other major American cities, most of the nation's medical facilities would be destroyed and the economy completely disrupted. Those who managed to survive the holocaust would find themselves in a desperate race to erect a new life-sustaining system before available supplies of food and other essential materials were exhausted. But, in the words of one physicist, "It is likely that the race would be lost."[44]

What would the consequences be if such a war spread beyond the confines of only two or a few industrial societies? Again, no one knows. We cannot even say with any confidence that our species would survive: some scientists believe that cockroaches and other insects, which can sustain far larger doses of radiation than either humans or the birds that keep insects in check, would be the ultimate victors. Another possibility is that the conflagration and the resultant radioactive fallout would spread until only the members of the most isolated societies were left alive. If advanced societies were eliminated and only very primitive ones (e.g., remote bands of Eskimo hunters and gatherers or South American horticulturists) survived, it would mean a complete reversal of all the trends produced by sociocultural evolution up to that point.

The outcome that is considered most likely after a widespread nuclear war, however, is the permanent regression of advanced societies to the horticultural or agrarian level of development, a return, perhaps, to the level of the Middle Ages, with scattered bands of people competing for scarce resources. The path to reindustrialization at some future date would probably be blocked forever, because, in order for industrialization to begin again, there would have to be substantial quantities of raw materials that could be obtained using only preindustrial tools and machines. Yet with every passing year, the quantity of fuels and minerals close to the surface of the earth, or otherwise easily accessible, is further depleted, and societies are forced to obtain their vital resources by methods that presuppose industrialization (e.g., setting up offshore oil rigs, smelting large quantities of low-grade ore). As one geophysicist sees it,

Our present civilization, itself the result of a combination of no longer existent circumstances, is the only foundation on which it seems possible that a future civilization capable of utilizing the vast resources of energy now hidden in rocks and seawater, and unutilized in the sun, can be built. If this foundation is destroyed, in all probability the human race has "had it." Perhaps there is possible a sort of halfway station in which retrogression stops short of a complete extinction of civilization, but even this is not pleasant to contemplate.[45]

Faced as we are with such a threat, the obvious solution would seem to be the creation of a world government that would not interfere with the internal affairs of societies, but which would have the authority, the mechanisms, and the sanctions necessary to monitor the production of military weapons and control their use. Although it would be enormously difficult to develop such a polity, it would be possible if the governments of all or most industrial and industrializing societies want it badly enough.

The most difficult problems in such an endeavor would probably stem from the great differences in economic development and standards of living between industrial and Third World societies. Recently, for example, per capita income in the United States was approximately $8,665, while for the world system as a whole it was only about $1,940.[46] Efforts to include Third World societies in a world polity would almost certainly be met by demands for a significant redistribution of world wealth and income. In exchange for their cooperation (e.g., permission to monitor military installations), developing societies would probably use the opportunity to press for substantial economic concessions. But this could easily kill the enthusiasm for world government by members of industrial societies: if world income were distributed equally among the world's population, per capita income would have to be reduced by nearly 80 per cent in the United States, for example, causing a decline in living standards to *one-fifth* their current level.

Although this is hardly an attractive prospect, some less extreme version of income redistribution might eventually be agreed on. Even if it still seemed harsh to advanced societies, they might consider it preferable to the continuing threat of nuclear warfare and its aftermath. If there is to be a viable compromise in the years ahead, however, governments must begin soon to narrow the economic gap between societies. Incentives must be provided industrializing societies to bring population growth to an end, so that standards of living can be improved, and industrial societies may have to sacrifice some of their own potential economic growth to provide these incentives and to reduce the gap between haves and have-nots. At present, however, the prospects for such action by the governments of industrial societies seem little better than the prospects for an end to population growth in the Third World.

What is more likely in the next few decades is a gradual strengthening of the United Nations, the closest thing to a world polity that now exists. The greatest obstacle to the effectiveness of that organization is probably the system of representation in the General Assembly, which provides an equal vote for the People's Republic of China, with its population of almost 1 billion people, and for the Democratic Republic of Sao Tome and Principe, which has only 80,000. The special powers vested in the Security Council, the veto power in particular, partly compensate for this, but the present organizational structure of the United Nations as a whole does not generate much confidence on the part of larger and more powerful nations.

Substantial changes will probably be needed if the United Nations is to become the basis of a future world polity. Until such a polity evolves, however, societies will continue to downplay the horrors of war, and humanity will continue to suffer from nationalism, which Albert Einstein once called "an infantile disease . . . the measles of mankind."[47]

Prospects: The Higher Goals

Early in this chapter, we reached the conclusion that sociocultural evolution has, more often than not, been accompanied by declining levels of freedom, justice, and happiness for the majority of people, but that the technological advances of the last 150 years have reversed this trend for the members of industrial societies. It would be gratifying to be able to predict that the increasing industrialization of the world system during the next quarter century would serve that same end for the world population as a whole. As our examination of population trends, the environment, war, and other matters has made clear, however, the prospects are dim for any significant improvement in humanity's higher goals in the decades immediately ahead.

In the Third World, we can expect a decline in individual freedoms to accompany an increase in the number of totalitarian regimes. This could have the effect of alleviating some human misery, however, since such regimes would be better able to control birthrates and thus perhaps lower the number of severely malnourished individuals in these societies. But even if this happens, there is not likely to be any great gain in either happiness or justice, since so many people will still be doomed to lives of abject poverty in the crowded slums of Third World cities. What is more, inflation, population growth, and shortages of vital resources will probably retard the pace of industrialization in many societies during the next few decades, delaying—perhaps for many years—the day when advances in productivity can begin to provide appreciable benefits for most of their members.

Although the prospects are brighter for advanced societies, continued improvement in terms of the higher goals is by no means inevitable. The members of some of these societies may well experience some decline in the level of freedom, although in most societies the likeliest prospect is that losses in some areas will be offset by gains in others. There is also the possibility that the level of suffering in some industrial societies will rise appreciably as a consequence of a growth in unemployment or other social problems (e.g., increasing numbers of elderly in nursing homes), or because of nuclear warfare.

Whatever difficulties human societies experience during the next few decades, however, they may suffer far more later in the next century. The levels of freedom, justice, and happiness are almost certain to decline seriously for the world system as a whole during that period—unless humanity begins soon to address its most basic problems. Our potential for shaping a better world is still, at this point, excellent—far greater, in fact, than it has ever been before. But this situation will not last: *the range of attractive options will decline with every year we fail to act.* Thus, the larger the human population becomes before growth is halted, the more likely it is that future political regimes will be harshly authoritarian, and individual freedoms severely limited. The further the biophysical environment deteriorates before that trend is reversed, the less likely it is that the human population as a whole will ever come to enjoy the enormous potential benefits of industrial productivity. And the longer sociocultural evolution continues to be shaped primarily by the blind forces of intersocietal selection, the more likely it is that our future will be shaped by convulsive changes that are forced on us by developments beyond our control.

The latter is, in fact, precisely the outcome predicted for human societies by many who have considered the problem. For example, Robert Heilbroner, long noted for his insightful analyses of the contemporary scene, has written a book entitled *An Inquiry into the Human Prospect* in which he forecasts such events as nuclear wars among societies that are experiencing severe population and environmental crises. He predicts, in effect, a future in which the forces of nature—including the irrational forces of our own genetic nature—produce the answers to the serious problems that *humanity failed to resolve with cultural resources.*

Heilbroner is not unaware of our species' remarkably adaptive capabilities. In fact, he believes that, in principle, we are capable of resolving our problems through cultural mechanisms. What he doubts, however, is our ability to do it *in time to avoid catastrophe.* He feels that it will require too long to alter certain dangerous behavior patterns—patterns that reflect our genetic tendencies toward individualism, self-centeredness, and expansiveness of needs, and which are reflected in our lack of cooperation, lack of concern for future generations and for the members of other societies, and our disinclination to deny ourselves. Heilbroner points out the futility of pinning our hopes on what we believe it is possible for humanity eventually *to become.* Rather, he says, we must consider what people are likely *to be* during the period in question, and he notes that the socialization process tends to produce individuals who are a generation or more behind the times, people who, tomorrow, will be prepared to respond to yesterday's problems.[48]

Even if one does not entirely agree with Heilbroner's pessimistic assessment, it is impossible to deny that certain aspects of our genetic heritage seriously handicap us in our efforts to solve our most urgent problems, or that the socialization process and other cultural mechanisms are often inadequate in helping societies to adapt to the conditions created by a rapidly changing technology. But while there is nothing we can do to alter our genetic mechanisms, at least in the immediate future, *we can alter our cultural mechanisms.*

If our hope is that humanity will be capable of handling the problems that confront it *tomorrow,* we must act *today* toward that end. Our decisions cannot be based on wishful thinking about the future; they must be based on cold, hard facts. We must come to recognize, for example, that the kinds of culturally derived needs and desires that develop in our children, and in theirs, will have to be different, in some respects, from those that motivated our parents or that are central in our own lives. We cannot rely solely on traditional solutions in shaping our actions: if we are to be responsible, we must be innovative; if we are to be compassionate, we must be rational and analytical.

In short, our values, ideals, and goals must become less and less unthinking responses to technological advance and more and more *rational mechanisms for controlling technological innovation and its applications*.

Of all the species on this planet, ours is the only one that is not doomed to have its evolutionary course shaped entirely by forces beyond its control. Thanks to culture, we can not only comprehend the evolutionary process, *we can chart for ourselves an evolutionary course within the limits set by our genetic heritage on the one hand and the natural constraints of the biophysical environment on the other*—a course that can provide a high degree of freedom, justice, and happiness.

But we also have the option to ignore this possibility until it is too late.

Glossary

Adaptation   The process of adjusting to, or changing, environmental conditions; hence, broadly, problem solving.

Agrarian era   The period in history when there were no societies technologically more advanced than agrarian societies (about 3000 B.C. to 1800 A.D.).

Agrarian society   A society that depends primarily on agriculture for the material necessities of life. *Advanced* agrarian societies have iron tools and weapons; *simple* agrarian societies do not.

Agriculture   The cultivation of fields using the plow.

Archaeology   The study of cultures of the past through their physical remains.

Arithmetic mean   The value that results when the sum of a set of items is divided by the number of items; a measure of central tendency.

Artisan   A craftsman. The term is usually applied to craftsmen in agrarian or maritime societies.

Ascribed role   A role which is assigned an individual (e.g., age, sex, race, kinship position) and which the individual normally finds difficult or impossible to discard or alter.

Association   A formally organized secondary group that performs some relatively specialized function or set of functions.

Autocracy   Rule by one person (compare with *Democracy, Oligarchy,* and *Theocracy*).

Autogenous   Self-generated; caused by internal forces.

Autonomous   Free from outside political control.

Band   A nomadic community at the hunting and gathering level.

Behavior   Any response by an organism to internal or external stimuli.

Biological evolution   The process of gradual genetic change and development through which every species of plant or animal has developed out of a preexisting species.

Biophysical environment   The biological and physical components of the environment.

Biotic   Pertaining to life and living things.

Bureaucracy   (1) The administrative component of a government or other association; (2) a system of administration characterized by a highly formalized division of labor, a hierarchical system of authority, and action oriented to a complex and formalized system of rules.

Capital goods   The goods in a society that are

devoted to the production of more goods (e.g., factories, machinery, tools, etc.).

Capital-intensive industry An industry in which the ratio of capital costs to other costs is high.

Capitalism An economic system in which the means of production are privately owned and the basic problems of production and distribution are settled by means of the market system, with minimal governmental regulation or control (see *Market economy*).

Civilization An advanced sociocultural system. The term is usually reserved for the cultures of societies with writing and urban communities.

Clan A kin group whose members claim descent from a common ancestor.

Class (1) An aggregation or group of people whose *overall* status is similar; (2) an aggregation or group of people who are alike with respect to some resource that affects their *access* to power, privilege, or prestige.

Clique A primary group organized around ties of friendship.

Command economy An economy in which the basic questions of production and distribution are decided by political authorities (contrast with *Market economy*).

Communication The exchange of information by means of signals or symbols.

Community A secondary group that is informally organized and whose members are united by a common place of residence or by a common subculture (see *Geographical community* and *Cultural community*).

Continuity The persistence of cultural elements in a society.

Cooperation Interaction by two or more individuals for mutual benefit.

Correlation coefficient A measure of the degree of association between two variables. Correlation coefficients range from 0.0, when there is absolutely no relationship between the variables, to ±1.0, when there is a perfect relationship (i.e., one value is a perfect function of the other).

Cultural community A community whose members are united by ties of a common cultural tradition (e.g., a racial or ethnic group).

Culture Symbol systems and the information they convey.

Customs Informal norms that define desirable or acceptable behavior in a society or a subgroup within society.

Democracy A type of political system in which sovereignty is vested in the people (contrast with *Autocracy*, *Oligarchy*, and *Theocracy*).

Demography The study of populations, their size, composition, and change.

Determinism The belief that a specific set of identifiable factors is sufficient to explain completely a given phenomenon.

Development The consequences of an increase in useful information for the various components of a system.

Diffusion Transmission of cultural elements from one society to another.

Discovery An innovation that results from a society's acquisition of new cultural information by means other than diffusion.

DNA Deoxyribonucleic acid; a chemical molecule that embodies genetic information.

Ecological-evolutionary theory Theory concerning (1) the relationships within and among human societies, (2) the relationships between societies and their biophysical environments, and (3) the processes of sociocultural change and development.

Ecology The science of the interrelationships of living things to each other and to their environments.

Economic surplus Production that exceeds what is needed to keep the producers of essential goods and services alive and productive.

Energy The capacity for performing work.

Environment Everything external to an entity (organism, population, society, etc.) that affects it, or is affected by it, in any way.

Era A period of time during which a particular type of society is the most advanced in existence (e.g., the agrarian era).

Ethnography The description of contemporary sociocultural systems.

Evolution In general, a process of long-term, cumulative, and pervasive change in which later stages emerge out of earlier stages (see *Biological evolution* and *Sociocultural evolution*).

Extended family A group of near relatives (e.g., cousins, aunts, uncles). More inclusive than the nuclear family, less inclusive than the kin group or clan.

Extinction The disappearance of elements from a sociocultural system; the elimination of human societies themselves.

Family A primary group organized around ties of kinship; a major institutional system in every society (see also *Nuclear family* and *Extended family*).

Feedback A special type of causal relationship in which part of the effect of an initial cause or event reverts back to its source, modifying or reinforcing it (i.e., A influences B, thereby causing B to exert an influence back on A).

Fishing society A society dependent primarily on fishing, or fishing and gathering, to obtain the material necessities of life.

Fixed costs Costs of production that remain more or less constant regardless of the number of units produced (contrast with *Variable costs*).

Freedom The availability of alternative courses of action.

Frontier society An agrarian society that is in the process of expanding into territories that are uninhabited, or inhabited by preagrarian societies.

Function (1) A characteristic activity of a person, a thing, or an institution; (2) a consequence of, or purpose served by, that activity; (3) a relationship in which changes in the magnitude of one variable are associated in a definite and determined way with changes in the magnitude of another variable.

Functional requisites Conditions that must be met if a society is to survive.

Fundamental innovation An invention or discovery that either (1) opens the way for many other innovations or (2) alters the conditions of human life so that many other changes become either possible or necessary.

Gathering Collecting wild fruits and vegetables.

Gene The basic unit of heredity; conveyer of genetic information.

Gene pool The genes of all the members of a population considered collectively.

Genetic constants Genetic attributes that are the same in every population of a species.

Genetic variables Genetic attributes that vary among the populations of a species.

Geographical community A community whose members are united primarily by ties of spatial proximity.

Governing class A largely hereditary class from which the political leaders of a society are recruited.

Gross domestic product Gross national product minus net income from other nations.

Gross national product The monetary value of the goods and services produced by a nation during a specific period (usually a year).

Group An aggregation whose members (1) act together to satisfy common, or complementary, needs; (2) have common norms; and (3) have a sense of common identity. The term is applicable to a society, an intersocietal unit, or an intrasocietal unit.

Guild A mutual aid association of merchants and artisans in the same trade (found in agrarian and maritime societies).

Headman The leader of a local community, usually in a preliterate society; one who leads rather than rules.

Herding society A society dependent primarily on herding to obtain the material necessities of life. *Advanced* herding societies are differentiated from

simple by the use of horses or camels for transportation.

Hominid A member of the genus *Homo*, which includes our own species as well as an undetermined number of humanlike species that preceded us and are now extinct.

Homo sapiens sapiens Genetically modern humans.

Horticultural era The period in history when there were no societies technologically more advanced than horticultural societies (about 7000 to 3000 B.C.).

Horticultural society A society that depends primarily on horticulture to obtain the material necessities of life. *Advanced* horticultural societies are differentiated from *simple* by the manufacture of metal tools and weapons.

Horticulture The cultivation of small gardens, in which a hoe or digging stick is the chief tool. Horticulture is differentiated from agriculture by the absence of the plow.

Human evolution The total evolutionary experience of our species, both biological and cultural.

Hunting and gathering era The period in history when there were no societies more advanced than hunting and gathering (to about 7000 B.C.).

Hunting and gathering society A society that depends primarily on hunting and gathering to obtain the material necessities of life.

Hybrid society A society that relies about equally on two or more of the basic modes of subsistence.

Hypothesis A proposition tentatively assumed to be valid until proven or disproven by testing.

Ideology Cultural information used to interpret human experience and order societal life. An ideology consists of a system of beliefs and related norms and values.

Industrial era The period in history when industrial societies have been dominant (from about 1800 A.D. to the present).

Industrialization Increasing reliance on inanimate sources of energy and the machines powered by them (compare with *Modernization*).

Industrial Revolution The revolution in technology that began in England in the eighteenth century, has since spread to most of the world, and is still continuing.

Industrial society A society that derives most of its wealth and income from productive activities dependent on machines powered by inanimate energy sources (i.e., coal, petroleum, natural gas, hydroelectric power, nuclear power). Currently, a society with a per capita GNP of $2,500 or more per year.

Information Experience as impressed on a memory system.

Innovation The process of introducing new cultural elements into a society; the new cultural element itself (see *Variations*).

Institution A system of social relationships and cultural elements that develops in a society in response to some set of basic and persistent needs.

Intelligentsia Well-educated persons; the upper part of the nonmanual class in East European societies (occasionally used to refer to the entire nonmanual class).

Intersocietal selection The process of selection *among* societies, whereby some survive while others become extinct; the basis of the primary trends of history.

Intrasocietal selection The process of selection *within* a society, whereby some of its cultural elements survive while others are eliminated.

Invention An innovation that results from a useful new combination of information already possessed by a society.

Labor-intensive industry An industry in which the ratio of labor costs to other costs is high.

Language A system of symbols.

Laws Norms sanctioned by the state or government.

Learning The process by which an organism acquires, through experience, information with behavior-modifying potential.

Legitimate That which is morally or legally justified by the norms or laws of a group.

Legitimize To make legitimate; to provide an ideological or legal justification for a practice that might otherwise be regarded as objectionable.

Macrosociology The branch of sociology that studies large social systems, especially total human societies.

Maritime society A society in which overseas commercial activity is the primary source of wealth and income.

Market economy An economy in which the basic problems of production and distribution are settled by the forces of supply and demand (see *Capitalism*, and contrast with *Command economy*).

Marxist society A society whose political elite is committed to Marxist ideology; a revolutionary socialist society.

Mass media Communications media developed in industrial and industrializing societies to reach the masses (especially TV, radio, newspapers, magazines, and movies).

Mean, arithmetic See *Arithmetic mean*.

Median The middle number in a series of numbers arranged in order from highest to lowest; a measure of central tendency.

Microsociology The branch of sociology that studies individuals and small social units, such as families and associations.

Mobility, vertical See *Vertical mobility*.

Modernization All the long-term changes associated with industrialization (compare with *Industrialization*).

Monopoly A commodity market with only a single seller.

Nation A society in which the administrative, legislative, and judicial functions of government are wholly or largely in the hands of full-time officials.

Nationalism An ideology that emphasizes the importance of the nation-state.

Neophilia The love of novelty or change for its own sake.

Nomad A member of a group that has no permanent settlement and moves about periodically (usually in a well-defined territory) to obtain food and other necessities.

Normative Of, or pertaining to, norms; having a moral and/or legal character.

Norms Definitions of acceptable and unacceptable behaviors for the members of a society in their various roles; norms may be formal (e.g., laws) or informal (e.g., customs).

Nuclear family A man, his wife or wives, and their unmarried children living with them.

Oligarchy The rule of the few (contrast with *Autocracy*, *Democracy*, and *Theocracy*).

Oligopoly A commodity market dominated by a few sellers.

Organism A living entity.

Peasant An agricultural worker in an agrarian society.

Per capita income National income divided by population. (This measure is somewhat misleading as a measure of the standard of living of the average person, since a small number of people with very large incomes can pull the average far above the median.)

Polity The political system of a group, especially of a society.

Population (1) Organisms of the same species that tend to interbreed because of their geographical proximity; (2) the members of a society, or a subgroup within a society, considered collectively.

Priest A religious functionary believed to have supernatural powers bestowed on him by an organized religious group; one who mediates between God, or a god, and humans (contrast with *Shaman*).

Primary group A small group in which face-to-face relations of at least a fairly intimate and

446

personal nature are maintained (see *Family* and *Clique*).

Primary industries Industries that produce or extract raw materials (especially farming and mining).

Primates The order of mammals that includes the prosimians (e.g., tarsiers and lemurs) and the anthropoids (e.g., monkeys, great apes, and humans).

Primitive Having limited sociocultural development.

Process A series of related events with an identifiable outcome.

Proletariat Marx's term for industrial workers in modern societies.

Race A breeding population in which certain traits occur with a frequency that is appreciably different from other breeding populations.

Religion The basic ideological beliefs of a group of people and the practices associated with those beliefs. The term can refer to nontheistic ideologies, such as communism and humanism, but is more often applied to ideologies that involve supernatural explanations.

Republic A nonmonarchical government.

Revolution Change that is unusually sudden, rapid, or far-reaching.

Role A position that can be filled by an individual and that has distinctive norms attached to it. The term may also be used to refer to the part a group, institution, or other social unit plays in the life of a society.

Sanction (1) A reward or punishment; (2) to reward or punish.

Secondary group Any group that is larger and more impersonal than a primary group.

Secondary industries Industries that process raw materials and turn out finished products.

Selection The process that determines the fate of the variations in a gene pool, in a sociocultural system, or in the world system of societies (see *Intersocietal selection, Intrasocietal selection,* and *Variations*).

Serf A peasant farmer who is bound to the land and subject to the owner of the land.

Shaman A person believed to enjoy special powers because of a distinctive relationship he or she has established with the spirit world; a medicine man. Not to be equated with *Priest*.

Signal An information conveyer whose form and related meaning are both determined genetically (contrast *Symbol*).

Social Having to do with the interactions among the members of societies.

Social controls Mechanisms that order societal life by controlling and regulating people's actions and relationships; norms and their related sanctions.

Social environment The other societies with which a society has contact.

Social institution See *Institution*.

Socialism An economic system in which there is little or no private ownership of the means of production (see *Capitalism*).

Socialist society A society in which there is little or no private ownership of the means of production (not applied to a society where a socialist party is in power if this condition is not met).

Socialization The process through which individuals become functional members of their society.

Social movement A loose-knit group that seeks to change the social order.

Social organization See *Social structure*.

Social structure The network of relationships among the members of a society or group.

Societal Of or pertaining to a society or societies.

Society, human An autonomous group of people engaged in a broad range of cooperative activities.

Sociocultural Contraction of *social* and *cultural*.

Sociocultural evolution The process of change and development in human societies that results from cumulative changes in their stores of cultural information.

Sociocultural system A system composed of a human population, its social structure, culture, and material products.

Sociology The branch of science that specializes in the study of human societies.

Stasis The condition of a society that neither develops nor regresses.

Status The relative rank of a person, role, or group, according to culturally defined standards.

Stratification Class or status differentiation within a population; hence, inequality.

Structural-functional theory Theory concerning the internal structures of societies, and the functions of their various parts.

Structure The arrangement of the parts of an entity.

Subculture The distinctive culture of a group within a society.

Subsistence The material necessities of life; also, the process by which they are obtained.

Subsistence technology The technology that is used by the members of a society to obtain the basic necessities of life.

Surplus See *Economic surplus*.

Symbol An information conveyer whose form is arbitrary and whose meaning is determined by those who use it (contrast with *Signal*).

System   An entity made up of interrelated parts.

Systemic   Having the basic qualities of a system.

Technology   Cultural information about the utilization of the material resources of the environment to satisfy human needs and desires.

Tertiary industries   Industries that perform services (e.g., retail trade, government).

Theocracy   A society ruled by a priesthood in the name of some deity or by a ruler believed to be divine.

Theory   An explanation of some aspect of the natural world; a set of assumptions and principles that has developed through testing in a field of inquiry and that serves as a framework for further inquiry.

Third World   The industrializing societies of the contemporary world.

Tribe   A preliterate group whose members speak a common language or dialect, possess a common culture that distinguishes them from other peoples, and know themselves, or are known, by a distinctive name.

Unilinear theory of evolution   A theory which assumes that all societies follow exactly the same path of evolutionary development.

Urban community   A community whose inhabitants are wholly or largely freed from the necessity of producing their own food, fibers, and other raw materials.

Values   Generalized moral beliefs to which the members of a group subscribe.

Variable   Any property that is capable of varying in degree.

Variable costs   Costs of production that tend to vary in proportion to the number of units produced (contrast with *Fixed costs*).

Variations   Products of the process of innovation (see *Innovation* and *Selection*).

Vertical mobility   Change of status, either upward or downward.

Working class   Members of modern industrial societies who belong to families headed by manual workers.

World system   The totality of human societies and their interrelationships.

Notes

Chapter 1

1. Carl Sagan, *Broca's Brain: Reflections on the Romance of Science* (New York: Random House, 1979), p. 13.
2. William R. Catton, Jr. *From Animistic to Naturalistic Sociology* (New York: McGraw-Hill, 1966).
3. Kingsley Davis, *Human Society* (New York: Macmillan, 1949), p. 27. See also Alfred E. Emerson, "Human Cultural Evolution and Its Relation to Organic Evolution of Insect Societies," in Herbert Barringer et al. (eds.), *Social Change in Developing Areas: A Reinterpretation of Evolutionary Theory* (Cambridge, Mass.: Schenkman, 1965), pp. 50–51.
4. Edward O. Wilson, *Sociobiology: The New Synthesis* (Cambridge, Mass.: Belknap, 1975), part III.
5. Ibid., p. 595.
6. George Gaylord Simpson, *The Meaning of Evolution* (New Haven, Conn.: Yale, 1951), pp. 283–284. Quoted by permission of Yale University Press.
7. This paragraph is based on Paul B. Weisz, *The Science of Biology*, 3d ed. (New York: McGraw-Hill, 1967), chap. 2.
8. Ibid., p. 19.
9. Simpson, p. 281.
10. This is a simplified summary of the basic principles of biological evolution as they are presently understood. It is based on Sir Julian Huxley, *Evolution: The Modern Synthesis* (London: G. Allen, 1942); George Gaylord Simpson, *The Major Features of Evolution* (New York: Columbia, 1953); Ernst Mayr, *Animal Species and Evolution* (Cambridge, Mass.: Harvard, 1963); Sol Tax (ed.), *Evolution after*

Darwin: The University of Chicago Centennial (Chicago: University of Chicago Press, 1960), vols. I and III; Weisz, op. cit.; G. G. Simpson and Anne Roe (eds.), *Behavior and Evolution* (New Haven: Yale, 1958); John Maynard Smith, *The Theory of Evolution* (Baltimore: Penguin, 1958); and Helena Curtis, *Biology,* 2d ed. (New York: Worth, 1976).

11. Curtis, pp. 796–798.
12. Ibid., p. 914.
13. J. Z. Young, *An Introduction to the Study of Man* (New York: Oxford University Press, 1971), pp. 470–472, and Curtis, pp. 914–916.
14. Curtis, p. 914.
15. This definition is a slightly modified version of that provided by W. H. Thorpe, *Learning and Instinct in Animals,* 2d ed. (Cambridge, Mass.: Harvard, 1963), p. 55.
16. Wilson, pp. 151–152.
17. Sherwood L. Washburn and David A. Hamburg, "The Implications of Primate Research," in Irven DeVore (ed.), *Primate Behavior: Field Studies of Monkeys and Apes* (New York: Holt, 1965), p. 613.
18. Sherwood Washburn, "The Evolution of Man," *Scientific American,* 239 (September 1978), p. 204; Dorothy Miller, "Evolution of the Primate Chromosomes," *Science,* 198 (Dec. 16, 1977), pp. 1116–1124. See also Mary-Claire King and A. C. Wilson, "Evolution at Two Levels in Humans and Chimpanzees," *Science,* 188 (Apr. 11, 1975), pp. 107–116.
19. Carl Sagan, *The Dragons of Eden: Speculations on the Evolution of Human Intelligence* (New York: Ballantine Books Inc., 1977), pp. 181–182, and John E. Pfeiffer, *The Emergence of Man,* 3d ed. (New York: Harper & Row, 1978), pp. 390–392.
20. Leslie White, "The Symbol: The Origin and Basis of Human Behavior," *Philosophy of Science,* 7 (1940), pp. 451–463.
21. Milton Singer, "Culture," in *International Encyclopedia of the Social Sciences* (New York: Macmillan and Free Press, 1968), vol. 3, p. 540.
22. This paragraph is based on Wilson, pp. 176–185.
23. See, for example, Francine Patterson, "Conversations with a Gorilla," *National Geographic,* 154 (October 1978), pp. 438–466, or Pfeiffer, pp. 373–381. For a more skeptical view of the ability of apes to use symbols, see Roger Brown, "Why Are Signal Languages Easier to Learn than Spoken Languages? Part Two," *Bulletin of the American Academy of Arts and Sciences,* 32 (December 1978), pp. 38–39.
24. Peter Marler, "Birdsong and Speech Development: Could There Be Parallels?" *American Scientist,* 58 November/December 1970, p. 671.
25. Pfeiffer, p. 381, citing Jane van Lawick-Goodall as authority.
26. J. S. Weiner, *The National History of Man* (Garden City, N.Y.: Doubleday Anchor Books, 1973), p. 83.
27. Leslie White, *The Science of Culture* (New York: Grove, 1949), pp. 37–39.
28. Robert Lord, *Comparative Linguistics,* 2d ed. (London: English Universities Press, Ltd., 1974), pp. 288–289.
29. John Locke, *An Essay Concerning Human Understanding* (New York: Dover, 1959, first published 1690).
30. Reinhold Niebuhr, *The Nature and Destiny of Man* (New York: Scribner, 1943), vol. I; Robert Heilbroner, *An Inquiry into the Human Prospect* (New York: Norton, 1974), chap. 4; and Jan Szczepanski, *Polish Society* (New York: Random House, 1970), p. 100 and chap. 9.
31. Theodosius Dobzhansky, *Mankind Evolving* (New York: Bantam, 1962), pp. 224–225, and Pfeiffer, chap. 18.
32. Pfeiffer, p. 354ff.
33. Rene A. Spitz, "Hospitalism," *The Psychoanalytic Study of the Child,* 1 (1945), pp. 53–72, and "Hospitalism: A Follow-up Report," ibid., 2 (1946), pp. 113–117.

34. Pfeiffer, pp. 429–430, and Sagan, *The Dragons of Eden*, pp. 47–48.

35. Stephen Jay Gould, "Human Babies as Embryos," *Natural History*, 85 (February 1976), p. 22ff.

36. Weisz, p. 819; Curtis, pp. 717–720.

37. Noam Chomsky, *Syntactic Structures* (The Hague: Mouton, 1957), *Aspects of the Theory of Syntax* (Cambridge, Mass.: MIT Press, 1965), and *Cartesian Linguistics* (New York: Harper & Row, 1966).

38. Pfeiffer, chap. 19.

39. Weisz, p. 819.

40. Dobzhansky, p. 354.

41. Thorstein Veblen provided the classic statement of this principle in his volume, *The Theory of the Leisure Class* (New York: Macmillan, 1899).

42. A. H. Maslow, *Motivation and Personality* (New York: Harper & Row, 1954), especially chap. 5. See also Wilson, p. 143.

43. William Graham Sumner, *Folkways* (New York: Mentor, 1960, first published 1906), p. 32.

44. For a good, brief summary of these developments, see Marvin Harris, *The Rise of Anthropological Theory* (New York: Cromwell, 1968), chap. 2.

45. For a good review of the early history of social research, see Bernard Lecuyer and Anthony R. Oberschall, "Sociology: The Early History of Social Research," in *International Encyclopedia of the Social Sciences,* vol. 15, pp. 36–53.

46. See, for example, Wlodzimierz Wesolowski, *Classes, Strata and Power* (London: Routledge, 1979); Eugen Pusić (ed.)., *Participation and Self-Management* (Zagreb: First International Sociological Conference on Participation and Self-Management, 1972); Murray Yanowitch and Wesley Fisher (eds.), *Social Stratification and Mobility in the U.S.S.R.* (White Plains, N.Y.: International Arts and Sciences Press, 1973); or Szczepański, op. cit.

47. Catton, chap. 3.

48. For pioneering statements of the newer ecological-evolutionary approach, see O. D. Duncan, "Social Organization and the Ecosystem," in R. E. L. Faris (ed.), *Handbook of Modern Sociology* (Chicago: Rand McNally, 1964), pp. 39–45; and Walter Goldschmidt, *Man's Way: A Preface to the Understanding of Human Society* (New York: Holt, 1959). See also Marvin Harris, *Cultural Materialism: The Struggle for a Science of Culture* (New York: Random House, 1979) for a more recent statement.

Chapter 2

1. Anatol Rapoport, "Systems Analysis: General Systems Theory," *International Encyclopedia of the Social Sciences* (New York: MacMillan and Free Press, 1968), vol. 15, p. 454.

2. From "The Mistress of Vision."

3. See, for example, David F. Aberle et al., "The Functional Prerequisites of a Society," *Ethics,* 60 (1950), pp. 100–111; or Talcott Parsons, *The Social System* (Glencoe, Ill.: Free Press, 1951), pp. 26–36.

4. Edward O. Wilson, *Sociobiology: The New Synthesis* (Cambridge, Mass.: Belknap, 1975), p. 510.

5. John E. Pfeiffer, *The Emergence of Man,* 2d ed. (New York: Harper & Row, 1973), pp. 296 and 330.

6. Carl Sagan, *The Dragons of Eden* (New York: Ballantine Books, 1977), p. 63, or Helena Curtis, *Biology,* 2d ed. (New York: Worth, 1975), chap. 39.

7. J. S. Weiner, *The Natural History of Man* (Garden City, N.Y.: Doubleday Anchor, 1973), p. 170.

8. Marvin Harris, *Culture, People, Nature,* 2d ed. (New York: Crowell, 1975), p. 98.

9. For brief but fascinating discussions of the relation between human physique and climate, see Theodosius Dobzhansky, *Mankind Evolving* (New York: Bantam, 1962), p. 287ff.; Weiner, p. 160ff.; and E. Adamson Hoebel, *Anthropology: The Study of Man,* 3d ed. (New York: McGraw-Hill, 1966), p. 214ff.

10. Weiner, p. 153.

11. Ibid., p. 167.

12. Dobzhansky, p. 158ff.

13. Harris, p. 107.

14. Paul R. Ehrlich and Richard W. Holm, *The Process of Evolution* (New York: McGraw-Hill, 1963), fig. 11.1, p. 253.

15. Fred Blumenthal, "The Man in the Middle of the Peace Talks," *Washington Post,* July 14, 1968.

16. Curtis, p. 159.

17. Hoebel, p. 35.

18. Karl G. Heider, *The Dugum Dani: A Papuan Culture in the Highlands of West New Guinea* (New York: Wenner-Gren Foundation, 1970), pp. 32–33.

19. Hoebel, p. 35.

20. Robert Lord, *Comparative Linguistics,* 2d ed. (London: English Universities Press, 1974), p. 316. For other interesting examples of changes in the meanings of words, see Charlton Laird, *The Miracle of Language* (Greenwich, Conn.: Premier Books, 1953), p. 54ff.

21. Edward Sapir, *Selected Writings in Language, Culture, and Personality,* David Mandelbaum (ed.), (Berkeley: University of California Press, 1949), p. 162.

22. See, for example, Dell Hymes, "Linguistics: The Field," *International Encyclopedia of the Social Sciences,* vol. 9., p. 22.

23. V. Gordon Childe, *Man Makes Himself* (New York: Mentor, 1951), p. 144ff.

24. This view of ideology borrows from Talcott Parsons's thesis that the prime function of religion is making sense out of the totality of human experience. If the term "religion" is defined to include nontheistic faiths (as we do in this volume), religion and ideology become almost indistinguishable. See Parsons, *The Structure of Social Action* (New York: Free Press, 1968), vol. II, pp. 566–567, 667–668, and 717.

25. See, for example, Robert S. Merrill, "Technology: The Study of Technology," *International Encyclopedia of the Social Sciences,* vol. 15, p. 576.

26. Ralph Turner, "Role: Sociological Analysis," ibid., vol. 13, pp. 552–557.

27. For a more extended discussion of classes, see Gerhard Lenski, *Power and Privilege: A Theory of Social Stratification* (New York: McGraw-Hill, 1966), pp. 73–82.

28. See Reinhard Bendix and Seymour M. Lipset (eds.), *Class, Status, and Power* (New York: Free Press, 1966), pp. 47–72.

29. Lenski, op. cit.

30. René Dubos, *So Human an Animal* (New York: Scribner, 1968), p. 28.

31. Ibid., p. 242. Quoted by permission.

32. Ibid., p. 28. Quoted by permission.

Chapter 3

1. This paragraph is based on Theodosius Dobzhansky, Francisco Ayala, G. Ledyard Stebbins, and James W. Valentine, *Evolution* (San Francisco: Freeman, 1977), chaps. 1 and 2; Helena Curtis, *Biology,* 2d ed. (New York: Worth, 1976), sec. 2; and Theodosius Dobzhansky, *Mankind Evolving* (New York: Bantam, 1962), chap. 2.

2. Patrick Malone, "Major Breakthroughs in Genetic Research," *The Washington Post,* Aug. 27, 1973, D3.

3. Dobzhansky, p. 175.

4. See, for example, Loren Eiseley, *Darwin's Century: Evolution and the Men Who Discovered It* (Garden City, N.Y.: Doubleday Anchor: 1961).

5. Leon Trotsky, *The History of the Russian Revolution* (Ann Arbor: University of Michigan Press, 1957, first published in Russian in 1933). For a more recent review of this idea, see W. F. Wertheim, *Evolution and Revolution* (London: Penguin, 1974), chap. 3.

6. A. L. Kroeber, *Anthropology* (New York: Harcourt, Brace, 1948), pp. 353–355. For other examples, see Howard A. Rush, "Right Time and Place: Many Medical Discoveries Found to Result from Series of Accidents," *New York Times*, June 8, 1969, and Irving Page, "A Sense of the History of Discovery," *Science*, Dec. 27, 1974, p. 1161.

7. Glynn Isaac, "The Food-Sharing Behavior of Protohuman Hominids," *Scientific American,* 238 (April 1978), pp. 90–108.

8. For an early discussion of this point, see William F. Ogburn, *Social Change* (New York: Viking, 1922), chap. 6.

9. Ogburn mentioned this factor briefly, but did not stress it. (Ibid., 1950, p. 110.)

10. Ralph Linton, *The Study of Man* (New York: Appleton-Century, 1936), pp. 326–327. Reprinted by permission of Prentice-Hall, Inc.

11. Basil Davidson with F. K. Buah, *A History of West Africa* (Garden City, N.Y.: Doubleday Anchor, 1966), pp. 8–9.

12. Ogburn, 1950, p. 107.

13. James K. Feibleman, *The Institutions of Society* (London: G. Allen, 1956), p. 52.

14. A. L. Kroeber, *Anthropology* (New York: Harcourt, Brace, 1948), p. 375.

15. Elman R. Service, *The Hunters* (Englewood Cliffs, N.J.: Prentice-Hall, 1966), pp. 6–7.

16. William H. McNeill, *Plagues and Peoples* (Garden City, N.Y.: Doubleday Anchor, 1976), chap. 4.

17. See William F. Cottrell, *Energy and Society* (New York: McGraw-Hill, 1955), p. 2, for a somewhat similar assertion concerning energy's impact on human life.

18. Scholars today estimate the world population of hunters and gatherers at 5 to 10 million around 7000 B.C. See, for example, Richard Leakey and Roger Lewin, *Origins* (New York: Dutton, 1977), p. 143. This indicates a minimum of 100,000 hunting and gathering societies.

19. Pitirim Sorokin, *Social and Cultural Dynamics* (New York: Bedminster Press, 1962), vol. III, chap. 10 and p. 352.

20. Thorstein Veblen, *The Theory of the Leisure Class* (New York: Macmillan, 1899).

21. F. G. Bailey, *Tribe, Caste, and Nation* (Manchester: Manchester University Press, 1960).

22. McNeill, chaps. 4 and 5.

Chapter 4

1. See Marvin Harris, *The Rise of Anthropological Theory* (New York: Thomas Y. Crowell, 1968), chap. 2, and Robert Nisbet, *Social Change and History* (New York: Oxford, 1969), chap. 4.

2. This method of classification is an expansion and modification of one developed earlier by Walter Goldschmidt in *Man's Way: A Preface to the Understanding of Human Society* (New York: Holt, 1959), chap. 6, and also reflects the influence of V. Gordon Childe, *Man Makes Himself* (New York: Mentor Books, 1951).

3. In Africa south of the Sahara, most societies have long manufactured iron tools and weapons but have had a horticultural base. This has been because of the diffusion of the techniques of ironmaking without a corresponding diffusion of the plow and agriculture. For purposes of analysis, these societies are classified as

advanced horticultural, since they fail to meet the minimal criterion for agrarian societies (i.e., the presence of the plow).

4. See Jacquetta Hawkes, *Prehistory* (New York: Mentor Books, 1965), chap. 6, for a good summary of archaeological finds relating to fishing. See also Grahame Clark and Stuart Piggott, *Prehistoric Societies* (New York: Knopf, 1965), chap. 7.

5. Robert Braidwood, "The Earliest Village Communities of Southwestern Asia Reconsidered," and Karl Butzer, "Agricultural Origins in the Near East as a Geographical Problem," in Stuart Struever (ed.), *Prehistoric Agriculture* (Garden City, N.Y.: Natural History Press, 1971), pp. 222 and 249.

6. James Mellaart, *Earliest Civilizations in the Near East* (London: Thames and Hudson, 1965), p. 105, and R. J. Forbes, *Studies in Ancient Technology* (Leiden: Brill, 1971–1972), vols. 8 and 9.

7. See, for example, Leslie Aitchison, *A History of Metals* (London: MacDonald, 1960), vol. 1, p. 41, and Forbes, op. cit.

8. E. Cecil Curwen and Gudmund Hatt, *Plough and Pasture: The Early History of Farming* (New York: Collier Books, 1961), p. 64.

9. Aitchison, pp. 102 and 111–113; and Forbes, vol. 9, chap. 3.

10. Mellaart, p. 20.

11. William H. McNeill, *The Rise of the West: A History of the Human Community* (New York: Mentor Books, 1965), p. 150.

12. The data which follow are, with three exceptions, based on Murdock's codes for the first 915 societies listed in the journal *Ethnology*, vols. 1–5. The classification of societies is explained in the Appendix to the 1970 edition of *Human Societies*, pp. 503–507. The first exception is explained in note 13 below. The second involves the data in Figure 4.4, which are based on only those societies included in both the *Human Societies* Appendix and the summary report in the April 1967 issue of *Ethnology*. The third exception is the data on industrial societies, which are our own estimates.

13. This particular code was not reported in the Ethnographic Atlas in *Ethnology* but in an earlier paper of Murdock's entitled "World Ethnographic Sample," *American Anthropologist*, 59 (1957), pp. 644–687. This paper provided data on a sample of 565 societies and offered a more limited range of information. The computations reported in the tables in this chapter are our own.

14. This method of classifying religious beliefs is based on work by G. E. Swanson in *The Birth of the Gods: The Origin of Primitive Beliefs* (Ann Arbor: University of Michigan Press, 1960), chap. 3.

15. Leslie White was the leading proponent of this point of view for many years. See, for example, his stimulating but extreme essay, "Energy and the Evolution of Culture," in *The Science of Culture* (New York: Grove Press, Inc., 1949), pp. 363–393.

16. Talcott Parsons is one of many who have consistently minimized the role of technology in the process of social change. Though not as extreme as some in his views, he has been very influential. See *Societies: Evolutionary and Comparative Perspectives* (Englewood Cliffs, N.J.: Prentice-Hall, 1966), especially pp. 113–114, for his views.

Chapter 5

1. For an example of the use of the term "analogous peoples," see Grahame Clark and Stuart Piggott, *Prehistoric Societies* (New York: Knopf, 1965), p. 133. On the value of inferences from ethnography, see Frank Hole and Robert Heizer, *An Introduction to Prehistoric Archeology* (New York: Holt, 1965), especially pp. 211–214 and chap. 16; or Grahame Clark, *Archeology and Society: Reconstructing the Historic Past*, 3d ed. (London: Methuen, 1957), pp. 172–174. In several

instances, contemporary hunters and gatherers have provided explanations for previously unexplained archaeological findings. See, for example, John E. Pfeiffer, *The Emergence of Man,* 3d ed. (New York: Harper & Row, 1978), chap. 15.

2. Clark, pp. 172–173. Quoted by permission of Methuen & Co., Ltd. See also Colin Renfrew, *Before Civilization* (Cambridge: Cambridge University Press, 1979), p. 254.

3. For more conservative estimates based on recent work in immunology, see Vincent Sarich and Joseph Cronin, "Molecular Systematics of the Primates," in Morris Goodman et al. (eds.), *Molecular Anthropology* (New York: Plenum, 1976), pp. 141–170, or Allan Wilson et al. (eds.), *Biochemical Evolution,* in Esmond Snell et al. (eds.), *Annual Review of Biochemistry,* 46 (1977), pp. 573–640. For estimates of earlier dates of speciation based on evidence from archaeology and paleontology, see Pfeiffer, prologue and chap. 2; and Richard E. Leakey and Roger Lewin, *Origins* (New York: Dutton, 1977), p. 56.

4. Pfeiffer, chaps. 3 and 4; and Leakey and Lewin, chap. 5.

5. J. S. Weiner, *The Natural History of Man* (Garden City, N.Y.: Doubleday Anchor, 1973), p. 50ff.

6. Glynn Isaac, "The Food-Sharing Behavior of Protohuman Hominids," *Scientific American,* 238 (April 1978), pp. 90–108.

7. Geza Teleki, *The Predatory Behavior of Wild Chimpanzees* (Lewisburg, Pa.: Bucknell University Press, 1973).

8. Jacquetta Hawkes, *Prehistory: UNESCO History of Mankind,* vol. 1, part 1 (New York: Mentor Books, 1965), p. 172. See also Clark and Piggott, p. 45, or Grahame Clark, *The Stone Age Hunters* (London: Thames and Hudson, 1967), p. 25.

9. William Laughlin, "Hunting: An Integrating Biobehavior System and Its Evolutionary Importance," in Richard Lee and Irven DeVore (eds.), *Man the Hunter* (Chicago: Aldine, 1968).

10. Pfeiffer, chap. 8, and Leakey and Lewin, p. 122.

11. H. V. Vallois, "The Social Life of Early Man: The Evidence of Skeletons," in Sherwood Washburn (ed.), *Social Life of Early Man* (Chicago: Aldine, 1961), pp. 214–235.

12. Pfeiffer, p. 153ff.

13. Ibid., p. 158.

14. S. A. Semenov, *Prehistoric Technology,* trans. M. W. Thompson (New York: Barnes & Noble, 1964), pp. 202–203.

15. E. Adamson Hoebel, *Anthropology,* 3d ed. (New York: McGraw-Hill, 1966), pp. 176–177, and Hawkes, pp. 212–213.

16. This and the following statements concerning the bow and arrow are based on Semenov, pp. 202–204.

17. Hawkes, p. 212.

18. J. G. D. Clark, *Prehistoric Europe: The Economic Basis* (London: Methuen, 1952), pp. 132–133.

19. Hawkes, pp. 184–188, and Pfeiffer, p. 194

20. Peter Ucko and Andreé Rosenfeld, *Palaeolithic Cave Art* (New York: McGraw-Hill, 1967); or Grahame Clark, *The Stone Age Hunters,* chap. 4.

21. Clark and Piggott, pp. 93–95.

22. Hawkes, pp. 293–294, including fig. 35b.

23. For good reviews of work on hunters and gatherers, see Richard Lee and Irven DeVore (eds.), *Man The Hunter* (Chicago:Aldine,1968); Carlton S. Coon, *The Hunting Peoples* (Boston: Little, Brown, 1971); and Elman Service, *The Hunters* (Englewood Cliffs, N.J.: Prentice-Hall, 1966).

24. This figure is based on Elkin's estimate that there were approximately 300,000 aborigines in Australia at the time of the first white settlement. This estimate was divided by 60, a very generous estimate for the average size of these societies. See A. P. Elkin, *The Australian Aborigines,* 3d ed. (Sydney: Angus and Robertson, 1954), p. 10.

25. See Martin Baumhoff, *Ecological Determinants of Aboriginal California Popula-tions,* University of California *Publications in American Archaeology and Ethnolo-gy,* 49 (Berkeley, 1963), especially pp. 227 and 231. See also Elkin, op. cit., and his estimate of an aboriginal population of 300,000 prior to white settlement. Since Australia contains nearly 3 million square miles, this means an average density of only 1 person per 10 square miles. In Alaska, there was only 1 per 25 square miles at the time of its purchase by the United States (Hawkes, p. 183).

26. Joseph Birdsell, "Some Predictions for the Pleistocene Based on Equilibrium Systems among Recent Hunter-Gatherers," in Lee and DeVore, p. 235, and Table 5.2 of this volume.

27. Gertrude E. Dole, *The Development of Patterns of Kinship Nomenclature* (unpub-lished Ph. D. dissertation, University of Michigan, 1957), p. 26, found an average life expectancy at birth in very primitive societies of only twenty-two years and also found that individuals who live to age fifty are rare. Holmberg, *Nomads of the Long Bow,* p. 85, reported that the average life-span among the Siriono was only thirty-five to forty years *even among those who survived infancy.*

28. Gini Bara Kolata, "!Kung Hunter-Gatherers: Feminism, Diet, and Birth Control," *Science,* 185 (Sept. 13, 1974), p. 934.

29. William Divale, "Systemic Population Control in the Middle and Upper Paleolith-ic: Inferences Based on Contemporary Hunters and Gatherers," *World Archaeolo-gy,* 4 (1972), fig. 11, p. 230, and John Whiting, "Effects of Climate on Certain Cultural Practices," in Ward Goodenough (ed.), *Explorations in Cultural Anthro-pology: Essays in Honor of George Peter Murdock* (New York: McGraw-Hill, 1964), table 9, pp. 528–533.

30. Don Dumond, "The Limitations of Human Population: A Natural History," *Science,* 187 (Feb. 28, 1975), p. 715.

31. Kolata, op. cit.

32. See, for example, John Garvan, *The Negritos of the Philippines* (Vienna: Ferdi-nand Berger, 1964), p. 27; or Edwin Loeb, *Sumatra: Its History and People* (Vienna: Institut für Volkerkunde, 1935), p. 283, on the Kubu.

33. Only one of the 15 nonnomadic hunting and gathering societies in Murdock's data set depended on hunting and gathering for as much as three-quarters of its subsistence, whereas more than half of the 136 nomadic hunting and gathering societies were in this category. The one exception among the nonnomadic societies (the Nomlaki) was located in the Sacramento Valley of northern California, a territory as favorable for a hunting and gathering people as any in the world (see Baumhoff, pp. 205–231).

34. Colin Turnbull, "The Mbuti Pygmies of the Congo," in James Gibbs (ed.), *Peoples of Africa* (New York: Holt, 1965), pp. 286–287.

35. James Woodburn, "Ecology, Nomadic Movement and the Composition of the Local Group among Hunters and Gatherers: An East African Example and Its Implications," in Peter J. Ucko, Ruth Tringham, and G. W. Dimbleby (eds.), *Man, Settlement and Urbanism* (London: Duckworth, 1972), p. 201ff.

36. Richard B. Lee, "Work Effort, Group Structure and Land-Use in Contemporary Hunter-Gatherers," in Ucko et al., pp. 181–184.

37. A. R. Radcliffe-Brown, "The Social Organization of Australian Tribes," *Oceania,* 1 (1930), pp. 44–46.

38. Elkin, p. 56 (Doubleday Anchor edition).

39. Service, *The Hunters,* p. 32ff. For some exceptions, see Colin Turnbull, *Wayward Servants, The Two Worlds of the African Pygmies* (Garden City, N.Y.: Natural History Press, 1965), pp. 109–112.

40. See, for example, Elkin, p. 50; Ivor Evans, *The Negritos of Malaya* (London: Cambridge, 1937), p. 254; and Garvan, p. 82.

41. Service, p. 42.

42. Coon, *The Hunting Peoples,* p. 192; Laughlin, "Hunting," pp. 318–320; Julian Steward, "Causal Factors and Processes in the Evolution of Pre-farming Socie-ties," in Lee and DeVore, pp. 332–333; and Elman Service, *Primitive Social*

Organization: An Evolutionary Perspective (New York: Random House, 1962), chap. 3, especially p. 61.

43. Service, *Primitive Social Organization*, p. 49.
44. See, for example, Elkin, pp. 134–137.
45. Garvan, p. 29.
46. Lorna Marshall, "The !Kung Bushmen of the Kalahari Desert," in Gibbs, pp. 257–258. Quoted by permission of Holt, Rinehart and Winston, Inc. See also Charles Hose and William McDougall, *The Pagan Tribes of Borneo* (London: Macmillan, 1912), pp. 190–191; Allan Holmberg, *Nomads of the Long Bow: The Siriono of Eastern Bolivia*, Smithsonian Institution, Institute of Social Anthropology, 10 (Washington, 1950), p. 11; or Loeb, p. 300.
47. See, for example, Walter Goldschmidt, *Nomlaki Ethnography*, University of California *Publications in American Archaeology and Ethnology*, 42 (Berkeley, 1951), pp. 333–335 and 417–428.
48. See, for example, Loeb, p. 294, or Holmberg, pp. 30 and 91.
49. Turnbull, pp. 287 and 297; Frederick McCarthy and Margaret McArthur, "The Food Quest and the Time Factor in Aboriginal Economic Life," in Charles Mountford (ed.), *Records of the American-Australian Expedition to Arnhem Land* (Melbourne: Melbourne University Press, 1960), pp. 190–191; Kenneth MacLeish, "The Tasadays: Stone Age Cavemen of Mandanao," *National Geographic*, 142 (August 1972), pp. 243–245; Richard B. Lee, "What Hunters Do for a Living, or How to Make Out on Scarce Resources," in Lee and DeVore, pp. 36–37.
50. See Service, p. 13, and Marshall Sahlins, "Notes on the Original Affluent Society," in Lee and DeVore, pp. 85–89.
51. Goldschmidt, p. 417. See also Asen Balicki, "The Netsilik Eskimos: Adaptive Responses," and the comments of Lorna Marshall and Colin Turnbull, in Lee and DeVore, pp. 78–82, 94, and 341, for challenges to the recent effort to portray life in hunting and gathering societies as idyllic and trouble-free.
52. See, for example, Lee, p. 40.
53. Coon, *The Hunting Peoples*, p. 176.
54. In the hunting and gathering societies in Murdock's data set, hunting was entirely a male activity in 97 per cent of the cases and predominantly a male activity in the rest. On the other hand, gathering was wholly or largely a female activity in 91 per cent of the societies and predominantly a male activity in only 2 per cent (in the remainder the activity was shared by both sexes).
55. Of the hunting and gathering societies in Murdock's data set, 57 per cent defined this as a male responsibility, 25 per cent as a female, and 18 per cent regarded it as appropriate to both sexes.
56. I. Schapera, *Government and Politics in Tribal Societies* (London: Watts, 1956), p. 93. See also Holmberg's description of the Siriono headman or chief quoted on p. 176, and Hose and McDougall, p. 190, on the Punan shaman. Other specialists, much less common, may include part-time workers in certain arts and crafts and occasionally an assistant to the headman. Such individuals are most likely to be found in settled communities that depend less than totally on hunting and gathering or in those with especially favorable environments. See, for example, Goldschmidt, pp. 331–332, and Elkin, p. 254ff.
57. See, for example, Turnbull, pp. 287–288; Evans, pp. 57 and 112–113; Garvan, p. 66; or Hose and McDougall, p. 191. Turnbull warns, however, that many scholars exaggerate the dependence of the Pygmies on the neighboring horticultural villagers. He maintains that they turn to the villagers only for luxuries and diversion. See *Wayward Servants*, pp. 33–37.
58. Gerhard Lenski, *Power and Privilege* (New York: McGraw Hill, 1966), pp. 95–96.
59. Occasionally there might be a second official. See, for example, Kaj Birket-Smith, *The Eskimos*, rev. ed. (London: Methuen, 1959), p. 145; Goldschmidt, pp. 324–325; and Frank Speck, *Penobscot Man* (Philadelphia: University of Pennsylvania Press, 1940), pp. 239–240.
60. Holmberg, pp. 59–60. Quoted by permission of the Smithsonian Institution Press.

Following an older usage, Holmberg referred to the leaders of Siriono bands as "chiefs." In current usage, such persons are usually referred to as "headmen," and the term "chief" is reserved for the leaders of tribes or other multicommunity societies. For this reason, the term "headman" has been substituted.

61. See, for example, John Cooper, "The Ona," in Julian Steward (ed.), *Handbook of South American Indians,* Smithsonian Institution, Bureau of American Ethnology, Bulletin 143 (Washington, 1946), vol. 1, p. 117; A. R. Radcliffe-Brown, *The Andaman Islanders* (Glencoe, Ill.: Free Press, 1948), p. 47; Hose and McDougall, p. 182, on the Punan of Borneo; Speck, p. 239, on the Penobscot of Maine; Schapera, *The Khoisan Peoples,* p. 151; and Roland Dixon, "The Northern Maidu," in Carleton S. Coon (ed.), *A Reader in General Anthropology* (New York: Holt, 1948), p. 272.

62. Baldwin Spencer and F. J. Gillen, *The Arunta: A Study of a Stone Age People* (London: Macmillan, 1927), vol. 1, p. 10.

63. Schapera, *Government and Politics,* p. 117. Quoted by permission of C. A. Watts & Co., Ltd. See also A. H. Gayton, *Yokuts-Mono Chiefs and Shamans,* University of Calfornia *Publications in American Archaeology and Ethnology,* 24 (Berkeley, 1930), pp. 374–376.

64. See, for example, Colin Turnbull, *Wayward Servants,* chaps. 11 and 12, or *The Forest People* (New York: Simon & Schuster, 1961), on the Mbuti Pygmies. As he indicates, the office of headman is sometimes found among these people, but it has been more or less forced on them by the Bantu villagers and is of little significance except in their contacts with these villagers.

65. See, for example, Schapera, *Government and Politics,* p. 193, or Turnbull, *Wayward Servants,* pp. 100–109.

66. See John Honigmann, *The Kaska Indians: An Ethnographic Reconstruction,* Yale University *Publications in Anthropology,* 51 (1954), pp. 90–92 and 96–97; Radcliffe-Brown, *The Andaman Islanders,* pp. 48–52; Schapera, *The Khoisan Peoples of South Africa* (London: Routledge, 1930), pp. 151–155; and Hose and McDougall, p. 182.

67. Schapera, *The Khoisan Peoples,* p. 152.

68. Radcliffe-Brown, *The Andaman Islanders,* p. 50.

69. Schapera, *The Khoisan Peoples,* p. 152.

70. See, for example, Goldschmidt, pp. 330–341.

71. See, for example, Evans, p. 21; Marshall, "!Kung Bushmen," p. 248; or Radcliffe-Brown, p. 29. For an exception, see Birket-Smith, pp. 145–146. For intermediate cases, see Honigmann, pp. 84, 88, and 96; Elkin, p. 45; and H. Ling Roth, *The Aborigines of Tasmania* (London: Kegan Paul, Trench, Trubner, 1890), p. 71.

72. Sometimes certain trees become the private property of an individual who stakes a special claim to them, but this is uncommon and the number of trees involved is generally small. See, for example, Radcliffe-Brown, *The Andaman Islanders,* p. 41, or Goldschmidt, p. 333.

73. See, for example, McCarthy and McArthur, "Aboriginal Economic Life," pp. 179–180; Schapera, *The Khoisan Peoples,* pp. 100–101; Radcliffe-Brown, *The Andaman Islanders,* p. 43; Hose and McDougall, p. 187; or Speck, p. 47.

74. Radcliffe-Brown, *The Andaman Islanders,* pp. 44–48.

75. See, for example, Goldschmidt, pp. 324–326.

76. Among the sample of hunting and gathering societies in Murdock's data set, 54 per cent had provision for the hereditary transmission of the office, usually to a son of the previous headman.

77. William D. Davis, *Societal Complexity and the Sources of Primitive Man's Conception of the Supernatural* (unpublished Ph.D. dissertation, University of North Carolina, Chapel Hill, 1971), chap. 5. Davis reports such beliefs in all but one of the eleven hunting and gathering societies he studied. See also Service, *The Hunters,* pp. 68–70.

78. See Service, *The Hunters,* p. 70.

79. For descriptions of shamans and their practices, see Evans, chaps. 19–20; Coon, *The Hunting Peoples*, chap. 16; Honigmann, pp. 104–108; Schapera, *The Khoisan Peoples*, pp. 195–201; Radcliffe-Brown, *The Andaman Islanders*, pp. 175–179; Elkin, chap. 11; or Gayton, pp. 392–398.

80. See, for example, Dixon, p. 282.

81. Ibid., p. 272.

82. Jacob Baegert, S. J., *Account of the Aboriginal Inhabitants of the California Peninsula*, in Coon, *A Reader in General Anthropology*, p. 79. See also Radcliffe-Brown, *The Andaman Islanders*, p. 177.

83. Turnbull, *The Forest People*, p. 130. Copyright, 1961 by Colin M. Turnbull. By permission of Simon & Schuster, Inc.

84. See, for example, Elkin, chap. 7; Marshall, "!Kung Bushmen," pp. 264–267; Turnbull, "The Mbuti Pygmies," pp. 306–307; or Coon, *The Hunting Peoples*, chap. 14.

85. Herbert Barry III, Irving L. Child, and Margaret K. Bacon, "Relation of Child Training to Subsistence Economy," *American Anthropologist*, 61 (1959), p. 263. See also Michael R. Welch, *Subsistence Economy and Sociological Patterns: An Examination of Selected Aspects of Child-Training Processes in Preindustrial Societies*((unpublished Ph. D. dissertation, University of North Carolina, 1980).

86. Some of the best evidence of religious motivation comes from Australia (see Elkin, pp. 191–192 or 232–234). For an example of art employed as an instrument of sympathetic magic, see Evans, p. 130ff.

87. Turnbull, "The Mbuti Pygmies," pp. 308–312, *The Forest People*, chap. 4, and *Wayward Servants*, pp. 259–267.

88. See, for example, Hose and McDougall, p. 192, and Speck, p. 270ff.

89. Turnbull, *The Forest People*, p. 135.

90. This definition is based on Hoebel, *Anthropology*, p. 572, and Elkin, *The Australian Aborigines*, p. 25.

91. Examples are provided by the Punan of Borneo (Hose and McDougall, p. 183) or the Mbuti Pygmies of Africa (Turnbull, *Wayward Servants*, pp. 100–109).

92. Schapera, *The Khoisan Peoples*, p. 76. Quoted by permission of Routledge & Kegan Paul, Ltd.

93. See, for example, Goldschmidt, p. 324.

94. For similar comparisons, see Grahame Clark, *The Stone Age Hunters*, op. cit.; and Pfeiffer, op. cit.

95. See, for example, Clark and Piggott, *Prehistoric Societies*, p. 130ff.; or Hole and Heizer, *Introduction to Prehistoric Archeology*, pp. 225–226.

96. Orlando Lizama, "Death of Woman Marked Tribe's End: First Seen by Magellan," *Washington Post*, Aug. 17, 1975, p. F3.

97. Marshall, p. 273.

98. Kolata, p. 932.

Chapter 6

1. Jack Harlan, "The Plants and Animals That Nourish Man," *Scientific American*, 235 (September 1976), pp. 89–97; Jack Harlan *Crops and Man* (Madison, Wis.: American Society of Agronomy, 1975); or Stuart Streuver (ed.), *Prehistoric Agriculture* (Garden City, N.Y.: Natural History Press, 1971), parts II and IV.

2. Lawrence Guy Straus et al., "Ice-Age Subsistence in Northern Spain," *Scientific American*, 242 (June 1980), pp. 142–152.

3. Marvin Harris, *Cannibals and Kings: The Origins of Cultures* (New York: Vintage Books, Inc., 1978), p. 31.

4. Ibid., p. 30.

5. Ibid.

6. The explanation underlying this model derives from the pioneering work of Kent Flannery. See, for example, "Origins and Ecological Effects of Early Domestication in Iran and the Near East," in P. J. Ucko and G. W. Dimbleby (eds.), *The Domestication and Exploitation of Plants and Animals* (Chicago: Aldine, 1969), pp. 73–100; or "The Origins of Agriculture," *Annual Review of Anthropology*, 2 (1973), pp. 270–310.

7. See, for example, Robert Braidwood and Bruce Howe, "Southwestern Asia beyond the Lands of the Mediterranean Littoral," in Robert Braidwood and Gordon Willey (eds.). *Courses toward Urban Life: Archeological Considerations of Some Cultural Alternatives* (Chicago: Aldine, 1962), pp. 137, 152–153, and 346; James Mellaart, *Earliest Civilizations of the Near East* (London: Thames and Hudson, 1965), pp. 12, 32–38, 47–50, and 81; or Barbara Bender, *Farming in Prehistory* (London: John Baker, 1975), chap. 6.

8. For a good description of the radiocarbon technique, see Frank Hole and Robert Heizer, *An Introduction to Prehistoric Archeology* (New York: Holt, 1965), pp. 145–150.

9. Braidwood and Howe, p. 140; Mellaart, chaps. 3ff.; V. Gordon Childe, "The New Stone Age," in Harry Shapiro (ed.), *Man, Culture, and Society* (New York: Oxford Galaxy, 1960), p. 103; E. Cecil Curwen and Gudmund Hatt, *Plough and Pasture: The Early History of Farming* (New York: Collier Books, 1961), p. 33.

10. Jacquetta Hawkes, *Prehistory, UNESCO History of Mankind*, vol. 1, part 1 (New York: Mentor Books, 1965), pp. 442–452; Mellaart, p. 42; Childe, "The New Stone Age," p. 107.

11. Childe, "The New Stone Age," pp.100–101.

12. See, for example, B. H. Farmer, "Agriculture: Comparative Technology," in *International Encyclopedia of the Social Sciences*, vol. 1, 204–205; or Curwen and Hatt, p. 68 and chap. 16.

13. V. Gordon Childe, *What Happened in History*, rev. ed. (Baltimore: Penguin, 1964), pp. 64–65.

14. Mellaart, pp. 50–51, or Jean Perrot, "Palestine-Syria-Cilcia," in Braidwood and Willey, pp. 156–157.

15. Hawkes, pp. 384–395; Childe, "The New Stone Age," pp. 104–105; or Perrot, pp. 154–155.

16. Hawkes, pp. 395–401; and Mellaart, pp. 40–42.

17. Mellaart, p. 47; and Bender, pp. 148–149.

18. Childe, "The New Stone Age," p. 105. Elsewhere Childe speaks of twenty-five to thirty-five households as "a not uncommon number" in central Europe and southern Russia. See *What Happened in History*, p. 66.

19. Mellaart, p. 36; or Hawkes, p. 310.

20. Mellaart, pp. 81–101.

21. See, for example, Childe, "The New Stone Age," p. 106, or *What Happened in History*, pp. 67–68. See also Braidwood and Howe, p. 138.

22. Mellaart, p. 36. See also p. 84 for his views on Catal Hüyük.

23. Childe, "The New Stone Age," p. 106.

24. Denise Schmandt-Bessert, "The Earliest Precursor of Writing," *Scientific American*, 238 (January, 1978), pp. 50–59.

25. Mellaart, pp. 43–44.

26. See Childe, *What Happened in History*, p. 67.

27. Childe, "The New Stone Age," p. 106, and *What Happened in History*, p. 67.

28. For a good review of these developments, see Hawkes, pp. 401–410 and 414–417; or V. Gordon Childe, *Man Makes Himself* (New York: Mentor, 1953), pp. 76–80.

29. Childe, "The New Stone Age," p. 107, or *What Happened in History*, p. 74.

30. Karl Heider, *The Dugum Dani: A Papuan Culture in the Highlands of West New Guinea* (New York: Wenner-Gren Foundation, 1970). See also the film "Dead Birds" based on the same society.

31. Childe, "The New Stone Age," p. 107.
32. For the ethnographic evidence, see Table 4.2, p. 91.
33. See Kwang-chih Chang, *The Archaeology of Ancient China* (New Haven, Conn.: Yale, 1963), pp. 130–131. See also Curwen and Hatt, pp. 16–18, on truths contained in ancient traditions.
34. The quotations in this paragraph are all from Chang. pp, 131–133, and are used by permission of the Yale University Press.
35. Mellaart, pp. 130–131, and V. Gordon Childe, *New Light on the Most Ancient East* (London: Routledge, 1952), p. 118ff.
36. Childe, *New Light,* p. 115; and Hawkes, p. 425.
37. Childe, *New Light,* p. 115.
38. Mellaart, p. 130.
39. Colin Renfrew, *Before Civilization* (Cambridge: Cambridge University Press, 1979), p. 167.
40. R. J. Forbes, *Studies in Ancient Technology*, 2d ed. (Leiden, Netherlands: Brill, 1972), vol. 9, p. 30, or Leslie Aitchison, *A History of Metals* (London: MacDonald, 1960), vol. 1, p. 21.
41. Forbes, pp. 32–34; or Aitchison, p. 40.
42. Ibid.; or Forbes, vol. 8, p. 26.
43. Childe, *Man Makes Himself*, p. 99.
44. V. Gordon Childe, *The Bronze Age* (London: Cambridge, 1930), p. 11.
45. See, for example, Childe, *New Light*, p. 116. There is still some uncertainty about this point.
46. William Watson, *The Chinese Exhibition* (a guide to the exhibition of archaeological finds of the People's Republic, exhibited in Toronto, 1974), p. 14.
47. Some bronze seems to have been manufactured accidentally a few centuries earlier as a result of using copper derived from ores containing tin, but the deliberate and conscious alloying of metals did not begin until after 3000 B.C. See Forbes, vol. 9, pp. 151–152. Recent research by scholars at the University of Pennsylvania suggests that the invention of bronze may have occurred in Thailand prior to 3600 B.C., which would explain why bronze was an integral part of advanced horticultural societies in China, but not in the Middle East.
48. William Watson, *China: Before the Han Dynasty* (New York: Praeger, 1961), p. 57.
49. Te-k'un Cheng, *Archaeology in China: Shang China* (Cambridge, England: Heffer, 1960), pp. 206–207.
50. Shang kings, for example, mounted "many military expenditions with an army of between 3,000 and 5,000 men." Ibid., p. 210; and Cho-yun Hsu, *Ancient China in Transition* (Stanford, Calif.: Stanford, 1965), p. 67.
51. See note 46 above.
52. Cheng, pp. 200–206.
53. Ibid., pp. 200–215 and 248. For a more detailed picture of the system of stratification in the Chou era, see Hsu, op. cit. In reading this book one must keep in mind that the Chan Kuo period, the "period of the warring states," is included, and by then, north-central China seems to have reached the agrarian level of development.
54. Watson, *China: Before the Han Dynasty*, p. 141, and Chang, p. 195ff.
55. Aitchison, p. 97.
56. Hsu, pp. 3–7 and chap. 4.
57. Chang, p. 150.
58. Watson, *China: Before the Han Dynasty*, p. 106. See also Hsu, p. 15ff., on the interrelations between religion and politics in Chou China.
59. Chang, pp. 150 and 159.
60. Ibid., p. 171.
61. Jesse D. Jennings, "Originis," in Jesse D. Jennings (ed.), *Ancient Native Americans* (San Francisco: Freeman, 1978), pp. 1–41.

62. For a recent survey of these developments, see pp. 212–228; for an extended survey of the three most highly developed cultures of the New World, the Aztecs, Mayas, and Incas, see Victor von Hagen, *The Ancient Sun Kingdoms of the Americas* (Cleveland: World, 1961).

63. For an alternative view, see Stephen C. Jett, "Precolumbian Transoceanic Contact," in Jennings, pp. 593–650.

64. Marvin Harris, *The Rise of Anthropological Theory* (New York: Crowell, 1968), p. 4.

65. Harris, ibid., p. 4. Emphasis added.

66. A careful comparison of societies in the two eras suggests that modern simple horticulturalists may be a bit less advanced than their prehistoric predecessors. For example, more than a third of those in Murdock's sample did not make pottery and more than half did not engage in weaving, both common practices in simple horticultural societies of prehistoric times.

67. Only 10 per cent of the hunting and gathering societies in Murdock's data set maintained fairly permanent settlements, and virtually all these relied on either fishing or horitculture as a secondary source of subsistence. By contrast, 87 per cent of the simple horticultural societies maintained such settlements.

68. A number of simple horticultural groups have built structures 50 or more feet long. See Gunnar Landtman, *The Kiwai Papuans of British New Guinea* (London: Macmillan, 1927), p. 5, or Gerhard Lenski, *Power and Privilege* (New York: McGraw-Hill, 1966), p. 121.

69. Lenski, pp. 124–125.

70. Ibid., p. 122.

71. See, for example, Steward and Faron's statement (op. cit., p. 300) with reference to villagers who occupied most of the northern half of South America that "kinship was the basis of society throughout most of this area." Many similar statements could be cited.

72. See E. Adamson Hoebel, *Anthropology*, 3d ed. (New York: McGraw-Hill, 1966), pp. 374–376, for a good brief summary of these functions.

73. For similar findings based on Murdock's earlier sample of 565 societies, see David Aberle, "Matrilineal Descent in Cross-cultural Perspective," in David Schneider and Kathleen Gough (eds.), *Matrilineal Kinship* (Berkeley: University of California Press, 1961), table 17.4, p. 677.

74. Aberle reached a similar conclusion (op. cit., p. 725). He states that "in general, matriliny is associated with horticulture, in the absence of major activities carried on and coordinated by males. . . ."

75. Multicommunity societies constitute only 2 per cent of all pure hunting and gathering societies (i.e., those in which fishing and horticulture are not important secondary sources of subsistence) but comprise 23 per cent of all simple horticultural societies.

76. Lenski, pp. 119–120.

77. For an early statement of this process, see Lewis Henry Morgan, *Ancient Society* (Cambridge, Mass.: Belknap Press, 1965, first published 1877), p. 109ff.

78. This dual role seems to have been quite common in South America. See Julian Steward and Louis Faron, *Native Peoples of South America* (New York: McGraw-Hill, 1959), p. 301, on the Indians of eastern Brazil and the Amazon Basin; or Julian Steward, "The Tribes of the Montaña and Bolivian East Andes," in Julian Steward (ed.), *Handbook of South American Indians*, Smithsonian Institution, Bureau of American Ethnology, Bulletin 143 (Washington, 1948), vol. III, p. 528. For a slightly different pattern in North America, see Irving Goldman, "The Zuni Indians of New Mexico," in Margaret Mead (ed.), *Cooperation and Competition among Primitive Peoples*, rev. ed. (Boston: Beacon Press, 1961), p. 313.

79. Robert Lowie, "Social and Political Organization," in Steward, *Handbook*, vol. V, p. 345. For examples of this, see Steward, *Handbook*, vol. III, pp. 85, 355, 419, and 478. See also Steward and Faron, p. 244.

80. See, for example, Alfred Métraux, *Native Tribes of Eastern Bolivia and Western Matto Grosso*, Smithsonian Institution, Bureau of American Ethnology, Bulletin 134 (Washington, 1942), p. 39, on the Araona; or Leopold Pospisil, "Kaupauku Papuan Political Structure," in F. Ray (ed.), *Systems of Political Control and Bureaucracy in Human Societies, Proceedings of the 1958 Meetings of the American Ethnological Society* (Seattle), p. 18.
81. For a more detailed discussion of these bases of status, see Lenski, pp. 126–131.
82. See Steward and Faron, pp. 302–303, on the former, and pp. 213–214, 243, and 248–249, on the latter.
83. Marvin Harris, *Cows, Pigs, Wars, and Witches: The Riddles of Culture* (New York: Random House, 1974), pp. 75–80.
84. William Divale, "Systemic Population Control in the Middle and Upper Paleolithic," *World Archaeology*, 4 (1972), fig. 9, p. 228.
85. Data provided by Leo Simmons, *The Role of the Aged in Primitive Society* (New Haven, Conn.: Yale, 1945), show that scalp taking or headhunting was a frequent practice in only one of five hunting and gathering societies but in thirteen of fourteen horticultural societies.
86. Alfred Métraux, "Warfare-Cannibalism-Trophies," in Steward, *Handbook*, vol. V, pp. 400–401. Quoted by permission of the Bureau of American Ethnology.
87. Sonia Cole, *The Prehistory of East Africa* (New York: Mentor, 1965), p. 299.
88. Meyer Fortes, in Meyer Fortes and E. E. Pritchard (eds.), *African Political Systems* (London: Oxford, 1940), p. 5.
89. In one study of twenty-two African horticultural societies, a correlation of 0.67 (Kendall's tau) was found between level of political development and level of social inequality (see Lenski, p. 163). See also Basil Davidson with F. K. Buah, *A History of West Africa: To the Nineteenth Century* (Garden City, N.Y.: Doubleday Anchor, 1966), p. 174.
90. See Lucy Mair, *Primitive Government* (Baltimore: Penguin, 1962), especially chap. 4. The discussion that follows is based largely on her work. See also Lenski, chaps. 6 and 7; Morton Fried, *The Evolution of Political Society* (New York: Random House, 1967); and Elman Service, *Origins of the State and Civilizations: The Process of Cultural Evolution* (New York: Norton, 1975).
91. Estimated from the map in Davidson, p. 68.
92. I. Schapera, *Government and Politics in Tribal Societies* (London: Watts, 1956), p. 169. See also the Swazi proverb that "nobles are the chief's murderers."
93. See, for example, Davidson, chap. 14.
94. See, for example, George Peter Murdock, *Africa: Its Peoples and Their Culture History* (New York: McGraw-Hill, 1959), p. 37.
95. See, for example, P. C. Lloyd, "The Yoruba of Nigeria," in James Gibbs (ed.), *Peoples of Africa* (New York: Holt, 1965), pp. 554–556.
96. For an example of a multicommunity society, see P. R. T. Gurdon, *The Khasis* (London: Macmillan, 1914). This author reports that these people were divided into fifteen small states averaging 15,000 in population and controlling about 400 square miles apiece (pp. 1 and 66).
97. Lenski, pp. 160–162. See also Davidson, pp. 76–77.

Chapter 7

1. V. Gordon Childe, *What Happened in History* (Baltimore: Penguin, 1964), p. 77.
2. Ibid., chap. 4.
3. This paragraph and the one that follows are based on B. H. Farmer, "Agriculture: Comparative Technology," in *International Encyclopedia of the Social Sciences* (New York: Macmillan and Free Press, 1968), vol. 1, pp. 204–205.
4. See Gudmund Hatt, "Farming of Non-European Peoples," in E. Cecil Curwen

and Gudmund Hatt, *Plough and Pasture: The Early History of Farming* (New York: Collier Books, 1961), pp. 217–218.

5. Childe, p. 89.

6. V. Gordon Childe, *Man Makes Himself* (New York: Mentor Books, 1951), p. 100.

7. Farmer, p. 205.

8. See Childe, *Man Makes Himself,* p. 100. In recent years, some have argued that horticulture is more efficient than agriculture in the tropics and that horticultural societies should not be considered less advanced than agricultural. Though there are some areas where horticulture is more efficient, these are rare (a 1957 study by the Food and Agriculture Organization of the United Nations showed that only 7 per cent of the world's population were using horticultural techniques, and often only because of ignorance of the alternative). Furthermore, horticultural societies clearly have not achieved the efficiency in other areas of technology or the complexity of social structure and ideology that agrarian societies have. Though we know of no single paper that provides a comprehensive, balanced analysis of this problem, we recommend R. F. Watter's excellent paper, "The Nature of Shifting Cultivation: A Review of Recent Research," *Pacific Viewpoint*, 1 (1960), pp. 59–99, especially pp. 77–95.

9. E. Cecil Curwen, "Prehistoric Farming of Europe and the Near East," in Curwen and Hatt, pp. 64–65; or C. W. Bishop, "The Origin and Early Diffusion of the Traction Plow," *Antiquity*, 10 (1936), p. 261.

10. Some scholars have argued that Egypt had no cities at this time. See, for example, John A. Wilson, "Civilization without Cities," in Carl Kraeling and Robert Adams (eds.), *City Invincible: A Symposium on Urbanization and Cultural Development in the Ancient Near East* (Chicago: University of Chicago Press, 1960), pp. 124–136; or William McNeill, *The Rise of the West: A History of the Human Community* (New York: Mentor Books, 1963), pp. 87–88. Although there were surely differences between Egyptian and Mesopotamian cities, it seems to be semantic gamesmanship to deny the point (see Kraeling and Adams, pp. 136–162). Especially telling was the comment of one Mesopotamian specialist, who noted that when the Assyrians came to Egypt, they spoke of "hundreds of cities" (Kraeling and Adams, p. 140). See also Tertius Chandler and Gerald Fox, *3000 Years of Urban Growth* (New York: Academic Press, 1974), p. 362.

11. Samuel Noah Kramer, *The Sumerians* (Chicago: University of Chicago Press, 1963), p. 123.

12. Childe, *Man Makes Himself,* pp. 143–144.

13. See, for example, Sir Leonard Woolley, *The Beginnings of Civilization*, UNESCO History of Mankind, vol. 1, part 2 (New York: Mentor Books, 1965), pp. 116, 119, 198, and 449ff.

14. Sir Leonard Woolley, *Prehistory* (New York: Harper & Row, 1963), vol. 1, part 2, p. 127. Reprinted by permission.

15. Margaret Murray, *The Splendour That Was Egypt* (London: Sidgwick & Jackson, 1949), p. 174.

16. On Mesopotamia, see Woolley, *Beginnings*, p. 356; or A. Leo Oppenheim, *Ancient Mesopotamia: Portrait of a Dead Civilization* (Chicago: University of Chicago Press, 1964), pp. 84–85. On Egypt, see Ralph Turner, *The Great Cultural Traditions: The Foundations of Civilization* (New York: McGraw-Hill, 1941), vol. 1, p. 187; or George Steindorff and Keith Seele, *When Egypt Ruled the East,* rev. ed. (Chicago: Phoenix Books, 1963), p. 83.

17. Robert Adams, "Factors Influencing the Rise of Civilization in the Alluvium: Illustrated by Mesopotamia," in Kraeling and Adams, p. 33.

18. See, for example, Kramer, pp. 88–89; Woolley, p. 125; or Kingsley Davis, "The Origin and Growth of World Urbanism," *American Journal of Sociology*, 60 (1955), p. 431. See also Oppenheim, p. 140, who, though declining to estimate size, reports Nineveh to have been larger than Ur (generally thought to have been over 100,000) and Uruk nearly as large; or Mason Hammond, *The City in the Ancient World* (Cambridge, Mass.: Harvard, 1972).

19. Woolley, *Beginnings*, p. 185ff.; or Steindorff and Seele, pp. 89–90.
20. Woolley, ibid., p. 188. Later armies were even larger.
21. Turner, p. 312.
22. McNeill, p. 68; Turner, pp. 310–311; Steindorff and Seele, chap. 9; Pierre Montet, *Everyday Life in Egypt: In the Days of Rameses the Great*, trans. A. R. Maxwell-Hyslop and Margaret Drower (London: E. Arnold, 1958), chap. 10; Oppenheim, pp. 70ff., 230ff., and 276–277.
23. Oppenheim, p. 276. As one writer reports, "Sumerian bureaucracy has left us a staggering number of texts; we are unable to venture a guess as to how many tablets beyond the far more than 100,000 now in museums may be buried in southern Mesopotamia."
24. Childe, *Man Makes Himself*, pp. 148–149, or Childe, *What Happened in History*, p. 144.
25. See especially Kramer, p. 231, or Samuel Noah Kramer, *It Happened at Sumer* (Garden City, N.Y.: Doubleday, 1959), p. 3.
26. See Turner, p. 263, or Childe, *What Happened in History*, p. 118.
27. Childe, *What Happened in History*, pp. 118–119.
28. See Turner's excellent treatment of this topic, pp. 317–323.
29. Adolf Erman, *Life in Ancient Egypt*, trans. H. M. Tirard (London: Macmillan, 1894), p. 128.
30. Childe, *Man Makes Himself*, p. 180, quoted by permission of C. A. Watts & Co., Ltd. See also McNeill, p. 53, or Childe, *What Happened in History*, p. 183ff.
31. *Man Makes Himself*, p. 181. Elsewhere, Childe adds a third innovation (or a fifth to the total list), the invention of glass in Egypt. See *What Happened in History*, p. 183.
32. See Childe, *Man Makes Himself*, chap. 9, for a classic discussion of this subject. The analysis that follows is heavily indebted to Childe's provocative discussion but varies in some details and emphasis.
33. See Childe, *What Happened in History*, p. 184.
34. For a classic statement of this principle, see Gaetano Mosca, *The Ruling Class*, translated by Hannah Kahn (New York: McGraw-Hill, 1939), p. 53.
35. For a good summary of the early history of iron, see Leslie Aitchison, *A History of Metals* (London: MacDonald, 1960), vol. 1, pp. 97–110. The discussion that follows is based largely on Aitchison.
36. Ibid., p. 113.
37. See, for example, Charles Singer's comparison of the level of technology in the ancient empires of Egypt and Mesopotamia prior to 1000 B.C. and later in Greece and Rome, in "Epilogue: East and West in Retrospect," in Charles Singer (ed.), *A History of Technology* (Oxford: Clarendon Press, 1956), vol. II, pp. 754–755.
38. Ibid., pp. 754–772.
39. This estimate was based on the known boundaries of these societies and on the fact that the Roman Empire, which was much larger and contained a much smaller percentage of uninhabitable land, had a maximum population of only about 70 million. See *The Cambridge Ancient History* (London: Cambridge, 1939), vol. XII, pp. 267–268. It is also noteworthy that in Roman times Egypt had a population of only 6 to 7 million. Even if allowance is made for the greater size of the Egyptian empire in the days of Egypt's independence, it is difficult to imagine a total population much in excess of 15 million. See Charles Issawi, *Egypt in Revolution: An Economic Analysis* (New York: Oxford, 1963), p. 20.
40. Chung-li Chang, *The Chinese Gentry: Studies on Their Role in Nineteenth-Century Chinese Society* (Seattle: University of Washington Press, 1955), p. 102.
41. On India, see Kingsley Davis, *The Population of India and Pakistan* (Princeton, N.J.: Princeton University Press, 1951), pp. 24–25; on Rome, see *The Cambridge Ancient History*, pp. 267–268; on Russia, see Blum, p. 278.
42. See, for example, Tertius Chandler and Gerald Fox, *3000 Years of Urban Growth* (New York: Academic Press, 1974).
43. Warren Thompson and David Lewis, *Population Problems*, 5th ed. (New York:

McGraw-Hill, 1965), p. 386; O. Andrew Collver, *Birth Rates in Latin America: New Estimates of Historical Trends and Fluctuations* (Berkeley, Calif.: Institute of International Studies, 1965), pp. 26–30; D. V. Glass and D. E. C. Eversley, *Population in History* (Chicago: Aldine, 1965), pp. 467, 532, 555, and 614. One of the lowest rates for an agrarian society prior to the twentieth century was for eighteenth-century Sweden, and it was nearly 36 per 1,000 (Glass and Eversley, p. 532).

44. See, for example, Horace Miner, *St. Denis: A French-Canadian Parish* (Chicago: Phoenix Books, The University of Chicago Press, 1963), p. 65; Coulton, *The Medieval Village*, p. 322; Manning Nash, *The Golden Road to Modernity: Village Life in Contemporary Burma* (New York: Wiley, 1965), pp. 265–266.

45. See, for example, John Noss, *Man's Religions*, rev. ed. (New York: Macmillan, 1956), pp. 227, 304ff., and 420–421; and Miner, pp. 65–66.

46. Miner, p. 170.

47. Harrison Brown, *The Challenge of Man's Future* (New York: Viking Compass, 1956), p. 75.

48. H. Hollingsworth, "A Demographic Study of the British Ducal Families," in Glass and Eversley, tables 2 and 5, pp. 358 and 360.

49. Brown, p. 75.

50. Warren Thompson, *Population Problems*, 3d ed. (New York: McGraw-Hill, 1942), p. 73.

51. M. C. Buer, *Health, Wealth, and Population in the Early Days of the Industrial Revolution, 1760–1815* (London: Routledge, 1926), pp. 77–78. Quoted by permission of Routledge & Kegan Paul, Ltd.

52. D. E. C. Eversley, "Population, Economy, and Society," in Glass and Eversley, p. 52.

53. Warren Thompson, p. 58. See also Brown, p. 32.

54. K. F. Helleiner, "The Vital Revolution Reconsidered," in Glass and Eversely, p. 79.

55. Turner, p. 911.

56. F. R. Cowell, *Cicero and the Roman Republic* (London: Penguin, 1956), p. 79. Quoted by permission of Penguin Books.

57. See, for example, Jerome Blum, *Lord and Peasant in Russia from the Ninth to the Nineteenth Century* (Princeton, N. J.: Princeton University Press, 1961), pp. 126 and 394–395, on Russia; or Ralph Linton, *The Tree of Culture* (New York: Vintage Books, 1959), p. 231, on China.

58. S. B. Clough and C. W. Cole, *Economic History of Europe* (Boston: Heath, 1941), p. 25.

59. Ibid. See also Blum, pp. 16 and 126.

60. Robert Heilbroner, *The Making of Economic Society* (Englewood Cliffs, N.J.: Prentice-Hall, 1962), p. 27. See also H. R. Trevor-Roper, "The Gentry 1540–1640," *The Economic History Review Supplements*, no. 1 (n.d.); or Marc Bloch, *Feudal Society*, trans. L. A. Manyon (Chicago: University of Chicago Press, 1962), who wrote of "that age when true wealth consisted in being the master" (p. 192).

61. Heilbroner, pp. 9–44.

62. A. H. M. Jones, *The Later Roman Empire 284–602: A Social, Economic and Administrative Survey* (Oxford: Blackwell, 1964), vol. I, p. 465.

63. See page 199 below on peasant revolts. See also G. G. Coulton, *The Medieval Village* (London: Cambridge, 1926), chaps. 11 and 24–25.

64. Blum, pp. 369–370.

65. Ibid., pp. 356–357.

66. Gideon Sjoberg, *The Preindustrial City* (New York: Free Press, 1960), p. 215.

67. See, for example, Chung-li Chang, *Income of the Chinese Gentry* (Seattle: University of Washington Press, 1962), pp. 37–51.

68. For a survey of these obligations, see Gerhard Lenski, *Power and Privilege* (New York: Mc-Graw Hill, 1966), pp. 267–270.

69. Ibid., p. 228.

70. See for example, Blum, p. 232, or W. H. Moreland, *The Agrarian System of Moslem India* (Allahabad, India: Central Book Depot, n.d.), p. 207.

71. George Sansom, *A History of Japan* (Stanford, Calif.: Stanford Press, 1963), vol. III, p. 29.

72. H. S. Bennett, *Life on the English Manor: A Study of Peasant Conditions, 1150–1400* (London: Cambridge, 1960), p. 236.

73. Ibid., pp. 232–236.

74. See, for example, Moreland, p. 147, on India; or Blum, pp. 163, 266–268, 309–310, and 552ff., on Russia.

75. Robert K. Douglas, *Society in China* (London: Innes, 1894), p. 354.

76. Blum, pp. 424 and 428, on Russia; and Gunnar Myrdal, *An American Dilemma* (New York: McGraw-Hill, 1964), p. 931, on the American South.

77. See Coulton, pp. 80 and 464–469; Blum, pp. 426–427; G. M. Carstairs, "A Village in Rajasthan," in M. N. Srnivas (ed.), *India's Villages* (Calcutta: West Bengal Government Press, 1955), pp. 37–38.

78. Bennett, p. 196; Coulton, pp. 190–191, 248–250, and 437–440.

79. G. G. Coulton, *Medieval Panorama* (New York: Meridan Books, 1955), p. 77, or Thompson, p. 708.

80. William Stubbs, *The Constitutional History of England* (Oxford: Clarendon Press, 1891), vol. I, p. 454n., Wolfram Eberhard, *A History of China*, 2d ed. (Berkeley: University of California Press, 1960), p. 32; and Yosoburo Takekoshi, *The Economic Aspects of the History of the Civilization of Japan* (New York: Macmillan, 1930), vol. I, pp. 60–63.

81. See Boak, *A History of Rome*, p. 127, or Cowell, *Cicero and the Roman Republic*, p. 64. For an example of the application of Cato's principle in medieval Europe, see Bennett, p. 283.

82. See, for example, Bloch, p. 337; or George Homans, *English Villagers of the 13th Century* (Cambridge, Mass.: Harvard, 1942), p. 229.

83. See, for example, Morton Fried, *The Fabric of Chinese Society: Study of the Social Life of a Chinese County Seat* (New York: Praeger, 1953), pp. 104–105; Moreland, pp. 168 and 207; and Bennett, pp. 100–101, 112–113, and 131ff.

84. See, for example, the franklins in thirteenth-century England (Homans, pp. 248–250).

85. May McKisack, *The Fourteenth Century* (Oxford: Clarendon Press, 1959), pp. 331–340; Philip Lindsay and Reg Groves, *The Peasants' Revolt, 1381* (London: Hutchinson, n.d.), pp. 30, 34, and 63; Charles Langlois, "History," in Arthur Tilley (ed.), *Medieval France* (London: Cambridge, 1922), pp. 150–151; and Paul Murray Kendall, *The Yorkist Age* (Garden City, N.Y.: Doubleday, 1962), p. 171ff.

86. Sjoberg, p. 83; Lynn White, *Medieval Technology and Social Change* (Oxford: Clarendon Press, 1962), p. 39; Henri Pirenne, *Economic and Social History of Medieval Europe* (New York: Harvest Books, n.d., first published 1933), p. 58; J. C. Russell, *British Medieval Population* (Albuquerque: University of New Mexico Press, 1948), p. 305; Blum, pp. 268 and 281.

87. See Sjoberg, pp. 108–116; or Samuel G. Stoney, *Plantations of the Carolina Low Country* (Charleston: Carolina Art Association, 1938), p. 36.

88. Kendall, p. 157.

89. Jerome Carcopino, *Daily Life in Ancient Rome* (New Haven: Yale University Press, 1940), p. 70.

90. Ibid.

91. See, for example, Sjoberg, p. 183ff. For an interesting example of the persistence of this pattern into the latter part of nineteenth-century England, see W. Somerset Maugham, *Cakes and Ale* (New York: Pocket Books, 1944), p. 29.

92. On acquisition by marriage, see Elinor Barber, *The Bourgeoisie in 18th Century France* (Princeton, N.J.: Princeton University Press, 1955), p. 89, or Sansom, vol. III, pp. 128–129. On confiscation, see B. B. Misra, *The Indian Middle*

Classes (London: Oxford, 1961), pp. 25–27; Takekoshi, vol. II, p. 251ff.; Kendall, p. 181; or Sir James Ramsay, *A History of the Revenues of the Kings of England: 1066–1399* (Oxford: Clarendon Press, 1925), vol. I, p. 58.

93. John Lossing Buck, *Secretariat Paper, No. 1, Tenth Conference of the Institute of Pacific Relations* (Stratford on Avon, 1947), reprinted in Irwin T. Sanders et al., *Societies around the World* (New York: Dryden Press, 1953), p. 65.

94. Clough and Cole, *Economic History of Europe*, p. 445.

95. See, for example, John Nef, *The Conquest of the Material World* (Chicago: University of Chicago Press, 1964), p. 69.

96. Cowell, p. 80. See also William Woodruff, *Impact of Western Man: A Study of Europe's Role in the World Economy* (New York: St. Martin's, 1966), p. 254.

97. Sylvia Thrupp, *The Merchant Class of Medieval London* (Ann-Arbor: Ann Arbor Paperbacks, University of Michigan Press, 1962), p. 9.

98. See, for example, Nef. p. 78.

99. Sidney Gamble, *Peking: A Social Survey* (New York: Doran, 1921), pp. 183–185.

100. Thrupp, pp. 19, 30, etc.

101. Ibid., pp. 23 and 29–31; James Westfall Thompson, *Economic and Social History of Europe in the Later Middle Ages, 1300–1530* (New York: Century, 1931), p. 398.

102. Gamble, p. 283.

103. In Asia many were sold into prostitution by their parents. See Gamble, p. 253. Many more, in every part of the world, were ignorant country girls seeking work in the city who were trapped by hired procurers, while still others were driven into prostitution by unemployment and lack of funds. See M. Dorothy George, *London Life in the XVIIIth Century* (London: Kegan Paul, Trench, Trubner, 1925), pp. 112–113.

104. See, for example, Frederick Nussbaum, *A History of the Economic Institutions of Modern Europe* (New York: Crofts, 1933); or Frank Aydelotte, *Elizabethan Rogues and Vagabonds* (Oxford: Clarendon Press, 1913), p. 4.

105. Lenski, pp. 197–198.

106. For the effect of war on the forms of government, see Herbert Spencer, *The Principles of Sociology* (New York: Appleton, 1897), vol. II, part 5, chap. 17; Pitirim Sorokin, *Social and Cultural Dynamics* (New York: Bedminister Press, 1962), vol. III, pp. 196–198; or Stanislaw Andrzejewski, *Military Organization and Society* (London: Routledge, 1954), pp. 92–95.

107. These figures were calculated from A. E. R. Boak, *A History of Roman Imperial Civilization* (Garden City, N.Y.: Doubleday Anchor, 1959), using Mattingly's list of emperors, pp. 351–355.

108. For figures on several other societies, see Lenski, p. 235.

109. Wolfram Eberhard, *Conquerors and Rulers: Social Forces in Medieval China* (Leiden, Netherlands: Brill, 1952), p. 52; and Blum, p. 558.

110. For an interesting popular account of the former, see Lindsay and Groves, op. cit.

111. Sorokin, vol. II, chap. 10, especially p. 352.

112. See, among others, Lenski, pp. 210–242 and 266–284, for more detailed documentation.

113. Douglas, p. 104.

114. See Max Weber, *The Theory of Social and Economic Organization*, trans. A. M. Henderson and Talcott Parsons (New York: Free Press, 1947), pp. 341–348; and Max Weber, *Wirtschaft und Gesellschaft*, 2d ed. (Tübingen: Mohr, 1925), vol. II, pp. 679–723.

115. Mattingly, p. 137. See also Turner, vol. II, p. 620, or Michael Rostovtzeff, *The Social and Economic History of the Roman Empire*, rev. ed. (Oxford: Clarendon Press, 1957), p. 54.

116. Hans Rosenberg, *Bureaucracy, Aristocracy, and Autocracy: The Prussian Experience 1660–1815* (Cambridge, Mass.: Harvard, 1958), pp. 5–6. Quoted by permission of Harvard University Press.

117. Chang, *The Income of the Chinese Gentry,* Summary Remarks, supplement 2, and chap. 1.

118. On the king's income, see Ramsay, vol. I, pp. 227 and 261. For the income of the nobility, see Sidney Painter, *Studies in the History of the English Feudal Barony* (Baltimore: Johns Hopkins, 1943), pp. 170–171. For the income of field hands, see Bennett, p. 121.

119. Lenski, pp. 219 and 228.

120. See, for example, Albert Lybyer, *The Government of the Ottoman Empire in the Time of Suleiman the Magnificent* (Cambridge, Mass.: Harvard, 1913); or Moreland, op. cit.

121. F. Pelsaert, *Jahangir's India,* trans. W. H. Moreland and P. Geyl and quoted by Misra, p. 47. Quoted by permission of W. Heffer & Sons, Ltd.

122. Lybyer, pp. 47–58 and 115–117.

123. See, for example, James Westfall Thompson's statement that "the medieval state was a loose agglomeration of territories with rights of property and sovereignty everywhere shading into one another," in *Economic and Social History of the Middle Ages* (New York: Appleton-Century-Crofts, 1928), p. 699. See also Bloch, especially chaps. 14–24; Blum, chap. 2; or Sidrey Painter, *The Rise of the Feudal Monarchies* (Ithaca, N.Y.: Cornell, 1951), and *Studies in the History of the English Feudal Barony,* op. cit.

124. See Kenneth Scott Latourette, *A History of Christianity* (New York: Harper, 1953), pp. 15–16.

125. See Robert Bellah, "Religious Evolution," *American Sociological Review,* 29 (1964), pp. 367–368.

126. See, for example, Lenski, pp. 7–9. See also Kendall, p. 232ff.

127. Lenski, pp. 257–258.

128. Ibid., pp. 262–266, gives a more detailed treatment of this aspect of religion.

129. J. W. Thompson, *Economic and Social History of the Middle Ages,* p. 684.

130. See, for example, Carlo Levi, *Christ Stopped at Eboli* (New York: Farrar, Straus, 1947), chaps. 11ff., for a good description of the role of magic in one agrarian community. On fatalism, see, for example, Edward Banfield, *The Moral Basis of a Backward Society* (New York: Free Press, 1967), pp. 36–37, 41, and 107ff.

131. Sjoberg, *The Preindustrial City,* p. 146ff.

132. Ibid., p. 155.

133. Ibid., p. 163ff.; Henry Orenstein, *Gaon: Conflict and Cohesion in an Indian Village* (Princeton, N.J.: Princeton University Press, 1965), pp. 53–57; Kendall, *The Yorkist Age,* chaps. 11 and 12; L. F. Salzman, *English Life in the Middle Ages* (London: Oxford University Press, 1927), pp. 254–256.

134. Bennett, p. 260. For other descriptions of the uses of leisure in agrarian societies, see Margaret Wade Labarge, *A Baronial Household of the Thirteenth Century* (New York: Barnes & Noble, 1966), chap. 10; Bennett, *Life on the English Manor,* chap. 10; or Coulton, *Medieval Panorama,* chaps. 8 and 44.

135. F. R. Cowell, *Everyday Life in Ancient Rome* (New York: Putnam, 1961), p. 173.

136. The data in this paragraph are drawn from Lenski, p. 212.

137. For further details on the expendables, see ibid., pp. 281–284.

138. See, for example, H. van Werveke, "The Rise of the Towns," in *The Cambridge Economic History of Europe* (London: Cambridge Press, 1963), vol. 3, pp. 34–37; L. Halphen, "Industry and Commerce," in Tilley, pp. 190–192; or Pirenne, *Economic and Social History of Medieval Europe,* pp. 187–206.

139. Amos H. Hawley, *Human Ecology* (New York: Ronald, 1950).

140. For important new analyses of the origins of ancient Israel, see Marvin Chaney, "Ancient Palestinian Peasant Movements and the Formation of Premonarchic Israel," *Biblical Archeologist,* forthcoming, and Norman K. Gottwald, *The Tribes of Yahweh* (New York: Orbis, 1979).

141. See, for example, Richard Tomasson, *Iceland: The First New Society,* (Minneapolis: University of Minnesota Press, 1980), chaps. 1 and 8; and Philip Longworth, *The Cossacks* (New York: Holt, Rinehart, 1970).

142. For the classic statement of the effect of frontier life, see Frederick Jackson Turner, *The Frontier in American History* (New York: Holt, 1920).
143. On the Incan empire, see Julian Steward and Louis Faron, *Native Peoples of South America* (New York: McGraw-Hill, 1959), pp. 115 and 121; on Songhay, see Basil Davidson with F. K. Buah, *A History of West Africa* (Garden City, N.Y.: Doubleday Anchor, 1966).
144. Chung-li Chang, *The Chinese Gentry* (Seattle: University of Washington Press, 1955), p. 102; *The Cambridge Ancient History*, pp. 267–268; and Blum, p. 278.

Chapter 8

1. According to Murdock's data, the Manus of New Guinea come as close to full dependence on fishing as any people in the world. See *Ethnology*, vol. 6, no. 2 (April 1967), pp. 170–230. Yet, as Margaret Mead indicates in her report, these people also depend heavily for their subsistence on garden products that they obtain through trade from neighboring peoples and to a lesser degree on pigs that they raise and obtain through trade. See Margaret Mead, *Growing Up in New Guinea* (New York: Mentor Books, 1953, first published 1930), especially pp. 173–174.
2. For an earlier discussion of this point, see Gordon Hewes's excellent paper, "The Rubric 'Fishing and Fisheries,'" *American Anthropologist*, 50 (1948), pp. 241–242.
3. See Table 4.2, p. 91.
4. For a good illustration of this, see Philip Drucker's excellent description of the Indians of the Pacific Northwest, in *Cultures of the North Pacific Coast* (San Francisco: Chandler, 1965).
5. The averages are hunting and gathering, 40; fishing, 60; simple horticultural, 95.
6. The percentages for permanent settlements are hunting and gathering 10; fishing, 49; simple horticultural, 87.
7. The percentages are hunting and gathering 10; fishing, 23; simple horticultural, 21.
8. Unless, perhaps, some evolved into maritime societies. To date, however, there is no real evidence that this ever happened. Maritime societies seem to have evolved out of advanced horticultural or agrarian societies.
9. See Hewes, pp. 240–241.
10. For an interesting account of one such group, see Wilmond Menard, "The Sea Gypsies of China," *Natural History*, 64 (January 1965), pp. 13–21.
11. See, for example, Lawrence Krader, "Pastoralism," in *International Encyclopedia of the Social Sciences* (New York: Macmillan and Free Press, 1968), vol. II, pp. 456–457; or Carleton Coon, "The Nomads," in Sydney Fisher (ed.), *Social Forces in the Middle East* (Ithaca, N.Y.: Cornell, 1955), pp. 23–42.
12. John L. Myres, "Nomadism," *Journal of the Royal Anthropological Institute*, 71 (1941), p. 20.
13. Krader reports that the average density of population in Mongolia was less than 1 per square mile, and among the Tuareg of Africa it was even lower (op. cit., pp. 458–459).
14. The percentages of single-community societies were 90, 78, 77, and 13, respectively, in Murdock's data set.
15. Found in 62 per cent of these societies as against 3 to 37 per cent of the rest.
16. For example, class stratification, by Murdock's definition, is present in 51 per cent of these societies.
17. This requirement is found in 93 per cent of these societies, compared to 37 to 86 per cent of other types.
18. This requirement occurs in 97 per cent of herding societies, compared to only 49 to 79 per cent of other types.

19. Among the rest, it is most common in advanced horticultural societies, but even there it occurs in only 16 per cent of the cases; in the other types, the frequency ranges from 2 to 10 per cent.

20. See William McNeill, *The Rise of the West: A History of the Human Community* (New York: Mentor Books, 1965), p. 126ff.; or Ralph Turner, *The Great Cultural Traditions* (New York: McGraw-Hill, 1941), p. 259.

21. For a good discussion of this important subject, see McNeill, p. 256ff.

22. Ibid., p. 111.

23. Immanuel Wallerstein, *The Modern World-System* (New York: Academic Press, 1974), p. 209ff.

24. On the less familiar Carthaginian empire, see Donald Harden, *The Phoenicians* (New York: Praeger, 1963), chaps. 5 and 6. The British empire, it might also be noted, was an *overseas* empire.

25. Compare, for example, the status of merchants and the rate of innovation for Europe during the sixteenth, seventeenth, and eighteenth centuries with the situation in India. Both were higher in Europe. Although this could have been coincidence, the evidence suggests a causal link.

Chapter 9

1. Charles Singer et al. (eds.), *A History of Technology* (Oxford: Clarendon Press, 1954–1956), vols. 1 and 2.

2. William H. McNeill, *The Rise of the West* (Chicago: University of Chicago Press, 1963), pp. 570–571.

3. S. B. Clough and C. W. Cole, *Economic History of Europe* (Boston: Heath, 1941), pp. 127–128.

4. Ibid.

5. R. H. Tawney, *Religion and the Rise of the West* (New York: Mentor Books, 1947), p. 117.

6. Immanuel Wallerstein, *The Modern World-System* (New York: Academic Press, 1974), especially chap. 2.

7. Tawney, p. 257.

8. James M. Wells, "The History of Printing," *Encyclopaedia Britannica*, vol. 18, p. 541.

9. Wells, pp. 541–542; and N. F. Blake, *Caxton: England's First Publisher* (New York: Barnes & Noble, 1976), chap. 1.

10. See, especially, Max Weber, *The Protestant Ethic and the Spirit of Capitalism*, trans. Talcott Parsons (New York: Scribner, 1958), or Reinhard Bendix, *Max Weber: An Intellectual Portrait* (Garden City, N.Y.: Doubleday, 1960), chaps. 3–8.

11. Tawney, pp. 92–93.

12. Clough and Cole, pp. 185–194.

13. Ibid., pp. 308–315.

14. See, for example, Robert Heilbroner, *The Making of Economic Society* (Englewood Cliffs, N.J.: Prentice-Hall, 1962), pp. 101–102.

15. See, for example, John Nef, *The Conquest of the Material World* (Chicago: University of Chicago Press, 1965), especially part 2.

16. If such refinements and improvements were included, it would be hard to avoid dating the start of the Industrial Revolution ten to fifteen thousand years ago, since technological progress of some kind, however slow, has been virtually continuous since then. One cannot use the criteria stated in the text above to date the *end* of the Industrial Revolution, since many societies have already reached the point where there is virtually no room for increase in the proportion of the population dependent on industrial activity or in the percentage of the gross national product obtained from this source, yet the revolution in the techniques and tools of

production is obviously continuing. The only standard we might use to mark the end of the Industrial Revolution would be a drastic slowing in the rate of technological innovation.

17. See especially Phyllis Deane and W. A. Cole, *British Growth 1688–1959: Trends and Structure* (London: Cambridge, 1962), chap. 2.
18. Paul Mantoux, *The Industrial Revolution in the Eighteenth Century*, rev. ed. (London: Cape, 1961), pp. 243–244.
19. Ibid., p. 312.
20. Earlier in the century, Thomas Savery and Thomas Newcomen invented the atmospheric engine, which laid the foundation for Watt's work. Its only practical use, however, was to pump water out of mines.
21. Deane and Cole, p. 212.
22. For 1788, see Clive Day, *Economic Development in Europe* (New York: Macmillan, 1942), p. 134; for 1840, see Deane and Cole, p. 225.
23. Deane and Cole, pp. 55 and 216.
24. W. S. Woytinsky and E. S. Woytinsky, *World Population and Production: Trends and Outlook* (New York: Twentieth Century Fund, 1953), p. 1147.
25. Ibid., tables 30 and 37.
26. U. S. Department of Commerce, Bureau of the Census, *Historical Statistics of the United States, Colonial Times to 1970*, series F238-239.
27. J. H. Clapham, *An Economic History of Modern Britain*, 2d ed. (London: Cambridge, 1930), vol. 1, pp. 391–392.
28. Clough and Cole, pp. 594–595.
29. Ibid., pp. 535–537.
30. Deane and Cole, p. 225.
31. Ibid., p. 216.
32. *Historical Statistics of the U.S.*, pp. 500–501.
33. Alfred D. Chandler, "Industrial Revolutions and Institutional Arrangements," *Bulletin of the American Academy of Arts and Sciences*, 33 (May, 1980), pp. 37–38.
34. Ibid., p. 38.
35. Clough and Cole, p. 538.
36. Calculated from Woytinsky and Woytinsky, p. 1003.
37. Chandler, pp. 40–45.
38. This figure is an estimate based on Clough and Cole's report of French production in 1902 (p. 773) and Woytinsky and Woytinsky's report of American production in 1900 and 1902 (p. 1168).
39. Woytinsky and Woytinsky, pp. 1165–1166, including fig. 328.
40. Ibid., p. 1164.
41. Ibid., p. 966.
42. The 1900 figure is estimated from information provided by Woytinsky and Woytinsky, pp. 897–900; the 1940 figure is from fig. 257, p. 897.
43. J. Frederic Dewhurst and Associates, *America's Needs and Resources* (New York: Twentieth Century Fund, 1955), p. 317; and U.S. Department of Commerce, Bureau of the Census, *Statistical Abstract of the United States, 1963*, p. 516.
44. Woytinsky and Woytinsky, p. 1171.
45. *Statistical Abstract of the U.S., 1963*, p. 586, and *Statistical Abstract of the U.S., 1979*, p. 667.
46. The 1938 figure is from United Nations, *Statistical Yearbook, 1951*, p. 261; the 1979 figure is from *UN Monthly Bulletin of Statistics*, 34 (February, 1980), pp. xxix and 80.
47. The figure for the late 1930s is based on Woytinsky and Woytinsky's statement about output in the United States and other countries in that period (p. 1201); the 1977 figure is from United Nations, *Statistical Yearbook, 1978*, pp. 306–309, but translated into short tons.
48. United Nations, *Statistical Yearbook, 1965*, p. 353.

49. *Statistical Abstract of the U.S., 1979*, p. 617.
50. *Newsweek,* June 30, 1980, p. 54.
51. Robert Cole, "The Japanese Lesson in Quality," *Technology Review,* 83 (July, 1981), p. 30
52. *Newsweek,* June 30, 1980, p. 55.
53. Figures for 1940 are from Woytinsky and Woytinsky, pp. 897, 966, and 1167; figures for 1980 are extrapolations from trends reported in *Statistical Abstract of the U.S., 1979*, p. 883.
54. J. L. Hammond and Barbara Hammond, *The Town Labourer: 1760–1830* (London: Guild Books, 1949, first published 1917), vol. 1, chap. 3.
55. Ibid., chaps. 2 and 6–9; or J. T. Ward (ed.), *The Factory System* (New York: Barnes & Noble, 1970), vols. I and II.
56. Hammond and Hammond, vol. I, pp. 32–33.
57. Compare and contrast the work of Hammond and Hammond, op. cit., or Eric Hobsbawm, "The British Standard of Living, 1790–1850," *Economic History Review,* 2d series, 10 (1957), pp. 46–61, with Thomas Ashton, "The Standard of Life of the Workers in England, 1790–1830," *Journal of Economic History,* 9 (1949), supplement, pp. 19–38.
58. *Historical Statistics of the U.S.,* series W-109; and *Statistical Abstract of the U.S., 1979*, p. 621.
59. See the high percentage of all research and development expenditures coming from the U.S. Department of Defense, *Statistical Abstract of the U.S., 1979*, table 1047.

Chapter 10

1. U.S. Department of Commerce, Bureau of the Census, *Historical Statistics of the United States: Colonial Times to 1970*, series D 152–153; and U.S. Department of Commerce, Bureau of the Census, *Statistical Abstract of the United States, 1979*, table 687.
2. J. Frederic Dewhurst and associates, *America's Needs and Resources* (New York: Twentieth Century Fund, 1955), p. 1116; and *Statistical Abstract of the U.S., 1979*, table 1008.
3. *Historical Statistics of the U.S.,* series S-1; and *Statistical Abstract of the U.S., 1979*, p. 600.
4. The 1750 figure is from W. S. Woytinsky and E. S. Woytinsky, *World Population and Production: Trends and Outlooks* (New York: Twentieth Century Fund, 1953), p. 1100; the 1970 figure is from *United Nations, Statistical Yearbook, 1971*, tables 121 and 122, and is converted to short tons.
5. The 1820 figure is from Woytinsky and Woytinsky, p. 1101; the 1970 figure is from *The World Almanac, 1976*, p. 109.
6. Production figures are from *The World Almanac, 1976*, p. 108. Per capita calculations are our own.
7. *Historical Statistics of the U.S.,* series F-3; and *Statistical Abstract of the U.S., 1979*, table 721.
8. Phyllis Deane and W. A. Cole, *British Economic Growth, 1688–1959* (London: Cambridge Press, 1962), tables 72 and 90; *Statistical Abstract of the U.S., 1979*, table 1554.
9. Robert Heilbroner, *The Worldly Philosophers*, rev. ed. (New York: Time Books, 1961), chap 3; and Jacob Viner, "Adam Smith," in *International Encyclopedia of the Social Sciences*, vol. 14, pp. 322–329.
10. Heilbroner, p. 47.
11. See, for example, Daniel Bell, "Socialism," in *International Encyclopedia of the Social Sciences*, vol. 14, pp. 506–532.
12. Maurice Duverger, *Political Parties: Their Organization and Activity in the*

Modern State, trans. Barbara North and Robert North (London: Methuen, 1959), pp. 118–119. Quoted by permission of Methuen & Company, Ltd.

13. Lewis Feuer (ed.), *Marx and Engels: Basic Writings on Politics and Philosophy* (Garden City, N.Y.: Doubleday, 1959), p. 127.

14. V. I. Lenin, *State and Revolution* (New York: International Publishers, 1932), p. 73.

15. Hans Kohn, "Nationalism," *International Encyclopedia of the Social Sciences*, vol. 11, p. 63–70.

16. Robert Bellah, "Civil Religion in America," *Daedalus*, 96 (Winter), pp. 1–21. See also Will Herberg, *Protestant-Catholic-Jew* (Garden City, N.Y.: Doubleday, 1955).

17. Thomas McKeown, *The Modern Rise of Population* (New York: Academic Press, 1976), p. 2.

18. Ibid., pp. 27–32.

19. *Statistical Abstract of the U.S., 1979*, table 96.

20. Ibid., table 99.

21. *The World Almanac, 1978*, p. 602.

22. For statistical analysis of data from contemporary societies, see Erich Weede, "Beyond Misspecification in Sociological Analyses of Income Inequality," in *American Sociological Review*, 45 (June 1980), pp. 497–501; for historical evidence, see Gerhard Lenski, *Power and Privilege* (New York: McGraw-Hill, 1966), chaps. 8–13.

23. *Forbes*, May 26, 1980, p. 137.

24. Edward Higbee, *Farms and Farmers in an Urban Age* (New York: Twentieth Century Fund; 1963).

25. Dan Morgan, "New Farming Frontier," *The Washington Post*, Oct. 20, 1974, pp. A1 and A4.

26. *Wall Street Journal*, Aug. 17, 1976, p. 1, and Apr. 7, 1977, p. 1.

27. Timo Toivonen and Stanislaw Widerszpil, "Changes in Socio-Economic and Class Structure," in Erik Allardt and Wlodzimierz Wesolowski (eds.), *Social Structure and Social Change: Finland and Poland* (Warsaw: Polish Scientific Publishers, 1978), p. 113.

28. *Statistical Abstract of the U.S., 1979*, table 670.

29. Ibid., tables 461 and 603.

30. Ibid., tables 512 and 519.

31. *Forbes*, op. cit.

32. U.S. Department of Labor, *Dictionary of Occupational Titles* (Washington, D.C.: Government Printing Office, 1965), vol. I, p. xv.

33. *Newsweek*, Mar. 26, 1973, p. 79.

34. Pehr Gyllenhammar, "Volvo's Solution to the Blue Collar Blues," *Business and Society* (Autumn 1973).

35. S. B. Clough and C. W. Cole, *Economic History of Europe* (Boston; Heath, 1941), pp. 693–698.

36. G. D. H. Cole, *A Short History of the British Working Class Movement* (New York: Macmillan, 1927), vol. II, p. 202; and Carroll P. Daugherty, *Labor Problems in American Industry* (Boston: Houghton Mifflin, 1941), p. 405.

37. G. Warren Nutter, "Industrial Concentration," in *International Encyclopedia of the Social Sciences* (New York: Macmillan and Free Press, 1968), vol. 7, p. 221.

38. Ben Bagdikian, "Why Newspapers Keep Dying," *Washington Post*, July 23, 1972, p. B-5.

39. John Kenneth Galbraith, *The New Industrial State* (New York: Signet, 1968), pp. 38–39.

40. Peter C. Dooley, "The Interlocking Directorates," *American Economic Review*, 59 (1969), pp. 314–323.

41. Paul Samuelson, *Economics*, 6th ed. (New York: McGraw-Hill, 1964), p. 36 and chaps. 8 and 9.

42. Clough and Cole, p. 148ff., or Edward S. Mason, "Corporation," in *International Encyclopedia of the Social Sciences,* vol. 3, pp. 396–403.
43. Statistics based on data in *Statistical Abstract of the U.S., 1979,* table 915.
44. *Forbes,* May 12, 1980, pp. 214 and 236.
45. See Robert A. Gordon, *Business Leadership in the Large Corporation* (Berkeley: University of California Press, 1961); or Edward S. Mason (ed.), *The Corporation and Modern Society* (Cambridge: Harvard Press, 1959) on American corporations; and P. Sargant Florence, *Ownership, Control, and Success of Large Companies* (London: Street and Maxwell, 1961); or David Granick, *The European Executive* (Garden City, N.Y.: Doubleday Anchor, 1964) on European corporations.
46. J. Frederic Dewhurst et al., *Europe's Needs and Resources* (New York: Twentieth Century Fund, 1961), pp. 436–440.
47. See, for example, Alec Nove, *The Soviet Economy,* rev. ed. (New York: Praeger, 1966), especially chap. 9; or Harry G. Shaffer, *The Communist World* (New York: Appleton-Century-Crofts, 1967), p. 226ff.
48. Nove, pp. 28–29.
49. Jan Szczepański, *Polish Society* (New York: Random House, 1970), p. 79.
50. Galbraith, chap. 9.
51. Hedrick Smith, *The Russians* (New York: Quadrangle, 1976), p. 239.
52. Ibid., chap. 9.
53. Robert J. Osborn, *Soviet Social Policies* (Homewood, Ill.: Dorsey, 1970), pp. 137–139; or Osborn, *The Evolution of Soviet Politics* (Homewood, Ill.: Dorsey, 1974), pp. 381–382.
54. Szczepański, p. 125. Quoted by permission.
55. Joseph Alsop, "Matter of Fact," *Washington Post,* Jan. 13, 1964, op-ed page.
56. Soviet scholars disagree sharply with this view. For their view, see Alex Simirenko (ed.), *Soviet Sociology* (Chicago: Quadrangle, 1966), pp. 327–339.
57. Jean Marchal and Bernard Ducros (eds.), *The Distribution of National Income* (London: MacMillan, 1968), pp. xiii–xiv and 274.
58. Richard Easterlin, "Economic Growth," in *International Encyclopedia of the Social Sciences,* vol. 4, p. 405.
59. Calculations based on United Nations, *Statistical Yearbook, 1965,* table 148, and *Statistical Abstract of the U.S., 1979,* table 1539.

Chapter 11

1. In Sweden, for example, property restrictions on the franchise were not finally eliminated until after World War I. See Dankwort Rustow, *The Politics of Compromise: A Study of Parties and Cabinet Government in Sweden* (Princeton, N.J.: Princeton Press, 1955), pp. 84–85.
2. Jan Szczepański, *Polish Society* (New York: Random House, 1970), p. 73; and Robert J. Osborn, *The Evolution of Soviet Politics* (Homewood, Ill.: Dorsey, 1974), p. 266.
3. Robert J. Osborn, *Soviet Social Policies* (Homewood, Ill.: Dorsey, 1970), chap. 4.
4. See, for example, Lidia Beskid, Antti Karisto, and Hannu Uusitalo, "Income and Consumption," in Erik Allardt and Wlodzimierz Wesolowski (eds.), *Social Structure and Change: Finland and Poland* (Warsaw: Polish Scientific Publishers, 1978), pp. 252–257.
5. William Welsh, "The Status of Research on Representative Institutions in Eastern Europe," *Legislative Studies Quarterly,* 5 (May 1980), pp. 275–308.
6. Maurice Simon, personal communication.
7. Kenneth A. Bollen, "Political Democracy and the Timing of Development," *American Sociological Review,* 44 (August 1979), pp. 572–587.

8. Many recent studies have documented the relationship between high rates of literacy and education on the one hand and democratic government on the other. See, for example, Daniel Lerner, *The Passing of Traditional Society: Modernizing the Middle East* (New York: Free Press, 1958), especially pp. 63–64 and 86–89; or S. M. Lipset, *Political Man* (Garden City, N.Y.: Doubleday, 1960), pp. 53–58.

9. On the relationship between democracy and the development of the mass media, see Lerner, op. cit., and Lipset, pp. 51–52.

10. See, for example, Kurt Shell, *The Transformation of Austrian Socialism* (New York: University Publishers, 1962), especially chaps. 6 and 7; Rustow, chap. 8; Albert Parry, *The New Class Divided: Science and Technology vs. Communism* (New York: Macmillan, 1966), chap. 7; and John Reshetar, *The Soviet Polity* (New York: Dodd, Mead, 1971), pp. 218–225.

11. Ivo Feierabend and Rosalind Feierabend, "Aggressive Behaviors within Polities, 1948–1962: A Cross-National Study," *Journal of Conflict Resolution*, 10 (1966), table 3. The measure used is Yule's Q. Results of this study suggest that rates of political instability are greatest in societies making the transition from agrarian to industrial, though results were not statistically significant. See the term "correlation coefficient" in the Glossary for an explanation of the coefficient 0.965.

12. The figures shown in Table 11.3 are based on our own calculations, using the following sources: Robert Alford, *Party and Society* (Chicago: Rand McNally, 1963), pp. 136, 202–203, 234–235, and 274–275; Richard Rose (ed.), *Electoral Behavior: A Comparative Handbook* (New York: Free Press, 1974), pp. 147, 294, 334, and 398; Hannu Uusitalo, "Class Structure and Party Choice: A Scandinavian Comparison," Research Report No. 10 (1975), Research Group for Comparative Sociology, University of Helsinki, p. 21; Roy Pierce, *French Politics and Political Institutions* (New York: Harper & Row, 1968), table 10; Richard Rose, "Class and Party Divisions: Britain as a Test Case," *Sociology*, 2 (1968), pp. 129–162; Erik Allardt and Yrjö Littunen (eds.), *Cleavages, Ideologies and Party Systems: Contributions to Comparative Political Sociology*, in a series entitled *Transactions of the Westermarck Society* (Helsinki: The Academic Bookstore, 1964), vol. 10, pp. 102 and 212; S. M. Lipset, *Political Man* (Garden City, N.Y.: Doubleday, 1960), pp. 225 and 227; Morris Janowitz, "Social Stratification and Mobility in West Germany," *American Journal of Sociology*, 64 (1958), p. 22; and *Gallup Political Index*, Report No. 17 (October 1966), p. 15 and inside back cover.

13. See, for example, Lipset, chaps. 2 and 4.

14. *Statistical Abstract of the U.S., 1979*, table 450; and *Historical Statistics of the United States: Colonial Times to 1970*, series Y 308. Similar trends are reported in other countries. In France, for example, civil servants increased from 3.7 per cent of the labor force in 1866 to 16.7 per cent in 1962. See Jacques Lecaillon, "Changes in the Distribution of Income in the French Economy," in Jean Marchal and Bernard Ducros (eds.), *The Distribution of National Income* (London: Macmillan, 1968), pp. 45 and 47.

15. *Statistical Abstract of the U.S., 1979*, table 509; and *Historical Statistics of the United States: Colonial Times to 1970*, series Y 332.

16. David Lane and George Kolankiewicz, *Social Groups in Polish Society* (New York: Columbia University Press, 1973), pp. 255ff. and 310–311; David Lane, *The Socialist Industrial State* (London: George Allen & Unwin, 1976), p. 29ff.; and Osborn, *The Evolution of Soviet Politics*, p. 281ff.

17. See, for example, the statements of Lenin and Trotsky, quoted by David Lane, *The End of Inequality?: Stratification Under State Socialism* (Baltimore: Penguin, 1971), p. 41; and Robert Osborn, *The Evolution of Soviet Politics* (Homewood, Ill.: Dorsey, 1974), p. 281.

18. *Encyclopaedia Britannica*, 23, pp. 716 and 800.

19. *Washington Post*, Nov. 9, 1976, p. 1.

20. On the lower classes in Soviet society, see Andrei Amalrik, *Involuntary Journey to*

Siberia, trans. Manya Harari and Max Hayward (New York: Harcourt, Brace, Jovanovich, 1970), chap. 5ff. On the more favored classes, see Roy Medvedev, *Let History Judge: The Origins and Consequences of Stalinism*, trans. Colleen Taylor, David Joravsky, and Georges Haupt (eds.) (New York: Knopf, 1971), pp. 540–541; or Smith, chap. 1.

21. Medvedev, p. 540.
22. Personal communication by informed East European social scientists.
23. See Szczepański, pp. 95 and 137–138.
24. Ibid., pp. 113–124.
25. These figures are our own calculations and are based on data in *Statistical Abstract of the U.S., 1979*, tables 772, 774, and 777.
26. One recent report indicates that one-third of the equity capital of the United States' publicly owned companies is owned by employee pension funds. See Peter F. Drucker, "American Business's New Owners," *Wall Street Journal*, May 27, 1976.
27. For the U.S., see Herbert E. Alexander, *Financing the 1972 Election* (Lexington Books, 1976), p. 77; for Japan, see Associated Press, "Japan's Parties Rake in Millions via Loophole," *The Washington Post*, Sept. 11, 1980, p. A26.
28. See Benjamin Bradlee, *Conversations with the President* (New York: Norton, 1975), p. 218.
29. On Canada, see John Porter, *The Vertical Mosaic: An Analysis of Social Class and Power in Canada* (Toronto: University of Toronto Press, 1965), part II, especially chaps. 7–9 and 12–13; on France, see Henry Ehrmann, *Organized Business in France* (Princeton, N.J.: Princeton University Press, 1957), chap. 5; on Britain, see Bernard Nossiter, "Cozy Conflicts of Interest in Britain," *Washington Post*, Nov. 25, 1975, p. A-15; on Japan, see the many accounts of the scandals involving former Prime Minister Tanaka.
30. See Lars Björn, "Labor Parties, Economic Growth, and the Redistribution of Income in Five Capitalist Democracies," *Comparative Social Research, 2 (1979)*, pp. 93–128.
31. Milovan Djilas, *The New Class: An Analysis of the Communist System* (New York: Praeger, 1959), especially pp. 37–39. For a more recent treatment of the subject by a Soviet author and former Party member, see Medvedev, op. cit. Although Medvedev focuses on the Stalin era, and refrains from using the term "new class," the situation he describes is strikingly similar to Djilas's description, and it is clear that he regards the problem as a continuing one.
32. Estimates of the number of *apparatchiki* range from 100,000 to 300,000. See Jerry Hough, "The Party Apparatchiki," in H. Gordon Skilling and Franklyn Griffiths (eds.), *Interest Groups in Soviet Politics* (Princeton, N.J.: Princeton University Press, 1971), p. 49; John Reshetar, *The Soviet Polity* (New York: Dodd Mead, 1971), p. 170; and Mervyn Matthews, *Class and Society in Soviet Russia* (New York: Walker, 1972), p. 213. With spouses and children, the group might total 750,000 at most, or 0.33 per cent of the population. For Poland, the comparable figures are 7,800 *apparatchiki* and perhaps 30,000 members of the immediate families, or 0.1 per cent of the total population. See Jerzy Wiatr and A. Przeworski, "Control Without Opposition," in J. Wiatr (ed.), *Studies of the Polish Political System* (Wroclaw: Ossolineum, 1967), p. 148.
33. Mervyn Matthews, *Privilege in the Soviet Union* (London: G. Allen, 1978), pp. 34–35.
34. David Granick, *The Red Executive* (Garden City, N.Y.: Doubleday Anchor, 1961), pp. 22–23.
35. Matthews, *Class and Society in Soviet Russia*, p. 226.
36. Ibid., p. 227ff.
37. See, for example, Amalrik, op. cit.; Medvedev, op. cit.; Zhores Medvedev and Roy Medvedev, *A Question of Madness* (New York: Knopf, 1971); or Alexander Solzhenitsyn, *The Gulag Archipelago* (New York: Harper & Row, 1974).

38. *New York Times*, June 10, 1964, p. 25.
39. See, for example, Senator Russell Long's comments on the hearings on the unethical conduct of Senator Thomas Dodd. He stated that at least half of the senators who were on the committee investigating Dodd could not stand a similar investigation. For an earlier study of the use of political power for private gain, see Harold Zink, *City Bosses in the United States* (Durham, N.C.: Duke, 1930), pp. 37–38. See also the evidence uncovered in the Koreagate and Abscam scandals.
40. See, for example, Maurice Duverger, *Political Parties*, trans. Barbara North and Robert North (London: Methuen, 1959), p. 114; or Angus Campbell et al., *The American Voter* (New York: Wiley, 1960), pp. 90–93.
41. *Statistical Abstract of the U.S., 1979*, table 835.
42. Osborn, *Soviet Social Policies*, chap. 4; Matthews, *Class and Society in Soviet Russia*, chap. 10; and Joseph R. Fiszman, *Revolution and Tradition in People's Poland* (Princeton, N.J.: Princeton University Press, 1972), chap. 3.
43. See, for example, Alexander Matejko, "From Peasant into Worker in Poland," *International Review of Sociology*, 3 (1971), pp. 27–75.
44. *Statistical Abstract of the U.S., 1979*, table 230.
45. See, for example, R. Barry Farrell, *Political Leadership in Eastern Europe* (Chicago: Aldine, 1970), table 5/1.
46. For a popular account of the role of the educational elite in Soviet society and its intrusion into politics, see Albert Parry, *The New Class Divided* (New York: Macmillan, 1966); and Skillings and Griffiths, chap. 7.
47. *Statistical Abstract of the U.S., 1979*, table 746.
48. Ibid.
49. Members of minority groups usually adopt the dominant group's prestige evaluations for groups other than their own. Sometimes they even adopt its evaluation of their own group. See, for example, Emory Bogardus, *Social Distance* (Yellow Springs, Ohio: Antioch Press, 1959), pp. 26–29.
50. See, for example, Everett C. Hughes, *French Canada in Transition* (Chicago: University of Chicago Press, 1943), especially chap. 7. See also Porter, *The Vertical Mosaic*, chap. 3.
51. Calculated from Donald Matthews, *U.S. Senators and Their World* (Chapel Hill: University of North Carolina Press, 1960), fig. 1.
52. W. Lloyd Warner and James Abeggien, *Occupational Mobility in American Business and Industry, 1928–1952* (Minneapolis: University of Minnesota Press, 1955), p. 30; and Mabel Newcomer, *The Big Business Executive* (New York: Columbia, 1955), p. 112.
53. Calculated from Morris Janowitz, *The Professional Soldier* (New York: Free Press, 1960), p. 63; and Robert Lampman, *The Share of Top Wealth-Holders in National Wealth: 1922–1956* (Princeton, N.J.: Princeton University Press, 1962), tables 48 and 49.
54. *Statistical Abstract of the U.S., 1979*, table 772.
55. William J. Goode, *World Revolution and Family Patterns* (New York: Free Press, 1963), p. 55.
56. Janet Schwartz, "Women Under Socialism," *Social Forces*, 58 (September 1979), table 1.
57. U.S. Department of Commerce, Bureau of the Census, *Historical Statistics of the United States: Colonial Times to 1957* (Washington, 1960), p. 71.
58. Calculations based on *Statistical Abstract, 1979*, tables 29, 644, and 651.
59. Ibid., table 687.
60. Hilary Land, "The Changing Place of Women in Europe," *Daedalus*, 108 (Spring 1979), p. 84.
61. Susan Okie, "Women Lagging in Medicine," *The Washington Post*, Aug. 7, 1975, p. A-4.
62. Schwartz, p. 75.
63. New York Times News Service release, Sept. 2, 1979.

64. Schwartz, p. 83.
65. Michael Pohoski, "Socio-Economic Achievement in Poland," unpublished manuscript.
66. Land, p. 80; Schwartz, p. 75; and *Statistical Abstract of the U.S., 1979*, table 691.
67. For a good summary of much of this, see Beth Vanfossen, *The Structure of Social Inequality* (Boston: Little, Brown, 1979), or Robert Rothman, *Inequality and Stratification in the United States* (Englewood Cliffs, N.J.: Prentice-Hall, 1978).
68. *Statistical Abstract of the U.S., 1979*, table 100.
69. See, for example, A. B. Hollingshead, *Elmtown's Youth* (New York: Wiley, 1949); St. Clair Drake and Horace Cayton, *Black Metropolis* (New York: Harcourt, Brace & World, 1945); Elliot Liebow, *Tally's Corner* (Boston: Little, Brown, 1967).
70. Calculated from U.S. Department of Commerce, Bureau of the Census, *Current Population Reports*, series P-23, no. 11 (May 1964), table 1.
71. A few surveys indicate an excess of downward mobility, but there is reason to believe that these results sometimes are owing to the failure to ensure that respondents report their father's occupation when he was *their* age. This is important, because mobility also occurs within careers, and here, too, upward mobility is more common than downward.
72. Gerhard Lenski, *Power and Privilege: A Theory of Social Stratification* (New York: McGraw-Hill, 1966), p. 228.
73. On the United States, see Edwin Sutherland, *White Collar Crime* (New York: Holt, 1949). On the Soviet Union, see Amalrik, op. cit.; or Medvedev and Medevdev, op. cit.
74. Lenski, pp. 308–313.
75. See ibid., pp. 313–318, for a more thorough discussion of this subject.
76. L. J. Zimmerman, *Poor Lands, Rich Lands: The Widening Gap* (New York: Random House, 1965), table 2.8, p. 38.

Chapter 12

1. Urie Bronfenbrenner, "The Disturbing Changes in the American Family," *Search* (Fall 1976), pp. 11–14.
2. U.S. Department of Commerce, Bureau of the Census, *Historical Statistics of the United States: Colonial Times to 1970*, p. 53.
3. This is our own calculation based on 603 hunting and gathering, horticultural, fishing, and herding societies in Murdock's data set of 915 societies (see p. 91). We have omitted 104 hybrid societies, most of which were preagrarian. If these were included, the figure would rise to 15 per cent.
4. U.S. Department of Commerce, Bureau of the Census, *Statistical Abstract of the United States, 1979*, table 80.
5. Calculations based on Warren Thompson and David Lewis, *Population Problems*, 5th ed. (New York: McGraw-Hill, 1965), p. 374; J. Bourgeois-Pichat, "The General Development of the Population of France Since the Eighteenth Century," in D. V. Glass and D. E. C. Eversley (eds.), *Population in History* (Chicago: Aldine, 1965), p. 498; and W. S. Woytinsky and E. S. Woytinsky, *World Population and Production: Trends and Outlooks* (New York: Twentieth Century Fund, 1953), p. 181.
6. Mary Jo Bane, *Here to Stay* (New York: Basic Books, 1976), table 2-2.
7. *Statistical Abstract of the U.S., 1979*, table 70.
8. Ibid.
9. In this section we have drawn heavily on suggestions provided by Joan Huber and on two of her papers, "Toward a Socio-Technological Theory of the Women's Movement," *Social Problems*, 23 (April 1976), and "The Future of Parenthood: Implications of Declining Fertility," in Dana Hiller and Robin Sheets (eds.),

Women and Men (Cincinnati: University of Cincinnati Press, 1976), pp, 333–351.

10. Hedrick Smith, *The Russians* (New York: Quadrangle, 1976), chap. 5.

11. United Press International news release, June 1, 1980, and Robin Morgan, "The First Feminist Exiles from the U.S.S.R," *Ms.* (November 1980), pp. 49–108.

12. Michael Getler, "Emancipation for E. German Women," *Washington Post,* Apr. 24, 1979, p. A-13, and Smith, p. 130.

13. Getler, ibid.

14. Ibid.

15. Joann Lublin, "As Women's Roles Grow More Like Men's, so Do Their Problems," *Wall Street Journal*, Jan 14, 1980, pp. 1 and 29.

16. Ibid.

17. Calculation based on *Statistical Abstract of the U.S., 1979*, table 222.

18. See, for example, Randall Collins, "Functional and Conflict Theories of Educational Stratification," *American Sociological Review*, 36 (1971), pp. 1002–1019.

19. In 1977, there were 245,000 babies born to unmarried teenage mothers in the United States (*Statistical Abstract of the U.S., 1979*, table 93). In addition, many more pregnancies were terminated by abortion.

20. Bronfenbrenner, p. 2.

21. Lynn Langway and William Schmidt, "A Youthquake in Russia," *Newsweek*, July 7, 1980, p. 46. See, also, Smith, chap. 7.

22. Walter Connor, *Deviance in Soviet Society: Crime, Delinquency, and Alcoholism* (New York: Columbia, 1972), p. 153.

23. *Statistical Abstract of the U.S., 1979*, table 311.

24. See, for example, Richard Quinney, *The Social Reality of Crime* (Boston: Little, Brown, 1970).

25. Connor, p. 93ff.

26. Ibid.

27. U.S. Department of Commerce, Bureau of the Census, *Social Indicators, 1976*, table 10/1.

28. Christopher Sterling and Timothy Haight, *The Mass Media: Aspen Institute Guide to Communication Industry Trends* (New York: Praeger, 1978), p. 374.

29. Bane, p. 15; and Bronfenbrenner, p. 13.

30. Erik Barnouw, *A History of Broadcasting in the United States*, vol. 3, *The Image Empire: From 1950* (New York: Oxford University Press, 1970).

31. Thomas E. Patterson, *The Mass Media Election: How Americans Choose Their President* (New York: Praeger, 1980). The information in this paragraph is based on a prepublication summary of the study, "The Role of the Mass Media in Presidential Campaigns," Social Science Research Council *Items*, 34 (June 1980), pp. 25–30.

32. See, for example, Walter Laqueur, *Terrorism* (Boston: Little, Brown, 1977), p. 109ff.

33. Barry Siegel, "TV on Trial," *The Washington Post*, July 8, 1980, p. A-6.

34. Emphasis added.

35. William Raspberry, "The Welfare Trap," *The Washington Post*, July 11, 1980, op-ed page; see also National Urban League, *Black Progress; Black Regression* (New York: National Urban League, 1980).

Chapter 13

1. These figures are medians. The calculations are based on United Nations, *Yearbook of National Accounts Statistics*, table 3, and Food and Agriculture Organization of the United Nations, *Production Yearbook, 1970,* table 5. Here, as

elsewhere in this chapter, we have ignored the new microstates such as Kuwait, Gabon, and Mauritania,

2. John Saar, "Indonesia Battles Disasterous Birth Explosion," *The Washington Post*, Dec. 18, 1975, p. A-20.

3. Manfred Halpern, *The Politics of Social Change in the Middle East and North Africa* (Princeton, N.J.: Princeton, 1963), p. 80.

4. Ibid.

5. See Glossary for an explanation of correlation coefficients. The study cited was Bruce Russett et al., *World Handbook of Political and Social Indicators* (New Haven, Conn.: Yale, 1964), p. 277, and was based on data from fifty-five societies.

6. Gladwin Hill, "View of the World's Shantytowns Less Grim," *New York Times*, June 9, 1976, p. 4.

7. Olga Tellis, "India Proposes Sterilization," *Washington Post*, Mar. 31, 1976, p. A-1.

8. Barry Kramer, "The Politics of Birth Control," *Wall Street Journal*, May 8, 1978, editorial page. See also Stuart Auerbach, "Family Planning—India's New Orphan," *The Washington Post*, Aug. 7, 1980, p. A-26.

9. Jay Mathews, "China Pressures Couples to Have Only One Child," *The Washington Post*, Feb. 28, 1980, p. A-20.

10. Ibid. See, also, Chen Muhua, "Birth Planning in China," *Family Planning Perspectives*, 11 (Nov/Dec., 1979), pp. 348–354.

11. June Shaplen and Robert Shaplen, "Taking on the Tide," *New York Times Magazine*, Aug. 27, 1976, p. 62.

12. Alex Inkles and David Smith, *Becoming Modern: Change in Six Developing Countries* (Cambridge, Mass.: Harvard, 1974, or Alex Inkeles, "Making Men Modern," *American Journal of Sociology*, 75 (September 1969), pp. 208–225.

13. Ray Vicker, "Arab Industrialization Adds to the Problems of Western Producers," *Wall Street Journal*, July 9, 1980, p. 1.

14. U.S. Department of Commerce, Bureau of the Census, *Statistical Abstract of the United States, 1979*, p. 895; also personal communication from Cuban-American sociologist following return visit to Cuba in 1979.

15. Marlise Simons, "Cuba Reviving Market Forces to Lift Economy," *The Washington Post*, May 29, 1980, p. A-15; Jay Mathews, "China Ventures into Shoals of Supply and Demand," ibid., Oct. 30, 1980, p. A-27.

16. See, for example, A. H. Hanson, *The Process of Planning: A Study of India's Five-Year Plans, 1950–1964* (London: Oxford University Press, 1966), part II, especially chap. 8; Peter Franck, "Economic Planners," in Sydney Fisher (ed.), *Social Forces in the Middle East* (Ithaca, N.Y.: Cornell, 1955), pp. 137–161; Louis Walinsky, *Economic Development in Burma, 1951–1960* (New York: Twentieth Century Fund, 1962), part V, especially chap. 29; or Lennox A. Mills, *Southeast Asia* (Minneapolis: University of Minnesota Press, 1964), chap. 11.

17. On Cuba, see Simons, op. cit.; on China, see Martin K. Whyte, "Destratification and Restratification in China," *Amsterdams Sociologisch Tijdschrift*, 5 (October 1978), p. 242–243; Jay Mathews, "China Propagandizes in Favor of Material Incentives," *The Washington Post*, Dec. 30, 1977, p. A-13; Robert Keatley, "China's New Economic Policy," *Wall Street Journal*, Sept. 22, 1977, editorial page; or Frank Ching, "Ex-Industrialists of Shanghai Contribute Money, Expertise to China's Development," ibid., Jan. 8, 1980, p. 6.

18. Elizabeth Becker, "Renewed Fighting Pushes Vietnam Deeper into Poverty," *The Washington Post*, Sept. 26, 1979, pp. A-1 and A-16.

19. Yilmaz Esmer, "Political Mobilization and Economic Development," in John Meyer and Michael Hannan (eds.), *National Development and the World System* (Chicago: University of Chicago Press, 1979), chap. 7; and Richard Rubinson, "Dependence, Government Revenue, and Economic Growth," ibid., chap. 12. See also David Apter, *The Politics of Modernization* (Chicago: University of

Chicago Press, 1965); S. M. Lipset, *The First New Nation* (New York: Basic Books, 1963); and Daniel Chirot, *Social Change in the Twentieth Century* (New York: Harcourt, Brace, Jovanovich, 1977).

20. International Labour Office, *Yearbook of Labour Statistics, 1971,* table 2A; and Food and Agriculture Organization of the United Nations, *Production Yearbook, 1970,* table 5.

21. See, for example, Myron Weiner, *Party Building in a New Nation: The Indian National Congress* (Chicago: University of Chicago Press, 1967).

22. Neil Smelser and S. M. Lipset (eds.), *Social Structure and Mobility in Economic Development* (Chicago: Aldine, 1966), p. 29ff. Statistics cited in this paragraph are from the same source.

23. John Meyer et al., "National Economic Development, 1950–70," in Meyer and Hannan, chap. 6, or Russett et al., p. 277.

24. Smelser and Lipset, p. 37, and Jan Szczepanski, *Polish Society* (New York: Random House, 1970), table 15, p. 115.

25. Smelser and Lipset, p. 37.

26. Halpern, p. 122.

27. Henry A. Landsberger (ed.), *Latin American Peasant Movements* (Ithaca, N.Y.: Cornell University Press, 1969).

28. For Latin America, see Robert E. Scott, "Political Elites and Political Modernization: The Crisis of Transition," in Lipset and Solari, p. 133.

29. See, for example, F. G. Bailey, *Tribe, Caste, and Nation* (Manchester, England: Manchester University Press, 1960), on the assimilation of hill tribes in India.

30. David Ottaway, "Tanzania Struggles in Vain to Meet the Needs of Its Poor," *The Washington Post,* Feb. 3, 1979, p. A-10.

31. *Statistical Abstract of the U.S., 1979,* table 1546.

32. Calculations are based on United Nations, *Demographic Yearbook, 1970,* table 9. The figures provided here are medians for eleven industrializing horticultural societies and thirty-three industrializing agrarian societies.

33. These calculations are our own and are based on data contained in *The World Almanac, 1978,* pp. 511–594.

34. *Statistical Abstract of the U.S., 1979,* table 1554.

35. See, for example, David Ottaway, "Ghana's Prosperity Feeds Corruption," *The Washington Post,* Jan. 29, 1978, p. A-27; or Leon Dash, "IMF Seeks to Aid Ruined Economy," ibid., Jan. 1, 1980, p. A-1.

36. Daniel Bell, "Socialism," *International Encyclopedia of the Social Sciences* (New York: Macmillan and Free Press, 1968), vol. 14, p. 529.

37. Ottaway, "Tanzania Struggles," op. cit.

38. See, for example, Gwendolen Carter (ed.), *African One-Party States* (Ithaca, N.Y.: Cornell, 1962), pp. 371ff. and 461ff; Guy Hunter, *The New Societies of Africa* (New York: Oxford University Press, 1964), chap. 9, especially p. 223ff.; International Bank for Reconstruction and Development, *The Economic Development of Uganda* (Baltimore: Johns Hopkins, 1962), pp. 23–24; or Ken Post, *The New States of West Africa* (Baltimore: Penguin, 1964), chap. 6.

39. Calculations based on *Statistical Abstract of the U.S., 1979,* table 1549.

40. Russett et al., table 65, provides data on the average annual increase in the rate of literacy for forty-three countries since about 1920. The median increase is 0.7 per cent per year; only nine of the forty-three countries had a rate in excess of 1 per cent.

41. Based on Inter-African Labour Institute, *The Human Factors of Productivity in Africa*, as summarized in William H. Lewis (ed.), *French-speaking Africa: The Search for Identity* (New York: Walker, 1965), p. 168. Many of these propositions were supported in papers presented to a recent conference on competing demands for labor in traditional African societies, cosponsored by the Joint Committee on African Studies of the Social Science Research Council, the American Council of Learned Societies, and the Agricultural Development Coun-

cil. See William O. Jones, "Labor and Leisure in Traditional African Societies," *Social Science Research Council Items*, 22 (March 1968), pp. 1–6.

42. See, for example, J. L. Hammond and Barbara Hammond, *The Town Labourer, 1760–1832* (London: Guild Books, 1949, first published 1917), especially chap. 2.

43. On the latter, see, for example, J. A. K. Leslie's fascinating study, *A Survey of Dar es Salaam* (New York: Oxford Univeristy Press, 1963).

44. Hunter, p. 85.

45. Ibid., p. 94.

46. See, for example, Aristide Zolberg, *One-Party Government in the Ivory Coast* (Princeton, N.J.: Princeton, 1964), pp. 202ff. and 286ff.; Hunter, pp. 286–298; or Lucy Mair, *New Nations* (Chicago: University of Chicago Press, 1963), pp. 114–122.

47. See, for example, Brian Weinstein, *Gabon: Nation-building on the Ogooue* (Cambridge, Mass.: M.I.T., 1966).

48. See Leslie, p. 32; or Merran Fraenkel, *Tribe and Class in Monrovia* (London: Oxford University Press, 1964), especially chap. 3.

49. See Apter, *The Politics of Modernization*, pp. 130 and 328–330; or Hunter, p. 289.

50. Mair, p. 122ff.

51. David Lamb "Africans Find Independence a Hard Road," *Los Angeles Times*, story reprinted in *Wall Street Journal*, Feb. 15, 1979, p. 15.

52. Ibid.

53. Ibid., p. 289. See also Bell, pp. 528–529.

54. *World Almanac, 1978*, pp. 517, 518, and 594.

55. The figure for Dar es Salaam is from Leslie, p. 210, and that for Tanzania from Russett et al., tables 74 and 75.

56. Fraenkel, p. 154; and Russett et al., tables 74 and 75.

57. From *A Survey of Dar es Salaam*, p. 211, by J. A. K. Leslie, published by Oxford University Press, 1963. By permission of the Oxford University Press.

58. Ibid., pp. 210–211.

59. Fraenkel, pp. 158 and 162.

60. Hunter, p. 74, provides numerous examples.

61. Carter, pp. 433–434. Copyright 1962 by Cornell University. Used by permission of Cornell University Press.

62. See, for example, Vittorio Lanternari, *The Religions of the Oppressed: A Study of Modern Messianic Cults*, trans. Lisa Sergio (New York: Knopf, 1963), chap. 1; or Mair, p. 171ff.

63. The same has been true of Sekou Touré's Democratic Party in Guinea. See, for example, Apter, p. 299, note 36.

64. Ibid., chap. 8.

65. L. A. Fallers (ed.), *The King's Men: Leadership and Status in Buganda on the Eve of Independence* (New York: Oxford University Press, 1964), p. 99.

66. From *A Survey of Dar es Salaam*, pp. 27–29, by J. A. K. Leslie, published by Oxford University Press. By permission of Oxford University Press.

67. Ibid., pp. 60–61; or Fraenkel, p. 127ff.

68. See, for example, Andre Gunder Frank, *Capitalism and Underdevelopment in Latin America* (New York: Monthly Review Press, 1969); Theotonio Dos Santos, "The Structure of Dependence," *American Economic Review* 60 (May 1970), pp. 231–236; or Celso Furtado, *Economic Development of Latin America* (Cambridge: Cambridge University Press, 1970).

69. Compare, for example, Frank, op. cit., with Johan Galtung, "A Structural Theory of Imperialism," *Journal of Peace Research*, 8 (1971), pp. 81–117.

70. See, for example, W. W. Rostow, *The Process of Economic Growth* (New York: Norton, 1962); Wilbert Moore and David Feldman, *Labor Commitment and Social Change in Developing Areas* (New York: Social Science Research Council,

1960); S. N. Eisenstadt, *Modernization* (Englewood Cliffs, N.J.: Prentice-Hall, 1966); Talcott Parsons, *The System of Modern Societies* (Englewood Cliffs, N.J.: Prentice-Hall, 1971); or Inkeles and Smith, op. cit.

Chapter 14.

1. See, for example, Jacques Ellul, *The Technological Society*, trans. John Wilkinson (New York: Vintage Books, 1967).

2. George R. Scott, *The History of Capital Punishment* (London: Torchstream Books, 1950), pp. 39–40.

3. Dover Wilson, *The Essential Shakespeare*, as quoted by Ivor Brown, *Shakespeare* (New York: Time Books, 1962), p. 112.

4. See, for example, Colin Turnbull, *The Forest People* (New York: Simon and Schuster, 1961); John Garvan, *The Negritos of the Philippines* (Vienna: Ferdinand Berger, 1964); or Kenneth MacLeish, "The Tasadays: Stone Age Men of the Philippines," *National Geographic*, 142 (1972), pp. 218–249.

5. Friedrich Engels, *Herr Eugen Dühring's Revolution in Science (Anti-Dühring)* (New York: International Publishers, 1939, first published 1878), as quoted by D. G. Brennan in Foreign Policy Association (ed.), *Toward the Year 2018* (New York: Cowles, 1958), p. 2.

6. M. King Hubbert, "Survey of World Energy Resources," in Lon C. Ruedisili and Morris Firebaugh (eds.), *Perspectives on Energy* (New York: Oxford, 1975), pp. 103–104.

7. Duncan Spencer, "Oceans, Pollution Prompting Weather Surprises," *Washington Star News Service*, Sept. 17, 1979, and Arlen J. Large, "Weather Report: More Heat," *Wall Street Journal*, Aug. 1, 1980, p. 12.

8. Jean A. Briggs, "Solar Power—for Real," *Forbes*, Oct. 13, 1980, pp. 142–146.

9. Wolfgang Sassin, "Energy," *Scientific American*, 243 (September 1980), p. 129.

10. Elias P. Gyftopoulous, "Energy: Everybody's Business," *Forbes*, October 27, 1980, p. 86.

11. Ibid., p. 88.

12. *Newsweek*, Sept. 22, 1980, p. 90.

13. Harrison Brown, *The Challenge of Man's Future* (New York: Viking, 1954), p. 114.

14. Jean Mayer, "The Dimensions of Human Hunger," *Scientific American,* 235 (September 1976), pp. 46–47, and Nevin Scrimshaw, as quoted by Anthony Lewis, New York Times News Service, Oct. 2, 1973.

15. John Saar, "Japan Looks to Future of Fish Farms," *Washington Post*, June 1, 1977, p. A-18.

16. Nevin Scrimshaw and Lance Taylor, "Food," in *Scientific American*, 243 (September 1980), p. 85.

17. Doug McInnis, "How Technology Altered NCR and Dayton," *Washington Post*, Jan. 8, 1978, p. F-2.

18. Jessica Tuchman Mathews, "Factories Too Tiny to See," ibid., Jan. 23, 1980, p. A-23.

19. Associated Press, July 22, 1980.

20. Mathews, op. cit.

21. Thomas O'Toole, "In the Lab: Bugs to Grow Wheat, Eat Metal," *Washington Post*, June 18, 1980, p. A-1.

22. See, for example, Marlise Simons, "Cuba Reviving Market Forces to Lift Economy," ibid., May 29, 1980, p. A-15.

23. Council on Environment Quality, *The Global 2000 Report to the President*, as quoted by *ZPG Reporter*, 12 (September 1980), p. 4.

24. Ibid., p. 2.

25. Spencer, op. cit.; Large, op. cit.

26. Spencer, op. cit.
27. *ZPG Reporter*, p. 4.
28. Ibid.
29. Clifford P. Case, III, "Why Do We Refuse to Recycle?" *Washington Post*, Apr 12, 1980, p. A-19.
30. Jay Mathews, "China Opts for Progress," ibid., Jan. 26, 1980, p. A10, and "Chinese Metals Plant Is Fined $1.3 Million for Water Pollution," *Wall Street Journal*, Mar. 18, 1980, p. 13.
31. *ZPG Reporter*, p. 1.
32. Ibid.
33. Ibid., p. 2.
34. Ibid.
35. Ibid.
36. Our own calculation based on the age distribution and life expectancy of the Mexican population, as reported in U.S. Department of Commerce, Bureau of the Census, *Statistical Abstract of the U.S., 1979*, tables 1585 and 1586.
37. United Press International news release, Sept. 11, 1977.
38. Ibid.
39. Lewis M. Simons, "India After Indira: Compulsory Sterilization Provokes Fear, Contempt," *Washington Post*, July 4, 1977, pp. A-1, 16, and 17.
40. Murray Marder, "A-War Estimate Held Too Low," ibid., Sept. 17, 1975, p. A-5.
41. Lee Lescaze, "Nuclear War Worse than People Imagine," ibid., Feb. 11, 1980, p. A-20.
42. Robert Heilbroner, *An Inquiry into the Human Prospect* (New York: Norton, 1974), p. 41.
43. Lescaze, op. cit.
44. Ibid.
45. Brown, p. 223.
46. Calculations based on *Statistical Abstract of the U.S., 1979*, table 895, in 1977 dollars.
47. Quoted by Carl Sagan in *Broca's Brain* (New York: Random House, 1979), p. 31.
48. Heilbroner, pp. 121–122.

Picture Credits

6.2 From Seton Lloyd and Fuad Safar, "Tell Hassuna," *Journal of Near Eastern Studies* (vol. 4, fig. 36). By permission of the University of Chicago Press.

6.3 Courtesy of Dr. James Mellaart, Institute of Archeology, University of London.

6.5 From W. Watson, *Early Civilization in China,* © 1970, Thames & Hudson Ltd, London.

6.6 Rene Burri/Magnum Photos, Inc.

6.7 Courtesy of The University Museum, University of Pennsylvania, Philadelphia.

6.8 By permission of the Smithsonian Office of Anthropology.

6.9 Courtesy of The American Museum of Natural History.

6.11 Napoleon Chagnon, *Yanamamö: The Fierce People,* copyright © 1968 by Holt, Rinehart & Winston, New York.

6.12 Napoleon Chagnon, *Yanamamö: The Fierce People,* copyright © 1968 by Holt, Rinehart & Winston, New York.

6.13 Courtesy of The American Museum of Natural History.

6.14 United Nations.

6.15 Courtesy of The American Museum of Natural History.

6.16 From Jacques Maquet, *Africanity, the Cultural Unity of Black Africa;* Oxford University Press, 1972, p. 112.

6.18 Reprinted from *The Ancient Maya,* third edition, by Sylvanus Griswold Morley; revised by George W. Brainerd, with the permission of the publishers, Stanford University Press. Copyright © 1946, 1947, and 1956 by the Board of Trustees of the Leland Stanford Junior University.

7.1 Courtesy of The Metropolitan Museum of Art.

7.2 Evans, Three Lion Photos, Inc.

7.3 Courtesy of The Metropolitan Museum of Art.

7.4 Courtesy of The Metropolitan Museum of Art, Museum Excavations, 1919—1920; Rogers Fund, supplemented by contribution of Edward S. Harkness.

7.6 United Nations.

7.8 Courtesy of Exxon Corporation.

7.9 Courtesy of Exxon Corporation.

7.11 United Nations.

7.12 United Nations.

7.13 From F. R. Cowell, *Everday Life in Ancient Rome,* G. P. Putnam's Sons, copyright © 1961. By permission of B. T. Batsford Ltd., London.

7.14 United Nations.

7.15 United Nations.

7.16 Courtesy of The Metropolitan Museum of Art, Bashford Dean Memorial Collection, 1929.

7.17 Courtesy of The Metropolitan Museum of Art, Rogers Fund, 1904.

7.18 United Nations.

7.19 Courtesy of Exxon Corporation.

7.20 Lauros-Giraudon.

7.21 Courtesy of the Kunsthistorisches Museum, Vienna.

7.22 From F. R. Cowell, *Everyday Life in Ancient Rome,* G. P. Putnam's Sons, copyright © 1961. By permission of B. T. Batsford Ltd., London.

8.1 United Nations.

8.2 P. F. Mele, Photo Researchers, Inc.

8.3 Monkmeyer Press Photo Service.

8.4 By permission of Institut Français d'Archéologie, Beirut, Lebanon.

8.5 Courtesy of The Metropolitan Museum of Art, Rogers Fund, 1906.

9.1 The Granger Collection.

9.2 From Fritz Rorig, *The Medieval Town,* copyright © by Propylaen Verlag; reprinted by permission of the University of California Press.

9.4 The Smithsonian Institution.

9.5 Historical Pictures Service, Chicago.

9.6 The Smithsonian Institution.

9.7 The Bettmann Archive, Inc.

9.8 Cary Wolinsky/Stock, Boston.

9.9 Courtesy of The Times, London.

9.10 Historical Pictures Service, Chicago.

10.1 © Joe Munroe/Photo Researchers, Inc.

10.2 Rene Burri/Magnum Photos, Inc.

10.3 The Bettmann Archive, Inc.

10.4 Courtesy of The New York Public Library.

10.5 Courtesy of the New York Convention and Visitors Bureau.

10.6 United Nations.

10.7 Cary Wolinsky/Stock, Boston.

10.8 Courtesy of The New York Public Library.

10.9 Elliot Erwitt/Magnum Photos, Inc.

11.1 Courtesy of The New York Public Library.

11.2 Ian Berry/Magnum Photos, Inc.

11.3 Wide World Photos, Inc.

11.4 "Grin and Bear It" by George Lichty, © 1981 Field Enterprises, courtesy of Field Newspaper syndicate.

11.5 Wide World Photos, Inc.

11.6 Cornell Capa/Magnum Photos, Inc.

11.9 Bruce Davidson/Magnum Photos, Inc.

11.10 United Nations.

11.11 United Nations.

12.1 Bill Brandt/Rapho/Photo Researchers, Inc.

Picture Credits

12.4	Howard Harrison.
12.5	Courtesy of Lincoln Center for the Performing Arts.
13.1	United Nations.
13.2	United Nations.
13.3	(a) United Nations.
13.4	Photograph by Arthur Galston; courtesy of Thomas Y. Crowell Co.
13.5	United Nations.
13.6	Courtesy of Moni Nag.
13.7	United Press International.
13.8	Mares/Monkmeyer Press Photo Service.
13.9	United Nations.
13.10	United Nations.

Author Index

Elkin, A. P., 455—459
Ellul, Jacques, 484
Emerson, Alfred E., 449
Engels, Friedrich, 337, 416, 484
Erman, Adolf, 465
Esmer, Yilmaz, 481
Evans, Ivor, 456—459
Eversley, D. E. C., 466, 479

F

Fallers, L. A., 483
Faris, R. E. L., 451
Farmer, B. H., 460, 463, 464
Faron, Louis, 462, 463, 470
Farrell, R. Barry, 478
Feibleman, James K., 453
Feierabend, Ivo, 476
Feierabend, Rosalind, 476
Feldman, David, 483
Feuer, Lewis, 474
Firebaugh, Morris, 484
Fisher, Sydney, 470, 481
Fisher, Wesley, 451
Fiszman, Joseph R., 478
Flannery, Kent, 460
Florence, P. Sargant, 475
Forbes, R. J., 454, 461
Fortes, Meyer, 161, 162, 463
Fox, Gerald, 280, 464, 465
Fraenkel, Merran, 483
Franck, Peter, 481
Frank, Andre Gunder, 483
Fried, Morton, 463, 467
Friedan, Betty, 350
Frost, Robert, 209n.
Furtado, Celso, 483

G

Galbraith, John Kenneth, 474, 475
Gallup, George, 414, 415
Galtung, Johan, 483
Gamble, Sidney, 468
Garvan, John, 456, 457, 484
Gayton, A. H., 458, 459
George, M. Dorothy, 468
Getler, Michael, 480
Gil, Federico, 190
Gillen, F. J., 458
Giner, Salvador, 190
Glass, D. V., 466, 479
Goldman, Irving, 462
Goldschmidt, Walter, 451, 453, 457—459

Goldsmith, Oliver, 192
Goode, William J., 478
Goodenough, Ward, 456
Goodman, Morris, 455
Gordon, Robert A., 475
Gottwald, Norman K., 469
Gough, Kathleen, 462
Gould, Stephen Jay, 451
Granick, David, 475, 477
Griffiths, Franklyn, 477, 478
Groves, Reg, 467, 468
Gurdon, P. R. T., 463
Gyftopoulous, Elias, 484
Gyllenhammar, Pehr, 474

H

Haight, Timothy, 270, 480
Halpern, Manfred, 481, 482
Halphen, L., 469
Hamburg, David, 450
Hammond, Barbara, 473, 483
Hammond, John, 473, 483
Hammond, Mason, 464
Hannan, Michael, 481, 482
Hanson, A. H., 481
Harden, Donald, 471
Harlan, Jack, 459
Harris, Marvin, 45, 150—151, 451—453, 459, 462, 463
Hatt, Gudmund, 454, 460, 461, 463, 464
Hawkes, Jacquetta, 110, 454—456, 460
Hawley, Amos H., 469
Heider, Karl G., 452, 460
Heilbroner, Robert, 441, 450, 466, 471, 473, 485
Heizer, Robert, 454, 459, 460
Helleiner, K. F., 466
Herberg, Will, 474
Hewes, Gordon, 470
Higbee, Edward, 474
Hill, Gladwin, 481
Hiller, Dana, 479
Hobbes, Thomas, 25
Hobsbawm, Eric, 473
Hoebel, E. Adamson, 452, 455, 459, 462
Hole, Frank, 454, 459, 460
Hollingshead, A. B., 479
Hollingsworth, H., 466
Holm, Richard, 452

Subject Index

Page numbers in **boldface** indicate the most basic references. Cross references to a particular subject *"under basic societal types"* refer to Agrarian societies; Horticultural societies; Hunting and gathering societies; Industrial societies; Industrializing agrarian societies; Industrializing horticultural societies.

A

Abortion, 112, 265, 278−279, 310, 352, 373, 426

Adaptive mechanisms, 6−7, 17, 408
   (*See also* Cooperation; Culture; Genetics; Learning; Societies, human; Symbols)

Africa:
   agrarian societies, 171−212
   fishing societies, 219
   frontier societies, 214−215
   hominid societies, 102−103
   horticultural societies, 160−164
   hunting and gathering societies, 111−129
   industrializing societies, 366−406

Age differentiation and stratification, 48−49, 332
   in agrarian societies, 208
   in horticultural societies, 156
   in hunting and gathering societies, 118, 123, 125, 130
   in industrial societies, 260, 319, **332−335,** 350−354

Age differentiation and stratification (*Cont.*):
   in industrializing societies, 382, 383, 385, 393, 400

Aging and the aged, 198, 212, 332−333, 383, 440
   consequences for social change, 71

Agrarian era, 90, 169ff.
   world system at close of, 228−231

Agrarian societies, 83−85, 128, **169−217**
   advanced, 88, 180−212
   basic characteristics, 212, 216
   communities: advanced, 182−185, 187−189, 193−198, 213
      fishing, 221
      permanence of, 93−94
      simple, 171, 173, 175, 177
      size, 91, 93, 173, 183
      specialized, 186−187
   defined, 84
   economy, 171, 173, **176−177,** 179, 180, 182, **186−198,** 207, 208
   education, 175−176, 262, 328, 341, 350

496

Polygyny, 115, 213, 247, 344, 399, 402
Population:
  as component of sociocultural system, **34—37,** 54
  as reproductive unit, 11—13, 16, 35
    tendency to overreproduce, **12,** 79, 430
  (*See also* Population variables; Surplus population)
Population control:
  industrial societies, 264—265, 278—279, 342, 344, 346
  industrializing societies, 373—374, 379, 391, 405, 421, 425, 431
  preindustrial era, 112—113, 156—157, 191
  prospects, 264—265, 406, 420—421, 430, 431, 439, 440
  (*See also* Abortion; Birthrates; Infanticide; *population under various societal types*)
Population variables, **36—37**
  age composition, 36, 431, 434
  consequences of technological advance, 68, 74, 80, 183, 217, 229, 260, 278—281
  density, 36, 111—112, 183
  rural-urban ratio, **260,** 280—281
    (*See also* Migration, intrasocietal)
  size and growth, 36—37, 91, 93
    consequences for innovation, 65—66, 68, 136, 261
    differences among preindustrial societal types, 91—93
  of world system (*see* World system, population)
  (*See also* Birthrates; Communities, size; Death rates; Life expectancy; Surplus population; *population under basic societal types*)
Poverty:
  agrarian societies, 185, 190—191, 197, 198
  industrial societies, 298, 319, 331, 335, 336, 356, 440
  industrializing societies, 367, 379—384, 397, 402, 431, 432
  relation to happiness, 413—414
  (*See also* Income per capita)
Primary groups, 50—51
  (*See also* Family and kinship)
Primary industries, 284—285
  (*See also* Agriculture)
Primates, 14—16, 22, 23n., 32, 102—103
Printing press, 90, 182, 238—240, 242, 265
Private enterprise:
  in Marxist societies, 296
  (*See also* Capitalism)
Probabilism, 96
  (*See also* Technological determinism; Variable concepts)
Problems, social (*see* Social Problems)
Property, ownership of (*see* Elites, propertied)
Proprietary theory of the state, 199—201, 378
Prostitution, 198, 336—337, 383

Protestant Reformation, 239—240, 242
  and democratic trend, 306—308
Protestants and Protestantism, 213, 308, 313, 332, 387, 426
  and work ethic, 240
Punishments (*see* Sanctions)
Purpose, role of:
  in cultural innovation, 61—63, 424—426, **441**
  in cultural selection, 69—70, 424

R

Race (*see* Ethnic-racial differentiation and stratification)
Racial traits, adaptive value of, 35—36
Railroads, 243, 247—248, 295—296, 404
Randomness (*see* Chance)
Recombinations:
  cultural, **65,** 68
  genetic, 12
Reductionism, 53—54
Regression, societal, 73, **75**
  prospects of, in future, 315, 438
Religion, 21, 44, 45, 55
  differences among preindustrial societal types, 95—96
  innovation in (*see* Ideology, innovation in)
  and population control, 183, 213, 310, 425n., 432
  prehistoric, 105, 109
  prospects, 424—425
  role of: in creation of surplus, 166, 171—173
    in Industrial Revolution, 239—240
    in intratype variations, 213
  secular, 271—278, 399—400
    (*See also* Communism; Marxism)
  trends in, 216—217
  (*See also* Ancestor worship; Animism; Buddhism; Catholicism; Christianity; Confucianism; Hinduism; Ideology; Judaism; Protestantism; Universal religions; *religion under specific societal types*)
Republican governments, 198—199, 212, 227—228, 308
Resources, natural, 30, 43, **46,** 47, 64, 83
  finite supply, 79, 264, 427—429
  (*See also* Energy: Environment, biophysical; *specific resources, such as* Coal; Petroleum)
Revolutionary socialism (*see* Marxism)
Revolutionary socialist societies (*see* Marxist societies)
Revolutions:
  agrarian, 169ff.

Social problems (*Cont.*):
  (*See also* Conflict, intrasocietal; *specific problems, such as* Divorce; Environment; Poverty; Unemployment; Warfare)
Social sciences, 25–27
  relation to biological science, 57–60
  relation of sociology to others, 27
Social species, 6–9, 13–17, 23
  (*See also* Cooperation; Mammals; Primates; Social insects; Societies, human)
Social structure:
  cause of technological slowdown, 179
  component of sociocultural systems, **47–53,** 90
  consequences of technological advance, 53, 91, 94, 98, 216, 229, 230, 363
  (*See also* Associations; Classes; Communities; Institutions; Stratification)
Socialism, **272–276,** 281
  prospects, 435
  in Third World, 378, 387, 388, 391, 397, 406
  (*See also* Communism; Democratic socialism; Marxism)
Socialist parties, 273–275, 310
Socialist societies, 281, 294–296, 299
  (*See also* Democratic societies; Marxist societies)
Socialization, **31,** 67, 71–72, 125, 341, 349, 441
  preagrarian societies compared, 125
  (*See also* Children; Education; Family and kinship; Infants)
Societal typology, **82–98**
  basis of, 82–87
    (*See also* Subsistence technology)
  (*See also* Theoretical perspective)
Societies; human:
  as adaptive mechanisms, 6–8, 14, 16
  biological foundation, 9–25
  change in, 61–72
    (*See also* Development, societal; Regression, societal; Sociocultural evolution)
  defined, 8–9, 55
  number of, 78, 436
  place in nature, 5–9
  size (*see* Geographical size of societies; Population variables, size and growth)
  systemic nature, 29ff., 53–55, 63, 64, 72, 130, 140
  types of, 82–98
  (*See also* Sociocultural systems; *various types of societies*)
Sociocultural evolution, **56–81**
  basic processes, 60ff.
    (*See also* Innovation; Selection; Variation)
  compared with biological evolution, 57–60
  defined, 60–61
  of individual societies, 37, 55, 60, **61–77**
    basic patterns of change, 73–75

Sociocultural evolution (*Cont.*):
  of world system, **77–81**
    to eve of Industrial Revolution, 228–231
    model of, 79–80
    prospects, 436–442
    (*See also* World system)
  (*See also* Change, sociocultural; Ecological-evolutionary theory; Trends in history)
Sociocultural systems, **28–55**
  basic components, 34–53
  process of change in, 61–77
  systemic nature, **29–30,** 53–55
  system-needs, 30–34
  (*See also* Societies, human)
Sociology:
  defined, 4
  goals and history, 25–27
  measurement in, 92
  theoretical perspectives in, 4–5, 26–27
  (*See also* Ecological-evolutionary theory)
Soviet society (*see* U.S.S.R.)
Specialization:
  communal and regional, 186–187
  occupational (*see* Occupational specialization)
  organization and institutional, 166, 205, 286–288, 303, 342–343
  societal, 363, 376–378, 391, 434
  trends in, 94, 186–187, 230, 260, 286–288, 363
Specialized societal types (*see* Environmentally specialized societies)
Speciation, **13,** 60
Species, biotic, 6ff., 59
  (*See also* Social species; Speciation; Homo sapiens)
Speech, human capacity for, 22–23
  (*See also* Language; Symbols)
Standards of living:
  in agrarian societies, 191, 195, 197, 283
  evolutionary trends, 264–265, 281–283
  in industrial societies, 215, 265, 281–283, 311, 361, 439
  in industrializing societies, 374, 378, 390, 402, 431, 439
  prospects, 433
  (*See also* Income per capita; Income distribution)
Stasis, societal, 73, **75**
State (*see* Government)
State enterprises:
  in capitalist societies, 295–296
  in Marxist societies, 294, **296–299,** 322
  (*See also* Proprietary theory of the state; Socialism)

Textile industry, 243—247, 376
Theocracies, 146, 172—173, 205
Theoretical perspective:
  on agrarian societies, 216—217
  on horticultural societies, 164—168
  on hunting and gathering societies, 129—133
  on industrial societies, 362—365
  on industrializing societies, 402—406
Theory in science, 4—5, 25—27
  (*See also* Ecological-evolutionary theory)
Third World, 76, 244, 256, 277, **366—406**
  industrialization in, 368—369, 371, 374—378,
    389—394, 402—406, 433
  population size and growth, 369—374, 390—391,
    404—405
  prospects, 406, 425—426, **429—432,** 434
  standard of living compared with U.S., 439
  (*See also* Industrializing agrarian societies;
    Industrializing horticultural societies)
Tools and weapons, 46—47, 77
  agrarian societies, 169—170, 180—182
  consequences for biological evolution, 102—104
  horticultural societies, 137—138, 140—148, 151,
    160, 166
  hunting and gathering societies, 102—110,
    118—120, 122, 129
  industrial and industrializing societies (*see* Military
    technology; *technology under these societal
    types*)
  in societal typology, 84ff.
  (*See also* Metallurgy; Technology; *specific tools and
    weapons, such as* Computer; Plow)
Trade and commerce, intersocietal:
  agrarian societies, 186—187, 205, 216—217, 227,
    236—237
  horticultural societies, 139—141, 151, 166—167
  hunting and gathering societies, 118
  industrial societies, 299—301
  industrializing societies, 376—378
  maritime societies, 86, 225—228
  role in intratype variation, 213—214
  world system, 299—301
Tradition and traditionalism, 189, 238, 271, 316, 380,
  386—388, 391, 393, 398—399, 403
Transportation:
  advances in, 86, 205, 224, 225, 236—238, 243,
    247—252, 261, 300, 437
  cost of different means compared, 197
  (*See also specific means, such as* Animals;
    Railroads)
Trends in history, 78, **80,** 90, 167, 216—217,
  228—231, 260—261, 363—364, 407—415
Tribes:
  in horticultural societies, 155—156
  in hunting and gathering societies, 126—127
  in industrializing horticultural societies, 393—397

Typology of societies, 82ff.

U

Unemployment, 198, 258, 273, 298, 306, 319, 353,
  372, 383
  prospects, 422, 434, 440
  (*See also* Labor surplus)
Unilinear theory of evolution, 60, 144, 160
U.S.S.R. (Union of Soviet Socialist Republics):
  agrarian era in Russia, 78, 183, 189, 199, 214, 217
  economy, 256, 296—299, 358—359, 435
  education, 305, 385—386
  family, 349, 350
  ideology, 365
    (*See also* Marxism)
  industrializing, 251, 252, 254, 259
  polity, 305, 306, 317, 358—359, 417—418,
    435—438
  revolution, 275, 382
  stratification, 319, 325—326, 330, 334, 335
  youth culture, 353—354
  (*See also* Marxist societies)
Unions (*see* Labor unions)
United Nations, 261, 301, 372, 435, 439
United States:
  agrarian era, 78, 214—215, 336
  economy and technology, 250—252, 255—256,
    262, 267—270, 281—295
  education, 328—330, 385—386
  energy consumption, 268—269, 419
  family, 340—350
  frontier effects on, 214—215, 278, 308
  GNP, 270
  ideology, 270—271, 276—277, 426
  income per capita, 281—282, 439
  and India, compared, 368
  industrialization, 247—254
  labor force composition, 268, 285—288
  labor movement, 290
  leisure and the arts, 354—355
  mass media, 356—358
  occupational specialization, 286
  polity, 303—304, 309—316, 324, 417—418,
    436—437
  population: age composition, 36—37, 434
    migration, 432
    rural-urban ratio, 280—281
  size, 278—279, 416
  religion, 271, 426